Harvard English Studies 12

Johnson and His Age

HARVARD ENGLISH STUDIES 12

Johnson and His Age
//

Edited by
James Engell

Harvard University Press
Cambridge, Massachusetts
and London, England
1984

Copyright © 1984 by the President and Fellows of Harvard College

All rights reserved

Printed in the United States of America

10 9 8 7 6 5 4 3 2 1

Library of Congress Cataloging in Publication Data

Main entry under title:

Johnson and his age.

  (Harvard English studies ; 12)
    1. Johnson, Samuel, 1709–1784—Criticism and interpretation—
Addresses, essays, lectures. 2. Johnson, Samuel, 1709–1784—
Contemporaries—Addresses, essays, lectures. 3. English literature—18th
century—History and criticism—Addresses, essays, lectures. I. Engell,
James, 1951–   . II. Series.
PR3534.J64 1984   828'.609   84-10732
ISBN 0-674-48075-9
ISBN 0-674-48076-7 (pbk.)

By the contributors to

W. JACKSON BATE

Biographer, Teacher,
Fellow Johnsonian

Preface

The hardest decision in editing this volume, published in the bicentennial of Johnson's death, was to choose a title. Many were acceptable, but none seemed fully adequate. Even a long, descriptive title page of the kind still popular in the second half of the eighteenth century could not characterize the literary variety and energy of that age. The term "neo-classicism," invented by scholars about a hundred years ago, fails to indicate essential changes taking place from Classic to Romantic. "Augustan" misses the mark chronologically; it usually describes a period and a group of writers somewhat earlier. Possible alternatives—and useful ones in many instances—include the Age of Sensibility or the Age of Sentiment (roughly equivalent in France to the Age of Rousseau), phrases that mark the premium placed on feeling and individuality in taste, social behavior, and ethical values. These labels suggest others, for instance the Früh- or pre-Romantic, still popular in Germany and at one time used extensively in English scholarship. But the sense this label gives of embryonic Romanticism or "anticipation," even while failing to cover many writers and works after 1770— Gibbon, for instance, or Crabbe—can also be stretched back to 1720. There has even been a recent engaging attempt to view the early eighteenth century, the Age of Pope and Swift, as "The Age of Passion." A common tag of *Kulturgeschichte*, the Age of Reason, does not fare particularly well as a signpost of English literature, which during the eighteenth century tested reason as well as trusting it. And although "English Literature of the Enlightenment" suggests a broader scope—and accommodates the great nonfiction prose characteristic of the time—it also extends to the earlier

1700s and includes, for example, Pope's *Essay on Man*; furthermore, we need to distinguish the English Enlightenment from that developed by the French *philosophes*— though, as Coleridge would remind us, to distinguish is not necessarily to divide: Hume and Gibbon help form a bridge to the Continent.

But in "The Age of Johnson" or "Johnson and His Age" the man remains preeminent: a man of letters, whom Eliot ranks as a major poet and whom many consider the best of English critics; a moral philosopher imbued with practicality and humor; and one of the most entertaining and provoking conversationalists and essayists in any national literature. At least one new edition of *Rasselas* has appeared each year since its publication in 1759. Individual aspects of Johnson's life and work (aspects that in other writers of his stature might not always attract our attention), his religious convictions and struggles, lexicography, travels and views on travel, political writing and journalism, poetic style, criticism, anecdotes—each of these has been the subject of several full-length studies, not just in the recent surge of academic criticism and scholarship, but continually since the late eighteenth century. There are few literary or historical figures in whom we find such power, depth, and combination of mind. To paraphrase Johnson's remark on the source of happiness, "multiplicity of agreeable consciousness," we find in him a multiplicity of powerful consciousness. As William Gerard Hamilton said shortly after December 13, 1784, "He has made a chasm, which not only nothing can fill up, but which nothing has a tendency to fill up.—Johnson is dead.— Let us go to the next best:—there is nobody; no man can be said to put you in mind of Johnson."

Johnson's contemporaries, in their love of descriptive nicknames ("Dictionary" Johnson, "Estimate" Brown, "Capability" Brown, or "Corsica" Boswell), gave him the additional honor, if at times a bit grudgingly, of phrases that have passed into legend. Johnson is "the great Cham of literature." Oxford awarded him the degrees of A.M. and LL.D. with a full awareness that although circumstances once prevented him from completing undergraduate studies, he had become worthy of the highest academic distinction many times over. Yet as *Ursa major* Johnson is accompanied by what Adam Smith, under a more northerly sky, referred to as a "constellation of genius." We need only recall Johnson's own remarks: Burke is "the first man everywhere"; "his stream of mind is perpetual." Richardson's *Clarissa* shows great knowledge of the human heart; Gray's "mind had a large grasp . . . his curiosity was unlimited"; every genre of literature Goldsmith touched he improved. And there were, of course, others. Boswell and Mrs. Thrale, inextricably linked to Johnson, bring the age to life—they give it form, intensity, and a dramatic texture so immediate that we feel no years separate us from their scenes. Johnson, a strong oak, stands in a forest of oaks.

An "ideal" reader of our period, born in 1740 and reaching four score, would already be completing formal education or receiving a university degree when Johnson's *Dictionary* (1755), Gray's *Bard* (1756), and Burke's *Enquiry* (1757) were appearing for the first time. But our reader would live also to enjoy the novels of Jane Austen, Keats's odes (1819), *Childe Harold* (1807–1819), and the *Biographia Literaria* (1817). *The Lives of the Poets* (1779–1781) would appear during our reader's early middle age, Wordsworth's *Descriptive Sketches* (1793) and Boswell's *Life* (1791) in the middle of the way, the *Lyrical Ballads*, with their famous Preface, in the sixtieth year. This life would span the anonymous publications of *Shamela* and *Frankenstein* and would cover the exuberant adolescence of that vital new genre, the novel.

Such a reader, or any reader of whatever age, would find it virtually impossible to give a terse, satisfactory account of the essentially metamorphic nature of later eighteenth-century literature: it was an age marked by great changes in literary form, and great changes in form go hand in hand with major shifts in thought and sensibility. We can witness the gradual but steady decline of the heroic couplet; the waning of satire and didactic poetry; the constant reappraisals of poetic diction and of the ideal of the epic or long poem; the resurgence of the lyric; the first comprehensive history of English literature and the first ancient history presented in a masterful literary style; the decline of classical mythology and the creation of new, more individualistic myths; a similar decline in classical rhetoric and—under the aegis of Thomas Campbell, Hugh Blair, and James Beattie—the establishment of a new rhetoric with its study of universal grammar and the arbitrary relation between words as signifiers and their significations. How could our reader classify Burns "following his plow" or "the marvellous Boy" Chatterton or define precisely the mark left on English prosody by what Coleridge calls Cowper's "divine chit-chat"?

Here is a literature not only metamorphic but also highly varied. It is not under the sway of authority, tradition, or convention. It is self-questioning, critical, aware of the past, interested in genius, and addressed to a rapidly expanding reading public. To find the right title for a volume of essays discussing this literature might become a dry routine, a chronology or periodization, but not if we remember that one of our essential pursuits is to ask the question, what makes a culture? And further, to ask how that culture views itself: What does it do with language and what does language do with it? What are its values, in appearance and in actuality, and how are these values reflected in its literature? What do its readers expect from literature and language, and how do writers both meet and change these expectations? How might we think of literary culture in general, and of the larger society with which it inevitably exists?

These questions are particularly valuable ones to ask about the later eighteenth century because they are the very questions the age asked of itself. Moreover, its own study of literature addresses the political, social, personal, and historical dimensions of experience as well as the more literarily formal concerns of criticism, poetics, drama, and narrative.

The study of literature is worthless unless it gives us pleasure or, as Johnson said of biography, something to put to use. If we distance ourselves from the present day and imaginatively recreate another time, other literary forms, and other writers, their motivations and their societies, it is in hope of returning to our own age refreshed by a sense of pleasure and delight or enlightenment and guidance—though at times we may come to realize how we are different as well as how we are the same, that what worked once will not work for us now. As Hans-Georg Gadamer says, almost as if he were quoting Burke, "Time is no longer a gulf to be bridged, because it separates, but it is actually the supportive ground of process in which the present is rooted."

The variety of contributions in this volume testifies to the direct engagement of literature in both the social and the individual life that we find in Johnson and his contemporaries. Together these essays bring into focus intellectual, emotional, and moral issues; they also deal with formal and rhetorical methods, with aesthetic and ethical problems. As in experience itself, all the issues must come together before we can begin to form a true picture of any age.

J. E.

Contents

A Critical Conspectus

Poets, Statesmen, Historians, Artists

The Novel

Johnson's Life and Thought

LAWRENCE LIPKING

Johnson and the Meaning of Life

What is the meaning of life? If anyone knows, it ought to be Samuel Johnson. Of all the great writers, none claims life as his subject more explicitly, more exclusively. Johnson thinks all other questions depend on this one. "The only end of writing," in his famous formulation, "is to enable readers better to enjoy life, or better to endure it."[1] Beyond the Horatian advice to instruct and delight, the somber phrasing insists that this author does not take his duty for granted. For many readers life must be a burden, with only a few thin pages of comfort to stand between them and despair. Hence writers must help them endure—not by creating a separate literary world but by making the best they can of the world as it is. "Books without the knowledge of life are useless," Johnson repeatedly told Mrs. Thrale; "for what should books teach but the art of *living*?"[2] Nor did he refuse his own challenge. A high proportion of his work deals directly with the art of living: essays and sermons on the conduct of life, fiction on the "choice of life," criticism on the relation of life to art, and those many biographies

1. Review of *A Free Enquiry into the Nature and Origin of Evil* (1757).
2. *Johnsonian Miscellanies*, ed. George Birkbeck Hill (Oxford, 1897), I, 324.

entitled lives. He is the expert on living. If Johnson cannot tell us the meaning of life, then where is the meaning of life to be found?

The most common answer today, of course, is "nowhere." Not many people feel confident, these days, about finding the meaning of life. To tell the truth, the whole issue seems a bit embarrassing, or even silly. The meaning of life? Surely that is not the sort of thing one talks about in polite company—at least not while sober. We might make jokes about it or, under provocation, annoy a philosopher or a clergyman by accusing him of not having anything to say about it either. We might tell a child who asked about it that she had better wait and ask again when she is older. By that time the whole problem, like sex, will probably have taken care of itself, with the aid of her little friends. But the meaning of life embarrasses modern grown-ups far more than sex does. We would not know how to teach it in the schools, nor even where to look for it. And very few people would now expect to find the answers in Johnson.

Indeed, not even Johnsonians, in the past few decades, have spent much time dealing with "life." The word, along with the kinds of issues it raises, has entered a period of semiretirement, when it is employed as a contrast to some words that seem more vivid—for instance, "art" and "death"—but is seldom paid much attention on its own. Despite the many books on Johnson as a moralist, a religious thinker, and a sage, "life" almost never appears in the index. There is no entry for it in the generous survey and bibliography by Clifford and Greene, in *The Critical Opinions of Samuel Johnson*, in the copious indices to the Yale Editions of *The Rambler, Idler* and *Adventurer*, writings on Shakespeare, or *Sermons*. To be sure, one might argue that the absence of the word testifies not to the neglect but to the ubiquity or omnipresence of what it signifies. Thus W. Jackson Bate's books on Johnson could hardly have put "life" in the index, referring to one page or another, since virtually everything in them refers to the one great question of how to live; "life" takes in all of the book. I intend to return to this point. Yet whether or not Johnsonians still read the master as a guide to the meaning of life, most of them now prefer to treat other issues. It is certainly very hard to write about life. A great wave of irony and presumption breaks over the author who sits down to do it. But perhaps that difficulty itself may provide us with a starting point. Why should questions about the meaning of life make us so uneasy? And why should we not trust Johnson to give us the answers?

There are three main ways of responding, I think, to each of these problems. The first and most obvious is ignorance, pure ignorance: we do not know enough; we have become increasingly conscious in the last two centuries of how little we know; and we have also learned that the sages who thought they knew the answers did not know enough either. The meaning of life is beyond us. Perhaps it is not even a meaningful phrase. In the age of space travel and the anti-utopia, post-Darwin, post-Marx, post-Freud, post-Einstein, and even post-man, the certainties of earlier ages vanish and leave us in the abyss. Or so we like to say—uttering our sense of the absurd like Rasselas in the Happy Valley, "with a plaintive voice, yet with a look that discovered him to feel some complacence in his own perspicacity, and to receive some solace of the miseries of life, from consciousness of the delicacy with which he felt, and the eloquence with which he bewailed them."[3] Many deep thinkers think the abyss their oyster. No refutation of the meaning of life seems more popular than what we might call the Argument from Astronomy: we are all of us marooned in space, clinging to a third-rate planet circling a mediocre star in a marginal quarter of the Milky Way expanding through one of many universes at nearly the speed of light toward the infinite reaches. What would Samuel Johnson say about that? Not much, I suppose, save to note that the relevance of an uninhabited void to human needs and duties is not obvious, that the idea of being lost in space would be

3. *Rasselas*, I, 2.

sensible only in relation to some other place where one might be found, that humility is endless, and that the speaker's reference to a "third-rate" planet, a "mediocre" star, and so on, seems to identify him with some first-rate planet or higher perspective that marks him as secretly proud.

I do not wish to imply that all modern assumptions—our skepticism about ultimate answers, our doubts that human life fulfills some purpose—can be dismissed abruptly with a grin. The interstellar spaces scare me as they scared Pascal. But the current notion that discoveries in science and philosophy have exposed the futility of any search for the meaning of life deserves to be regarded skeptically in turn. Too often it reveals not thought but intellectual arrogance—specifically the arrogance of assuming that all minds in earlier ages were credulous and dogmatic. Our claims of sophistication require them to be naive.

Johnson affords an excellent case in point. As modern scholarship has shown again and again, the nineteenth-century caricature of a violently prejudiced, superstitious old Tory reflects a picture of nineteenth-century fears having little to do with Samuel Johnson himself. Yet the caricature survives. It is especially popular among philosophers. If they and the general public know one thing about Johnson (and frequently that one thing is all they know), they remember that he "refuted" Berkeley by kicking a stone. That incident crops up obsessively in philosophical writing and conversation. During the past year, as a matter of fact, I have heard three philosophers refer to it in public lectures. They needed it, presumably, as an example of a blind and stubborn faith, an antiphilosophical attitude so deep-rooted that it casts off reasoning itself in favor of immediate primal experience. A good many people *like* this attitude; often Johnson is praised for preferring the direct intuition of concrete reality to any kind of thought. But philosophers seldom concur. Usually they point out that the immaterialist argument, which holds that all we can know is our own sensations, can hardly be refuted by insisting on those sensations. Johnson has committed a vulgar fallacy; perhaps the archetype of all vulgar fallacies. His kick is a shorthand for all who kick against the traces of abstract reasoning. It is significant that the only book in recent years to attempt a full and serious discussion of the meaning of life—Robert Nozick's ambitious *Philosophical Explanations*—mentions Johnson just once, carrying the Berkeley anecdote to a further stage of dogma: "Would even Dr. Johnson have said, 'How do I know I am not dreaming? By seeing what is in front of me'?"[4] We all know that "Dr." Johnson. He is the man who clings obstinately to his illusions, insisting that they are facts, and will not see that he himself has made the world on which he rests his case. He is the old believer, the practical English spirit at its most obtuse.

Like most of the better-known fables, this pocket view of Johnson doubtless contains a tiny grain of truth. He *did* mistrust all systems raised on abstract thought alone; he *did* reject philosophies that seemed inimical to common sense or Christian faith. Yet the usual construction placed on the incident of the stone is (if you will pardon the word) sensationally mistaken. As H. F. Hallett argued as long ago as 1947 in a trenchant article, Johnson's refutation of Berkeley, however casual, is by no means superficial. It rests not on a vulgar fallacy (that our sensations of objects prove that they exist) but on two points: that objects demonstrate their independent existence by resisting and affecting *us* ("striking his foot with mighty force against a large stone, till he rebounded from it"—the stone moves Johnson, not vice versa) and that actions occur independently of our perceptions of them (to kick with the foot or to see with the eye is not the same as to perceive the foot or the eye—the eye does not see itself).[5] A longer exposition would be tedious. In any case it would probably not deter philosophers from applying the anecdote improperly (Hallett did not succeed), since what they require is not a legitimate argument but a

4. Cambridge: Harvard University Press, 1981, p. 233.
5. H. F. Hallett, "Dr. Johnson's Refutation of Bishop Berkeley," *Mind*, 56 (1947), 132–147.

straw man to beat with a stick—"I refute Johnson *thus.*"
But the implications about Johnson's habitual modes of reasoning should not be allowed to go unchallenged. As anyone
who has actually read his writings must be aware, it is ludicrous to think ourselves superior to Johnson on the grounds
that we are more inquisitive than he or more conscious that
virtually everything we think we know may be an illusion.
On these grounds he cannot be bettered. Thus he refutes
Berkeley's skepticism about the material world by extending
his own skepticism to Berkeley's first assumptions. His
questioning mind never flags. Nozick's fancy about Johnson
as someone who might deny that he was dreaming seems
peculiarly unfortunate, since the fancy that life itself may be
a dream is a favorite of Johnson. Such skepticism encom-
passes much of what *we* take on faith. Hence, whatever
answers Johnson provides about the meaning of life, he cannot be said to overlook one reason why many of us do not
ask the question: our suspicion that for creatures so limited
and infirm, creatures like us, life may be meaningless.

The concept of meaninglessness, however, might be
thought to apply more properly to words than to things, and
a second reason why so many people become uncomfortable
at talk about the meaning of life may be that they think it an
empty verbal gesture. One might as well try to discover the
meaning of blue. To define the meaning of life, we should
first have to know what "life" means, or at any rate the context in which it occurs, and because the possibilities are
innumerable and indeterminate the question itself soon
breaks into hundreds of pieces. How could any group of
people ever agree on *the* meaning of life? A more sensible
course would be to begin by setting more limited terms. For
instance, we might decide whether the object under investigation is the *meaning* of life, or the meaning of *life*, or *the
meaning of life* (that is, the whole set of assumptions we call
into play by employing the phrase). This exercise, to be
sure, would presumably lead to still further verbal distinctions, and would require so much clarity in formulating the
problem that no room would be left in which to venture an
answer. But that would be no great loss. If "life" is only a

word, then what higher purpose could be expected of it than to find its place amidst the network of words?

To put this another way: in the opinion of many modern intellectuals, disputes over such questions as "what is the meaning of life?" inevitably resolve into arguments about what vocabulary will be used. Allow me my "abyss" and you can keep your "God." From this point of view, the history of philosophy consists of a struggle in which each successive antagonist tries to substitute his own vocabulary for those of his predecessors: "idea" deposed by "entelechy," "dialectic" by "will," and "being" by "différance"—words without end, forever and ever. The only conflict that cannot be negotiated arises between the metaphysicians (those who believe that their vocabularies provide a unique and irresistible means of arriving at final truth) and the intellectuals (those who are never quite sure that any other vocabulary might not serve quite as well).[6] Thus "the meaning of life," in intellectuals' eyes, affords a perfectly satisfactory way of talking for those who like to talk that way, provided that no one pretends that this way of talking has any authority over anyone who prefers to talk some other way. That is a tolerant view. It begins to break down, however, when faced with someone like Johnson. The author of *The Rambler* employs his vocabulary with such majestic certitude, such confidence that his moral discriminations reflect the universal nature and experience of mankind, as to be the envy and despair of less positive minds. In the last number, for instance, he expresses some satisfaction that, throughout all two hundred and eight essays, he has avoided arbitrary criticism by "establishing all my principles of judgment on unalterable and evident truth." Can a modern intellectual forgive a writer so sure he commands the truth? Many cannot, and Johnson goes further yet. "Truth indeed is always truth, and reason is always reason; they have an intrinsick

---

6. Much of Richard Rorty's *Consequences of Pragmatism* (Minneapolis: University of Minnesota Press, 1982) enlarges on this "opposition between mortal vocabularies and immortal propositions" (p. xli).

and unalterable value; and constitute that intellectual gold which defies destruction."[7] But gold does not last forever. A thinker who views it instead as an item of barter, shaped into coins of various sizes and passed from hand to hand until it becomes so worn as to lose its value, will trade it with caution. Perhaps Johnson's own vocabulary is now somewhat tarnished, if not altogether worn out. The "life" he relies on may be an archaic term.

Johnson himself was fully aware of this problem. To some extent he may even be said to have popularized or disseminated it, since as the author of the first important English dictionary on historical principles he spread the word that words change their meaning and force with each generation. The meaning of "life," considered strictly as a word, cannot remain stable. Significantly, Johnson's most eloquent statement of the power of usage (like that of Horace before him) specifically compares the life of words with the vicissitudes of human life. "When we see men grow old and die at a certain time one after another, from century to century, we laugh at the elixir that promises to prolong life to a thousand years; and with equal justice may the lexicographer be derided, who being able to produce no example of a nation that has preserved their words and phrases from mutability, shall imagine that his dictionary can embalm his language, and secure it from corruption and decay, that it is in his power to change sublunary nature, and clear the world at once from folly, vanity, and affectation."[8] As this sentence develops, the relation of language to human nature becomes so intimate that words seem almost to take upon themselves the blight of original sin. The corruption and decay of vocabulary reflect the ancient folly of the race, and the god of mutability rules over language. Thus the meaning of "life" as a word can be no purer than the mixed motives and vicious purposes of those who use it. Johnson's

---

7. "Life of Cowley," in *Lives of the English Poets*, ed. George Birkbeck Hill (Oxford, 1905), I, 59. Hereafter cited as *Lives*.

8. Preface to the *English Dictionary* (London, 1755); cf. Horace, *Ars Poetica*, 60–72.

Dictionary cannot repair the faults of mankind. Nor can it restore words to the simple origins of unequivocal meaning.

If we ask Johnson for a literal answer to "what is the meaning of life?", in fact, his reply will be very complex. The first edition of the *Dictionary* includes no fewer than fifteen definitions of the word (later editions added a few more), and several of these definitions subtly qualify or contradict each other. There are also several surprises. A modern reader fresh from Boswell or *The Oxford Book of Death* (where Johnson ranks second in the number of quotations) may be taken aback to find that the *Dictionary*, unlike any recent one I have inspected, never mentions death at all in defining life. The primary meaning of "life" for Johnson and his contemporaries is "Union and co-operation of soul with body," a vital chain properly opposed not to death but to an inanimate state, when the link has not been forged or has been broken.[9] In this respect Johnson comes closer than we do to the Indo-European root of the word: "*leip-*. To stick, adhere; fat." Life is a kind of glue, in this derivation, the sticky stuff that pastes matter and spirit together. More important, what life is *not*, for Johnson, is the battle against death, the project for death, the interval in death, or the desperate denial of death, that furnishes so many modern philosophies of life with their principle of analysis and their sense of urgency. The ultimate psychological melodrama of the nuclear age, the war of life against death, gains its force from definitions unavailable in the eighteenth century. No power can destroy the soul, according to Imlac, except for the Being that made it. Hence Johnson's fear of death is more properly fear of the afterlife, in our terms, and death neither gives life its meaning nor takes it away.

Yet "life" is not simple for Johnson. A good deal of his writing might be charted as the play among different senses of the word or an exploration of its ambiguity. For instance,

---

9. On the contemporary context see Robert G. Walker, *Eighteenth-Century Arguments for Immortality and Johnson's "Rasselas"* (Victoria, B. C.: English Literary Studies, 1977).

the much disputed question of "the choice of life" in *Rasse-las*, where the phrase originally functioned as the working title of the book, may be clarified by noting an implicit tension between two definitions of "life" in the *Dictionary*: "5. Conduct; manner of living with respect to virtue or vice. 6. Condition; manner of living with respect to happiness and misery." Rasselas' hope of making his "choice of life" need not be considered ironic in regard to conduct, since the choice of virtue over vice, Johnson would remind us, is always within our power. But "nature sets her gifts on the right hand and on the left," and the choice of happiness over misery requires the cooperation of higher powers. Despite his unlimited wealth, Rasselas can hardly alter his condition. The confusion between the choices he can make and the choices he cannot supplies the book with much of its air of comic frustration.[10] Meanwhile he is carried along by life in its other aspects, where choice has no part: "10. General state of man. 11. Common occurences; human affairs; the course of things." Here nothing is ever concluded. Life will go on, whether or not Rasselas partakes of it, and it will obey his will no more than the stars obey the astronomer, or the river the fish who swim in it. Johnson is swimming there too.

This last sense of "life," however, may suggest a third reason why so few people think they can find the meaning of life or trust Johnson to find it. The word seems not only complex and ambiguous, like so many other words, but uniquely ungraspable, as if it were the residue left over from all other definitions. Life surrounds us and escapes us even in the act of defining it. Thus the search for the meaning of life cannot be satisfied by temporary expedients and partial solutions. It drives toward infinity and teleology, toward the

---

10. The arid modern debate about whether *The Vanity of Human Wishes* and *Rasselas* are best understood as "satiric" or "tragic" results from stressing one kind of choice over another. But Johnson makes room for both. Unlike those "swelling moralists" who boast that "happiness is the unfailing consequence of virtue" (*Adventurer* 120), he refuses to blame victims for their own misery except when it results from vice or self-deception.

meaning left when all other meanings have ended. Life is always defined by something beyond it: our death, our children, the memory we leave behind, the survival of the race, the last judgment. Nor does this process ever reach a stop. If humanity were extinguished, for instance, the meaning of its collective life could still be recovered a billion years hence by some other life form, which sifted through the artifacts and concluded that, all things considered, a nuclear arms race might not be such a good idea. Contemporary writers have not overlooked the ironic possibilities of this theme, as in Kurt Vonnegut's speculation that our species was created in order to manufacture a spare part for a passing spacecraft—a whimsy anticipated, to some extent, by Johnson's own review of Soame Jenyns. But the ironies inherent in defining the meaning of life as something fundamentally unrelated to the purposes and experiences of those who live it have tended to discourage the whole investigation. Not many people are willing to wait a billion years to find out whether what they are doing has any meaning.

It is not only extension into unlimited future time, the cosmic amortization of significance, that renders the meaning of life so hard to grasp. A still more intractable problem occurs in the present. I refer to the question of whether life is a field of vision or all the minute particulars that swarm in that field—the river or the motions of the fish within it, the container or the thing contained. Perhaps this problem can be made clearer by looking at one of the most famous modern definitions of life as it appears (or should appear) to the artist, the beautiful and influential postulates of Virginia Woolf. "Life is not a series of gig-lamps symmetrically arranged; life is a luminous halo, a semi-transparent envelope surrounding us from the beginning of consciousness to the end. Is it not the task of the novelist to convey this varying, this unknown and uncircumscribed spirit, whatever aberration or complexity it may display, with as little mixture of the alien and external as possible?"[11] The project

11. "Modern Fiction" (1925), in *Collected Essays* (London: Hogarth

is truly inspiring. But just how does one go about drawing a
semitransparent envelope or catching an unknown spirit or
determining what is external to it? Woolf's life work tries to
provide an answer. Above all she opposes "gig-lamps symmetrically arranged," an image referring in context to the art
of Arnold Bennett but, more broadly, to a state of mind she
associates with the eighteenth century. Orlando encounters
it during her memorable night ride through London with
Alexander Pope. "Lamp-posts lit with oil-lamps occurred
every two hundred yards or so, but between lay a considerable stretch of pitch darkness. Thus for ten minutes Orlando
and Mr. Pope would be in blackness; and then for about half
a minute again in the light. A very strange state of mind was
thus bred in Orlando."[12] Bemused by this partial enlightenment, she imagines in the darkness that Mr. Pope is handsome and that whatever is, is right, only to be shocked
awake each time they pass a lamp. A better artist, Woolf
implies, would have to carry a flashlight or a halo by which
she could see in the dark. Pope and Bennett and Johnson
see only by gig-lamps, in brilliant but partial insights controlled by the prearranged forms and understandings that
blind them to what falls between.

Yet Woolf's alternative does not solve the problem. If
life is a semitransparent envelope, then the artist who claims
to capture it is doomed to disappointment. Inevitably she
will fill her pages with the contents of the envelope, with the
objects of consciousness rather than its essence, or at best
with some specially treated matter, opaque and undifferenti-
ated enough so that at times one may glimpse the shadow of
a halo flitting across it. Woolf succeeds at this project if anyone can. But not every reader would want to call it "life."
Some might reserve the term for the spirit itself, the laws
and principles that run through all the variations of behavior
and hold it steady. Some would identify "life" instead with
all the unpredictable, ceaselessly created materials that

Press, 1966), II, 106.
   12. *Orlando* (London: Hogarth Press, 1928), p. 185.

cannot be reduced to any rule. Some, like Woolf herself, might try to find a third term such as consciousness that takes in both spirit and matter, both the container and the thing contained.[13] (The "blood consciousness" of D. H. Lawrence, a secret of life that spills up from under rather than down from over, is another such third term.) Yet only a very few authors have faced the problem squarely, founding their search for the meaning of life on a full awareness of the difficulty: life is both a halo and what the halo illumines, an envelope and what it envelops, a narrative and the incidents it describes, a person's story and everything that resists being put into a story, the outside of experience and the inside. Samuel Johnson, I think, is one of those authors. And if, despite all the reasons that keep us from searching for the meaning of life or trusting those who do, I still maintain that Johnson's answers to the question are rich and interesting, one reason is that he does not underestimate the problem of how someone enclosed within life can see life as a whole.

Consider, as an epitome, one of his briefest and most explicit statements about life, *Rambler* 102. Like *The Vision of Theodore the Hermit*, which Johnson once called the best thing he ever wrote, it takes the form of an allegory. That form is not original. Johnson is clearly indebted to Addison's popular "Vision of Mirzah" (*Spectator* 159), and beyond that to the work that many scholars consider the most important single influence on eighteenth-century fiction, the so-called "Table of Cebes, or Picture of Human Life."[14] Nor did Johnson first invent the image that shaped

13. Woolf's struggles with the problems inherent in her definition of "life" have been used as the central organizing principle of her work by such critics as James Naremore, *The World Without a Self* (New Haven: Yale University Press, 1973).

14. See Carey McIntosh, *The Choice of Life* (New Haven: Yale University Press, 1973), pp. 109–116; Earl R. Wasserman, "Johnson's *Rasselas*: Implicit Contexts," *Journal of English and Germanic Philology (JEGP)*, 74 (1975), 1–25; and Lawrence Lipking, "Learning to Read Johnson: *The Vision of Theodore* and *The Vanity of Human Wishes*," *ELH,* 43 (1976), 517–537.

his vision. What then is life as he sees it? First of all, despite what you may have heard, life is definitely not a fountain—except in certain sections of the Far East. Life is of course a journey, and also a dream. The Rambler describes himself as falling asleep while meditating on a passage in Seneca, and reflecting "on the state of man, the incessant fluctuation of his wishes, the gradual change of his disposition to all external objects, and the thoughtlessness with which he floats along the stream of time."[15] Such musings on fluctuation and floating inevitably lull him into a reverie about the great ocean where all of us sail, trusting to infirm vessels and doomed to shipwreck. Some boats are borne into darkness or swept into whirlpools; others shatter on the Rocks of Pleasure. Hope offers false consolations, and Reason, the pilot, can extricate only a few. The picture is certainly grim. By substituting a sea voyage for the customary land journey of life, Johnson increases the hazards and minimizes the rewards. "The only advantage, which, in the voyage of life, the cautious had above the negligent, was, that they sunk later, and more suddenly."

Two points of this vision deserve special emphasis, for, although hardly unique to Johnson, they do recur in his allegories more often than in anyone else's. The first is the lack of any destination. The Rambler stays within the ancient form of his allegory, and does not allow his sailors to steer for the Isles of the Blest: "all that Hope ventured to promise, even to those whom she favoured most, was, not that they should escape, but that they should sink last." These pilgrims do not progress. Whether we attribute the darkness of Johnson's vision to his refusal to pollute sacred truths with fiction or to the native pessimism of which many contemporary readers accused the Rambler, he does not encourage much hope that the meaning of life will be found at its end. This admonition is quite consistent in Johnson.

15. *The Rambler*, ed. W. J. Bate and Albrecht B. Strauss, vol. 4, *The Yale Edition of the Works of Samuel Johnson* (hereafter cited as *Works*), (New Haven: Yale University Press, 1969), p. 179.

In an age when many people were obsessed by deathbed conversions and famous last words, when Boswell haunted Hume's bedside on the chance of hearing his soul recant as it flew out, and when Edward Young based his theory of criticism on Addison's Christian version of the dying Cato, Johnson regards such stories as pleasing fables—neither to be rejected nor accepted out of hand. The issue remains in God's hands, and earth is not the right place to look for guarantees of happiness.[16] In general, Johnson's *Lives* are notably reserved about drawing conclusions. They tend not to speculate about the "meaning" or ultimate happiness of the lives they survey; they report the death gravely and simply, without further words. Johnson saves his most brutal irony for the notion that human hopes can be fulfilled. Thus John Philips, after his first success, "grew probably more confident of his own abilities, and began to meditate a poem on *The Last Day*, a subject on which no mind can hope to equal expectation." Only one sentence can follow: "This work he did not live to finish."[17] The voyage of life arrives at no shelter or harbor. Nor did Johnson consider himself immune from this vision. No more than others did he know where he was going. As he wrote to his friend John Taylor, "Is not mine a kind of life turned upside down? Fixed to a spot when I was young, and roving the world when others are contriving to sit still, I am wholly unsettled. I am a kind of ship with a wide sail, and without an anchor."[18]

16. A few scholars, most recently Donald Greene, have used Sermon 5 as evidence that Johnson believes "that of course the good life is possible here on earth" (Greene, "Johnson, Stoicism, and the Good Life," in *The Unknown Samuel Johnson*, ed. John J. Burke, Jr., and Donald Kay [Madison, Wisconsin: University of Wisconsin Press, 1983], p. 32). But as Paul K. Alkon remarks, the optimism of this sermon "is only the most extreme of Johnson's various homiletic departures from his more characteristic attitudes" (*Samuel Johnson and Moral Discipline* [Evanston: Northwestern University Press, 1967], p. 204).

17. *Lives*, I, 314.

18. November 16, 1775, in *The Letters of Samuel Johnson*, ed. R. W. Chapman (Oxford: Clarendon Press, 1952), II, 90.

Thus Johnson imagines his life in terms of his own allegory. Rather than use his dream as a defense against the world, he wakes to find it truth. That is a second recurring feature of Johnson's visionary mode: the tendency of the vision to dissolve, abolishing the distance between reader and subject or author and text. The name of the dream is life. Hence *Rambler* 102 concludes not with shipwreck but dreamwreck, as the author becomes a character in his own fiction. "As I was looking upon the various fate of the multitude about me, I was suddenly alarmed with an admonition from some unknown Power, 'Gaze not idly upon others when thou thyself art sinking. Whence is this thoughtless tranquillity, when thou and they are equally endangered?' I looked, and seeing the Gulph of Intemperance before me, started and awaked." The voyage was "only" a dream. But unlike the standard effect of this device, relief at having escaped the cul-de-sac of a nightmare, Johnson's effect increases anxiety by projecting the nightmare beyond the moment of waking. The true dreamers are those who do not think that they are participating in this dream. It surrounds us through all our lives, encompassing both the reader and what he reads, the author and his fiction. We lift our eyes from the page to the voyage around us.

At the same time, Johnson turns to discredit fiction itself. The dream has lulled the dreamer despite its truth. By associating his vision with idle gazing, and perhaps with the fatal Intemperance that swallows all who luxuriate in their dreaming, the Rambler renounces any claim of superiority to the victims he has described. Indeed, his own abilities do not suffice even to wake him from idleness or convey a proper moral. The use of "some unknown Power" for that purpose may seem inartistic, a casual *deus ex machina*. Yet Johnson does not trust human beings to reach the truth in any other way (*The Vision of Theodore* ends with a similar admonition from a heavenly "Protector"). Fiction cannot cure fiction nor dreaming wake dreamers. Caught within life, or reading with "thoughtless tranquillity," both author and reader struggle in vain to win some better perspective. A limitless gulf opens at the moment that writing ends, when the claim that the author has "awaked" remains to be proved by his future conduct. Thus Johnson's vision teaches the futility of visions, unless some Power should intervene to carry revelation into a waking state. The irony goes deep into Johnson's view of life. It includes not only the special circumstances of allegory, whose technique of saying one thing while meaning another sometimes arouses his doubts, but the predicament of every form of writing. Stated most radically, the predicament is this: life consists of everything that cannot be known from books. By definition, therefore, the author removes himself from the mainstream of life in the process of sitting down to write about it, and the reader abandons living in order to read. Literature stands apart from the passing world. This point is enforced in the *Dictionary* by both quotations that Johnson selects to illustrate the sense of "life" as "common occurences; human affairs; the course of things":

> This I know, not only by reading books in my study, but also by experience of *life* abroad in the world.
> —Ascham

> Not to know at large of things remote
> From use, obscure and subtile; but to know
> That which before us lies in daily *life*,
> Is the prime wisdom.

The choice of this last quotation, from Book VIII of *Paradise Lost*, is especially droll, since Johnson likes to regard Milton himself as the perfect type of a bookish author, out of touch with ordinary life: "He had read much and knew what books could teach; but had mingled little in the world, and was deficient in the knowledge which experience must confer."[19] Not all Milton's learning, nor Adam's, amounted to much with their wives.

19. *Lives*, I, 189.

The opposition between books and life strikes Johnson with a force that writing cannot contain. He views it not only as the most difficult predicament of authorship but as the major moral predicament of authors' lives. Like Milton, most men of learning and men of letters seem all too ready to mistake their reading for wisdom. They reduce the meaning of life to hermeneutics. Johnson's most eloquent statement of this situation, Sermon 8, on the text "Be not wise in your own conceits," specifically associates the temptations of men of learning with the hazards on the voyage of life. "As they are, by their abstraction and retirement, secluded from the gaieties, the luxuries, and the pageantries of life, they are willingly persuaded to believe, that because they are at a great distance from the rocks on which conscience is most frequently wrecked, that therefore they sail with safety, and may give themselves to the wind, without a compass."[20] They are of course wrong; the rocks that await them are subtle but very sharp. Every scholar can profit from reading this sermon. Yet Johnson does not mean to disparage book learning. What he stresses, instead, is that books and life depend on each other in spite of their divorce. An odd or impossible couple, they quarrel and embrace, they support and contradict one another at the same time. Thus books cannot teach us about life but alone can define its meaning, and life stays outside of books but is responsible for everything valuable in them. They contain each other and are the thing contained.

This paradoxical logic helps to account for much of Johnson's own effort as an author. In the face of his knowledge that imaginative literature is as distinct from life as dreams from reality or the golden world of legend from the quotidian world, he tries to build commerce between them. It is a heroic task. Indeed, according to one prevailing modern view of writing, the task seems Herculean not only in its difficulty but in its impossibility or foolishness, since writing can refer only to other writing and "life," as

20. *Sermons*, ed. Jean Hagstrum and James Gray, *Works* (1978), XIV, 87.

soon as it enters a text, collapses into a word among words, one more object for textual analysis. Johnson asks writing to be something other than itself, to do something it is not equipped to do. Thus Paul Fussell's engaging book *Samuel Johnson and the Life of Writing* betrays, in its very title, a slipping away from Johnson's enterprise. The life of writing is not life; it depends on "the force of genre" and must not be mistaken for the unformed, illiterate life that may or may not exist outside of writing. Starting from this premise, Fussell naturally finds Johnson often confused or "richly inconsistent." All the modern critic's affection for his subject cannot keep his tone from sounding patronizing at times. But Fussell himself creates the inconsistencies he finds.[21] Few authors are more consistent than Johnson. The contradiction between life and writing where the modern critic ends is the point at which Johnson begins, the problem he sets out to solve. And if Johnson cannot be said to have solved that problem once and for all, neither can it be said that modern theories of intertextuality have proved very satisfactory at accounting for Johnson. We need some opening to life that texts do not close off.

One limited way to describe Johnson's effort would focus on matters of style. As he himself viewed his place in English literature, and more particularly as a periodical writer, he judged his contribution less as the discovery of truth than as the development of a style to convey that truth to readers. He took pride in his labors to refine the language. "Something, perhaps, I have added to the elegance of its construction, and something to the harmony of its cadence."[22] Earlier authors had had an easier task. Before Addison, for instance, "if the writers for the theatre are excepted, England had no masters of common life." The authors of that generation, therefore, were obliged only

---

21. See James L. Battersby, *Rational Praise and Natural Lamentation* (Rutherford, N. J.: Fairleigh Dickinson University Press, 1980), pp. 63–105.
22. *Rambler* 208, in *Works*, V, 319.

to teach readers about life as clearly as possible. Swift had excelled in this style and thus deserved praise, "though perhaps not the highest praise," according to Johnson. "For purposes merely didactick, when something is to be told that was not known before, it is the best mode, but against that inattention by which known truths are suffered to lie neglected it makes no provision; it instructs, but does not persuade."[23] Johnson adapted his own style to persuasion. He had to find new methods or new cadences to refresh the meaning of life for those who had forgotten or neglected it. One of the best of Johnson's early critics, George Gleig, follows this line of thought to a properly Johnsonian conclusion: "There are very few moral truths in the *Spectator* or in the *Rambler* of which the reader can be totally ignorant; but there are many which may have very little influence on his conduct, because they are seldom the objects of his thought. If this be so, that style should be considered as best which most rouses the attention, and impresses deepest in the mind the sentiments of the author: and therefore, to decide between the style of Addison and that of Johnson, the reader should compare the effects of each upon his own memory and imagination, and give the preference to that which leaves the most lasting impression."[24] On these grounds, Gleig implies, Johnson will win the palm.

Are the grounds valid, however? The ambition to rouse the attention and impress the mind of the reader seems noble, but it also relies on the reader's cooperation. Not every modern reader considers Johnson's style especially compelling. Indeed, of the acknowledged masterpieces in English, one might venture to guess, perhaps none has been read through lately by fewer readers than *The Rambler.* If the test of style is to shock us into attention, then many current masters of English far surpass Johnson (the criterion of a lasting impression is of course another matter).

23. *Lives*, III, 52.
24. *Johnson: The Critical Heritage*, ed. James T. Boulton (London: Routledge & Kegan Paul, 1971), p. 73.

Moreover, Johnson's and Gleig's firm distinction between style and truth (or form and content) has fallen into bad repute since the eighteenth century. Surely style and truth modify each other in the very process of composition, as the Romantics insisted and almost every freshman composition teacher now repeats. If Johnson had nothing new to say, all the style in the world could not tempt us to read him. Finally, modern theorists might point out that Gleig's criteria appeal to something outside literature—not only to readers but to "moral truths" and "conduct"—as the test of literature. Once again we are thrown back on *life*. But style pertains to qualities of writing, and writing has no means of transcending itself.

All these objections make sense in their own terms, and they also pose in different ways the relation of container to thing contained that is so central to my argument about the meaning of life. Yet as Johnson would say, an appeal is always open from theory to experience, and the experience of reading the *Rambler* essays does indeed support the grounds invoked by Gleig. We cannot respond to these essays merely as pieces of writing. They ask instead for an active reading, absorbed and reflective, in which the reader at every point compares his or her own way of living with the life described in the text. Thus an essay like *Rambler* 11, on the folly of anger, will have failed of its effect for someone who regards it as the sort of thing that happens only to other people, like Ajax. The essay begins to work only when the reader enters and entertains it, associating its analysis with some half-forgotten private experiences and realizing, perhaps with surprise, his or her own susceptibility. Johnson helps us locate each of the vices somewhere in ourselves. Just how he does this is not easy to determine. He does not confess his own failings in any overt way (though the constant, almost imperceptible undercurrent of self-reference is one of the traits that most endear these essays to Johnsonians), nor does he lure us in with many anecdotes or vivid pictures of evil. The best reason I can give for the success of these essays is simply their moral intelligence. That is, they persuade us we are capable of doing wrong by showing us the logic of our involvement with terrible clarity, tracing the passion firmly from its birth to its consequences, and never allowing us to feel superior to either the victim or the moralist. The teachings themselves are familiar but not the intelligence with which they are rendered. As with Rilke's torso of Apollo, there is no place that the steady gaze does not see us, quietly insisting that we must change our lives.

The effect I have been trying to register may appear not only extra-literary but rather banal. It has become a commonplace of reader-response criticism, in recent years, to sketch the process by which authors like Spenser, Shakespeare, or Milton lure their readers into an identification with sin, thus proving the moral warning on their own pulses. Personally I have never been convinced by such arguments. With a subtlety of thematic and rhetorical analysis that not even modern readers can agree on, they project contemporary sophistications back into history and assume that earlier readers were as unsuspecting as young Americans of their own sinfulness. Surely Milton must have had a hard time surprising someone who had already read St. Augustine with a sense of original sin. Moreover, the mingling of fiction with sacred truth, so often reproved by Johnson, would become much more pernicious if the author conceived his work as seducing the audience into sympathy (however temporary) with Duessa or Iago or Satan. Such responses might contaminate imaginative literature itself. The Rambler sets himself a sterner task. He never makes vice attractive for an instant (that is one reason, of course, why many people do not read him today), and he takes great pains to distinguish it from virtue even in the hardest cases (like that of Richard Savage). Rather than seduce his readers, he tries to dispel all illusions, leaving all us poor sinners naked. Worse yet, he calmly persuades us to strip ourselves.

Thus Johnson attempts to pursue his readers beyond the page, back into daily life. As a periodical writer, entitled to the attention of his subscribers twice a week over a period of two years, he assumes the role of a seasoned companion, whose calls to conscience are hardly to be avoided even during vacations. As a writer of lives, he does not allow the public to linger on a vision of greatness, but issues constant reminders that poets stub their minds on petty domestic grievances as frequently as the rest of mankind. As a literary critic, he holds Shakespeare himself accountable to "the writer's duty to make the world better," and praises him above all for drawing his characters from life rather than from the closet, "a vigilance of observation and accuracy of distinction which books and precepts cannot confer."[25] As a poet, he directs us to turn our eyes from dreams of glory to the world of patrons and jails, returning us to the daily vexations that most poetry tries to escape. Sermons, in Johnson's canon, do not occur only on Sundays. The reader must be followed into the street, the marketplace, the coffeehouse, and the private chambers of the soul as it kills time on Monday and Tuesday. Johnson seems to be watching over our shoulders.

The reader that Johnson molds, therefore, will carry him everywhere and attend to his tutelage even after the particular works that convey it have been forgotten. The text is consumed and passes, the lesson continues. The best Johnsonians learn not only snappy quotations—the random change of his life—but how to think like him and how he views life as a whole. That is what W. Jackson Bate means, I suppose, when he concludes that "it does not minimize Johnson's criticism or indeed his writing on human experience itself to say that his ultimate greatness lies in the example they provide."[26] The writing erases itself to diffuse through the reader. Hence Johnson becomes the container and thing contained: simultaneously a mode of thinking and the object of that thought, an example of something and the something it exemplifies, an instance of life and the life that gives it meaning. We wake from a book like *Rasselas* to discover that we are in it.

25. "Preface to Shakespeare" (1765), in *Johnson on Shakespeare*, ed. Arthur Sherbo, *Works* (1968), VII, 88.
26. *The Achievement of Samuel Johnson* (New York: Oxford University Press, 1955), p. 233.

But what is the *meaning* of life? Insofar as this analysis rings true at all, it suggests that a full Johnsonian answer would focus not only on the particular trials and duties that test us at every hour (the sort of answer that finds the meaning of life in the effort to be a decent human being) nor on the ultimate truths in whose light our petty problems fade away (the sort of answer that finds the meaning of life in the love that moves the sun and the other stars) but on the unending tension and commerce between them (the sort of answer that finds the meaning of life in the peculiar human tendency to try to reconcile individual behavior with universal law). That is why Johnson thinks that the injunction to *know thyself* "may be said to comprise all the speculation requisite to a moral agent. For what more can be necessary to the regulation of life, than the knowledge of our original, our end, our duties, and our relation to other beings?"[27] To be acquainted with oneself requires the ability to view life at once from the inside and the outside, in the light of one's private motives and final ends. And it also requires the will to act on that knowledge.

Thus Johnson tests the sages by what they do. One of the most poignant and comic moments of *Rasselas* occurs in chapter 18 when "the prince finds a wise and happy man," a professor who proves by inexorable logic that the man of reason "walks on calmly through the tumults or privacies of life, as the sun persues alike his course through the calm or the stormy sky." A few days later the death of a daughter has sunk this philosopher into inconsolable grief. "'Have you then forgot the precepts, said Rasselas, which you so powerfully enforced? Has wisdom no strength to arm the heart against calamity? Consider, that external things are naturally variable, but truth and reason are always the same.' 'What comfort, said the mourner, can truth and reason afford me? of what effect are they now, but to tell me, that my daughter will not be restored?'" The moral is painfully clear. As Imlac points out, the teachers of morality

27. *Rambler* 24, in *Works*, III, 130.

"discourse like angels, but they live like men." Yet we should not be too quick to put Johnson on the side of the angels. The philosopher's pain is not the end but the beginning of wisdom. Rather than discrediting his teaching, it pushes it back into life, where truth and reason endure a trial by combat. Such trials go on forever. That is the meaning of life.

How useful is Johnson's conception? Does it still provide a perspective from which a discourse about the meaning of life might be renewed, without embarrassment or irony, to guide not only what we study but how we live? I will not pretend that I can answer those questions. To state only one objection: what is the perspective that allows an author to view his own perspective from outside? When the Rambler wakes at the end of his vision of life, is he not himself a higher power that has invented the higher Power that wakes him? How can this circle be broken? Such problems have haunted our thought for at least a century, and not even Johnson can prove that we are dreaming. So be it. No one promised us that life would be easy.

Yet the use of "life" as a favored term of analysis, if not as a privileged answer to all questions, does have its advantages; with them I shall conclude. Much of the history of philosophy, we remarked before, might be viewed as a war over terms. The supreme maneuver of these battles consists of outflanking; that is, the philosopher tries to prove that *his* terms surround and include all the others. More recently, a strategy has been developed that denies that the crucial terms are terms at all, or words like other words. Thus Nietzsche described first the Dionysian, and later the will to power, as something prior to and ungraspable by language; Heidegger fiercely resisted the whole course of history that had blasted the root of *Sein*; and Derrida (surely one of the most gifted outflankers of all time) has somewhat puzzlingly denied that "différance which was not a word before he used it, could ever be reduced to a word in the future. All these terms (if terms they are) serve a double purpose: they point to the imprisonment or binding of thought by the frame of language, and they try, by "thinking" that frame in turn, to achieve some perspective upon it. It is not my business here to weigh their success. But it *is* my business to try to think about life, or even to "think life," and Johnson may help me to think what that thinking means.

The strength of "life," from this point of view, lies in its passive resistance to any fixed meaning. Life is the question we ask, the answer to that question, and whatever is missing from the answer; the container, the contained, and the uncontainable. Hence the meaning of Johnson's allegory of voyage might be considered the series of disasters it pictures, the picture itself as an "image of life," or the postwaking state in which new and unpredictable disasters will shortly occur. We cannot limit such meanings. When life is outflanked it takes in the outflanker as well as the formless events that have no flanks. The price of such flexibility, of course, is a flirtation with meaninglessness. Perhaps the ultimate difficulty (and fascination) in finding the meaning of life stems from a definition of life as precisely that which does not mean but *is.* No wonder that philosophers and literary theorists do not want to talk about it. It breaks the conversation by denying that anything at all—the light streaming through the seminar curtains, the pipes on the table, the politics of the participants, the unborn, the bottom of the sea—can be excluded as irrelevant. And it also invites all the people outside the room, however unqualified at making sense, to compare what is being said with their own experiences. The experts on life are surely a motley crew. Francis Barber, Mrs. Williams, Robert Levet—can we allow faces like this around our table?

Samuel Johnson does. For the final advantage in using "life" as a term of analysis is not its defensiveness but its generosity, not its strategic imperviousness to being captured but its willingness to surrender to any questioner who is not too proud or foolish to admit being part of the voyage. To ask for the meaning of life, to criticize language for what it leaves out, may entangle us in absurdities, or even in The

Absurd.[28] But what does it mean to fail to ask the question? We do not find our way by closing our eyes. The modern tendency to sort things by function or structure, to parse "life" according to grammar, has had its own brilliant successes. Yet a different light falls as soon as we leave the room. There Johnson is waiting for us. He does not intend to relieve us of problems, or even to whisper a secret. The meaning of life is no secret. It is the confusion we live in, as well as the answers we find, and the test of the one by the other. We will not solve it but live it, and sometimes enjoy and endure. Perhaps Samuel Johnson can help.

28. According to Greene, "Johnson, Stoicism, and the Good Life," p. 31, no one has yet applied the term "absurd" to Johnson, and that is proper so long as we equate the term with the notion that "life is pointless and therefore not worth living." But few authors have examined "The Absurd" more thoroughly than Johnson, if we adopt Thomas Nagel's definition of the term as "the collision between the seriousness with which we take our lives and the perpetual possibility of regarding everything about which we are serious as arbitrary, or open to doubt" (*Mortal Questions* [Cambridge: Cambridge University Press, 1979], p. 13).

MARTINE WATSON BROWNLEY

Johnson's *Lives of the English Poets* and Earlier Traditions of the Character Sketch in England

James Boswell in *The Life of Samuel Johnson* noted Johnson's habit of "quite unexpectedly" producing "one of the many sketches of character which were treasured in his mind" and praised "the strong, yet nice portraits which he often drew" of the varied characters he had met.[1] Frances Reynolds, too, wrote that "Dr. Johnson seem'd to delight in drawing characters; and when he [did so] *con amore*, delighted everyone that heard him."[2] What Johnson did so effectively in conversation he did equally well in writing. With his wide knowledge of human nature, his psychological insight, his powers of observation, his sympathetic imagination, and his powerfully condensed expression, he found the character sketch a form particularly congenial to his abilities. Thus when he wrote the *Lives of the English Poets*, he

---

1. *Boswell's Life of Johnson*, ed. George Birkbeck Hill, rev. L. F. Powell, 6 vols. (Oxford: Clarendon Press, 1934–1950), III, 20; hereafter cited as *Life*.

2. "Recollections of Dr. Johnson by Miss Reynolds," *Johnsonian Miscellanies*, ed. George Birkbeck Hill, 2 vols. (1897; reprint, New York: Barnes and Noble, 1966), II, 270.

produced character sketches which far surpassed previous
efforts in earlier collections.

By the time Johnson's series of lives appeared, the basic
tripartite structure which he used—a chronological life, a
character sketch, and a section on the author's works—was
not uncommon. In addition to Fontenelle, among Johnson's
English predecessors, Giles Jacob, Elizabeth Cooper, and
Robert Shiels ("Theophilus Cibber" et al.) show at least
traces of the form in some of their entries.[3] Even John
Ward's *Lives of the Professors of Gresham College* (1740),
which Johnson owned,[4] employed this kind of structure. But
most of the sections on character in such collections, in
many cases merely scattered remarks or a line or two, were

3. Paul Hanchock ("The Structure of Johnson's *Lives*: A Possible
Source," [*Modern Philology*, 74 {1976}, 75–77]) notes that among classical
writers, only Diogenes Laertius uses the tripartite structure, although he
slightly overstates the consistency of its appearance in the *Lives of the Philosophers*. Because of Johnson's own remark about the French Miscellanies in
the prefatory note to the *Lives* (*Lives of the English Poets*, ed. George Birkbeck Hill, 3 vols. [Oxford: Clarendon Press, 1905], I, xxvi; hereafter cited
within the essay by volume and page number), Hawkins' reference to the
Countess D'Aunois and Langbaine, Winstanley, and Jacob (*The Life of
Samuel Johnson, LL.D*, ed. and abr. Bertram H. Davis [New York: Macmillan, 1961], p. 237), and Johnson's discussion of Shiels in the "Life of Ham-
mond" (II, 312), either Fontenelle's *Recueil* or Shiels has tended to be
credited as the source of Johnson's structure. A single source is unlikely,
because of the number of precedents—at least skeletally—for his format.
On Fontenelle, see Lawrence Lipking, *The Ordering of the Arts in Eighteenth-
Century England* (Princeton: Princeton University Press, 1970), pp.
415–417, 419, 422. For other precedents, see Lipking, pp. 417–419,
422–428; Robert Folkenflik, *Samuel Johnson, Biographer* (Ithaca: Cornell
University Press, 1978), pp. 97–117; William R. Keast, "Johnson and
'Cibber's' *Lives of the Poets*, 1753," in *Restoration and Eighteenth-Century
Literature: Essays in Honor of Alan Dugald McKillip*, ed. Carroll Camden
(Chicago: University of Chicago Press, 1963), pp. 89–101; Walter Raleigh,
Six Essays on Johnson (Oxford: Clarendon Press, 1910), pp. 98–127; James
L. Battersby, "Johnson and Shiels: Biographers of Addison," *Studies in
English Literature*, 9 (1969), 521–537.

4. Donald Greene, *Samuel Johnson's Library: An Annotated Guide*, ELS
Monograph Series, no. 1 (Victoria: University of Victoria, 1975), p. 115.
Ward does, however, usually cover the works in a list and sometimes adds
accounts of the surviving family at the end of entries.

rudimentary compared to Johnson's. For parallels with his practice in the *Lives*, critics have turned to earlier sketches, particularly those developed in English during the seventeenth century: Theophrastan characters, portraits by historians and biographers, and the characters of John Dryden in *An Essay of Dramatic Poesy*.[5] Seeing Johnson's knowledge of his predecessors who wrote character sketches, and comparing their practices with his, can suggest some of the ways in which he worked with and against traditional conventions to evolve a form in the *Lives* uniquely suited to convey his own beliefs about human character and its presentation in biography.

As English collections of literary biographies developed from the catalogues of John Leland, John Bale, and John Pits, and from the abbreviated notices of Edward Phillips and William Winstanley, the character sketch was a natural addition. The common structure of biographical accounts was a chronicle of the deeds and events of a man's life followed by a section on his character. By the early 1680s, John Evelyn in his *Life of Mrs. Godolphin* referred to this bipartite organization as the "Usual Method."[6] Many of Johnson's own biographies before the *Lives* use this format, whether he adapted them from sources (Sarpi, Baratier) or composed them himself (Savage, Cave, Browne, Ascham). Indeed, with the brief consideration of writings at the end of the character, the account of Browne very roughly suggests the basic structure which the *Lives* would take. Johnson's reference to himself at the end of his character sketch of Milton as "he who has now attempted to relate his [Milton's] Life" (I, 160) emphasizes his view of the character sketches as part of his biographical endeavors in the *Lives*, as does his comment in a letter: "I have undertaken to put before each

---

5. See, for example, Jean H. Hagstrum, *Samuel Johnson's Literary Criticism* (1952; reprint, Chicago: University of Chicago Press, 1967), pp. 38–41; Lipking, *Ordering of the Arts*, pp. 409, 420; Folkenflik, *Samuel Johnson*, pp. 100–101, 107.

6. Ed. Harriet Sampson (London: Oxford University Press, 1939), p. 84.

authour's works a sketch of his life, and a character of his writings."[7]

In England the practice of following a life with a separate character developed from the close connections of secular biography with historical writing; the saints' lives, in which deeds were the essence of character, had required no such distinction. Bacon, Dryden, and other commentators noted that lives were considered one branch of history, and throughout the seventeenth century there was a good deal of confusion and overlap between the two. (Even early in the eighteenth century, Edmund Smith describes Sprat as the "historian" of Cowley [I, 320].) When early seventeenth-century writers of history began to find the chronicle and the annal increasingly unsatisfactory forms, their most popular alternative was to structure works in terms of an individual monarch's life and reign. In 1633 Thomas May wrote that "It has beene a custome of old Historians, when they record the actions of great Princes, to deliver also some Characters of their persons and peculiar dispositions."[8] May's reference is probably not so much to his English predecessors as to the classical sources—Plutarch, Tacitus, Sallust, Suetonius, and others—from whom the various kinds of character sketches in English histories developed. Although Plutarch incorporated his depictions of character within the chronological framework of deeds, Suetonian biography provided some precedents for the division of public and private concerns. In the seventeenth century, Bacon, William Habington, and others enhanced their histories with a final set piece summarizing the monarch's character. Biographers, in turn, followed the historians' lead.

The bipartite organization reflected biography's dual task of providing both a historical account of the external facts of a person's life and a psychological interpretation of the inner workings of his or her personality. Johnson himself believed

7. *The Letters of Samuel Johnson*, ed. R. W. Chapman (Oxford: Clarendon Press, 1952), II, 186.

8. "The Description of King Henry the Second," in *The Reigne of King Henry the Second* (London: A. M., 1633), n.p.

that either approach alone was insufficient. He described biography as more than "a chronological series of actions or preferments,"[9] and he censured Sprat for giving only "the character, not the life of Cowley" (I, 1). The formal separation of life and character reflected certain assumptions about human beings expressed as early as Aristotle's *Poetics*, where the tragic character's role as an agent is distinguished from his traits as a person.[10] But the artificiality which the distinction could produce was emphasized by some early English biographies and histories in which the summary of facts about a life and the character sketch were written by two different authors.[11] Occasionally, writers objected to the assumption implicit in the format that what a person had done could be understood apart from a knowledge of what a person was. After his account of events in *The Life and Raigne of King Henry the Eighth*, Lord Herbert of Cherbury wrote that the king's "History will be his best Character and description."[12] Boswell similarly asserted at the end of the *Life* that "The character of SAMUEL JOHNSON has, I trust, been so developed in the course of this work, that they who have honoured it with a perusal, may be considered as well acquainted with him."[13] But for both writers the precedents were too strong. Lord Herbert somewhat grudgingly provided a character sketch of Henry, and even Boswell, so confidently revolutionary in many of his biographical practices, acquiesced in what he described as "expected" and

9. *Rambler* 60, in *The Rambler*, ed. W. J. Bate and Albrecht B. Strauss, *The Yale Edition of the Works of Samuel Johnson* (New Haven: Yale University Press, 1969), III, 322.

10. Aristotle, *Poetics*, trans. Ingram Bywater, in *Rhetoric and Poetics* (New York: Modern Library, 1954), pp. 231–232; see also O. B. Hardison, Jr., "A Commentary on Aristotle's *Poetics*," *Aristotle's Poetics* (1968; reprint, Tallahassee: University Presses of Florida, 1981), pp. 82–83, 123–126, 199.

11. Donald A. Stauffer, *English Biography Before 1700* (Cambridge: Harvard University Press, 1930), pp. 271–272.

12. (London: E. G., 1649), p. 570.

13. *Life*, IV, 424–425.

went on to "endeavour to acquit myself of that part of my
biographical undertaking."[14]

Even more problematical in early biographies than the
character's formal status as an almost autonomous and sometimes awkward appendix to *res gestae* was its tendency,
because of the association of biography with ethical instruction, to become hagiographical. In presenting Sir Matthew
Hales' character, Gilbert Burnet found "so much here to be
commended, and proposed for the imitation of others, that I
am afraid some may imagine I am rather making a picture of
him, from an abstracted idea of great virtues and perfections,
than setting him out as he truly was."[15] The effect Burnet
feared was precisely what most biographers produced in their
sketches of character. Roger North wrote that "One may
walk in a Gallery, and extract as fair an account from the air
of their Countenances or the cut of their whiskers" as from
"the many Scetches [*sic*] or profiles of great mens [*sic*]
lives."[16] Again, this tendency derives partly from early historians' practices; Bacon draws Henry VII in his character
sketch as a model politician. Johnson's description of Walton, one of his favorite writers, as a "great panegyrist"[17] and
his disapproval of Sprat's "funeral oration" for Cowley, with
its few details obscured by "the mist of panegyrick," show
his recognition of the pervasive tendency of biographers to
lose the real in the ideal (I, 1).

Much more realistic were the short sketches of individual
characters inserted in seventeenth-century histories, which
had appeared in England as early as Polydore Vergil and were
used by William Camden, Edward Hall, and others. These
developed directly from classical sources, particularly from
Tacitus, the single most important influence on the

14. *Life*, IV, 425.

15. "The Life and Death of Sir Matthew Hale," in *The Works, Moral and
Religious, of Sir Matthew Hale* (London: R. Wilks, 1805), I, 50.

16. Quoted from manuscript by James L. Clifford in "Roger North and
the Art of Biography," in *Restoration and Eighteenth-Century Literature*, p.
283.

17. *Life*, II, 364.

seventeenth-century historical character. Johnson knew the classical writers of the brief character, for he named Xenophon's "delineation of *characters* in the end of the first Book" of the *Anabasis* as "the first instance of the kind that was known."[18] (He was probably referring to the series of sketches of generals at the end of book 2 rather than to the single portrait of Cyrus near the end of book 1.) But as a whole, he seems to have been less interested in this kind of character sketch as such than in other more general methods of the classical writers. Plutarch and Suetonius, two of the writers who most influenced the *Lives*, do not usually write small set sketches of character. Although he had three editions of Tacitus in his library, Johnson disliked the style—he felt that Tacitus had written "notes for an historical work" rather than a history—and seems never to have mentioned Tacitus' characters.[19] He did admire one of Tacitus' own major influences, Sallust, and translated part of his *Bellum Catalinae*.[20] However, Sallust's extant writings contain relatively few brief characters. The *Cataline* includes sketches only of Sempronia and Cataline himself, along with a comparative sketch of the characters of Caesar and Cato (thereby providing yet another possible model for Johnson's famous comparison of Pope and Dryden, already overloaded with multiple imputations of influence). Although these characters are very fine, Sallust employs other methods of characterization—the set speech or the depiction of a typical action, for example—which are equally important, and in view of Johnson's general outlook toward classical depictions of character, it is quite likely that in Sallust he was particularly responding to these. But if Johnson showed little interest in the brief character sketches of the classical writers, the seventeeth-century English historians whom he praised are famous for their use of the form. Although he recognized the problems in Clarendon's style, he would

18. *Life*, IV, 31–32.
19. *Life*, II, 189.
20. *Rambler* 60, III, 321; *Life*, IV, 383, n. 2; see also *Life*, II, 79.

allow neither Robertson nor Hume "to be more to Clarendon, than a rat to a cat," and particularly commended "the
variety, distinctness, and strength of his characters."[21] Ber-
gen Evans points out that *Idler* 84, second only to *Rambler*
60 as a major source for Johnson's ideas of biography, was
probably suggested by the publication of Clarendon's *Life*.[22]
Its strength is in its characters, most of which are longer and
more finely crafted than those in Clarendon's original *History*. Despite a style which Johnson described as "mere
chit-chat," he considered Burnet's history "very entertaining" and especially praised the first part of it, which contains
many of Burnet's best characters.[23] Significantly, Burnet's
sketches are the most realistic (if the least artistic) among
those of the historians. Johnson also liked Raleigh, and
above all, he praised Knolles and noted his effective descriptions of character.[24]

Johnson's enthusiasm for these historians was thoroughly
justified. What they rendered in their sketches were men as
individuals, not general types or saintly models for emula-
tion. The historians' characters were not without occasional
moral overtones—the memorialist traditions of history
served partly emulative purposes, and Tacitus himself was
often viewed as a moralist in the seventeenth century—but
moral concerns seldom stifled realistic ones. These historians made the most important advances in the description of
complex human beings in English prose before the

21. *Life*, V, 57–58, n. 3; *Rambler* 122, IV, 290; see also *Life*, III,
257–258; IV, 311; II, 79.
22. "Dr. Johnson's Theory of Biography," *Review of English Studies*, 10
(1934), 301.
23. *Life*, II, 213; *Boswell's Journal of A Tour to the Hebrides*, ed. Frederick
A. Pottle and Charles H. Bennett (New York: Literary Guild, 1936), p. 253.
24. *Rambler* 122, IV, 289, 290. Knolles wrote the greater part of his history in terms of the lives of individual rulers, which often contain character
sketches at the end. Among the seventeenth-century historians, Johnson
also knew and liked Thuanus (Jacques Auguste de Thou) (*Rambler* 60, III,
321; *Life*, IV, 410). Although French influences on the character sketch,
from the romances and other sources, are important during the century,
Johnson seems to have been more interested in the English writers.

eighteenth-century novelists. Nevertheless, despite their achievements, they did not usually develop the whole character. Fully rounded depictions were unnecessary for establishing the roles individuals played in events, and overly detailed descriptions would disrupt rather than enhance the historical narrative. Clarendon's depiction of Waller in the *History of the Rebellion*, for example, focuses on the personal traits relevant to his political actions; he never mentions that Waller was a poet. For his "Life of Waller," Johnson turned to the more personal portrait in Clarendon's autobiography. The historians as a whole managed to distance the character sketch from hagiography, but their purposes limited their delineations in other ways.

The Theophrastan character, the succinct depiction of a type produced by early seventeenth-century writers, is inevitably mentioned in connection with Johnson's characters. The form is actually more important as an analogue and as one manifestation of a widespread approach to character than as a direct influence. Its extremely rapid rise and development—the first Theophrastan collection in English, Joseph Hall's, appeared in 1608, and Benjamin Boyce calls the form "perfectly developed by 1632"[25] —suggest both the self-contained quality and the lack of flexibility which limited its further applications. Johnson undoubtedly knew Theophrastus' characters, for Theophrastus himself makes an appearance in *Rambler* 173, and the "Life of Addison" (II, 95) mentions Eustace Budgell's Preface to *The Moral Characters of Theophrastus*. In various capacities Johnson also knew most of the English Theophrastans. He several times refers to "the famous Hall" as a satirist and controversialist, and he knew at least something of Sir Thomas Overbury from Savage's tragedy.[26] In the Hebrides he quoted from one of the characters in Samuel Butler's *Remains*, although he

25. *The Theophrastan Character* (Cambridge: Harvard University Press, 1947), p. 287.

26. *Lives*, I, 102, 229, 466; III, 251; II, 338–341.

does not mention Butler's characters in the *Life*.[27] The only notable—and rather surprising—omission seems to be the greatest English character writer, John Earles, whose stature as a Royalist ecclesiastic would also have appealed to Johnson. Nor does Johnson seem to have commented specifically on either Theophrastus' characters or the English ones. His lack of recorded interest in the form probably stemmed from the same attitudes that led him to object to decorum of type in drama in the "Preface to Shakespeare" and to the concept of the "ruling passion" in the "Life of Pope" (III, 173–175). The Theophrastan character, like dramatic characters drawn (and often quartered) by the rules or satirical characters shaped to reveal one motivation, oversimplified human beings. It was too artificial in its focus on one trait to be a "just representation" of the actual nature of every person as an individual. Johnson criticizes Fenton for giving Roscommon's writings "a character too general to be critically just."[28] In accounts of personal character, too, he disliked general rather than specific treatments.

What would have pleased Johnson about the Theophrastan character was its traditional association with morals. Although modern classicists see Theophrastus as a natural scientist recording his observations of human beings as descriptive data, the older critical view of him was as a moralist, the follower of Aristotle who illustrated his master's doctrine of the golden mean.[29] Isaac Casaubon, whose late sixteenth-century editions made Theophrastus widely available, claimed that Theophrastus' sole motivation

27. *Boswell's Journal*, p. 37; see *Life*, V, 57, n. 2.

28. *Early Biographical Writings of Dr. Johnson*, ed. J. D. Fleeman (Westmead: Gregg International, 1973), p. 387. Johnson corrects this literary character with his own, seconding "the judgment of the publick" (I, 239), at the end of the "Life of Roscommon".

29. Warren Anderson, *Theophrastus: The Character Sketches* (Kent: Kent State University Press, 1970), pp. xii-xviii; see also Boyce, *Theophrastan Character*, pp. 11–14.

for writing characters was the improvement of morals,[30] and Hall's and Earle's religious and spiritual emphases strengthened the moral connections. The very limitations of the Theophrastan character which lessened its realistic depiction of human beings made it useful for moral purposes, for its constricted focus could increase the monitory effect. In this sense it was similar to the characters traditional in religious writings, dating as far back as the portrait of the good woman in the last chapter of Proverbs and extending through medieval hagiography and the one-dimensional characters in morality plays to those in many sermons. With the homiletic and devotional writers Johnson was of course very familiar. William Law, the greatest eighteenth-century character writer in this tradition, is the obvious example. Johnson himself used such characters mainly when he wanted directly "to point a moral"—in his sermons, for example, and in characters such as the scholar in *The Vanity of Human Wishes.* Jean Hagstrum has noted that Imlac's description of the poet in *Rasselas* has affinities with the Theophrastan character, which was often extended in the seventeenth century to incorporate descriptions of occupational groups.[31]

With the character sketches attached to biographies, the short historical portraits, and the Theophrastan characters, the seventeenth century developed three ways of depicting character which differed in the numbers and kinds of traits they emphasized and thus in their degree of realism. Precisely establishing the literary influence which each form of the character separately exerted is extremely difficult, in some cases because of overlapping conventions and in others because of problems in ascertaining the relationships between the various branches of the character. The biographical character sketches and those in histories, for example, have some common roots in the classical writers, but because their differing purposes led to different kinds of development in each, their later effects on each other tend to

---

30. Boyce, *Theophrastan Character*, p. 160.
31. Hagstrum, *Samuel Johnson's Literary Criticism*, p. 40.

be general rather than specific. The rather stubbornly
independent Theophrastan form particularly illustrates the
overlaps. In addition to the homiletic characters, which are
themselves similar to certain depictions in Plutarch's
Moralia, the Theophrastan form has affinities with humor
characters in drama, which developed independently about
the same time, and also with later characters drawn in terms
of the theory of the "ruling passion." As Theophrastan
writers quickly exhausted the standard types and sought others, their portraits of professional and economic groups had
some resemblances to the earlier "Literature of the
Estates."[32] But despite the similarities, specific ties between
all of these forms remain unclear. Nor is it possible with any
certainty to limit particular influences to the Theophrastan
character. Rhetoric included formulas for depictions of
character—*effictio*, *notatio*, *ethopoeia*, *prosopopoeia*, and
descriptio, varying according to the commentator—and writing
a character had long been a common rhetorical exercise.[33]
Had the Theophrastan never appeared in England, the
humor characters and other forms would probably have produced many of the same effects in literature. It played a role
in encouraging succinctness in character depiction, but the
historical character, which almost surely would have
appeared without the Theophrastan, would have similarly
encouraged economy. The same is true for the polemical
characters of John Cleveland and others at midcentury,
which have strong ties to both the Theophrastan and the historical character. The constant qualifications necessary in
dealing with specific influences from the various kinds of
characters lead mainly to literary dead ends. It is of course
possible to see in a limited way the effects some individual
writers of characters had on each other. The historical character received enormous impetus early in the eighteenth century from the posthumous publication of Clarendon's

---

32. Boyce, *Theophrastan Character*, pp. 58–59, 67–69.
33. Ibid., p. 129; A. M. Kinghorn, *The Chorus of History* (London: Bland-
ford Press, 1971), p. 27; F. P. Wilson, *Seventeenth Century Prose* (Berkeley:
University of California Press, 1960), p. 13.

history: Burnet went back to his own history, still in manuscript, and revised his characters after reading Clarendon. Similarly, William Law's vivid characters in the *Serious Call* are reflected in certain of Johnson's characters in the *Rambler* and also occasionally in the *Idler*, which as a whole shows the lighter tones and more social emphases of Addison's and Steele's characters. These writers in their turn, as Johnson recognized, reflect La Bruyère, but when Gibbon in his *Memoirs* associates La Bruyère with Law,[34] the cycle is complete and the specific traditions increasingly indistinguishable.

Fortunately, clearer and much more important are certain general influences which the different kinds of character sketches exerted collectively. The seventeenth-century character writings reflected the assumptions of the period about the nature of human beings, but they also conditioned the ways in which subsequent authors would for a time treat character. Certain conventions in all of the sketches exerted literary pressure on other depictions of character, even as descriptions of characters in early eighteenth-century novels and biographies became longer and more complex. There was, for example, a tendency to show a moral bias, which came simultaneously from the Theophrastan character's association with morals, the biographical character's function as a model, and the emulatory and memorialist traditions of the historical character. The great strength of the character sketch as a genre was its ability to create a single unified impression of a person, whether as an individual or a type. The succinctness essential for producing this effect carried inherent limitations. Character sketches tended to be reductive. Each of the early forms, for differing reasons, oversimplified the human beings they depicted. The biographical character moved toward hagiography; the historical portrait emerged as *homo politicus*; the Theophrastan form could verge on caricature. All of the major forms of the

34. Edward Gibbon, *Memoirs of My Life*, ed. Georges A. Bonnard (New York: Funk and Wagnalls, 1969), p. 22.

character were in certain ways arbitrary, and all involved a certain level of abstraction, because of the deductive method writers usually employed. An author's concept of a character was imposed and illustrated, rather than exposed inductively. The brevity made complexity difficult to achieve; Henry Gally, in "A Critical Essay on Characteristic-Writings" (1725), emphasized that "An Author, in this Kind, must not dwell too long upon one Idea: As soon as the masterly Stroke is given, he must immediately pass on to another Idea."[35] Increasing the general tendency to sacrifice life to art in the character was the witty, aphoristic prose style traditionally associated with it. Hugh Blair pointed out that "characters are generally considered, as professed exhibitions of fine writing," and Gally quoted Casaubon's observation that the form was "a Medium between Moral Philosophy and Poetry."[36] Poetry too often tended to predominate. The stylistic demands of the genre as it evolved combined to pressure all writers on character to make their depictions more coherent and consistent than actual human nature could ever be.

The major writers of characters between the originators of the form in English and Johnson recognized that more effective depiction in character sketches would require greater individualization of their subjects. In poetry Pope and even Young in their satires presented more fully rounded characters, although, as Coleridge was one of the first to note, Pope's tendency to proceed deductively limited his effects.[37] Satire itself as a genre encouraged simplification of character and caricature. In the character sketch proper, La Bruyère, Addison, and Steele made enormous strides toward greater realism, introducing more variety and detail

---

35. In *The Moral Characters of Theophrastus* (London: John Hooke, 1725), p. 39.

36. Hugh Blair, *Lectures on Rhetoric and Belles Lettres* (Philadelphia: T. Ellwood Zell, 1833), p. 405; Gally, "Critical Essay," p. 7.

37. *Table Talk of Samuel Taylor Coleridge*, ed. Henry Nelson Coleridge (London: George Routledge, 1884), pp. 167–168.

into the genre.[38] Johnson knew these writers well and appreciated their accomplishments. Arthur Murphy called Johnson a "professed admirer" of La Bruyère,[39] whom Johnson praised for his "liveliness of description and justness of observation" (II, 93). One of Johnson's projected works, appropriately reflecting his interest in both classical and contemporary characters, was "Maxims, Characters, and Sentiments, after the manner of Bruyère, collected out of ancient authours, particularly the Greek, with Apophthegms."[40] Johnson emphasized the greater realism of characters in the *Spectator* and *Tatler* by pointing out that they were "not merely ideal," but "known, and conspicuous in various stations" (II, 95). Placing Addison "perhaps first of the first rank" as a "describer of life and manners," Johnson praises him with generous fullness in the *Life* (II, 148).

Despite Johnson's accolades, for his own purposes even these well-drawn characters retained traces of the shortcomings of the character sketch as a genre. He analyzed Addison's problems in developing the complexities suggested by the original presentation of Sir Roger de Coverley's character. At first Sir Roger is described as "having his imagination somewhat warped"; however, because "The variable weather of the mind"—always a subject of consuming interest to Johnson—"requires so much nicety to exhibit," Addison could not finally do creative justice to his conception (II, 97). Despite their increased individuality, the characters of La Bruyère, Addison, and Steele still showed traces of the type and derived part of their value as representatives of classes. For Johnson, they were also deficient in a certain

38. On these, see Edward Chauncey Baldwin, "La Bruyère's Influence Upon Addison," *PMLA*, 19 (1904), 479–495, and Margaret Turner, "The Influence of La Bruyère on the 'Tatler' and the 'Spectator'," *The Modern Language Review*, 48 (1953), 10–16.

39. "An Essay on the Life and Genius of Samuel Johnson, LL.D.," in *Johnsonian Miscellanies*, I, 416. Boswell described Johnson as drawing "the character of a rapacious Highland chief with the strength of Theophrastus or La Bruyère" (*Boswell's Journal*, p. 372).

40. *Life*, IV, 382, n. 2.

seriousness and depth, the nature of which is suggested by
his chastising Hester Thrale for "preferring La Bruyère to
the Duc de Rochefoucault."[41] Even as he lauded Addison
and Steele as "master[s] of common life" who "taught . . .
the most important duties and sublime truths" (II, 93, 96),
many of his descriptions suggest the limitations he saw in
their approach. They were "judge[s] of propriety"; they
"adjusted . . . the unsettled practice of daily intercourse by
propriety and politeness"; their aims were "To teach the
minuter decencies and inferior duties, to regulate . . .
conversation, to correct those depravities which are rather
ridiculous than criminal" (II, 93, 95, 92). The connections
are primarily Horatian. The word "elegance," a term of
high praise but also with certain limits for Johnson, recurs in
his commentary.[42] As the type character became more indivi-
dualized, the danger was that the concern with morals traditional in the character sketch could degenerate into a concern
with manners. What Johnson viewed as less essential elements in man would come to the fore. In discussing contemporary novels and plays, he noted that "there is all the
difference in the world between characters of nature and
characters of manners"; though he considered characters of
manners "very entertaining," he felt that they required less
ability than characters of nature, where "a man must dive
into the recesses of the human heart."[43] He described
Addison as knowing "the heart of man from the depths of
stratagem to the surface of affectation" (II, 121). Johnson
knew these same areas of the human heart, but he also knew
far deeper levels of consciousness where the comedy and
farce of Addison's "stratagem" and "affectation" became

41. Hester Lynch Piozzi, *Anecdotes of the the Late Samuel Johnson, LL.D.*,
in *Johnsonian Miscellanies*, I, 334.

42. Hagstrum, *Samuel Johnson's Literary Criticism*, pp. 130–131; 134–135;
196–197.

43. *Life*, II, 48–49. See also *Johnson on Shakespeare*, ed. Arthur Sherbo,
The Yale Edition of the Works of Samuel Johnson (New Haven: Yale University Press, 1969), VIII, 973–974.

stark tragedy. For his characters, like his essays, he found in Addison and Steele models not entirely sufficient.

One particular advantage the character sketch had for Johnson as he began to write his own in the *Lives* was that through a century of development, it had remained a fairly open form in content and internal structure. No rigid rules dictated either what could be included in it or the order in which information had to be given. Descriptions of appearance, for example, often surfaced first, but this procedure seems to reflect the natural human tendency to move from the exterior to the interior, from the most obvious to the more complex, rather than any critical dicta on organization. Thus the form of Johnson's sketches could be adapted to whatever information he had or wanted to use for his own purposes. For Collins, he simply went back to the memoir he had written for *The Poetical Calendar* in 1763. Though most of his character sketches occur between the life and the criticism, a few appear at the end, and occasionally, as in the "Life of Pitt," Johnson mixed life, character, and criticism throughout. He used the character sections in a variety of ways. Not all of the *Lives* include character sketches. Sometimes, as he often expressly regretted, he lacked enough information to draw a character (Denham, Butler, Otway, Pomfret, Blackmore, Somerville, West, and Dyer). In the cases of the rather ironic duo of Watts and Rochester, Johnson viewed the poet's character as so central in the life that his biographical section covered it thoroughly enough to make a separate sketch unnecessary. In addition, with Rochester, as perhaps also with Akenside, Johnson had no desire to review the character in detail. He inserted a physician's account of Lyttleton's death to "spare me the task of his moral character" (III, 454). In the "Life of Sprat," an anecdote from Johnson's father about Sprat's and Burnet's sermons replaced the character sketch. With Halifax and Granville, he used the section to discuss how praise due to a person or his position sometimes redounds upon his work. Johnson seldom worried about proportions. One sentence quoted from Pope covered the ineffectual Gay, while two sentences served for Dorset.

In his *Dictionary* Johnson had defined character as a
"representation of any man as to his personal qualities,"[44]
and his sections on character in the *Lives* are sketches not so
much of writers as of men. The famous discussion of Pope's
"intellectual character" (III, 216), which culminates in the
comparison with Dryden, has tended to obscure the fact that
the great majority of Johnson's character sketches cover only
personal concerns. His critical sections include a number of
succinct reviews of the major literary traits of a poet, which
Johnson occasionally calls "characters": various summaries
within the "Life of Cowley"; the "general character" of
Waller's poetry and of Addison's (I, 294; II, 127); the
"character" of Hughes's genius (II, 164); the "general survey of Dryden's labours" (I, 457); the final paragraphs in
the *Lives* of Sprat, Sheffield, John Philips, and Shenstone;
and many more. These literary characters are influenced by
Dryden's practice, particularly in the character of Shakespeare which Johnson so admired (I, 412). Dryden's
literary characters occupy a small side plot in the middle
ground between the Theophrastan and the historical character; realistic in their focus on an individual, like the Theophrastan they are limited to one characteristic and its
ramifications. But, because Dryden depicts minds and
talents rather than personalities, drawn primarily from the
works rather than the man,[45] his examples were useful to
Johnson in his character sections only with the few figures
for whom he includes strictly literary concerns (notably
Pope, Addison, Swift, and Savage). Although he is always
interested in an individual's mind, and he often includes a
poet's work habits, studies, and knowledge of literature,
Johnson's sketches are never primarily literary or intellectual. Several fine studies have shown how Johnson focuses
on one or a few important traits throughout all three sections

44. *A Dictionary of the English Language* (1755; reprint, New York: Arno
Press, 1979), fourth definition.
45. Hagstrum, *Samuel Johnson's Literary Criticism*, p. 41; his whole discussion of Johnson and these characters (pp. 38–41) is very good.

of certain individual *Lives*,[46] and there are relationships
between some of the authors' personal characteristics and
their works. John Philips' narrow and blameless life as
presented in his character sketch has obvious parallels with
his poetic achievement; the opening sentence of Parnell's
specifically literary character—"The general character of Parnell is not great extent of comprehension or fertility of
mind" (II, 54)—is meant to suggest the man as well as his
poems. But the exclusively personal emphases of most of
his character sketches are yet another reflection of Johnson's
extreme hesitancy in directly connecting a man's life and his
works.[47]

Certain conventions of the character sketch, such as the
satirical strokes and the antithetical style, were especially
congenial to Johnson's own literary tendencies. Characteristic of him, too, was the emphasis on morals associated with
the character, which he naturally reflected in these *Lives*
"written I hope in such a manner, as may tend to the pro-
motion of Piety."[48] If in Walton and other early biographers
Johnson had recognized how moral purpose could dilute
realistic depiction, from Law he learned how both could
combine to produce entertaining characters that also
instructed. In only a few sketches does Johnson fail to
render at least some kind of a moral judgment on any aspect
of the writer's behavior. He remarks that Gray's contempt is
"often employed, where I hope it will be approved, upon

46. Leopold Damrosch, Jr., *The Uses of Johnson's Criticism* (Charlottes-
ville: University Press of Virginia, 1976), pp. 133–134; 167–220 (Dryden,
Pope); Folkenflik, *Samuel Johnson, Biographer*, pp. 165–170 (Milton); James
L. Battersby, "Patterns of Significant Action in the 'Life of Addison'"
Genre, 2 (1969), 28–42. Lipking's treatment of the character sketch as a
narrative device for transition in the *Lives* is particularly good (*Ordering of
the Arts*, pp. 419–422), as are his sections on individual *Lives*.
47. On his hesitancy, see Hagstrum, *Samuel Johnson's Literary Criticism*, pp.
39–40; Lipking, *Ordering of the Arts*, p. 420; Damrosch, *Uses of Johnson's
Criticism*, pp. 126–127; Folkenflik, *Samuel Johnson, Biographer*, pp. 118–173.
48. *Diaries, Prayers, and Annals*, ed. E. L. McAdam, Jr., with Donald and
Mary Hyde, *The Yale Edition of the Works of Samuel Johnson* (New Haven:
Yale University Press, 1958), I, 294.

scepticism and infidelity," and inserts Gray's negative
account of Shaftesbury; he notes his own pleasure at
"recording the fraternal kindness of Thomson" (III, 432,
295). Even the single-sentence summaries to which the
characters of Tickell and King are reduced include moral
judgments. Moral concerns actually shape the structure of
the character sketches in certain *Lives*. Aside from his
appearance and conversation, the rest of Mallet's character
"sink[s] into silence" (III, 410) for moral reasons. One-
third of the entire sketch of Fenton is devoted to the story
of his kindness to an unfortunate relative, which Johnson
feels "ought not to be forgotten" (II, 263).

Johnson told Boswell that the "chief excellence" of family portraits was in their verisimilitude,"[49] and his strong
natural inclination toward the moral emphases of the character sketch was matched by his response to its realistic elements. Sallust, Suetonius, parts of Plutarch, the
seventeenth-century historians, La Bruyère, Addison, and
Steele offered specific examples of how to render the
significance of small details of character. The great strength
of Johnsonian biography is its insistence both on human
similitude—the basic "uniformity in the state of man"[50]
—and on human individuality—"The delicate features of the
mind, the nice discriminations of character, and the minute
peculiarities of conduct" (II, 116). Through both he powerfully combines the familiar and the novel to appeal simultaneously to man's self-love and his fascination with the
alien other. The biographical sections and the character
sketches in the *Lives* include both elements, but in general,
the uniformity among men tends to be more emphasized in
the events of a life and human individuality in the character
sketch. When in conversation about the *Lives* Johnson
explained that the "business" of an "exact biographer" was
"to give a complete account of the person whose life he is
writing, and to discriminate him from all other persons by

49. *Boswell's Journal*, p. 181.
50. *Rambler* 60, III, 320.

any peculiarities of character or sentiment he may happen to have,"[51] he seems to have been reflecting what he saw as the primary task of each of the first two sections of his biographies. The character sketches are used to preserve the small miscellaneous details of personality which, as Johnson lamented, were so easily forgotten that they had in the past too often been lost.[52] He particularizes in order to humanize, portraying the living man and his "behaviour in the lighter parts of life": "the private life and domestic manners," "social qualities," "familiar practices," "petty peculiarities," "slight amusements" (II, 198; I, 410; III, 206; II, 197; III, 197; I, 408). There is John Philips' "addiction to tobacco," Prior's "propensity to sordid converse," Swift's "muddy complexion," Ambrose Philips' "bravery and skill in the sword," Dryden's "great confidence" in astrology, Thomson's "very unskilful [*sic*] and inarticulate manner of pronouncing any lofty or solemn composition" (I, 316; II, 200; III, 55; III, 323; I, 409; III, 297). In offering what Johnson so admired in biography, "relations which are levelled with the general surface of life,"[53] the character sections depict everyday affairs with which the reader can identify, but they do so mainly to emphasize each poet's unique personal attributes. Even the assertion that Pope "passed through common life . . . with the natural emotions of common man" (III, 210) functions partly to highlight certain peculiarities in Pope's professed attitudes. Giles Jacob wrote in the preface to the second volume of his earlier collection of literary biographies that "If one considerable Character happens to resemble another in the following Work, where there are so many, 'tis no more than what is natural to

51. "Apophthegms, &c., from Hawkins' Edition of Johnson's Works," in *Johnsonian Miscellanies*, II, 3.

52. *Rambler* 60, III, 321–323; *Lives*, II, 116; "The Life of Sir Thomas Browne," in *Early Biographical Writings*, p. 452.

53. Samuel Johnson, *Idler* 84, in *The Idler and the Adventurer*, ed. W. J. Bate, John M. Bullitt, L. F. Powell, *The Yale Edition of the Works of Samuel Johnson* (New Haven: Yale University Press, 1963), II, 262.

expect."[54] Johnson's *Lives* produce no such effect, mainly because, as he infuses his sketches with particulars, the character section becomes his major vehicle for discriminating among the poets as individuals.

Johnson uses abundant particulars to heighten realism, but he manipulates details to create markedly different effects from those traditionally produced by the character sketch. His methods not only distinguish each poet as an individual, but they also specifically highlight the complexities and contradictions within each individual. His character of Sheffield, who got his religion from Hobbes, his attitudes toward women from the court of Charles II, and his principles about property from the gaming table, is naturally enough negative, but Johnson ends by mentioning Sheffield's tenderness and his willingness to apologize. He carefully deploys his information to undercut the static effect generally created in character sketches. Swift's personal and ecclesiastical attitudes toward money are delineated as a complex mixture of parsimony and generosity. He considers Pope's finances and Dryden's conversation twice in each character sketch, with varying emphases. Because Johnson prefers complexity over consistency in presenting characters, his method is consciously inductive rather than deductive. He never opens with an overview of character which is then systematically illustrated. Even in the characters of major writers, where critics have noted his emphasis on dominant traits picked up from the biographical section which are also reflected in the criticism, Johnson tries to avoid tailoring the depiction to focus only on those traits. He shows Addison's timidity, but he also points out that a man "cannot be supposed very inexpert in the arts of conversation and practice of life, who, without fortune or alliance," attained positions as high as Addison's in both the political and social worlds (II, 119). Although emphasizing Milton's violent independence, Johnson defends him for his omission of scheduled

---

54. *The Poetical Register; Or, The Lives and Characters of All the English Poets* (London, 1723), II, xiv.

prayers and exonerates him from at least one tyrannical imposition on a daughter. Like Waller's life and work, the poet's character shows a general lack of strength, but he is unwavering in his support of monarchy. In pointing up the inadequacies of Fenton's poetical character of Roscommon, Johnson remarks: "But thus it is that characters are written: we know somewhat, and we imagine the rest" (I, 235). Always sensitive to the needs and capacities of the human imagination, Johnson in writing his own sketches of personal character in the *Lives* seeks to stimulate the imaginations of his readers toward complex conceptions of the characters of individuals.

In emphasizing complexity Johnson is trying not only to be fair to each individual poet by presenting all of the available evidence about him but also to be honest in his rendering of the general complexity of all human beings. What he deliberately avoids is the single unified impression of a person that the character sketch had traditionally rendered. His treatment of his own sketches and those of others shows him actively undercutting any such effect in the *Lives*. After his own negative "character of Swift as he exhibits himself to my perception" (III, 63), he ends the character section with Delany's more positive character. Witnesses are introduced to modify the sketches: Burnet amplifies Clarendon's observations on Waller's "parliamentary eloquence" (I, 280), as Johnson himself does in comments on financial matters; Mason further explains his own remarks on Gray's effeminacy. No sketch is allowed to stand as final. In the "Life of Rowe," he opens with Welwood's character, "apparently given with the fondness of a friend," moves to Pope's positive testimony, slightly darkens the general effect with "less advantageous" comments from Pope reported by Warburton, and complicates any final assessment with his own warning at the end: "Few characters can bear the microscopick scrutiny of wit quickened by anger" (II, 74, 75). The "Life of Smith" illustrates his dissatisfaction with the character as a form. He begins with William Oldisworth's overly panegyrical character of Smith and shows its inadequacies in his own section on character not by

producing an alternative sketch, but by offering a series of
"minute memorials" (II, 20) only loosely related, if at all, in
topic. The effect is to emphasize not only Oldisworth's, but
any man's inability to render satisfactorily the portrait of an
entire human being in one condensed summary. That some
can do so better than others he shows when he relents by
giving the magnificent sketch of Walmsley at the end, but
his basic point has been made. Justice to the inveterate individuality of any man requires more than the character sketch
as a genre can provide. In this sense perhaps the best parallels to Johnson's approaches in the character sketches in the
Lives can be found in certain of Gibbon's characters in later
books of the *Decline and Fall.* Although with some early
figures he often finds a single trait (such as Augustus' hypo-
crisy) useful as a personal index and narrative tool and
presents the character entirely in terms of it, later characters
such as Mohammed are drawn to emphasize the multiple
dimensions of personality: "Could I truly delineate the portrait of an hour, the fleeting resemblance would not equally
apply to the solitary of mount Hera, to the preacher of
Mecca, and to the conqueror of Arabia."[55] Like Johnson,
Gibbon uses the character sketch in ways which point up the
inadequacies of the form itself.

W. Jackson Bate has emphasized the dual tendencies in
Johnson's thought toward reductionism and openness, pointing out that the reductiveness which often characterizes his
conversation seldom appears unqualified in his writing.[56] The
natural ability to sum up a man succinctly which Boswell and
Reynolds noted in Johnson's conversation is shown to a certain extent in his character sketches, but more importantly,
the sketches also reflect, as all of his writings do, his lifelong
recognition of the contradictions and complexities of men.
Retaining those conventions of his predecessors in the genre
which were especially congenial to his own mind, he applied

55. Edward Gibbon, *The Decline and Fall of the Roman Empire*, ed. J. B.
Bury, 3rd. ed. (London: Methuen, 1908), V, 375.
56. *Samuel Johnson* (New York: Harcourt, Brace, Jovanovich, 1977), pp.
489–497.

others in ways which systematically undermined the residual level of generality which the character sketch had retained throughout its development. As a static, basically ornamental form became a means of emphasizing the dynamic psychology of each individual, Johnson was able to suggest the ultimate inadequacy of the genre itself to do justice to human complexity and the fullness of individual life. In his hands the character sketch emerged as a tool for reflecting an essential truth about the nature of man and about the limitations of one common biographical method for depicting it. Those involved with recent critical trends would perhaps point out that what Johnson does in the *Lives of the English Poets* is a kind of deconstruction of the character sketch. Given a chance to respond, Johnson himself, never one for trends and particularly not for trends which isolated art from human concerns, might well answer—metaphorically kicking the rock to ground speculation in the real—that his formal procedure was simply the best way he knew to offer his readers that "truth to life" which he believed that the best literature always rendered.

Johnson and Mrs. Thrale: The Beginning and the End

Biographers of Johnson have always been fascinated by his relationship with Mrs. Thrale, whose kindness "soothed twenty years of a life radically wretched." Those often-quoted words, written by Johnson himself in his last letter to Mrs. Thrale at the time of her second marriage to Gabriel Piozzi, have served as a melancholy coda to the story of their intimacy. No biographer in our time has done more to explore and illuminate the relationship than W. Jackson Bate, whose enthralling *Samuel Johnson* (1977) provides a richly detailed and sympathetic account. If I may be allowed a brief personal reminiscence, it was Jack Bate, in his lectures on "The Age of Johnson" almost twenty years ago, who awakened my own interest in Johnson and Mrs. Thrale and prompted me to read Mrs. Thrale's *Anecdotes of Johnson* for the first time. A decade later, I published a short inquiry into the biographical facts and problems of their last years together.[1] Since that time I have continued to think about the ways in which Mrs. Thrale "soothed" Johnson—what

---

1. "Johnson's Last Years with Mrs. Thrale: Facts and Problems," *Bulletin of the John Rylands University Library of Manchester*, 57 (Autumn, 1974): 196–212.

she did, how and why it affected him—with a particular view
to understanding, in psychological terms, his repudiation of
her when she married Piozzi: "If you have abandoned your
children and your religion, God forgive your wickedness; if
you have forfeited your Fame, and your country, may your
folly do no further mischief."[2] Why did he react so
violently? Here I must confess that none of the explanations offered by scholars seems to me fully adequate. In this
essay I should like to reexamine some of the evidence and
call attention to a fundamental change in their relationship
which occurred before its final years.

Johnson first met Mrs. Thrale and her husband at their
house next to the Thrale brewery in Southwark on January
9, 1765. The laconic entry in his diary for this date reads
simply, "At Mr Trails."[3] But Mrs. Thrale, writing in her
own diary *Thraliana* a dozen years later, recalled how the
meeting came about and what happened:

It was on the second Thursday of the Month of January 1765.
that I first saw Mr Johnson in a Room: [Arthur] Murphy whose
Intimacy with Mr Thrale had been of many Years standing, was
one day dining with us at our house in Southwark; and was zealous
that we should be acquainted with Johnson, of whose Moral and
Literary Character he spoke in the most exalted Terms; and so
whetted our desire of seeing him soon, that we were only disputing
how he should be invited, *when* he should be invited, and what
should be the pretence. at last it was resolved that one [James]
Woodhouse a Shoemaker who had written some Verses, and been
asked to some Tables, should likewise be asked to ours, and made
a Temptation to Mr Johnson to meet him: accordingly he came,
and Mr Murphy at four o'clock brought Mr Johnson to dinner—
We liked each other so well that the next Thursday was appointed
for the same Company to meet—exclusive of the Shoemaker, and

---

2. *The Letters of Samuel Johnson, with Mrs. Thrale's Genuine Letters to Him*,
ed. R. W. Chapman (Oxford: Clarendon Press, 1952), III, 174 (July 2,
1784). Hereafter cited as *Letters*.

3. Samuel Johnson, *Diaries, Prayers, and Annals*, ed. E. L. McAdam, Jr.,
with Donald and Mary Hyde (New Haven: Yale University Press, 1958), p.
84. Hereafter cited as *Diaries*.

since then Johnson has remained till this Day, our constant Acquaintance, Visitor, Companion and Friend.[4]

Johnson was fifty-five at the time of their meeting, the most eminent man of letters in England even though his long-awaited edition of Shakespeare had yet to appear. Mrs. Thrale was a woman of not quite twenty-four—easily young enough to be his daughter—and Henry Thrale was some twelve years older than his wife. The Thrales had been married little more than a year.

It is a well enough established fact that Johnson was then approaching a kind of nervous breakdown, an emotional disturbance whose seriousness is alluded to in Boswell's *Life of Johnson* but nevertheless underestimated. "About this time [1764]," Boswell informs us, "he was afflicted with a very severe return of the hypochondriack disorder, which was ever lurking about him. He was so ill, as, notwithstanding his remarkable love of company, to be entirely averse to society, the most fatal symptom of that malady." Boswell had first mentioned the matter of Johnson's "morbid melancholy" under the year 1729, when the twenty-year-old Johnson, forced to leave Oxford for financial reasons, had become "overwhelmed with . . . a dejection, gloom, and despair, which made existence misery."[5] The psychological origins of this early breakdown are by no means well known, but it has been cogently argued, I think, that the crisis he experienced, in the months after his return home to his aging parents in Lichfield, had much to do with an

---

4. *Thraliana: The Diary of Mrs. Hester Lynch Thrale (Later Mrs. Piozzi) 1776–1809*, ed. Katharine C. Balderston, 2nd ed. (Oxford: Clarendon Press, 1951), I, 158–159. The account of their first meeting in her *Anecdotes of the Late Samuel Johnson LL.D.* (1786) is substantially the same but more detailed; it is reprinted in *Johnsonian Miscellanies*, ed. George Birkbeck Hill (Oxford: Clarendon Press, 1897), I, 232–233. Hereafter cited as *Anecdotes, Johns. Misc.*

5. *Boswell's Life of Johnson*, ed. George Birkbeck Hill, rev. L. F. Powell (Oxford: Clarendon Press, 1934–1964), I, 483, 63. Hereafter cited as *Life*.

unresolved inner conflict concerning his mother and (to a lesser extent) his father.[6] "I did not respect my own mother," he revealed to Mrs. Thrale many years later, "though I loved her."[7] Undoubtedly there were other factors as well, such as the hard realization of his meagre prospects for the future, which contributed to Johnson's depression. In any event, it seems almost certain that what he began to fear for the first time was the actual loss of his sanity, and his terror became so intense that he is said to have contemplated suicide.[8]

"From this dismal malady," Boswell continues, "he never afterwards was perfectly relieved; and all his labors, and all his enjoyments, were but temporary interruptions of its baleful influence."[9] It had taken Johnson several years to get over this first episode. Now, well advanced into middle age, with the productive decade of the 1750s behind him but feeling more lonely than ever after the deaths of his wife and mother, he was increasingly beset with what he called "vain scruples" and feelings of guilt over "time spent in idleness." "I have led a life so dissipated and useless, and my terrours and perplexities have so much encreased," he wrote in his diary for Easter Eve, 1761, "that I am under great depression and discouragement." The "terrours" did not subside, and we find another reference to them in a prayer he composed three years later. There can be hardly any doubt here that Johnson was again plagued by fears of insanity. Though he was capable of putting up a bold front in the company of most people, his diary for these years records his constant

6. See George Irwin, *Samuel Johnson: A Personality in Conflict* (Auckland: Auckland University Press and Oxford University Press, 1971), chap. 1. Irwin's well-informed and persuasive study deserves to be better known. Bate interprets Johnson's relationship with his parents rather differently, arguing that his father "intensified" the struggle with his own "internal self-demand" while his mother indulged him and provided security; see *Samuel Johnson* (New York: Harcourt Brace Jovanovich, 1977), pp. 18–21.

7. *Anecdotes, Johns. Misc.*, I, 163.

8. See James L. Clifford, *Young Sam Johnson* (New York: McGraw-Hill, 1955), p. 129.

9. *Life*, I, 63–64.

anxiety and inner torment. "A kind of strange oblivion has overspread me," he confessed in April, 1764, "so that I know not what has become of the last year."[10]

Such was Johnson's dismal state of mind when he was introduced to the Thrales. "When I knew him first," Mrs. Thrale noted, he seemed to be a man who had "looked on Life till he was weary" and was "sincerely sick" of his existence as he continued to view it.[11] But the meeting went off so well that "from that time he dined with us every Thursday through the winter [of 1765]."[12] Arthur Murphy, who had arranged the introduction, was later pleased to point out that this was the year when Johnson gained the "resource, which contributed more than any thing else to exempt him from the solicitudes of life." And even Boswell, whose literary rivalry with Mrs. Piozzi after Johnson's death caused him to belittle her as much as possible in print, was forced to admit, "Nothing could be more fortunate for Johnson than this connection":

He had at Mr. Thrale's all the comforts and even luxuries of life; his melancholy was diverted, and his irregular habits lessened by association with an agreeable and well-ordered family. He was treated with the utmost respect, and even affection. The vivacity of Mrs. Thrale's literary talk roused him to cheerfulness and exertion . . . for he found here a constant succession of what gave him the highest enjoyment: the society of the learned, the witty, and the eminent in every way, who were assembled in numerous companies, called forth his wonderful powers, and gratified him with admiration, to which no man could be insensible.[13]

Yet Boswell had very little communication with Johnson during the mid-1760s; and even if he had, it is most unlikely that he would ever have discovered the true basis of the intimacy that developed between Johnson and Mrs. Thrale.

10. *Diaries*, pp. 70, 73, 76, 77–78.
11. *Thraliana*, I, 206.
12. *Anecdotes, Johns. Misc.*, I, 233.
13. Murphy, *An Essay on the Life and Genius of Samuel Johnson LL.D.* (1792), in *Johns. Misc.*, I, 422; *Life*, I, 495–496.

It had little to do with creature comforts, domestic harmony, or intellectual sport.

Though they made friends with each other quickly, it naturally took time for them to become intimate. The friendship began with Johnson's weekly dinners at the Thrales' in Southwark. Johnson flattered Mrs. Thrale's literary penchant by collaborating informally with her on translations of Boethius and by engaging her in lively conversations. Then the family (by this time the Thrales had an infant daughter) moved to Streatham, their country house outside London, for the spring and summer. Johnson apparently visited them there from time to time, but for the most part he was busy in London completing his Shakespeare edition (published in October) and seeing it through the press. This was the summer when he and his domestic "inmates" moved to a house at No. 7 Johnson's Court. When he was unable to join the Thrales at Brighton in August, he wrote to Mrs. Thrale (the first of his surviving letters to her): "I hope that the week after the next, will be the end of my present business. When business is done what remains but pleasure? and where should pleasure be sought but under Mrs Thrale's influence?"[14] When Johnson finally arrived at Brighton, the Thrales had already returned to London so that Henry Thrale could prepare to stand for election to Parliament. Johnson was angry and disappointed, but Arthur Murphy interceded and brought them back together. "From that time his visits grew more frequent," Mrs. Thrale relates, "till in the year 1766 his health, which he had always complained of, grew so exceedingly bad, that he could not stir out of his room in the court he inhabited for many *weeks* together, I think months."[15]

Having finished *Shakespeare*, Johnson had begun "engaging in politicks" with William Gerard Hamilton. Little is known about this employment, which may not have occupied much of his time. We do know from Mrs. Thrale as well as

14. *Letters*, I, 174 (August 13, 1765).
15. *Anecdotes, Johns. Misc.*, I, 233–234.

from Johnson's diary that during these months he sank ever deeper into "doubts," "vain terrours," and "perplexity."[16] According to Bate's reckoning, it was in May of 1766 that "Johnson's breakdown was at its worst."[17] Because he became so disinclined even to leave his room, the Thrales decided to call on him; "[our] attentions . . . became so acceptable to him, that he often lamented to us the horrible condition of his mind, which he said was nearly distracted." Johnson evidently believed that he had been insane, or at least hovering on the edge:

and though he charged *us* to make him odd solemn promises of secrecy on so strange a subject [that is, his supposed insanity], yet when we waited on him one morning, and heard him, in the most pathetic terms, beg the prayers of Dr. Delap, who had left him as we came in, I felt excessively affected with grief, and well remember my husband involuntarily lifted up one hand to shut his mouth, from provocation at hearing a man so wildly proclaim what he could at last persuade no one to believe; and what, if true, would have been so very unfit to reveal.

Henry Thrale, deeply horrified at Johnson's condition, withdrew from the scene, leaving his wife alone with Johnson but urging her to "prevail on him to quit his close habitation in the court and come with us to Streatham"—"where," Mrs. Thrale continues, "I undertook the care of his health, and had the honour and happiness of contributing to its restoration."[18]

This last statement almost makes it sound as if Mrs. Thrale went about restoring Johnson's mental health according to a specific plan or regimen, but this was surely not the case. Rather, her "therapy" at this crucial time apparently was to serve as a sympathetic and discreet listener who could inspire Johnson's complete confidence. This in itself may not seem very remarkable, but I would go further in

16. *Diaries*, pp. 98, 107 (Nov., 1765; Mar. 29, 1766).
17. *Samuel Johnson*, p. 419.
18. *Anecdotes, Johns. Misc.*, I, 234.

identifying Mrs. Thrale's role—as far as he was concerned, at a subconscious level—as essentially that of a mother or mother-substitute.[19] It is not necessary, I think, to pursue an elaborate psychoanalytic hypothesis in order to recognize this. The evidence for it is fragmentary but highly suggestive.

Moved by Mrs. Thrale's concern, Johnson stayed at Streatham "more than three months," from late June to the first of October.[20] It was this extended stay that probably did more than anything else to "domesticate" Johnson in the Thrale family. We have few details of how the summer actually went, but several references in Mrs. Thrale's *Anecdotes* ("one day that he was totally confined to his chamber," "one other day that he was very ill") seem to indicate that it was a while before Johnson was well enough to join in the family's daily routine. On such days, when he "felt his fancy, or fancied he felt it, disordered," he would try to divert himself with mathematical calculations. Sometimes Mrs. Thrale would initiate a conversation, "knowing what subject he would like best to talk upon."[21] Clearly she did her best to make herself available to him in this way at any time, whether during the day or (as was often the case) late at night. Gradually she gained his trust and began to draw him out of himself. As Bate has astutely observed, "he was plainly so helpless that, besides the respect she gave

19. The notion of Mrs. Thrale as a mother figure has of course been advanced by others, notably George Irwin (n. 6 above). Using a psychoanalytic model, Irwin refers (p. 128) to the "transference relationship" which, he believes, Johnson "had unconsciously sought but failed to establish with his wife and also with Hill Boothby [but which] was at last to be realized and completely fulfilled [with Mrs. Thrale]." This and other aspects of their relationship have been assessed by Martine Watson Brownley in a valuable study published after my essay was completed; see Brownley, "'Under the Dominion of *Some* Woman': The Friendship of Samuel Johnson and Hester Thrale," in *Mothering the Mind: Twelve Studies of Writers and Their Silent Partners*, ed. Ruth Perry and M. W. Brownley (New York and London: Holmes and Meier, 1984), pp. 64–79.

20. *Diaries*, p. 111 (October 3, 1766).

21. *Anecdotes, Johns. Misc.*, I, 200–201.

him, she also began to baby him, though he was thirty-one years older than she. Johnson, ordinarily so fiercely scrupulous and self-examining, in turn began to accept this without quite knowing he was doing so."[22] He was treated as a member of the family, and in time he came to feel like one of them—an experience he had not had since his boyhood, and then under much less comfortable circumstances.

When Johnson returned to London in October, his progress toward recovery had begun. Thereafter he had an arrangement with the Thrales whereby he would spend a good part of each week with them (except, of course, when he or they went away on trips) at their house in Southwark or Streatham, each of which had an apartment fitted up for his use. The salutary effect of this adopted family on Johnson can be glimpsed in a letter he sent to Mrs. Thrale the following summer from Lichfield, where he had gone to attend the last illness of an old family servant. "Though I have been away so much longer than I purposed or expected," he wrote, "I have found nothing that withdraws my affections from the friends whom I left behind, or which makes me less desirous of reposing in that place which your kindness and Mr Thrale's allows me to call my *home*."[23] In time Johnson would regularly address Mrs. Thrale as "dearest Madam." Henry Thrale, to whom he always showed a kind of filial respect and devotion, became "my Master" and likewise Mrs. Thrale was "my Mistress."

Johnson's long "exile" at Lichfield in 1767 had been difficult for him nonetheless. As he wrote to his friend Robert Chambers, the new Vinerian Professor at Oxford whom Johnson had been helping to write his law lectures, "I have passed this summer very uneasily. My old melancholy has laid hold upon me to a degree sometimes not easily supportable." It is not unreasonable to wonder if his long separation from Mrs. Thrale had allowed his troubles to return in force. Johnson comes close to admitting as much

---

22. *Samuel Johnson*, pp. 415–416.
23. *Letters*, I, 198 (July 20, 1767).

in a letter to her the following April, when he was "very
much disordered" during another long visit to Oxford. All
along, of course, his ills had been physical as well as mental,
and it may well be that some of these were psychosomatic.
"But whithersoever I may wander," Johnson wrote to her in
June of 1768, "I shall not, I hope, leave behind me that gratitude and respect, with which your attention to my health
and tenderness for my weakness have impressed my
heart."[24] "Impressed my heart": the phrase carries with it
the sense that Mrs. Thrale's solicitude had touched him as
few others' had, so that now there were few, if any, feelings
he would be unable to share with her.

It is impossible to know exactly when Johnson entrusted
her with "a Secret far dearer to him than his Life"—the
belief that he had, for a time, been insane. Writing in her
diary in 1779, Mrs. Thrale could not be sure about the date
of his disclosure: it was "about the Years 1767 or 1768."
But she felt certain that "he has never since that Day regretted his Confidence, or ever looked with less kind Affection
on her who had him in her Power." "Johnson," she
observed in contradiction to the cynical maxim of La Roche-
foucauld, "is more a Hero to me than to any one—& I have
been more to him for Intimacy, than ever was any Man's
Valet de Chambre."[25] The strong likelihood is that he
imparted his "secret" to her not long after a brief tour
through Kent with the Thrales in September, 1768—a time
when Johnson was feeling "great perturbation" and
"distress."[26]

Mrs. Thrale's startling entry in her diary, it may be
recalled, was one of the principal exhibits in Katharine
Balderston's famous essay "Johnson's Vile Melancholy," in
which she argued the case for Johnson's erotic masochism
underlying certain suspected episodes in their relationship.
There is no need to review here all the evidence presented

24. *Letters*, I, 200, 210, 221 (c. October 8, 1767; April 19, 1768; June 17,
1768).
25. *Thraliana*, I, 384–385 (entry dated May 1, 1779).
26. *Diaries*, p. 119 (September 18, 1768).

by Balderston or the inferences she draws from it. In his biography of Johnson, Bate provides a circumspect analysis of the same evidence and has shown that her conclusions are unwarranted.[27] Everyone who is interested in this question should read his discussion carefully. He makes it perfectly clear, for example, that "Johnson's padlock," which (Mrs. Thrale specified) was "committed to [her] care in the year 1768," had nothing to do with a *masochistic* desire on Johnson's part to be chained up by her. He had doubtless acquired a padlock and fetters as a last resort, to restrain himself in the event that he felt his "madness" was going beyond his control. His surrendering of these items to Mrs. Thrale was an act expressing his complete trust in her, for in doing so he was acknowledging the "Secret far dearer to him than his Life" and he was empowering her to use the padlock and fetters if they were needed.

Two other points need to be stressed. The first is that the "secret" Johnson confessed to her was not simply his *fear* of going insane, but rather his conviction that he had actually *been* insane—for the awareness of having gone over the brink was what shattered and humiliated him and added greatly to his feelings of guilt. The second point is that Johnson's conviction was based on his own (not someone else's) peculiar notion of what constitutes insanity. His views on this subject are scattered throughout his writings, but nowhere does he express them more succinctly than in the famous forty-fourth chapter of *Rasselas* on "the dangerous prevalence of imagination." There he has Imlac the philosopher declare unequivocally that "All power of fancy over reason is a degree of insanity; but while this power is such as we can controll and repress, it is not visible to others, nor considered as any depravation of the mental faculties: it is not pronounced madness but when it comes

---

27. See Katharine C. Balderston, "Johnson's Vile Melancholy," in *The Age of Johnson: Essays Presented to Chauncey Brewster Tinker* (New Haven: Yale University Press, 1949), pp. 3–14, and Bate, *Samuel Johnson*, pp. 384–389, 439–441.

ungovernable, and apparently influences speech or action."[28] Although many of Johnson's contemporaries might not have agreed with him, this was how he defined insanity, and from his point of view he was convinced that he had been "mad."

Thus Johnson in effect committed himself to Mrs. Thrale's care and was thereby, no doubt, relieved of a crushing psychological burden. At the same time, even though he might still have an "insane thought about foot-fetters and manacles" (as he apparently did in 1771),[29] he secured for himself a sense of Mrs. Thrale's protection that must have helped to dispel his fears. Most important, her sympathetic acceptance of his "secret" and her concern never to betray it gave him the strongest possible proofs of her esteem for him—the kind of esteem that one might ordinarily expect to have only from one's mother. This in turn would have given him the measure of self-acceptance he desperately needed in order to free himself of his debilitating feelings of guilt and unworthiness.

With rare exception, Johnson wrote to Mrs. Thrale frequently and regularly when they were separated by traveling. Had more of their correspondence survived, we would have a clearer picture of Johnson's gradual recovery over the next few years. In the letters that have been preserved, one is struck by the need and concern that he openly expresses for her. In June, 1769, while she was confined by another pregnancy, Johnson waited impatiently "to be informed that your trouble is over, and that you [are] well enough to resume your care for that which yet continues, and which your kindness may sometimes alleviate." A year later, when Johnson was away at Ashbourne and learned that she was not well, he immediately responded: "I hope your complaint, however troublesome is without danger, for your danger involves us all, when you [were] ill before, it was agreed that if you were lost, hope would be lost with you, for such another there was

28. *Rasselas*, ed. Geoffrey Tillotson and Brian Jenkins (London: Oxford University Press, 1971), p. 114.
29. See *Diaries*, p. 140.

no expectation of finding."[30] These are but two of many such passages that reveal his fear of losing her at a time when he, as well as her family, required her "care."

On his sixtieth birthday (September 18, 1769) Johnson felt well enough to acknowledge in his diary "a slow progress of recovery" over the past year and his "hope of health both of mind and body." That his recovery was sustained rather than temporary is confirmed by a similar entry exactly two years later: his mind was now "less encumbered" and he was "less interrupted in mental employment." He continued to improve, and on Easter morning 1772 he offered thanks to God "for the deliverance which thou hast granted me from diseases of mind and body."[31] Of course there were bound to be relapses—times when circumstances made the old psychological patterns reassert themselves—for Johnson's troubled mind was never to be wholly at peace with itself. Such an episode seems to have occurred in May, 1773, when Johnson stayed at Streatham while Mrs. Thrale's mother, Mrs. Salusbury, lay dying of cancer. It was then that Johnson sent Mrs. Thrale the "curious letter written in French," as Balderston called it, which has been the subject of so much misinterpretation. Since this letter and Mrs. Thrale's reply to it are so revealing of the persistent mother-child element in their early relationship, we must briefly examine what happened.

The context in which Johnson's letter was composed is crucial to our understanding of it. Although fully aware that Mrs. Salusbury was fatally ill and that Mrs. Thrale, distraught with worry, was devoting herself to nursing her mother, Johnson nevertheless wanted to be with her at Streatham. In a childlike way he had almost from the beginning competed with Mrs. Salusbury, a woman close to his own age, for her daughter's attention. In a letter of May 29, he openly expressed his wish to be there and added: "I hope I shall not add much to your trouble, and will wish at least to give

30. *Letters*, I, 226–227, 243 (June 21?, 1769; July 20, 1770).
31. *Diaries*, pp. 122–123, 142–143, 149.

you some little solace or amusement. I long to be under your care."[32] Knowing that Johnson himself had not been well physically, Mrs. Thrale acquiesced. But when Johnson arrived she could not give him much of her time, and Henry Thrale (who had decided to remain at the brewery in Southwark) was not there to help out. Johnson understood all this well enough and probably felt guilty about being in the way, but his own feelings of hurt and neglect evidently got the better of him. He made a show of retiring to his room for hours at a time, hoping, no doubt, that Mrs. Thrale would soon recognize her neglect. When his voluntary confinement went virtually unnoticed, he felt the need to make some kind of protest.

But the delicacy of the situation and probably his own feelings of embarrassment made him resort to communication by letter—moreover, a letter written in French that would allow him the mock-formality he required as well as making it impossible for the servants in the house to read. It is, as Bate has aptly characterized it, an "extraordinary document—self-defensive, ironic, coy, disguising complaint under the appearance of excessive courtesy and self-abasement, and filled with signals asking for reassurance that he was not in the way but rather a cherished member of the family."[33] While ostensibly asking Mrs. Thrale to tell him how he should conduct himself during this difficult time—whether he should confine himself to his room or move freely about the house—what he really seeks is her approval and reassurance that he is still "digne, comme auparavant, des soins et de la protection d'une ame si aimable par sa douceur." He would like it if she would take charge of things, spare him "la necessitè de me contraindre" by enforcing the rules of the household herself, and not forget her promises of help to the extent that he has had to make

32. *Letters*, I, 331 (May 29, 1773).
33. Bate considers the French letter in detail in *Samuel Johnson*, pp. 387–388, 439–441. For Balderston's very different analysis, see her essay (n. 27 above), pp. 6–8. Both discussions include the complete text of the letter, which is also printed in *Letters*, I, 323–324.

"tant de solicitations reiterèes que la resouvenance me fait horreur." Addressing her as "ma patronne," he says he wishes that her "autoritè me soit toujours sensible" and that she will keep him "dans l'esclavage que vou scavez si bien rendre heureuse." Far from revealing a masochistic desire to be dominated, his wish expressed his need to feel the kind of authority that a parent or governess ("patronne") has over a child, and he alludes to the happiness or security that a child commonly feels in having acceptable limits of behavior clearly defined by his guardian.[34]

Mrs. Thrale's reply, which in its tone and outlook is not unlike that which a parent or governess might write to a child, shows that she understood completely the essence of Johnson's plea but was unwilling to indulge him any further. "What Care," she asks, "can I promise my dear Mr Johnson that I have not already taken? what Tenderness that he has not already experienced?" She notes that she has been reproached by him for neglect and "by myself for exciting that generous Confidence which prompts you to repose all Care on me." Clearly she thought that she had done all she could for him in her role as mother-substitute or governess; it was time for him to take charge of himself and no longer turn to her for "care" and protection. If they are to "go on together," he must accept his confinement during that time her dying mother requires her attention. But she believes the best thing would be for him to seek diversion elsewhere. "Mr Boswell will be at last your best Physician," she suggests, referring to Johnson's proposed tour of the Hebrides. "For the rest you really are well enough now if you will keep so; and not suffer the noblest of human Minds to be tortured

---

34. Johnson's use of the word "patronne" in addressing Mrs. Thrale can be even more clearly understood in the perspective of a letter he wrote to her about six months earlier. In recent letters to him she had used flattery—perhaps in an effort to increase his self-esteem—but he admonished her against it: "You have read of heroes and princes ruined by flattery, and I question if any of them had a flatterer so dangerous as you. Pray keep strictly to your character of governess." *Letters*, I, 293 (November 23, 1772).

with fantastic notions which rob it of all its Quiet." Answering directly his appeal to her "authority," she concludes: "Farewell and be good; and do not quarrell with your Governess for not using the Rod enough."[35] The implication here is surely not, as Balderston supposed, that Mrs. Thrale was accustomed to administering physical discipline. The meaning of her remark, when considered in its proper context, is simple enough: she does not wish to be reproached for not being stern with him when he was sulking and making himself a nuisance.

In her letter Mrs. Thrale expressed her confidence in Johnson's ability to carry on without her special care, and this seems to have given him the reassurance he needed. That the episode passed quickly is an indication that he was, as she had said, "well enough now." At her death in mid-June, Johnson and Mrs. Salusbury parted tenderly. Following Mrs. Thrale's advice, he went forward with plans for the long-contemplated trip to Scotland, and by early August he was on his way. Johnson had always relished traveling in an unfamiliar place, and the Hebridean journey afforded him much of interest and entertainment. This we know well from Boswell's published account of it, but neither the *Tour* nor even his *Life of Johnson* shows any awareness of the real intimacy that had grown up between Johnson and Mrs. Thrale. What Boswell gives us instead is the "Johnson of legend" who was now embarking on a period of relative stability and well-being that lasted more or less until the death of Henry Thrale in 1781. It would be wrong to imply that these years, while Johnson passed from his mid-sixties to early seventies, were without problems and difficulties, but they were probably the happiest of his life. He continued to enjoy the comforts and diversions of the Thrale household, traveled with them to Wales and to France, and crowned his literary career with the *Lives of the Poets*.

35. *Letters*, I, 331–332. R. W. Chapman conjecturally dated her letter c. May 30, 1773, as if it were the reply to Johnson's letter of May 29, quoted above. But she is clearly answering his letter in French, which was probably written in early June after he had been at Streatham a few days.

Mrs. Thrale, on the other hand, felt the worries and frustrations of her own life mounting up. Her marriage to Henry Thrale had never been a love match, but she had tried to make the best of it. Of the twelve children she bore him, only four lived to maturity; the death of young Harry, Thrale's only remaining son, in 1776 was a blow from which he never recovered. Thereafter he grew increasingly stubborn, withdrawn, and lethargic. His reckless speculating and overproduction at the brewery led to more than one financial crisis which Mrs. Thrale herself, with Johnson's help, had to resolve. And a growing irritation to her, from 1778 onward, was Thrale's undisguised infatuation with the beautiful and accomplished Sophia Streatfeild. Through all of this, until the ripening of her friendship with Fanny Burney, Mrs. Thrale had no female companion with whom to share her distresses. As her biographer, James L. Clifford, remarks, her only confidant during these difficult years was the journals she kept, her "Children's Book" and *Thraliana*.[36]

Johnson was a ready source of advice and moral support, but she could not always turn to him for sympathy. Since the time when he had ceased to be emotionally dependent on her, their relationship, though outwardly much the same, had undergone a significant change. It involved a fundamental reversal of roles. No longer was he like a child coming to his mother for tender loving care; as befitted his age and experience, he was now like an elderly father, wise and well-intentioned but at times fretful and demanding, who looked forward to having the attention of a favorite and dutiful daughter in his declining years. To a great extent, Mrs. Thrale accepted and participated in this reversal of roles, as a particular entry in *Thraliana*, written in February, 1782, suggests: "Here is Mr Johnson very ill, ill indeed; & I do not see what ails him: 'tis repelled Gout I fear fallen on his Lungs, & Breath of course, what shall we do for him? If I

36. *Hester Lynch Piozzi (Mrs. Thrale)*, 2nd ed. with corr. (Oxford: Clarendon Press, 1968), p. 173. Like all recent writers on Mrs. Thrale, I am much indebted to Clifford's biography.

lose *him* I am more than undone: Friend, Father, Guardian,
Confident! God give me Health & Patience—what shall I
do?"[37] But if Mrs. Thrale revered Johnson as a father and
inalienable friend, this did not mean that she was willing to
devote herself to him exclusively. Indeed, when she made
this entry in *Thraliana*, she was torn between her filial sense
of duty toward the ailing Johnson and her growing desire for
romantic escape with her lover, Gabriel Piozzi.

The event that drastically altered the course of Mrs.
Thrale's life with Johnson was Henry Thrale's death in
April, 1781, the result of several strokes he had suffered
over the previous two years. Johnson's letters to her at
Brighton, where she went to recover from the shock, show
how deeply he felt the loss. "I am not without my part of
the calamity," he wrote. "No death since that of my Wife
has ever oppressed me like this." A few days later he told
her: "I feel myself like a man beginning a new course of
life. I had interwoven myself with my dear Friend."[38]
According to Boswell, Johnson "did not foresee all that
afterwards happened"—meaning Mrs. Thrale's love affair
and eventual marriage with Piozzi—but he was "sufficiently
convinced that the comforts which Mr. Thrale's family
afforded him, would now in a great measure cease."[39] Johnson may naturally enough have feared the loss of these
"comforts," but as yet Mrs. Thrale had given him no reason
to expect it.

In any event, gossip concerning the wealthy widow's
future immediately sprang up, and rumors began to circulate
in London that she might marry Johnson. Boswell himself
contributed to the speculation by composing, in execrable
taste, a satirical epithalamium the day after Thrale's burial
and then reciting it in mixed company, although he withheld
publication of the scurrilous *Ode* until 1788. The same
week, in a private conversation with the eminent lawyer

37. *Thraliana*, I, 528 (February 1, 1782).
38. *Letters*, II, 415, 418 (April 5 and 11, 1781). Thrale died on April 4.
39. *Life*, IV, 85.

William Scott at Johnson's house, Boswell "agreed that it
was possible Mrs. Thrale might marry Dr. Johnson, and we
both wished it much."[40] Both of these incidents indicate how
poorly Boswell—not to mention the world at large—
understood Mrs. Thrale's relationship with Johnson, for certainly she never even remotely considered marrying him.[41]

The sale of the brewery at the end of May provided Mrs.
Thrale with a handsome regular income and placed her, as
she remarked, in the "restored Character of a
Gentlewoman."[42] No longer the wife of a man in "trade,"
she was now a well-to-do and admired lady of fashion, just
forty years old. As she began to get some perspective on her
situation, she felt the uncertainties of her new independence
while having to deal with a succession of everyday details.
She had five daughters to look after, the youngest but three
years old. And as Johnson's physical ills increased, she was
obliged to tend him patiently at Streatham. Still, she seems
to have been happy enough to go forward in this way until
(as Boswell hinted in the *Life*) her attachment to Johnson
was "divided by another object."[43] After she had fallen in
love with Piozzi, her "perpetual confinement" with Johnson,
as she later called it, became "irksome" and frustrating.[44]

She had met Piozzi at a party given by Johnson's friend
Dr. Burney, the music historian, in February of 1778. During the summer of 1780 at Brighton, where she had gone
with her husband for his health, she saw Piozzi again and
engaged him to give singing lessons to her eldest daughter,
Queeney. He had quickly become a favorite. "I am
ashamed to say how fond I am grown of Piozzi," she wrote
to Fanny Burney in August, "but he is so sensible, & so

40. *Boswell, Laird of Auchinleck, 1778–1782*, ed. Joseph W. Reed and
Frederick A. Pottle (New York: McGraw-Hill, 1977), pp. 316–321, 324
(April 12 and 15, 1781).
41. See Clifford, *Hester Lynch Piozzi*, p. 200.
42. Quoted in *Hester Lynch Piozzi*, p. 202 (Mrs. Thrale to Mrs. Lambart,
June 3, 1781).
43. *Life*, IV, 158.
44. *Anecdotes, Johns. Misc.*, I, 341.

discerning. One cannot but help wishing for his good Opinion: his Musick too is tender & tasteful, and helps to sooth sorrow charmingly."[45] Thrale's death the following spring removed, in her own words, the "yoke my husband first put upon me"[46] and opened up new possibilities in her life. By the fall of 1781, when Johnson went off to the Midlands for his autumn visits, Mrs. Thrale felt emotionally drawn toward Piozzi and grew more and more preoccupied with thoughts of him. He was soon to return from Italy, and when Johnson heard the news he wrote to her from Ashbourne: "Piozzi, I find, is coming . . . and when *he* comes and *I* come, you will have two about you that love you; and I question if either of us heartily care how few more you have. But how many soever they may be, I hope you keep your kindness for me." Here Johnson made no distinction between the deep affection and regard he felt for Mrs. Thrale and Piozzi's "love" for her. Yet only two weeks later, just before returning to Streatham, he seemed to reveal for the first time a fear that Piozzi might come between them: "This you may know at present, that my affection for you is not diminished, and my expectation from you is encreased. Do not neglect me, nor relinquish me. Nobody will ever love you better or honour you more."[47]

During 1782 Johnson's health deteriorated to such an extent that, as Boswell observed, "the history of his life this year, is little more than a mournful recital of the variations of his illness."[48] In February Mrs. Thrale wrote in *Thraliana* (in the entry quoted earlier in full): "Here is Mr Johnson very ill, ill indeed . . . what shall we do for him?" It was she, after all, who bore the responsibility for nursing him and hearing his complaints when he stayed with her at the house she had rented in London for the winter or at

45. Mrs. Thrale to Fanny Burney, Brighthelmstone [August 1780], MS in the Burney Papers, Berg Collection, New York Public Library, quoted by kind permission of the curator, Lola Szladits.

46. *Anecdotes, Johns. Misc.*, I, 341.

47. *Letters*, II, 451, 454–455 (November 24 and December 8, 1781).

48. *Life*, IV, 136.

Streatham over the summer. The tensions of their life together increased as he struggled to regain his health and she inwardly debated the alternatives of her future. If she did remarry, she told herself, it would be for love and nothing else.[49] The scandalmongers continued to plague her with false reports of her marital plans, and even Johnson joked about it in her presence. But the fear of losing her had not left him. In late April, while away from Streatham, he implored her in a letter: "Do not let Mr. Piozzi nor any body else put me quite out of your head, and do not think that any body will love you like [me]."[50]

To be sure, Piozzi was much on her mind during the summer. For some time she had thought of taking her older daughters on an extended tour of Italy, with him along as guide and companion. When the outcome of a costly property suit suddenly reduced her regular income, she determined on making the trip abroad, where she could live more cheaply and rid herself of scandalmongers. But the thought of leaving Johnson behind, as if she were abandoning an infirm and elderly parent, troubled her conscience. When at last she mustered up the courage to tell him her plan, he astonished her by unselfishly approving it—for she had imagined that Johnson "could not have existed without me forsooth."[51] It was decided to let Streatham to a tenant, Lord Shelburne, for three years, and in early October they dined there for the last time. With a doleful sense of finality, Johnson composed a moving prayer for the Thrale family and made his "parting use of the library."[52]

In the company of Fanny Burney, Johnson and the family then went off to Brighton for six weeks. By this time Mrs. Thrale knew she was in love with Piozzi, and she was seriously considering marriage. When at last she had resolved on it, she confessed her passion to both Fanny and Queeney, but Fanny was disapproving and Queeney withheld her

49. See *Thraliana*, I, 531 (April 17, 1782).
50. *Letters*, II, 477 (April 24 or 25, 1782).
51. *Thraliana*, I, 540 (August 22, 1782).
52. *Diaries*, pp. 337–339 (October 6–7, 1782).

consent. Johnson was kept totally ignorant, though he probably sensed that something momentous had happened. "He has been in a terrible severe humour of late," Fanny noted in her diary. "To me only I think he is now kind, for Mrs. Thrale fares worse than any body."[53] In late November they returned to London, and Mrs. Thrale moved into another house which she had rented for the winter. Johnson was with her less frequently than in the past. She had given Piozzi some encouragement, but before long the question of their marriage developed into a crisis, and she found everyone around her (Johnson, of course, excluded) united in their opposition to it. This persuaded her, with the greatest reluctance, to give up her own hopes in the best interests of her daughters. The Italian trip was dropped, and in late January (1783) she tearfully informed Piozzi of her decision.

Mrs. Thrale agonized over Piozzi's dismissal as he prepared to leave England permanently. Finally, she decided to quit London for Bath, where (as she tried to explain in her *Anecdotes*) she "found it convenient, for every reason of health, peace, and pecuniary circumstances, to retire"— "where I knew Mr. Johnson would not follow me, and where I could for that reason command some little portion of time for my own use."[54] Johnson was never consulted about any of this, for she undoubtedly feared his disapproval and did not want to disobey his wishes openly. Yet he could hardly have been completely unaware of what was going on. In early April, when Mrs. Thrale was about to depart for Bath with three of her daughters, Johnson wished her well and "took leave" of her after "some expostulations" that very likely concerned Piozzi. "I was much moved," he wrote in his diary. "She said that she was likewise affected."[55]

53. *Diary and Letters of Madame D'Arblay*, ed. Austin Dobson (London: Macmillan, 1904–1905), II, 122 (November 7, 1782).

54. *Anecdotes, Johns. Misc.*, I, 340.

55. *Diaries*, pp. 358–359 (April 5, 1783).

Johnson mourned her absence and wrote to her regularly, but she was too distraught over her separation from Piozzi to reply in kind. She nurtured the hope that someday she might be reunited with her lover. In June, when Johnson suffered a stroke temporarily depriving him of speech, he wrote her a long and "querelous" letter describing his condition. Accusing her and pleading with her by turns, he could not hold back a direct appeal for her sympathy: "'I have loved you with virtuous affection, I have honoured You with sincere Esteem. Let not all our endearment be forgotten, but let me have in this great distress your pity and your prayers. . . . do not, do not drive me from You, for I have not deserved either neglect or hatred.'"[56] Mrs. Thrale, still anguishing over Piozzi, was in no mood to nurse Johnson through yet another ailment, and she remained at Bath, the victim of her own hypochondria and self-pity. In this way she gradually grew more distant from Johnson. Her despondency over her "perduto sposo" (as she referred to him in her letters to Fanny Burney) eventually brought her in November to the verge of collapse. Seeing the real threat to her mother's health, Queeney at last gave way and, on the advice of Mrs. Thrale's physicians, agreed that Piozzi should be recalled from Italy.

Whatever Johnson may have known or suspected thus far about the Piozzi affair, he continued to delude himself—right up to the time of her announcement—with the hope that the marriage might not take place. During the early months of 1784 he was confined to his quarters by illness, but at some point he learned the truth. Mrs. Thrale almost certainly saw him, if briefly, when she returned to London for a week in early May to make arrangements for the marriage, though she would have carefully avoided making any mention of her plans. When Boswell visited him later in the week, however, "he talked of Mrs. Thrale with much concern, saying, 'Sir, she has done every thing wrong, since Thrale's bridle was off

---

56. *Letters,* III, 35 (June 19, 1783). Boswell, who quotes most of the letter in the *Life of Johnson,* omits this passage.

her neck,'" and he was about to explain himself when he was interrupted by the arrival of another caller.[57] On July 1st Johnson learned of Mrs. Thrale's definite intention to marry Piozzi in a letter from Queeney, which he read "with anguish and astonishment, such as I never felt before." Although the news cannot have taken him by surprise, the reality of it was still a tremendous shock. "I had fondly flattered myself," he admitted to Queeney, "that time had produced better thoughts."[58]

Mrs. Thrale's formal announcement, sent to Johnson in his capacity as one of the legal guardians of the Thrale daughters, arrived from Bath the next day. It was enclosed with a letter, begging his pardon "for concealing from you a Connection which you must have heard of by many People, but I suppose never believed." She tried briefly to justify her behavior toward Johnson over the course of her love affair: "Indeed, my dear Sir, it was concealed only to spare us both needless pain; I could not have borne to reject that Counsel it would have killed me to take; and I only tell it you now, because all is *irrevocably settled*, & out of your power to prevent. Give me leave however to say that the dread of your disapprobation has given me many an anxious moment." Her concluding words strike the chord of their relationship during their troubled last years together. "I feel as if I was acting without a parent's Consent," she told him, "—till you write kindly to your faithful Servt."[59] The failure of Johnson's biographers to recognize the full significance of her remark is, I believe, due to a failure to understand the fundamental "reversal of roles" that I have described earlier.

"Madam / If I interpret your letter right, you are ignominiously married": the violence of Johnson's reaction was a result of, and is largely explained by, that reversal of roles.

---

57. *Life*, IV, 277 (May 16, 1784). For a detailed discussion of how much Johnson knew about the Piozzi affair at various dates, and the evidence for Mrs. Thrale's last meeting with Johnson, see my article (n. 1 above), pp. 206–209.

58. *Letters*, III, 173 (July 1, 1784).

59. *Letters*, III, 172–173 (June 30, 1784).

It was precisely because of the particular intimacy and delicacy of their early relationship that Johnson, after the parent-child roles became reversed, felt so outraged and betrayed. In his "rough" reply to Mrs. Thrale, written the same day he received her letter, he charged her with abandoning her children, her religion, her reputation, and her country.[60] But he could not bring himself to tell her what hurt him most deeply and directly: her abandonment of him. His letter was the outcry of a parent whose intimacy and love over many years had, so he believed, secured a daughter's endearment and devotion to him for the rest of his life—only to find that she had "done every thing wrong" (as he told Boswell) and had, in effect, committed the ultimate act of disobedience.

The rest of the story is too well known to require much elaboration. Mrs. Thrale wrote a firm and dignified response, defending Piozzi's character and her choice of him as a husband; she wished to have no more correspondence with Johnson until he changed his opinion of Piozzi. Johnson had asked to see her "if the last act is yet to do," but she feared any interference and so she declined the meeting. On July 8 Johnson resignedly offered her his benediction, bravely asserting that what she had done had "not been injurious to me." Here Johnson was not deceiving himself, but he was still unable to admit to her his true feelings. "Whatever I can contribute to your happiness," he assured her, "I am very ready to repay for that kindness which soothed twenty years of a life radically wretched." He "presumed" to offer her some advice—again, the sort of advice a well-meaning father might give to his daughter—and this was that she should settle with Piozzi in England, where her "dignity" and "security" would be greater than in Italy. In soliciting her "good wishes," he evidently hoped their correspondence would continue.[61]

60. *Letters*, III, 174 (July 2, 1784).
61. *Letters*, III, 175, 177–178 (July 4 and 8, 1784).

To Fanny Burney, who had been her trusted confidante
during the entire affair, Mrs. Thrale then reported this climactic exchange of letters: "Dr. Johnson wrote me a most
ferocious Letter in ansr. to that you saw the Copy of, but
when he read my Reply to it, he softened at once; has sent
Prayers and Wishes for mine and my Piozzi's happiness—&
behaved with all the Tenderness you can imagine. . . . [He]
is going to Derbys—and in very good humour with me I am
sure: This Moment [July 12] I wrote again to him with
Piozzi's Coms. &c."[62] On July 17, only six days before her
marriage took place in London, she wrote to Fanny once
again. "You can scarce imagine how *very* little I think about
what the Guardians [of her daughters] say," she insisted;
"they none of them say any thing to me good or bad, except
Dr. Johnson, who wrote me an affectionate Letter." Her
happiness, she said, depended "wholly on the health & continued Attachment of my Husband," and she hoped that
"the Storms are past."[63] As these two letters show, Mrs.
Thrale trusted, or at least had convinced herself, that she
was back in Johnson's good graces and was parting with him
on amiable terms. Her conscience was put at ease, and she
could now become completely absorbed in her new life.

What Johnson really felt was evidently something quite
different, as Fanny Burney herself discovered a few months
later. When she called on Johnson at Bolt Court in late
November, less than three weeks before his death, she could
not resist asking if he ever heard from Mrs. Piozzi. " 'No,'
cried he, 'nor write to her. I drive her quite from my mind.
If I meet with one of her letters, I burn it instantly. I have

62. Mrs. Thrale to Fanny Burney, Bath, July 12, 1784, MS in the Burney
Papers, Berg Collection, New York Public Library (see n. 45 above). For
Mrs. Thrale's last letter to Johnson (written on the 12th but postdated by
her "15: July 1784" and sent from Bath, in order to conceal from Johnson
the fact that she was then in London, still unmarried), see *Letters*, III, 184.
63. Mrs. Thrale to Fanny Burney, "Saturday" [July 17, 1784] (misdated
in another hand "July 18: 1784"), MS in the collection of Miss Paula
Peyraud, Chappaqua, New York. I am very grateful to Miss Peyraud for
permission to quote from this letter, which was long missing and only
recently came to light.

burnt all I can find. I never speak of her, and I desire never to hear of her more. I drive her, as I said, wholly from my mind.' ''[64] The bitterness and resentment that poured forth on this occasion were strong evidence that he still felt keenly the injury he had received from Mrs. Thrale. Well might he have lamented with Lear that

> I loved her most, and thought to set my rest
> On her kind nursery.

He had wished her happiness but, unlike Lear, found himself unable to forgive her.

---

64. *Diary and Letters of Madame D'Arblay*, II, 271 (November 28, 1784, recording the meeting on November 25).

Thomas Hollis and Samuel Johnson

A brief passage in Boswell's *Life of Johnson* set the tone for most subsequent commentators on Thomas Hollis of Lincoln's Inn (1720–1774), defining him as a curious but relatively harmless eccentric, probably a revolutionary, and perhaps an atheist. Eccentric he surely was, but he was just as surely a deeply religious man although a dissenter, and he was an ardent supporter of his country and the house of Hanover. His quarrel was with established religion and the infringement of civil and religious liberty by the misdeeds of government ministers. Because he chose to work anonymously and refused public office of any kind, his accomplishments were seldom perceived in his own time, and posterity has been generally content to value him at Johnson's estimate. Boswell's pivotal anecdote about him deserves close scrutiny not merely on Hollis's account, but also because it sheds some light on an obscure period of Johnson's life.

The comment on Hollis in the *Life* occurs in the entry for Friday, April 20, 1781, which Boswell recalled as "one of the happiest days that I remember to have enjoyed in the whole course of my life." He and Johnson, with Miss Hannah More, Mrs. Edward Boscawen, Mrs. Elizabeth Carter, Sir Joshua Reynolds, and Dr. Charles Burney were invited to dine in the Adelphi by Mrs. David Garrick, her first social occasion since the death of her husband three months

earlier. Boswell writes, "The general effect of this day
dwells upon my mind in fond remembrance; but I do not
find much conversation recorded. What I have preserved
shall be faithfully given." He then goes on,

"One of the company mentioned Mr. Thomas Hollis, the strenuous Whig, who used to send over Europe presents of democratical
books, with their boards stamped with daggers and caps of liberty.
Mrs. Carter said, "He was a bad man. He used to talk uncharitably." JOHNSON. "Poh! poh! Madam; who is the worse for
being talked of uncharitably? Besides, he was a dull poor creature
as ever lived. And I believe he would not have done harm to a
man whom he knew to be of very opposite principles to his own. I
remember once at the Society of Arts, when an advertisement was
to be drawn up, he pointed me out as the man who could do it
best. This, you will observe, was kindess to me. I however slipt
away, and escaped it."
    Mrs. Carter said of the same person, "I doubt he was an
Atheist." JOHNSON. "I don't know that. He might perhaps
have become one, if he had had time to ripen, (smiling.) He
might have *exuberated* into an Atheist."[1]

Boswell's rough journal, kept at the time of this event and
his source for the anecodote, reveals slight but significant
differences.

Before dinner Hollis was talked of. Mrs. Carter said he talked
uncharitably of people. Dr. Johnson *with* great sophistry said,
"Who is the worse for being talked of uncharitably? Hollis *was* a
dull, poor creature as ever lived." He said he beleived [!] Hollis
*woul*d not have DONE harm to a Man of opposite principles.
"Once at the Society of Arts when an Advertisement was to be
drawn up, he pointed me out as a Man who would do it best. This
was kindness to me. I *however* slipt away." Mrs. Carter doubted
he was an Atheist. "I don't know that," said the D*octo*r, smiling.
"He might perhaps have become one if he had had time to ripen.

    1. *Boswell's Life of Johnson*, ed. George Birkbeck Hill and L. F. Powell
(Oxford: Clarendon Press, 1934), IV, 96–98. Hereafter cited as *Life*.

He might have exuberated into an Atheist."[2]

The two versions are remarkably close, but not identical. In reworking the journal entry for the *Life*, Boswell incorporated a recollection of Hollis's striking emblematic bindings, which he had seen in the public library at Bern in 1764.[3] He added a few minor embellishments and made other small changes designed to convey a sense of actual conversation. Johnson was described as "*the* man who *could* do it best," rather than "a Man who would do it best." The later version is also notable for the ommission of the words, "with great sophistry." Why had Boswell, fresh from the scene, applied that phrase to Johnson's remark? And, even more puzzling, how did Thomas Hollis, a plain man who had courted obscurity, and who had died more than seven years earlier, come to be a topic of discussion in that select company? The answer to these questions appears to lie in the publication in 1780 of Archdeacon Francis Blackburne's monumental and anonymous (and according to Horace Walpole, deadly dull[4]) *Memoirs of Thomas Hollis, Esq.*

In itself this book can hardly have interested them much, and seemed unlikely to invite the condescension (and sophistry?) of Dr. Johnson and the spite of Mrs. Carter. But one part of it cannot have seemed dull to Johnson and his friends. Blackburne had planned a lengthy appendix to the *Memoirs* containing, among other things, biographical notices of the Commonwealth heroes whom Hollis had revered and whose works he had caused to be republished for the benefit of eighteenth-century readers. Leading them all was John Milton, whose writings had been the single greatest influence on Hollis's life. In the appendix as first printed, Blackburne's notes on Milton consisted mainly of comments

2. *Private Papers*, ed. Geoffrey Scott and F. A. Pottle (Mt. Vernon, N. Y.: privately printed, 1928–1934), XIV, 14. Hereafter cited as *Boswell Papers*.
3. *Boswell Papers*, IV, 46–47.
4. *Memoirs of the Reign of King George the Third*, ed. Sir Denis Le Marchant, Bart. (London, 1845), III, 331 n. 2. Walpole wrongly dates Hollis's death as 1764 rather than 1774.

on earlier biographers and critics, whom he was at pains to
correct when he thought it necessary.

In 1779, after the text and appendix of the *Memoirs* had
been set and printed but before its publication, Johnson published the first volumes of his *Lives of the Poets*, and in
Volume II appeared his controversial account of John Milton, generally acknowledged to be the most biassed of all the
Lives. As Johnson's bibliographers put it, "The political side
of Milton's life aroused the antipathy of Johnson; the ways
and habits of the shrinking recluse at Cambridge did not
attract the sympathy of a man who had battled with poverty
for many a year and had passed his days amid the turmoil of
Fleet Street."[5] Johnson could not deny Milton's literary
eminence, but he seized every opportunity to disparage him
personally. The asperities of Milton's family life, William
Lauder's old and discredited claim that Milton had been the
agent for inserting Pamela's Prayer in the text of *Eikon Basi-
like*, the charge that he was a paid hack writing for
Cromwell's government—these and many such topics were
the subject of acid comment.

Admirers of Milton and ardent Whigs were not slow in
responding, none more bitingly than the man who was on
the verge of publishing his own very different view of Milton. Blackburne was a skillful and experienced political and
religious polemicist, one of a small group of such writers
whom Hollis had kept supplied with ammunition for their
forays against established religion and Tory politics. During
the late summer and early autumn of 1779 he wrote a spirited defense of Milton that was also a blistering attack on
Samuel Johnson. Fifty-four quarto pages were inserted at
the end of the original section on Milton in the appendix to
the Hollis *Memoirs*; repeated and starred pagination and

5. William Prideaux Courtney and David Nichol Smith, *A Bibliography of
Samuel Johnson*, reissue of the 1915 edition (Oxford: Clarendon Press,
1925), pp. 129–140, esp. p. 137.

signature-marks make the insertion obvious.[6] The last leaf of the preface to the *Memoirs* was also replaced by a cancel to insert another unfavorable reference to Johnson's work. Meantime the text of Blackburne's addendum was reprinted in small octavo similar in size to Johnson's *Lives,* presumably to range beside them on the shelf. The octavo edition added texts of two of Hollis's favorites among Milton's prose essays: *Of Education* and *Areopagitica.*

Blackburne freely acknowledged Johnson's literary stature, but then took the position that it made his attack on Milton all the more reprehensible. And, canny debater that he was, he turned Johnson's own words and actions back against him when he could. He dwelt at length on Johnson's preface to Lauder's fabricated charges of plagiarism against Milton; when Johnson wrote disparagingly of Milton's having run a "boarding-school," Blackburne inserted a footnote quoting Johnson's advertisement for his own school in the *Gentleman's Magazine* for 1736, citing the very page on which it appeared. Of Johnson's political pamphleteering he wrote, "Having tasted the honey of a pension for writing ministerial pamphlets, would he feel no regret in returning once more to hunger and philosophy?" — almost an exact quotation of Johnson's own remark on Milton's situation at the time of the Restoration. And in an afterthought to the addendum, written several months later but still squeezed in, Blackburne envisioned a future monument to Johnson's "vast exploits" on which some "humorous drole" would have inscribed "with a homely pencil of charcoal, HERE LYES THE GRAND EXEMPLAR OF LITERARY PROSTI-TUTION." To justify these harsh words, he recalled in detail Johnson's change of political sentiments since his early

6. Francis Blackburne, in *Memoirs of Thomas Hollis, Esq.,* the 54 leaves are inserted between pp. 532 and 533 and paged 533*-*576, *577*-*584*, 579*-*580. Their irregularity points to at least two stages of revision before publication. Hereafter cited as *Memoirs.*

life of Savage and finished by attacking him for writing on
behalf of the unfortunate Dr. Dodd.[7]

Of all the responses to Johnson's life of Milton,
Blackburne's was clearly the one that stung. Arthur Murphy, a close friend of Johnson, devoted some 18 (out of
187) pages of his *Essay on the Life and Genius of Dr.
Johnson* (1792) to defending the treatment of Milton, spending more
time on Blackburne's *Remarks* than on any other attack.[8] He
tells how John Nichols showed the "libellous" passage about
Lauder to Johnson, who read it "with attention, and
instantly wrote on the margin: 'In the business of Lauder I
was deceived, partly by thinking the man too frantic to be
fraudulent'"—not, perhaps, the strongest of defenses.
Johnson also denied that he had been the author of an
anonymous "Poetical Scale" comparing the supposed merits
of various writers, published in the *Literary Magazine* for
1758 and attributed to him by Blackburne. There can be no
question that Johnson read Blackburne's *Remarks* and read
them with care. Obviously the attack troubled him to an
unusual degree. His friends must have been equally aware
of it and scandalized by it, and the association of it with the
Memoirs must have been what brought Hollis to mind on
April 20, 1781.

How well did Johnson know Hollis, that he could characterize him as "a dull poor creature as ever lived" while
attesting to his lack of malice? And when was their association? Two main sources of information survive: Hollis's
unpublished diary for the years 1759 to 1770, and the
records, published and unpublished, of what Johnson called
"The Society of Arts"—the full name of which was the
Society for Promoting (alternatively, for the Encouragement

7. A *terminus a quo* for the first and longest portion of Blackburne's
addendum is provided by a reference to the *Critical Review* for May 1779,
on p. 539* of the *Memoirs*; for the last few pages, by a reference to the
Gentleman's Magazine for October 1779, on p. *581*. On Johnson and
Dodd, see A. D. Barker, "Samuel Johnson and the Campaign to Save William Dodd," *Harvard Library Bulletin*, 31 (1983), 147–180.

8. Pp. 59–67, 177–186, esp. pp 66–67, 183–185.

of) Arts, Manufactures and Commerce, abbreviated by contemporaries as S.P.A.C.[9] It is known today as the Royal
Society of Arts, and occupies quarters on John Adam Street
in the Adelphi, not far from where it was founded and close
to the scene of Mrs. Garrick's dinner party.

The idea of such a society was conceived in 1753 by William Shipley for the purpose of establishing a fund for
awarding premiums "for the promoting of improvements in
Liberal Arts, Sciences, Manufactures, etc." Its first organi-
zational meeting took place in a coffee house in Covent Garden in 1754. It adopted a constitution and elected officers in
1755. Thereafter its list of premiums rapidly grew in scope
and quantity, while its membership increased in numbers
and distinction. From 1755 to 1760 its rolls swelled from
104 subscribing members to 1,350. As its bicentennial historians remark, "it might almost seem easier to compile a
list of the eminent men of the mid-eighteenth century who
were *not* members."[10] Merchants and artisans took an active
part in its affairs alongside noblemen, eminent commoners,
wealthy amateurs, and artists.

In the year of its conception, Thomas Hollis had just
returned from two consecutive grand tours of Europe that
had lasted six years in all. He was filled with patriotic ardor

9. The MS records of the society are in its library in London. I am
indebted to its curator-librarian, D. G. C. Allan, Esq., for access to them
and for answering many questions about the society. References to its
records are by the title (e.g., *General Minutes*) and volume numbers and the
foliation supplied by the library. The MS Diary of Hollis (hereafter cited as
Diary) was presented to the Houghton Library, Harvard University in 1962
by Mr. Arthur A. Houghton, Jr., and is shelved as MS Eng 1191; since it
remains unpublished, references are by date of entry. I am presently
engaged in preparing a fresh and annotated transcript of it. I am indebted
to Rodney G. Dennis, Curator of MSS, for permission to publish excerpts.
10. Derek Hudson and Kenneth W. Luckhurst, *The Royal Society of Arts,
1754–1954* (London: John Murray, 1954), p. 28. In 1980 Mr. D. G. C.
Allan prepared an excellent *Bibliographical and Tabular Supplement* to Hudson and Luckhurst, published by the society in photocopy. See also Sir
Henry Trueman Wood, *A History of the Royal Society of Arts* (London: John
Murray, 1913), who prints a selected list of eminent early members, pp.
28–46.

and a desire to promote the interests of England, particularly against the competition and indeed hostility of the French. The new society was intended for just such purposes, and he soon joined its ranks. He was proposed by a friend, Thomas Major, the engraver, and elected on March 17, 1756.[11] He became a life member in 1759. From 1757 until the Spring of 1763 he attended as many of the weekly general meetings as he could, together with the committees that interested him or to which he was appointed. At times he was in the society's rooms as often as five or six days in the week. Few members were more active or more faithful until a meeting early in 1763, probably in March or April, when one Mr. Shirley seriously affronted him "in full Society, uncontradicted by one single person." The records of the society reveal neither the exact date nor the nature of the affront, but because of it, Hollis resolved that he could no longer "in decency attend that Society in person."[12] Nonetheless he continued to take an active part in society affairs, though at second hand; Dr. Peter Templeman, its secretary, now began coming to Hollis to seek his counsel and it was freely given. Hollis's enthusiasm for the principles of what he commonly referred to as "the Society, the NOBLE Society" was unabated, but he would not come to meetings and committees, though he appeared at the rooms occasionally to view exhibitions. Late in 1769, his wounds apparently healed by the passage of time, he began attending occasional meetings once more.

Samuel Johnson's membership in the S.P.A.C. was junior to Hollis's by some eight months. He was proposed by James Stuart and elected on December 1, 1756.[13] But more than shared membership linked Hollis and Johnson. Hollis had been an early patron and supporter of "Athenian"

11. *General Minutes*, I, 105–106. See John L. Abbott, "Thomas Hollis and the Society 1756–1774," *Journal of the Royal Society of Arts* (hereafter *JRSA*), 119 (1970–71), 711–715, 803–807, 874–878.

12. *Diary*, September 28, 1763.

13. *General Minutes*, I, 184–185. See John L. Abbott, "Dr. Johnson and the Society," *JRSA*, 115 (1966–67), 395–400, 486–491.

Stuart. They had met as early as February 11, 1751, when Hollis wrote home from Venice to his revered tutor, Dr. John Ward of Gresham College, transmitting a manuscript prospectus for a proposed work on the classical remains at Athens, to be compiled by Stuart and Nicholas Revett.[14] Such support must have been encouraging to the two young architects, who were then virtually unknown and whom the Turks had not yet permitted to set foot in Greece to carry forward their great project. The friendship between Hollis and Stuart developed into collaboration after both were back in England, when they worked together on the design for the society's first premium medal as well as the series with which the S.P.A.C. celebrated the victories of the Seven Years' War.[15] The iconography that they employed had much in common with the emblems Hollis adopted for the "Liberty" prints that he commissioned and the tools he had caused to be designed for his bookbindings. Later Hollis offered to allow Stuart to publish two Greek owls from his personal collection in *The Antiquities of Athens*, and his name was in the list of subscribers when the first volume was published in 1762.[16] Stuart lived in St. James's Square just around the corner from Hollis, and Hollis's diary shows that they enjoyed evenings of conversation together quite apart from their discussions about design.

14. The original is in the British Library, London, MS. Add. 6210, f.133; its proper date may be 1752, because in that year England adopted the New Style calendar and one cannot be sure which system Hollis was employing. Another letter from Hollis to Ward referring to Stuart and Revett is dated December 25, 1752 (f.139).

15. *General Minutes*, II, 7; III 72–73, 76, and elsewhere. *Diary*, October 8, 1759, August 30, 1760, May 26, 1761, September 17, 1761, and elsewhere.

16. *Diary*, June 12, 1760. Stuart does not seem to have depicted the owls in the *Antiquities*, but one of Hollis's favorite symbols, the owl with outspread wings, clutching a palm-leaf, appears in the gilt design on the front cover of several special copies of the book; see the Houghton Library copy, Typ 705.62.811P v.1.

Thus Stuart may have actually introduced Johnson and Hollis at the society. But even if he did not, the society was so small when they joined that two such striking figures must have been well aware of each other at any meeting both attended. In the early days meetings averaged about twelve and seldom exceeded twenty participants; by 1758 the average attendance was thirty-eight with an occasional peak of about sixty. Johnson's unusual appearance and manner are sufficiently familiar to modern readers to require no detailed description here. As for Hollis, he was characterized by his artist-friend G. B. Cipriani as Herculean in size—over six feet tall—muscular and well proportioned; a man to stand out among his generally much smaller contemporaries.[17]

As far as one can tell from the surviving records of the S.P.A.C., Johnson was by no means as faithful a member as Hollis. There are lacunae in the minutes, and the identification of participants is frequently ambiguous, but on March 2, 1757 it seems certain that both Hollis and Johnson attended the same regular meeting, and they may also have done so on February 1, 1758.[18] At a meeting on May 17, 1758 both were appointed to a large committee to consider proposals for a charity house for prostitutes, but it is not certain whether either was present, and no records of the committee survive.[19] After that date there are no further

17. Giovanni Battista Cipriani is quoted at length on Hollis's appearance, *Memoirs*, p. 503.

18. *General Minutes*, II, 143–146.

19. *General Minutes*, III, 16 and 42. The proposal was evidently deemed inappropriate as a function of the S.P.A.C., and it was organized instead as the Magdalen House or Hospital, with its own independent membership and officers. See the pamphlet by Saunders Welch, a metropolitan magistrate who was also a member of S.P.A.C., *A Proposal to render effectual a Plan to remove the Nuisance of Common Prostitutes from the Streets of this Metropolis* (London, 1758), and the organization's own *Plan of the Magdalen House for the Reception of Penitent Prostitutes* (London, 1758). Hollis subscribed twenty guineas to become a life governor, though he said "the name given to it [was] exceptionable" (*Diary*, April 26 and July 29, 1759). He continued to support the charity, giving twenty guineas on October 22, 1767 towards the building of a new house for it (see *Diary*).

references to Samuel Johnson in 1758 or 1759, although Hollis's attendance at meetings and committees continued unabated. In February 1760, Johnson did, however, assist the artist members of the society in persuading it to permit an exhibition to be held. In fact Johnson's dues were then in arrears, and he made them up in April 1760, possibly so that he could be eligible to vote for his friend Robert Dossie, who had just been proposed.[20] Later in the same year Johnson took part in several affairs of the society that did not involve Hollis, who was as busy as ever about other aspects of the S.P.A.C.

In 1761 Johnson was named to two committees. The first was directed to examine a proposed method of "preserving Water sweet and wholesome," and included Benjamin Franklin in its roster. Johnson certainly met with it twice, on November 27, 1761 and January 11, 1762, but probably not again. The committee slowly faded away as its experiments showed that there was little to recommend the scheme.[21] The second committee was viewed somewhat more seriously by the society. It was set up to judge a competition for the best essay on "The Arts of Peace," evidently intended to celebrate the aims that the society had been established to foster. Committee members included not only Johnson and Franklin, but also Hollis and his close friend Thomas Brand.[22] On January 26, 1762 Johnson attended a meeting of the committee, but Hollis does not seem to have been present; on February 2 Hollis attended, but apparently not Johnson.

During the early part of 1762 Samuel Johnson served on one more committee that does not seem to have included Hollis, and he proposed three new members who were elected to the society: Richard Bathurst of Gray's Inn, John

20. Abbott, "Dr. Johnson and the Society," pp. 397–398.
21. Ibid., p. 487.
22. *General Minutes*, VII, 60; Abbott, "Dr. Johnson and the Society," pp. 487–488. D. G. C. Allan, who has examined the miscellaneous committee minutes with this in mind, assures me that Hollis and Johnson do not appear ever to have both been present at any meeting of this committee.

Bell of Hart Street, Bloomsbury, and Edmund Allen, printer, of Bolt Court.[23] At the meeting of March 31, 1762 when Johnson proposed Allen, Hollis proposed Linnaeus for Corresponding Membership.[24] Members could be proposed by letter, so the nomination implies nothing about the presence or absence of either man on that occasion. After this date Johnson's name appears no more in the records of the society, and his membership lapsed. Nevertheless, years later when James Barry adorned the Great Room of the Society with a mural, Johnson's portrait was included among other worthies, but Hollis was forgotten.

Hollis and Johnson, then, were brought together by the S.P.A.C., but they do not appear to have met there frequently. Hollis's diary, however, suggests contacts under other circumstances. The difficulty, as pointed out by James L. Clifford in his *Dictionary Johnson* (1979) and elsewhere, is that Hollis customarily referred to people by last name only.[25] The same problem besets anyone trying to interpret the records of the S.P.A.C., in which Samuel Johnson was the only member of that surname until the second half of 1760. Then Robert, William, and James Johnson were all elected in rapid succession, with resultant confusion. References to "Mr. Johnson" in Hollis's diary, as in the records of the S.P.A.C., prior to July 1760 may reasonably be identified with Samuel, but thereafter only if there is corroborative evidence. Peeling away the other Johnsons may help to confirm genuine encounters between Hollis and Samuel Johnson.

For example, on July 25, 1760 Hollis recorded, "Dined at a Tavern with Mr. Hewet, and Mr. Johnson. Induced the latter to become a member of the Society for promot. arts and commerce." This was certainly not Samuel, who was

23. Abbott, "Dr. Johnson and the Society," p. 488.
24. *General Minutes*, VII, 125.
25. James L. Clifford, "Some Problems of Johnson's Obscure Middle Years," in *Johnson, Boswell and Their Circle* (Oxford: Clarendon Press, 1965), pp. 101–106; *Dictionary Johnson* (New York: McGraw Hill, 1979), p. 235.

already a member, but rather Robert Johnson of Cavenham Hall, Suffolk, proposed by Hollis for membership on August 6 and elected on the twentieth.[26] With few exceptions, references in Hollis's diary to "Mr. Johnson" after that date are probably to Robert, who was the eldest son of the colonial governor of South Carolina, Robert Johnson (ca. 1676–1735).[27] It is too bad, because for several protracted periods over the next few years Hollis reported dining almost nightly with "Mr. Johnson," often in the company of John Hewett, William Lloyd, and Thomas Brand; after which they sometimes went for walks through the City and the surrounding suburbs, or visited Ranelagh, or attended a performance by Samuel Foote. All these diversions are well known to have appealed to Samuel Johnson, but it appears to have been Robert who shared them with Hollis, as verified when "Mr. Johnson" turns up with a nephew, "Mr. Izard." Ralph Izard (1741/2–1804) was the son of Robert Johnson's sister Margaret, and was proposed by Hollis for membership in S.P.A.C. as "of Trinity College, Cambridge" on March 22, 1762 and elected on March 29.[28] Other identifiable Johnsons in Hollis's diary are the son of the well-known collector, Maurice Johnson of Spalding, whose cabinet of coins and medals was viewed by Hollis on tour on August 6, 1761, and a bookseller in Ludgate Street whose shop he visited on November 24, 1763—almost certainly E. Johnson of 4 Ludgate Hill.[29]

When we strip such references away, there remains a small but significant residue. A cluster of early entries in the diary records five dinners in unidentified taverns with "Mr. Johnson" in July 1759, almost certainly Samuel Johnson. The earliest, on Saturday the twenty-first, strikes an

26. *General Minutes*, VI, 10, 15.
27. On the colonial governor, see article in the *Dictionary of American Biography (DAB)*, references to the Johnson family.
28. *General Minutes*, VII, 114, 121; article on Ralph Izard in *DAB*.
29. H. R. Plomer, *A Dictionary of the Printers and Booksellers . . . in England . . . from 1726 to 1775* (Oxford: Bibliographical Society, 1932), pp. 140–141. Other Johnsons listed by Plomer seem less likely.

unpromising note: "Dined at a tavern with Mr. Johnson, and found him the same Selfist, Reptile, as ever." Devout Johnsonians may boggle at such a characterization, but many of Johnson's contemporaries judged him difficult if not unpleasant. Thus W. J. Temple in 1762 reported him "surly, morose, Dogmatical [and] imperious," while Horace Walpole remarked that his manners were "sordid, supercilious and brutal."[30] *Selfist* and *reptile* would not be over-strong terms in Hollis's vocabulary to describe such behavior; whenever the diarist strayed from a strictly factual report of events, his language could be surprisingly frank and incisive. The entries cannot be dismissed out of hand, and if the identification is correct, the entry quoted shows that Hollis and Johnson had been acquainted for some time—and were not temperamentally attracted to each other. Nevertheless they dined again on Monday the twenty-third and walked out together in the evening, dining also on the twenty-sixth, twenty-seventh, and twenty-ninth. Hollis, alas, recorded no details of where they went or what they talked about.

Their next point of contact cannot be doubted and was the most important. Late in 1759 the victories of the British over the French in the Seven Years' War—the same victories that Stuart, Hollis, and the S.P.A.C. were celebrating with commemorative medals—brought into England growing numbers of French prisoners, destitute except for the clothes on their backs and the small ration allowance customarily

---

30. Quoted by A. Lytton Sells, *Oliver Goldsmith* (London: George Allen & Unwin, 1974), p. 96. The *New English Dictionary* defines *selfist* as "A self-centered or selfish person" with the earliest example of use in 1649; *reptile* sb.2 as "A person of a low, mean, grovelling, or repulsive character," quoting Fielding in 1749 and Johnson's *Rambler* 170 in 1751. Johnson's *Dictionary* does not list *selfist* and defines *reptile* as "An animal that creeps upon many feet." [!] The word *selfist* is clearly written in the *Diary*, but both Clifford ("Some Problems," cited above, n. 25) and Caroline Robbins, "The Strenuous Whig, Thomas Hollis of Lincoln's Inn," *William and Mary Quarterly*, 7 (1950), p. 422, misread it as "selfish." But the reading *selfist* is reinforced by a parallel construction in a letter of Hollis of 1757, probably to his Swiss friend Rodolph Vallbravers, in which he writes of "SELFISM, steril[!], exterminating SELFISM," *Memoirs*, p. 66.

granted such unfortunates. The French crown had evidently written them off. Many had been captured in warmer climes or during the summer, and their suffering was great in the English winter. A movement began to solicit contributions all over England to provide warm clothing for the captives. Newspapers spread the word in London and elsewhere.

The response to the appeal was generous, so much so that on December 18, 1759 a public meeting was held at the Crown and Anchor Tavern in the Strand to discuss how the funds might be managed. At a second meeting two days after a committee of twenty-five was constituted to oversee the actual work of distributing warm clothing to the sufferers. It was headed by Mr. Serjeant (later Sir George) Nares and included both Hollis and Thomas Brand, and it continued to meet publicly once a week at the Crown and Anchor. The committee published advertisements in newspapers describing the progress of its work and listing the gifts it received.[31] A formal report was to be issued when its mission was accomplished, summarizing the committee's activities, listing contributions, and printing a section of grateful responses from the recipients of its bounty. One of its members, Samuel Smith, wrote an introduction for the proposed pamphlet.

The charity did not escape criticism, some of it savage. Letters supporting and attacking it appeared in the public prints. The most vicious onslaught was an unsigned letter in the *London Chronicle* for January 19–22, 1760. Its tone was set in the first paragraph: "It is certain, that true Charity is one of the most amiable of Virtues, that is, when

---

31. For an advertisement, see the *London Chronicle*, January 12–15, 1760, p. 51; for an interim report, ibid., January 17–19, 1761, p. 67. On the Preface to the *Report*, see *Life*, IV, 491; and Allen T. Hazen, *Johnson's Prefaces & Dedications* (New Haven: Yale University Press, 1937), pp. 189–193. It may be worth noting that, according to J. A. Cochrane, *Dr. Johnson's Printer: the Life of William Strahan* (Cambridge: Harvard University Press, 1964) p. 104, the *London Chronicle* "was the only newspaper which Johnson took in regularly," so he must have been aware from the start of the differing views concerning this charity.

administered under the directions of prudence; otherwise it may prove a Vice, as it may nurse Sloth, and support Fraud and Debauchery. A humane temper and a soft heart, directed by a weak head, may become injurious to society. I was led into these reflections by observing proposals to collect money for the relief of French prisoners." A torrent of invective followed, filling three and a half columns. The French were enemies to Britain's "Religion, Liberty, and Trade"; as Papists they "would imbrue their hands in the blood of all who refuse to join in their senseless superstitions"; they loaded their cannon with *langrage*, the eighteenth-century equivalent of fragmentation grenades and dum-dum bullets; they treated British prisoners "with the greatest barbarities"; and the French prisoners would use the money collected "to live in riot, or what is worse, to carry our property into their own country." The writer argued that it would be far better to raise funds to alleviate the lot of the poor and elderly in Britain, to say nothing of the families of distressed British captives. Why not threaten reprisals against French prisoners if British prisoners continued to be maltreated? Pampering them would only lead their rulers to think that the British were weak and fearful. In any event, the scheme had been originated by "a notorious Jacobite" (unidentified), and it sprang either from "egregious weakness and folly, or consummate wickedness and malice."

On January 28 Hollis attended the regular meeting of the committee, and recorded the following in his diary: "A scandalous libel against the Committee, and the subscribers to this Charity was read, which libel was published anonimously, by way of letter, in the London Chronicle, jan. 22, 1760. Resolved unanimously That the Chairman be desired to send for the publisher of such libel, and to reprehend him sharply & to commence a prosecution against him for such publication unless he discover the author of the libel, or ask solemn pardon of the Committee & Subscribers, in print, for having published it." In its issue of January 29 the *Chronicle* printed a letter signed "S. G." responding to the attack, along with a letter dated January 22 by "T.S." in general support of the charity, but these were unrelated to the committee's action and scarcely enough to offset the damage that had been done. Certainly Hollis did not think so. On February 2 he dined with the chairman, Nares, and they had "much conversation" about the libel and the refusal of John Wilkie, publisher of the *London Chronicle*, to acknowledge his error in printing it; and on the fourth, the committee met again and confirmed its earlier resolution. Hollis, who evidently had principal responsibility for seeing the committee's report into print (he designed its title page and general layout, and probably wrote some of it), decided that more should be done, and that the place for it was at the head of the published report.

Samuel Smith's introduction to the report has not survived. We may surmise that Hollis did not think it powerful enough to answer the libel in the *Chronicle*. But he knew someone "of very opposite [political] principles to his own," who nevertheless shared his humanitarian concerns, and was "the man who could do it best." Through their mutual friend, John Payne, the bookseller and publisher, he commissioned Samuel Johnson to write a concise and masterly preface that met and defeated the anonymous libeller on all points. Through Payne, Hollis paid five guineas for it at a time when Johnson must often have wondered where the next shilling was coming from.[32] It was a familiar pattern for Hollis, who helped many an artist of his acquaintance over a rough spot with a generous and well-timed commission. Payne turned Johnson's manuscript over to Hollis on the evening of June 19, 1760. During the next ten days Hollis called on every member of the committee then in town, manuscript in hand, to gain individual agreement to replace Smith's introduction with Johnson's. He also sent a copy to Brand at his country home and received his approbation by

32. *Diary*, December 17 and 23, 1761. Johnson's part in this is discussed and his preface analyzed by Donald J. Greene, "Samuel Johnson and the Great War for Empire," in John H. Middendorf, ed., *English Writers of the Eighteenth Century* (New York: Columbia University Press, 1971), pp. 36–65, especially pp. 63–65. Greene was not aware of Hollis's role or the letter in the *London Chronicle* of January 19–22, 1760.

mail. On June 30 Payne informed Hollis that Samuel Smith, having learned of the universal approval for Johnson's paper, "had approved it likewise, and in a handsome manner." On July 23 Hollis recorded in his diary, "Dined with Mr. Johnson at a Tavern. At a Committee for the Relief of French prisoners of war held at the Crown and Anchor in the Strand. Settled everything ultimately for the intended publication; and among other Resolutions agreed that Mr. Johnson's Mscript should serve as an Introduction to the Publication in the place of Mr. Smith's." Johnson's preface is a remarkable piece of writing, standing on its own as an eloquent plea for humane treatment of helpless prisoners, but it gains enormously in power and immediacy when placed beside the scurrilous letter it so ably answers.

Dinner on July 23, 1760 may well be the last time that Johnson sat down with Hollis, or indeed met him unless casually or by accident; and twenty years later at Mrs. Garrick's party, he forgot the preface and its welcome honorarium. What he remembered was the competition already mentioned, last in the list of premiums of the S.P.A.C. for 1760:

165. A Gold Medal will be given for the best Treatise on the Arts of Peace, containing an historical Account of the progressive Improvements of Agriculture, Manufactures, and Commerce, in that Part of *Great Britain* called *England*, with the Effects of those Improvements on the Morals and Manners on the People, and pointing out the most practicable Means for their future Advancement.[33]

Entries were to be handed in not later than the second Wednesday in December 1761, and as we have seen, the large committee of judges included Johnson as well as Hollis, Brand, and Benjamin Franklin.

As it turned out, the entries were disappointing. At first there appeared to be only one. It was examined by the committee on December 16, but it failed to meet expectations

---

33. *Premiums Offered by the Society . . .* , (London, 1760), pp. 52–53.

and was rejected at a meeting on December 22, 1761. Then the secretary discovered that he had failed to recognize a second entry because of the title its author had given it. On January 26, 1762 the committee was not favorably impressed after reading its first twelve pages, and after completing the reading on February 2 they voted to return it to its author as unsuitable.[34]

But the topic was central to the concerns of the society, and the failure of what he thought was the single entry had disturbed Hollis enough for him to become personally involved even before the second entry had been discovered and judged inadequate. Again he thought of "the man who could do it best," and he recorded in his diary for December 17, 1761, "At Mr. Payne's to desire him to engage Mr. Johnson to write a Dissertation on the polite and liberal arts; their use and benefit to civil life and manners, and to commerce; the noble Society for promoting arts and commerce in respect to them; the success of those views already, and the future expectations from them. Gave him Five Guineas to present to Mr. Johnson for writing the Dissertation, and one Guinea for himself." Hollis knew that the competition carried only a medal as its prize, and he was probably aware that Johnson was still chronically short of money. As before, an approach through a publisher seemed more tactful than a direct commission. On December 21 Hollis recorded that Payne paid him a visit "to acquaint me, that Mr. Johnson declines writing the desired Dissertation as Not sufficiently informed of the several matters to which it must relate. On considering the matter farther with Mr. Payne, desired him engage Mr. Hawksworth to write it." This was, of course, the occasion when Johnson "slipt away." Perhaps he had no wish to appear to be entering a contest for which he was already on the committee of judges, or to rouse himself from his habitual sloth in order to write an essay so closely to someone else's specification. Very likely he saw

<hr />

34. John L. Abbott, "John Hawkesworth and 'The Treatise on the Arts of Peace,'" *JRSA*, 115 (1966–67), 645.

through the polite subterfuge, for years later he could recall
that Hollis was behind the proposal. And, as it turned out,
Hollis was no luckier in his second choice. On January 3,
1762, according to the diary, "Mr. Payne [was] with me for
an hour in the morning to read to me the Dissertation written by Mr. Hawksworth, mentioned dec. 21, in which,
unhappily, he has not succeeded." No more is heard of it
thereafter.

No incident or argument separated Hollis and Johnson,
simply their wide divergence in temperament and philosophy. Hollis was unlikely to offer further commissions to a
man who had refused one, and before the year was out,
Johnson was secure in his government pension. Both were
shortly to end their direct participation in the affairs of the
S.P.A.C. Yet it would be remarkable if each had not continued to be aware of the other, perhaps Hollis more so than
Johnson. In the relatively small society of London in the
eighteenth century they must surely have encountered one
another in the ordinary course of their perambulations of the
town, particularly as they frequented some of the same
taverns and coffee houses, to say nothing of bookshops and
printing houses, but such chance meetings are not a matter
of record. They certainly had numerous friends and acquaintances in common, many but not all of them through the
Society. All the men present at Mrs. Garrick's dinner party
had been members, though Boswell's membership was tenu-
ous at best and of short duration. Hollis visited both Reynolds and Hogarth in their studios; Hogarth once gave him
one of his prints. Goldsmith, accompanied by Mr.
Chamier—possibly Anthony, member of The Club, but
perhaps John, who later went out to India as a merchant —
visited Hollis on March 1, 1760 to solicit his vote for the
secretaryship of S.P.A.C., but he shortly withdrew his name
when Garrick threatened to vote against him. Over the years
Hollis and Goldsmith evidently became well acquainted, for
when they met accidentally in the Temple on April 11, 1767,
Hollis recorded that he "enduced him in our prate to throw
off an ironical Squib in one of the public prints, for which he
is singularly able, against the dull Citizens of London, for

intending to Convert Gresham College into an Excize Office." Garrick served on several committees on the society with Hollis, as did the eminent architect, Sir William Chambers. Dr. William Rose, the translator and schoolmaster of Kew and Chiswick, said to be one of the very few who bested Samuel Johnson in verbal combat, became a close friend of Hollis in the late sixties; he was also a member of the S.P.A.C.[35] Another member known to both was John Wilkes, whose conversation was sometimes relished by Johnson although his politics were abhorrent.[36] Hollis, on the other hand, applauded Wilkes' fight for civil and especially electoral liberties, though he distrusted his glibness. On their first recorded meeting, he called him "a man of much low art, & a W[a]lp[o]l[ea]n philosopher."[37] Other possible points of contact of this kind could no doubt be multiplied.

Another interesting mutual acquaintance was the Jesuit Padre Rudyer Josip Boscovich, the learned scientist of Ragusa (Dubrovnik), whom Johnson astonished with the fluency of his Latin conversation. Hollis could converse with Boscovich in Latin, too; but on a more practical level, he saw to it that Boscovich's Latin poem on Newtonian science was published in London, and probably even had a hand in designing its title page. Hollis was undoubtedly inspired by his veneration of Sir Isaac Newton, in his opinion the scientific genius of his age; for example, he assembled and sent to Harvard College a nearly complete series of Newton's works, all in bindings bearing the emblems he used to symbolize wisdom and peace. But he was probably just as interested in sponsoring a learned man who was experiencing difficulty finding a publisher.[38]

35. On Johnson's acknowledging Rose's victory, see Murphy, *Essay*, pp. 94–95; *Life*, IV, 509. Hollis and Rose shared concern about the establishment of a Roman Catholic school for Protestant youth in Kensington, and frequently consulted about countermeasures.

36. *Life*, III, 183.

37. *Diary*, October 9, 1759.

38. Rudyer Josip Boscovich, *De solis ac lunae defectibus libri V* (London, 1760); *Life*, II, 125, 406; *Diary*, August 30, 1760, September 29, 1761, January 12, 1768. Hollis persuaded Millar to take part in publishing the poem.

With his many Italian contacts, it was inevitable that
Hollis should come to know another member of Johnson's
circle, Giuseppe Baretti, who had come to England in 1751.
When they met is not recorded, but on March 16, 1760
Hollis wrote in his diary, "Signor Baretti with me to pass the
evening. Much Conversation concerning his own schemes,
Mr. Da Costa's benefaction to the B[ritish]. Musuem, Mr.
Johnson etc. etc." It was neither the first nor the last evening that they spent in conversation, but the only one on
which Hollis recorded Johnson as a topic of discussion.
They continued to correspond when Baretti returned to Italy.
When he came back to England and got into the unfortunate
scuffle with a ruffian in Haymarket leading to his arrest and
trial for murder in 1769, Hollis visited him in prison with
both moral support and material comforts. Johnson, of
course, testified in court for Baretti,[39] but Hollis took no
direct part in the proceedings, his help having been yet again
material rather than verbal.[40] It was through Baretti that the
last distant contact between Hollis and Johnson had taken
place some years before, while Baretti was still in Italy.
Hollis wrote in his diary on March 23, 1766,

. . . Mr. Joseph Baretti having been pleased to send me from
Ancona, six copies of a work of his, in sheets, printed in Italy,
anonimously, & called *La Frusta Letteraria*; busied the morning
about them, in order to their dispersion, bound, to the following
Persons & Places.
Mr. Johnson.
Mr. Cipriani.
The British Musaeum.
Williams's Library.
The Radcliffe Library, Oxford.
Christ College, Cambridge.

39. *Life*, II, 96–98, esp. p. 97 n. 1.
40. *Diary*, October 11, 13, 20, 1760. Hollis gave Baretti twenty guineas
toward expenses: "He treated me rather coolly, yet thanked me for the
present, and expressed a desire, that I should attend his trial" — which
Hollis did not do.

There is no evidence that Johnson knew the intermediary through whom Baretti's periodical was transmitted, but he certainly was familiar with the work, and acknowledged a reference to himself in it.[41] Hollis never mentioned Dr. Johnson again, and as far as we know Johnson never referred to Hollis until Mrs. Garrick's dinner party, long after Hollis's death.

It is not surprising; they had little more in common. Hollis must have been alienated when Johnson accepted the pension from Lord Bute in 1762, as he was later outraged when the elder Pitt received a pension and a peerage through the same agency.[42] And as the years went by, Johnson became increasingly hostile to Whigs and to anyone sympathizing with the North American colonies. Like the relationship between Boswell and Mrs. Thrale, theirs was an impossible friendship,[43] but of much shorter duration and for quite different reasons.[44]

41. *Life*, III, 173, 503.

42. Among other things, Hollis had a medal honoring Pitt reengraved to read "WILLIAM PITT / LOST IN PARCHMENT / AND BVTISM / IVY XXX MDCCXVI" (*Diary*, October 8, 1766); but in later years, he and Pitt became close personal friends.

43. On Mrs. Thrale and Boswell, see Mary Hyde, *The Impossible Friendship* (Cambridge: Harvard University Press, 1972).

44. I am grateful to the John Simon Guggenheim Memorial Foundation for a grant relieving me from regular duties for a year and enabling me to pursue research on Thomas Hollis in Europe and America. And I owe much to the doyenne of Hollis studies, Professor Caroline Robbins, for generously sharing the fruits of her devoted labors.

The Vision of Theodore: Genre, Context, Early Reception

Apparently Dr. Johnson's first piece of allegorical fiction, *The Vision of Theodore, Hermit of Teneriffe*, was composed, on the authority of Thomas Tyers, "in one night" after the author had finished "an evening in Holborn."[1] Such a statement is consonant with reports of Johnson's speed in writing the *Life of Savage, Rasselas*, and the fairy tale *The Fountains*, among other works. The *Vision* was one of Johnson's contributions to Robert Dodsley's two-volume textbook *The Preceptor*, published on April 7, 1748, which was designed for the instruction of youthful readers and seemingly intended to compete with John Newbery's more extensive collection, *The Circle of the Sciences* (1745–46?).[2] *The Preceptor*

1. "A Biographical Sketch of Dr. Samuel Johnson," *Gentleman's Magazine*, 56 (December 1784), 901. Tyers's revised "Sketch" appeared as an independent pamphlet in 1785.
2. For a discussion of Johnson's connection with *The Preceptor* and the evidence (a notice in the *General Advertiser*) for the publication date of the work, see Allen T. Hazen, *Samuel Johnson's Prefaces and Dedications* (New Haven: Yale University Press, 1937), pp. 171–172; cited hereafter as Hazen, *Prefaces and Dedications*. To support his inference regarding the relationship between *The Preceptor* and *The Circle of the Sciences*, Hazen quotes this passage from Johnson's preface to the former: "It must not be expected, that in the following Pages should be found a complete Circle of

contains a dedication, a preface (also by Johnson), and twelve parts: "READING, SPEAKING, and WRITING LETTERS"; "ARITHMETIC, GEOMETRY, and ARCHITECTURE"; "GEOGRAPHY and ASTRONOMY"; "CHRONOLOGY and HISTORY"; "RHETORIC and POETRY"; "DRAWING"; "LOGIC"; "NATURAL HISTORY"; "ETHICS, or MORALITY"; "TRADE and COMMERCE"; "LAWS and GOVERNMENT"; and "HUMAN LIFE and MANNERS."[3]

Some of the materials making up the two volumes were original; some were borrowed from other works.[4] *The Vision* appears as the second section of the final part, "Human Life and Manners." In the initial section, the speaker, or "preceptor," urges his "dear Pupil," who has been "conduct[ed]" during the course of the two volumes "into the first Entrance . . . of the Temple of Science" (II, 517), to "Pause . . . at the Portal of Life" and add "Wisdom" to his "other Acquirements" (II, 518). Certain "Precepts" "may facilitate" the "Attainment" of wisdom and the tutor therefore "advise[s]" the student "to divide the study of yourself into the three distinct Subdivisions of *Habits, Sentiments,* and *Passions.*"

"By HABIT," the teacher continues, "is meant such a custom of doing any particular Action, as to fall into it involuntarily and without thinking, or to repeat it so frequently as to render it almost a part of our Nature, not to be subdued without the greatest Difficulty." "*Swearing*" is an instance of the "*first* sort" of habit, "*Drinking*" "of the *second.*" Having commented on both instances, the "preceptor" "mention[s] . . . *Idleness* and *Sauntering.*" "*Indolence,*" he says, citing "an Eastern Writer, is the Daughter of *Folly,* the Sister of *Vice,* and the Mother of *Misfortune.* Whoever

---

the Sciences." The tentative publication dates of the first edition of *The Circle of the Sciences* are drawn from the General Catalogue of the British Library.

3. The headings of these twelve parts are reproduced from the title page of Vol. I of the third edition of *The Preceptor* (2 vols.; London, 1758), and subsequent quotations (located by page numbers in the text of this essay) are drawn from Vols. I and II of the same edition.

4. For a list of the known borrowed materials, see Hazen, pp. 173–174.

suffers himself to fall into this pernicious Habit, cannot hope
to make much Progress in Learning or Knowledge of any
Kind . . . . WISDOM is not to be won without great Assiduity
and constant Application . . . ." Thus he "intreat[s]" his
"dear Pupil" "to take particular Care how you contract *bad
Habits* of any kind," for, "in spite of all your Endeavours to
shake them off, they will hang upon you to your Destruction." "I will illustrate this Subject," he concludes, "and
close my Advice to you on this Head, with a beautiful and
instructive Fable, communicated to me by a Friend for this
Purpose" (II, 519–520). Then follow the title and text of
The Vision (II, 520–530).

Related in the first person by the hermit himself and
addressed to "*SON* of Perseverance, whoever thou art" (II,
520), the eleven-page narrative tells how Theodore, having
retired to the foot of Mount Teneriffe, decides to climb to
the top of the Peak in the forty-eighth year of his retreat.
Becoming weary on his ascent, he "resign[s]" himself "to
Sleep" when a supernatural Protector appears before him
and directs him to "survey" the allegorical Mountain of
Existence and "be wise" (II, 520–521). Obeying, Theodore
observes at the bottom of the mountain a multitude of men
and women attended by the Virgin Innocence. As the group
advances upward, Education replaces Innocence and later
Reason (preceded by her mistress, Religion) succeeds Education as the monitor. A "Troop of Pygmies"—human
habits—also accompany the travelers, sometimes smoothing
their progress but often binding them with chains of
appetites and passions. Some of the pilgrims, guided by
Religion, make their way up to the Temple of Happiness at
the summit of the mountain. Others fall into the clutches of
vicious habits and are lost to Ambition, Avarice, Intemperance, Indolence, Despair, and so on. While Theodore is
"musing on this miserable Scene," his Protector speaks:
"Remember, *Theodore*, and be wise, and let not HABIT prevail against thee." The hermit concludes, "I started and
beheld myself surrounded by the Rocks of *Teneriffe*; the
Birds of Light were singing in the Trees, and the Glances of
the Morning darted upon me" (II, 527, 529–530).

After the presentation of Johnson's *Vision*, the teacher turns to the second of the "three distinct Subdivisions" into which he had previously distinguished the "Study" of the pupil's self. Limiting his treatment to "a few of the most useful or dangerous" passions "as they commonly appear in Human Nature," he briefly discusses Admiration or Wonder, Fear, Pride, Anger, and Love (II, 530, 531–533). His conclusion resembles his introduction of *The Vision*: "As I clos'd the last Part with a modern Allegory, so I chuse to finish and illustrate this with one of the most beautiful Fables in all Antiquity" (II, 533). Then follows "The CHOICE of *Hercules*," "composed by *Prodicus*," the tutor remarks later, "and . . . related by *Xenophon* in his *Memorable Things* of *Socrates*"; "it is here cloath'd in a new Dress by a very eminent Hand, and retains all the native Elegance and Simplicity of the Prose Original, heighten'd with all the Graces of Poetical Ornament" (II, 534–544, 544).[5]

The tutor next "proceed[s] to the *third* Rule, which I laid down for the Attainment of Human Happiness, which you [the pupil] may remember was the Acquisition of wise and prudent SENTIMENTS and OPINIONS" (II, 544). A paragraph of didactic observations ensues, and then the teacher says, "I will close the whole of my Instruction to you on this Head, and finish your Education in general with the celebrated Picture of Human Life, by *Cebes* the *Theban*, a Disciple of *Socrates*, and one of those who assisted him in his last Hours; which I earnestly recommend to your most serious Study and frequent Perusal. It is translated into *English*, by a Person considerably distinguished in the Republic of Letters, and is as follows" (II, 545).[6] The text of "The Picture of HUMAN LIFE" (II, 545–560) brings *The Preceptor* to an end.

Its title, contents, and immediate context all serve to identify the generic classification and literary background of *The Vision of Theodore*. Like its companion pieces, and in the

---

5. The "very eminent Hand" was Bishop Robert Lowth (Hazen, p. 173), whose version of *The Choice* is cited hereafter in the text of this essay.

6. The "Person" was Joseph Spence (Hazen, p. 173), whose version of *The Picture* is cited hereafter in the text of this essay.

words of the preceptor, the work is a "fable" (defined— under sense 1—in Johnson's *Dictionary* [4th ed., 1773] as "A feigned story intended to enforce some moral precept") or an "allegory" (defined in Johnson's *Dictionary* as "A figurative discourse, in which something other is intended, than is contained in the words literally taken; as, *wealth is the daughter of diligence, and the parent of authority*"). Unlike its companion pieces, *The Vision* is cast in the form of a dream. *The Choice of Hercules* by Prodicus and *The Picture of Human Life* attributed to Cebes the Theban were its most significant classical forebears, which—famous in ancient times, largely ignored during the Middle Ages, rediscovered by numerous writers and painters during the Renaissance, and employed frequently as school texts—possibly attained the height of their enormous popularity in the eighteenth century.[7] Besides their inclusion in *The Preceptor*, another indication of their midcentury appeal was the appearance of *The Picture of Human Life* in Robert Dodsley's *Museum* (1747) and of *The Choice of Hercules* both in Joseph Spence's *Polymetis* (1747) and Dodsley's *Collection of Poems* (1748).[8] Furthermore, at the beginning of the century, Addison, who influenced his

7. Prodicus of Ceos was a contemporary of Socrates (469 B.C. – 399 B.C.); *The Choice* was transmitted through Xenophon's *Memorabilia*. Cebes of Thebes may have lived in the fourth century B.C.; his supposed "Picture" or "Table" was probably composed in the first century A.D. For other details see *The Oxford Classical Dictionary* (Oxford: Clarendon Press, 1949), pp. 177, 733.

The principal bases of my statement on the fortunes of *The Choice* and *The Picture* are two illuminating studies: Edwin Christian Heinle, "The Eighteenth Century Allegorical Essay" (Ph.D. diss., Columbia University, 1957), esp. chap. 4 "The 'Choice' Theme': Prodicus and Cebes," pp. 78 – 106; and Earl R. Wasserman, "Johnson's *Rasselas*: Implicit Contexts," *Journal of English and Germanic Philology*, 74 (1975), 1–25, esp. 6–9, 12–16. See also Wasserman's "The Inherent Values of Eighteenth-Century Personification," *PMLA*, 65 (1950), 437–439; and Carey McIntosh's revealing *The Choice of Life: Samuel Johnson and the World of Fiction* (New Haven: Yale University Press, 1973), pp. 110–111.

8. Heinle, "Eighteenth Century Allegorical Essay," pp. 99–100. For other eighteenth-century translations of *The Choice* and *The Picture*, see Wasserman, "Johnson's *Rasselas*," p. 7, n. 12; p. 13, n. 21.

contemporaries and successors in so many ways, had undertaken the "revival" of allegory as "practised by the finest Authors among the ancients"—authors who certainly included Prodicus and Cebes.[9] Earlier, too, the Third Earl of Shaftesbury had composed a substantial essay on "A Notion of the Historical Draught or Tablature of the Judgment of Hercules," had commissioned a painting and engraving based on Prodicus' "fable," had translated the allegory by Cebes, and had planned for it a "literary and artistic treatment" similar to that accorded Prodicus.[10] In 1735 Johnson himself had placed "Cebes" and "Xenophon" (which contains Prodicus' *Choice*) on the list of Greek writers recommended as pre-university reading to his cousin Samuel Ford,[11] and in his preface to *The Preceptor* he remarked that the two "Fables . . . were of the highest Authority, in the ancient *Pagan* World" (I, xxx). Lastly, shortly before the publication of *The Preceptor*, the Scots Professor David Fordyce, in the first volume of his *Dialogues Concerning Education* (London, 1745; 2nd ed. also 1745), had warmly praised the instructional virtues of the two pieces.[12]

The first of these embodies a theme which is also present in the second and was to loom large in numerous eighteenth-century allegorical essays.[13] *The Choice of Hercules*

9. See Donald F. Bond, ed., *Spectator*, 5 vols. (Oxford: Clarendon Press, 1965), IV, 275 (No. 501) (cited hereafter as *Spectator*); *Guardian*, ed. John Calhoun Stephens (Lexington: University Press of Kentucky, 1982), p. 497 (No. 152). Addison provides an English version of *The Choice* in *Tatler* 97 and mentions it again in *Spectator* 183 (*Spectator*, II, 221); he also mentions *The Picture* in the *Tatler*, ed. George A. Aitken, 4 vols. (London: Duckworth, 1898), III, 250 (No. 161).

10. For more details, see Heinle, "Eighteenth Century Allegorical Essay," pp. 48–49, 90, 91–91.

11. *The Letters of Samuel Johnson*, ed. R. W. Chapman, 3 vols. (Oxford: Clarendon Press, 1962), I, 7; *Boswell's Life of Johnson*, ed. George Birkbeck Hill and L. F. Powell, 6 vols. (Oxford: Clarendon Press, 1934–1950), I, 99–100 (cited hereafter as *Life*).

12. See pp. 368–369, 375, 376, 392, 410, 411.

13. Dividing them into four groups—"The Choice of Ladies," "The Forked Path," "The Allegorical Mountain," and "The Procession" (p. 107)—Heinle discusses many of these essays in his fifth and sixth chapters,

depicts the allurements proffered the youthful Greek hero (retired to a "lonely Vale" [II, 534]) via a succession of speeches by two beautiful women (personifying Virtue and Sloth respectively) who interrupt his contemplation, and then represents the hero's choice—of Virtue naturally—between the two. At the end of "the glorious Path" of Virtue is Happiness, the product of "a Life well-spent: / In which no Hour flew unimprov'd away; / In which some generous Deed distinguish'd every Day." Among the concomitants of Sloth, on the other hand, belong Riot, Indolence, grief, and shame (II, 542, 540). The Path of Virtue is a "rough" "steep Ascent" requiring arduous "Toil" and dangerous acts for its traversal; the "Way" of Sloth is "fair, easy, smooth, and plain" (II, 542, 536, 538, 539). Four features, then, the "pictorial setting,"[14] the "choice" theme, the association of happiness with self-discipline and misery with sensual indulgence, and the metaphorical notion of the ascending path of virtue, although certainly not unique to the form, suggest a significant generic connection between the fable by Prodicus and that by Johnson.

The Vision of Theodore exhibits still more—and more striking—resemblances to Cebes' *Picture of Human Life*. Presented (after a short introduction) as a dialogue, *The Picture* relates an Old Citizen's explanation, given to a group of young Strangers, of a puzzling picture hanging "in the Temple of Saturn" (II, 546, 545). Before beginning his interpretation, however, the Citizen emphasizes the importance of the lesson taught by the picture, which, he says, "includes all the Doctrine of what is Good in Life, what is Bad, and what Indifferent." The entire work portrays "the CIRCUIT OF HUMAN LIFE." At the bottom, a "great Number of People standing before the Portal, are those who are to enter into Life." "By the entrance," a "GENIUS . . . directs all that are going in, what they should do after they are enter'd into

---

pp. 107–160.

14. I borrow this phrase from Heinle, who points out (ibid., p. iv) that a pictorial setting is one of the three common elements—the other two being a dream and a guide—in many eighteenth-century allegorical essays.

Life; and shews them which Way they ought to take in order
to be happy in it" (II, 546, 547).

The remainder of the picture depicts three "Inclosures,"
arranged in an ascending direction, and, at the very top and
accessible by a path or "Way," a "high Edifice" towering
like "a Citadel . . . above all the Buildings in a City" (II,
554). Among other figures and places in the first enclosure
are Intemperance, Luxury, Avarice, Flattery, Voluptuous-
ness, Punishment (holding a "Scourge in her Hand"), Sorrow, Anguish of Mind, Repining, and his Sister Despair, the
House of Misery, and Repentance (II, 549–550). Among
those in the second enclosure are False Science; some
"Poets, some Rhetoricians, some Logicians . . . Pleasurists,
Peripatetics, Critics"; and "Intemperance, and her Companions" (again) (II, 550–551). A "small Track," "rough and
stony, and difficult," "with very few People" on it, leads
upward to a "high Cliff." In the third enclosure appear a
"beautiful meadow," Science (who gives the traveler "a
Draught" to "drive out" "all the evil Impressions and
Habits that he had contracted in his Passage thro' the first
Inclosure"), and "Knowledge, and the other Virtues" (II,
551, 552, 553). The Virtues conduct the traveler to "their
Mother" Happiness, who sits "on a Throne in the Portico"
(II, 554) of the building situated at the summit of the pic-
ture.

Later, the Old Citizen tells the strangers, the Virtues take
the person "to the Place that he had left, and bid him
observe those who continue there, amidst what Difficulties
and Troubles they pass their Time . . . or are conquered, and
led along like Captives, some by INTEMPERANCE . . . or any
other of the VICES: whose Chains they are in vain striving to
get loose from, that they might escape, and get to this Place
of Rest . . . And all this they suffer from their mistaking the
right Way, and forgetting the Orders given them by the
Directing GENIUS" (II, 555). After a further exchange of
questions and answers, the Old Citizen remarks: "To close
all, my Friends, what I would entreat of you is, to think over
every thing I have said to you, to weigh it well in your
Minds, and to practise accordingly. Get a Habit of doing

right, whatever Pain it costs you; let no Difficulties deter you, in the way to VIRTUE . . . Then will the Lesson that I have taught you, prove to yourselves a Lesson of HAPPI-NESS'' (II, 560).

The similarities between *The Picture* and *The Vision* cause a reader to wonder whether Johnson had Cebes' allegory in mind when he composed his own.[15] Both works feature a wise guide who informs and instructs stationary listeners-viewers (of an allegorical picture and an allegorical moun-tain, respectively). Both portray human life as a physical ascent and happiness as the ultimate goal of the individual's upward movement—in Cebes, from birth at the bottom of the picture to the ''Edifice'' of Happiness at the top; in *The Vision*, from Innocence toward the foot of the Mountain of Existence to the Temple of Happiness at the summit (II, 554, 522, 527). Both specify ''intemperance,'' sensuality, and ''despair'' among the other psychological states—gathered under the general category of ''OPINIONS, DESIRES, and PLEASURES'' (II, 547) for Cebes, under ''appetites'' and ''passions'' for Johnson—which obstruct the traveler's pro-gress on the road to happiness. Again, although the Greek work, unlike the English, spends only a few words on the topic, both fables stress the cultivation of good, and the avoidance of bad, habits: at the end of *The Picture*, the Old Citizen says, ''Get a Habit of doing right, whatever Pain it costs you''; at the end of *The Vision*, the ''Protector'' ''call[s] out . . . 'Remember, *Theodore*, and be wise, and let not HABIT prevail against thee' '' (II, 560, 530). Moreover, although it, unlike *The Vision*, does not explicitly apply the figures of ''chains'' and ''captivity'' to the formation and power of habits, *The Picture*, as noted above, mentions the

15. In Heinle's opinion, ''the model for [the] system of roadways [in *The Vision*] is undoubtedly the long road of Cebes'' (ibid., p. 141). McIntosh, *Choice of Life*, states flatly that ''many of Johnson's allegories are modeled after Prodicus and Cebes'' (p. 112). And in his study of *Samuel Johnson's Allegory* (The Hague: Mouton, 1971), Bernard L. Einbond concludes that ''Johnson may well have taken the germ of his idea [for habits in *The Vision*] from Cebes' *Table*'' (p. 64).

plight of those unfortunate mortals who are "led along like Captives, some by INTEMPERANCE, and others by ARRO-GANCE; here by COVETOUSNESS, and there by VAIN-GLORY, or any other of the VICES: whose Chains they are in vain striving to get loose from" (II, 555). Finally, the brief appearance of Repentance in *The Picture* resembles that of Conscience in *The Vision*, for both personifications induce the restoration of aberrant persons on the upward path to happiness.

If we admit the probability of Johnson's indebtedness to Cebes, however, we must also immediately acknowledge the marked divergences between *The Picture* and *The Vision*. For additional anticipations of assorted aspects of the latter, we may turn to examples of the long-lived, widely cultivated genre commonly called the dream vision. Its English members, exceedingly diverse, include the Middle English *Pearl*, various works by Chaucer, the *Vision of William Concerning Piers Plowman*, at least one version of Prodicus' *Choice of Hercules* (in Alexander Barclay's *Ship of Fools*), Bunyan's *Pilgrim's Progress* ("delivered under the similitude of a dream"), and a host of eighteenth-century allegorical prose pieces, the most famous of which is Addison's "Vision of Mirzah" (*Spectator* 159).

The Vision of Theodore clearly belongs to the same literary family. In his *Dictionary*, Johnson defined the fourth sense of *vision* as "dream; something shewn in a dream" and then adds: "A dream happens to a sleeping, a vision may happen to a waking man. A dream is supposed natural, a vision miraculous; but they are confounded."[16] With some of its

16. Most commentators have assumed that Theodore experiences his vision while he is asleep. What the Hermit says, however, is that "an irresistible Heaviness suddenly surprized me; I laid my Head upon the Bank and resigned myself to Sleep: when methought I heard the [sic] Sound as of the Flight of Eagles, and a Being of more than human Dignity stood before me" (II, 521). At the end of *The Vision*, he says, "While I was musing on this miserable Scene, my Protector called out to me . . . I started, and beheld myself surrounded by the Rocks of *Teneriffe*" (II, 530). One can thus conclude that Theodore's vision takes place while he is semiconscious and that, strictly speaking, the distinction made in the *Dictionary* between a

medieval predecessors, *The Vision* shares a number of traits, notably a heavily didactic theme, the convention of a guide for the dreamer, and such personified figures as Reason, Religion, and Avarice.[17] Like *Pilgrim's Progress*—one of only three books, according to Johnson, readers "ever" "wished longer"[18] —it pictures human life as an upward "pilgrimage" (Johnson's term) and stresses the dreadful power of the "cruel tyrant" Despair (compare the Giant Despair in *Pilgrim's Progress*). Like Addison's Mirzah, a resident of "Bagdat," Johnson's Theodore, Hermit of Mount Teneriffe, having ascended a considerable distance up a peak (Mirzah actually climbs to the top of a mountain), composed himself to sleep (Mirzah begins to "muse"), and being "instructed" by a supernatural "protector" (called a "Genius" by Addison), observes, on looking eastward, an allegorical vision of human life (represented as a mountain by Johnson; a combination of a vale, a tide, a bridge, and paradisiacal islands by Addison).[19] Finally, Johnson's employment of an allegorical mountain continued a convention previously used in essay visions by such authors as Addison, Steele, Parnell, and Fielding—to quite different ends.[20]

Most of the separate ingredients forming *The Vision of Theodore* thus display likenesses to elements in the classical allegories by Prodicus and Cebes and earlier English dream visions. Still another part of Johnson's composition—the geographical setting—can also be connected to a limited kind of literary, or "allusive," tradition. The "Peak" constituting a portion of Teneriffe, largest of the Canary Islands, had

---

dream and a vision also obtains in the allegory.

17. It should be noted, however, that, as Heinle points out ("Eighteenth Century Allegorical Essay," pp. 1–8, 17–28), most eighteenth-century English allegorists imitated the classical works by Prodicus and Cebes rather than medieval and Renaissance allegories, which tended to be condemned or ignored.

18. *Life*, I, 71, n. 1. The other two books were *Don Quixote* and *Robinson Crusoe*.

19. *Spectator*, II, 122–126.

20. See, for example, *Tatler* 81; *Spectator* 460, 514, 558, 559; *Champion* for December 13, 1739.

never apparently provided the locale of an allegorical vision before Johnson's Theodore retired there. But the mountain, long renowned for its height (about 12,000 feet), which caused some commentators to rank it among the tallest in the world, had become a symbol, a designation of immense height for English writers as early, at least, as the seventeenth century. Milton, Marvell, Sir Thomas Browne, Abraham Cowley, and numerous others refer to the towering "Pike," as it was sometimes spelled, in various works.[21] During the next century, similar allusions were equally, perhaps even more, common. Only a year before the appearance of *The Vision*, Thomas Warton, Jr. published his poem *The Pleasures of Melancholy*, which begins: "MOTHER of musings, Contemplation sage, / Whose grotto stands upon the topmost rock / Of Teneriff." Johnson himself commented humorously in *Rambler* 117: "That a garret will make every man a wit, I am very far from supposing; I know there are some who would continue blockheads even on the summit of the Andes, or on the peak of Teneriffe." And a well known passage in Hume's "Of the Standard of Taste" (1757) declares that "whoever would assert an equality of genius and elegance between Ogilby and Milton, or Bunyan and Addison, would be thought to defend no less an extravagance, than if he had maintained a mole hill to be as high as Teneriffe, or a pond as extensive as the ocean."

By his choice of a setting for *The Vision*, Johnson initiated a pattern he was to repeat with variations in his other extended pieces of fiction, *Rasselas* and *The Fountains*.[22] For

---

21. *Paradise Lost*, IV, 11. 985–987; Marvell, "On the Victory Obtained by Blake over the Spaniards, in the Bay of Sanctacruze, in the Island of Tenerif," 11. 77–80; Browne, *Pseudodoxia Epidemica, The Works of Sir Thomas Browne*, ed. Geoffrey Keynes, 4 vols. (Chicago: University of Chicago Press, 1964), II, 451; Cowley's essay "Of Greatness," in *Essays, Plays, and Sundry Verses*, ed. A. R. Waller (Cambridge: Cambridge University Press, 1906), p. 433.

22. For other possible reasons for Johnson's selection of the setting, see Lawrence Lipking's suggestive essay, "Learning to Read Johnson: *The Vision of Theodore* and *The Vanity of Human Wishes*," *ELH*, 43 (1976), 524–525.

each, he selected a famous mountainous site, actual, not fictional: the Peak of Teneriffe; the prison for royalty (an elevated valley surrounded by mountains)[23] in Amhara, a kingdom of Abyssinia; the Welsh Mount Plinlimmon. In or near this location he placed central characters—an elderly hermit, a youngish prince, an unmarried woman—whose experiences, active and observational (not all of them occurring, of course, in the original setting), dramatize the choices human beings make as they pursue earthly happiness. Supernatural personages—a "protector" and a fairy—are partly responsible for the experiences of the first and third characters. Pervading a sizable amount of Western art and literature,[24] this "choice" theme can be traced back, as indicated above, to Greek works.

Since *The Preceptor*, of which Johnson's allegory makes up a segment, was apparently designed to compete with a somewhat similar collection, *The Circle of the Sciences*, one may well inquire whether the latter includes anything which might further illuminate the contemporary context of *The Vision*. The answer is no. But volume two of David Fordyce's *Dialogues Concerning Education*, which appeared the same year (London, 1748)[25] as *The Preceptor*, contains a section that invites comparison with Johnson's composition. In Dialogue 16 ("On Dreaming"), Sophron relates a dream vision—prompted, as he says, by his "musing" on "the *celebrated Picture of Cebes*, that eminent *Moral* Limmer" (p. 259).

23. In its precise configuration, Johnson's "Happy Valley" differs markedly, of course, from the actual "mount" in Amhara where the Abyssinian princes were imprisoned.

24. For specific studies of the artistic and literary manifestations of the "choice" theme, see Heinle, "Eighteenth Century Allegorical Essay," p. 79 n.; Wasserman, "Johnson's *Rasselas*," pp. 6, n. 6; 7–8.

25. Subsequent quotations from Vol. II of the *Dialogues* are located by page numbers in the text of this essay. Heinle, "Eighteenth Century Allegorical Essay," also describes (pp. 127–130) the "vision" related in the *Dialogues*; in addition, he summarizes (pp. 143–145) a supplementary "vision" in Fordyce's *The Temple of Virtue* (1757).

"Wandering," so we are told, "upon a Wild . . . on which" run "numberless Roads . . . leading different Ways" and "frequented" by various "Travellers," Sophron (a member of a group bound for "the Abode of *Happiness*") meets "an old Man . . . pointing . . . to the different Paths, and showing Travellers where they terminated." This character, named "the GENIUS of EDUCATION," warns his auditors to "follow" his "Directions" and take the "Path," "known only to" him, which leads to "the Temple of Virtue" (p. 260). Instead, lured by the female figures of Credulity and Deceit, Sophron and his companions "very readily" move along the "Way" to the Bower of Bliss. Soon left alone, Sophron encounters Lady Pleasure, who, together with Lady Admiration, guides him to her palace, "where," she assures him, "no gloomy Cares or corroding Sorrows enter, where neither sullen Rules nor Stoical Pride are admitted to damp the jocund Humour of the Inhabitants" (p. 265). In the palace he observes a large assortment of allegorical individuals, including Vanity, Intemperance, Luxury, Cruelty, Incontinence, Indolence, Remorse, and Shame. "VARIOUS Petitioners presented themselves before the Throne, and humbly offered their Suits to the jolly Goddess [Pleasure]" (p. 272). After the last—a hypocritical roué—of these petitioners (none of them admirable) has appeared, Sophron asks Simplicius to interpret his dream. But Simplicius refuses, saying, "I can no more think of unfolding those Nocturnal Scenes, than I would attempt to explain the Sense of an *oracular* Answer." To which Sophron replies that Simplicius "shall have no more of my Dreams" (p. 291).

Striking dissimilarities obviously separate the Vision of the Palace of Pleasure, as it may be called, and *The Vision of Theodore*. Yet certain features suggest a common bond between the two pieces. Both are heavily didactic allegories, cast in the mold of dream visions, which delineate the "choice" theme. Both exhibit strong affiliations with the allegories by Prodicus and Cebes. Both form parts of educational works (whose contents are otherwise quite different) published at about the same time. Therefore, without implying a direct causal connection of any sort between the two compositions, we may remark that Johnson (assuming his responsibility for the presence of *The Vision* in *The Preceptor*) was not unique among his contemporaries in employing the exceedingly popular genre of the allegorical dream vision within the confines of an avowed educational work. Fordyce, indeed, we should note further, seems to have recommended the issuance of the kind of collection exemplified a little later by *The Vision, The Choice*, and *The Picture*: in the first volume (1745) of Fordyce's *Dialogues*, one of the speakers comments that, since "Fable, Allegory, and similar pleasant Dialogue" are "the best and most successful Method we can use in the EDUCATION of CHILDREN . . . it might be of considerable Use in Education, if the most beautiful and interesting of those Allegories, whether *Ancient* or *Modern*, which have or might have been mentioned [including, of course, *The Choice* and *The Picture*], were collected into one Volume, and exhibited to the Youth, as so many *Philosophical Pictures* of human Life" (pp. 406–407). What Fordyce proposed, Johnson, or Dodsley, or both, actually realized in the final part of *The Preceptor.*[26]

It is impossible to measure the real efficacy of *The Preceptor*, and of *The Vision* in particular, as an instrument of education. But at an unspecified date (presumably between 1756 and March 12, 1760), Johnson himself, so Thomas Percy reported, "attribute[d] the Palm over all he ever wrote" to the "little allegorical Piece." Although such an appraisal seems excessive today, the unusual esteem bestowed on the essayistic dream vision during the eighteenth century, the immense vogue of the genre, and *The Vision's* physical parity (at least) with the admired productions of Prodicus and Cebes all help to explain the apparent eccentricity of

---

26. The possibility of some kind of connection between Fordyce and Johnson during this period should be mentioned briefly. As Hazen points out (*Prefaces and Dedications*, p. 172), Johnson's association with *The Preceptor* may have included editorial duties. Part 9, "On Ethics, or Morality," contains the initial publication of Fordyce's *Elements of Moral Philosophy*, which came out separately in 1754. Thus Johnson and Fordyce may have communicated with each other one or more times.

Johnson's judgment.[27] Moreover, Bishop Percy concurred with Johnson's high estimate, adding that the work "far excells" the production of Cebes.[28] In addition, several of Johnson's contemporaries expressed unreserved commendations of the piece. For example, Joseph Towers, in his *Essay on the Life, Character, and Writings of Dr. Samuel Johnson* (1786), labels it "a beautiful and instructive allegory." Another *Life of Dr. Samuel Johnson*, probably composed by James Harrison and also published in 1786, goes much further. *The Vision*, we are informed,

is one of the finest moral allegories, if not the very finest, that ever proceeded from the pen of man. This is a bold assertion, but it is not a hasty one: and those who peruse the Vision . . . with attention; consider its excellent adaptation to the work [*The Preceptor*]; and reflect on the valuable precepts it inculcates; if they are at all zealous for the virtue of the rising generation, and the consequent felicity of their fellow-creatures, will not deem any encomium too great for its deserts.[29]

Neither Mrs. Piozzi's *Anecdotes of Samuel Johnson* (1786) nor Sir John Hawkins' *Life* (1787) assesses *The Vision*;[30] but Boswell, characteristically more evaluative than his rivals,

27. For additional suggestions regarding the reasons for Johnson's high estimate of *The Vision*, see Lipking, "Learning to Read Johnson," pp. 517–537.

28. Cleanth Brooks, ed., *The Correspondence of Thomas Percy & William Shenstone*, vol. 7 (1977) of *The Percy Letters* (New Haven: Yale University Press), pp. 57, 58. In his *Life* (I, 192), Boswell remarks: "The Bishop of Dromore heard Dr. Johnson say, that he thought [*The Vision*] was the best thing he ever wrote." Percy and Johnson apparently met first in 1756 (*Life* I, 48, n. 2). The date of Percy's letter to Shenstone is March 12, 1760.

29. For the passages from these two lives of Johnson, see *The Early Biographies of Samuel Johnson*, ed. O M Brack, Jr., and Robert E. Kelley (Iowa City: University of Iowa Press, 1974), pp. 215, 268.

30. Mrs. Piozzi does not mention *The Vision*; Hawkins (*Life of Samuel Johnson*, p. 381 n.) instances it, "the work of one sitting," as a specimen of Johnson's rapidity of composition.

calls the piece "a most beautiful allegory of human life."[31] And Robert Anderson, in his *Life of Samuel Johnson*, repeats Boswell's comment, remarking also that the work "is indeed truly excellent."[32]

The *Vision*'s appearances both within and outside *The Preceptor* during, roughly, the first half-century of its existence supplement the testimonials to its merit offered by Johnson's early biographers. In all likelihood, nine London editions of *The Preceptor* were issued at fairly regular intervals—in 1748, 1754, 1758, 1763, 1764, 1769, 1775, 1783, and 1793. Moreover, Dublin editions came out in 1761 and 1786, and a German translation in 1765–67.[33] As a small part of the two-volume collection, Johnson's allegory surely exerted only a negligible influence on the sales of the complete work; nonetheless, it is noteworthy that the collection itself evidently remained available for at least fifty years.

The earliest separate reprinting of *The Vision* occurred in the April 1748 number of the *Gentleman's Magazine*, where a postscript calls the allegory "beautiful" and a specimen of the "crowning" part of *The Preceptor*.[34] Thereafter the piece appeared in the following places and possibly elsewhere: *Grand Magazine of Magazines* (August-September 1750); *De Hollandsche Wysgeer*, Part I (1759; a Dutch translation); Thomas Davies, ed., *Miscellaneous and Fugitive Pieces*, I (1773); *Lloyd's Evening Post* for May 18, 1774 (an extract); *Lady's Magazine* (September-October 1777), which recommends *The Vision* to those "who superintend the Education of Youth"; *Weekly Miscellany, or Instructive Entertainer* (1781); Harrison's *New Novelist's Magazine, or Entertaining Library*, I (1786); Hawkins' edition (1787) of Johnson's

31. *Life*, I, 192.
32. 3rd ed. (Edinburgh, 1815), p. 122.
33. For information about the London and Dublin editions and the German translation of *The Preceptor*, I have relied on the *New Cambridge Bibliography of English Literature*, II, col. 1144. Hazen (*Prefaces and Dedications*, p. 175) lists only eight London editions (omitting 1764) and notes the possibility of a Dublin edition in 1750.
34. 18 (1748), 159–163, 164.

works; the 1792 edition (prefaced by Arthur Murphy's *Essay on the Life and Genius of Samuel Johnson*) of Johnson's works; and *Aberdeen Magazine, or Universal Repository* (1797).[35]

Surveying the various signs of its reception, one may say that *The Vision* enjoyed a steady if unspectacular existence between 1748 and 1800 largely because of its inclusion in successive editions of *The Preceptor*. At the same time, the allegory's independent appearances denote its own moderate appeal to a reading public whose appetite for prose "visions" was both settled and strong. Several members of that public united in applying the epithet "beautiful" to the work. Altered literary tastes would probably prevent most critics from using the term today, but for the reader, young or old, willing to be persuaded of the potency of human habits, *The Vision of Theodore* still provides vivid instruction and sage counsel.[36]

35. For information about the appearance of *The Vision* in the *Grand Magazine of Magazines, Lloyd's Evening Post,* and *Lady's Magazine,* I have drawn on Helen Louise McGuffie, *Samuel Johnson in the British Press, 1749–1784: A Chronological Checklist* (New York: Garland, 1976), pp. 11, 127, 214; for information about its appearance in *De Hollandsche Wysgeer* and Harrison's *New Novelist's Magazine* I have drawn on *NCBEL*, II, col. 1144; and for information about its appearance in the *Weekly Miscellany,* 15 (1781), 505–509, 532–538 and the *Aberdeen Magazine,* 2 (1797), 482–486, 536–540, I am indebted to Professor Robert Mayo of Northwestern University. The allegory appears on pp. 80–94 of Vol. I of Thomas Davies' *Miscellaneous and Fugitive Pieces* (1773); pp. 145–162 of Vol. XI of the 1787 works, and pp. 398–415 of Vol. II of the 1792 works.

36. In Lipking's opinion, "All that [*The Vision*] teaches us—the central importance of education, the view of life as a heroic journey, the Christian applications of Prodicus and Cebes, the power of habit in the author's mind, and the ambivalent attitude toward vision itself—informs [Johnson's] later work" ("Learning to Read Johnson," p. 527). For Einbond, "the omnipresent threat of habit is the heart of Johnson's message," and the "figures of Habit [are] the most entertaining of allegorical beings" (*Samuel Johnson's Allegory,* p. 61).

JOHN H. MIDDENDORF

Steevens and Johnson

Johnson once disagreed with Boswell's definition of a friend as "one who supports you and comforts you while others do not" by replying, "Many men would not be content to live so (I hope I should not be content), but would wish to have a friend with whom to compare mind[s] and cherish private virtues."[1] His reply provides a way to consider his relationship with George Steevens. Broadly speaking, we can think of the people in Johnson's orbit as mainly in one of three groups: those to whom he opened his soul, like Mrs. Thrale, who knew what he was about, and possibly John Taylor, who probably did not know as acutely what Johnson was about but who was said by Johnson to be "better acquainted with my *heart* than any man or woman now alive."[2] In a second group belong, on a wide spectrum, those like Richard Bathurst, Joshua Reynolds, and John Hawkesworth, with whom he could compare minds and cherish private virtues. And, in a third group, I would place those with whom he could compare minds and—stretching his remark a bit—

1. Joseph W. Reed and Frederick A. Pottle, eds., *Boswell, Laird of Auchinleck, 1778–1782* (New York: McGraw-Hill, 1977), p. 98.
2. *Boswell's Life of Johnson*, ed. George Birkbeck Hill, revised and enlarged by L. F. Powell, 6 vols. (Oxford: Clarendon Press, 1934–1950; Vols. V and VI [2nd ed.], 1964), I, 26 n. 1. Hereafter cited as *Life*.

whose accomplishments he could admire but with whom the opportunities of cherishing private virtues were less frequently available or sought, if at all. Clearly these admittedly rough distinctions will allow for many gradations and permutations, enough, I would hope, to accommodate others closely associated with Johnson, like Boswell, John Hawkins, and Oliver Goldsmith. Certainly George Steevens belongs in group three.

From the abundance of evidence concerning the Johnson-Steevens relationship, a few details suggest its nature. They first met at the Temple when they were both living there, sometime between 1763 and 1765, and their association lasted for the rest of Johnson's life. Among the many who saw them there together was Garrick, who refers to meeting Steevens—"a frisking young caller"—in Johnson's quarters. The association of the two on the edition of Shakespeare began at this time. Steevens (on Croker's identification) worked in Johnson's room when Johnson was writing his preface to Shakespeare.[3] Steevens' contributions to the Appendix have long been known, as have his contributions to the edition of 1773. From the mid-1760s until Johnson's death (Steevens was among Johnson's last callers, and he walked in the funeral procession), the two met with what may at times have been daily frequency. Steevens included Johnson's morning levees as a regular part of his walking excursions from his home in Hampstead Heath to London and back.[4] He occasionally attended the theater and other public events with Johnson. He went with him and Joseph Cradock to Marylebone to see the burletta attributed to Pergolesi, *La Serva Padrona*. He attended the performance of Foote's *The Maid of Bath* at the Haymarket in 1771 with Johnson. Steevens himself (admittedly not the most trustworthy of witnesses) tells us that he went with Johnson to Marylebone on another occasion to see

3. George Birkbeck Hill, ed., *Johnsonian Miscellanies*, 2 vols. (New York: Harper and Bros., 1897), II, 328, n. 2.
4. Ibid.

the fireworks display of Signor Torré sometime between 1772 and 1774, a visit, Steevens says, that resulted in Johnson's starting a riot.[5] Johnson proposed Steevens to the Club, and he was elected in 1775. Boswell refers to Steevens at the Club a number of times when Johnson was there. Later Johnson included Steevens among the first members of the Essex Head Club in 1783. Steevens helped Johnson with revisions of the *Dictionary*[6] and with the *Lives of the Poets.* In short, the evidence suggests that the two met frequently, in public and private, over a period of about two decades.

Steevens' nickname was "the asp." Garrick, whose relationship with Steevens fluctuated (this was true of almost all of Steevens' relationships), referred to him at various times as spiteful, malicious, malignant, "the pest of society." Mrs. Thrale asserted that Steevens was "ever prepared to injure those he cannot hate," and Topham Beauclerk declared that he "deserves to be hanged" and "certainly ought to be *kicked*."[7] Lord Mansfield thought one might safely believe half of what Steevens said, and Johnson sensibly responded to this: "Ay, but we don't know *which* half to believe. By his lying we lose not only our reverence for him, but all comfort in his conversation."[8] John Nichols, close to Steevens, spoke of his jealousy of other men's knowledge, his capriciousness, the fickleness of his attachments, his cynical asperities. Edmond Malone said that Isaac Reed and Richard Farmer were the only friends Steevens ever had with whom he did not quarrel. Dr. Parr said the same, but

5. Hill, *Johnsonian Miscellanies*, II, 410; George Winchester Stone, Jr., *The London Stage, 1660–1800*, Part 4 (Carbondale: Southern Illinois University Press, 1962), p. 1556; *Life*, IV, 324.

6. James H. Sledd and Gwin J. Kolb, "The History of the Sneyd-Gimbel and Pigott-British Museum Copies of Dr. Johnson's *Dictionary*," *Papers of the Bibliographical Society of America*, 54 (1960), 286.

7. *Life*, III, 281 n. 3; Katharine C. Balderston, ed., *Thraliana: The Diary of Mrs. Hester Lynch Thrale (Later Mrs. Piozzi), 1776–1809*, 2 vols., (Oxford: Clarendon Press, 1942), II, 785.

8. *Life*, IV, 178.

added himself.[9] At one time or another (to mention only the better known of his targets), Steevens incurred the dislike of Thomas Percy, Arthur Murphy, Garrick, Malone, Hawkins, and Boswell. The number of lesser lights is legion, including all those victims of his love of hoax and deception, the best known of whom is Erasmus Darwin, taken in by Steevens' report of the famous upas or poison tree, and Richard Gough, Director of the Society of Antiquaries, fooled by Steevens' "discovery" of an "ancient" fragment of stone with the "epitaph" of Hardicanute, who was supposed to have died after drinking a flagon of wine.[10] For much of his trickery Steevens relied upon the newspapers. Boswell once observed to Johnson that Steevens was a great writer in the newspapers and then added (as he says, "thoughtlessly"), "What pleasure can he have in that?" "Nay," said Mr. Johnson, "*you* can best tell that."[11]

Steevens' quarrelsomeness, trickiness, and unreliableness were not enough to prevent his remaining an active member, throughout most of his life, of the intellectual and literary world of his time. For there is another side to the coin. Before being stung, Percy praised Steevens' diligence, the breadth of his scholarship, his "openness and generosity of heart," and his "liberal mind."[12] Garrick at one point welcomed Steevens to the use of his library, treated him as a member of the household, and even gave him keys to the garden and the library, though this was an arrangement broken by Steevens' ridicule of Garrick as Steward of the Shak-

9. Edward L. Hart, *Minor Lives* (Cambridge: Harvard University Press, 1971), p. 61; *Life*, II, 487, III, 281, n. 3.

10. Bertrand H. Bronson, *Joseph Ritson: Scholar at Arms*, 2 vols. (Berkeley: University of California Press, 1938), II, 546.

11. Charles Ryskamp and Frederick A. Pottle, eds., *Boswell: The Ominous Years, 1774–1776* (New York: McGraw-Hill, 1963), p. 146.

12. Cleanth Brooks, ed., *The Correspondence of Thomas Percy & Richard Farmer* (Baton Rouge: Louisiana State University Press, 1946), pp. 101–103.

espeare Festival.[13] Nichols writes of Steevens' "rare insight into human character, his ever fixing his good opinion only on men of honor and genius." He was, said Nichols, "a most pleasant tête-à-tête companion."[14] Boswell speaks of Steevens' generosity, his fullness of mind, his animated powers of communication; Dr. Parr, of his wisdom; William Cole, of his gentlemanly qualities: good breeding, civility, obligingness.[15] Evidence to establish Steevens' powers of mind, learning, generosity, conversational ease and wit, and high moral standards could be readily augmented.

Bertrand Bronson is quite correct when he says, of Steevens' meeting Johnson after he had done most of the work for his Shakespeare, that the "arrival of George Steevens on the scene was unhappily mistimed; five years earlier would have made all the difference."[16] The difference, of course, would have been brought about by Steevens' energy, eye for detail, antiquarian learning, and diligence, especially in examining and collating the early editions of Shakespeare that Johnson had neglected. That Johnson found Steevens' help and work satisfactory is evident when we recall his encouragement of Steevens' *Twenty Plays* of Shakespeare, published in four volumes in 1766. Steevens' precise contributions to the edition of 1773 have been charted by Arthur Sherbo,[17] though from time to time evidence may still emerge to add to our knowledge of the possible extent of Steevens' anonymous assistance. Suffice to say that in addition to his own notes and the list of

13. Garrick's relationship with Steevens resumed somewhat shakily a number of years later. See Evelyn Wenner, "George Steevens and the Boydell Shakespeare" (Ph.D. diss., George Washington University, 1952), p. 22.

14. Hart, *Minor Lives*, p. 52.

15. *Life*, III, 100, 281, n. 3; Reed and Pottle, *Boswell, Laird*, p. 298; Hart, *Minor Lives*, p. 53.

16. "Introd.," *Johnson on Shakespeare*, ed. Arthur Sherbo, vols. 7 and 8, *The Yale Edition of the Works of Samuel Johnson* (New Haven: Yale University Press, 1968), VII, xxv.

17. Arthur Sherbo, *Samuel Johnson, Editor of Shakespeare. With an essay on "The Adventurer"* (Urbana: University of Illinois Press, 1956).

translations available to Shakespeare, Steevens assumed the major task of seeing the edition through the press, determining the order of the printing, and correcting galleys. Johnson generously acknowledged Steevens' diligence and sagacity in a paragraph added to the Preface for 1773. During the early years of the 1770s, Steevens was also assiduously helping Johnson in the revisions for the fourth edition of the *Dictionary*. All the evidence points to a close, continuing collaboration, with Steevens taking an especially active part in the emendation of illustrative quotations from Shakespeare, offering new quotations, explaining words and phrases, and at times drawing attention to corruptions in quotations used in the earlier editions.[18] The appearance in 1773 of revisions of two of Johnson's greatest works thus owed much to Steevens' industry and careful, informed attention. How relieved Johnson must have been to have had such a resourceful and energetic collaborator.

Four or five years later Johnson no doubt recalled Steevens' earlier help, for he now enlisted it again in writing the *Lives of the Poets*. To be sure, he also called upon others, notably Nichols and Reed. The proof sheets of the first edition of the *Lives* at the Victoria and Albert acknowledge Nichols' help in a marginal note for the life of Collins, but unfortunately supply no information for Steevens. But other evidence of assistance exists. Boswell tells us that Johnson asked Steevens to "castrate" Rochester's poems for the first edition, and Johnson tells us that he had forgotten to mention Young's tragedies until Steevens reminded him.[19] Perhaps Steevens himself had been reminded of them because of his work for Reed on the revision of the *Biographica Dramatica* (1782). Steevens may have brought William Shenstone's *Miscellany* of 1737 to Johnson's attention. When we know with some certainty the sources Johnson

18. I am indebted to Allen Reddick, of Columbia University, for this information about Steevens' role in the revision of the *Dictionary*.

19. *Life*, III, 191; George Birkbeck Hill, ed., "Life of Young," in *Lives of the English Poets*, 3 vols. (Oxford: Clarendon Press, 1905), III, 396, par. 162.

used for a particular life, and then find a detail or details in the printed life not found in a source, it is reasonable to suppose that he may have received information from Steevens. But then Nichols or Reed are just as good candidates. In the life of Hughes, for example, Johnson gives a detail not found in his sources—that Hughes' edition of Spenser was not reprinted for thirty years. And in the life of Ambrose Philips the date of Philips' death, not found in the sources, may have come from the obituary in the *Gentleman's Magazine* dug up by a helper. When the first edition of the *Lives* was printed, Johnson, as a token of gratitude, wrote to Nichols asking that a full set be sent to Steevens.[20]

In a letter now at the Morgan Library dated October 27, 1780, Steevens writes to Johnson giving details of Pope's difficulties with William Broome's translations. In his *Anecdotes*, Nichols prints a letter from Steevens dated September 18, 1782 for Johnson's use, in which Steevens includes a letter from Pope to Broome on the subject of Elijah Fenton's death.[21] What these letters clearly indicate is that Steevens continued to help Johnson in the preparation of his revisions. Johnson's anxiety to get to the end of his labors is well known. That anxiety must have been made more bearable by the knowledge that he could call upon Steevens' ready assistance. It is revealing that he acknowledges only Steevens in the Advertisement to the third, corrected edition of 1783.

In his journal entry for April 19, 1779, Boswell noted attending the hanging of the Reverend Hackman, accused of shooting Martha Ray, mistress of the Earl of Sandwich. Boswell writes: "Steevens there; disagreeable [when] unrestrained by Johnson."[22] In the anecdotes of Johnson that Steevens sent to Boswell, Steevens observes that "it is unfortunate . . . that [Johnson's] particularities and frailties can be more distinctly traced than his good and amiable

20. R. W. Chapman, ed., *The Letters of Samuel Johnson*, 3 vols. (Oxford: Clarendon Press, 1952), II, 429 (Letter 731).
21. "Life of Fenton," in *Lives*, II, 265–266.
22. Reed and Pottle, *Boswell, Laird*, p. 93.

exertions" and goes on to refer to Johnson's "many boun-
ties . . . studiously concealed . . . many acts of humanity . . .
performed in private," and to conclude that if they had been
displayed "with equal circumstantiality, his defects would be
so far lost in the blaze of his virtues, that the latter only
would be regarded." At another point he told Boswell that
"it was a pity Mr. Johnson is so rough, as it prevented many
people from knowing his excellence."[23] Substitute different
qualities for roughness, and the same might well have been
said about Steevens.

Steevens was justifiably proud of his association with
Johnson. "This is a distinction which malevolence cannot
obscure, nor flattery transfer to any other candidate for public favour," he wrote in the Advertisement of the edition of
Shakespeare in 1793. When Johnson was in the Hebrides,
Steevens wrote to Garrick: "Do you not long to hear the
roarings of the old lion, over the bleak mountains of the
North?"[24] These and other remarks suggest a respect and
pride energized by something close to deep affection. And
they prompt a query: Did Johnson perhaps judge Steevens
when he was at his best, at times willingly, at other times
unwillingly?

And now what of Johnson? The best known evidence of
his opinion of Steevens' aspishness is in the *Life*. After
Beauclerk had asserted that Steevens deserved hanging—at
least kicking—for speaking behind the backs of those with
whom he was on good terms, and attacking them in the
newspapers, Johnson replied, "Sir, we all do this in some
degree. *'Veniam petimus damusque vicissim.'* To be sure it
may be done so much, that a man may deserve to be kicked
. . . No, Sir; he is not malignant. He is mischievous, if you
will. He would do no man an essential injury; he may,
indeed, love to make sport of people by vexing their vanity."
He then continued with a reference to someone who was
"absolutely malignant," who really "wished evil to others

23. *Life*, IV, 325.
24. *Life*, II, 284, n. 2.

and rejoiced at it."[25] Boswell's journal entry for this account is essentially the same, though the evil man is here identified as Meynell (Littleton Poyntz).[26] Boswell gives other versions of the conversation, with no indication of its earlier date, in his journal for March 28, 1781, and again for May 15, 1784, where Johnson is said to reply "from a spirit of contradiction": "Come, come, this is not so terrible a crime. He means only to vex them a little. I do not say that I should do this. But there is a great difference. What is fit for Hephaestion is not fit for Alexander."[27] Leaving aside the implications of Johnson's comparison of himself to Alexander, never a favorite of *his*, we cannot overlook the fact that Hephaestion was *Alexander*'s favorite.

It seems clear that Johnson, at the least, thought well of Steevens, tolerated his faults, did not take his "malignant" habits very seriously. This is in character. Johnson's bearishness is well known, but, as Steevens recognized, his capacity for love and his forbearance, unless mightily provoked, are less frequently remembered. Johnson himself was not above vexing his friends—witness his mockery of Percy—though it must be added that he never fell to Steevens' level and certainly did not engage in anonymous paper warfare. Perhaps the most appropriate explanation of his attitude toward Steevens is suggested in his own words about two other Shakespearians, in the Preface to his edition of Shakespeare. Speaking of Warburton's chief "assailants," Thomas Edwards and Benjamin Heath, he says of the first that he "stings like a fly, sucks a little blood, takes a gay flutter, and returns for more; the other bites like a viper, and would be glad to leave inflammations and gangrene behind him."

25. *Life*, III, 281.
26. Charles McC. Weis and Frederick A. Pottle, *Boswell in Extremes, 1776–1778* (New York: McGraw-Hill, 1970), p. 278.
27. Reed and Pottle, *Boswell, Laird*, p. 298; Irma S. Lustig and Frederick A. Pottle, eds., *Boswell: The Applause of the Jury, 1782–1785* (New York: McGraw-Hill, 1981), p. 211. See also *Life*, IV, 274.

But then he adds: "Let me however do them justice. One is a wit, and one a scholar."[28]

To Johnson, who let the little dogs bark and snap, the world of newspaper warfare was a world that he could not accept with great seriousness. One can imagine his saying, like Pope, that paper attacks were his amusement, but not, like Pope, contorting his features in repressed rage when he read them. The rhetoric of eighteenth-century paper warfare established it as a kind of game: "skulking friend," "infamous scoundrel," "malignant spirit," "pitiful cavaler," "literary hangman." The language is so severe as no longer to carry force. It teeters on the edge of self-parody and suggests that its writers enjoyed the game, had "fun," to use Steevens' own word to describe his often outrageous activities. One can imagine these controversialists beginning the day with a question: Let's see, what can I call him today?

In a sense, the rhetoric represents, albeit in exaggerated form, the spirit of the Club, a spirit that allowed for very blunt statements (according to modern standards) that not infrequently led to wounds and hurt feelings, but wounds and hurt feelings that were soon enough healed or softened by the love of intellectual exchange, parry and thrust, and by respect for one's opponent and his accomplishments. (Smith and Gibbon were obvious exceptions.) More important to Johnson than Steevens' aspishness, I believe, were his learning, his powers of mind, the cut of his wit, perhaps also his solid reputation as an upholder of religion and the Established Church.[29] An outlaw of society Steevens may have been (the description is Johnson's),[30] but then so was Savage and, in his way, Johnson himself. The qualities of mischievousness in Steevens that angered others did not stir Johnson very much, especially since their anger often reflected their vanity and pretentiousness. Indeed, Johnson may have secretly grinned at some of Steevens' antics even

---

28. Bronson, "Introd.," *Johnson on Shakespeare*, ed. Sherbo, VII, 100.
29. Wenner, "Steevens and the Boydell Shakespeare," p. 6.
30. *Life*, II, 375.

as they were being censured by his companions.

In sum, Steevens had much going for him with Johnson. He helped Johnson in his work when he needed help, and Johnson's gratitude, once given, was given for life. He was one of Johnson's younger friends, and Johnson was tolerant of the young. Steevens' wild side gave no evidence of a joy in evil. But then Steevens could never have been one with whom Johnson could seriously cherish private virtues. He was aware of Steevens' untruthfulness at least as early as 1769, when Mrs. Thrale told him that she, not Steevens, as he had claimed, had written the doggerel verses *Political Alphabet*. She says that Johnson, on hearing her, "did not utter a word, and we never talked about it any more."[31] The feelings prompting his silence must have included disappointment, regret, anger, perhaps bewilderment and sadness that such obvious talent could be so misused and flawed. Surely his feelings then and later, despite Steevens' intellectual and scholarly powers and energy, prevented him from taking Steevens to his heart. Just as Steevens regretted that Johnson's roughness prevented others from seeing his virtues, so Johnson must have regretted that Steevens' love of mischief often prevented others from seeing *his* virtues — and, more importantly and poignantly, all too often overwhelmed them.[32]

31. Balderston, *Thraliana*, I, 122 and n. 4. See also James L. Clifford, *Hester Lynch Piozzi (Mrs. Thrale)* (Oxford: Clarendon Press, 1941), p. 73.
32. A version of this paper was delivered at the annual meeting of the MLA in New York City in December 1981.

JAMES G. BASKER

Minim and the Great Cham: Smollett and Johnson on the Prospect of an English Academy

The idea of founding an English Academy of Letters was still very much alive in the mid-eighteenth century, and one of its most interesting—and unlikely—proponents was Tobias Smollett. Sometime in late 1755 Smollett proposed what he described as "an extensive Plan . . . for a sort of Academy of the belles Lettres."[1] Of course his proposal, like those of Dryden, Sprat, Defoe, and Swift before him, was never realized and the episode is hardly known (if at all) beyond the circle of Smollett specialists. It is not listed, for example, in Allen Walker Read's excellent survey, "Suggestions for an Academy in England in the Latter Half of the Eighteenth Century."[2] For lack of information it is usually mentioned as a mere footnote to Smollett's other activities. But further investigation of his proposal and its reception not only adds a new dimension to our sense of Smollett's literary achievement, but also broadens our understanding of important currents in contemporary thought. Smollett's proposal

1. Smollett to John Wilkes, August 3, 1756, *The Letters of Tobias Smollett*, ed. Lewis M. Knapp (Oxford: Clarendon Press, 1970), p. 46.
2. *Modern Philology*, vol. 36 (1938–1939), pp. 145–156.

linked him with a century-long tradition of opinion in favor of an English academy. It also, unfortunately, made him the standard bearer for an idea that was relentlessly opposed by Samuel Johnson, the man whose growing authority in the literary world Smollett himself ironically acknowledged when he dubbed him the "great Cham of Literature."[3] As Smollett's experience would attest, Johnson's achievements and attitudes formed the greatest obstacle to founding an academy any time between 1755 and his death in 1784.

Smollett's idea had venerable precedents. Thomas Sprat, in his *History of the Royal Society* (1667), outlined a plan for a possible academy and its benefits, the details derived in part from discussions with Dryden, Roscommon, and other members of the Royal Society with whom Sprat had served on a committee appointed to pursue such ends.[4] That Smollett was familiar with Sprat's idea is evident: he measured Sprat's book against Thomas Birch's *History of the Royal Society* in a review he wrote at the beginning of 1756.[5] Undoubtedly Smollett was also familiar with other works by major authors that contained proposals and expressions of support for an academy: Defoe's "Of Academies" in his *Essay on Projects* (1697), Addison's *Spectator* 135 (August 4, 1711), Swift's *Proposal for Correcting, Improving and Ascertaining the English Tongue* (1712), and Voltaire's essay "On the Royal Society and Academies" in his *Letters on England* (1733), which Smollett later included in his edition of the *Works of Voltaire* (vol. 12, 1762). Thus Smollett was consciously following in a tradition of ideas distinguished by such spokesmen, hoping to bring to fruition the work they had

3. Smollett to John Wilkes, March 16, 1759, *Letters of Smollett*, p. 75.

4. Ed. Jackson I. Cope and Harold Whitmore Jones (St. Louis, Missouri: Washington University, 1958), pp. 39–45. See also Oliver Farrar Emerson, "John Dryden and a British Academy," *Proceedings of the British Academy*, 10 (1921), pp. 45–58, reprinted in *Essential Articles for the Study of John Dryden*, ed. H. T. Swedenberg, Jr. (Hamden, Conn.: Archon Books, 1966), pp. 263–280.

5. Tobias Smollett in *Critical Review*, 1 (1756), 41.

scarcely begun—an indication both of his idealism and of his sense of his own powers.

In 1755 the thirty-four-year-old Smollett was best known as a novelist and translator. Fielding's death in 1754 left Smollett, chiefly on the strength of *Roderick Random* (1748) and *Peregrine Pickle* (1751), England's greatest living comic novelist, a reputation bolstered by the success of his translations of *Gil Blas* (1748) and *Don Quixote* (1755), which remained best sellers for generations. Few could be expected to remember the seriousness with which he had embarked on a literary career, arriving in London in 1739 with his hopes riding on a formal verse tragedy (like James Thomson and Johnson before him, though with less success, as Smollett never got his *Regicide* staged), and after an interlude as a surgeon in the Royal Navy, resuming his literary activities with two formal verse satires in imitation of Juvenal, *Advice* (1746) and *Reproof* (1747). But whether Smollett had arrived at some sort of professional crisis, perhaps brought on by the poor reception of his most recent novel *Ferdinand Count Fathom* (1753), or was simply enacting a long-held design, in 1755 he turned his energies to the most ambitious project of his career.

Although Smollett does not seem to have got to the point of publishing his proposals (if he did, none have survived), and thus details are frustratingly scarce, it is clear that in late 1755 and early 1756 Smollett was actively soliciting support for his academy project. In a letter of August 3, 1756, he announced to his friend John Moore in Glasgow that his newly founded literary journal the *Critical Review* was but "a small Branch of an extensive Plan which I last year projected for a sort of Academy of the belles Lettres, a Scheme which will one day, I hope, be put in Execution to its utmost Extent. In the meantime the Critical Review is conducted by four Gentlemen of approved abilities, and meets with a very favourable Reception."[6] In addition to spreading word about his projected academy among his Scottish friends, Smollett

6. *Letters of Smollett*, p. 46.

discussed it with various literary friends in London, including the poet-physician John Armstrong and the politician John Wilkes, with whom Smollett remained close friends until the *Briton-North Briton* paper wars in 1762–63. Armstrong expressed skepticism in a letter to Wilkes in January 1756 —"Smollett imagines he and I may both make Fortunes by this project of his [but] I'm afraid he is too sanguine"[7] —but nonetheless joined the staff of the *Critical Review* at the outset, as did fellow Scot Patrick Murdoch, a member of the Royal Society and minor littérateur.[8] There is no evidence that Wilkes was an active participant in the project, although he is known to have been negotiating for the institution of another kind of academy—an academy of art (which emerged in 1760 as the Society of Artists)—at about this time.[9] Another friend Smollett consulted about his plan was Dr. George Macaulay, husband of the historian Catherine Macaulay. In April 1756 Smollett wrote Macaulay to ask for help in the form of a loan to cover a financial embarrassment, saying: "This disgrace hovers over my imagination so that I shall be rendered incapable of prosecuting my scheme."[10]

But it can be seen now that word about Smollett's academy proposal had reached a wider audience than just his immediate circle of friends. An anonymous article in the March 1756 issue of the *Universal Visiter*, which was edited by Christopher Smart and Richard Rolt—and to which, interestingly, Johnson was a contributor[11] —attacked Smollett and his staff of writers on the *Critical Review* as "a hug-

7. Unpublished ms. letter in British Museum, Br. Mus. Add. MS 30867, ff. 113–113a, quoted from Lewis M. Knapp, *Tobias Smollett: Doctor of Men and Manners* (Princeton: Princeton University Press, 1949), p. 174.

8. Derek Roper, "Smollett's 'Four Gentlemen': The First Contributors to the *Critical Review*," *Review of English Studies*, n.s. 10 (1959), pp. 38–44.

9. William T. Whitley, *Artists and Their Friends in England 1700–1799* (London: The Medici Society, 1928), pp. 165–166.

10. April 6, 1756, *Letters of Smollett*, p. 45.

11. Roland B. Botting, "Johnson, Smart, and the *Universal Visiter*," *Modern Philology*, 36 (1938–1939), 293–300.

bug-rub-drug, pug-scrub, *Acad. &c. Soc.*"[12] Obviously a
barbed reference to Smollett's academy project, this curious
and cryptic epithet suggests that some figures in the literary
world resented, if not the idea of an academy itself, then at
least Smollett's presumption in proposing it. Not all
responses, however, were negative. Smollett's friend and
former colleague on the *Monthly Review*, Theophilus Cibber,
endorsed the academy project enthusiastically in his "Two
Dissertations on Theatrical Subjects," which he first began
delivering as public lectures in January 1756 and then published in book form later that year.[13] The central theme of
Cibber's "Dissertations" is the degeneracy of contemporary
literature, particularly as manifested in the theater. In
describing a possible remedy, Cibber gives an account of the
academy scheme then in the air:

I have heard of an Academy,—intended to consist of a select
Number of Gentlemen, eminent for their Taste of the *Belles Let-
tres*; and some, whose Works have the deserv'd Estimation of the
Public:—On which Plan it will be propos'd, to support Authors of
Merit;—to give Praise to the Deserving, and due Censure to the
Dull and Presuming;—to shew the many why they are pleas'd:—
May that laudable Scheme succeed, and prevent the Depravity we
are falling into, by rescuing sound Sense and Morality, from the
barbarous Attacks of Ignorance and Gothism! . . . Thus may the
encroaching Power of [theater] Managers be properly check'd, and
rational Entertainments alone become the polite Amusement of the
town . . . 'Till this Plan is put in Execution,—and I hope the
interim will be but short,—permit me humbly to propose an
Expedient, for the immediate Correction of Theatrical
Misconduct.[14]

12. "From *Edmund Curl*, to the principal Author of a *Thing*, called the
Critical Review," *Universal Visiter*, 1 (1756), 139.

13. See also Philip H. Highfill, Jr., et al., *A Biographical Dictionary of
Actors, Actresses, Musicians, Dancers, Managers and Other Stage Personnel in
London, 1660–1800* (Carbondale: Southern Illinois University Press, 1975),
III, 258.

14. *Two Dissertations*, pp. 61–62.

In view of Cibber's uneven reputation, Smollett may have had mixed feelings about his support, but there was no denying the extent of the publicity he provided. Cibber's remarks about the proposed academy even made the front page of a newspaper, *The Evening Advertiser* for January 8, 1756.

As late as 1759 another writer recalled Smollett's academy proposal, but hardly with approval. A ropemaker by trade but playwright by avocation, Joseph Reed was an avowed enemy of Smollett's who in mid-1759 published a pamphlet attack: *A Sop in the Pan for a Physical Critick: in a Letter to Dr. Sm*ll*t.* In the course of his tirade against Smollett and the *Critical Review*, he harks back mockingly to Smollett's academy scheme:

In the close of the Year 1755, a certain *Caledonian* Quack, by the Curtesy of *England,* call'd a *Doctor of Physick,* whose real, or assum'd Name was FERDINANDO MAC FATHOMLESS, form'd a Project for initiating and perfecting the Male-Inhabitants of this Island, in the Use and Management of the *linguinary Weapon,* by the Erection of a *Scolding Amphitheatre.* For this Purpose, he selected, and engag'd, on weekly Salary, about a Dozen of the most eminent Professors of *Vociferation* in this Academy: but, after he had been at a considerable Expence, the unfortunate *Emperic* could not get his Project licenc'd.

The Doctor was greatly mortified at his unexpected Disappointment, but being resolved that *his own,* and the *Sisterhood's* Talents should not be lost to the World, *he* set about publishing a periodical Work, called the *Hyper-Critical Review.*[15]

Despite the animosity and sexual innuendo, it seems clear that Reed was taking up point by point some of the actual details of Smollett's original proposal, in order to goad him on what he knew to be a sore subject.

These accounts must, of course, be treated with caution, but they offer enough clues to reconstruct a basic outline of what Smollett had termed his "extensive plan." The

15. P. 5.

academy was to consist of a "select number" (Reed set it at twelve) of eminent literary figures, operating under some kind of "license"—perhaps a Royal charter or the sponsorship of a noble Lord—a license that Smollett, according to Reed, had been unable to get. Their function was to be at least fourfold. The first, which Reed emphasizes, was to be the exercise of authority over the English language— "initiating and perfecting on the Male-Inhabitants of this Island, in the Use and Management of the *linguinary Weapon*"—a central feature in most academy proposals, but usually described in terms more like Swift's idea of "correcting, improving and ascertaining the English tongue." Second, they were to have some sort of critical authority (though certainly not absolute censorship) over the publishing world, with a mandate "to give Praise to the Deserving, and due Censure to the Dull and Presuming." This is very similar to a feature of the academy proposed by Thomas Sprat in his *History of the Royal Society*, which would have established a board of critics "according to whose Censure, all Books, or Authors should either stand or fall."[16] It was undoubtedly this purpose that gave rise to the *Critical Review*, merely "a small branch" (as Smollett had said) of his larger plan. The scale of his plan is further suggested by the grand title he had originally set for his journal, but abandoned just before publication: "The Progress or Annals of Literature and the Liberal Arts."[17] Third, the academy would pay particular attention to the theaters, exerting its influence to correct "theatrical misconduct" and to ensure that "rational Entertainments alone become the polite Amusement of the town." This was Cibber's favorite aim, and perhaps Smollett's too, for Smollett in 1755 was still smoldering over sixteen years of frustrated attempts to get one of his own plays staged. Though for less personal reasons, authority to reform the theaters had also been a key point in Defoe's proposal for an academy in 1697. The fourth

16. P. 43.
17. *Public Advertiser*, December 19, 1755.

function would be (in Cibber's words) "to support authors of merit," meaning, presumably, financial support in the form of pensions, stipends, and perhaps subsidies for major projects. Smollett was probably looking for his example to Europe, particularly France, where academies supported authors in various ways and where one government-subsidized journal, the *Mercure de France*, even rechanneled its profits into grants-in-aid for writers.[18] This point too had featured in Sprat's proposal, whereby the academy would finance and supervise worthy literary projects. Perhaps it was something like this that Smollett had in mind when he assured Armstrong they would "both make fortunes by this project." (Ironically the generous Edward Cave had sought just this kind of assistance for Samuel Johnson—later a great foe of an English Academy—when in 1741 he appealed to Thomas Birch and the Society for the Encouragement of Learning to finance the publication of Johnson's *Irene*.)[19] Finally, in both Reed's and Cibber's accounts, the academy scheme was linked with some kind of periodical publication, presumably a journal not unlike the *Critical Review* in which the learned body would publish its transactions and critical dictates.

Smollett was not alone among his contemporaries in thinking that England needed a central authority in the world of letters. In 1752 the anonymous author of the *True Briton* called for an authoritative body to recommend "proper books" to the public and to combat the corruption of classical texts by supervising their publication.[20] In the same year, as Read has pointed out, Dr. George Harris proposed that Parliament establish an academy to standardize and regulate

18. Raymond F. Birn, *Pierre Rousseau and the Philosopher of Bouillon*, vol. 29, Studies on Voltaire and the Eighteenth Century, ed. Theodore Besterman (Genève: Institut et Musée Voltaire, 1964), p. 21 n. 2.

19. *Boswell's Life of Johnson*, ed. George Birkbeck Hill, revised and enlarged by L.F. Powell (Oxford: Clarendon Press, 1934), I, 153 and n. 2. Hereafter cited as *Life*.

20. Vol. 4 (1752), 10.

by force of law all English spelling.[21] In 1753 William White-
head (soon to become Poet Laureate) suggested to the
authors of *The World* that they assume the role of censors
and adjudicate on the merits of contemporary fiction.[22] In
1755 a female voice joined the chorus: in response to a
letter signed only "T.S." (perhaps Smollett himself?),
Frances Brooke devoted the December 6 issue of her periodical essay *The Old Maid* to the lamentable state of contemporary theater. She, too, felt an academy was the answer:
"As I think a good critic a friend both to authors and actors,
I could wish a society of real judges were incorporated, by
way of an academy, to take the theatres under their inspec-
tion."

Despite the preponderance of historical and current opinion behind him, however, events were no kinder to Smollett
than they had been to his predecessors. No patronage was
secured, no plan put into action, and (needless to say) no
academy established. Several factors contributed to the
failure of Smollett's proposal: his relative youth (aged
thirty-four), his Scottish origins, and especially his lack of
either real stature in the literary world or powerful connections in the political world. But his greatest misfortune was
an accident of history: proposing an English academy in the
very year that Johnson published his *Dictionary*. This long-
awaited event had the double effect of seeming to obviate
the need for an English academy—after all, Johnson already
had fulfilled its primary purpose of standardizing the
language—and lending unique authority to Johnson's growing opposition to the whole idea.

To compare Johnson's achievement in the *Dictionary* with
those of whole academies in France and Italy was an
immediate and widespread reaction. As James Sledd and
Gwin Kolb point out, Johnson himself had invited the comparison, both in his *Plan of a Dictionary* (published in 1747)

---

21. *Observations upon the English language in a Letter to a Friend* [1752], pp.
13–14, quoted in Read, "Suggestions for an Academy," pp. 145–146.
22. "To Mr. Fitz-Adam," *The World*, no. 19 (May 10, 1753).

and in the Preface to the *Dictionary* itself.[23] Reviewers followed suit. Adam Smith, in his well-known article on the *Dictionary* in the *Edinburgh Review*, wrote:

When we compare this book with other dictionaries, the merit of its author appears very extraordinary. Those which in modern languages have gained the most esteem, are that of the French academy, and that of the academy Della Crusca. Both these were composed by a numerous society of learned men, and took up a longer time in the composition, than the life of a single person could well have afforded. The Dictionary of the English language is the work of a single person, and composed in a period of time very inconsiderable, when compared with the extent of the work.[24]

Johnson soon adopted the explicit comparison in his own descriptions of what he had accomplished. He opened the Preface to the 1756 octavo edition of the *Dictionary* with this statement: "Having been long employed in the study and cultivation of the English language, I lately published a dictionary like those compiled by the academies of Italy and France, for the use of such as aspire to exactness of criticism or elegance of style."[25] It was precisely to this point that a writer in the *London Chronicle* spoke when, in 1757, he pronounced that the *Dictionary* "hath supplied the Want of an Academy of Belles Lettres, and performed Wonders towards fixing our Grammar."[26]

Such a public reaction, which was gaining momentum in the very months that Smollett was trying to persuade people that an academy was much needed, must have cut the wind from his sails. Moreover, Johnson was not simply an overshadowing presence. He was an outspoken critic of the idea of an English academy whose opposition grew stronger as his influence became greater. Johnson first touched on

23. James H. Sledd and Gwin J. Kolb, *Dr. Johnson's Dictionary: Essays in the Biography of a Book* (Chicago: University of Chicago Press, 1955), p. 25.
24. *Edinburgh Review*, 1 (1755), 61–62, quoted from Sledd and Kolb, *Johnson's Dictionary*, p. 10.
25. I, [iii].
26. "The Theatre," *London Chronicle*, April 12–14, 1757.

the subject in an early version of the "Life of Roscommon" he contributed to the *Gentleman's Magazine* in 1748. There he contented himself with quoting Elijah Fenton's description of how Roscommon had tried unsuccessfully to found an academy in the 1660s, including Fenton's skeptical comment that it was "a design, of which it is much easier to conceive an agreeable idea, than any rational hope ever to see it brought to perfection."[27] (This was a line of argument—the impracticability of academy schemes—that Johnson was to pursue with a vengeance in his expanded "Life of Roscommon" thirty years later.)

By the mid-1750s, Johnson's attitude had hardened. Warm with pride in his achievement, Johnson confronted the prospect of an English academy defiantly in his Preface to the *Dictionary* in 1755:

> If an academy should be established for the cultivation of our stile, which I, who can never wish to see dependance multiplied, hope the spirit of *English* liberty will hinder or destroy, let them, instead of compiling grammars and dictionaries, endeavour, with all their influence, to stop the licence of translatours, whose idleness and ignorance, if it be suffered to proceed, will reduce us to babble a dialect of *France*.[28]

The vehemence of his rhetoric notwithstanding, this is the only instance in his career where Johnson treated as a real and present possibility the institution of an English academy; he even recommends the specific issues that such an academy, if over his objections it should come into existence, might usefully take up. It is tempting to speculate whether Smollett's academy proposal had something to do with the fact that Johnson, who in 1748 had written that since Swift's proposal of 1712 the idea of founding an academy "has never been mentioned," should now in 1755 take the question of an academy so seriously. For whatever

27. "Life of the Earl of Roscommon," *Gentleman's Magazine*, 18 (1748), 216.
28. P. [xii].

reasons, the academy issue remained on Johnson's mind for years to come. He returned to it in 1759 in one of his *Idler* essays on Dick Minim (no. 61), and again in 1779 in three of his *Lives of the Poets*, those of Prior, Swift, and Roscommon, all of which may be better understood in light of further events in the late 1750s.

In addition to their differences of opinion about an academy, at the close of 1755 Smollett and Johnson suddenly found themselves in a position of more direct rivalry. Unbeknownst to either, but with many of the same ideas in mind, each was about to launch a new literary journal: Johnson his *Literary Magazine*, Smollett the *Critical Review*. The coincidences are remarkable. Each journal was scheduled to begin publishing the first of February 1756; each grew out of similar perceptions about the inadequacy of contemporary English review journalism; and each announced very similar editorial policies and purposes. In compiling the *Life*, Boswell discovered important clues about Johnson's intentions: "In one of his little memorandum-books I find the following hints for his intended Review or Literary Journal: '*The Annals of Literature, foreign as well as domestick.* Imitate Le Clerk - Bayle - Barbeyrac. Infelicity of Journals in England. Works of the learned. We cannot take in all. Sometimes copy from foreign Journalists. Always tell.' "[29] The prospective title Johnson jotted down here closely resembles the title Smollett had first proposed, "The Progress or Annals of Literature and the Liberal Arts." Johnson's note on the "infelicity of Journals in England" shows a dissatisfaction with contemporary literary journalism that Smollett expressed more violently in a tirade against the only review journal then in print, Griffiths's *Monthly Review*, which he damned as "a contemptible Manufacture . . . carried on by wretched Hirelings, without Talent, Candour, Spirit, or Circumspection."[30] Both Johnson and Smollett seemed especially intent on covering foreign literature, Johnson with his

29. *Life*, I, 284–285.
30. *Public Advertiser*, December 19, 1755.

note on "copying" from foreign journals, and Smollett with the system of foreign correspondence he featured in advertisements for the *Critical Review* and published as a distinct section of each issue. Advertisements for the *Literary Magazine* and the *Critical Review* both emphasized their intention to provide reviews of all English publications, to encourage authors of merit, to redeem criticism from commercial influences, and to promote a more refined public taste.

Thus when advertisements for Smollett's journal first began appearing in the *Public Advertiser* on December 19, 1755, there were immediate and rather sharp reactions from the proprietors of the *Literary Magazine.* They rushed their first advertisement into print on December 25. In it they mocked Smollett's emphatic claims for his journal's objectivity, quoting sarcastically from the advertisement for the *Critical Review,* and tacitly reproving him for his attacks on the *Monthly Review*:

> The Gentlemen concerned in the Undertaking [i.e., the *Literary Magazine*] don't pretend to have "*no Connections to warp their Integrity, no Prejudices to influence their Judgment,*" honestly acknowledging themselves vastly inferior, in this Repsect, to those exalted Intelligences (see Public Advertiser for Friday last) the *Monthly Annalists* [i.e., the *Critical Review*]; nor do they take upon them to censure the Productions of those who are concerned in Undertakings of the same kind.[31]

But the early rivalry between the two journals in fact came to very little. Although Johnson provided some interesting book reviews and articles, he was compiling the *Literary Magazine* by himself and could not hope to match the comprehensive coverage of the *Critical* or *Monthly* reviews, with their staffs of writers. Other problems arose and within a few months Johnson had left the *Literary Magazine*, which soon shifted its focus to politics and lost any claim to literary preeminence. It failed altogether in 1758. For Smollett, on the other hand, the successful establishment of the *Critical*

31. *Public Advertiser*, December 25, 1755.

Review (which lasted well into the nineteenth century) provided some consolation for the stillborn academy scheme. It gave him a forum from which he could satisfy, at least in part, his desire to wield influence in the literary world.

Although the snappish advertisements for their journals did not lead to open hostilities—certainly not of the kind that Grub Street was used to—there continued to be signs of tension between Johnson and Smollett over the next three years. Johnson never mentioned the *Critical Review* by name in the *Literary Magazine*, apart from a single sentence defending his friend Arthur Murphy's *Apprentice* from harsh reviews in it and the *Monthly Review*.[32] But he did become quite openly critical of the reviews in other contexts. He used an article in the *Universal Visiter* in 1756 to disparage the recent proliferation of new magazines and review journals, comparing them to "wolves in long winters [who] are forced to prey on one another."[33] A year later, Johnson observed that the lack of a good literary journal had been "for a long Time, among the Deficiencies of English Literature, but," he added sardonically, "as the Caprice of Man is always starting from too little to too much, we have now, amongst other Disturbers of human Quiet, a numerous Body of *Reviewers* and *Remarkers*."[34]

If Johnson was less than impressed by the *Critical Review* and its ilk, Smollett made it equally clear that he was not overawed by Johnson's authority, whether as critic or lexicographer. In reviewing Joseph Warton's *Essay on Pope*, for example, Smollett firmly defended one of Pope's couplets from the criticism of both Warton and Johnson:

Notwithstanding the demonstration of the Rambler, which is so convincing to our author, we think the sound is admirably adapted to the sense in these lines—

32. "An Occasional Prologue . . . by Mr. Murphy," *Literary Magazine*, 1 (1756), 29.
33. "To the *Visiter*," *Universal Visiter*, 1 (1756), 164.
34. [Untitled editorial], *London Chronicle*, January 1, 1757.

'Soft is the strain when *Zephyr* gently blows,
And the smooth stream in smoother number flows.'

That there is not much volubility in the first of these, we own; but, surely he must have an undistinguishing ear who does not in the *soft strain, &c.* recognize the sound of *Zephyr* rustling among the leaves of the vernal grove; and as for the consonants in the other line, they roughen the verse just enough to produce an agreeable murmur, without which the current would be altogether unperceived.[35]

In the same passage, Smollett disputed another of Johnson's criticisms: "The Alexandrine, which gave umbrage to the critic of the *Rambler*, might have been lightened with a greater number of short syllables—But as it stands, it exhibits a fine, gay, fleeting picture; and the length of the line, implies the length of space through which *Camilla* passed with such velocity—'Flies o'er th'unbending corn, and skims along the main.'" Johnson, who was very likely to have read this review because he was himself reviewing Warton's *Essay* for the *Literary Magazine*, cannot have been pleased with Smollett's remarks, especially the insinuation that he had "an undistinguishing ear" for poetry. Indeed (as will be seen) Johnson seems to have remembered well Smollett's brand of practical criticism when he set about creating his parody of the coffee-house critic, Dick Minim.

In 1759 Smollett's irreverence in another of his *Critical Review* articles finally roused Johnson to an angry response. Smollett was engaged in a running feud with the hack writer James Grainger who, in a typically ranting pamphlet (*A Letter to Tobias Smollet*), tried to vindicate his works by citing Johnson's expressions of approval. In reviewing this pamphlet, Smollett chastised Grainger's use of Johnson, "on whose genius and learning poet Grainger comes abroad like a puny dwarf mounted on the shoulders of a giant," and

35. *Critical Review*, 1 (1756), 231–232. The couplet, as well as the Alexandrine discussed below, are from Pope's *Essay on Criticism*, 11. 366–367 and 373.

explained away Johnson's endorsement very politely: "We can easily conceive how a good-natured man should be influenced to speak civilly of a bad performance, written by a humble admirer and officious adherent."[36] But unfortunately Smollett also chose to demonstrate that Johnson's *Dictionary*, which Grainger had invoked, was not without flaws:

We have looked into that work, and found, that even Johnson is not infallible. He has, for example, mistaken the word *aloft* for *aloof*, and misquoted Milton for his authority . . . We have likewise seen his definition of a *dab-chick*, which he calls a chicken newly hatched; though in fact it is a water-fowl; and perhaps what is more extraordinary, we find him giving *Sabbath* and *Sabaoth* as synonimous words, though every old woman that reads her prayers can tell, that the first signifies *rest*, and the other *hosts* or *armies*. We seek not to swell the catalogue of such mistakes; neither will we, in imitation of critic Grainger, affirm that none but ignorant blockheads could mistake so grossly the meaning of an English word. Remember, however, that as your great oracle, Mr. Johnson, the dictionary-writer, has been caught tripping more than once, even when deliberately walking in his own beaten path; we, in the hurry of a monthly publication, may sometimes stumble, without incurring the imputation of ignorance and presumption.[37]

Smollett was right about the errors in Johnson's *Dictionary*. Johnson corrected the definition of "dab-chick" in the 1760 octavo edition of the *Dictionary* and of "sabaoth" in the 1765 folio edition, although the disputed definition of "aloft" and what is indeed a misquotation from *Paradise Lost* (Book III, l. 577) persisted in later editions well into the nineteenth century. But pulling down Johnson to excuse his own mistakes was ungenerous of Smollett, to say the least. Johnson complained of this treatment in a note to Smollett's printer, a note Smollett read and dismissed without a trace of remorse as "a very petulant Card . . . concerning an Article

---

36. *Critical Review*, 7 (1759), p. 156.
37. *Critical Review*, 7 (1759), p. 155.

in the last Review."[38] Clearly, as Smollett told Wilkes in the same month that Johnson sent his angry note, he and Johnson "were never cater-cousins."[39] This became even more evident a few weeks later when Johnson drew on details from Smollett's career to create his parody of the prototypical pseudocritic, Dick Minim, in *Idler* essays 60 and 61 (June 9 and 16, 1759).

This is not to contend that Dick Minim "is" Smollett: Minim is of course a composite caricature, his traits and critical commonplaces drawn from various "types" and generalized to make the satire more effective and anything but personal. Several details that one could connect with Smollett—such as each having served an apprenticeship in his youth, Minim to a brewer, Smollett to a surgeon—would apply just as readily to hundreds of other literary dabblers. In his day and since, Johnson's satiric art has generally resisted efforts to discern specific "originals" he may have had in mind when he created Minim. But after tracing the history of both Smollett's academy proposal and his relations with Johnson, it now seems possible to identify Smollett as the source for two details: Minim's ridiculous mode of poetic criticism and his grandiose academy scheme. Like Smollett in his defense of Pope's lines against Johnson's criticism (cited above), Minim "is particularly delighted when he finds '*the sound an echo to the sense*'" (Idler, no. 60). Johnson then "quotes" Minim's close reading of some lines from *Hudibras*, of which one passage will suffice to show Minim's over-enthusiastic adherence to Pope's maxim: "It is impossible to utter the two lines emphatically without an act like that which they describe: *bubble* and *trouble* causing a momentary inflation of the cheeks by the retention of the breath, which is afterwards forcibly emitted, as in the practice of *blowing bubbles*." This and the rest of the passage are a skillful parody of Smollett's sometimes overwrought

38. Smollett to John Wilkes, April 1, [1759], *Letters of Smollett*, p. 77.
39. Smollett to John Wilkes, March 16, 1759, *Letters of Smollett*, p. 75.

"scrutinist" criticism and a deft (though delayed) retort to
Smollett's comments in the Warton review in 1756.

But the most outstanding parallel is the academy scheme,
the height of Minim's aspirations:

> Minim professes great admiration of the wisdom and
> munificence by which the academies of the Continent were raised,
> and often wishes for some standard of taste, for some tribunal, to
> which merit may appeal from caprice, prejudice, and malignity. He
> has formed a plan for an academy of criticism, where every work
> of imagination may be read before it is printed, and which shall
> authoritatively direct the theatres what pieces to receive or reject,
> to exclude or revive.
>
> Such an institution would, in Dick's opinion, spread the fame of
> English literature over Europe, and make London the metropolis of
> elegance and politeness . . . where nothing would any longer be
> applauded or endured that was not conformed to the nicest rules,
> and finished with the highest elegance.
>
> Till some happy conjunction of the planets shall dispose our
> princes or ministers to make themselves immortal by such an
> academy, Minim contents himself to preside four nights in a week
> in a critical society selected by himself, where he is heard without
> contradiction, and whence his judgment is disseminated through
> the great vulgar and the small.[40]

Minim's plan for an "academy of criticism" contains many
echoes of Smollett's academy scheme: the establishment of
a critical tribunal, the patronage of neglected merit, the regulation of the theaters, the reformation of public taste, and
the refinement of English letters to European standards.
Moreover, Minim's experience closely resembles Smollett's.
Unable to secure patronage or support for his academy
scheme, he is forced to settle for a lesser undertaking, a critical society selected by himself whence his opinions are
disseminated. The only detail missing to complete the

40. *The Idler*, 61, *Universal Chronicle*, 2 (June 16, 1759), 185; quoted from
The Idler and The Adventurer, ed. W. J. Bate, John M. Bullitt, and L.F.
Powell, vol. 2, *The Yale Edition of the Works of Samuel Johnson* (New Haven:
Yale University Press, 1963), p. 190.

parallel is a literary journal like the *Critical Review*. But perhaps this was deliberate on Johnson's part, to avoid pointing the satire specifically at Smollett. Johnson rarely indulged in personal attacks of that kind and it would have been especially inopportune in mid-1759 when he was still seeking Smollett's help in securing his servant Frank Barber's release from the Navy. Nevertheless, for Smollett, as for Dick Minim, the *Idler*'s reading of the stars was accurate. The obstacles to organizing an academy proved insurmountable and no miraculous "conjunction of the planets" ever occurred to make his dream come true.

But if as the years passed Smollett gradually resigned himself to the futility of his own academy proposal, he certainly did not abandon his belief that some such institution was a good and necessary thing for England. Under Smollett's editorship from 1756 to 1763, the *Critical Review* repeatedly editorialized on the subject of academies. In a review of a French-English dictionary in October 1759, the writer lamented the irregularity and mutability of the English language, concluding "It were to be wished for the honour of this country, that an academy were established, and vested with full power and authority to reform these abuses, and fix the volatility of the English tongue, which is so fluctuating and mutable."[41] Many other reviews repeated the call for some authority to regulate pronunciation, orthography, grammar, and every other element of the language. Indeed, in their reviews Smollett and his colleagues were so consistently severe on language and style—detecting barbarisms, neologisms, Scotticisms, and other flaws—that Robert Spector has justly likened their conduct of the *Critical Review* to that of an "English Academy *de facto*."[42] Other possible benefits of an academy were not forgotten. Smollett praised the voluminous *Universal History* as a work "not unworthy of the most eminent and learned academy that ever flourished in

---

41. *Critical Review*, 8 (1759), 323.
42. *English Literary Periodicals and the Climate of Opinion during the Seven Years' War* (The Hague: Mouton, 1966), p. 328; see also pp. 324–327.

Europe."[43] Not simply a puff for a project he had helped edit, his review succeeded in pointing to the lack of an academy in England: "We are astonished, when we reflect that a set of private booksellers could be found to engage in such an enterprize."

In 1760, while summarizing the progress of society in the reign of George II in the *Continuation* of his *History of England*, he returned to the theme yet again. He compared the achievements of the Society for the Encouragement of the Arts, a body of private citizens, to those of the academies of Europe, and he lamented the failure of the Crown or Parliament to provide any such institutions in England: "No Maecenas appeared among the ministers, and not the least ray of patronage glimmered from the throne. The protection, countenance, and gratification, secured in other countries by the institution of academies, and the liberality of princes, the ingenious in England derived from the generosity of a public, endued with taste and sensibility, eager for improvement, and proud of patronizing extraordinary merit."[44] Elsewhere in the *Continuation*, he resumed his lament about the neglect of learning and letters by the great: "Never was the pursuit after knowledge so universal, or literary merit more regarded, than at this juncture by the body of the British nation; but it was honoured by no attention from the throne, and little indulgence did it reap from the liberality of particular patrons." Many authors of this age, added Smollett, "whose merit was the most universally acknowledged, remained exposed to all the storms of indigence, and all the stings of mortification."[45] Undoubtedly he included himself among the neglected. But more than a personal complaint, these passages describe a national disgrace—in Smollett's view, one of his country's greatest failings thus far in its history.

43. *Critical Review*, 7 (1759), 1.
44. *Continuation of the Complete History of England*, II (1760), 412.
45. *Continuation*, IV (1761), 128–130.

Other writers continued to express sentiment in favor of
an academy throughout the "Age of Johnson." Goldsmith,
in his "Account of the Augustan Age of England," wrote
that Queen Anne had died "before any plan of an academy
could be resolved on" and that "meanwhile, the necessity of
such an institution became every day more apparent."[46]
Arthur Murphy, Thomas Sheridan, and a host of lesser
known writers echoed these opinions throughout the second
half of the eighteenth century, as Read has shown. In fact,
Read concluded, "the consensus of stated opinion during
this period was clearly in favor of an academy."[47]

Perhaps Johnson sensed this, which would explain why in
compiling his *Lives of the Poets* in the late 1770s, he took the
trouble to elaborate and justify his views on the academy
issue in both his life of Swift and especially his life of Roscommon. One textual detail in the latter suggests as much.
In his 1748 version of "Roscommon" (in the *Gentleman's
Magazine*), Johnson mentioned that Swift's *Proposal* in 1712
had revived the Restoration scheme for an English academy,
"but," he noted, "since that time it has never been
mentioned."[48] In expanding and rewriting this brief biography for inclusion in the *Lives* thirty years later, Johnson
repeated the line almost verbatim, with one subtle but
revealing alteration: the design "was revived by Dr. Swift
. . . but it has never since been *publickly* mentioned" (italics
added).[49] With this careful qualification Johnson tacitly acknowledged his awareness of private suggestions for an
academy that had never been published or formally taken up.
Interestingly, in his revisions Johnson also deleted his con-
jecture that no academy had been founded since Swift's time
"because the statesmen who succeeded [Oxford] have not
had more leisure for literary schemes." He thus eliminated

---

46. *The Bee*, 8 (November 24, 1759), in *Collected Works of Oliver
Goldsmith*, ed. Arthur Friedman (Oxford: Clarendon Press, 1966), I, 503.
47. Read, "Suggestions for an Academy," p. 156.
48. *Gentleman's Magazine*, 18 (1748), 216.
49. "Roscommon," *Lives of the English Poets*, ed. George Birkbeck Hill
(Oxford: Clarendon Press, 1905), I, 232. Hereafter cited as *Lives*.

any possibility of inferring that he felt statesmen with leisure *should* take up such literary schemes—quite the opposite of Smollett's sentiments on government intervention.

Johnson's treatment of the academy topic in his lives of Swift and Roscommon show him at his best, weighing the imagined benefits of an academy against the dictates of common sense and experience. He faults Swift's *Proposal* for being "written without any accurate enquiry into the history of other tongues," which in turn led Swift to assert an unfounded confidence in the power of an academy to perfect and forever fix the English language: "The certainty and stability which, contrary to all experience, he thinks attainable, he proposes to secure by instituting an academy; the decrees of which every man would have been willing, and many would have been proud to disobey, and which, being renewed by successive elections, would in a short time have differed from itself."[50]

In his life of Roscommon Johnson argued the same grounds, but more thoroughly and more fairly. He conceded that "such a society might perhaps without much difficulty be collected" and that "the Italian academy seems to have obtained its end," having "refined and . . . fixed" the language. But then follow his counterarguments, one after another. The French academy had failed in its efforts to fix the language; the appointment of members would be subject to political favoritism and corruption; members thus appointed would be negligent and uncooperative; disagreement would divide and paralyze the academy; and even if agreement were reached and decrees issued, there would be neither power to enforce nor inducement to obey them. In Johnson's mind, the question was beyond dispute, the issue settled: "nothing is left but that every writer should criticise himself."[51]

50. "Swift," *Lives*, III, 16.
51. "Roscommon," *Lives*, I, 232–233.

Johnson had drawn on his deep understanding of human psychology to argue an academy an impracticable undertaking. But whatever the strength of his reasoning, it did not—indeed it could not, as his knowledge of human nature should also have told him—quell the persistent expressions of support for an academy. Shortly after his *Lives* were published, a critic harangued Johnson about this very passage in "Roscommon": "If the Italian Academy has obtained its end, why should not an English Academy have the same success? The Doctor had better say at once—My Dictionary has fixed the English Language; an Academy to fix it is therefore totally useless. —Yet where is the man that can possibly understand the Doctor's definitions? They have puzzled England, enraged Scotland, and confounded Ireland."[52] Even Johnson's admiring friend and biographer, Arthur Murphy, disagreed with him on the academy question. In his *Essay on the Life and Genius of Samuel Johnson, LL.D.* (1792), Murphy digressed at length on the advantages that would have accrued, and the evils that would have been avoided, had there been an English academy. Concerning Johnson's view, Murphy seemed embarrassed: "It is needless to dissemble, that Dr. Johnson, in the Life of Roscommon, talks of the inutility of such a project." Murphy proceeded to refute Johnson's objections one by one, after which he renewed the call: "An Academy of Literature would be an establishment highly useful, and an honour to Literature . . . The minister, who shall find leisure from party and faction, to carry such a scheme into execution, will, in all probability, be respected by posterity as the Maecenas of letters."[53] But still, as Smollett had stated of an earlier period, "no Maecenas appeared."

52. [?Reverend Beilby of Ferriby], *Remarks on Dr. Johnson's Lives of the Most Eminent English Poets* (1782), reprinted in *On the Lives of the Poets 1781–1782*, vol. 12 of Johnsoniana, (New York: Garland Publishing, 1975), p. 12.
53. Pp. 117–119.

A nineteenth-century admirer said of Smollett that "for a short period during the interregnum between Pope and Johnson he was a kind of literary Protector."[54] Others, including Johnson himself, probably considered him more of a "young pretender" who tried to vault himself into authority even as Johnson was rising to the role of literary arbiter of his age. Johnson's prediction that an academy would never succeed for practical reasons proved self-fulfilling: Johnson himself became the practical obstacle that could not be converted or overcome. Ultimately, however, though neither Smollett nor Johnson backed away from his position, their differences did not permanently estrange them. Smollett praised Johnson lavishly in his *Continuation* in the 1760s and a decade later Johnson insisted on writing a Latin inscription for a memorial to Smollett.[55] The academy question did not, of course, die with either of them.[56] Among those who took it up in the nineteenth century was Matthew Arnold, who, in his essay "The Literary Influence of Academies"—an essay that Henry James felt marked Arnold's coming into his own as a critic—tried to assess the consequences for English literary history of not having had an academy. Without taking up the sorts of commonsensical objections Johnson raised, Arnold nevertheless offered a kind of benediction on the impasse that the academy debate had produced in Johnson's age and in others: "When a literature has produced Shakespeare and Milton, when it has even produced Barrow and Burke, it cannot well abandon its traditions; it can hardly begin, at this late time of day, with an institution

54. Thomas Seccombe, *The Age of Johnson* (London, 1900), p. 171.
55. IV, 127–128; *Life,* V, 366–367.
56. Nor has it died in the twentieth century. Harry Levin, for example, raised the issue by way of inquiring into the historic differences between the English and French languages, in his essay "The War of Words in English Poetry," *Contexts of Criticism* (Cambridge: Harvard University Press, 1957), p. 214. See also John Barrell's excellent discussion of the socio-political implications of the academy debate, "The Language Properly So-Called: The Authority of Common Usage," *English Literature in History 1730–80: An Equal, Wide Survey* (London: Hutchinson, 1983), pp. 110–175.

like the French Academy."[57] Nearly forty more years were to pass, adding their weight to his judgment, before an academy with far more modest aims was founded, in the form of the British Academy in 1902.

57. *Cornhill Magazine* (Aug. 1864), quoted here from *Essays in Criticism*, 2nd ed. (London: Macmillan, 1869), p. 73. For James's comment, see *Literary Reviews and Essays by Henry James*, ed. Albert Mordell (New York: Twayne, 1957), pp. 348–349 and 401.

Johnson, Traveling Companion, in Fancy and Fact

In spite of its benignity, *Rasselas*, measured on the scale of life's rational goods, offers little to make the heart leap with joy. In a series of probing trial runs, it becomes apparent that under the sun "the race is not to the swift, nor the battle to the strong, neither yet bread to the wise, nor yet riches to men of understanding, nor yet favor to men of skill; but time and chance happeneth to them all." In the face of this generally disillusioned view of the human lot—most powerfully expressed in his greatest poem—the only positive recommendation Johnson has to offer comes as a prayer "for patience sov'reign o'er transmuted ill." This is expanded in the religious assurance of *Idler* 89: "That misery does not make all virtuous experience too certainly informs us; but it is no less certain that of what virtue there is, misery produces far the greater part. Physical evil may be therefore endured with patience, since it is the cause of moral good; and patience itself is one virtue by which we are prepared for that state in which evil shall be no more."[1] In the same

---

1. *The Idler and the Adventurer*, vol. 2, *The Yale Edition of the Works of Samuel Johnson*, ed. W. J. Bate, et al. (New Haven: Yale University Press, 1963), p. 278.

essay, Johnson tells us: "If the senses were feasted with perpetual pleasure, they would always keep the mind in subjection. Reason has no authority over us, but by its power to warn us against evil."[2] But if to human misery we— "helpless man, in ignorance sedate"—are obliged for the greater part of what virtue there is, we must not be driven to conclude that Johnson thinks we ought to be thankful for human misery. In his manly essay, *Rambler* 32, he makes very clear that he does not minimize the reality of our suffering, but only strives to instruct us how best to bear it.

Let us move to a closer reading of *Rasselas*. It is probably of slight consequence, but nevertheless a fact, that *Rasselas* contains *two* imaginary sojourns, one within the other, but the first one twenty years long. I mean the probatory tour of Imlac's *Wanderjahre*, which Johnson first traces, no doubt to establish Imlac's right to our confidence in him as a trustworthy guide for youth. Imlac's father had envisioned for him the career of a merchant prince, since, being himself already possessed of great wealth, but yet a man "of mean sentiments and narrow comprehension," the accumulation of riches was the limit of his horizon. Nevertheless, he allowed his son the advantage of a liberal education before launching him into the world. Imlac, however, was quickly seduced by the love of learning, and at the age of twenty, equipped with a stock of ten thousand pieces of gold, he repudiated his father's art of growing rich and opted for science and the pursuit of knowledge in foreign climes. He took ship on the Red Sea for Surat, and, conforming to the *Drang nach Osten* that overcame so many eighteenth-century travelers, struck off into the interior of India as far as Agra, where he learned the language, conversed with the learned, and gained credit with the Great Mogul before going on to Persia. Here he found sociable people, examined the "remains of ancient magnificence, and observed many new accommodations of life," tracing human nature in characters and manners. From Persia he made his way into Arabia, where he studied

2. P. 277.

a nation both pastoral and warlike, ever in motion, restless and quarrelsome. In these countries, he made poetry his special study, committing much of it to memory; ultimately determined to be an original poet, he crammed his mind with images—the naturally beautiful and dreadful, the "awfully vast or elegantly little"—and familiarized himself "with all the modes of life."

Next he traveled through Syria and reached Palestine, where he lingered for three years, grew acquainted with Europeans and learned about the sources of power and knowledge among the Western nations. Thence he moved to Cairo, where also he stayed a long time, before heading finally to Suez, and so by the Red Sea back to the port whence he first set out years before, and by caravan home to Abyssinia.

Years later, hearing that the Thrales had just received £14,000, Johnson wrote to Mrs. Thrale: "If I had money enough, what would I do? Perhaps . . . I might go to Cairo, and down the Red Sea to Bengal, and take a ramble in India . . . Half fourteen thousand would send me out to see other forms of existence, and bring me back to describe them."[3]

When Imlac reached home, he found that his father had been dead for fourteen years. We should not forget the filial preoccupations and pressures under which Johnson was suffering as he wrote *Rasselas*. He could hardly avoid having his father in mind, as well as his mother, during the week when he was composing. There might have been a personal shadow in the reference to the "narrow comprehension," if not the "mean sentiments." The long hours of childhood, during which the parents wrangled fecklessly about money and the endless burden of undischarged debt must have left ugly traces. We know he had an abiding sense of guilt toward both his parents. No one can forget his self-imposed penance of standing bareheaded in the rain, in the market-place at Uttoxeter, to atone for his prideful refusal to attend

3. *The Letters of Samuel Johnson*, ed. R. W. Chapman (Oxford: Clarendon Press, 1952), II, 61–62.

his father's bookstall fifty years earlier. With his mind on
these early days, it does not seem to me a wild surmise that
he would like to insert some private testimony into the book.
I do not know that it has been suggested before, but I suggest it now: Johnson's invention of his central character's
name was an obeisance to Michael Johnson. The spelling of
the name is negotiable. In the Warwickshire Register of
Michael's marriage to Sara Ford, June 19, 1706, his name is
entered as Mickell. Not to belabor the point, my notion is
that Michael is easily reduced to an alternative spelling. *Ch*
is equivalent to a hard *c*, and the *e* is frequently dropped in
foreign equivalents of the name. So we get MICAL and its
transpositional anagram, IMLAC.[4]

There are other telltale clues of where his thoughts were
roving. Recall the echoes of his early years in Stourbridge
and Lichfield, of Cornelius Ford and his niece Olivia Lloyd,
of Gilbert Walmsley and the town's best families, that W.
Jackson Bate has brought into vivid prominence, and compare Imlac's references: "They admitted me to their tables,
heard my story, and dismissed me. I opened a school, and
was prohibited to teach . . . [There was] a lady that was fond
of my conversation, but rejected my suit, because my father
was a merchant."[5]

If one estimates the book's rating on the thermometer of
human satisfaction with the human lot—call it content or
discontent—I think it must be placed near the bottom of the
scale of hope. Irony, as Agostino Lombardo emphatically
.pointed out on the two hundredth anniversary of *Rasselas*, is
at the very heart of the book: "This is, after all, the history

---

4. Had he needed it, Johnson could have found an analogy in the name
of perhaps the most famous club in Georgian London: Almack's. Report
has it that this is an anagram of the name of its proprietor. I quote
Webster's *Biographical Dictionary*: "William Almack, d. 1781. Scottish
founder of the famous Assembly Rooms, King St., St. James's. His surname said to be a syllabic transposition of original patronymic McCaul, or
McCall."

5. Samuel Johnson, *The History of Rasselas, Prince of Abyssinia*, ed.
Geoffrey Tillotson and Brian Jenkins (London: Oxford University Press,
1971), p. 35.

of a search which we know to be useless." The conclusion, "in which nothing is concluded," is already implicit in the opening sentence, which as we remember w-rns the listener that "the whispers of fancy," "the phantoms of hope," and the promise of the morrow are doomed to disappointment.[6] By Imlac's very entrance into the Happy Valley years before the story opens, he had tacitly signified his conviction that earthly happiness is an illusion, and that the rational way to meet that fact is to turn one's back on the pursuit of happiness. In encouraging Rasselas to escape and in accompanying his flight, was Imlac expecting anything other than a repetition of the old lesson? If the answer is—as it must be—no, is that negative conclusion not equally and still more decisively true of Imlac's creator, for whom the alter ego is only a thin disguise? Johnson cannot plead Rasselas' ignorance before he left the valley, when the youth's old tutor told him that if he had ever seen the miseries of the outside world, he would set a right value on his present state. "I shall long," was the prince's answer, "to see the miseries of the world, since the sight of them is necessary to happiness." Nor can Johnson allow himself the luxury he permits to the prince, the Rousseauan complacency of "consciousness of the delicacy with which he felt, and the eloquence with which he bewailed" the miseries of life. Did not Johnson express an aversion for "feelers"? But he can and does express the profound irony of Imlac's disclosures to Rasselas, that there is no one of all the prince's attendants "who does not lament the hour when he entered this retreat." Later in the story, to the friends assembled inside the Great Pyramid, Imlac offers his ultimate justification of its erection, and of all other human endeavor: "It seems," says he, "to have been erected only in compliance with that hunger of imagination which preys incessantly upon life, and must be always appeased by some employment."

6. Agostino Lombardo, "The Importance of Imlac," *Bicentenary Essays on Rasselas*, collected by Magdi Wahba, Supplement to *Cairo Studies in English* (Cairo, 1959), p. 41.

But the imaginary travels comprising the work as a whole contain a partial and temporary alleviation of unhappiness and disillusion in the eager welcome of new experience enjoyed by the young and unjaded travelers being guided through life's novelties by the knowing Imlac—discreet, helpful, and forbearing toward intelligent ignorance. Nor does Imlac personate a neutral observer, bent merely on confirming conclusions already reached. He shares in the inquiry both by prompting further investigation and by a sympathetic interest in the impact of each event on his companions. He resembles, though far less energetically, Johnson in his own demeanor on the imaginative and observant journey through the Highlands with Boswell.

That Johnson had not lost his zest for experience becomes abundantly clear when we pass from his imaginary journeying to its imaginative counterpart, to which we now turn our attention: the translation into actual living, unforgettably and doubly documented in the contrasting masterpieces, *A Journey to the Western Islands of Scotland*, and Boswell's *Journal of a Tour to the Hebrides with Samuel Johnson, LL.D.* That for Johnson this was in a true sense an adventure into country foreign both in place and figuratively in time is manifest throughout his book, in the terms in which he thinks, speaks, and writes of the journey.

Very early in their friendship, Johnson and Boswell talked about the Western Islands, and Johnson said that his interest had been aroused when he was very young by his father's putting into his hands Martin Martin's *Description*. He remembered that his father had then called to his attention Martin's account of the St. Kilda man who, when asked what he had thought of the high Church in Glasgow, answered that yes, it was a *large* rock, but that St. Kilda had higher rocks; yet he allowed that the caves inside the Church, with their supporting pillars and arches, were the best he had ever seen—conceiving that the structure had been hollowed out of the rock. We are all aware today of the eighteenth-century passion for grottoes; but this perhaps is to carry the obsession to an extreme! The fancy, at any rate, had stuck in Johnson's mind. Ever since reading that book, he said, he had wanted to visit the region. He now told Boswell, in an outburst of enthusiasm, that he would go with him to the Hebrides, unless some fit companion should offer to accompany Johnson to the North before Boswell got home from his imminent foreign travel.

It will be remembered that, as early as their third rendezvous, by his manifest hunger for whatever guidance, intellectual and moral, Johnson would bestow, and by his own ingenuous and spontaneous self-disclosure, Boswell had won a place in his sage's capacious affections. Among other confidences, he described to him Auchinleck, his family situation, his father's position in the legal and social world in Scotland, and his own natural expectations as heir to the estate. Johnson's notion, Boswell writes, "of the dignity of a Scotch landlord had been formed upon what he had heard of the Highland Chiefs," and with this preconception Johnson declared: "Sir, let me tell you, that to be a Scotch landlord, where you have a number of families dependent upon you, and attached to you, is perhaps, as high a situation as humanity can arrive at. A merchant upon the 'Change of London, with a hundred thousand pounds, is nothing: an English duke, with an immense fortune is nothing: he has no tenants who consider themselves as under his patriarchal care, and who will follow him to the field upon any emergency."[7]

I think it is clear that Johnson's primary purpose in undertaking the Highland expedition was to consolidate his opinions, test his earlier conjectures, and formulate his judgment by firsthand observation of the merits and demerits of a system of life which he had long idealized. In a true sense, he was projecting an imaginary journey into the past, into the ways of another age, a feudal society and a strange environment that would literally transport him from the familiar and contemporary and enable him to make valid comparisons

---

7. *Boswell's Life of Johnson*, ed. George Berkbeck Hill, revised and enlarged by L. F. Powell (Oxford: Clarendon Press, 1934–1959), I, 409.

with a different system of life against which he could measure the worth of familiar actualities. When, toward the end
of his adventures a decade later, he came to summarize what
he had learned, we can see by the tenses he uses in his analyses, how reluctant he was to surrender the past to the
present or give over what he had hoped to find. He writes:

> The laird is the original owner of the land, whose natural power
> must be very great, where no man lives but by agriculture; and
> where the produce of the land is not conveyed through the
> labyrinths of traffick, but passes directly from the hand that gathers
> it to the mouth that eats it. The laird has all those in his power
> that live upon his farms. Kings can, for the most part, only exalt
> or degrade. The laird at pleasure can feed or starve, can give
> bread, or withhold it. This inherent power was yet strengthened by
> the kindness of consanguinity, and the reverence of patriarchal
> authority. The laird was the father of the clan, and his tenants
> commonly bore his name. And to these principles of original com-
> mand was added, for many ages, an exclusive right of legal jurisdic-
> tion.
>   This multifarious, and extensive obligation operated with force
> scarcely credible. Every duty, moral or political, was absorbed in
> affection and adherence to the chief. Not many years have passed
> since the clans knew no law but the laird's will. He told them to
> whom they should be friends or enemies, what king they should
> obey, and what religion they should profess.[8]

He then turns to describe the swift disintegration consequent
upon the defeat at Culloden and the strict imposition of
English law and order:

> Their [native] pride has been crushed by the heavy hand of a
> vindictive conqueror, whose severities have been followed by laws,
> which, though they cannot be called cruel, have produced much
> discontent, because they operate upon the surface of life, and make

---

8. *A Journey to the Western Islands of Scotland*, vol. 9, *The Yale Edition of the Works of Samuel Johnson*, ed. Mary Lascelles (New Haven: Yale University Press, 1971), pp. 85–86.

every eye bear witness to subjection. To be compelled to a new dress has always been found painful.

Their chiefs being now deprived of their jurisdiction, have already lost much of their influence; and as they gradually degenerate from patriarchal rulers to rapacious landlords, they will divest themselves of the little that remains. . . .

The last law, by which the Highlanders are deprived of their arms, has operated with efficacy beyond expectation . . . The supreme power in every community has the right of debarring every individual, and every subordinate society from self-defence, only because the supreme power is able to defend them . . . These islands might be wasted with fire and sword before their sovereign would know their distress . . . It was observed by one of the chiefs of Sky, that fifty armed men might, without resistance, ravage the country. Laws that place the subjects in such a state, contravene the first principles of the compact of authority: they exact obedience, and yield no protection.[9]

I have cited only a fraction of Johnson's really superb and, on the whole, evenhanded survey of the plight of Scotland in his half-century, and none of what he says of the gains, because I wished to illustrate how deeply his sympathies were involved in the Highlanders' loss of their traditional mode of existence. He saw with equal clarity the ensuing benefits yet to be realized. But it is Old Scotland, especially in the Highlands and Western Islands, that seizes his imagination and holds his attention throughout the tour.

Boswell starts his published *Journal* with a superlative tribute to Johnson's fertile imagination. But what strikes us first and last in Johnson's printed *Journey* is the other half of his power: "a most logical head." We are impressed by his vigilant observation, and the gift, to use J. L. Lowes's favorite phrase, of "putting facts on their inferences." In writing his book, Johnson felt the weight of his responsibility as a faithful reporter, aware of what he would and did ask of other travelers in their published accounts. He allows scant room for the play of fancy.

9. *Journey to the Western Islands*, pp. 89–91.

But the latter was an asset seldom dormant in him as a traveling companion; and to see him in the round (if the phrase may be forgiven), Boswell's daily record of what passed in his company is essential, especially if we wish to get a sense of what it was like to be with him in unfamiliar conditions—out of context, as it were, and divested of his normal stage properties. It is worthwhile, therefore, to attend to facets of his nature spontaneously surfacing in sallies of imaginative fun or wit, evoked by circumstance or the remarks of conversational interchange. Of course, the range of topics arising in casual talk and the breadth of reference and allusion, are breathtaking and everywhere evident in the ampler *Life.*

But his readiness to join at every innocuous level of mental play with responsive companions is more conspicuous in Boswell's *Journal of a Tour* than anywhere else. The zest for living with which he commences this expedition is evident on the very day of setting out from Edinburgh, when he *sets the pace* for the group, asking no concessions from his juniors. Crossing the Firth, he insists on landing on the quite uninviting island of Inch Keith, with its high rocky shore. Neither of his companions had ever thought it worth a visit. They coast about and find an inlet on the northwest side. They clamber up a very steep ascent, through a profusion of thistles, but finding some good grass and a small herd of black cattle—Aberdeen Angus, I should like to think. One can only be startled by the bravado of this initial challenge by the heavy, sixty-four-year-old man. "He stalked," says Boswell, "like a giant among the luxuriant thistles and nettles." Not content with the physical exertion and the exploratory examination of the fort, Johnson next set Boswell a joculatory task, daring him to write a typical traveler's account of their discovery of this island, with minute particulars, "stating the grounds on which we concluded that it must have once been inhabited, and introducing many sage reflections . . . so as to induce people to come and survey it. All . . . might be true, and yet in reality there might be nothing to see." Then his fancy leaps forward. "I'd have this island," he declares. "I'd build a house, make a good landing-place, have a garden, and vines, and all sorts of trees. A rich man, of a hospitable turn, here, would have many visitors from Edinburgh." The subject unexhausted for him as the boat pushed off, he challenges Boswell: "Come, now, pay a classical compliment to the island on quitting it." And Boswell rose to the occasion: "I happened luckily, in allusion to the beautiful Queen Mary, whose name is upon the fort, to think of what Virgil makes Aeneas say, on having left the country of his charming Dido: 'Invitus, regina, tuo de littore cessi.' 'Very well hit off!' said he."[10] Could Harry Bailey himself have contrived a livelier, more *allegro* setting forth than this? "This gooth aright; unbokeled is the male."

Clouds gather over St. Andrews. Johnson "was affected with a strong indignation while he beheld the ruins of religious magnificence. I happened [says Boswell] to ask where John Knox was buried. Dr. Johnson burst out, 'I hope in the highway. I have been looking at his reformations' . . . He wanted to mount the steeples, but it could not be done . . . One of the steeples, which he was told was in danger, he wished not to be taken down; 'for,' said he, 'it may fall on some of the posterity of John Knox; and no great matter!'"[11] But he lamented the evidence of recent deterioration and neglect more even than the destruction formerly wrought by Knox and his followers. The visitors were well treated by the faculty and properly appreciative of the courtesies paid to them. Johnson's thanks, in their published form, are well worth listening to: "by the interposition of some invisible friend, lodgings had been provided for us at the house of one of the professors, whose easy civility quickly made us forget that we were strangers; and in the whole time of our stay we were gratified by every mode of kindness, and entertained with all the elegance of lettered

10. James Boswell, *The Journal of a Tour to the Hebrides with Samuel Johnson, LL.D.*, vol. 5, *Life*, pp. 55–56.
11. *Journal*, pp. 61–63.

hospitality."[12] But they left, says Johnson, with "the uneasy remembrance of an university declining, a college alienated, and a church profaned and hastening to the ground."[13]

It stuck in Boswell's memory that Dr. Blair had told him that on calling on Dr. Johnson in his chambers in Inner Temple Lane, he had "found the Giant in his den"; and as soon as Boswell grew well enough acquainted, he told Johnson that he had had this image in his mind when he first knocked at his door. He repeated Blair's expression, and Johnson "was diverted at this picturesque account of himself." The reason for adverting to the comparison will at once appear. At Aberdeen the travelers were invited to tea at the house of Boswell's cousin, where a little girl, Stuart Dallas, niece of the cousin, was staying. The conversation was light and lively. Johnson soon made friends with the little girl, and Boswell overheard him inventing a role in which he was a giant and saying, in a hollow voice, that he lived in a cave and had a bed in the rock, and that he would take her with him, and she should have a little bed cut opposite to his in the rock. Boswell, with ears erect, reported no ensuing alarm, and we may quiet our latterday fears and assume that the youngsters enjoyed their game.

Next morning a learned delegation arrived at the inn to accompany Johnson to the colleges and escort him to the magistrates in the town hall, where the provost was to present him with the freedom of the town before a numerous company. "It was striking," says Boswell, "to hear all of them drinking 'Dr. Johnson! Dr. Johnson!' in the town-hall of Aberdeen, and then to see him with his burgess-ticket, or diploma, in his hat, which he wore as he walked along the street, according to the usual custom."[14]

In the evening there was a distinguished dinner company at Sir Alexander Gordon's. Boswell found the assembly "but barren," the professors afraid to speak; so he started a

---

12. *Journey to the Western Islands*, p. 5.
13. Ibid., p. 9.
14. *Journal*, pp. 90–91.

topic, the difference between one genius and another, hoping to engage Dr. Gerard and Dr. Johnson in what he called "a disquisition." He mentioned as a curious fact that Locke had written poetry. Johnson took the bait: "I know of none, sir, but a kind of exercise prefixed to Dr. Sydenham's Works, in which he has some conceits about the dropsy, in which water and burning are united and how Dr. Sydenham removed fire by drawing off water, contrary to the usual practice, which is to extinguish fire by bringing water upon it. —I am not sure that there is a word of all this; but it is such kind of talk."[15] Boswell adds a note to the reader: "All this, as Dr. Johnson suspected at the time, was the immediate invention of his own lively imagination; for there is not one word of it in Mr. Locke's complimentary performance" —and to prove the point, Boswell quotes forty-eight lines of Locke's Latin elegiacs.

Three days later the tourists crossed the heath near Elgin, where tradition placed Macbeth's encounter with the witches, and Johnson repeated a good deal of that part of the play, with "grand and affecting" recitation. He then turned to his companion: "All hail Dalblair! hail to thee, Laird of Auchinleck!" They reached Fores after dark that night, and, says Boswell, "found an admirable inn, in which Johnson was pleased to meet with a landlord who styled himself 'Wine-Cooper, from London.'" We may suppose that the Doctor slept the sounder, if not on English casks. Only three days out of Edinburgh he had said to Boswell, apropos of the reversal of customs, religious especially: "Sir, we are here, as Christians in Turkey."

Inevitably, alien manners were a frequent topic of conversation. Just what lay behind Johnson's choice of Turkey for his simile we cannot guess, but Turkey carried a cloud of popular and fabulous allusion throughout the century. G. P. Marana's "L'Espion Turc" (1686) was the bellwether of a flock of pseudoveridical histories or chronicles in foreign dress of local scandal, social and political gossip and satire.

15. *Journal*, pp. 93–94.

It was immediately translated into English as *The Turkish Spy* and was reprinted, adapted, and imitated over many years. Defoe produced a "Continuation of Letters Written by a Turkish Spy in Paris" (1718). Ned Ward's *London Spy* (1698–1700) is an offshoot. Mrs. Haywood's *Letters from the Palace of Fame* (1727) and her *The Invisible Spy* (1754) follow the pattern, more or less. Johnson was obviously already familiar with *The Turkish Spy* when he ran across a copy in Mull at a house where he and Boswell dined. He thereupon gave his opinion "that it told nothing but what every body might have known at that time [that is, Paris in the last quarter of the seventeenth century]; and that what was good in it, did not pay you for the trouble of reading to find it."

At dinner in Dunvegan Castle, in a conversation of much greater moment, Johnson alluded to the author of the acknowledged masterwork of the genre, the *Persian Letters*. M'Leod started, according to Boswell—who might well have started it himself—the subject of making women do penance in the church for fornication. Johnson at some length pronounced his approval of this. He said, in part:

I would not be the man who would discover it, if I alone knew it, for a woman may reform; nor would I commend a parson who divulges a woman's first offence; but being once divulged, it ought to be infamous. Consider, of what importance to society the chastity of women is. Upon that all the property in the world depends. We hang a thief for stealing a sheep; but the unchastity of a woman transfers sheep, and farm and all, from the right owner. I have much more reverence for a common prostitute than for a woman who conceals her guilt. The prostitute is known. She cannot deceive: she cannot bring a strumpet into the arms of an honest man, without his knowledge.

Boswell:

There is, however, a great difference between the licentiousness of a single woman, and that of a married woman.

Johnson:

Yes, sir; there is a great difference between stealing a shilling, and stealing a thousand pounds; between simply taking a man's purse, and murdering him first, and then taking it. But when one begins to be vicious, it is easy to go on. Where single women are licentious, you rarely find faithful married women.

Boswell:

And yet we are told that in some nations in India, the distinction is strictly observed.

Johnson:

Nay, don't give us India. That puts me in mind of Montesquieu, who is really a fellow of genius too in many respects; whenever he wants to support a strange opinion, he quotes you the practice of Japan or of some other distant country, of which he knows nothing. To support polygamy, he tells you of the island of Formosa, where there are ten women born for one man. He had but to suppose another island, where there are ten men born for one woman, and so make a marriage between them.[16]

Johnson's allusion here may have pointed rather to *L'Esprit des lois* than to the *Persian Letters*. The question is unimportant. In spite of the good talk and what Boswell describes as princely entertainment — venison pasty, most excellent roast beef, abundance of good things "genteelly served up" — the Castle was stormbound for several days, with unrelenting wind and rain. "Every room in the house smoked but the drawing-room. We began tonight a comfortable custom of retreating to the drawing-room, where we took our glass warmly and snugly." But the affairs of the Clan were not in good order financially, the members ungenerous and indisposed to the chief. Johnson was suffering from a heavy cold; but he was persuaded to put on a large

16. *Journal*, p. 209.

flannel nightcap that one of the ladies made for him and to drink a little brandy on going to bed, and next morning he was in high spirits. He walked out to see the cascade of Rorie More. But ideas of escape were in the back of everyone's mind. Boswell said he would like to go to Sweden and see the king, and Johnson said he would go with him. It was natural for their thoughts to wander: Boswell's, as we learn from the original journal-text, to his pride in being admitted to distinguished company—"Member of the Club at the Turk's Head," and so on. Johnson's drifted in another direction:

After the ladies were gone from table, we talked of the Highlanders not having sheets; and this led us to consider the advantage of wearing linen. *Johnson*:

> All animal substances are less cleanly than vegetables. Wool, of which flannel is made, is an animal substance; flannel therefore is not so cleanly as linen . . . I have often thought, that, if I kept a seraglio, the ladies should all wear linen gowns, —or cotton; —I mean stuffs made of vegetable substances. I would have no silk; you cannot tell when it is clean: It will be very nasty before it is perceived to be so. Linen detects its own dirtiness.

Boswell's fancy had not wandered farther toward the East than the Turk's Head, and he could not restrain his mirth. He continues: "To hear the grave Dr. Samuel Johnson, 'that majestick teacher of moral and religious wisdom,' while sitting solemn in an arm-chair in the Isle of Sky, talk, *ex cathedra*, of his keeping a seraglio, and acknowledge that the supposition had *often* been in his thoughts, struck me so forcibly with ludicrous contrast, that I could not but laugh immoderately."[17] And here we must advert to the original journal. "Mr M'Queen asked him if he would admit me. 'Yes,' said he, 'if he were properly prepared; and he'd make

17. *Journal*, p. 216.

a very good eunuch. He'd be a fine gay animal. He'd do his part well.' 'I take it,' said I, 'better than you would do your part.' "[18] We revert to the 1793 print. "He was too proud to submit, even for a moment, to be the object of ridicule, and instantly retaliated with such keen sarcastick wit, and such a variety of degrading images, of every one of which I was the object, that . . . I . . . found myself so much the sport of all the company, that I would gladly expunge from my mind every trace of this severe retort."

It is amusing, and I think endearing, that Johnson's fancy of owning his own Scottish island—and being, as it were, himself a Highland chief—keeps recurring like a leitmotif during the course of their tour. Before the end of it, he once or twice all but enacts the role. "One night," says Boswell—"One night, in Col, he strutted about the room with a broad-sword and target, and made a formidable appearance; and, another night, I took the liberty to put a large blue bonnet on his head. His age, his size, and his bushy grey wig, with this covering on it, presented the image of a venerable *Senachi*: and, however unfavourable to the *Lowland* Scots, he seemed much pleased to assume the appearance of an ancient Caledonian."[19]

The notion developed most exuberantly when the comforts of Dunvegan have made Johnson confess that he "had tasted lotus, and was in danger of forgetting that [he] was ever to depart." Boswell writes:

There is a beautiful little island in the Loch of Dunvegan, called *Isa*. M'Leod said, he would give it to Dr. Johnson, on condition of his residing on it three months in the year; nay one month. Dr. Johnson was highly amused with the fancy . . . He talked a great deal of this island; —how he would build a house there, —how he would fortify it, —how he would plant, —how he would sally out, and *take* the isle of Muck; —and then he laughed with uncommon glee, and could hardly leave off . . . M'Leod encouraged the fancy of Dr. Johnson's becoming owner of an island; told him, that it

18. *Life*, Appendix D, V, 538.
19. *Journal*, p. 324.

was the practice in this country to name every man by his lands;
and begged leave to drink to him in that mode; "*Island Isa*, to
your health!" —Ulinish, Talisker, Mr. M'Queen, and I, all joined
in our different manners, while Dr. Johnson bowed to each, with
much good humour.[20]

(Recall that Johnson touched no whiskey during the tour.)

At the end of the sojourn, at Inchkenneth, where he
wrote a stately ode in Latin elegiacs to the island, he comes
back once more to what had by then, and in spite of genuine
hardships endured, become a haunting idée fixe. "Having,"
writes Boswell, "expressed a desire to have an island like
Inchkenneth, Dr. Johnson set himself to think what would
be necessary for a man in such a situation. 'Sir, I should
build me a fortification, if I came to live here; for, if you
have it not, what should hinder a parcel of ruffians to land in
the night, and carry off every thing you have in the house,
which, in a remote country, would be more valuable than
cows or sheep? add to all this the danger of having your
throat cut'" (October 18, 1773). We observe that in all
such flights Johnson was never content with only *passive*
enjoyment. He had to *possess* his island fully, develop its
possibilities, and set them to work with patriarchal oversight
and protection. During the visit to Inchkenneth, where the
travelers were in the capable hands of Sir Allan M'Lean,
whose island it was, Dr. Johnson, says Boswell, "here
shewed so much of the spirit of a Highlander, that he won
Sir Allan's heart: indeed, he has shewn it during the whole
of our Tour."

Sir Allan, who was the chief of his clan, had the means of
conveying his guests during their stay with him to the island
of Icolmkill by "a strong good boat with four stout rowers."
This was a cruise of considerable length. They started early
in the morning, coasting along the shore of Mull, but landing to examine Mackinnon's Cave. They entered it, ventur-
ing with candlelight to a depth of nearly five hundred feet,
with a clear flame and pure air. The roof was arched and

20. *Journal*, pp. 249–250.

very lofty, but they could not estimate the height. They thought it best to retreat, lest their single candle fail and they be left darkling. Dr. Johnson, by now an expert spelunker—for at Ulinish he had already examined a vast island cave (180 feet long, 30 feet broad, and 30 feet high)—declared that "this was the greatest natural curiosity he had ever seen." Having again embarked, they could see Staffa not far off, but the surge was too high for them to land; so they proceeded along the coast, stopping in the afternoon for a "cold repast." The liquor supply of the public house nearby had been exhausted because of a recent funeral; but Sir Allan sent out an SOS to a neighboring tacksman of the Duke of Argyle, who promptly relieved their drought with a liberal donation. They followed the coastline to a distance of about forty miles while the night drew on. "As we sailed along by moonlight, in a sea somewhat rough, and often between black and gloomy rocks, Dr. Johnson said, 'If this be not roving among the Hebrides, nothing is.'" Reaching the village of Icolmkill at last, they found accommodation only in a large barn and lay down fully clothed on some good hay, with each his portmanteau for a pillow. Says Boswell: "When I awaked in the morning, I could not help smiling at the idea of the chief of the M'Leans, the great English Moralist, and myself, lying thus extended in such a situation."

This was to be one of the supreme moments of the tour, and Johnson's words to impart his emotions upon "treading that illustrious Island," properly echoed by Boswell, are too celebrated to need repeating but still deserve it.

Whatever withdraws us from the power of our senses, whatever makes the past, the distant, or the future, predominate over the present, advances us in the dignity of thinking beings. Far from me, and from my friends, be such frigid philosophy as may conduct us indifferent and unmoved over any ground which has been dignified by wisdom, bravery, or virtue. That man is little to be envied, whose patriotism would not gain force upon the plain of

Marathon, or whose piety would not grow warmer among the ruins of *Iona!*[21]

The party devoted the morning to examining the sacred ruins. Boswell recalled an altercation between Sir Allan and a tenant that would have impressed Johnson, had he heard it. Sir Allan was incensed because he had been informed, and mistakenly believed, that the man had refused to send him some rum. " 'You rascal! (said he,) don't you know that I can hang you, if I please? . . . Refuse to send rum to me, you rascal! Don't you know that, if I order you to go and cut a man's throat, you are to do it?' —'Yes, an't please your honour! and my own too, and hang myself too.' " Boswell continues: "His making these professions was not merely a pretence in presence of his Chief; for after he and I were out of Sir Allan's hearing, he told me, 'Had he sent his dog for the rum, I would have given it: I would cut my bones for him.' "[22]

This, though the island had now passed from M'Lean to the Duke of Argyle, and M'Lean had not been on it for fourteen years. Sir Allan had no more doubts of his right to command than the tenant of his duty to obey; and Boswell declares himself "most willing to contribute what I could towards the continuation of feudal authority. 'Why, (said Sir Allan,) are they not all my people?' 'Very true,' said I." We can only guess what Johnson would have said; but would it not have puzzled him to assent?

It seems almost impossible that Boswell and Johnson jogged on together so comfortably as they did. There are few recorded occasions when Boswell got on Johnson's nerves simply by being himself. One was Johnson's explosion when Boswell innocently rode ahead to the inn at Glenelg to make provision for Johnson's reception. He was in a passion at being left behind, and said, "Sir, had you gone on, I was thinking that I should have returned with you

---

21. *Journal*, p. 334.
22. *Journal*, p. 337.

to Edinburgh, and then have parted from you, and never spoken to you more." The next morning he owned he had spoken to Boswell in passion. He added, "Let's think no more on't."

Another outburst occurred on the island of Col. They had been forced by the violence of a storm to land there unintentionally. The weather continued generally foul, they were uncomfortably lodged; their hosts were inconvenienced and uncongenial; and they had been forced to remain almost a fortnight. There was a break: they made a start for the harbor, but were driven back, and Boswell was soaked, having fallen into a brook and been wet to the middle, with his boots full of water. They kill time, talk little, and spend another night together perforce. In the morning they are told that the day is good for the passage to Mull, and they hurry to get ready. Johnson, says Boswell, "was displeased at my bustling and walking quickly up and down." The phrase evokes the whole scene, and Johnson certainly must have expressed his displeasure more fully than we are told: "He said 'It does not hasten us a bit. It is getting on horseback in a ship. All boys do it,' said he, 'and you are longer a boy than others.'" Again Boswell finds the word that reflects his own self-image in characterizing Johnson: "He himself has no alertness . . . so he may dislike it, as *Oderunt hilarem tristes*."[23]

Besides Boswell, once in a while others felt a well-aimed retort to their self-complacency. For example: the travelers had had a heavy dose of brutal weather, continuous rain and wind and near disaster in a storm at sea. If they were irritable on the subject, that is hardly surprising. The day before they left the islands, Sir Allan M'Lean, their kind host and companion to Iona, "began," says Boswell, "to brag that Scotland had the advantage of England, by its having more water." This was more than Johnson could accept quietly. "Sir," said he, "we would not have your water, to take the vile bogs which produce it. You have too much! . . . Your

23. *Journal*, pp. 307–308.

country consists of two things, stone and water. There is, indeed, a little earth above the stone in some places, but a very little; and the stone is always appearing. It is like a man in rags; the naked skin is still peeping out."[24]

This salvo was fired on the last day of Johnson's stay on the Islands, where he and Boswell had been buffeted by vile weather during eighteen days out of the seven weeks they spent there, and once, between islands, had been in real danger of drowning.

Yet, in Johnson's philosophical perspective, the physical discomforts of the journey found a place of relative insignificance in the overall increment of valuable experience. Surely they infused the whole expedition with a higher seasoning, and its recollections with a keener zest. In his casual allusions to the sojourn, he quite ignores them. Three years later he wrote to Boswell: "The expedition to the Hebrides was the most pleasant journey that I ever made. Such an effort annually would give the world a little diversification."[25] More than six years later the impression had not faded, for in the spring of 1783, Johnson declared: "I got an acquisition of more ideas by it than by any thing that I remember."[26]

Boswell records Goldsmith's saying to Johnson on a day undetermined that he "wished for some additional members to the Literary Club ... for (said he,) there can now be nothing new among us: we have travelled over one another's minds. Johnson seemed a little angry, and said, 'Sir, you have not travelled over *my* mind, I promise you.'" The metaphor invites us to juxtapose our views of Johnson as an imaginary traveler in Eastern lands and as the actual tourist whom we know through his and Boswell's reports of their journey among the Highlands and Western Islands of Scotland.

24. *Journal*, p. 340.
25. *Letters*, II, 153.
26. *Life*, IV, 199.

Rasselas, we know, was written by Johnson in the shadow of his mother's death. It opens, nonetheless, with the picture of an earthly paradise, the "Happy Valley," surrounded on every side by overhanging mountains, from which rivulets descended to fill the valley with verdure and fertility. The slopes were covered with trees; the brooks were banked with flowers and fruits that flourished all the year. Flocks and herds fed in the pastures, and all the harmless creatures frisked and gamboled in play.

The journey to the Western Islands properly begins with the travelers, about noon, entering "a narrow valley, not very flowery, but sufficiently verdant . . . I sat down on a bank, such as a writer of Romance might have delighted to feign. I had indeed no trees to whisper over my head, but a clear rivulet streamed at my feet. The day was calm, the air soft, and all was rudeness, silence, and solitude. Before me, and on either side, were high hills, which by hindering the eye from ranging, forced the mind to find entertainment for itself."[27]

It is not long before Rasselas, in his boredom and unhappiness, learns from Imlac that every inmate of the "Happy Valley" secretly laments "the hour when he entered this retreat." But, says Imlac, if Rasselas knew what it was like outside, battered by violence, treachery, wrongs, frauds, anxieties, and competitions, he would soon be reconciled to "these seats of quiet." " 'Do not seek to deter me from my purpose,' said the prince: 'I am impatient to see what thou hast seen . . . I am resolved to judge with my own eyes of the various conditions of men.' "[28]

Johnson's mind, forced to find entertainment for itself because of the surrounding calm, the restricted prospect, and the rude barrenness and solitude of the scene, like Imlac, contemplates its opposite. He writes:

We were in this place at ease and by choice, and had no evils to

27. *Journey to the Western Islands*, p. 40.
28. *Rasselas*, p. 37.

suffer or to fear; yet the imaginations excited by the view of an unknown and untravelled wilderness are not such as arise in the artificial solitude of parks and gardens, a flattering notion of self-sufficiency, a placid indulgence of voluntary delusions, a secure expansion of the fancy, or a cool concentration of the mental powers. The phantoms which haunt a desert are want, and misery, and danger; the evils of dereliction rush upon the thoughts; man is made unwillingly acquainted with his own weakness, and meditation shows him only how little he can sustain, and how little he can perform . . . Whoever had been in the place where I then sat, unprovided with provisions and ignorant of the country, might . . . have wandered among the rocks, till he had perished with hardship, before he could have found either food or shelter.

And then his mind, figuring how much of the earth is wild, uninhabited and uncultivated, leaps to magnify the present scene to its ultimate extreme, and he exclaims: "Yet what are these hillocks to the ridges of Taurus, or these spots of wildness to the desarts of America?"[29]

> The mind, that ocean where each kind
> Does straight its own resemblance find
> Yet it creates, transcending these,
> Far other worlds and other seas.

Four years after this event, Johnson wrote to Boswell (July 22, 1777): "Our ramble in the islands hangs upon my imagination." But that was the day, September 1, 1772, and that the hour, when he "first conceived the thought of this narration," *A Journey to the Western Islands of Scotland.*

It was the same mind that conceived the two contrasting journeys:

> That ever with a frolick [Johnson's own word] welcome took
> The thunder and the sunshine . . .
> Come, my friends,
> 'Tis not too late to seek a newer world.

---

29. *Journey to the Western Islands*, pp. 40–41.

This is where the imagination and the imaginary fuse: where Imlac and Johnson join hands, perhaps to meet on Island Isa, with that unappeasable "hunger of imagination" which can force everyone "to hope or fear beyond the limits of sober probability."

A Critical Conspectus

JOHN D. BOYD, S. J.

Some Limits in Johnson's Literary Criticism

The limits of Johnson's literary criticism have for some time now been too well known to need merely another recital. More importantly, if Samuel Johnson's achievement as a critic were not so massive and secure, we would have little interest in its limiting factors, especially at this distance in time. If these limiting factors had not, indeed, derived from an excess of a good thing, his criticism and its limits would hardly be worth our consideration now. The good thing I refer to is Johnson's haunting awareness and constant urging of the close relationship between literature and life, which we may call literature's vibrant affinity with life in all its density. I have written elsewhere of Johnson's central critical achievement, sketchily mentioning some of its limits and hinting at their causes.[1] Here I shall attempt to study further

1. See my *The Function of Mimesis and Its Decline*, 1st ed. (Cambridge: Harvard University Press, 1968), 2nd ed. paperback (New York: Fordham University Press, 1980), chapter 7, especially pp. 290–295. The present article is more an essay in interpretation than one of research. The facts involved have been known for some time, as have been the general forces in Johnson's mind and personality. In this effort I am in general debt to W. Jackson Bate, *The Achievement of Samuel Johnson* (New York: Oxford University Press, 1955) and *Samuel Johnson* (New York and London: Har-

the matter of its limits, the better to understand them and to appreciate Johnson's abiding contribution to literary criticism, namely his assertion of a rich humanism, which was both the source and the fruit of his perception of this affinity. Finally I shall say a word about the staying power of his model of this humanism, which the attrition caused by the work of some prominent recent critics cannot readily efface, at least among more thoughtful men and women.

In Johnson's view the main value of literature is, to echo Gerard Manley Hopkins, in the realer and rounder replies to life that it affords the reader. We readily recall, for example, that at its best in Shakespeare, the poet of nature, we find a faithful mirror of manners and of life, "from which a hermit may estimate the transactions of the world, and a confessor predict the progress of the passions." Such insights were supplied by what today we more readily would call the transforming vision of the poet's imagination, a blend of aesthetic and human interests, the work of the poet as both maker and seer at once, of the one through the other, what one might see as the amalgam of the *dulce* and the *utile*, had not the history of this formula been so unfortunate even as early as its origins in Horace. Johnson's very concept of "general nature," as he develops it with more empirical relevance from Aristotle's "probability," is a fusion of his aesthetic and real-life concerns. This transformed blend argues at its best an intrinsic openness of literature to life, a nourishing potential in each for the stability and maturity of both. That real-life and aesthetic elements are not identical or univocal, nor hostile or equivocal, argues that the two are meant to be in healthy dynamic tension, hence forming with each other an intrinsic analogy.

This balance is as difficult to maintain as it is to speak about adequately. In Johnson's day and for some time previous to it, the balance was often poorly honored by the

---

court, Brace, Jovanovich, 1977); James Engell, *The Creative Imagination: Enlightenment to Romanticism* (Cambridge: Harvard University Press, 1981); and Charles E. Pierce, *The Religious Life of Samuel Johnson* (Hamden: Shoe String Press, 1983).

critics, especially in theory. This was due in good part to the leveling influence of the new science and the philosophies germane to it on the already limited neoclassical critical tenets, including in a special way the tendency to confuse poetry with rhetoric. The larger picture, when the mimetic tradition finally declined, presented a split into formalism in literary interests and moralism or didacticism in relating literature and life.[2] For the most part Johnson held out for the desired balance, though where he failed, one can see a dim reflection of this same split. He was able to keep the balance not because of any delicately honed theoretical position but because of his admirable personal sensitivity and competence. Though fully schooled in the classical and neoclassical critical traditions and in ready agreement with their healthy spirit, he regularly saw the need to appeal to real life and its experience to erase the limit of rule and tenet: witness his reasoning on mixing the comic with the tragic and his demolition of the fairly-established unities of time and place in the drama. This strong appeal from criticism to nature, to life as it is to be lived, somewhat reminiscent of the ringing Pauline *Caesarem appello* in another context, pinpoints the true focus of Johnson's critical efficacy and sanity, namely his strongly personal, intuitive, and existential center, something larger and more important than common sense, yet its constant source and stability. His critical soundness in reading the deep affinity of literature and life thus derives in a transcending fashion from his own personal investment in life, and from the pains and satisfactions its stakes occasion.

This intensely personal, highly informed realism, in no way at odds with general nature as literature's reward but rather intensifying it, is, I think, the key to his critical skill in finding the rich humanistic values which literature achieves, well beyond the merely technical perfection of art, much as it was one significant source of his keenly felt anxieties over the pressures of life that accounted for his clear

2. Boyd, *Function of Mimesis*, chs. 2 and 4.

critical limits. However, to avoid thinking of his abilities as
a simple balance of plus and minus, we should remember
that the pressures were of greater magnitude and frequency
than the times of peace; for this reason the positive richness,
depth, and wisdom of his criticism were the more far-
reaching and impressive for his persistent victory over such
turmoil.

Perhaps one can liken Johnson's view of literature's place
in human life to Shakespeare's image of Prospero. The
magician's most potent art was for the enchantment of life,
just as life offered needed substance and occasion for its
proper exercise. Each had a value in itself, and so enjoyed
an intrinsic autonomy. Johnson the serious moralist could
say: "The only end of writing is to enable the readers better
to enjoy life, or better to endure it."[3] Again: "As there is
no necessity for our having poetry at all, it being merely a
luxury, an instrument of pleasure, it can have no value
unless when exquisite in its kind."[4] At times, however, this
autonomy could be exaggerated: Ariel could be over-
demanding of his freedom. Was not the dukedom lost for
such a reason? Life's greater seriousness made Prospero
break his staff and bury it certain fathoms in the earth, and
drown his book; for the stability of truth must be sought at
all costs. Yet Johnson could be restless and further disturbed in the face of such a demand, for there were windows
into the truth of life that could indeed terrify, which poetry
at its most serious could supply and open: "We read Milton
for instruction, retire harassed and overburdened, and look
elsewhere for recreation; we desert our master, and seek for
companions."[5] Here we may begin to see a hint of the varied
restlessness Johnson saw at the heart of experience itself,
that was ultimately the root of the limits of his criticism. At

3. Samuel Johnson, *The Works of Samuel Johnson* (Oxford, 1825), VI, 66.
4. James Boswell, *Boswell's Life of Johnson*, ed. George Birkbeck Hill and
L.F. Powell (Oxford: Clarendon Press, 1934–50), II, 351–352.
5. Samuel Johnson, "Milton," in *Lives of the English Poets*, ed. George
Birkbeck Hill (Oxford: Clarendon, 1905), I, 183–184. Further references to
Lives will be made in the text by volume and page number.

times Ariel may be given his fling or even eventually dismissed, but there is always Caliban to reckon with inside and outside of art. Shakespeare hinted this strongly but Johnson grappled with it. Prospero saw this especially at the end of the play; Johnson, his entire career as a critic.

Guiding Critical Factors

One can easily recognize three principal factors in Johnson's criticism, closely linking life and literature as its imitation and testing their close affinity in author, subject matter, and audience. In differing ways they guide both his successful as well as his more limited criticism. These are (1) the hegemony of reason, (2) in its broadest sense, a strong moral concern with human life, and (3) the restlessly active imagination. Though abstractly isolated here for the purposes of discussion, they must be seen in Johnson's view as vital dynamic forces, engaged in endless interaction. It is difficult to isolate any priority of instigation in this interaction, each force being fairly simultaneously responsible for it. In the bulk of Johnson's criticism reason, moral concern, and imagination form a triangle—its lines and angles mutually aiding and sustaining each other, especially because of the strong personal center spoken of above. For a variety of reasons this massive triangle casts a smaller, shadowy triangle, which can account for Johnson's critical limits. To vary the image a bit, it is something of a Bermuda triangle. Under the storm of prejudice and anxiety his more stable principles go awry, and some valuable freight is lost.

The Hegemony of Reason. As a man of the classical tradition, Johnson was a man of reason. The breadth of his approach to life, often even when harassed by the storms, made him much more nuanced and reasonable than the Enlightenment rationalist of the clear and distinct idea. Though benefiting from the Lockean empirical stress, his classical sense of *nous* kept him the true Western realist in breadth and depth of interest. Common sense was the fruit of this much richer vitality of mind. All this was a guide to his view of what was humanly important in the regulation of life, both interior and public. Human goals were the challenge to a broadly conceived reason, whose governance was the program of the classical realist.

This was especially true of literature and its criticism, and their appeal to real life, for their true evaluation was only an intensification of this reasoned activity. Since the days of the Greeks, mimesis in this matter was reason's special voice. Though Aristotle's *Poetics* best accounted for what this entailed, criticism in the Renaissance and the Enlightenment was in great part Aristotelian in letter more than in substance and spirit, as I have shown elsewhere.[6] Johnson, however, precisely because of his realism, was essentially Aristotelian, especially in his "Preface to Shakespeare." He saw the drama as a structured imitation of life that released a significant insight into it, transforming it from being a merely factual likeness to it. Others frequently delivered characters that were individual, Shakespeare regularly presented a species. The stage-deception theory behind the unities was seen for what it was; the narrow principles of John Dennis and Voltaire were too concerned with the factual and the documentary and not with valid general nature, with the drapery in the painting and not the substantial human figure.

Though all art is dramatic (that is, the structured meaning of the poet as a maker), nevertheless mimesis, especially for Aristotle, best fitted the drama, which in its structure was most like on-going life, much as the theater verified the classical mind's object-orientation (*theasthai* meaning to look upon). For these reasons he also thought drama the most fully developed genre and the most perfect form of mimesis. Yet he did apply the concept to other genres, such as the epic and the elegy. Johnson's use of mimesis is critically most fruitful when he is speaking of the drama and of Shakespeare in particular. But it is curious that on occasion he falls into the common errors of the time, which he rejects in the "Preface," namely demanding either a more

---

6. *Function of Mimesis*, pp. 35–36, 191–192, for example. This theme is verified in most of the book.

documentary-like realism (at which he had poked fun in speaking of Voltaire's claim that Shakespeare's senators were not senatorial enough) or, on the other hand, an idealized view of reality as the Platonists and Neoplatonists were wont to expect (instead of general nature, namely the poet's culling and heightening of the real state of sublunary nature—idealization versus ideation). When Johnson's criticism appears thus limited, something more like an Enlightenment rationalism seems to be at work than the broader Johnsonian reasonableness. This critical rationalism in turn frequently accompanies a similar rationalism in his coping with anxieties of a moral sort or with aberrant imagination.

Strong Moral Concern. The second and probably the most powerful source of Johnson's critical judgments was his strong moral concern with human life. "Moral" is used here in its broad and inclusive sense. W. Jackson Bate wrote: "It is as a moralist, in the broad sense of the word, that Johnson regarded himself. In the moral writings as a whole during this period of his life—from the age of thirty-nine (1748) when he wrote *The Vanity of Human Wishes*, to the age of fifty-one (1760)—we have the essence of Johnson."[7] This concern deals, to be sure, with the life of reason but with special emphasis on its comprehensive object. This included the entirety of human life, the place of human beings in nature as well as their differences from and oppposition to it, and the transcendent dimension of religion and God. It very much included the life of the mind as pilot at the center of all this concern, its appetitive and affective aspects and not merely its more readily thought of cognitive aspect. As Bate has well noted, this process of learning and growing demanded an assimilative strength, consisting of a massive honesty, an unrivaled, if often desperate courage, compassion, and a refreshing humor.[8] Moral, then, for Johnson was much broader than a narrowly-conceived ethic, though surely it included the very important dimension of ethics in human

7. *Samuel Johnson,* p. 296.
8. Ibid., pp. 296–297.

living. In this respect he should be distinguished from moralistic critics who are really didactic in their concern with literature. Didactic poetry was at best for Johnson a minor genre and when successful a cause for surprise. For him as for all true humanists the good of the person must be first the good of the mind broadly conceived, and not bypassed for whatever fallacious pretext. Nor was this a plea from an ivory tower. The stability of truth was needed for the truly all-important human and ethical action.

This, of course, is Johnson at his most usual and his best. But just as his strong moral concern was the most influential source of his best critical judgments, based upon reason as the most substantive source so, when straitened by anxiety, its narrowing focus could render a view of human values hardly commensurate with the moral breadth just spoken of. The prime cause of this was psychological, but since the psychological was the center of his dealing with the human in both literature and life, its ramifications were far-reaching indeed, especially in their ethical and religious implications. His massive anxieties and their consequent compulsions, lethargies, and depressions have been fully and richly explored by Bate and should be recalled here as the foundations and imbalances of some of his criticism. What Johnson saw only too well of the terror as well as of the tedium of life, where it did not spur him to further depths in his mastery of them, tended to block out the attraction of a better contemplative understanding, and to turn his judgment, so uncharacteristically, in a puritanical direction. As a result we find too quick and impatient an appeal of ethical and religious imperatives of a more severe rather than a liberating sort. Of course, at work here, too, was his fear of the restless and unruly imagination, a force difficult to extricate from this psychological factor.

A word may be warranted here about Johnson's religious experience in this psychological context. Bate and, more recently, Max Byrd and Charles E. Pierce have discussed in detail Johnson's religious center and its peculiar psychological coloring. For most of his mature life he was a committed Christian, and he finally achieved, in good part by a kind of spiritual counterpunching, a genuine, if unconventional, Christian integration. Apart from his many positive practices of prayer, frequenting the Sacraments, reading of the Scripture and of the theological masters, penances, and a permeating and sincere dedication, his religious experience was in great part anxiety-ridden. His upset was also affected by his imagination and by an imperious rationalistic spirit. His understanding of faith, for example, seemed in practice more a Pelagian struggle of the conscious mind rather than the reasonable, if mysterious, cooperative venture of human effort with divine grace, as seen in Christian experience, however darkly, both in faith's effectiveness and in the peace it usually finally engenders. (We recall on a purely natural human level an instructive parallel in his impatience with myth and romance, for example.) One dimension seriously lacking in Johnson's theological and religious tradition was the confidence to be derived from the theologies of St. John and St. Paul in the intrinsically transforming operation of the Holy Spirit in the person of the believer, making him a New Creature and a child of God. Nor was he habitually aware of the cultural implications for a Christian of the Incarnation as source and archetype of God's closeness to men. His religion, more morally demanding than contemplative, was rather one of overpowering awe and fear. This naturally affected his criticism, as it touched upon matters germane to religion and belief.[9]

The Restlessly Active Imagination. If the hegemony of reason was the most substantial and his strong moral concern the most influential factor in his critical judgments, we may say that Johnson's awareness of the impact of the imagination was his most sensitive. In his own experience and his observation of others he found it a most active and relentless agent. For him its influence was rarely absent, whether in life or in art, and with respect to the latter both in its composition and in its expected audience.

---

9. See my review of Charles E. Pierce, *The Religious Life of Samuel Johnson* in *America*, 149 (1983), 34–36.

At this point a few important details should be recalled. First of all, in a technical and formal sense, the word "imagination" for Johnson was still defined in the older classical and neoclassical sense. In his *Dictionary* we find it "the power of forming ideal pictures; the power of representing things absent." It was not yet the creative faculty of mind about its unifying and poetic business, that it would be, say, for Coleridge, the soul that is everywhere. Reason was still in charge in the making of poetry, though dependent upon imagination in its use of "invention," an operation still shared with the art of rhetoric. Second, imagination was closely allied with emotional interests in both life and art, often acting as their voice in the endless quest for novelty. But Johnson's focus in the matter was not primarily on system or theory but on the dynamic process of life as he found it, hence for him imagination merited much greater importance than the abstract accounting might suggest; hence in practice his view of imagination resembled that of the Romantics.[10]

Third, in either of these considerations, though especially in the latter, the positive function of imagination made man something of a "self-starter." It instigated his quest for that novelty of which the mind is always in search. If we associate originality with the romantic view of the faculty, we should do so also in the case of Johnson: his interest in genius was clear and celebrated. But his interest in imagination and its originality also saw in them important aids to the mind to get to the origin of things in the seemingly endless quest for the stability of truth. Finally, given the turmoil in life that he personally experienced and that he saw as clearly our lot in general, there is a strongly negative influence of the imagination in human affairs. It was restless and never satisfied but also at times clearly aberrant and downright dangerous.[11]

10. James Engell, *The Creative Imagination*, pp. 57ff.
11. Ibid., pp. 58, 60.

Keeping in mind these three inclusive critical influences on Johnson's judgments of literature, both negative and positive, we may now turn to some of the more specific limits of his criticism. Although all three critical influences can, in general, be seen in each of them, these limits may profitably be reviewed in a gamut that begins with a literary or aesthetic interest and moves toward a moral concern. As mentioned earlier, the resultant split resembles the more evident and pronounced split marking so much of the breakdown of neoclassical criticism. It was a split that caused in this small corner of Johnson's work a wilting of the tension constituting a healthy sense of the affinity of literature and life. Though Johnson was clearly Aristotelian in his central reading of literature—for example, his pervasive realism, its dramatic implications for mimesis, and his preference for tragedy over epic in an all but singular voice at the time— one can easily think of F. L. Lucas' summary of Plato's objections to poetry as describing Johnson's limited critical judgments of it: that it was unreal, unrestrained, and unrighteous. In fact in this respect Johnson is a Christian Plato.[12]

Some Specific Limits

Romance and Mythology. Johnson was not unique in his time in being critical of myth, the wonderful, and romance. These in general offended the classical and neoclassical instinct for verisimilitude, which, as we have seen, for Johnson was best achieved in the drama. At worst this distrust was the voice of the Enlightenment that decried the mysterious and supplied us with our modern misapprehension of the root meaning of *myth* itself. Johnson's rational turn of mind, linked with his unusual fear of life's uncertainties, worked against developing any appetite for the marvelous. Dealing with it taxed his sense of the real and his quest for

12. F. L. Lucas, *Literature and Psychology*, rev. American ed. (Ann Arbor: University of Michigan Press, 1957), p. 269.

general nature, yet at times it ironically turned this quest in the direction of the merely empirical or factual as normative. Granted the absurdity of many situations in the romances, there was always the example of Shakespeare's work of fantasy that was a sure source of realistic wisdom, a point Johnson himself saw: he approximates the remote, and familiarizes the wonderful.

Johnson's critique of Gray's *The Bard* is an example of his distrust of myth. Though he finds in it "more force, more thought, and more variety," still "to copy is less than to invent, and the copy has been unhappily produced at a wrong time . . . [Such a] revival disgusts us with apparent and unconquerable falsehood." Then precisely to his point: "he that forsakes the probable may always find the marvellous" ("Gray," *Lives*, III, 438). In the "Life of Waller" we find a similar judgment in principle, namely that romances, which were factually improbable and hence read with wonder, were morally useless, for in them "virtue is unattainable, is recommended in vain; that good may be endeavoured, it must be shown to be possible,"—thus doing Aristotle one better with an improbable impossibility! (*Lives*, I, 295). Throughout the issue is clear: Johnson's rationalism has gotten the better of his hegemony of reason by asking of mimesis something of a factual realism rather than the richer realism of general nature. And the voice of moral concern together with that of the fear of uncertainties, an easy prey to the imagination, join in, even if somewhat mutedly.

The Pastoral. Akin to Johnson's distrust of the preternatural in literature was his clear dislike of the pastoral: "easy, vulgar, and therefore disgusting" ("Milton," *Lives*, I, 163–164). Demand for a greater realism was still his motive. No more friendly than this comment on *Lycidas* was his dismissal of Lyttelton's *Progress of Love*: "it is sufficient blame to say that it is pastoral" (*Lives*, III, 456). This remark has regularly drawn sympathetic smiles from many over the years, when the poorer efforts in the genre and our burden of having to read them are remembered. As in the case of the mythological, Johnson was impatient with the distant removal of this genre from real life: it glorified country life, while Johnson was for London; learned shepherds were out of date and out of character in expressing political, literary, and theological opinions; their language was staid, their psychology escapist, and their imitation slavish. Yet at bottom Johnson was denying the potential of art to reveal a deeper view of the underlying reality of life through the mimetic process. F. L. Lucas has rightly found Achilles more real than Alexander, and W. K. Wimsatt has seen that poetry gives us a view that is more lively, if less lifelike, than life itself.[13]

More particularly at stake here is the fact of convention, surely to Johnson an important literary structure and a significant part of the more broadly accepted tradition of decorum. While a convention usually has some naturalistic basis, its value lies in its ability to reach well beyond this to deliver meaning otherwise unavailable. Its aesthetic potential somewhat resembles what later, more subjective critical attention pointed to, namely persona, voice, and mask. All such forms must keep their vitality, largely achieved through social approval; otherwise, of course, they die. By Johnson's time, no doubt, some death throes had begun to attach to the pastoral form. One can easily appreciate his all-but-exasperation in these remarks: "A Pastoral of an hundred lines may be endured; but who will hear of sheep and goats, and myrtle bowers and purling rivulets, through five acts? Such scenes please barbarians in the dawn of literature, and children in the dawn of life" ("Gay," *Lives*, II, 284–285). Yet one remembers that Milton's *Lycidas* from the start has pleased many and pleased long. Once again Johnson's realism has overshot itself, not without an assist from his starved imagination and his concern for moral values in poetry.

---

13. Ibid, p. 267; W. K. Wimsatt, "Northrop Frye: Criticism as Myth," in *Northrop Frye in Modern Criticism*, ed. Murray Krieger (New York: Columbia University Press, 1966), p. 79.

Some Questions of Imagery. Mention of *Lycidas* naturally
brings to mind another limit, which also links those touching
the mythological and the pastoral, namely some of Johnson's
understanding of the ways of imagery in poetry, especially
nondramatic poetry. Waller, he says, "borrows too many of
his sentiments and illustrations from the old mythology, for
which it is vain to plead the example of ancient poets: the
deities which they introduced so frequently were considered
as realities, so far as to be received by the imagination, whatever sober reason might even then determine" (*Lives*, I,
295). In a similar vein we read of Milton's *Lycidas*, after
Johnson has expressed some displeasure with the pastoral
form: "This poem has yet a grosser fault. With these
trifling fictions are mingled the most awful and sacred truths,
such as ought never to be polluted with such irreverent combinations. The shepherd is now likewise a feeder of sheep,
and afterwards an ecclesiastical pastor, a superintendent of a
Christian flock. Such equivocations are always unskilful; but
here they are indecent, and at least approach to impiety, of
which, however, I believe the writer not to have been conscious" (*Lives*, I, 165). The point in both cases is the blending of pagan with Christian imagery.

One immediately senses a strong religious motive for
these judgments, though in the case of *Lycidas* Johnson's
personal bias against Milton is evident in addition. But also
effectively involved—and working as well through these
same concerns—is Johnson's strong homing tendency toward
the factual, almost documentary-like as the matter of
mimetic decorum, rather than toward his more dramatically
conceived realism of general nature. Linked with this was
his tendency to think of imagery as a decoration of the
theme. Nowadays, at least, we see in a critical way what Milton seems to have seen intuitively as a poet, that an image
is essentially as much a structure of a poem as a plot is of a
drama, and hence quite rightly to be deemed the source of
thematic revelation. What, we may ask, then, could be more
natural and a matter of mimetic decorum than to link a
series of shepherd images from the pastoral tradition that
denote a variety of leadership with the long tradition of

Scripture, in which the leaders of God's people and indeed God Himself are denoted by the same image that is taken from a purely human occupation? Add to this that Milton was here developing not so much the theme of Edward King's death and loss as that of his own poetic, that of the Christian poet as shepherd, the significant cultural leader of his people (not the least eligible poet among them being John Milton himself, and at that in conflict with the established ecclesiastical shepherds).

Metaphysical Poetry. Johnson's famous qualifications about Metaphysical Poetry derive from essentially similar sources as those we have been discussing, though with some differences of a literary critical sort worth noting; and his nonliterary objections are more psychological than religious. His treatment of the matter in the "Life of Cowley" is well known. Though it is generally critical of this kind of poetry, it is the source of the popular name given to it since, Metaphysical, and the source, too, of the description of its characteristic wit image, the conceit, *discordia concors,* which has occasioned so much speculation on the nature of this kind of writing. In it, too, Johnson does praise some of the conceits for occasioning insight and thought in the reader; their maker's labor was not wasted, "they likewise sometimes struck out unexpected truth; if their conceits were farfetched, they were often worth the carriage" (*Lives,* I, 21).

"These writers . . . cannot be said to have imitated any thing: they neither copied nature nor life; neither painted the forms of matter nor represented the operations of intellect" (I, 19). "They were not successful in representing or moving the affections . . . Their courtship was void of fondness and their lamentation of sorrow" (I, 20). Johnson clearly wants a verisimilitude that is close to the factual, the immediate, something closer to the materials of the drama, as has already been seen when discussing imagery. Here he finds added offense, since the materials used are abstract and distorted. "They left not only reason but fancy behind them; and produced combinations of confused magnificence that not only could not be credited, but could not be imagined" (I, 21). This combined with thoughts that lacked the genuine general nature he so valued. "They never attempted that comprehension and expanse of thought which at once fills the whole mind, and of which the first effect is sudden astonishment, and the second rational admiration. Sublimity is produced by aggregation, and littleness by dispersion. Great thoughts are always general" (I, 20–21).

Johnson centers his attack on the kind of wit the Metaphysical Poets' conceit contains. At its noblest wit is both natural and new, the kind one acknowledges to be just and is surprised he never thought of himself. Their conceit, however, is new but seldom natural. Far from wondering why one had not himself thought of it, one "wonders more frequently by what perverseness of industry they were ever found" (I, 20). Whether this judgment fits the better Metaphysical Poetry can be argued, but Johnson's argument in this respect: "Great thoughts are always general" (I, 21), leads one to think that an intrinsic weakness, at least in his present application, of his notion of general nature has the concept veer in the direction of the philosophic universal rather than the poetic. He seems to have missed in the better poems of Donne, say, and George Herbert, the metonymy of mind at work in the conceit, wherein a single and at times singular insight is immensely powerful in illumining a whole swath of the human situation. This characteristic is not limited to the Metaphysical Poets but often seen in some Romantics and in our own day in the deceptively simple poetry of metonymy of Robert Frost. His "Fragmentary Blue," for example, is a poem that grows to true generality from quite a singular sense of detail, in developing its theme of the importance of metonymous thinking.

Religious Poetry. The judgment of Johnson, religious man and poet, on religious poetry lies about halfway in our gamut of the influence of literary or aesthetic and of moral factors. His objection to the phenomenon derives about equally from both sources, though the vigor of his argument is more religiously based. Under "Sacred Poetry" Joseph Epes Brown's *The Critical Opinions of Samuel Johnson* lists a dozen entries, all disfavoring religious poetry.[14] The "Life of Waller" represents his position most clearly and copiously. We read there, for instance: "Contemplative piety, or the intercourse between God and the human soul, cannot be poetical. Man admitted to implore the mercy of his Creator and plead the merits of his Redeemer is already in a higher state than poetry can confer . . . Omnipotence cannot be exalted; Infinity cannot be amplified; Perfection cannot be improved" (*Lives*, I, 291 – 292). Faith, thanksgiving, repentance and supplication are above poetic embellishments. Simplicity is the key to religious sublimity, Brown summarizes; then Johnson again: "All that pious verse can do is to help the memory and delight the ear, and for these purposes it may be very useful; but it supplies nothing to the mind. The ideas of Christian Theology are too simple for eloquence, too sacred for fiction, and too majestick for ornament; to recommend them by tropes and figures is to magnify by a concave mirror the sidereal hemisphere" (*Lives*, I, 292 – 293).

The literary consideration here is from Renaissance Neoplatonic theory, of which, for example, Rosemond Tuve writes approvingly in her *Elizabethan and Metaphysical Imagery*.[15] Imagery is not a part of the poem's organic structure but a decoration, which enhances and celebrates the central idea, in Johnson's words: exalts, amplifies, and improves it. It is important to see that this approach to imagery and theme is diametrically opposed to the method of Aristotle's *Poetics*, which derives theme from structures, which are "made." Johnson's general nature of the "Preface" and *Rasselas*, we recall, is the result of dramatic induction, not the blend of the Neoplatonic philosophic universal and rhetorical decoration.[16]

14. Joseph Epes Brown, *The Critical Opinions of Samuel Johnson* (New York: Russell & Russell, 1961), pp. 226 – 229.

15. Rosemond Tuve, *Elizabethan and Metaphysical Imagery* (Chicago: University of Chicago Press, 1947), pp. 388 – 398.

16. See Jean H. Hagstrum, *Samuel Johnson's Literary Criticism* (Minneapolis: University of Minnesota Press, 1952), p. 75.

Though this approach to imagery was not unique with Johnson at the time nor unusual for Johnson himself, it was especially useful for his overriding concern here, namely the subject matter of religious poetry. Although it could be satisfying to use a literary or aesthetic reason to reject what he found religiously objectionable, the latter was in itself much more urgent. Johnson's religious temperament was one of profound awe and reverence, yet this temperament was laced with anxieties and dread of the Almighty. Granted that religious poetry often fails, largely because it is bad art or it comes from poets with very limited religious sensibility, it still deserves its proper place, if it is truly the result of human experience, as is all genuine poetry, and not considered an effort to improve on the Infinite God. But religious experience itself was for Johnson so awesome that it precluded the touch of poetry; it is of a higher state, as he put it. True enough, in a very important and even absolute sense, religious experience does transcend in value the aesthetic experience, yet this does not *close* it as a human experience to the reflective gaze of the imagination. It remains a central paradox of Johnson's life, that one so alert to the ways of both poetry and religion should find no place for their alliance.

The autonomy of the claims of poetry and of religion can amicably meet through an active sense of analogy, and they meet for the Christian in a culture that sees the Incarnation as an archetype of this analogy in a special way. Had Johnson, in consequence of this belief, enjoyed something of the religious and cultural climate more open to the sacramental view of the universe, as did Dante, Donne, Hopkins, and Eliot, his views in this matter might have been different.

Literature and Morals. Two other topics suggest themselves at this point and may be mentioned here, namely poetic justice and the Horatian please-and-teach formula. Given the welter of moralism and didacticism in the critical tradition in which Johnson found himself, he kept a reasonably even keel regarding both these matters. While there was some ambiguity deriving from his larger moral earnestness, he managed to sense wisely literature's value and its autonomy and not prostitute it in principle in these matters to a cheap understanding of means and ends. With respect to poetic justice, though he was attracted to it as a pragmatic convention, as when he chided Shakespeare in the "Preface" for making no just distribution of good and evil, still he does not make it a critical tenet. He disagrees with Dryden's urging that Milton's Adam cannot be deemed a hero because he is not successful, in saying that heroes are successful only by established practice. Despite his strong tug in the direction of poetic justice, several plays having it left him cold. Bate has said well that, though Johnson was undeniably attracted to it through a rather pathetic tug toward wish fulfillment, he never lets it serve as a primary critical norm by which to accept or reject.[17] In principle, then, he sees the need for literature to function in its own terms, despite some passing ambiguity in the matter.

The Horatian formula is a large order, of which I have written at length elsewhere. On the balance sheet Johnson is seen clearly to respect the autonomy of literature, again most richly in the context of the "Preface to Shakespeare." Even when practical moral considerations tend to tip the scales toward a more narrow moralism, a broader and more solid base is evident. In noting that Johnson altered the traditional Horatian phrase to "instruct by pleasing," Bate wisely says: "We are dealing with a conception of form that is altogether functional, and in a massive and reassuring sense of the word. In fact, it evolves from Johnson's conception of the function of literature itself, and is completely dependent on it." Enlightenment and growth in awareness is not apart from the process of pleasing but rather by reason of it.[18] Though in agreement with this perceptive comment, I think Johnson might have been more forceful in keeping the formula away from its very frequent rhetorical understanding at the time, had he said rather "to please by instructing, or

---

17. Bate, *The Achievement of Samuel Johnson*, pp. 201–202.
18. Ibid., pp. 206–207.

revealing," the pleasurable contemplation which is implied in the satisfaction offered by the stability of truth.

The Bawdy. The last specific limit to be considered here and surely the one closest to the polarity of moral concern is Johnson's attitude toward the bawdy. This is no surprise when one recalls his earnestness in this matter. Though his treatment of the material in this case is somewhat narrow, the concern is as broad as his concern for human life and hence it touches on author, audience, and the earnest image of the human scene he considers literature is to achieve. But the audience was for him a special focus of interest in this matter. In this he echoes the seriousness of Plato's problem, and so tends to slight the nature of literature. Johnson's somewhat jaunty characterization of the audience of the new genre of the novel as the young, the ignorant, and the idle had a straitening seriousness when there was question of the bawdy. Here again, besides this moral concern, the unruly powers of the human imagination are at work and together they affected his practical judgment of literature itself.

Dryden, Pope, Swift, Fielding, and even Shakespeare were all rebuked. Of Swift he writes: "The greatest difficulty that occurs, in analysing his character, is to discover by what depravity of intellect he took delight in revolting ideas from which almost every other mind shrinks with disgust. The ideas of pleasure, even when criminal, may solicit the imagination; but what has disease, deformity, and filth upon which the thoughts can be allured to dwell?" (*Lives*, III, 62). Pope along with Swift "had an unnatural delight in ideas physically impure" (*Lives*, III, 242); and in Dryden such degradation of genius "cannot be contemplated but with grief and indignation" (*Lives*, I, 398–399). He says that Shakespeare sacrifices virtue to convenience and makes no just distribution of good and evil. Finally, his broadside against "immoral writers" in *Rambler* 77: "What punishment can be adequate to the crime of him who retires to solitudes for the refinement of debauchery; who tortures his fancy, and ransacks his memory, only that he may leave the world less virtuous than he found it; that he may intercept the hopes of the rising generation; and spread snares for the soul with more dexterity?"[19]

The questions that touch upon the relations of art and morality, wherein the valid claims in both directions are respected, are not easy to deal with. Newman, serious divine that he was, wisely observed that our literature is by necessity about a fallen race.[20] In our own day W. K. Wimsatt, himself a serious, moral and religious man, and a Johnsonian, too, has argued cogently for the value of even an immoral imaginative point of view, that has achieved such structure as to reveal a significant insight into the human condition, that would be otherwise unavailable, thus distinguishing between philosophic or moral truth and the truth of aesthetic perception.[21] When one remembers Johnson's view in the matter, especially of Swift and Shakespeare, one misses this more expansive dealing with the legitimate claims of imaginative literature. There are, of course, limits to taste. There are times, surely, when one thinks that enough of Swift is enough, though, of course, a good case can be made for his catching rather sharply in such writings a genuine sense of Original Sin.[22] But with Shakespeare things tend to be different. Here one feels closer to normalcy, closer to a reasonable sense of Johnson's prized general nature. The more placid judgment of Coleridge on this aspect of Shakespeare was that in his work there were no innocent adulteries and no interesting incests.[23] At all

19. Samuel Johnson, *The Rambler*, ed. W. J. Bate and Albrecht B. Strauss (New Haven and London: Yale University Press, 1969), II, 43 – 44.

20. John Henry Cardinal Newman, "English Catholic Literature," in *The Idea of a University*, ed. C. F. Harrold (New York: Longmans, Green, 1947), pp. 274 – 275.

21. "Poetry and Morals: A Relation Reargued," in *The Verbal Icon: Studies in the Meaning of Poetry* (Lexington: University of Kentucky Press, 1954), pp. 85 – 100.

22. See James L. Tyne, S.J., "Gulliver's Maker and Gullibility," in *Criticism*, 8 (1965), 151 – 167, especially 158.

23. S.T. Coleridge, "Summary of the Characteristics of Shakespeare's Dramas," in *The Selected Poetry and Prose of Samuel Taylor Coleridge*, ed. Donald A. Stauffer (New York: Random House, 1951), p. 434.

events, seeing the genuine potential in such matter for satire
and comedy—in humor, irony, wit, and fancy—which our
state of sublunary nature regularly supplies us with, we can
only regret Johnson's treatment of the subject. What would
the world be, once bereft of Shakespeare's bawdy, and of
Chaucer's, too?

This brief review has emphasized the powerful force of
Johnson's human preoccupations. In each case of limited
judgment specific critical concerns were involved, but the
cumulative effect is of their being overpowered by his moral
urgency. Though this split in him in one sense reflected the
critical split of the age at large between formalism and moralism, in Johnson's case it was finally much more like a complete takeover by the moral imperative, more narrowly
conceived. Even in his critical limits he reveals his intense
center, a personal critic genuinely committed to the all-
important human value of literature, struggling in his intense
way to assert the affinity and harmony of literature and life,
which indeed at his best he so eloquently and massively did.
From a perspective more searching than its original context,
this is his appeal from criticism to nature, to human life, of
which literature is finally and significantly a part. It is an
assertion of a personal philosophy of existence—though
surely not of the Sartrean kind—over mere philosophies of
essence or of concept, and much more over one of merely
empirical phenomena with its schematisms, to which we see
so much criticism reduced these days.

The mention of these critical straits may serve to suggest
that, even amid his limits, Johnson the critic still has something healthy to say to us. He not only vitally professed the
mimetic realism of the classical tradition, but he also showed
himself open in so many ways to its more subjective
developments of the age of Romanticism just dawning. Now
two centuries after his death he is still a lively witness to the
importance of this realism, the deep affinity of literature with
human life. His assertion of the needful human center and
purpose of art and of the critic as humanly involved and
committed can offer us a starting point again. When we witness literature being painted into a corner by our own

inhuman devisals, a captive of the deterministic yet ineffective and nonreferential behavior of language, parentless and exclusively the ward of the critic, it is time for us not so much to be apprised of something new as to be reminded of the obvious. There is always an appeal from criticism to nature, to human life, as a point of departure.[24]

24. I have developed a modern theory of the mimetic in "A New Mimesis," which is scheduled to appear (1984) in *Renascence*, published by Marquette University, Milwaukee. It is part of a book-length study of modern criticism, *Mimesis Revisited*, in preparation.

EMERSON R. MARKS

The Antinomy of Style in Augustan Poetics

From one literary period to another ideals of poetic language have tended to oscillate, in very rough fashion, between the poles of simplicity and ornateness. They involve vocabulary, tropical usages, syntax, and sometimes degrees of metrical regularity. The period of English poetry spanning the careers of Dryden and Dr. Johnson, despite its own initial reaction against the baroque involutedness of metaphysical verse, is generally regarded as favoring the pole of ornateness. "Poetry requires ornament," wrote Dryden, whom Johnson a century later praised for having supplied the "elegances or flowers of speech" which properly set it apart from prose.[1] One of the triad of fatal poetical blemishes mentioned in *Rambler* 122 is "impropriety of ornament."[2]

The concept of poetry as elegant discourse was of course neither an eighteenth-century discovery nor exclusively English, but an age-old commonplace. Four centuries earlier

1. Dryden, *Of Dramatic Poesy and Other Critical Essays*, ed. George Watson, 2 vols. (New York: Dutton, 1962), II, 252; Johnson, *Lives of the English Poets*, ed. George Birkbeck Hill, 3 vols. (Oxford: Clarendon Press, 1905), I, 420.

2. *The Rambler*, ed. W. J. Bate and Albrecht B. Strauss, vol. 4, *The Yale Edition of the Works of Samuel Johnson* (New Haven: Yale University Press, 1969), p. 288. Hereafter cited as *Works*.

Dante had ascribed the beauty of his *Canzoni* to their orna-
mented words, though he was careful to assign primary value
to their moral teaching ("la bontà è nella sentenza, e la *bel-
lezza* nell' ornamento delle parole").[3] In his *Éléments de lit-
térature* (1787) Johnson's French contemporary Jean Fran-
cois Marmontel could put it with dogmatic finality: "Le style
de l'orateur et celui du poète a besoin d'être orné."[4]

Romantic poetics opens with a violent swing to the opposite pole in Wordsworth's prefaces to *Lyrical Ballads*, in
which the term *poetic diction*, honorific since its currency was
initiated by John Dennis in 1696, suddenly labels a poetic
vice. Thereafter critics tend increasingly to admit stylistic elaboration only when what is being said defies literal directness, and they have scant patience with the notion of a select
poetic vocabulary. The older view was embodied in the traditional vestiary metaphor, the poet's thoughts "dressed" in
attractive verbal garb. The organicist aesthetic orientation of
the nineteenth century, hostile to so bald a severance of
form and content, abandoned this metaphor. Words, Wordsworth observed, thinking primarily of poetry, are not the rai-
ment but the incarnation of thoughts.[5] Elegance, the central
term of approval in the lexicon of European neoclassical
literary theory, gradually acquired the faintly pejorative overtones it still retains. (The conceptual alteration in question
here pertains to theory, not necessarily to the poets' actual
practice.)

What I've just summarily characterized is a familiar topic
exhaustively explored by literary historians. A related issue,
which for lack of a less unwieldy phrase I will call *the antin-*

---

3. *Il Convito di Dante Allighieri*, ed. Giambattisto Giuliani (Firenze, 1874),
p. 138.
4. Marmontel is quoted in Ernst Robert Curtius, *European Literature and
the Latin Middle Ages*, trans. W. R. Trask (New York: Pantheon Books,
1953), p. 71.
5. *Literary Criticism of William Wordsworth*, ed. Paul M. Zall (Lincoln:
University of Nebraska Press, 1966), pp. 125, 163.

omy of poetic style,[6] though it too has a history coterminus with that of poetics itself, has received nothing like the scrutiny it deserves. It consists in the fact that the very features of expression which give fine verse its special power and allure may also constitute the vices and defects that mark poetic mediocrity and even downright trash. A problem of both composition and theory in every age, it takes on special cogency during the eighteenth century, when the pendulum of theory was in the decorative sector of its arc.

This mysterious phenomenon receives attention in the earliest Western critical texts. In Longinus and Quintilian eighteenth-century writers found especially influential warnings against the betrayal of their inspiration to the attractions of a stylistic siren decked out in every charm of the maidenly muse. In "that high flying liberty of conceit proper to the Poet" their respected predecessor Sir Philip Sidney had apparently sensed no inherent destructive potential but only "some divine force," though in one place even he blames imitative poets for dressing up Matron Eloquence like a prostitute.[7] In Quintilian's *Institutes of Oratory*, however, there are repeated condemnations of fancy phrase-making, deliberate striving after gilded verbiage, even though a whole section of that work is devoted to the many devices of stylistic heightening that orators and poets alike must master. For "where ornament is concerned," he observes, "vice and virtue are never far apart," and the anomaly becomes more piquant but no nearer solution when he adds that utter barbarisms in prose can actually be attractive in verse, a peculiarity sporadically noted in discussions of verse and prose from Aristotle's *Rhetoric* to modern structuralism.[8] That the

6. It will become obvious from what ensues that although my focus throughout is on the language of verse, the antinomy operates only less crucially in oratory and other forms of aesthetically valuable prose.

7. *Elizabethan Critical Essays*, ed. G. Gregory Smith, 2 vols. (London: Oxford University Press, 1904), I, 154, 202.

8. 4 vols. (Cambridge: Harvard University Press, 1963), III, 188, 215. I quote from the translation supplied for this Loeb Classics edition by H. E. Butler. Though the *Institutes* is a rhetoric, not a poetics, much of its teaching, especially in book 8, is clearly relevant to poetry, as Quintilian's illustra-

attributes of a vicious style often bear a resemblance of near identity to those of effective composition had been a staple of classical literary discussion well before Quintilian's time. For the three levels of good style first laid down in the *Rhetorica ad Herennium*, there are, says its author, faulty styles very closely related to them (*finitima et propinqua vitia*). What he calls the swollen style is easily mistaken for the grand, the loose for the middle, the meager for the simple.[9] Similarly, for each of the four kinds of style roughly delineated in the Greek treatise *Peri hermeneias* (*On Style*) by one Demetrius, the author identifies corresponding "perversions":[10] for the stately, the frigid; for the plain, the arid; for the forceful, the disagreeable. "In the same way," in Rhys Roberts' version, "there is a defective style perilously near to the elegant," namely the affected. Like others, Demetrius sees an analogy to the propinquity of his opposed styles in the similar relation of the moral virtues and vices. Courage, he notes, is next neighbor to rashness.[11]

The paradox is most forcibly stressed in the Greek rhetorical treatise that became a near-sacred text for many of Johnson's contemporaries, Longinus' *On the Sublime*. "For our virtues and vices spring from much the same sources. And so while beauty of style, sublime expression, yes, and agreeable phrasing all contribute to successful composition,

---

tive citations of Virgil and Horace alone suffice to show.

9. [Cicero], *Rhetorica ad Herennium* (Cambridge: Harvard University Press, 1954), pp. 262–266.

10. So rendered by T. A. Moxon in *Aristotle's Poetics, Demetrius on Style, Longinus on the Sublime* (New York: Dutton, 1963), pp. 91 *et passim.* Hereafter cited as Moxon. W. Rhys Roberts, in *Aristotle the Poetics, "Longinus" on the Sublime, Demetrius on Style* (Cambridge: Harvard University Press, 1932), hereafter cited as Roberts, makes it "distorted varieties" and "defective style" (pp. 373, 417). Demetrius' phrase is *diemarteménos charákter.* Since even the best translation betrays, it may help to note that *diemarteménos* derives from *hamartánein*, "to miss the mark."

11. Moxon, pp. 91, 117, 131; Roberts, p. 417. Roberts' "perilously near," for Demetrius' *parakeitái* ("lies adjacent") perfectly captures the antinomial quality of the phenomenon. CF. the *finitima et propinqua vitia* just cited from the *Rhetorica ad Herennium*.

yet these very graces are the source and groundwork no less of failure than of success." The author therefore assumes it to be a part of his instructional duty to suggest how aspiring writers can "avoid the faults that go so closely with the elevated style." Beyond the admonition sounded at the outset, that sublimity, the great quality he is analyzing, bears a fatal likeness to its aesthetic opposite, tumidity, he detects the duplicity even in the individual figural devices that account for much of its appeal. Periphrasis is "a risky business"; hyperbole, overdone, "produces the opposite effect to that intended," and so on.[12]

Ancient authorities, however, could supply no objective rationale to account for this disturbing trick of literary language. Instead, they offered psychological explanations of how authors fell victim to it and how readers could detect it. For the latter this meant having good taste, a criterion which in this application as in every other bears the curse of circularity. The generally assigned cause of the fault was a poet's overconscious art, his substitution of deliberate striving for the unsought promptings of genuine inspiration. The idea of self-defeating creative effort is so strongly emphasized by Longinus that we may conclude, in parody of his famous aphorism, that tumidity echoes the straining of a puny soul. Horace, in the *Ars poetica*, refines on this motif of compositional psychology. Most of us poets, he confesses, fall into obscurity by striving for concision, become flaccid by aiming at smoothness, and produce bombast by reaching for grandeur. Our well-intended efforts to avoid certain faults lead ironically not to their opposed beauties but to the vices kindred to those beauties, if we haven't properly learned our trade (*si caret arte*).[13]

According to the author of the *Rhetorica ad Herennium*, Horace, and Demetrius, the plain style is as prone to this risk as the ornate. The eighteenth century, too, knew something of both cases. Pope tried to distinguish genuine

12. Roberts, pp. 137, 207, 231.
13. *Ars poetica*, lines 24–31.

simplicity from its fraudulent mimic, which he dubbed rusticity (he was speaking of pastorals), and everyone remembers his neat sample of it, adopted from Dryden's *Essay of Dramatic Poesy*: "And ten low Words oft creep in one dull line."[14] But neoclassical theory held the main difference between verse and prose to consist in the cultivation of lexical and figurative embellishment in the one and its relative avoidance in the other. It is therefore not surprising that Johnson and David Hume—to instance only the more eminent—saw in the age's preponderant relish for poetry of excessive dictional refinement and imagistic elaboration the risk of "affectation" (Johnson), portending a "degeneracy of taste" (Hume).[15] It is essential to keep in mind that neither of these men can even remotely be considered a harbinger of any Wordsworthian poetics of plain talk. On the contrary, both fully subscribed to the doctrine of their time that elegant turns of phrase and choice words, advisable in many kinds of prose, were virtual requirements in verse. "If his language be not elegant," Hume wrote, no author can please his readers. As for the much touted simplicity, he admits it can have no appeal if not "accompanied with great elegance and propriety."[16] Yet precisely therein, he argues, lies the menace. So too Johnson. Writers on topics "probable and persuasory," a category inclusive a fortiori of poets, must be able "to recommend them by the superaddition of elegance and imagery, to display the colors of varied diction, and pour forth the music of modulated periods." He regards those writers as neither useless nor contemptible whose main effort is not to say anything new but to enhance familiar ideas "by

14. *Pastoral Poetry and An Essay on Criticism*, ed. E. Audra and Aubrey Williams, vol. 1, *The Poems of Alexander Pope* (New Haven: Yale University Press, 1961), pp. 32, 278. Hereafter cited as *Poems of Pope*.

15. Johnson, *The Idler and the Adventurer*, ed. W. J. Bate, John M. Bullitt, L. F. Powell, vol. 2, *Works* (1963), p. 198; Hume, "Of Simplicity and Refinement in Writing," in *On the Standard of Taste and Other Essays*, ed. John W. Lenz (New York: Bobbs-Merill, 1965), p. 47.

16. "Of Simplicity and Refinement in Writing," pp. 43, 47.

fairer decorations."[17] Yet within a few years of saying so he felt impelled to alert the public to the danger (Hume used the same word) inherent in this very process.

It would seem that in no other kind of human endeavor is it so true that there can be too much of a good thing as in the art of literature, and that the criticism of no other period is so pervaded by a troubled awareness of this fact as that produced in the eighteenth century. A kind of stylistic *nihil nimis*, locating excellence in a mean between extremes, is a constantly recurring theme. The mediating description of what makes for an effective ode set forth in Edward Young's "On Lyric Poetry" typically pairs its several qualities with their defective excesses. "To sum up the whole: Ode should be peculiar, but not strained: moral, but not flat; natural, but not obvious; delicate, but not affected; noble, but not ambitious; full, but not obscure; fiery, but not mad; thick, but not loaded in its numbers."[18] The recommended moderation was not confined to the lyric. In every genre, as Henry Pemberton wrote, precisely because artful expression is necessary, "care must be taken to avoid excess."[19]

No theory providing a set of terms for isolating and possibly resolving this aesthetic puzzle, from which the poets and readers of this rule-conscious literary era might have distilled appropriate rules, was ever devised. The futility of any attempt to do so is implied by the many endorsements, repeated to the century's end, of Longinus' recourse to the ineffable standard of an intuition nourished by experience. In the seventh of his *Discourses on Art*, Joshua Reynolds had no hesitation in prescribing the "ornaments" of meter and metaphor as indispensable to poetry. Yet "how far figurative or metaphorical language may proceed, and when it begins to be affectation"—did Reynolds have his friend the Rambler's admonitions in mind?—can be determined only by taste,

17. *The Idler and the Rambler*, pp. 460, 495.
18. In *Eighteenth-Century Critical Essays*, ed. Scott Elledge, 2 vols. (Ithaca: Cornell University Press, 1961), I, 414.
19. *Observations on Poetry* (London, 1738), p. 101.

which, to compound the problem, he regards as itself a cultural variable.[20]

To name everyone who warned against meretricious verbal embellishment during the ages of Pope and Johnson would come near a roll call of major eighteenth-century critics. It was almost inevitably included in the many academic compendia of poetic rules and principles, like the Latin lectures delivered at Oxford by Joseph Trapp in 1711. Trapp found Ovid frequently guilty of inappropriate or excessive ornamentation, Homer himself occasionally so, the impeccable Virgil (*qui nil molitur inepte*) never.[21] The views of the Trapps and the Pembertons tell us much. But with an aesthetic issue of such subtlety as this there is more profit in the witness of those who encountered it in their own creative practice, especially poets of the first rank who happen also to be critically articulate. We can be sure that Pope's inspired and agonized labors at an English Homer, including his study of the earlier translations he hoped to supersede, contributed to his discovery that the "sublime style is more easily counterfeited than the natural; something that passes for it, or sounds like it, is common in all false writers." But how distinguish the counterfeit from the real? Though Pope knows it is vital to do so, no more than anyone else can he find a touchstone. He repeats the familiar principle of propriety: avoid grand expressions with low or simple subjects. In both his Preface to the *Iliad* and his Postscript to the *Odyssey*, however, his language confesses that the problem is too complex and elusive to yield to any such critical rule of thumb. When "to be plain and when poetical and figurative" he calls "a great Secret" and "the great point of

20. Edited Robert R. Wark (San Marino: Huntington Library, 1959), p. 136.
21. *Lectures on Poetry, Translated from the Latin by William Bowyer* (London, 1742), pp. 56, 78. Trapp's transference of Horace's ascription of perfection, *qui nil molitur inepte* (*Ars poetica*, line 140), from Homer to Virgil typifies the Virgil-worship of the age. Pope's estimate of Homer's preeminence is a notable exception.

judgment." Had he himself discovered the secret? All he
tells us is that poets can learn it from Homer, whose epics,
Pope constantly reminds his readers, furnished Longinus
with the finest examples of the true sublime.[22]

Johnson's complaints that the studied elegance of modern
poets too often crossed the line of mere ostentation are
matched by Joseph Warton's denunciations of their "false
refinement."[23] More arresting is James Beattie's excoriation
of the "finical style" of poets who concoct verses out of
such periphrastic stereotypes as "syren song," "oaten reed"
and the like. Its appearance in the very work in which he
analyzes in detail, and advocates, the various devices of verbal elaboration essential to poetry bespeaks again their antinomial nature. Like the classical rhetoricians, he urges
special care in the use of hyperbole, so efficacious in elevating discourse, because "employed injudiciously" it brings
about the exactly opposite effect.[24] In this figure above all,
the sublime and the ludicrous reveal their common source.
Of course the double-edged potency of literary language can
be intentionally exploited, given the requisite talent, to produce delightful comic parody. Its repulsive twin is the kind
of unintentional parody to which these eighteenth-century
writers were calling attention.

What, in abstract terms, distinguishes injudicious rhetorical usage from its admired counterpart, or eloquent simplicity from the pedestrian, remained even more obscure to
neoclassical inquirers than it has become since, and the mystery is still far from clarification. Hume judged it to be hard
if not impossible "to explain by words where the just
medium lies between the excesses of simplicity and
refinement, or to give any rule by which we can know pre-

---

22. *The Odyssey*, ed. Maynard Mack, vols. 9–10 (1967), *Poems of Pope*, X,
389, 387; *The Iliad*, ed. Maynard Mack, vols. 7–8 (1967), *Poems of Pope*,
VII, 18.
23. *Eighteenth-Century Critical Essays*, II, 758.
24. *Essays on Poetry and Music* (Edinburgh, 1778), pp. 259, 273.

cisely the bounds between the fault and the beauty."[25] The violation of the rule of propriety they came to see as at best but one type of the error, not its universal condition. Besides, that rule itself, derived from the classical doctrine of high, middle, and low styles first enunciated in the *Ad Herennium*, was already being challenged.

One aspect of that challenge has direct bearing on the antinomy of poetic expression. It was noticed that even if a trivial theme forbade ornate treatment,[26] the corollary that serious subjects could never admit unadorned poetic style was patently untrue. It was recognized that a small but significant amount of excellent verse on weighty topics was actually devoid, or nearly devoid, of the usual embellishments. Beattie's citation of the moving lines spoken by King Lear on regaining consciousness and sanity is perhaps the most compelling instance in neoclassical discussion.[27]

>   Pray do not mock me:
> I am a very foolish fond old man,
> Fourscore and upward, not an hour more nor less;
> And, to deal plainly,
> I fear I am not in my perfect mind.
> Methinks I should know you and know this man,
> Yet I am doubtful; for I am mainly ignorant
> What place this is, and all the skill I have
> Remembers not these garments . . .

This sparse style was referred to as "easy poetry," a label singularly inept since, as Johnson observed in *Idler* 77, it is the hardest to write. The quality of ease, he notes, inheres mainly in the diction, which must be free of all artifice. The modern poets' "ambition of ornament and luxuriousness of imagery," he feels, has discouraged a proper appreciation of

---

25. "Of Simplicity and Refinement in Writing," p. 45.

26. Even this prohibition had its dissenters. Addison, to name one, pointed to Virgil, who in his *Georgics* "raised the natural rudeness and simplicity of his subject" by the "pomp of verse," breaking clods and tossing dung "with an air of gracefulness." *Eighteenth-Century Critical Essays*, I, 6.

27. *Essays on Poetry and Music*, p. 267.

a style which, "tho' it excludes pomp, will admit greatness."
By no means confined to "minute subjects," it is as well
adapted to tragic declamation as to the pithy epigrammatic
wit of a stanza by Cowley. Many lines of the soliloquy
delivered by the hero in the last act of Addison's *Cato* Johnson finds to be "at once easy and sublime."[28]

Johnson's illustration of the style which is diametrically
opposite to easy poetry is no other than the four opening
lines of Pope's *Iliad*:

> Achilles' *wrath*, to Greece the direful *spring*
> Of woes unnumber'd, *heav'nly* Goddess, sing,
> The [That] wrath which hurl'd to Pluto's *gloomy reign*
> The souls of *mighty* chiefs untimely slain.

When we recall that some twenty years later, in his final
maturity, Johnson was to rate Pope's *Iliad* as "certainly the
noblest version of poetry" ever written, a "poetical
wonder," the severity of the censure he pronounces on these
lines is somewhat startling. "In the first couplet," he
declares, "the language is distorted by inversions, clogged
with superfluities, and clouded by a harsh Metaphor; and in
the second there are two words used in an uncommon sense,
and two epithets inserted only to lengthen the line; all these
practices may in a long work easily be pardoned, but they
always produce some degree of obscurity and ruggedness."[29]

Some of Johnson's disapprobation here may conceivably
be ascribed to special pleading induced by his immediate
purpose—to win appreciation for simplicity—some, but I
think not much. It seems more likely that he shared the
curious vacillation of his coevals on the subject of poetic
figuration, in one breath prescribing it as necessary, in
another conceding, even insisting, that the greatest emotional force can be embodied in the plainest words. In his
popular *Lectures on Rhetoric and Belles Lettres* (1783) Hugh
Blair taught that "Figures form *the constant Language of*

28. *Works*, II, 239, 240, 241.
29. *Lives of the English Poets*, III, 119, 236; *Works*, II, 240.

poetry" (my italics). To see why, he suggested, we have
only to compare the trite expression "the sun rises" with the
magnificence of James Thomson's version of the same
thought:

> But yonder comes the powerful king of day,
> Rejoicing in the east. . . .

Blair has apparently forgotten that only four pages earlier he
had solemnly declared that often the most moving passages
of verse, Virgil's for example, are "expressed in the simplest
language."[30] His shifts of ground are of a piece with
Johnson's unfavorable references to the excessive verbiage
of the very translation he elsewhere extolled. The censori-
ous tone of his curt anatomy of Pope's lines precludes the
explanation that he meant only to suggest that the
translator's style, though admittedly admirable, was less
suited to Homer's august matter than the "easy" style would
have been. And surely—one cannot help remarking by the
way—one item in his indictment, that the first couplet is
"clogged with superfluities," comes awkwardly from the
man whose finest poem opens, as Coleridge's gleefully malicious paraphrase of it lays bare, with triple-decked repetition:

> Let Observation, with extended View
> Survey Mankind from China to Peru.[31]

The clashing ideals of poetic diction reflected in the speculations of neoclassical critics may well owe something to an
imperfect accommodation of the reigning theory to the
experience of readers. Although they may have comprised
only a discriminating minority at the time, many lovers of
poetry delighted both in the elegance of gorgeous verbal

30. Ed. Harold F. Harding, 2 vols. (Carbondale: Southern Illinois University Press, 1965), I, 285–286.
31. See Coleridge, *Shakespearean Criticism*, ed. Thomas Middleton Raysor,
2 vols. (New York: Dutton, 1960), II, 89: "as much as to say, 'Let observation with extensive observation observe mankind extensively.' "

array and the "naked elegance"—to use Johnson's oxymoron-skirting phrase—of easy poetry. The orthodox doctrine had always recognized the appropriateness of even the most literal directness in certain kinds of prose, but poetry, as Dryden had said, demanded ornament. If admissible at all in verse, undecorated expression was confined to the humbler genres and subjects. To use it with tragic or epic material was, as Demetrius taught, to fall into its corresponding vice, aridity. Post-Romantic theory, having either totally abandoned this hierarchical stylistic, or else greatly relaxed it, presented no such impasse to a reader's actual experience of poetic beauty being attainable throughout the entire spectrum of verbal complexity. As a result critics have long been able to avoid the inconsistencies that troubled the earlier poetics. But these speculations would require for their full validation a range of evidence too digressive for my present concern.

To put the problem in a way more relevant here, the existence of easy poetry would seem to authorize a far more sweeping challenge to the decorative theory of poetic discourse than that entailed by the antinomy. The one protests only that the much prized devices of specialized diction, deviant syntax, and figurative expression (not to mention meter) by which poets beautify their speech may equally make it repellent. But the fact that great verse can apparently dispense entirely with these formalities supports the logical inference of the radical Wordsworthian conclusion: use only the language of common speech or of prose. Unfortunately, *experience*, to which Johnson argued all theory must finally yield, makes this position as untenable as the one it would replace. Eighteenth-century readers, critics, and poets, like those in ages before and since, could point to a vast body of poetry whose enduring appeal was obviously, perhaps even demonstrably, referable to its highly elaborate linguistic structure. For this too is a fact, whether the elaboration is appreciated as attractive "clothing" of paraphrasable ideas or as itself an "incarnation" of ideas expressible in no other way, as modern theory generally holds.

So the quandary of the stylistic antinomy persists. Luckily, my aim is not to propose a solution but only to take note of its main manifestations during a century much given to literary theorizing. One of the most interesting is an aspect of neoclassical Longinianism which lent powerful support to the antidecorative thrust of easy poetry. Although the *Peri hypsous* had been published in 1554 and appeared in an English translation by John Hall as early as 1652, its appreciable influence on English critical thought begins only with the French translation by Nicolas Boileau in 1674. The brief explicative preface by which he introduced the work to his readers may well have done more to bring the problematic nature of poetic style to the bemused awareness of Britons than Longinus' own remarks about the antinomy. Boileau well knew the bias toward ornate writing among the French *literati* of the time, who he feared might simply laugh at Longinus' laudatory citation of passages "qui bien que très sublimes, ne laissent pas d'être simples et naturels." And so he sets himself to explaining to an audience prone to equate fine writing with fancy phrasing "ce que Longin entend par Sublime." He does this by sharply separating "le Sublime" from "le style sublime." Whereas the sublime style depends on verbal pomp ("de grands mots"), the sublime itself, by which readers and hearers are irresistibly transported, consists in a single thought, image, or turn of phrase ("seule pensée . . . seule figure . . . seule tour de paroles"). The antinomy lying at the heart of the issue thus surfaces in Boileau's manipulation of his author's central term, because his two uses of it are not merely distinguished as to designation but set in mutually exclusive opposition. To enforce his point he rewords, in the "style sublime," the celebrated example of sublimity which Longinus cites from Genesis. "Le souverain Arbitre de la nature d'une seule parole forma la lumière," Boileau maintains, totally lacks the majesty of the stark scriptural form: *Dieu dit: Que la lumière se fasse, et la lumière se fit.*[32]

---

32. *Oeuvres complètes*, ed. Françoise Escal (Paris: Gallimard, 1966), p. 338.

Any careful student of the Greek treatise will see that Boileau's reading replaces its total thesis with a reductive extrapolation from one portion of it. Nonetheless, his is the interpretation predominant in the eighteenth-century concept of the sublime in England, which placed almost exclusive stress on Longinus' two innate sources of elevated discourse, noble thought and vehement feeling. The various figures of speech and thought which make up the three acquired sources were disregarded or even rejected outright. The sublime, Hugh Blair affirmed, cannot be attained "by hunting after tropes, and figures, and rhetorical assistances."[33] The theoretical confusion certainly not caused, but much aggravated, by Boileau's preface was considerable. One senses a kind of tendentious irrelevancy in Beattie's imitation of Boileau's ploy. With proper acknowledgment of his French source, Beattie holds up for a comparison in Milton's disfavor that poet's elaboration of Jehovah's terse decree in *Paradise Lost* (VII, lines 243 ff.):

> "Let there be light," said God, and forthwith light
> Ethereal, first of things, quintessence pure
> Sprung from the deep, and from her native east
> To journey through the airy gloom began,
> Sphered in a radiant cloud, for yet the sun
> Was not. . . ."[34]

Perhaps the most revealing evidence of the French critic's impact on the ambivalent evaluation of the poet's medium that prevailed during the ensuing century is provided by John Husbands, one of several who exalted the Hebrew poetry of the Old Testament. Husbands rejoices to find the scriptural style perfectly answerable to the traditional requirements, according to which, he writes, the *essence* of poetry

---

33. *Lectures*, I, 277.
34. *Essays on Poetry and Music*, p. 270. The inconsistent attitude toward poetic adornment existed in Boileau himself, who speaks of "cette élégance qui faict proprement la poésie." *Lettres à Racine et à divers* (Paris: Société des Belles Lettres, 1943), p. 114.

inheres in lively discourse "adorn'd with Figures, varying according to the Greatness, Nature, and Quality of the Subject." Since their subject was nothing less than the mighty works of God, the Hebrew writers were especially favored by having lived in precivilized times. One article of the cultural primitivism of the Enlightenment held that pristine conditions of life fostered highly rhythmic and metaphorical expression. "No wonder therefore," Husbands reasons,

that their Diction is something more flourish'd and ornamental, more vigorous and elevated, more proper to paint and set Things before our Eyes, than plain and ordinary Recital. . . .

The Scripture abounds with a vast Variety of . . . beautiful Expressions, which breathe the true Spirit of Poetry. The Dawning of the Day the Hebrew expresses by *the Eyelids of the Morning.* Corners of the Earth are *Wings of the Earth.*[35]

Yet with no attempt at reconciling the discrepancy, or even apparently noticing it, within a few pages Husbands grounds the superiority of the sacred writings over all other literature on the two "Beauties" of *simplicity* and *sublimity*, as being appropriate to momentous themes, which eschew "all Dress, and adventitious Ornament." Predictably, he then invokes Boileau's observations on the passage from Genesis adduced by Longinus (himself repeatedly named). From the same book of the Bible Husbands chooses his own samples of the plain sublime. In one he finds the "whole passion of Love" concisely and movingly conveyed: "And Jacob served seven years for Rachel, and they seemed unto him but a few Days, for the Love he had unto her." The beauty of such a passage, Husbands points out, "does not consist in a Flourish of Words, or Pomp of Diction, not in the *ambitiosa ornamenta*

---

35. Preface to *A Miscellany of Poems by Several Hands* (Oxford, 1731) [no pagination]. Among other curiosities in this volume is a Latin verse translation of Pope's *Messiah*, done as a college exercise by "Mr. Johnson, a Commoner of Pembroke-College, in Oxford," which Professor Bate identifies as "the first surviving publication of any of his works." *Samuel Johnson* (New York: Harcourt Brace Jovanovich, 1977), p. 93.

of Rhetorick."[36] This after having just founded the essence and true spirit of poetry precisely in such verbal decoration.

The tone and language of the proponents of this strand of the eighteenth-century sublime suggest that it may represent a kind of unconscious evasion of the antinomial stylistic trap. Since legitimate embellishment is so prone to betrayal by its fraudulent double, and since the plain style is found to be consistent with the greatest expressive power, why not dispense with embellishment altogether? Yet this question, as noted, is readily answered out of common experience. Besides, the aesthetic ravishment examined by Longinus himself was also effected by passages in a style as remote as possible from plainness, by the periodic sentences of sustained involution in oratory or the enjambed verse paragraphs breathlessly piling image on image in epic or dramatic poetry. In fact to cap the contradiction, among the English Longinians themselves the favorite modern example of poetic sublimity was *Paradise Lost.* And in this judgment they were supported by many who were immune to the more outré symptoms of the Longinian fever, like Johnson, who named sublimity as the "characteristick quality" of Milton's epic.[37]

The linguistic perversity that led Longinus to assign poetic vices and virtues to "much the same sources" is perhaps only the lexical form of a broader aesthetic ambivalence. Or is there, in literary art, beneath the aesthetic a moral incentive at work, a deep-seated suspicion that the smoke of verbal overplus conceals the flames of deception or insincerity? Jane Austen makes a sense of this very impulse an ingredient in the finely tuned sensibility of the heroine of *Persuasion.* At one point Anne Elliot checks her skepticism toward her snobbish family's boasts of social triumph. "She heard it all under embellishment. All that sounded extravagant or irrational in the progress of reconciliation might have

36. *A Miscellany of Poems.*
37. *Lives of the English Poets,* I, 177.

no origin but in the language of the relators."[38] However it
may be, deep within the most discriminating readers' love of
poetry there does seem to lurk an "antipoetic" motive. (It is
not, typically, philistines who are repelled by manneristic
flourish.) For this reason the ambiguities that mark neoclassical theory of poetic discourse retain more than historical
interest. True, its two chief strategies for dealing with the
antinomy, the bans on excessive and inappropriate ornamentation, too often fail the test of poetry itself. Yet ambiguities
and strategies alike are symptomatic of a perennial condition
of our intercourse with the verbal arts. One of Samuel
Johnson's several complaints about blank verse was that it
could "hardly sustain itself without bold figures and striking
images."[39] For most readers today his generalization, even
where it holds, will not seem a valid objection. Yet it may
contain its germ of truth. For some readers at any time, I
suspect, the distaste of a more cynical moralist,
Shakespeare's Jaques, touches a sympathetic chord even as
they smile at the irony of its context: "Nay, then, God be
wi' you, an you talk in blank verse."

38. Jane Austen, *Persuasion* (New York: Oxford University Press, 1930),
p. 157.
39. *Lives of the English Poets*, I, 237.

JAMES ENGELL

The Source, and End, and Test of Art: Hume's Critique

My tastes are very simple. —I am always satisfied with the best.

Oscar Wilde

"A Criticism of Criticism"

Even a casual glance at critics from Hobbes through Coleridge reveals their search for objective principles and for an accompanying, though admittedly elusive, standard of taste. The hope was to guide taste with systematic criticism and to reinform critical precepts with empirical knowledge and exercised judgment. Thus the critic and the general reader would merge, with criticism and taste bearing somewhat the same relation to each other as tailoring and sewing. When Johnson concurred with the popular estimate of Gray's *Elegy*, "rejoice" really did describe his feeling that a professional critic such as himself could suspend "the dogmatism of learning" long enough to agree with the "common reader . . . uncorrupted with literary prejudices."[1]

1. *Lives of the English Poets*, ed. George Birkbeck Hill, 3 vols. (Oxford: Clarendon Press, 1905), "Life of Gray," III, 441.

Although Dryden rejected formulas and arbitrary authority, he nevertheless insisted that critics acquire special
knowledge and understanding. As he explained, it is not
enough to enjoy or to appreciate, "Nor is every man, who
loves tragedy, a sufficient judge of it; he must understand
the excellencies of it too, or he will only prove a blind
admirer, not a critic."[2] Of course the concern over principles
and the standard of taste echoed a preoccupation with the
larger question of "rules of art" and the social function of
literature. These issues could not be taken up separately—
and this essay aims in part to show that any debate about
critical principles or evaluation becomes meaningless unless
it is founded on assumptions about the role of literature in
society. During the eighteenth century an increasing suspicion of traditional, didactic rules governing artistic creativity
and the formal or generic characteristics of literature was
paradoxically yoked to a growing mandate for more exact
"scientific" and "systematic" principles of criticism. We are
still living with this paradox.

To put our discussion in perspective, it would help to note
that "taste" or "judgment" as used in the eighteenth
century—and as generally understood since then—really
amount to the same thing as the more abstract, polysyllabic,
latinate term "evaluation," which is at times felt to carry
overtones of academic, even demonstrable, precision and
dispassionate method. So much in criticism is a turning of
the semantic kaleidoscope. We might remind ourselves, too,
that to evaluate goes one step beyond the learning or intellectual *sprezzatura* that we bring to bear on a work; it means
to judge that work according to values, which may include
more than formal or stylistic ones. To evaluate, to exercise
taste, urges the critic or reader to consider *what values* and
what standards form the criteria of judgment.

2. Sir Walter Scott, ed., *The Works of John Dryden*, rev. and corr. George
Saintsbury, 18 vols. (Edinburgh: William Paterson, 1883), Preface to *All
for Love* (1678), V, 332.

Whatever worth the massive eighteenth-century attempt to clarify standards and to formulate "objective" criticism holds for us, it lies not so much in any number of specific principles we have inherited and revere, as in that century's brilliant critique on the very possibility and limits of system and principles in general. (It may be noted, though, that we continue to use approaches developed in the eighteenth century, such as literary history, a modern view of rhetoric, interest in myth, and the critical union of biography, psychology, and literature.) As René Wellek explains, Kant, in expounding "a theory of taste very similar to Hume's," would arrive "at an impasse." Yet Hume, in "On the Standard of Taste," first "poses the antinomies of Kant's *Critique of Judgment* and resolutely raises the problem of criticism as such. Actually it is a criticism of criticism."[3] Striving to construct or to extract "principles," Hume and later critics were becoming acutely aware of the limitations of such an enterprise. Coleridge, for example, began his "Essay on Taste" in 1810 with a tentatively optimistic statement: "The same arguments that decide the question, whether taste has any fixed principles, may probably lead to a determination of what those principles are."[4] But he aborted the essay after three paragraphs.

Our eighteenth-century legacy hands down to us at least two lessons. The first is that any system or theory built on purely formal qualities of genre, type, and kind of composition (as many neoclassical theories were) may succeed in describing a given body of literature, but its principles will not hold up under the natural variety and change that continually modify literary forms and the taste of readers, especially in a society where readership expands in pluralistic fashion. In "The Modern Mind," Eliot notes, "So our

3. René Wellek, *History of Modern Criticism*, 4 vols. to date (New Haven: Yale University Press, 1955–), I, 109; cf. Ernst Cassirer, *The Philosophy of the Enlightenment*, trans. F. C. A. Koelln and J. P. Pettegrove (Princeton: Princeton University Press, 1951), pp. 275–278.

4. *Biographia Literaria*, ed. John Shawcross, 2 vols. (Oxford: Oxford University Press, 1907), II, 247.

criticism, from age to age, will reflect the things that the age demands; and the criticism of no one man and of no one age can be expected to embrace the whole nature of poetry or exhaust all of its uses. Our contemporary critics, like their precedessors, are making particular responses to particular situations." The second lesson is that principles having a chance of succeeding beyond a generation or two are based on formal qualities in active confluence with other disciplines and with a sense of psychology, history, and the study of language—rhetoric, linguistics, philology, and semiotics.

Neoclassic theory had, in fact, offered internally consistent rules. But Hobbes, Butler, Dryden, Addison, Pope—even Rymer—and later Johnson and Reynolds rejected many of them as dry conventions imposed *ab extra*. Johnson praised Dryden "as the writer who first taught us to determine upon principles the merit of composition," but not according to "a dull collection of theorems." His criticism "is the criticism of a poet."[5] Samuel Butler abhorred the critic who examined new plays "precisely by the rules of the ancients" as much as he detested the solipsistic "modern critic" who "is not bound to proceed but by his own Rules."[6]

Despite these powerful voices, the itch for critical system remained. Johnson stated that by the latter part of the century Addison had lost respect as a critic because he was viewed as unstructured or "experimental" and had neglected "rules" considered "scientific."[7] Explaining why Shakespeare remained so popular despite his technical "faults," Johnson would revert to the distinction between "principles demonstrative and scientific" and those principles more open to experience and perception—and therefore generally more applicable to literature as an imitative art. He worried that

5. *Lives*, "Life of Dryden," I, 410, 412.

6. *Satires and Miscellaneous Poetry and Prose*, ed. Rene Lamar (Cambridge: Cambridge University Press, 1928), "Upon Critics Who Judge of Modern Plays Precisely by the Rules of the Antients," pp. 60–62; and in Butler's *Characters*, ed. A. R. Waller (Cambridge: Cambridge University Press, 1908), "A Modern Critic," p. 32.

7. *Lives*, "Life of Addison," II, 145.

criticism in his own time was spending too much effort in the direction of method and system, a state of affairs expressed at its narrowest in the coffeehouse dogmas of Dick Minim. As minima became maxima they grew less satisfactory, and eighteenth-century critics eventually turned the principles of criticism into the principles of the imagination itself. Critics began to equate—or, depending on one's point of view, to confuse—imagination with taste, so that the two became nearly inseparable.[8] Richard Payne Knight, Alexander Gerard, Archibald Alison, and even Reynolds view taste as the product of an organizing play of mind that combines the passive perception of what Hume calls "objects, as they really stand in nature," with the active structuring of objects in a larger associational and contextual framework of yet other objects, personal experiences, sympathy, and the power of suggestion or—as Burke phrased it—"obscurity." (Shaftesbury had envisioned a comprehensive play of all faculties and sensibilities earlier in the century, and his work would help shape views of taste, genius, and imagination developed in Germany between Baumgarten's *Aesthetica* and Schelling's *Philosophie der Kunst.*) Burke had emphatically urged the fusion of two concepts once considered quite different: "to cut off all pretence for cavilling," he says in the "Introduction: On Taste" to his *Enquiry*, "I mean by the word Taste no more than that faculty, or those faculties of the mind which are affected with, or which form a judgment of, the works of the imagination and the elegant arts."[9] Taste and imagination were increasingly treated as synonyms. Of course this increased the subjective, psychological element in aesthetic judgment. And this tendency helps to explain, in a nutshell, much critical activity from Johnson through Coleridge. In the course of this development we commonly find judgments such as Goldsmith's on Spenser:

8. W. Jackson Bate, *From Classic to Romantic: Premises of Taste in Eighteenth-Century England* (Cambridge: Harvard University Press, 1946), pp. 113–114.

9. Ed. J. T. Boulton (New York: Columbia University Press, 1958), p. 13.

"However, with all his faults, no poet enlarges the imagination more than Spenser."[10] In a quest for the source, and end, and test of art, the principles of criticism moved from nature and the ancients toward the modern artist's imagination.

It is first "in Hume," says Ernst Cassirer, that "the whole battlefront of aesthetic controversy is reformed . . . Feeling no longer needs to justify itself before the tribunal of reason . . . Reason not only loses its position of dominance; even in its own field, in the domain of knowledge, it has to surrender its leadership to the imagination," which "is now treated as the fundamental power of the soul."[11] As Coleridge would say, "The *rules* of the IMAGINATION are themselves the very powers of growth and production," and so it was a central object of the *Biographia* to present the "deduction of the imagination, and with it the principles of production and of genial criticism in the fine arts."[12] The focus of principles had changed considerably since Dryden's time, but the desire for them remained.

One reason Coleridge wrote the *Biographia* (so he says in the book itself) was not only to distinguish his views on poetry from Wordsworth's but also to refute or at least to rectify Wordsworth's critical "sentiments" by replacing them with genuine "principles."[13] Sixty years earlier in his essay on the standard of taste—which might also be referred to as an essay on the lack of such a standard, or at least on its elusiveness—Hume had also distinguished between "principles" and "sentiments." Hume's essay is one of the sharper eighteenth-century tests of the possibility and limits of

10. *Works*, ed. Peter Cunningham, 4 vols. (London: John Murray, 1854), IV, 203. The sentence occurs in a contribution to *The Critical Review* attributed, but not with certainty, to Goldsmith. *The Collected Works*, ed. Arthur Friedman, 5 vols. (Oxford: Clarendon Press, 1966), omits this review of Ralph Church's edition of *The Faerie Queene*.

11. *Philosophy of the Enlightenment*, p. 305; see also pp. 311–312.

12. Samuel Taylor Coleridge, *Biographia Literaria*, eds. James Engell and W. Jackson Bate, 2 vols. (Princeton: Princeton University Press, 1983), II, 84; I, 264.

13. *Biographia*, eds. Engell and Bate, II, 9–11, 119.

objective standards in art and criticism, and with the background just outlined, perhaps we can see its detail in the larger perspective of "a criticism of criticism."

A Bisociative Act

"Of the Standard of Taste," which Hume published in 1757, confronts the difficulty of establishing a standard by which to judge works that arouse our sentiment and imagination as much as they accommodate our sense of the matter-of-fact. Hume thus explores a problem that recalls Plato's charge that the poet falsifies reality. But he treats the problem with wider scope and psychological acuity: how can critics find a "standard" that is to be shared and understood logically, when that standard must apply to works that are imaginative and emotional (and hence often "original")?

In other words, a barrier in the way of critical principles may arise from the nature of imaginative art as it addresses the whole mind. For on one side of the psyche we tend to arrange judgment and the understanding, faculties that shape what Hume calls "opinion" or "science," and that guide us in matter-of-fact knowledge, which Hume associates with reason and the understanding. On the other side of the psyche we tend to place matters of "taste" and "sentiment" of our likes, dislikes, and feelings. These are self-referential or, as Hume says, they are—according to some—"always real" or always "right: Because no sentiment represents," or pretends to represent, "what is really in the object." No "sentiment" sees the object as it really is. The dominant faculty here is passionate imagination. As Hume spreads out the dichotomy, reason "discovers objects, as they really stand in nature," while taste "has a productive faculty, and gilding or staining all natural objects with the colours, borrowed from internal sentiment, raises, in a manner, a new creation." A dilemma emerges when we assign our critical faculty either solely to judgment and understanding or solely to sentiment and imagination ("The difference, it is said, is very wide between judgment and sentiment").[14] Hume believes that emphasizing one more than the other is lopsided.

When Romantic criticism began to base itself on sympathy and the imagination, it was, in a sense, attempting not to exclude judgment and understanding but to synthesize them with sympathy and imagination. But in doing so it also magnified the subjective element to the extent that the personal and idiosyncratic—either the work or the criticism of it—could become self-indulgent. This was the chief complaint Hazlitt lodged against the poetry of his own day. Critical principles of any worth must be rationally grasped, understood, and applied, but now what was increasingly wanted emerged as the imaginative and original, not the understandable or "correct."[15]

In fact, one crucial issue of modern poetics was developing into something like the following: is human nature (and hence experience or even truth itself) essentially divided between an inner *I am* of personal, visionary feeling and perception responsible for creating "fictions," and an equally inner *it is* fitted to understand the external world of cause, effect, and matter-of-fact? (We might recall Blake railing against Wordsworth's "fitted and fitting.") This is one way to read Keats's question, "Do I wake or sleep?" Are these states mutually exclusive? If the poet indulges imagination, is he in danger of becoming, as Keats himself wondered, a fever of himself, a useless thing? Is there no third possibility, no waking dream, no willing suspension of disbelief? Is the soul or its dream vision separate from the reasonable

14. "Concerning Moral Sentiment," in *Essays Moral, Political, and Literary*, ed. T. H. Green and T. H. Grose, 2 vols. (London: 1882; reprint, Aalen: Scientia Verlag, 1964), II, 265, 268 (vol. IV of *The Philosophical Works*).

15. The potential split between genius cultivated with a reflexive, self-conscious understanding and that of a more spontaneous, "natural" gift runs through eighteenth-century criticism—e.g., Addison's *Spectator* 160, Alexander Gerard's *Essay on Genius*, and Schiller's *Naive and Sentimental Poetry*.

self, or antithetical to it—or is human nature more of a unity in which soul and self, imagination and reason, inner vision and external experience exist in *discordia concors*?[16] Moreover, simply because all these questions are not about the self and nature so much as about the condition of the self alone, might we not expect as many different answers as there are selves? How, in matters of taste, can there be any consensus? These are the basic and persisting questions that Hume poses.[17]

Add to this Hume's admission that "when critics come to particulars . . . it is found that they had affixed a very different meaning to their expressions," and we see that the imprecision of language further clouds and hampers the issue. Even "the seeming harmony in morals" found among writers may be an illusion created by "the very nature of language." Yet, despite these observations and a warning that "variety of taste" may be "still greater in reality than in appearance,"[18] Hume maintains that a standard of taste does exist, much in the same way Eliot affirms, near the close of "The Modern Mind," that "Amongst all these

16. For discussion in light of recent critical theory, see Frank Lentricchia, *After the New Criticism* (Chicago: University of Chicago Press, 1980), ch. 2, "Versions of Existentialism," esp. pp. 35–60. This potential psychic split is discussed by Paul de Man with regard to Yeats in *Blindness and Insight* (New York: Oxford University Press, 1971), pp. 170–172, and by Jean Hagstrum with reference to "wit" in "Johnson and the Concordia Discors," in *The Unknown Samuel Johnson*, eds. John J. Burke, Jr., and Donald Kay (Madison: University of Wisconsin Press, 1983), pp. 39–53, esp. pp. 51–52.

17. For Hume's persisting relevance see Murray Cohen, "Eighteenth-Century English Literature and Modern Critical Methodologies," *The Eighteenth Century: Theory and Interpretation*, 20 (1979), 5–23, esp. 11–15; and Mary Carman Rose, "The Importance of Hume in Western Aesthetics," *The British Journal of Aesthetics*, 16 (1976), 218–229. Rose contends that Hume made vital "contributions to modern aesthetics" (p. 220) and that "the aesthetic inquiry of twentieth-century American and British language philosophers has explicitly been an appropriation but also a development of Hume's empirical approach to aesthetics" (p. 224).

18. "Of the Standard of Taste," in *Essays Moral, Political, and Literary*, 1, pp. 266, 267, 266. Hereafter cited as "Standard."

demands from poetry and responses to it there is always some permanent element in common, just as there are standards of good and bad writing independent of what any of us happens to like and dislike."[19]

Hume's analysis anticipates many critical stances in which two faculties, one basically rational and the other nonrational, either square off against each other (as in Shelley's *Defense* with its initial split between reason and imagination, Blake's similar division, Yeats's mirror and lamp, Wallace Stevens' "fictions," Eliot's "dissociation of sensibility," and Richards' "intellectual" *versus* "emotional belief") or are united by a third, synthesizing element (such as *Spieltrieb* in Schiller's *Philosophische Briefe*, the poetic imagination in Coleridge, Arnold's "imaginative reason," and Newman's "illative sense"). The potential dualism—essentially one between imagination and judgment—has been treated by poets themselves, Keats in *Lamia*, for instance, or Tennyson in *The Palace of Art*.

Hume's affinities rest with a line of English poet-critics that includes Sidney, Dryden, Johnson, Coleridge, Arnold, and Eliot. He appeals to "experience," that is, to *all* experience, which includes both art and "reality." He concludes that the mind is not inherently cleft between the literary equivalent of right and left hemispheres: "It appears," he says, "amidst all the variety and caprice of tastes, there are certain general principles of approbation or blame, whose influence a careful eye may trace in *all* operations of the mind."[20] There exists a natural tension, much like the one separating the horses that draw Plato's chariot of the soul, but there is no unharnessed tug-of-war.

A literary physiologist might say that Hume affirms a *corpus colosum*, a connecting body, between judgment and sentiment. In fact, he explicitly states this as his overall purpose: his "intention in this essay is to mingle some light of

---

19. *The Use of Poetry and the Use of Criticism* (London: Faber and Faber, 1933), pp. 141–142.

20. "Standard," p. 271, emphasis added.

the understanding with the feelings of sentiment."[21] Hugh Blair would later echo and amplify Hume:

The difference between the authors who found the standard of Taste upon the common feelings of human nature ascertained by general approbation, and those who found it upon established principles which can be ascertained by reason, is more an apparent than a real difference. Like many other literary controversies, it turns chiefly on modes of expression . . . These two systems . . . differ in reality very little from one another. Sentiment and Reason enter into both; and by allowing to each of these powers its due place, both systems may be rendered consistent.[22]

Such a mingling, not an emphasis on sentiment or understanding alone, is Hume's critical basis.[23] The critical act becomes a bisociative one. True, the object of poetry is "to please by means of the passions and the imagination" and not by means of the understanding, but "every kind of composition, even the most poetical, is nothing but a chain of propositions and reasonings; not always, indeed, the justest and most exact, but still plausible and specious [able to be seen], however disguised by the colouring of the imagination." As examples Hume gives the events and characters in tragedy and epic poetry, and though his case may be vitiated to some extent by the rise and eventual dominance of the lyric, his stance is wide: "It seldom, or never happens, that a man of sense, who has experience in any art, cannot judge of its beauty; and it is no less rare to meet with a man who

21. Ibid., p. 272.
22. *Lectures on Rhetoric and Belles Lettres*, 2 vols. (London: W. Strahan, 1783), I, 32 n.
23. For interplay of sense and sentiment, reason and feeling, see Ralph Cohen, "The Rationale of Hume's Literary Inquiries," in *David Hume: Many-sided Genius*, ed. Kenneth R. Merril and Robert W. Shahan (Norman: University of Oklahoma Press, 1976), pp. 99, 105; Teddy Brunius, *David Hume on Criticism* (Stockholm: Almquist & Wiksell, 1952), pp. 37, 39, 53; and Nicholas Capaldi, "Hume's Theory of the Passions," in *Hume, A Reevaluation*, ed. Donald W. Livingston and James T. King (New York: Fordham University Press, 1976), pp. 172–190, esp. pp. 175–176.

has a just taste without a sound understanding."[24] These criteria imply that poet-critics will both be better poets for being critics and better critics for being poets.

Accepting criticism as a bisociative act, we see the familiar and much abused term "common sense" in a new light. Hume wants common sense to mingle the illumination of mirror and lamp, of "the understanding *and* the colouring of the imagination." True *common* sense becomes the mediating ground of experience drawn from imagination or sentiment and from our understanding of the matter-of-fact. It is common to both and combines them.[25] This is what Hume means when he admits that the latitude in subjective tastes, "by passing into a proverb *[de gustibus non disputandum]*, *seems* to have attained the sanction of common sense," but—and it is a very big "but"—"there is certainly a species of common sense which opposes it, at least serves to modify and restrain it."[26] Such an attitude had already been broached by one of Hume's acquaintances, Adam Smith. In his *Lectures on Rhetoric and Belles Lettres* delivered at the University of Glasgow in 1762–1763 (most likely an expanded version of his Edinburgh lectures of 1748–1751), Smith rather bluntly asserted, "If you will attend to it, all the rules of criticism and morality, when traced to their foundation, turn out to be some principles of common sense which every one assents to."[27] Significantly, Johnson would write in his "Life of Gray" that "by the *common sense* of readers uncorrupted by literary prejudices . . . must be finally

---

24. "Standard," pp. 277–278.
25. Capaldi notes that for Hume, "the test of all philosophical speculation is its relevance to our common experience. Common sense is not something to be explained away but something which calls for explanation" (p. 176).
26. "Standard," p. 269, emphasis added.
27. *Lectures*, ed. John M. Lothian (London: Thomas Nelson and Sons, 1963), p. 51; see also pp. xiii-xvi and Cassirer, *Philosophy of the Enlightenment*, p. 308.

determined all claim to poetical honours."[28] It is intriguing to see Hume, the most radical skeptic in the English tradition, oppose a skeptical view of taste, of all things, in favor of a finer "species of common sense," the lineage of which is as mixed as experience itself.

"The Key with the Leathern Thong"

But Hume remains troubled that sentiment and judgment rarely appear to coincide. He admits the scarcity of his preferred stock of common sense. "Those finer emotions of the mind" on which art and poetry rest "are of a very tender and delicate nature, and require the concurrence of many favourable circumstances to make them play with facility and exactness, according to their general and established principles."[29] How does he imagine such a "concurrence"? The answer may first be suggested by his vocabulary, in which we encounter, repeatedly: "tender," "delicate," "exactness," "discrimination," "notice," "nice," "finer" and "minute qualities," "particular flavours," "particular feelings," and "delicacy of taste."

Although Hume probably owes a debt to Bouhours' aesthetic of *délicatesse*, the point here is not to pull up the roots of Hume's essay but to see it as a crucial, representative document in the history of taste and "the criticism of criticism." Hume stresses that repeated perusals give rise to interlocking sets of comparisons; minute particulars become connected at many interstices—we structure; judgment and feeling come together as a network or matrix. Immersion in reading, interpreting, and appreciating art will form the organs of taste and observation until they become susceptible to all possible shades (see Kinbote) and particulars of what we read. Hence "nothing tends further to increase and

28. *Lives*, III, 441, emphasis added. For philosophically oriented discussion, see Chester Chapin, "Samuel Johnson and the Scottish Common Sense School," *The Eighteenth Century: Theory and Interpretation*, 20 (1979), 50–64, esp. 51, 64.

29. "Standard," p. 270.

improve this talent"—this delicacy—"than *practice* in a particular art, and the frequent survey or contemplation of a particular species of beauty." The whole key is experience, thorough and complete. "But allow him to acquire experience," Hume says, and like a weathervane the critic will point judgment in the right direction. "So advantageous is practice to the discernment of beauty" that every object or work of art must be repeatedly "surveyed in different lights." A work of art is a structured object, a made object, and we must try to see it in all its possible perspectives, not to demand that it appear in, or by, one light.[30]

Hume's example of *délicatesse* from *Don Quixote* (part II, chapter 13) relates how two of Sancho Panza's kinsmen taste a certain wine and pronounce it excellent. But one detects a hint of leather, the other a hint of iron. Both men withstand ridicule until the drained hogshead reveals an old key tied to a leather thong. "The great resemblance betwen mental and bodily taste," says Hume, "will easily teach us to apply this story." Any standard requires *"delicacy of taste."* And to "produce these general rules or avowed patterns of composition is like finding the key with the leathern thong, which justified the verdict of Sancho's kinsmen, and confounded those pretended judges who had condemned them."[31]

One might ask, Has it ever been otherwise? Isn't Hume operating from neoclassical premises, from what he calls "general and established principles" or "avowed patterns," which he assumes his audience shares, and isn't he then simply saying that the application of these principles becomes clearer with practice and repetition?

What if two descendants of Sancho were to read Allen Ginsberg? Both might discern nuances and, comparing Ginsberg's work with others', earn minute knowledge of it.

---

30. "Standard," pp. 274, 275. Ralph Cohen, "David Hume's Experimental Method and the Theory of Taste," *ELH*, 25 (1958), 270–289, remarks, "The most significant element of Hume's essay on taste is its insistence on method, of the introduction of fact and experience into the problem of taste" (p. 270).

31. "Standard," p. 273.

But if the premises of Sancho's kin were to differ, one might praise the poet and the other reject him. "Where these doubts occur," says Hume, "men can do no more than in other disputable questions, which are submitted to the understanding: They must produce the best arguments, that their invention suggests to them."[32] For nowhere in his essay does Hume attempt to describe what the standard of taste actually is or should be. He will only say that it *exists.* He also wants to make clear that taste is not completely relative—which would be the case if there were no standard.[33] One unavoidable result of this postulate is that some literary views are, in *fact*, better than others, but *which ones* cannot be demonstrated.[34] This is analogous to Hilary Putnam's argument that we cannot prove a statement's truth *a priori*, but neither can we demonstrate that there are no *a priori* truths. The two descendants of Sancho, Hume would say, "must acknowledge a true and decisive standard to exist somewhere, to wit, real existence and matter of fact; and they must have indulgence to such as differ from them in their appeals to this standard. It is sufficient for our present purpose if we have proved, that the taste of all individuals is not upon an equal footing."[35]

32. "Standard," p. 279. See Brunius, *David Hume on Criticism*, where Brunius sees Hume "creating a dialog about the great questions to which there are no definite answers" (p. 15).

33. On Hume's relativism limited by his insistence on a standard or common cultural framework, see Cohen, "Hume's Experimental Method," p. 278, and "The Rationale," p. 114; also Brunius, *David Hume on Criticism*, pp. 75, 85.

34. Ernest Campbell Mossner, "Hume's 'Of Criticism,'" in *Studies in Criticism & Aesthetics: Essays in Honor of Samuel Holt Monk*, ed. Howard Anderson and John S. Shea (Minneapolis: University of Minnesota Press, 1967), pp. 232–248, puts the case bluntly: "In the realm of matter of fact, demonstration cannot be reached" (pp. 234–235).

35. "Standard," p. 279. Cohen, "Hume's Experimental Method," states: "It has sometimes been overlooked that Hume's explicit purpose . . . was to prove that some tastes are better than others and to provide a basis for this distinction" (p. 272).

The standard of taste becomes a presence that is, in a sense, an absence, what Hazlitt calls an Ideal of Taste, a fact that can no more be denied than it can be exactly determined. No one can be proved to have attained it. But in the attempt to attain such a standard (which has, I believe, something to do with that volatile literary value "sincerity"), the reader must exercise empathy with the work of art itself, which, as Hume says, "in order to produce its due effect on the mind, must be surveyed in a certain point of view, and cannot be fully relished by persons, whose situation, real or imaginary, is not conformable to that which is required by the performance." Here Hume sounds like Pater or Arnold—or like Pope's *Essay on Criticism* or Johnson's "Life of Dryden": the reader needs to make an effort to overcome prejudices ingrained by his own time, milieu, and personal experience. The "different humours of particular men," says Hume, and "the particular manners and opinions of our age and country," as well as speculative beliefs, especially religious, always distort taste.[36] Hume's ideal reader or critic will ferret out, assess, and minimize these predilections.[37]

Although not our major interest here, it might be instructive to compare Hume's position—that of an atheist skeptical of the Western philosophical tradition in metaphysics—with the position of someone as recent as Jacques Derrida, whom E. D. Hirsch calls a cognitive atheist. For Hume is saying that in matters of taste, although there is very definitely at any given time in history a center or a standard, we cannot define or find that center—at least we cannot precisely agree what it is. Yet Hume continues to uphold that such a center or standard does exist and that it is grounded on the totality and delicacy of all our experience. In what seems an analogous statement, Derrida says that the "absent" center is to

36. "Standard," pp. 276, 280.
37. Cohen, "The Rationale," thus speaks of the critic undergoing a "*de-conversion*" (pp. 109–110).

be interpreted *"otherwise than as loss of the center."*[38] If one were to take the radical stance that neither center nor standard exists, there could be no judgment whatsoever, *only* pleasure or displeasure of the text, only individual prejudice confirming itself.

Hume is less neoclassical and rigid than he appears at first. Gerald Chapman remarks, "The conviction of mid-century critics like Burke and Kames that rules cannot be drawn from dogmatic tradition owes much to Hume's example."[39] Hume recognizes no authority, no defined rules or dicta. And, like Johnson in *Rambler 3*, he stakes a modest claim for the critic's power; time makes the final judgments. But all critics and interpretations are not equally good. The realm of taste may be a democracy and its voters may be created equal, but the votes cast are not equally well informed, and the candidates vary in quality. In a critical version of Kurt Gödel's Incompleteness Theorem, all demonstrative arguments concerning taste are ultimately circular, but the radius of some is more extensive, the center more accurately plotted.

When it comes to principles of criticism, Hume and Johnson are not far apart. Both believe that literature should please and that it should also examine values of behavior and virtue that rise above changes in customs and manners. The good critic, well read but not merely bookish, writes a forceful and agreeable style, is informed by history, delights in language, and reads human character with charity and insight.

---

38. "Structure, Sign, and Play in the Discourse of the Human Sciences," in *The Structuralist Controversy: The Languages of Criticism and the Sciences of Man*, ed. Richard Macksey and Eugenio Donato (Baltimore: Johns Hopkins University Press, 1972), p. 264.

39. Ed., *Literary Criticism in England: 1660–1800* (New York: Knopf, 1966), p. 273 (from Chapman's "The Anglo-Scots Inquiry," pp. 265–276). On Hume's breaking the neoclassical mold, see also Cohen, "Hume's Experimental Method," p. 280, and Mossner, "Hume's 'Of Criticism,'" pp. 237, 239. No recent commentator identifies Hume with neoclassical criticism.

A Principle of Art

Hume assumes, beneath his position, one essential fact or principle—and it is not, strictly speaking, a principle of criticism. In contradistinction, he calls it a "principle of art," or, rather, the assumed postulate that art does have "avowed principles" or purposes, that there is an end to art, that art is teleological or purposive, and that it is not hermetically sealed nor completely autonomous. "Even poets and other authors," says Hume, "whose compositions are chiefly calculated to please the imagination, are yet found, from Homer down to Fénelon, to inculcate the same moral precepts and to bestow their applause and blame on the same virtues and vices."[40]

"To produce," then, "general rules" of criticism and of composition "is like finding the key with the leathern thong." This is done by showing the "bad critic" what

40. No other single issue has led to more disagreement than Hume's views relating aesthetics to morality. William H. Halberstadt, "A Problem in Hume's Aesthetics," *The Journal of Aesthetics and Art Criticism*, 30 (1971), 209–214, remarks, "There are good grounds for maintaining . . . that Hume treated aesthetics and ethics similarly" (p. 213)—though independently (?), as Mary Carman Rose in "The Importance of Hume" contends: "Hume interprets both the development and the functioning of the individual's moral nature as independent of the development and functioning of his aesthetic sense" (p. 223). Mossner states, "Hume's 'Of Criticism,'" "Morality, for Hume, may legitimately enter into the critical judgment of art" (p. 238). Cohen, in "Hume's Experimental Method," says that Hume's procedure "helped separate art from morals," but it also implied that "no critic should give up his ideas of morality and decency in order to relish the work of art" (pp. 276, 277).

Compare Philip Flynn, "Scottish Aesthetics and the Search for a Standard of Taste," *Dalhousie Review*, 60 (1980), 5–19, esp. 9: "Hume, Kames, Blair, Gerard, and Beattie noted that a just taste in the fine arts and a keen sense of virtue are not *always* joined in the same person. But most of the Scottish aestheticians agreed that art is an important force for moral instruction, operating more often through our sympathetic emotions than through our reason's grasp of moral principles." See also A. M. Kinghorn, "Literary Aesthetics and the Sympathetic Emotions—A Main Trend in Eighteenth-Century Scottish Criticism," *Studies in Scottish Literature*, 1 (1963), 35–47.

Hume calls "an avowed principle of art" (not "of criticism"); once we have won acceptance for such an avowed principle we can proceed, as it were, to empty the hogshead. At that point the bad critic "must conclude, upon the whole, that the fault lies in himself, and that he wants the delicacy, which is requisite to make him sensible" of beauty and excellence. In the end, a set of "avowed" or established principles of art determines the principles of criticism and assures the existence of a standard of taste. And the first postulate or "principle of art" concerns the purpose or function of art in society and culture.[41]

If art is "autonomous," unanchored in any other valuations of experience, if art has *no* purpose—the MGM motto above the roaring lion *ars gratia artis*, or Ortega y Gasset's reductive "just Art" at the end of *The Dehumanization of Art*—if art has no ends outside itself, there can not exist any standard of taste. The most exciting area will be an avant garde perpetually struggling to maintain its identity while becoming absorbed and conventionalized at an ever more rapid rate. The only principle of art then becomes the imagination or "fictions" of the artist, who is judged in his own court under his own laws. Criticism will stress only how we read, not how we judge what we read.

All this helps us to see why Aristotle and Coleridge—and countless other critics and poets—define poetry, a poem, and the nature of the poet not in formalistic or linguistic terms alone (though these are always included) but in terms of their functions, their immediate pleasure and their eventual truth. In the simple phrasing of Tolstoy: what is art? Hume's analysis—and all such analyses or debates over principles of taste and criticism—devolves to this question about

41. "Standard," pp. 273–274. See Flynn, "Scottish Aesthetics," pp. 7, 11; Cohen, "The Rationale," p. 114; and Peter Jones, "Strains in Hume and Wittgenstein," in *Hume, A Re-evaluation*, pp. 191–209, and—in the same volume—"Cause, Reason, and Objectivity in Hume's Aesthetics," pp. 323–342. Jones discusses a social and communal foundation of Hume's "general inalterable standard, by which we may approve or disapprove of characters and manners" (p. 330).

the nature and purpose of art.[42] If we feel there is no answer to Tolstoy's question, or that there are as many answers as there are authors, then all principles of criticism vanish. As Hume wrote to George Cheyne in 1734, under such conditions philosophy and criticism exhibit "little more than endless disputes, even in the most fundamental articles."[43] One of many qualities giving Keats's poetry and letters so fresh an appeal is that he never stopped asking Tolstoy's question—what should a poet do, what is poetry? Keats had answers but he was not sure of them, an uncertainty that adds to his gifts, perhaps because he does not force the answers on us but invites us to consider them with him.

Although the formulation is simple it may be overlooked: until the critic answers—or attempts to answer—the questions What is art and What is the function of art in society and culture, no standard of taste can operate, and the only "principles" that can exist will deal with formalistic or linguistic considerations. Objective principles seem to be the *Ding-an-sich* of criticism. Whether they exist, no one can prove with certainty, though no one can prove they do not. They are regulative, and perhaps ultimately constitute a social idea as much as an aesthetic one. In "The Polite Learning of England and France Incapable of Comparison," Goldsmith remarks, "Truth is a positive, taste a relative excellence."[44] Most sentiments and fashions in criticism do not last; the permanence and objectivity of any critical system or set or principles remains elusive. But such principles and the standard of taste they imply, if associated with a

---

42. Jones, "Cause, Reason, and Objectivity," p. 331: "Hume also claims that certain fundamental 'rules of art are founded on the qualities of human nature.'" Cohen wrestles with the issue in "The Rationale": "Perhaps one way to approach these inquiries is to ask why Hume does not undertake to define art . . . to him, art is important only in the sense that it engages human beings" (p. 101). But "Art was . . . for Hume . . . an enhancement of man's values" (p. 107) and "It was the value of art that in the end constituted the rationale of Hume's literary inquiries" (p. 115).

43. Quoted by Chapman, *Literary Criticism in England*, p. 273.

44. *Works*, ed. Friedman, I, 294 and n., which connects Goldsmith's remark with Hume's essay "The Sceptic."

sense of how art affects education and society, may exist as an absence that has the force of a presence, a missing capstone that serves to ventilate the smoke of provincial controversy: a vacancy at the top that cannot be filled but that, like heaven, we guess at—as Keats said—"from forth the loftiest fashion of our sleep."

JOHN L. MAHONEY

The Anglo-Scottish Critics:
Toward a Romantic Theory of Imitation

Spanning the eighteenth century—early and late—is a remarkable group of English and Scottish critics, aestheticians, and philosophers, perhaps not major figures by the usual standards, but interesting and original in their ideas and approaches. They are enormously varied in their preoccupations but are generally concerned with examining and, more often than not, widening the scope of artistic inquiry. They are loosely united by a concern with forces of the inner rather than the outer life, with faculties of the mind, with beauty and power as forces of the mind, and with the ways by which art is created and affects. Empirical in their orientation, strongly critical of metaphysics, they stress combinations of concrete sensations and associations as sources of knowledge and aesthetic pleasure, and emphasize the stimulation of imagination and emotion as the great power of art.

In this essay I shall examine a key idea in a representative selection of these writers. The idea is the ancient one of art as imitation, and the emphasis is on new shadings as they begin to fill out and enrich the idea. I also argue for a consequent force given to a new defense of subjectivity in literature and art. Why focus on the idea of imitation? There is, to be sure, no dearth of books and articles dealing with the recurring critical concept of poetry—indeed, of art generally—as mimetic, as imitative of men and women in action. Such studies follow the idea from its origins in Plato and Aristotle to its codification in Roman critics like Horace, to its medieval phase where it takes on sharply didactic and religious overtones, to its neoclassical restatement—in conservative Renaissance theorists like Sir Philip Sidney and more flexibly and openmindedly in Restoration and eighteenth-century critics like Dryden, Pope, and Johnson.

There is certainly no need to rehearse the premises of earlier studies, although those premises will prove central to an overall understanding of the argument to be developed.[1] My argument will instead see the Anglo-Scottish critics as not so

1. See, among others, Erich Auerbach, *Mimesis: The Representation of Reality in Western Literature*, trans. Willard Trask (Garden City: Doubleday, 1957); M. H. Abrams, *The Mirror and the Lamp* (New York: Oxford University Press, 1968); John Boyd, *The Function of Mimesis and Its Decline* (Cambridge: Harvard University Press, 1968), p. x; the pioneering work of R. S. Crane on classical criticism and on British criticism from 1650 to 1800 in his *Critics and Criticism (Abridged Edition)* (Chicago: University of Chicago Press, 1952), and Richard McKeon's valuable essay, "Literary Criticism and the Concept of Imitation in Antiquity," in Crane's anthology, pp. 147–175. See also Crane's "English Neoclassical Criticism: An Outline Sketch" in the anthology and his "On Writing the History of English Criticism, 1650–1800," *University of Toronto Quarterly*, 22 (1953), 376–391.

See also John Draper, "Aristotelian 'Mimesis' in Eighteenth-Century England," *PMLA*, 36 (1926), 372–400, and Goran Sorban, *Mimesis and Art: Studies in the Origin and Early Development of an Aesthetic Vocabulary* (Stockholm: Svenska borkfrlaget [Bonnier], 1966), p. 128.

Wider ranging but no less important works which deal with the idea of imitation at various points in its history are Jean Hagstrum, *The Sister Arts: The Tradition of Literary Pictorialism and English Poetry from Dryden to Gray* (Chicago: University of Chicago Press, 1958); Walter Hipple, *The Beautiful, the Sublime, and the Picturesque in Eighteenth-Century British Aesthetic Theory* (Carbondale: University of Southern Illinois Press, 1957); G. N. Giordano Orsini, *Organic Unity in Ancient and Later Poetics: The Philosophical Foundation of Literary Criticism* (Carbondale: University of Southern Illinois Press, 1975); M. A. Goldberg, *The Poetics of Romanticism* (Yellow Springs, Ohio: Antioch Press, 1969); and Wallace Jackson, *The Probable and the Marvelous: Blake, Wordsworth, and the Eighteenth-Century Critical Tradition* (Athens, Georgia: University of Georgia Press, 1978), and also his *Immediacy: The Development of a Critical Concept from Addison to Coleridge* (Amsterdam: Rodopi NV, 1973).

much abandoning the idea, but rather—carrying forward a tradition of subjectivity originating in Dryden, Addison, and Burke—struggling to widen its possibilities. Such a widening seems demanded by the rapid psychological and aesthetic developments of the age, developments which do not so much deny the validity of external nature as see the equal or even greater validity of the inner life—the feelings, the imagination—and of the literature which attempts to represent this life. If imitation in its classical roots means the capturing of what is essential in the events and actions of human life—so goes a new question—cannot it also involve the capturing of what is central to the workings of the inner life, with all its nuances? And cannot such imitation, conveyed in language and imagery of power, be said to imitate the truth of reality? More often than not, imitation comes to be seen in a broader perspective, suggesting the representation of the whole external and internal universe or the interaction between them.

As early as Anthony Ashley Cooper, third Earl of Shaftesbury, a philosopher-critic who in many ways exemplifies the traditionalism of neoclassicism, we can observe a more decidedly subjective view of art.[2] Coming from a family actively involved in politics, Shaftesbury, who was often in poor health, became interested in philosophy and art and published his key ideas in his *Characteristics of Men, Manners, Opinions, Times* (1711). Nature was for him not simply the materials of empirical reality but those materials touched by the human mind, by a highly perfected taste. "A

2. Martin Price pays elaborate tribute to Shaftesbury and his defense of art in *To the Palace of Wisdom: Studies in Order and Energy from Dryden to Blake* (Garden City: Doubleday, 1964), p. 98: "Shaftesbury's theory of art seems to have developed out of his use of the analogy of aesthetic and actual experience in the *Characteristics*, and, with the fragments that make up the *Second Characters*, it is the most complete and impressive theory recorded by an English writer of the age." Citations from Shaftesbury are from *Characteristics of Men, Manners, Opinions, Times, Anthony, Earl of Shaftesbury*, ed. John M. Robertson, with an introduction by Stanley Green, 2 vols. (Indianapolis and New York: Bobbs-Merrill, 1964).

painter," he says, discussing the issue of imitation, "if he has any genius, understands the truth and unity of design; and knows he is even then unnatural when he follows Nature too close, and strictly copies life. For his art allows him not to bring all nature into his piece, but a part only. However, his piece, if it be beautiful, and carries truth, must be a whole, by itself, complete, independent, and withal as great and comprehensive as he can make it" (I, 94).

Only the artist, the virtuoso with the innate moral sense and taste, can create the great work; "if he has not at least the idea of perfection to give him aim, he will be found very defective and near in his performance" (I, 214). Such an artist probes the heart and explores the geography of the soul; he imitates the inner life. Even the artist who imitates a certain outward grace and beauty seems to discover, in the midst of false manners and unrefined styles, a "true and natural one, which represented the real beauty and Venus of the kind. 'Tis the like moral grace and Venus which, discovering itself in the turns of character and the variety of human affection, is copied by the writing artist." Lacking this discovery, he can never capture the fullness of life whether he stays close to the outlines of the actual or whether he indulges a more daring and wide-ranging imagination in his representations (I, 217).

In "*Soliloquy*: or, Advice to an Author," Shaftesbury develops further the theme of imitation of the inner life, using a fascinating metaphor to advance his idea of the particularly mimetic quality of art and to convey his advice on how the artist should proceed. It is highly emotional advice for an early eighteenth-century theorist to be offering, not urging the writer to abandon an awareness of the world around him, but strongly advising him to "set afoot the powerfullest faculties of his mind, and assemble the best forces of his wit and judgment, in order to make a formal descent on the territories of the heart, resolving to decline no combat, nor hearken to any terms, till he has pierced into its inmost provinces and reached the seat of empire" (I, 228–229).

Such an approach to the artist and his work implies a sense of art as relatively autonomous, as somewhat free from the restraints of philosophy and religion. Art for Shaftesbury, rationalist though he be in many ways, is a form of knowing, a way of giving energy to the truths of experience. The artist, he says, can "give to an action its just body and proportions." Elevating the artist to the status of a "second maker, a just Prometheus under Jove," and articulating the organicism of Coleridge's descriptions of the secondary imagination, he sees this artist as forming "a whole, coherent and proportional in itself, with due subjection and subordination of constituent parts" (I, 136).[3] Still operating within the limits of a neoclassical vocabulary, Shaftesbury nevertheless—now with echoes of Plato, Plotinus, and the seventeenth-century Cambridge Platonists, and now with anticipations of the Romantic critics—advances a more subjective view of the artist and of art as expressive of the heart's penetration of the inner world. Though early in the process, he is a force in the evolution of a more personal mimesis and a more inward aesthetic.

There are few more thorough and provocative discussions of imitation in eighteenth-century literary theory than Alexander Gerard's *Essay on Taste*. A Scot to the core, he was born in 1728 in Aberdeenshire, the son of a minister. After gaining his M.A. from Marischal College, Aberdeen, he went on to study theology at Aberdeen and Edinburgh and later held the chair of philosophy and became professor of divinity at Marischal. In 1771 he became professor of divinity at King's College, Aberdeen. Active in philosophical circles, especially among followers of the Common-Sense philosophy opposed to the dominant empiricism of David Hume and others, he published his influential *Essay on Taste* in 1759

---

3. Ernest Tuveson, in "Shaftesbury and the Age of Sensibility," *Studies in Criticism and Aesthetics, 1660–1800*, ed. Howard Anderson and John S. Shea (Minneapolis: University of Minnesota Press, 1967), p. 85, develops at great length these phrases describing the artist and the implications of these phrases for a new way of talking about the mimetic dimension of art.

and *Essay on Genius* in 1774. Gerard is clearly a major figure in what has come to be known as the Scottish intellectual Renaissance.

Gerard's *Essay on Taste* is important here for a number of reasons, but chiefly because it sees poetry as both imitative and non-imitative when measured against traditional criteria. With Gerard we see a careful distinction made between the mode of representation in the several arts and a consequent sharpening of the mimetic power of poetry. Put perhaps too crudely, poetry is not imitative if by that term we mean a kind of art—witness painting and sculpture—which represents exactly by its medium a reality beyond the mind. It is, however, even when the term seems weak and ambiguous and cries out for another, imitative in the sense that Aristotle suggests in the *Poetics*. Poetry, by its use of language, with its vagueness and at times even confusion, invades, to go back to Shaftesbury's image, the territories of the heart. It communicates not an exact but certainly a probable representation of the persons, actions, and attitudes of life as conceived by the poet.

The growing interiority of much British criticism can be felt at the beginning of Gerard's *Essay*. "Taste," as his definition goes, "consists chiefly in the improvement of those principles which are commonly called the *powers of imagination*, and are considered by modern philosophers as internal or reflex senses, supplying us with finer and more delicate perceptions than any which can be referred to our external organs."[4] True imitations for Gerard are not copies in the familiar sense. They consist not in "exactness," but in the "excellence which they represent; and the gratification which these copies afford, may almost as properly be ascribed to beauty or sublimity as to imitation" (p. 49). If

---

4. *An Essay on Taste (1759) Together With Observations Concerning The Imitative Nature of Poetry by Alexander Gerard.* Facsimile Reproduction of the Third Edition (1780) with an Introduction by Walter J. Hipple, Jr. (Gainesville: Scholar's Facsimiles and Reprints, 1963), pp. 1–2. All references to Gerard are to this splendid edition. I am greatly indebted to Hipple's introductory essay.

such premises are granted—and we note in the above a foreshadowing of Hazlitt's ideas of poetry and imitation—ordinary ideas of imitation must give way. The "rudest rocks and mountains"; "objects in nature that are most deformed"; "disease and pain"—we often hear echoes of Addison and Burke—are phenomena that can acquire beauty when skillfully imitated in painting. As a matter of fact, Gerard continues, it is the imitation of what are usually regarded as "imperfections" and "absurdities" that can bring a pleasure deeper than mere copying of what is considered "good" and "proper." In an argument that seems like a modernization of Aristotle's idea of imitation leading to catharsis, and at times like Hazlitt's and Keats's view of Shakespearean tragedy as offering an intensity of representation whereby "all disagreeables evaporate," he addresses Shakespeare to illustrate his point:

> A perfect imitation of characters morally evil, can make us dwell with pleasure on them, notwithstanding the uneasy sentiments of disapprobation and abhorrence which they excite. The character of Iago is detestable, but we admire Shakespeare's representation of it. Nay, imperfect and mixt characters are, in all kinds of writing, preferred to faultless ones, as being juster copies of real nature. The pleasant sensation resulting from imitation is so intense, that it overpowers and converts into delight even the uneasy impressions which spring from the objects imitated. (p. 51)

Gerard is one of several critics and theorists who, in challenging poetry's right to be called imitative, actually proceed to redefine imitation, to recast Aristotle's idea in eighteenth-century terms. In the process two things stand out: (1) a widening of the objects of imitation; and (2) a more psychologically sophisticated consideration and defense of the particular ways by which poetic imitation is carried out. Painting and sculpture are seen as the "most perfect" imitations because, on an obvious level, they produce the "most perfect likeness" (p. 53).

In this sense poetry is "more imperfectly mimetic" than the other arts—"imitating by instituted symbols no wise resembling things" (p. 55), but, ironically, in this very imperfection resides its peculiar merit, its uniqueness, its power to engage the heart and draw it to a more intense perception of reality. In a statement all the more remarkable given its midcentury date, Gerard does not avoid the term "mimetic" and adopt a new one like "expressive," but rather gives a new shape and fullness to the old Aristotelian term. The superiority of poetry to all its sister arts, he argues, "is its peculiar and unrivalled power of imitating the noblest and most important of all subjects, the calmest sentiments of the heart, and human characters displayed in a long series of conduct." The premise underlying this claim is not just "the excellence of the instruments or manners of imitation claimed by all the sister-arts, but also the moment of what they imitate, and the value of the 'ends' to which they are adapted" (p. 55). Gerard lends greater complexity to this question of what are the objectives of imitation. The representation of a psychologically rich experience, blending things new and natural, enlightened by the power of fiction and a rich variety of imagery, is poetry's unique claim to excellence, and such a claim is central to the new defense of poetry.

In the appendix to the essay called "Concerning the Question, Whether Poetry be properly an Imitative Art? and if it be, In what sense is it Imitative?" Gerard cites Aristotle as the father of the idea of poetry as imitation and complains about the lack of any clear definition or description of the nature of this imitation. He further cites contemporary theorists like Lord Kames who deny that poetry is imitative, arguing only for painting and sculpture. These other arts capture the form and shape of visible objects and communicate the resemblance to the appropriate senses. Even dramatic poetry may be considered properly imitative, not simply describing but exhibiting conversations and actions. Lyric poetry—where "the poet, in his own person, describes or relates," where the urgency of emotion is expressed—presents the problem. Here the poet struggles with language in order to articulate the complex rhythms of the heart. Such language, such signs, of course, "bear no resemblance to the things signified by them; and therefore the poem can

have no proper resemblance to the thing described in it"
(pp. 277–278).
Yet poetry is imitative if in a quite different and striking
way, the way in which painting of a certain kind is.

But suppose that a painter, instead of copying an individual object
with which he is acquainted, invents a subject, suppose for
instance, that he paints a Hercules, from a standard idea in his own
mind; in this case, the picture is not an imitation, as being a copy
or resemblance of any one individual existing in nature. It is still
an imitation, but in a quite different sense; the subject itself is an
imitation; it is, not a real individual, but a general representation of
the make of a strong man. The imitation made by poetry, is of this
very kind. The poet conceives his subject; and this subject is an
imitation; it is not, in all its circumstances, a thing which really
exists in nature, or a fact which has really happened; it only resembles things which exist, or which have happened. (pp. 280–281)

Gerard builds solidly on the Aristotelian distinction
between history (things as they are) and poetry (things as
they may be). Poetry represents the probable; the poet, in
imagining his subject, is, in that very action, imitating. Like
many other theorists of the time, Gerard will often use the
term "description" to suggest more precisely the imitation of
the inner life. He consistently separates mere adherence to
the real thing, accompanied by fanciful, adorning imagery,
from that which is most distinctive of true poetry, namely,
its simultaneity with the processes of nature. This is surely
the kind of defense of literature to be seen in force fifty
years later in the criticism of Wordsworth and Coleridge.
"In a word," says Gerard, "poetry is called an imitation, not
because it produces a lively idea of its immediate subject, but
because this subject itself is an imitation of some part of real
nature" (p. 283).

It is what the interior universe of the artist brings to the
world outside that constitutes great art. It is the imagination
of the artist which invents and creates the language, signs,
symbols which may not have a resemblance to the subject in
and of itself but which excite "an idea of the object
described, as conceived by the poet" (pp. 277–278). In the

Iliad Homer "only takes his hints from the real events of the Trojan war; he introduces the heroes who served in it; but he engages them in whatever combats he thinks proper; he feigns those circumstances, those turns of success, and those consequences of the several combats, which produce the best effects on the imagination and the passions . . . The subject of every poem, is to a certain degree a *fable*; and to the very same degree, it is an imitation" (p. 283). Gerard has taken the idea of imitation in a new direction and justified a literature more subjective but no less real.

James Beattie, celebrated author of the exuberantly romantic poem *The Minstrel* and professor of philosophy at Marishal College, Aberdeen, is also important as a literary theorist who discusses the imitative aspect of art and defends a new kind of poetry. Although not as direct as some contemporaries in his references to Aristotelian themes, he nevertheless reveals a full awareness of these themes. In his most famous work, *Essays: On Poetry and Music as They Affect the Mind; On Laughter, and Ludicrous Composition; On the Usefulness of Classical Learning* (1762), he stresses, in the tradition of neoclassical criticism, the teaching and pleasing functions of literature but goes on to distinguish sharply poetry from history and philosophy.[5] Unlike the others, "the poet must do a greater deal for the sake of pleasure only; and if he fail to please, he may indeed deserve praise on other accounts, but as a poet, he has done nothing" (pp. 9–10). Indeed, pleasure communicated through the engagement of the inner life is the vehicle through which poetry achieves its unique educative power. Poetry is not concerned with "merely the communication of moral and physical truth" (p. 19).

Beattie grounds his idea of imitation in this emphasis on pleasure as a central purpose of poetry. Since we do not derive pleasure from the unnatural, he argues, poetry must proceed in accordance with nature. But it must not simply

5. James Beattie, *Essays: On Poetry and Music . . .* (London, 1779).

duplicate nature; it must, without distorting the essential, see
its more vital meanings in new ways. In so doing, it is more
pleasurable because we grant greater freedom to its fictions
and modes of expression, and "consequently that poetry
must be, not according to real nature, but according to
nature improved to that degree, which is consistent with probability, and suitable to the poet's purpose. And hence it is
that we call Poetry, "AN IMITATION OF NATURE." An
"imitation," properly so called, has within it something *not*
in the original. "If the prototype and transcript be exactly
alike, if there be nothing in the one which is not in the
other; we call the latter a representation, a copy, a draught,
or a picture of the former; but we may never call it an imitation" (pp. 86–87). Only when it readily puts one in mind of
the thing imitated can art be called imitative (p. 129).

Beattie continues to widen the concept of imitation already
noted and, in so doing, anticipates Romantic manifestoes. In
a passage that catalogues the objects of imitation—a passage
that underlines the quest of art for "the highest possible
perfection"—he pays a great deal of attention to the
representation of the inner life. Poetical representations, he
says, must rival the highest excellence they are capable of
achieving. External nature must be more picturesque; action
more vigorous; "sentiments more expressive of the feelings
and character, and more suitable to the circumstances of the
speaker" (p. 54). This pattern of perfection is not to be
found in real nature, but in the mind of the poet, ultimately
shaped by an informed imagination. The poet, in addressing
the reader, in trying to evoke joy or sorrow, admiration or
terror, "generally copies an idea of his own imagination, an
idea rooted in concrete experience" (p. 56). What Beattie is
doing is stressing an older emphasis on poetry's attempt to
capture the universal in the particular, to complete nature,
including in that universal an area of life—emotional,
imaginative—often neglected in previous and even contemporary discussions.

Beattie uses two striking literary examples to point up his
emphasis on the imitation of the inner life in poetry. We
can observe a strong suggestion of a theory of the lyric with

emphasis on the speaker, state of mind, and the nature of expression. He considers Anacreon, the Greek lyric poet, and Thomas Gray's eloquent bard in the poem of the same name and treats them as speakers of their respective poems. Anacreon warbles his songs in the midst of flowers, his mind and spirit indolent and caught up in objects of his pleasure. Gray's bard, surrounded by the sublime desolation of mountains and streams, curses Edward I, persecutor of bards, and, caught up in fits of passions, prophesies disaster for the king and his descendants. "If perspicuity and simplicity," says Beattie in comparing the two lyric voices, "be natural in the images of Anacreon, as they certainly are, a figurative style and desultory composition are no less natural in this inimitable performance of Gray" (p. 269).

In Beattie and other critics of the age, there is an interest in the character of the poet, to be sure—the intensity of feelings, the activity of imagination, the depth of sympathy with nature. There is further a new, and profoundly psychological, concern with the audience. The good work of art, the successful poet, by a figured representation of strong feeling, must of necessity draw the audience closer to the external and internal universe, must provoke them to feel the beauties of sea, sky, and mountain, to share sympathetically joy and sorrow, exaltation and pain, and consequently to widen their awareness. In language that strongly suggests Hazlitt's idea of gusto, Beattie argues that if the true poet would move "the passions and sympathies of mankind," his own must be moved, that many passions, by their very nature, "increase the activity of the imagination" (pp. 266–267). In provoking them thus, the poet is an educative force in society, and his art is moral in the noblest sense. To share intensely the condition of another person, whether it be pleasurable or painful, is healthful and constructive. "Hence the good of others becomes in some measure our good, and their evil our evil; the obvious effect of which is to bind men more closely in society, and prompt them to promote the good, and relieve the distresses of one another" (p. 193).

Richard Hurd, for twenty-eight years Bishop of Worcester and celebrated chiefly for his pioneering justification of the Gothic in his *Letters on Chivalry and Romance*, needs also to be considered in any treatment of the shifting focus of imitation. A classical scholar, Hurd edited Horace's *Ars poetica* in 1794 and *Epistola ad Augustum* in 1751. To the latter he added "A Discourse Concerning Poetical Imitation." Another essay of importance—"A Letter to Mason, on the Marks of Imitation"—appeared in 1757.[6]

Hurd is quite specific in talking about imitation. In "Dissertation III on Poetical Imitation," he cites Aristotle's view of poetry as "the noblest and most extensive of the mimetic arts; having all creation for its object, and ranging the entire circuit of universal being" (p. 111). Interesting in this rather straightforward statement is the emphasis on a range of imitation, on poetry's world as an extensive and inclusive wealth of universal being. Hurd proceeds to amplify on this matter of the breadth of poetry's concern as he outlines the materials over which the active imagination of the poet travels. There is, of course, the material world. But—and this is more significant for our purposes in this essay—there is a strong focus on the poet, on the "*internal workings of his own mind, under which I comprehend the manners, sentiments, and passions,*" or, moving beyond poetry, on "*those internal operations, that are made objective to sense by the outward signs of gesture, attitude, or action*" (pp. 115–116).

In this area of imitating—"in imitating the *marks* of vigorous affection," writers differ considerably. The challenge is great. Not only must artists capture the wondrous variety of the world around them, but also the vast complexity and richness of the world within. Hurd has widened the circumference of nature to include external and internal reality and the interaction of the two. Great art must explore the subjective as well as objective if it is to fulfill its chief

---

6. *The Works of Richard Hurd, D.D. Lord Bishop of Worcester, in Eight Volumes* (London, 1811), II.

mission of imitation. The movements of the inner life, if not visible to the eye, are no less real than *"permanent, external existences"*; "to succeed in this work of painting the *signatures of internal affection*, requires a larger experience, or quicker penetration, than copying after *still life"* (p. 148).

Lest he be seen as advancing the idea of a highly subjective, idiosyncratic form of imitation and of art, Hurd is careful, in a summing-up statement like the following, to stress the classical notion of the persistence of the subjects of great art, extending those subjects, however, to include not just significant human actions but also human emotions that do not change essentially over the centuries. Anticipating the Romantic idea of the creative imagination, he stresses the power of mind. Experience, he says, provides the materials of imitations just as it provides the stuff of human knowledge, but "it is in the *operations* of the mind upon them, that the glory of *poetry*, as of *science*, consists" (pp. 176 – 177).

Pleasure comes ultimately from activity of the mind, and it is this activity that the best poetry stimulates. As he puts it, in graphic language and imagery that seem to look ahead to the later *Discourses* of Sir Joshua Reynolds, pleasure "is the ultimate and appropriate end of poetry." But, unlike other kinds of writing which are under the control of reason and which *"buckle and bow the mind to the nature of things,"* poetry "accommodates itself to the desires of the mind" and seeks to "gratify" those desires. For pleasure, he contends, comes not from the calm recognition of some objective idea or beauty beyond the self but from the engagement of the mind by a recognition in a work of art of what it passionately seeks but cannot completely find in the ordinary business of living. Poetry gratifies the mind's desires, but in a vitally unique way, a way that challenges and outdistances the ways of philosophy, history, and other forms of knowledge (pp. 3 – 4).

Lest one feel that there is anything like a consensus on the idea of imitation in eighteenth-century Anglo-Scottish criticism, it might be useful to look at either different shadings of opinion or in some cases strongly negative reactions to any suggestion that poetry is, in Aristotle's terms, imitative. To several critics the chief objection is rooted in the idea that any genuine imitation must have a natural resemblance to the thing imitated. Hence poetry, with the fertile but ambivalent medium of language, cannot match the immediacy of sculpture and painting, which evoke more directly the objects of imitation. Often the activity of poetry is described as "description," and the effect created is called "sympathy," although it seems relatively clear that these words represent an attempt to give more scope to the term "imitation" and that they reveal the critic's struggle to come to terms with a widening of human consciousness and the need to represent it. Hugh Blair in *Lectures on Rhetoric and Belles Lettres* is a good example.[7] Born in 1718, Blair was part of a Scottish literary circle that included David Hume and Adam Smith. A minister noted for his sermons, he was also a professor of rhetoric at the University of Edinburgh. His rhetorical writings were enormously influential during the century in England and America.

Citing both Aristotle and Addison as sources in his *Lectures*—examples of both classical and Romantic views of imitation—Blair complains of the lack of precision in contemporary critical language and contends, "Neither discourse in general, nor poetry in particular, can be called altogether imitative arts" (p. 94). The distinction between "Imitation" and "Description" must be made. Sounding like Addison on the pleasures of the imagination, he argues that poetry derives its great power from "significancy of words" (p. 96). The power, however, is one of description, not of imitation, description being "the raising in the mind the conception of an object by means of some arbitrary or instituted symbols, understood only by those who agree in the institution of them; such are words and writing" (p. 94). In another

---

7. *Lectures on Rhetoric and Belles Lettres by Hugh Blair, D.D.*, 2 vols. ed. Harold F. Harding, foreword by David Potter (Carbondale and Edwardsville: Southern Illinois University Press, 1965), I.

treatise, *A Critical Dissertation on the Poems of Ossian*, Blair, an ardent supporter and defender of James Macpherson's wildly romantic Ossian poetry, stresses the power of primitive poetry to capture "the most natural pictures of ancient manners." What these pictures offer is not simply a historical account—surely a less valuable record—but "the history of human imagination and passion." Such a history provokes sympathy, makes us "acquainted with the notions and feelings of our fellow creatures in the most artless ages."[8]

The same kinds of reservations about a more traditional concept of imitation can be found in Henry Home, Lord Kames, in his celebrated *Elements of Criticism in Three Volumes* (Edinburgh, 1762), an attempt to construct a full-blown aesthetics and a work that was widely read in Scotland, on the Continent, and in America.

Connecting criticism to the heart as well as the head, Kames sees his principles as drawn "from human nature." Like Blair, he regards only painting and sculpture as by their very nature imitative (I, 16). "Language," he says, "has no archetype in nature, more than music or architecture; unless where, like music, it is imitative of sound or motion" (II, 234). Sounding again like Addison on the secondary pleasures of the imagination—those pleasures not in bodies but in the mind—he contrasts the order and regularity of beauty with the ruggedness and power of grandeur and sublimity. The latter "generally signify the quality or circumstances in the objects by which the emotions are produced; sometimes the emotions themselves" (I, 266). Using the word "description" as a matter of course, and using it to suggest a wider ranging kind of representation, he praises the power of art, of language, to convey more than reality itself. Vivid and accurate description raises ideas no less distinct. "I have not words to describe this act, other than that I perceive the thing as a spectator, and as existing in my presence" (I,

---

8. Hugh Blair, *A Critical Dissertation on the Poems of Ossian, the Son of Fingal* (London, 1765), p. 1.

108). Language, never completely adequate to the great task of evoking a sense of reality, of what Kames calls "ideal presence," has nevertheless a power to suggest in the mind the nuances of experience often not apparent in a matter-of-fact account. It yields up the riches of creation in a way history cannot. In offering lively and distinct images, it stirs the reader's passions by throwing him into "a kind of reverie, in which state, losing the consciousness of self and of reading, his present occupation, he conceives every incident as passing in his presence, precisely as if he were an eyewitness" (I, 112).

Built into Kames' aesthetic of representation is a new defense of fiction. Not merely a fanciful creation, not simply an adorning of everyday experience, it holds meaning in the confines of its language and imagery. Man's intellectual faculties can take him a distance, but they lack that quality of sympathy which enables him to enter into and share the fullness of experience. They simply cannot "dive far even into his own nature" (I, 105). Only the emotions, the faculties addressed by the fictions of art, can confront the complexity of human experience and convey a sense of ideal presence. Language, "by means of fiction, has the command of our sympathy for the good of others. By the same means, our sympathy may also be raised for our own good." For Kames no other discipline does more to make virtue habitual, to drive its truth home not just to the head, but to the heart— to the full range of human awareness. Fiction holds a power over the mind that affords "an endless variety of refined amusement," and such amusement "is a fine resource in solitude, and by ... sweetening the temper, improves society" (I, 126–127).

Sir William Jones, one of the great scholars of the age, a linguist fluent in thirteen languages and a specialist in oriental languages and literatures, is the author of two striking essays appended to his *Poems, Consisting Chiefly of Translations from the Asiatic Languages* (1772).[9] One of them, "On the Arts Commonly Called Imitative," is especially important for our purposes, taking the position, as it does, that "though poetry and music have, certainly, a power of imitating the manners of men and several objects in nature, yet their greatest effect is not produced by imitation, but by a very different principle, which must be sought for in the deepest recesses of the human mind" (II, 872). Here again we see the theorist challenging the Aristotelian mimetic designation and posing the problem of the inwardness of poetry. The artist is not so much an imitator of nature as the voice of nature herself, and the true subject matter of poetry is the inner life, passion, and sympathy. Consequently, Jones is primarily concerned with lyric poetry, with the Song of Solomon, the Prophets, the lyrics of Alcaeus, Alcman, and Ibycus, the hymns of Callimachus, the elegy of Moschus on Bion, with a kind of poetry where there is no real imitation as Aristotle conceived it. Even though some kinds of painting are strictly imitative in that they capture exactly in line and color their subjects, the greatest picture—the various representations of the Crucifixion, Domenichino's painting of the martyrdom of St. Agnes— "cannot be said to imitate, but that its most powerful influence over the mind arises, like that of the other arts, from sympathy" (II, 879).

Like other critics in this section, Jones is puzzled by the challenge of dealing with a new problem—how to designate a poetry that represents not the world around us but that within us, how to find a vocabulary that will enable one to talk about the lyric. Grounded in the classics and in the classical views of Aristotle, he cannot, at least on the surface, think of lyric poetry as imitative. Words and sounds "have no kind of resemblance to visible objects; and what is an imitation but a resemblance of some other thing?" (II, 879).

---

9. Sir William Jones, in *Eighteenth-Century Critical Essays*, ed. Scott Elledge, 2 vols. (Ithaca: Cornell University Press), II, 838–848.

At the same time, however, Jones is keenly aware of the power of the inner life and the need to represent it in poetry. What results is not so much the rejection of the idea of imitation, but rather the search for language to describe more adequately the representation of passion, especially in lyric poetry. Predictably, the two most common words are "description" and "sympathy," and the approach taken is very much that of Addison when he discusses the secondary pleasures of the imagination. One cannot help noticing in Jones's analysis that he is struggling to deal with how, psychologically, feeling is communicated by the artist and received by the audience. What is being expressed, it would seem, is an aesthetic of imitation as it relates to the inner life, an aesthetic that might be described as follows: (1) since the emotions are vital aspects of human life, art must represent them; (2) but such emotions do not lend themselves to the kind of direct imitation that one might find in painting and sculpture; (3) therefore, strong and vital language and imagery are needed to trigger in the minds of the audience an awareness of and a sympathy with the feelings expressed.

In a fascinating section at the end of his essay, Jones argues for the superiority of imitation by sympathy over imitation by exact description. Such exact description—not that description already considered in this essay—is, he contends, "the meanest part" of both poetry and music, for true imitation lies in resemblance, not duplication. He then creates a scene in which a poet, musician, and painter are attempting to convey to a friend or patron the pleasure each has felt at the sight of a beautiful prospect. The poet "will form an agreeable assemblage of level images which he will express in smooth elegant verses of a sprightly measure; he will describe the most delightful objects, and will add to the graces of his description a certain delicacy of sentiment, and a spirit of cheerfulness." The musician will similarly create strong effects by utilizing the many resources of his medium. The painter, however, will, by the very nature of his medium, fall short of his competitors; his pencil may "express a simple passion" but cannot paint a thought or draw the "shades of sentiment." The painter can, however, achieve his own success with graceful and elegant landscapes, rich and glowing colors, striking perspective, and great variety. Once again—this time in Jones—we see the strong emphasis on poetry, as well as other art, as conveyor of the passions. The finest art moves beyond mere duplication to suggest the possibilities of nature and to draw readers and spectators to those possibilities with a strong and genuine sympathy.

In James Harris (1709–1780), whose uncle was the Earl of Shaftesbury, we find another eighteenth-century figure who explores aesthetics in new and interesting ways. After graduating from Wadham College, Oxford, he pursued legal studies at Lincoln's Inn, acted as magistrate for the County of Wiltshire, and later served as a lord of the Admiralty (1762), a lord of the Treasury (1763), and secretary and comptroller to the queen (1774). He wrote in the course of his career on a variety of topics, but it is the aesthetic that concerns us here.

In 1744 Harris published his *Three Treatises: I. Concerning Art. II. Concerning Music, Painting, and Poetry. III. Concerning Happiness.*[10] In the first two Harris conducts a systematic examination of the foundation of art, an account of its manifestations in music, painting, and poetry, a detailed analysis of the mimetic power of poetry, and a defense of its moral force in society. In the first treatise, dedicated to Shaftesbury and using the techniques of the aesthetic dialogue so often employed by the philosopher, the speakers agree on a wideranging subject matter for art. "If this, continued he, be true, it should seem that the common or universal subject of art was, all those contingent natures which lie within the reach of the human powers to influence.—I acknowledge, said I, it appears so" (p. 11). In an extraordinary statement, Aristotelian in its force, the

10. *The Works of James Harris, Esq. with an account of his life and character by his son The Earl of Malmesbury* (London, 1841).

speakers agree on the final cause of art—a cause neither didactic nor aesthetic. In language that suggests art's power to do more than entertain or instruct in the narrow sense, to outdo nature and hence to reveal it in its essential outlines, the dialogue proceeds. The first speaker argues that art is created and all its operations are brought to bear by "the want or absence of something appearing good; relative to human life, and attainable by man, but superior to his natural and uninstructed faculties." And the second speaker quickly agrees that "the account appeared probable" (pp. 16–17).

In the second treatise, still in an Aristotelian vein, Harris clearly assumes that the informed reader is familiar with classical and neoclassical assumptions about imitation. There is also a desire to push forward, to explore all shadings of those assumptions, to advance a contemporary view of imitation responsive to the realities of nature and the psychological complexity of the human person. Again the force of Addison's views seems a strong one. First, there is the emphasis on sensation, on the mind being "made conscious of the natural world and its affections, and of other minds and their affections, by the several organs of the senses." Then there is the widening of the process of imitation; the arts of music, painting, and poetry "imitate either parts or affections of this natural world, or else the passions, energies, and other affections of mind." These arts, then, are "all mimetic or imitative" and differ only as they imitate by different media, "painting and music, by media which are natural; poetry, for the greatest part, by a medium which is artificial" (p. 28).

Poetry, according to Harris, has up to this time received attention for "mere natural resemblance" (p. 33), an inferior form of imitation, and one that is carried off better by painting and music. Poetry's medium of words renders it "less similar, less immediate, and less intelligible" than painting (p. 35), and yet poetry aspires to rival the imitations of painting and music. Language, for all its inadequacies, is the magical medium to convey the complex rhythms of human feeling. Actually "in manners and passions there is no other which can exhibit them to us after that clear, precise, and definite way, as they in nature stand allotted to the various sorts of men, and are found to constitute the several characters of each" (p. 38). For Harris poetry is "much superior to either of the other mimetic arts," equally excellent in the accuracy of its imitation" and in its "subjects which far surpass, as well in utility, as in dignity" (p. 39).

Certainly one of the most interesting pieces of criticism in the eighteenth century is the *Lectures on the Sacred Poetry of the Hebrews* (1753, trans. 1787) by Bishop Robert Lowth.[11] It is, of course, a splendid example of a concern with ancient religious poetry as illustrative of those qualities of spontaneity and sublimity that tend to be minimized in more polished and sophisticated eras. It also reveals a new consideration of the Old Testament more as a poetic text than as a religious document. Lowth, born in 1710, succeeded Joseph Spence in the prestigious Oxford Chair of Poetry in 1741. His lectures on a variety of topics, from imagination to allegory, the sublimity of the Old Testament, and ideas of the lyric were collected in his *Lectures*, a work for which Oxford gave him a honorary degree. The magnum opus of this scholar, clergyman, and member of the Royal Society was written in Latin but translated into English in 1787; it became very influential.

For Lowth poetry, in accordance with Aristotle's definition in the *Poetics*, is at root an imitation, although the matter imitated is as varied as *Oedipus the King* and The Book of Job. Lowth sees poetry as the imitation not just of actions but also of emotions; not just of the deeds of great heroes, but also of the inner turmoil of God's creatures. So strong is the emphasis on expression of emotion that M. H. Abrams groups him with his expressive tradition of criticism, constructing a line from Lowth to John Keble and ultimately to

---

11. *Lectures on the Sacred Poetry of the Hebrews by Robert Lowth, D.D.*, trans. from the original Latin by G. Gregory, F.A.S. A New Edition with Notes by Calvin E. Stowe, A.M. (Boston, 1829).

Herder, who claimed Lowth as his source in his *Vom Geist der ebraischen* published in 1782.[12] Abrams is, of course, right to see the expressive dimension of Lowth's criticism, although it is, I think, more fruitful to see what we might call the amplification of the mimetic in his reading of Aristotelian terminology and his formulation of a distinctive idea of imitation that connects him with his eighteenth-century heritage and prepares the way for the Romantics.

Lowth's Lecture 33, "The Poem of Job Not Perfect Drama," uses Aristotle's theory of tragedy as a springboard; it compares *Oedipus the King* and Job—one perfectly Greek and the other thoroughly Hebrew—to illustrate the former's emphasis on plot and action, and the latter's on character and emotion. The documents selected are suggestive not simply because one is more expressive than the other, but because in moving from one to the other, one can see the range of experience—from the external to the internal; from men in action to men in inner turmoil—which Lowth finds in Aristotle's idea of nature.

Lowth's great emphasis is on the sublimity of Hebrew poetry—not merely a sublimity of "objects" charged by powerful imagery and diction, "but that force of composition, whatever it be, which strikes and overpowers the mind, which excites the passions, and which expresses ideas at once with perspicuity and elevation" (pp. 112–113). Taking Longinus as his guide, he focuses sharply on poetry as revelatory of intense feeling and on language as the strong conduit of that feeling. He distinguishes between "the language of reason," with its care and clarity, and "the language of passions," which is completely different; "the conceptions burst out into a turbid stream, expressive in a manner of the inter-

---

12. See especially in *The Mirror and the Lamp*, p. 77: "While Lowth exemplifies a fairly common tendency in the criticism of his day to emphasize the poetic representation of passion, rather than of people and actions, he is notable for conceiving the poem as a mirror which, instead of reflecting nature, reflects the very *penetralia* of the poet's secret mind."

nal conflict; the more vehement break out in hasty confusion; they catch (without search or study) whatever is impetuous, vivid, or energetic" (p. 113).

Whereas the mind speaks straightforwardly and literally, the passions express themselves poetically. He describes the mind when impassioned as struggling to get beyond some kind of exact or literal mode of expression and to find one agreeable to its sensations, more able to communicate concretely the urgency and depth of its feelings. The passions "are naturally inclined to amplification; they wonderfully magnify and exaggerate whatever dwells upon the mind, and labor to express it in animated, bold, and magnificent terms" (p. 113). This expression may take one of two forms. The first is the old-fashioned method of imagery illustrating the subject. The other, more in keeping with the new turning inward of literary and psychological theory, employs "new and extraordinary forms of expression, which are indeed possessed of great force and efficacy in this respect especially, that they in some degree imitate or represent the present habit and state of the soul" (p. 113). Interestingly, the words "imitate" and "represent" are stressed, as is the "state of the soul." Art is for Lowth, the historian and critic of ancient Hebrew poetry, still an imitation, although the subject matter has become increasingly personal.

No study of eighteenth-century literary theorists can be complete if it neglects Adam Smith, who is known best for his economic treatise, *The Wealth of Nations*, but is also crucial for an understanding of a whole range of critical issues in the age. Born in Glasgow and educated at the university and later at Oxford, he went on to lecture at Edinburgh, where he knew important philosophers like Lord Kames and David Hume. For twelve years he was professor of logic at the University of Glasgow, a time during which he wrote his celebrated philosophical treatise, *The Theory of Moral Sentiments* (1759). In this we find his pioneering work on psychological response to the arts, especially on the concept of the sympathetic imagination so central to the Romantic theory of Hazlitt and Keats.

Smith was interested in the foundation of the arts, and particularly in the imitative dimension, as can be seen in a remarkable piece "Of the Nature of that Imitation which takes place in what are called the Imitative arts" in his *Essays on Philospohical Subjects.*[13] Imitation is the heart of the creative process, according to Smith, and close resemblance is not the best kind of imitation. Although the copy may derive some merit from its reminder of an original, "an original can certainly derive none from the resemblance of its copy" (p. 178). Poetry, with its powerful vehicle of language, can express many things fully and distinctly which dance can catch only imperfectly, things "such as the reasonings and judgements of the understanding; the ideas, fancies, and suspicions of the imagination, the sentiments, emotions, and passions of the heart" (p. 189).

Music, however, has a special imitative power, to be matched by none of the other arts. It, of course, strives to make a thing of one kind resemble something of a different kind, shaping and bending as it does the measure and melody so as to capture on the one hand the special tone and language of conversation and on the other hand the special accents and styles of emotion and passion. But the power of music and words in expressing strong passions outdoes every form of discourse which lacks the special graces of music. "Neither Prose nor Poetry," he says, "can venture to imitate those almost endless repetitions of passion." They may describe, but they do not fully imitate. The music of a passionate air, however, frequently does, "and it never makes its way so directly or so irresistibly to the heart as when it does so" (pp. 191 – 192).

Little is known about Thomas Twining beyond the information supplied by editors of his work. A fellow of Sidney Sussex at Cambridge University, a clergyman and rector of

13. Adam Smith, "Of the Nature of that Imitation," in *Essays*, ed. W. P. D. Wightman and J. C. Bryce with *Dugald Stewart's Account of Adam Smith*, ed. I. S. Ross. General editors D. D. Raphael and A. S. Skinner (Oxford: Clarendon Press, 1980).

St. Mary's in Colchester, a devotee of literature and music, a classical scholar praised by contemporaries, his most celebrated work was *Aristotle's Treatise on Poetry, Translated: With Two Dissertations, on Poetical and Musical Imitation* (1789).[14]

As an end-of-the-century theorist, Twining is especially interesting as he looks back on earlier critics. His aim, he tells us, is to clear up a gathering confusion brought about by the writings of many of the critics we have been considering. Like the schoolmaster, he sets out at once, in "On Poetical Imitation," to make distinctions between proper and improper uses of the term. In its proper sense it must meet two conditions—"the resemblance must be immediate, i.e. between the *imitation, or imitative work, itself,* and the object imitated; and, it must also be *obvious.*" In sculpture, painting, mimicry, voice, gesture, "the resemblance is *obvious*; we recognize the object imitated; and it is, also *immediate*—it lies in the imitative *work*, or *energy, itself*, or in other words, in the very materials, or *sensible media*, by which the imitation is conveyed. All *these* copies, therefore, are called strictly and intelligibly imitations" (pp. 4−5).

With poetry the situation is different. Here words are the medium, and, strictly speaking, they imitate only to the extent that there is a resemblance of "words considered as mere sound, to the *sounds* and *motions* of the objects imitated." In a wider sense, however, with words as medium, "the resemblance is so faint and distant and of so general and vague a nature, that it would never, *of itself*, lead us to recognize the object imitated. We discover not the *likeness* till we know the *meaning*" (I, 5−6). The relationship of word and thing is arbitrary or conventional, then; much depends on certain qualities of suggestiveness in the language. Such resemblances, however delicate and suggestive, "are yet a source of real beauties, of beauties *actually*

14. *Aristotle's Treatise on Poetry, trans. with notes on the translation and on the original; and Two Dissertations on poetical and musical imitation by Thomas Twining, M.A.*, 2 vols. (London, 1812).

felt by the reader, when they arise, or appear to arise, spontaneously from the poet's feeling, and their effect is not counteracted by the obviousness of cool intention and deliberate artifice" (I, 7–8).

Poetry, then, first of all is imitative in that its language is not so much sounds and sounds only, but "sounds significant." Sounding Addisonian, Twining regards merely descriptive poetry, like landscape painting, as only a part of artistic imitation conveying, as it does, only a clear idea of its object. Poetry is truly imitative "only in proportion as it is capable of raising an ideal *image* or *picture*, more or less resembling the reality of things" (I, 12–13). Hence it is the imagination of the artist which creates a language and imagery able to elicit the ways in which nature affects the mind. The passion is described by its sensible effects. Twining puts it succinctly when he says that while merely descriptive imitation may offer clear and distinct but also less forceful representation; in the other—he calls it imitative description—the image is only the occasion for effecting the principal aim of such description, "the emotion, of whatever kind, that arises from a strong conception of the passion itself. The image carries us on forcibly to the feeling of its internal cause." Summing up this point, Twining offers his view of the truly imitative as "*this* of passions and emotions, by their *sensible* effects" (I, 23).

Continuing, Twining discusses a third kind of imitation produced by fiction, that in which a new relationship is set up—a resemblance between the ideas raised and still other ideas, the ideas raised being in some ways copies or resemblances, but, strictly speaking, new combinations of those general ideas in the poet's mind. Whereas in description, imitation "is opposed to actual *impression*, external or internal: in fiction, it is opposed to fact." While illusion is a key part of the effect of both, it is a different kind of illusion in each. "Descriptive imitation may be said to produce *illusive perception*; fictive, *illusive belief*" (I, 28).

If one follows the Aristotelian ideas closely, says Twining, only the fourth and final kind of imitation—dramatic or personative poetry—is proper, possessing, as it does, both immediate and obvious resemblance, with speech imitating speech. At the same time he warns against the notion that Aristotle, deeply influenced by the predominance of tragedy in his age and hence understandably stressing the dramatic element, ruled out the descriptive, sonorous, or fictive kinds of imitation. Indeed, the whole tenor of his essay suggests an openness to a broader concept of imitation while stressing the roots of the word in the Plato-Aristotle dialogue in Greek culture. After all, it was early in his essay when he spoke of descriptive imitation as quite properly imitative in its representation of the "emotions, passions, and other internal movements and operations of the mind" (I, 22). It was he who, in the spirit of the sensationalistic philosophies of his time, emphasized the imitative quality of operations of the mind upon experience. So also did he stress the imitative power of the fictive with its capacity to capture truth more vividly and to produce "illusive belief."

This wide-ranging end-of-the-century essay captures much of the speculation of the age. It is, to be sure, conservative in its respect for the tradition going back to Plato and Aristotle and in its desire to develop categories for talking about a proper imitation. Yet it is never exclusive, never closed to the possibilities of Addison's "pleasures of the imagination" or Burke's "sublime," with their emphasis on the centrality of mind in the capturing and presenting of beauty. Twining stresses the gap that has developed in the late eighteenth century between those critics who understand "in what senses, and from what original ideas, Poetry was *first* called imitation by Plato and Aristotle" and those who, still finding poetry designated as imitative, nevertheless "instead of carefully investigating the original meaning of the expression, have had recourse, for its explication, to their own ideas, and have, accordingly, extended it to every sense which the widest and most distant analogy would bear" (I, 58). He is a reconciler of the claims of the traditional and the new, emphasizing poetry's new claim to capture a wider ranging view of nature—both the object and the subject responding to it. He also defends the power of poetry to convey truth as seen by the eyes, understood by the head, and felt by the heart.

A remarkable group of eighteenth-century aesthetician-critics were increasingly preoccupied with the psychological dimensions of art and criticism and often concerned with the idea of art as imitation. These critics—and we have seen a representative if not by any means an exhaustive sampling—offer no one "best" point of view. Some argue that poetry can no longer be regarded as imitative in any traditional sense and must be described with new terminology like "descriptive" or "expressive." Others would broaden the scope of the Aristotelian term to include works of art that represent the widest variety of human experiences. All were eager to find ways of describing a new area of artistic inquiry—the subjective—and to justify this inquiry as worthy of the most advanced critical concern.

Adam, Tinker, and Newton

"You and Newton and I," Chauncey Tinker wrote to R. B. Adam II in 1921, "some trio,"[1] and A. Edward Newton said, "Between us, that is between you and Tinker . . . and [me], we have put Boswell, Johnson, and Company on the map, by God we have!"[2]

In 1909 Chauncey Brewster Tinker, then assistant professor of English literature at Yale, met R. B. Adam II, an eminent book collector and president of a large department store in Buffalo, New York. Tinker was thirty-four and Adam was forty-six the summer that Tinker came to Buffalo to select books from Adam's collection to display in Yale's exhibition celebrating the two hundreth anniversary of Samuel Johnson's birth. In November, when the event was over, Tinker thanked the generous lender and told him that the show had been "largely attended, and highly enjoyed . . . One professor of English in Princeton [Charles Osgood] came all the way to New Haven simply to see your books. He remarked that the forthcoming exhibition at the Grolier

1. CBT to RBA, August 22, 1921. Ms. correspondence of Adam, Tinker, and Newton is in the Adam Archive (Hyde Collection, Somerville, New Jersey). Rosenbach correspondence is in the Rosenbach Museum and Library, Philadelphia.
2. AEN to RBA, February 2, 1923.

Club would be a sad anticlimax after our rich display."
Tinker ended his letter by saying, "Perhaps you will at some
future time again permit me to trespass on your courtesy,
and ask for the favor of making a more extended examination of the books in Buffalo."[3]

Adam was glad to further the acquaintance, and not one
visit but several followed. Tinker's scholarship, appreciation,
and good manners endeared him to the household at 46 Norwood Avenue. He was gracious to Lena Adam, R. B.'s wife,
a charmer in her own right; he paid proper attention to the
two pretty little daughters, Harriet and Florence; and he
formed a life-long friendship with R. B. As collector and
scholar they worked hand in hand, a wonderful relationship
when it occurs. Tinker alerted Adam to purchases and gave
good counsel; Adam loaned Tinker books and manuscripts
for long periods of time; original manuscripts, because this
was before the day of photocopying. Adam even acquired
unpublished material expressly to help Tinker with his work
on "a complete edition of Boswell's correspondence . . .
[also his work on a planned] biography."[4]

"[Y]ou have spoiled me, I now shamelessly ask you for
anything," Tinker wrote in July 1918. And later that year,
"[I]t would be best to tell [Mr. Blue, a Canadian, who
threatened to write a Boswell biography] that you had given
me the right to print the unpublished letters." There were
continual thanks: "I am in my chronic state of gratitude to
you"; "[s]ometimes I think you and I are the only ones in
the world really interested in Boswell's correspondence"; on
receiving the gift of a Boswell letter, "I kiss your foot"; for
another gift, "[l]et me be your worm"; and another, "I
resume my place at your feet. You are Roberto the
Magnificent."[5] But Tinker could also be very stern, as when
he reprimanded Adam for annotating his letters with memos
such as bonuses . . . income tax . . . storm windows . . .

3. CBT to RBA, November 8, 1909.
4. CBT to RBA, October 27, 1918.
5. CBT to RBA, July 29, 1918; October 27, 1918; July 27, 1919;
December 4, 1920; November 24, 1928; May 21, 1926; March 16, 1924.

baby's milk for two days . . . bells on elevators. He would order him not to annotate his letters.

Business man to business man was the very different relationship between Adam and A. Edward Newton, the Philadelphia book collector, author, and president of the Cutter electrical circuit breaker company. They met in 1918,[6] and Tinker did not introduce them, though he knew Newton well through Osgood. Characteristically, Newton introduced himself, simply going to Adam's office one day when he was in Buffalo on business. All his book collecting life he had heard of Adam's library, for George Birkbeck Hill, the celebrated editor of Boswell's *Life of Johnson*, had referred to it in glowing terms in the 1890's as the finest collection of Johnson and Boswell on either side of the Atlantic. When Newton sent in his card, he expected to be greeted by a gentleman in his mid-eighties. He was astounded when he was ushered into the presence of a man about his own age. They were, indeed, exact contemporaries, born in 1863, Adam in July, Newton in August; when they met, they were fifty-four.

Newton said that he had hoped to see the Johnson collection, but he was bitterly disappointed. " 'So soon?' [said Adam], 'how is that?' 'Why' [said Newton], 'I expected to meet a man old enough to be my father. I thought it possible that some day your collection, or part of it, would come to the auction block. Judge how disappointed I am to meet a man as young . . . [as] myself.' 'Ah!' said Mr. Adam with a smile, 'you were thinking of my father!' "[7] Adam explained that R. B. Adam I was actually his uncle who in 1857, in his midtwenties, had emigrated from Scotland with his wife. After working for a thread manufacturing company in Boston for ten years, he moved to Buffalo where he founded a small dry goods store. His name was synonymous with honest

---

6. AEN to RBA, January 3, 1919.

7. Newton's "Preface" in *The R. B. Adam Library Relating to Dr. Samuel Johnson and his Era. Catalogue*, 3 vols. (Oxford University Press, printed in Buffalo, 1929).

dealing, and his store prospered. In time, he became one of the first citizens of Buffalo, public spirited and much loved.

The Adams regretted having no children, and in 1872 the first Adam brought to Buffalo and legally adopted his namesake nephew, Robert Borthwick Adam Scott, nine years old, son of his sister Jean and John Scott, principal of the Academy of Berwick-upon-Tweed. The little boy was personable, adaptable, and bright, but not strong, though later, Adam said, "tough as a hickory nut." But early on he was kept out of school two separate years "or I [would] have been ready for Yale or Harvard by sixteen. I planned to go to Harvard," he wrote to his friend R. W. Chapman in 1927.[8] As it turned out, when young Robert was ready for college, his uncle determined against higher education. R. B. I had had schooling only to the age of ten, and he believed Robert should lose no time in learning the merchandise trade, so R. B. II's career in the store began. During the next few years he served behind the counters of every department and for ten years wrote all the advertising copy for the company.[9]

Newton's early life had followed much the same pattern. He was earning his own living before he was fifteen, and when he went to Cutter, he wrote the ads for the electrical appliances; this developed his style of writing, he later claimed. For Newton and Adam, their libraries were not only relaxation and pleasure, they were their universities. The senior Adam and young Newton had been active book buyers in this country and in England in the 1880's. Newton went to London for the first time in 1884 and there, he said, "I fell under the lure of Dr. Johnson and Charles Lamb. After that, the deluge."[10] His ambition was to have a "first issue of every great, superlatively great book in English

8. RBA to RWC, November 26, 1927.
9. *Rochester Democrat Chronicle*, September 6, 1936.
10. *Amenities of Book Collecting* (Boston: Atlantic Monthly Press, 1918), p. 10.

literature."[11] The first Adam's ambition was perhaps more modest but still on a grand scale. He wanted to have the finest collection of Burns, the finest collection of Ruskin, and the finest collection of Johnson. Birkbeck Hill was his advisor in the last field.

It was the Johnson collection that prompted Newton's call, and he knew from the first Adam's 1895 catalogue exactly what he wanted to see: Johnson's MS "Plan of the Dictionary"; the proof sheets of Johnson's "Life of Pope," with manuscript corrections by Johnson and an inscription to Fanny Burney; Goldsmith's *Traveller* and *Deserted Village*, annotated by Boswell; and Boswell's revised proof sheets of the *Life of Johnson*. Two of the manuscripts mentioned, and hundreds of others, were in the magnificent volumes of Birkbeck Hill's five standard books on Johnson, twelve volumes, extended by the first Adam's extra-illustration (letters, documents, portraits, and views bound in) to thirty-eight volumes, and after the first Adam's death in 1904, further extended to fifty-nine volumes by the second Adam. The set, in full brown morocco, elaborately tooled in gold, was a masterpiece of the Club Bindery and is still considered one of the most spectacular examples of extra-illustration in existence.

Newton saw a few books and manuscripts on his first visit, and on subsequent visits he came to know the library well. The two businessmen understood each other, had the same philosophy of life, point of view, judgment, sense of humor, and the same enjoyment in a number of things which were an anathema to Tinker: such as traveling for pleasure, meeting all manner of new persons, entertaining and being entertained, and joining clubs. They were as clubbable as Johnson himself.

Newton encouraged Adam to join the Grolier Club,[12] and proposed him for life membership in the Lichfield Johnson

11. A. E. Newton, *End Papers* (Boston: Little, Brown, 1933), p. 27.

12. R. B. Adam I, a clubbable man also, was elected to Grolier membership in 1892. Newton, thirty years his junior, was elected in 1890.

Society; Adam himself soon had the pleasure of making his infant son and namesake, of whom he was very proud, a life member as well. As for the Johnson Club of London, Adam was the first American member.

Friends meant much to Adam, and he liked to share his pleasure in books with them. In 1919 he began his series of Christmas keepsakes with a facsimile of his important purchase at the recent Morrison sale, Boswell's manuscript notebook, a diary thought to be an unique manuscript source for the *Life of Johnson.* Adam had fifty copies of the little notebook printed, and Newton, an old hand at Christmas booklets, suggested a few names for his list of recipients: obvious institutions, himself of course, and Tinker (who was overjoyed to have the Boswell treasure in Adam's possession), Beverly Chew, Amy Lowell, Christopher Morley, and Johnsonian professors Robert Rodgers and Charles Osgood—also Dr. A. S. W. Rosenbach.[13]

Newton had recently brought Adam and the Doctor together, and the voluminous correspondence of these two had begun; personal notes, invitations, thank you's and, every few days, letters from the Rosenbach Company offering books and manuscripts.

Newton had not yet been able to introduce Osgood, but when Adam asked if he knew who could lecture on Ruskin in Buffalo, Osgood was one of those Newton suggested. Arrangements were made and it was a "fine" occasion, Adam said. "[W]e were all charmed with your friend Osgood and his lecture was beautifully done and I have heard nothing but praise for him and I feel that I have made a friend indeed through you." Adam sat in the front row of the hall and "heard every other word distinctly."[14] In 1920 he was already deaf. As soon as possible he took Osgood back to the library at Norwood Avenue, where he could hear every word and they talked about Johnson till the early hours of the morning.

13. AEN to RBA, November 18, 1919.
14. RBA to AEN, May 10, 1920.

"What is this I hear of Osgood?" wrote Tinker, "I wake with a start to realize that I have a hated rival! My mistake was ever the flat transgression of a school-boy, who, being overjoyed with finding a bird's nest, shows it [to] his companion, and he steals it? I didn't know that, like Newton, you went in for college-professors as a genus. But perhaps I shall have to forgive Osgood after all, in as much as he introduced *me* to Newton. He is a wonderful fellow."[15] Adam agreed, and he asked Osgood to write the Introduction for a second Adam library catalogue which he was preparing. Osgood was honored to comply.

Shortly before Osgood's lecture, Adam had received a letter from Dr. R. W. Chapman, secretary of the Oxford University Press and editor of Jane Austen, who was now at work on a new editon of Johnson's letters. Chapman wrote, "Prof. Chauncey Tinker encourages me to believe that you will be so very good as to help me in a Johnsonian project I have in mind." Chapman needed "any copies of, or information about, any letter of Johnson's whether published or unpublished."[16] Adam paid no attention to this request. In the summer, however, Tinker was in England, searching for more unpublished Boswell letters, and he saw a good deal of Chapman, whose press he hoped would some day produce his book. Tinker told Chapman to write again. So he did, beginning his letter, "Prof. Chauncey Tinker encourages me to trespass on a courtesy well known to scholars." The new edition of Johnson's letters, which Chapman contemplated, he explained, is "not in any way designed to rival the great work of Birkbeck Hill" (whom he knew Adam admired). It was designed "to supplement it by giving a fuller and in some places a more accurate text." He hoped that Adam would help him "out of the stores of [his] unrivalled

15. CBT to RBA, May 10, 1920.
16. RWC to RBA, March 15, 1920.

collection and from [his] knowledge of the collections of others in the United States."[17]

This time Adam gave in and invited Chapman to visit. Four months later Chapman announced that he was coming to the United States on Oxford Press business and hoped to see Dr. Rosenbach's Johnson letters in Philadelphia and also journey to Buffalo to avail himself of Mr. Adam's "very kind invitation [to] come and see [his] treasures."[18] As the time drew closer, Chapman, always diplomatic with the fair sex, said he was eager to meet the literary Mrs. Adam and the daughters, "young ladies, who I doubt not are the brightest ornaments of your collection!"[19] The two day visit was "as pleasant as it was profitable," Chapman said truthfully in his thank-you note.[20] During his visit he had copied out the texts of all the unpublished Johnson letters in Adam's library, some thirty, and he now noted that these, added to Newton's similar number, and his other transcripts, totaled two hundred new letters for his edition.

Chapman, who was not retiring, but like Tinker a strong personalilty and a redoubtable scholar, soon became an influential friend. Adam gave access to his treasures and, in return, Chapman gave scholarly advice. Also, as he made his own search for Johnson letters, reading book catalogues and haunting bookshops and auctions, Chapman would send information to Adam. He often acted as his agent and sometimes even tempted Adam with the possibility of selling books from his own collection. Chapman's correspondence with Adam is extensive, running from March 1920 to November 1936. Almost all of his letters are written in his indecipherable, infuriating scrawl, which Newton thought he did on purpose.

Newton also helped Adam acquire material, and one amusing incident must have pleased collectors and pained dealers. On March 5, 1920, Boswell's fragmentary "first"

17. RWC to RBA, July 19, 1920.
18. RWC to RBA, November 17, 1920.
19. RWC to RBA, December 8, 1920.
20. RWC to RBA, December 20, 1920.

proof sheets of *Life of Johnson* were to be sold at the American Art Association in New York. These were the perfect supplement to the "revised" proof sheets already in Adam's library, and he wanted them badly. "Now, listen attentively to what I suggest," Newton told Adam. Pay no attention to Bryne Hackett's offer to bid, and withdraw the bid from Gabriel Wells, because, said Newton, "I have reason to believe that George Smith is going to buy the volume in any event, and if he makes up his mind, he will not let anyone outbid him." George Smith, Newton went on to say, was under obligation to him, so that if Smith got the proof sheets he would turn them over to Newton, and Newton would turn them over to Adam at the same price. So, Newton said, that shows you "how much fonder I am of you than I am of Boswell."[21]

Adam did as he was told, but then Newton, at the moment of giving his bid, read in the paper that George Smith had died! Having told everyone that he was not in the market for the lot himself and to complete the deception, having arranged to lunch with Dr. Rosenbach in Philadelphia at the hour of the sale, he could not very well bid himself. So he sent a man from his office to New York. In the excitement which prevailed when the Boswell proof sheets were knocked down, Newton's man, instead of following directions and giving his own name, gave Newton's, "which created some sensation. Now, two or three men are going to call me a liar." No matter, said Newton, "Altogether, I think it was a very pretty plot."[22]

The proof sheets were acquired in the nick of time to include an entry and two full page illustrations in Adam's new catalogue. This single volume, privately printed in Buffalo, appeared in March 1921. It had been compiled entirely by Adam—a massive labor. He said in his Justification, which preceded Osgood's Introduction, that he owed much to Newton "for his interest and encouragement"

21. AEN to RBA, March 3, 1920.
22. AEN to RBA, March 8, 1920.

and that he was "greatly indebted" to Osgood and Tinker. His purpose, Adam stated, was to share the pleasure of his collection with others. The catalogue described manuscripts, letters, books, and "ana" of Johnson and Boswell, also non-Johnsonian autograph letters in the collection. At the end of the volume was a personal touch, an appealing photograph of Adam and his small son, Robert Jr., both dressed for a Buffalo winter; the picture was captioned, "Life Members of the Johnson Society of Lichfield, England." Originally, Adam had thought of a catalogue in two volumes but, in the end, he and Newton agreed that it would be better in one, therefore the print was small. And, for some reason, the pages were unnumbered.

No written comment on the catalogue is in Tinker's file but Newton gave full praise: "It's certainly a corker,"[23] and, on the subject of Osgood's Introduction, "I think it perfectly delightful and I confess to you, and to no one else, that I have a feeling that I have influenced the literary style of both Tinker and Osgood for the better."[24] Seriously, the book "is a noble monument to its past and present owner."[25]

Chapman gave his thanks for the catalogue in person when the Adam family came to London in the spring of 1921. A while later, he boldly inquired if, since the "first" and "revised" proof sheets of the *Life* had been recorded and photographed, might they be consulted by one L. F. Powell, who was working on the revised edition of Birkbeck Hill for the Oxford Press. "What I should *like* to do," Chapman said, "is to look through the *whole* of the proofs and revises and extract all plums. But that would be a biggish job and I don't see how to do it unless I had the books here—which I hesitate to suggest!"[26]

Adam, trusting and generous, wrapped up his volume of "first" proof and two volumes of "revised" proof and sent them to Oxford. Here they remained for several years, their

23. AEN to RBA, March 29, 1921.
24. AEN to RBA, April 10, 1921.
25. AEN to RBA, May 2, 1921.
26. RWC to RBA, October 25, 1923.

present shabby condition silent testimony to the rigors of scholarship and, as Chapman himself confessed, frequent rides in his bicycle basket.

Scholars from all over were making requests for transcripts or asking to visit the Buffalo library. Adam was his own librarian, and he had other responsibilities—a store and a bank to manage. The library demands became impossible. Furthermore, the scholar usually referred to the kind purpose Adam had expressed in his Justification, of desiring to share his books with others, and this placed him in an awkward position.

The worst offenders were Tinker's graduate students. Adam had the matter out, and Tinker wrote stiffly after one visit, "Since I saw you, I have called off all my graduate students; so if you are bothered by new applicants, they are not set on you by me, whatever they say."[27] Despite Tinker's assurance, requests kept coming and Adam protested in despair, wasn't Tinker himself bothered as a collector? Newton was. Tinker replied, "I read your letter with much laughter . . . I am not a sufficiently eminent collector to be troubled this way." It was Adam's own fault, he said—his good nature and his catalogue. "You come before the world and boast of your possessions, and then get sore because the world is interested in what you have. *What, pray, did you expect?*" Tinker went on to say, "I am sorry you chose my nice boy, Hilles, to jump on, because he is a gentleman as well as a scholar . . . Oh, if you were only as easy to manage as Ned is!"[28]

A few months later, Tinker, disregarding his promise, wrote, "Please let me know if you can let F. A. Pottle into your library for an hour or two. 'Can you' means *will you*? He has completed his bibliography of Boswell, except for the work that remains to be done in Buffalo. He is very much afraid of you. I tell him not to be, but must admit that you

27. CBT to RBA, May 14, 1925.
28. CBT to RBA, November 25, 1925.

are at moments a little awe-inspiring."[29] Adam agreed to
receive Pottle, and Tinker answered, "You will, I am sure,
like Pottle, though not, perhaps, for his prowess on the
golf-course. He knows more of J.B. than any man alive, and
is, I must say, a far more accurate scholar than I. He is
afraid of you, so don't put on all your terrors when he comes
. . . comme toujours, toujours à vos pieds."[30] The visit went
off well, and Pottle wrote a warm letter of thanks, "I do wish
to tell you, just as simply and sincerely as I can, how deeply
I feel your kindness in letting me see and use your great collection, and how grateful I am for your fine and genial hospitality. I have never had any pleasure in literature quite like
that of turning over the manuscripts in the great *Letters*
volumes." Pottle went on to say that he would like to make
the translations that were needed for the French and Latin
autograph letters, "partly to discharge in some measure my
present debt of gratitude to you, and partly because I need a
great deal of such exercise."[31]

In many parts of the country Tinker's graduate students
were distinguishing themselves, and his own star shone
above them. His *Young Boswell* had been published by the
Atlantic Monthly Press in 1922, a collection of essays, based
largely on unpublished Adam material. Tinker dedicated his
book to R. B., though in phrases very different from his
affectionate style in letters. Newton criticized the formality
of the dedication. "But," he said, "the book itself is admirably done; it is the best book on Boswell without a doubt."[32]

Early in 1924 Tinker's two volume collection of *Boswell
Letters* was published by the Oxford Press. There were two
hundred new letters and, as the Preface said, the book contained "the largest amount of information regarding James
Boswell which is to be found outside the *Life of Johnson*."
The book was received with acclaim, establishing Tinker as
the outstanding Boswell authority. "[T]hat terrible Blue

29. CBT to RBA, May 10, 1926.
30. CBT to RBA, May 21, 1926.
31. FAP to RBA, May 30, 1926.
32. AEN to RBA, March 24, 1922.

person"[33] had given up; Boswell studies were the undisputed domain of Tinker.

So it seemed, but there was a presence in London—ominous for Tinker—though he did not realize it at the time, nor did anyone else. Newton was reporting a simple encounter when he wrote Adam in December 1923, "Oh by the way I met a man the other day who has a great collection of J. and B. Makes *mine* look like thirty cents."[34] Ralph Isham, thirty-three. "American. Joined the English Army and finished as Lieut. Colonel on Haig's staff. He says he's poor but he rides around in a Rolls Royce."[35] "I am very anxious for you to meet."[36]

Lacking foreknowledge, Tinker was not concerned about Isham; what he was concerned about was Adam's talk of selling material from his library—not Johnson and his circle—but other things. "Are you really going to sell the Burns stuff?" Tinker inquired plaintively. "Why not *give* it to Yale as a memorial to your father?"[37] Adam did not accept this suggestion, and in October 1924 he sent his Burns collection to Dr. Rosenbach to sell;[38] his Ruskin collection had gone to the Doctor the year before and was being offered to Henry Huntington.[39]

Adam was in a building mood. He was considering a new store, and he was moving to a fine new house at 780 West Ferry Street —Georgian, red brick, with imposing white pillars. On the ground floor there was a handsome library room for which Newton had all manner of ideas. The two friends discussed them by letter and also had several talks in the mellowing atmosphere of tobacco and brandy. One Newton inspiration was for the style of the room to be "strictly

33. CBT to RBA, September 16, 1919.
34. AEN to RBA, December 4, 1923.
35. AEN to RBA, January 13, 1924.
36. AEN to RBA, October 6, 1924.
37. CBT to RBA, October 6, 1923.
38. RBA to ASWR, October 29, 1924.
39. Rosenbach Co to RBA, March 8, 1924.

Adam.''[40] This suggestion was not followed, but Newton's
sketch for a new, purely Johnson bookplate was accepted and
continues to be admired, the Bartolozzi profile of Johnson on
an oval leather label. (Incidentally, Newton's celebrated
Temple Bar bookplate was designed by Osgood.[41])

In 1926, despite Tinker's objections, Adam decided to
auction his non-Johnsonian material (and even some splendid bits of Johnsoniana). He sent over four hundred lots to
the Anderson Galleries to be sold on February 15 and 16.
The time has come, he wrote in his Introduction to the sale
catalogue, "to separate my special, and some of my miscellaneous books, from that great period of literature, the
eighteenth century, in which my chief interest endures, and
to give what I can spare of what remains to me of my days
and nights to the study of the Johnsonian era."

Chapman, who had dedicated his Oxford edition of
Johnson's and Boswell's Hebrides journals to Adam in 1924,
wrote "I am sorry to hear you are having a sale—because
parting is always sad . . . but as long as you don't sell Johnson I can bear it."[42] Newton was not sad, he was ecstatic.
He had never expected such an opportunity, and he wrote
Adam, "I can see that my bank account is going to be damn
badly bent."[43] To Mitchell Kennerley, manager of the
Anderson Galleries, he wrote, "Short of ruining myself, I
want to do everything in my power to make the Adam sale a
success." Would Kennerley arrange a little supper party at
the Plaza, "supply the guests, I will sign the check."[44]

The supper party was a triumph and so was the sale, as
the signatures in Adam's bound copy of the auction catalogue attest: Jerome Kern, Carl Pforzheimer, Owen D.
Young, A. S. W. Rosenbach, Lathrop Harper, Walter Hill,

40. AEN to RBA, June 23, 1924.
41. Newton, *Amenities*, pp. 60–61.
42. RWC to RBA, January 25, 1926.
43. AEN to RBA, December 18, 1925.
44. AEN to MK, December 29, 1925.

Bryne Hackett, Gabriel Wells, Christopher Morley, Seymour de Ricci—and Osgood, Tinker, and Isham. Adam's friends were there, and they gave him strong support.

Once the excitement was over, Adam came back to his library, which now had more available shelf space; he put his books in order and began to plan a monumental catalogue—for Johnson. Adam had not been overly excited by the rumors which had been going around for several years—that Boswell's manuscript archive might still survive, owned, it was said, by Lord Talbot de Malahide, Malahide Castle, near Dublin. When the rumors were confirmed shortly after the publication of Tinker's volume of *Letters*, Adam accepted the fact philosophically that *his* collection of Boswell was no longer the finest, in fact, it was insignificant. However, he had no interest in trying to acquire the Malahide papers. He was committed to Johnson—not Boswell. He was simply an interested bystander, a sad fact for Tinker but one he had to accept.

Tinker's situation was tragic. His recently applauded book was rendered a mere sampling of Boswell's letters, and, unless he could gain free access to the new mass of material, he could not retain his position as doyen of Boswell studies.

Newton urged him "to go to Dublin . . . and run the story down, taking with him every possible credential, and securing the material, if it existed, against all comers."[45]

Tinker made a gallant try. Without any backing, he went alone to Ireland in the summer of 1925. He penetrated Malahide Castle and met briefly with the Talbots. "Everything here and nothing to be touched," he wrote to Newton, "I have been on the rack. Sinbad and the Valley of Diamonds is the correct metaphor."[46]

Newton now encouraged Isham, that "fascinating devil," as he called him. And Isham made *his* try the next summer. He had asked Newton and he had asked Rosenbach to go half with him in the venture, but both had refused. So

45. AEN to RBA, July 13, 1925.
46. Repeated by AEN to RBA, July 13, 1925.

Isham, on his own, went to Ireland in June of 1926. With impeccable credentials he called on the Talbots, had tea and social conversation and, though nothing was promised, he had a hunch that he could get the papers, if he could get the money. In January 1927 he auctioned a large number of his books and, with a small profit from the sale and all the funds he could raise by other means, he returned to Ireland.

Rosenbach and Bryne Hackett, independent of each other, were to deal with the Talbots, but Isham was the only person able to make a single purchase. He's bought "a wonderful Goldsmith letter," Newton told Adam in February;[47] and by September Newton sent the great tidings from London, that Isham now possessed all the Boswell papers except the journals. "I have seen them."[48]

Isham was planning to publish the papers, and his obvious choice for an editor was Tinker. Isham found the professor in London and invited him to his suite at Claridge's; there, the two spent hours examining the mass of material from Malahide. The more Tinker saw, the more depressed he became. He knew that he was temperamentally unable to do scholarly work under anyone's direction—particularly under Isham. But he also knew that by refusing, he was sacrificing his world eminence as the authority on Boswell—a devastating end to his years of scholarly labor.

Tinker went away from the meeting in misery and, not long after, he heard that Isham had engaged Geoffrey Scott, a British scholar, to be his editor. Newton tried to cheer Tinker up by holding a reception for him at Johnson House in Gough Square. "Preposterous," Tinker wrote to Adam, "but you know Ned."[49]

When Tinker sailed for home in October he was in deep depression. "My name is MUD, and Isham has christened

47. AEN to RBA, February 7, 1927.
48. AEN to RBA, September 1, 1927.
49. CBT to RBA, September 12, 1927.

me," he cried to Adam.[50] By November, however, he was
able to advise Newton that he was now "absolutely at peace
regarding Isham. A beautiful calm has descended on me. I
am finishing a lovely book to be called *The Good Estate of
Poetry* . . . My graduate students are becoming professors all
over 'the length and breadth of this great land,' and they rise
up and call me blessed because I treated 'em like human
beings and not like graduate students. Why then should I
worry myself into the grave because Isham bought my mistress with his money? He did, and knows he did. Let him
see how much he can make—he and his Mr. Scott."[51]

By the beginning of 1928 Tinker was able to report progress on *The Good Estate of Poetry.* "I like it better than
anything I have ever done. I hope my friends will. I had to
do something to take my mind off Isham and the rest. (I
hear now that he has also purchased the MS journal. Gods,
gods!)"[52]

In Oxford meanwhile Chapman was paying special attention to Adam's Johnson catalogue, which was to be printed
by the Oxford Press. The job of translating the foreign
letters had not been given to Pottle, but to L. F. Powell
"and his minions"[53] (his wife, his son, the Reader of
French, and the Lecturer of Italian). In June 1928 Chapman
was delighted by the "good news" that Adam was coming
over and bringing the manuscript of the catalogue with him.
"It is no use asking a printer to say how long he will take to
produce a book he has not seen; and remember that all your
friends want to read the proofs."[54]

Adam looked forward to a leisurely working stay in
Oxford and a sociable visit to Lichfield at the time of the
annual Johnson birthday dinner. He wanted to honor Chapman, this year's president, and he hoped to enjoy all his
Johnsonian friends. This was not to be, for Mrs. Adam's

50. CBT to RBA, October 12, 1927.
51. Quoted by AEN to RBA, November 9, 1927.
52. CBT to RBA, January 9, 1928.
53. RWC to RBA, January 25, 1928.
54. RWC to RBA, June 29, 1928.

mother died and all plans for the trip were canceled. In November, when Adam could see no prospect of coming to England, he began to think he should have his catalogue printed in Buffalo. Chapman protested, it would be a great disappointment if it were not printed in Oxford. However, if it could not be, he pleaded "do give me a chance: 1) to read the proofs before it is too late for suggestions; 2) to help you design the book. The old book [the 1921 catalogue] is terribly difficult. People want to quote it (Powells and Pottles) and there is no means of reference."[55] Chapman promised he would continue to press Powell for the translations but could not at the moment, for "he is gone to be interviewed by the Boobies of Birmingham. The Boobies want a University librarian."[56] Powell, to the lasting gratitude of all Johnsonians, did not defect to Birmingham. He remained in Oxford and continued to devote himself to the revision of Hill's edition of Boswell's *Life of Johnson*. He was now working on volume 3.

Chapman, himself, was plugging away at his edition of *Johnson's Letters* in the time he could spare. "I must finish next year," he wrote to Adam in December of 1929, "or I shall be a laughing-stock."[57] (Little did he realize that *twenty-three more years* would elapse before *Johnson's Letters* would finally appear in 1952!)

Unlike Chapman, Newton had no trouble bringing out two books between 1927 and 1929, albeit not scholarly works, *The Busted Bibliophile* and *The Book Collecting Game*, but both were selling well, and so were his electrical circuit breakers, which allowed him to build an attractive and expansive addition to this house. This included two spacious bedrooms to make his guests more comfortable, and what with the five libraries, "the house is now an architectural

55. RWC to RBA, November 16, 1928.
56. RWC to RBA, November 17, 1928.
57. RWC to RBA, December 22, 1929.

maze," Tinker wrote Adam after a November visit to Oak Knoll.[58]

Through the 1920s all was well with business and family for Newton and Adam. Both men were able to enjoy their books and have leisure without anxiety. For the Adams it was Pinehurst in the winter, and, as Tinker put it, "migration" to the seashore in the summer. The beautiful daughters were young ladies now and by the midtwenties Junior was in school. For the Newtons, it was just A. E. and Babette, since Swift had come through World War I unscathed and was now married, and Caroline had embarked on her independent career. The Newtons usually spent several months in London, often taking a service flat (their favorite was at 71 Jermyn Street). They also made extended trips to distant lands.

They were in Egypt when the Jerome Kern auction took place in New York (January 7–10, 1929). The sale was successful beyond expectation (Kern realized large profits and, wisely he *thought*, put the money at once into the stock market). The Kern sale prices were "so wildly inflated," Adam felt, that he acquired very little beyond Johnson's manuscript review of Grainger's *Sugar Cane* and his contract for the 12mo *Rambler*. Newton commented from Rome that "Jerry Kern's books sold too well, if anything," and he gathered that Tinker "did not get a smell." Newton went on to say that his promise to write a Preface for Adam's Johnson catalogue was very much on his mind and that it would be the first job to be tackled when he came home in April.[59] He was true to his word.

By May of 1929 two volumes of Adam's catalogue had been printed and sent to the binders, the third volume was still at press. In the same month Pottle's bibliography came out, *The Literary Career of James Boswell* (dedicated to Tinker). "Excellent," Newton found it and so did Adam.

---

58. CBT to RBA, January 9, 1928.
59. AEN to RBA, February 7, 1929.

Powell called it "a great work,"[60] and Geoffrey Scott expressed "profound admiration—amazement rather—at the total achievement."[61] Also in May six volumes of Isham's *Boswell Papers* appeared, edited by Scott, an extraordinary feat to accomplish in such a short time. "I like everything about them except the [shiny red] binding" wrote Newton.[62] It's "a magnificent piece of work."[63]

Tinker's *Good Estate of Poetry* appeared in 1929 as well, and those not au courant with Boswell news were surprised to see the distinguished authority turning to so different a subject, but they were not disappointed for it was a good book.

Tinker, with determination, was creating a new life for himself; his academic interest was to be poetry, and his even more important university interest was to be rare books in Yale's collections—a crucial project for the new University Library which was being planned.

Adam wished to support Tinker in his library efforts and gave him a generous gift. He took back his Ruskin collection, still lying unsold at the Rosenbach Company, and presented it to Yale in honor of R. B. Adam I. "Everybody is 'jubilant,'" Tinker said in a letter of thanks, and "[y]ou may be sure that [the Ruskin] will be kept together and properly cared for."[64]

By the last week of October the Adam catalogue, an edition of five hundred copies, was almost ready to ship. The book had been printed in Buffalo by the Volksfreund Press, though it bore an Oxford imprint. No cost had been spared in production: sumptuous binding, handsome paper, fine type, and profuse illustration, some eight hundred facsimiles of manuscripts, letters, portraits, and views.

60. LFP to RBA, December 31, 1929.
61. GS to FAP August 1929, printed in Isham "Announcement" for continuation of *Boswell Papers* under editorship of Frederick A. Pottle, November 7, 1929.
62. AEN to RBA, May 20, 1929.
63. AEN to RBA, July 16, 1929.
64. CBT to RBA, May 3, 1929.

Newton's Preface was in volume 1, preceding the Introduction by Osgood, who was honored to have his essay
included and "to know that you think of me kindly from
time to time cannot but cheer me on."[65] Unfortunately,
however, Osgood's 1921 essay was reproduced without
correction and now the statement that all of Boswell's papers
had been destroyed, save Adam's "Notebook," was ludicrous.

Volume 1 of the catalogue was devoted to manuscripts
and letters of Johnson, Boswell, and other eighteenth-
century writers; volume 2, books by the same authors; and
volume 3, miscellaneous autographs. Along with the literary
portraits in the three volumes were personal photographs: R.
B. Adam I and Birkbeck Hill; Newton and Osgood; Tinker;
Dr. Rosenbach; Chapman; Powell; Nichol Smith (this
eminent Oxford scholar-collector, like Chapman was supplying Adam with Johnson material from England); Aleyn Lyell
Reade, the Johnsonian "gleaner"; Sir Charles Russell, the
collector; Arundell Esdaile of the British Museum; and Cecil
Harmsworth, who had preserved Dr. Johnson's only surviving house in London and was turning it over to a trust
(Adam, Newton, and Chapman were among those asked to
be governors). At the end of volume 3 was a picture of R.
B. and Junior in riding togs, also a picture of the Adams'
stately home on West Ferry Street. The volume concluded
with four pages of "Corrections and Additions." If the
catalogue could have been printed in Oxford, Adam's
friends, as Chapman suggested, would have spotted the
errors; also Oxford could easily have supplied an index, item
numbers, and consecutive page numbers. Adam was sadly
aware of these defects and had written Chapman in January,
"I still and probably always will regret not publishing at
Oxford. But it could not be helped and I felt too old to
wait."[66] Regardless of its faults, Adam knew that his catalogue was an important and delightful book, and he was

65. CGO to RBA, December 28, 1928.
66. RBA to RWC, January 11, 1929.

generous with his complimentary copies. Chapman thought too generous and protested, "I see no reason at all why you should give a copy to every member of the Johnson Club, a number of the members are lucky enough to be members and certainly don't deserve a bonus."[67] But Adam was in high spirits and his generosity was not to be curbed.

This happy state of affairs came suddenly, shockingly, to an end, even before Adam received Chapman's letter. For on Tuesday, October 29, 1929 came the stock market crash in New York City—a national humiliation, a crippling, devastating blow to business throughout the country. Halycon days were over for Adam; he no longer had time for leisure and travel, nor the means to be generous and hospitable; he had no more time for the absorbing pleasures of book collecting.

The praise which poured in for his three-volume Johnson catalogue was now ironic. There were tributes from friends, scholars, and institutions all over the world, and uniformly enthusiastic reviews: "a feast for Johnsonians . . . a masterpiece of scholarship and devotion," *New York Times*;[68] "a work of reference indispensable to Johnsonian scholars," L. F. Powell in *Review of English Studies.*[69]

Business now controlled totally. Adam was working ten hours a day, having lunch at his desk, worrying about the store and about the bank, which was a department of the store. He could not sleep, felt unwell, and was growing increasingly deaf.

Two days after the stock market crash, Adam wrote to Dr. Rosenbach in a covering letter for the Johnson catalogue which was on its way, "I expect to be in N.Y. within two weeks, and I want to speak to you on a subject that has not yet passed my lips—the disposition of this collection. You will be as silent I know. Let me know, if you will, whether

67. RWC to RBA, October 30, 1929.
68. September 7, 1930.
69. April 1936, pp. 230–235.

or not you are likely to be in town.''[70] An immediate answer came from the Doctor, he would meet Adam at any time that was convenient to discuss the "absolutely confidential" matter.[71] They met and Adam empowered Rosenbach to act as his sole agent to *sell* the treasured Johnson library.

Three years after Adam had written that he planned to dedicate his remaining days and nights to the study of the Johnsonian era, his great Johnson library was for sale.

What happened to Adam during the depression? To his business and his books? How did Tinker try to set a course for his friend? Was Newton in the same situation? What about their libraries? There *is* more to the story, but it must wait for another time.

70. RBA to ASWR, October 31, 1929.
71. ASWR to RBA, November 4, 1929.

Poets, Statesmen, Historians, Artists

HOWARD D. WEINBROT

Gray's "Progress of Poesy" and "The Bard": An Essay in Literary Transmission

Gray's odes long have been the poor relations in a family dominated by its elegiac patriarch. When they are studied, they may be cited as exemplars of the uncertainty of poetic reputation, as instances of Gray's visual imagination, as episodes in midcentury visionary concerns, or most recently, as paradigms of the anxiety of influence.[1] On this hypothesis,

1. For some relevant studies, see William Powell Jones, "The Contemporary Reception of Gray's Odes," *Modern Philology*, 28 (1930), 61–82; R. W. Ketton-Cremer, *Thomas Gray: A Biography* (Cambridge: Cambridge University Press, 1955), pp. 116–157; Jean H. Hagstrum, *The Sister Arts: The Tradition of Literary Pictorialism and English Poetry from Dryden to Gray* (Chicago: University of Chicago Press, 1958), pp. 301–314; Arthur Johnston, "Gray's Use of the Gorchest y Beirdd in *The Bard*," *Modern Language Review*, 59 (1964), 335–338; F. I. McCarthy, "*The Bard* of Thomas Gray: Its Composition and Its Use by Painters," *National Library of Wales Journal*, 14 (1965), 105–113, and plates 4–11; Arthur Johnston, *Thomas Gray and the Bard: An Inaugural Lecture Delivered at the University College of Wales, Aberystwyth* (Cardiff: University of Wales Press, 1966); Patricia Meyer Spacks, *The Poetry of Vision: Five Eighteenth-Century Poets* (Cambridge: Harvard University Press, 1967), pp. 103–114; Irvin Ehrenpreis, "The Cistern and the Fountain: Art and Reality in Pope and Gray," in *Studies in Criticism and Aesthetics 1660–1800: Essays in Honor of Samuel Holt Monk*, ed. Howard

Gray exemplifies the weak poet who cows before his betters
and surrenders what shreds of originality he loosely grasps.
Such a fate, alas, seems endemic to the eighteenth-century
poet. One recent commentator argues that "the Augustans
sought to avoid direct rivalries with the ancients by limiting
themselves beyond the limitings already present in the classical writers."[2] Another sees the consequences of such a debilitating approach for Gray himself: "It is unwise to assume
that Gray wishes to add so much as a grace note to the vocal

Anderson and John S. Shea (Minneapolis: University of Minnesota Press,
1967), pp. 158–170; four essays in *Fearful Joy: Papers from the Thomas Gray
Bicentenary Conference at Carlton University*, ed. James Downey and Ben
Jones (Montreal and London: McGill-Queen's University Press, 1974) —
Arthur Johnston, "Thomas Gray: Our Daring Bard," pp. 50–65; Eli Man-
del, "Theories of Voice in Eighteenth-Century Poetry: Thomas Gray and
Christopher Smart," pp. 103–118, George Whalley, "Thomas Gray: A
Quiet Hellenist," pp. 153–155, and James Steele, "Thomas Gray and the
Season for Triumph," pp. 218–224; Mary I. Oates, "Jonson, Congreve, and
Gray: Pindaric Essays in Literary History," *Studies in English Literature*, 19
(1979), 387–406. This partial selection must neglect studies in which Gray
and his odes are incidental. The list can be augmented by familiar studies
of the "progress poem" and the larger context of the eighteenth-century
ode, especially Norman Maclean's "From Action to Image: Theories of the
Lyric in the Eighteenth Century," in *Critics and Criticism Ancient and
Modern*, ed. R. S. Crane (Chicago and London: University of Chicago
Press, 1952), pp. 408–460.

2. Peter Thorpe, "Harold Bloom's Revisionary Ratios and the Augustan
Satirists," *The Southern Humanities Review*, 13 (1979), 196, n. 30. See also
his view that, for the eighteenth century, "Culture has steadily decayed
since the Golden Age of Athens and Rome, and all bids for immortality by
the moderns will be futile" (p. 187). "The better satirists of the eighteenth
century knew from the outset that they could not begin to compete with the
Romans" (p. 188). Comparable adaptations of "anxiety" permeate Paul S.
Sherwin, *Precious Bane: Collins and the Miltonic Legacy* (Austin: University
of Texas Press, 1977). The ur-text is Professor Bloom's *Anxiety of Influence:
A Theory of Poetry* (New York: Oxford University Press, 1973), and its view
that all poetry after the Renaissance "*is a history of anxiety and self-saving
caricature, of distortion, of perverse, wilful revisionism without which modern poetry as such could not exist*" (p. 30). Subsequent applications and fine-tuning
of the theory appear in *A Map of Misreading* (1975), *Kabbalah and Criticism*
(1975), *Poetry and Repression* (1976) and, among other works, *Agon:
Towards a Theory of Revisionism* (1982).

harmony of his precursors." Gray, indeed, "is a paradigm of what Harold Bloom would call a 'weak poet'; what Gray screens out [in his Pindarics] in order to reformulate his psychic distance is not the consciousness of strong origins, but rather the threatening idea that originality is strength."[3]

My scepticism regarding this view is independent of the theory on which it wobbles, and its related notions regarding Augustanism and a critic's wisdom. It seems to me that Gray's "Progress of Poesy" and "The Bard" are both original and traditional in almost any positive sense of those words. The odes contribute to midcentury reconsideration of the conventions and utility of Pindarics; they also contribute to midcentury reconsideration of the utility of ancient Graeco-Roman culture for a modern northern European nation. "They" do so, because these poems lose much of their meaning when studied individually rather than as sister odes in which one poem extends and fulfills the other, while exemplifying the superiority of the British to the Pindaric ode in the modern world.

The danger or irrelevance of classical culture in a putative neoclassical age is not one of the more attractive paradoxes of literary history. Nonetheless, commentators in the Restoration and eighteenth century often suspected, or knew, that the classical models sometimes foisted on them were inappropriate for their own culture. This suspicion was enhanced by the abundant political rhetoric in the paper wars between the Walpole administration and its opposition. Here, marginally relevant "parallel History" often was used to savage each side's leaders for their assumed likeness to some classical scoundrel or another.[4] Awareness of the incongruity of Mediterranean and Atlantic cultures, however, had a long precedent. Hobbes's *Leviathan* (1651), ii. 29, and the final lines of dialogue three of *Behemoth, or The Long*

3. Paul H. Fry, *The Poet's Calling in the English Ode* (New Haven and London: Yale University Press, 1980), pp. 79, 85.

4. The term "parallel History" comes from the *London Journal*, June 29, 1734.

Parliament (1682) both insist on the dangers of adherence to republican, antimonarchic classical writers. By 1727 Defoe was equally impatient with the classical world as a norm for the modern. In the *History of the Principal Discoveries and Improvements in the Several Arts and Sciences* he thus says that "Looking into Antiquity, is a Dry, Empty, and Barren Contemplation, any farther than as it is brought down to our present understanding; and to bear a steady Analogy of its parts, with the Things that are before us." Modern times are as exemplary as the "most early Times," even though their ignorance allowed even more to be discovered and improved (pp. 4–5). A few years later, the anonymous author of *Power and Patriotism* (1746) urges that "it would be a Thing of great Consequence" if British youth studied British history with the same rigor that they study the histories of Greece and Rome. Though it would be wrong to ignore those, it is "if possible the greater Fault" to ignore one's own past. He also amplifies Hobbes's remarks regarding the classics. That author, he says, believed that "our last Civil War was in a great Measure owing to our great Men's studying *Greek* and *Latin* Writers, and endeavouring to introduce the Maxims inculcated by them, into the Management of our Affairs, without duly considering the Difference between the Nations and their Civil Constitutions" (p. 4). The author of *Reflections on Ancient and Modern History* (1746) makes the same point. After reviewing ancient governments, he concludes that "there is not the least resemblance or Conformity between their Arts of Life and Government, and our own," and that it is therefore "unsafe in Civil Affairs, to propose Antiquity for a Guide" (pp. 20, 24). By 1752 Lord Bolingbroke, who was a leader in the earlier application of parallel history, had come to accept the need to be selective regarding the uses of the past, which should be dealt with the way a modern free imitator deals with a classical poem. "History is the ancient author: experience is the modern language ... We translate the sense and reason, we transfuse the spirit and force: but we imitate only the particular graces of the original; we ... are far from affecting to copy them servilely."[5] Edward Burnaby Greene is commonplace when, in 1779, he complains that praise of Rome often is used "intentionally to degrade . . . *our* Country." Burnaby Greene is among many in the eighteenth century who know that "the history of Rome is little applicable to ours," and that, in any case, heathen rapacious Rome is inferior to modern Britain.[6]

Increased affection for national history was consistent with increased affection for national letters. One familiar approach was that applied to Graeco-Gallic criticism and drama, in which Aristotle's rules and models were held up as standards designed to shame the crude English. Dryden's "Heads of an Answer" to Thomas Rymer's *Tragedies of the Last Age* (1677) argues that English writers must please an English audience. With the exception of plot, those moderns write "more beautifully" and with a greater "genius in tragedy" than the ancients. Aristotle himself is a dubious guide if he insists that pity and terror "are either the prime, or . . . the only ends of tragedy." He "drew his models of tragedy from Sophocles and Euripides; and if he had seen ours, might have changed his mind."[7] Dryden and others of course were thinking of Shakespeare, who frequently was used to counter the claims of the ancients and their rules. Hence Pope's Preface to his edition of Shakespeare (1725) insists that "To judge . . . of *Shakespeare* by *Aristotle*'s rules, is like trying a man by the Laws of one Country, who acted under those of another. He writ to the *People*."[8]

5. Bolingbroke, *Letters on the Study . . . of History* (London, 1752), I, 67.

6. Burnaby Greene, *The Satires of Persius Paraphrastically Imitated, and Adapted to the Times* (London, 1779), p. 16 n.

7. For the "Heads" see *John Dryden: Of Dramatic Poesy and Other Critical Essays*, ed. George Watson (London and New York: Dent, Dutton, 1967), I, 215, 218.

8. Pope, *Eighteenth-Century Essays on Shakespeare*, ed. D. Nichol Smith, 2nd ed. (Oxford: Clarendon Press, 1963), p. 47.

Commentators also soon became aware that on qualitative grounds Milton was at least the equal, and on moral grounds the superior, of his epic forbears. As early as 1674 Samuel Barrow applied Propertius, *Elegies*, ii. 34, 65, to Milton, saying *cedite Romani scriptores, cedite Graii!* —give way, you bards of Rome, give way, you of Greece—words originally applied to the *Aeneid*.[9] In 1688 Dryden makes a comparable judgment and places it under the engraving of Milton in the fourth edition of *Paradise Lost* (1688):

> Three *Poets*, in three distant *Ages* born,
> *Greece, Italy*, and *England* did adorn.
> The *First* in loftiness of thought Surpass'd;
> The *Next* in Majesty; in both the *Last*.
> The force of *Nature* cou'd no farther goe:
> To make a *Third* she joyn'd the former two.[10]

Addison's first *Spectator* paper on *Paradise Lost*, No. 267, January 5, 1712, resurrects Propertius' line, and on January 16, 1712, No. 409, Addison observes that Milton is "the greatest Poet which our Nation or perhaps any other has produced."[11]

Partisans of British literature soon would expand this discussion to the Spenserian epic, once regarded as negatively gothic, irregular, and insufficiently classical to please the discerning. Richard Hurd's *Letters on Chivalry and Romance* (1762) speaks congenial and increasingly familiar truths when it censures the slaughter of the classical epic, praises the greater love and friendship of the gothic (p. 47), and insists that the *Faery Queene* must be "read and criticized" (p. 56) on its own and not on classical terms, which often

9. See Donald F. Bond, ed., *The Spectator* (Oxford: Clarendon Press, 1965), II, 537 n-538 n for the reference to Barrow's "In Paradisum Amissam Summi Poetae Johannis Milton" prefatory to the second edition of *Paradise Lost*. Bond also mentions Propertius.

10. *Poems 1685–1692*, ed. Earl Miner and Vinton A. Dearing, vol. 3 of The Works of John Dryden (Berkeley and Los Angeles: University of California Press, 1969), p. 208.

11. See Bond, *Spectator*, III, 530 for Addison's generous praise of Milton.

are inferior to the gothic (pp. 60–62). "Classic ideas of Unity . . . have no place here; and are in every view foreign to the purpose" (p. 65). Spenser's supernatural world is better than the classical in evoking both the imagination and the sublime (pp. 93–95). Above all, Hurd makes clear that there is no inherent reason to prefer the classical before the native tradition.

This discussion of course easily could include Pope's imitations often critical of Horace, Johnson's rejection of Juvenal in *The Vanity of Human Wishes* (1749) and, in general, the emulative cast of mind that encouraged the eighteenth-century author to compete with his literary ancestor. Charles Gildon's *Miscellaneous Letters and Essays on Several Subjects* (1694), for example, bemoans "a *biggotted* [sic] Veneration for a former Age," berates Rymer's archaic and unpatriotic aesthetics, and bravely insists that no Englishman should yield to Greece or Rome "the Honor of *Arms*, or the Wisdom of our Laws," or "the precedence in *Poetry*" (sigs. A2^v–3^r). "*We have the Honor to have more and better* Poets *than ever* Greece *or* Rome saw" (sig. A8^r). John Ames later adds that English poets, like English generals, contest the noblest glories of the past in combat with their respected predecessors. To do otherwise, he claims, is "injustice to ourselves, and them."[12]

Indeed, British writers so often argued that their own literary, and other, national achievements equalled or surpassed those of the ancients that their pride was noticed and questioned by sceptical French observers: Voltaire knew Dryden's praise of Milton and thought it excessive.[13] In 1753 the Abbé Antoine Yart regards British confidence as amiable self-delusion. "La plûpart des Anglois placent leurs grands Poëtes sur le Parnasse, au-dessus des Poëtes de toutes les Nations: leur Milton, par exemple, leur Shakespeare, & leur

---

12. *Belgrade. A Poem* (London, 1717), p. 4.
13. Voltaire, *An Essay upon the Civil Wars of France* (1727), 4th. ed. (London, 1731), pp. 73–74.

Pope, au dessus d'Homère, de Sophocle, & de Virgile; c'est
un erreur agréable dont il ne faut point les disabuser."[14]

The Pindaric ode was not immune from this solid judgment or agreeable error, as the case may be. Several writers
at several times in the eighteenth century tried to show that
Cowley's putative Pindarics lacked the regularity and coherence of Pindar's own efforts. Even Congreve, Trapp, West,
and Johnson, however, could not banish the tenacious view
of Pindaric flights beyond the scope of reason.[15] Thus as late
as 1773 Percival Stockdale's *The Poet* characterizes Pindar as

> Now in the clouds, now in the low profound;
> Now in the circus, now in Jove's abode,
> Parent of nonsense, in the shape of ode. (p. 25)

Hence, one reason for the British ode's superiority to Pindar
is its superior coherence. In 1786 Gilbert Wakefield says
that "in grandeur of imagery and regularity of thought [Pin-

14. Yart, *Idée de la poësie Angloise* (Paris, 1749–1756), IV (1753), 271.

15. Congreve, "A Discourse on the Pindarique Ode" prefatory to *A Pindaric Ode on the Victorious Progress of Her Majesties Arms* (London, 1706);
Joseph Trapp, *Praelectiones Poeticae* (1711–1719), trans. William Bowyer
and William Clarke as *Lectures on Poetry Read in the Schools of Natural Philosophy at Oxford (London, 1742), pp. 203–204, 206–207, 216–217; Gilbert
West, trans., The Odes of Pindar. . . . To which is added a Dissertation on the
Olympick Games* (1749), 2nd ed. (London, 1753), I, iii-xiii; Johnson, "Life
of Cowley" (1779) in *Lives of the English Poets*, ed. George Birkbeck Hill
(Oxford: Clarendon Press, 1905), I, 42–48; "Life of Congreve" (1781), II,
234. For a few other contemporary sources, see John Dennis, Preface to
The Court of Death (1695), and Edward Niles Hooker's remarks—quoting
René Rapin and Basil Kennett—in *The Critical Works of John Dennis*, ed.
Edward Niles Hooker (Baltimore: The Johns Hopkins Press, 1939–1943),
I, 42–43, 510–511, respectively. Norman Maclean discusses eighteenth-
century attitudes towards Pindaric regularity in his "From Action to Image"
(see note 1, above), pp. 423–428. See also Robert Shafer, *The English Ode
to 1660: An Essay In Literary History* (Princeton: Princeton University
Press, 1918), pp. 149–157; Arthur H. Nethercot, "The Relation of
Cowley's 'Pindarics' to Pindar's Odes," *Modern Philology*, 19 (1921–1922),
107–109, and Nethercot, *Abraham Cowley: The Muses' Hannibal* (London:
Oxford University Press, 1931), pp. 136–141.

dar] is surpassed by *Mr. Gray.*"[16] Stockdale later observes that "The Progress of Poesy" is matchless in its kind. "It has all the boldness, and fire of Pindar; with a more connected series of fine, and affecting sense, and sentiment." Similarly, "The Bard" is "superior in vigour, and in ornament, to the most animated odes of Horace." It includes "all that is legitimately bold, and striking in Pindar, without his wildly abrupt, and rhapsodical transitions."[17]

Many British commentators also found that the typical Pindaric subject could not light a wise man's fire. John Oldham evokes the ghost of Spenser, who tells an aspiring poet that he himself would prefer to be an unknown street hawker

> Rather than He, who sung on *Phrygia* 's Shore,
> The *Grecian* Bullies fighting for a Whore:
> Or He of *Thebes*, whom Fame so much extols
> For praising Jockies, and *New-Market* Fools.[18]

Oldham's Restoration judgment found later counterparts, for it required Gilbert West's response in 1749. His extensive "Dissertation on the Olympick Games" is written, in part, to correct the belief that Pindar's odes glorify a set of athletes whom readers "may look upon only as so many *Prize Fighters* and *Jockeys.*"[19]

16. Wakefield, *The Poems of Mr. Gray. With Notes* (London), p. 74.

17. Stockdale, *Lectures on the Truly Eminent English Poets* (London, 1807), II, 573, 589.

18. I found Oldham's remark in Eric Rothstein's distinguished *Restoration and Eighteenth-Century Poetry, 1660–1780* (London and Boston: Routledge & Kegan Paul, 1981), p. 7; see pp. 93–95 for his discussion of Gray's Pindarics. Oldham's words from "Spencer's Ghost," called "A Satyr concerning Poetry" in the volume's Table of Contents, are in *The Works of Mr. John Oldham, Together with his Remains* (London, 1684); new title page for *Poems and Translations. By the Author of The Satyrs upon the Jesuits*, p. 167.

19. See West's *Odes of Pindar* (note 15, above), I, xiii. This caution was repeated in William Rose's review of West in the *Monthly*, 1 (1749), 43. For the attribution, see Benjamin Christie Nangle, *The Monthly Review First Series, 1749–1789. Index of Contributors and Articles* (Oxford: Clarendon Press, 1934), p. 220.

Pindar also was deemed vulnerable, and hence capable of
being transcended, because his triumphant jockies were, after
all, ancient Greeks engaged in ancient Greek games. The
British odist enjoys subjects specifically relevant to a modern
nation's character. Edward Young at least twice adapts his
odes to his countrymen's achievements. In *Ocean* (1728) he
tells the king that this is "A truly *British* Theme I Sing," and
that neither Greece nor Rome can "triumph o'er a Northern
Isle."[20] More specifically, his theme is one unattempted by
the ancients:

> Durst *Homer*'s Muse,
> Or *Pindar*'s chuse
> To pour the Billows on his String?
> No, both defraud
> The tuneful God;
> Scarce more sublime, when JOVE they sing. (II, 7)

Shortly thereafter, Young turns to an ode in praise of merchants. *Imperium Pelagi: A Naval Lyric: Written in Imitation
of Pindar's Spirit* (1729), nonetheless disputes the crown with
its apparent inspiration. The merchant, Young believes, is
indeed a name and subject worthy of Pindar (II, 80); the
modern chiefs he sings are so distinguished that the earlier
Olympic heroes will not "*grudge to* Britons *bold their* Theban
Song" (II, 114). Upon mature reflection, however, Young
thinks his own topic worthier than Pindar's.

---

20. *The Poetical Works of the Reverend Edward Young, LL. D.* (London,
1741), II, 35. Subsequent citations are given in the text. The image in the
stanza immediately quoted—"To pour the Billows on his String?"—is
sufficiently wretched for Young to have banished it when he revised the
poem for the 1757 edition. The student of the ode should see Young's
"Essay on Lyric Poetry" which prefaces *Ocean*. He there insists that his
"Subject is in its own Nature, noble, most proper for an *Englishman*; never
more proper than on this Occasion; and (what is strange) hitherto unsung"
(II, 23–24). As a relevant aside, *Imperium Pelagi* was retitled *The Merchant*
for the Dublin 1730 text.

> *Not* Pindar's *Theme with mine compares,*
> *As far surpast as* useful *Cares*
> *Transcend diversion* light, *and Glory* vain:
> *The Wreath phantastic, shouting Throng,*
> *And panting Steed* to *Him belong,*
> *The* charioteer'*s, not* Empire'*s golden Rein.*
>   (II, 114)

The Reverend Mr. Stephen Duck, then Rector of Byfleet, generalized British praise beyond the merchant's role in imperial expansion. He will

> Let lofty Pindar sing the Grecian steed,
> Britannia glories in as choice a breed:
> As gallant heroes too adorn her coast,
> As fam'd Olympia's plain could ever boast.[21]

By 1760 the outdoing of Pindar was familiar enough to be subject to parody. The elder George Colman's and Robert Lloyd's *Two Odes* mock Gray, Mason, and perhaps Collins, and show that

> . . . each Bard with eager speed
> Vaults on the Pegasean Steed:
> Yet not that Pegasus of yore
> Which th' illustrious Pindar bore,
> But one of nobler breed.
> High blood and youth his lusty veins inspire.
> From Tottipontimoy He came,
> Who knows not, Tottipontimoy, thy name?[22]
>   (pp. 8–9)

---

21. *Caesar's Camp. Or, St. George's Hill. A Poem* (London, 1755), p. 4.

22. Gray was aware of the parody, and discussed it in several of his letters. See *Correspondence of Thomas Gray,* ed. Paget Toynbee and Leonard Whibley (Oxford: Clarendon Press, 1935) II, 674–675 and notes, 681, 690. See also Johnson's remarks in *Boswell's Life of Johnson,* ed. George Birkbeck Hill, and rev. L. F. Powell (Oxford: Clarendon Press, 1934–1950), II, 334, and 334 n; and [ ] *A Cursory Examination of Dr. Johnson's Strictures on the Lyric Performances of Gray* (London, 1781), pp. 13–14.

The splendid stallion wins races at Northampton, Lincoln, Oxford, York, and Newmarket before arriving at Cambridge and inspiring the "self-complacent" poet there (p. 11).

Such parody to the contrary, Gray's odes evoked pleasure in part because of the local and historical color which refurbished the threadbare costume of the Pindaric. Contrast the remarks by, say, Hobbes and Burnaby Greene with these by an unidentified critic whom William Mason quotes in 1775. He admires "The Progress of Poesy" and, especially, "The Bard," for they strike native chords: "Can we in truth be equally interested, for the fabulous exploded Gods of other nations (celebrated in the first half of ['The Progress']) as by the story of our own Edwards and Henrys, or allusions to it? Can a description, the most perfect language ever attained to, of the tyranny expelling the muses from Parnassus, seize the mind equally with the horrors of Berkley Castle, with the apostrophe to the tower?"[23]

This context of confident revision in light of modern needs may illumine some of Gray's achievement in the poems that he and others once thought his major accomplishment, and about which John Pinkerton said—"Pindar stood without a rival till Gray appeared."[24]

23. William Mason, *The Poems of Mr. Gray. To which are Prefixed Memoirs of his Life and Writings*, 2nd ed. (London, 1775), pp. 88–89 of Gray's poems. Observations regarding British history in "The Bard" were familiar in commentary upon it. See James Beattie, "An Essay on Poetry and Music, as they Affect the Mind. Written in the Year 1762," in *Essays* (Edinburgh, 1776), I, 560, and Wakefield's *The Poems of Mr. Gray*, p. 107 (see note 16).

24. *Letters of Literature. By Robert Heron* [pseud. for Pinkerton], (London, 1785), p. 33.

The information in the first part of this essay of course is intended to be suggestive rather than exhaustive; it is prolegomena to a longer study of the rise of British and the decline of classical literature and values during the Restoration and the eighteenth century. This should appear sometime before the second coming.

"The Progress of Poesy" was completed in 1754, but Gray resisted the temptation to issue it separately. The ostensible reason was his dislike for the frequently published individual poems that briefly gained public attention and soon disappeared into the limbo of pie crusts and curlers. I suspect that there was another reason as well—namely, that "The Progress" and "The Bard" comment upon one another, and that one poem could be genuinely finished only when the other was. In this case, that was May of 1757, when Gray heard a blind Welsh harper in Cambridge, he was moved to complete "The Bard," and by implication complete "The Progress" as well. Gray later said that "I felt myself the bard," and in a key sense is as accurate as he is melodramatic, for that poem allows Gray to investigate his own literary role.[25] In the process, "The Bard" alludes to epic tradition, and helps to reestablish the sublime ode in mid-century Britain. Much of this is subsumed under Gray's use of the ode to celebrate British mythic history through a poet's prophetic, visionary, voice; but that celebration is incoherent until we see its relationship to the poem whose manuscript gestation took three years before its bardic midwife induced labor.

"The Progress of Poesy" begins with references to Greece and to the variety of poetic kinds that stem "From Helicon's harmonious springs."[26] The pastoral, the vocal ode, the georgic, and the sublime epic are among its "thousand rills" (l. 4). Poetry, Gray insists, is a benevolent master who is sovereign, parent, enchanter, and controller (ll. 13–16), but

25. See *Correspondence*, I, 420, for Gray's reluctance to publish the "Progress" alone, and II, 501–502 for the visit of John Parry, the Welsh harper. Gray equates himself with the Bard in *Correspondence*, III, 1290, as reported in Norton Nicholls' "Reminiscences of Gray," written in 1805.

26. Line 20, as in *The Complete Poems of Thomas Gray. English, Latin and Greek*, ed. H. W. Starr and J. R. Hendrickson (Oxford: Clarendon Press, 1966). Subsequent citations are given in the text. I have also profited from the editions of Roger Lonsdale, *The Poems of Gray, Collins, and Goldsmith* (London and New York: Longman, Norton, 1969), and Arthur Johnston, *Selected Poems of Thomas Gray and William Collins* (Columbia: University of South Carolina Press, 1970).

only of those with a "willing soul" (l. 13). Hence, with
such a responsive audience, poetry induces peace and contentment, and pacifies the eagle of war (ll. 20–24):

> On Thracia's hills the Lord of War,
> Has curb'd the fury of his car,
> And drop'd his thirsty lance at thy command.
> (ll. 17–19)

The arms of war yield to the arms of woman, and poetry and
its myths evoke amiable sexual passion and, presumably,
propagation. Venus appears, and "O'er her warm cheek, and
rising bosom, move / The bloom of young Desire, and pur-
ple light of Love" (ll. 40–41). That happy vision ends the
first triad or unit of three verse paragraphs and its strophe,
anti-strophe, and epode that include classical mythology and
show the strength and power of poetry in the world of willing
souls.

The second unit and its classical mythology transport us to
a world in which poetry has a different role—as compensa-
tion for man's physically and morally fallen state, and consequent labor, pain, disease, sorrow, and death (ll. 43–45).
Gray now introduces his first major allusion to Milton, as he
asks his song to negate such a view, "And justify the laws of
Jove" by means of "the heav'nly Muse" (ll. 47–48). Poetry is the sun that scatters the spectres of the night; even in
the frigid north and savage south, the Muse can cheer or can
encourage glory (ll. 57, 64) and "Th' unconquerable Mind,
and Freedom's holy Flame" (l. 65). This important line
concludes the middle paragraph, or anti-strophe, of the
second unit, and is the transitional device to the epode and
the beginning of the poem's conventional "progress"
through time and space based on a familiar theory of causa-
tion. Greece was the source of poetic inspiration until her
"evil hour" (l. 77) when liberty collapsed and the Muses
departed for Italy, where the pattern ultimately was repeated
and poetry and liberty emigrated to England. In the poem's
final triad, Gray begins to discuss English poetic forms and
audiences, and, not surprisingly, starts with Shakespeare as

the darling child of nature (l. 84) rather than of classical learning. England's Avon thus replaces the Greek Helicon, and England's Mother Nature replaces the Roman Venus. Nature teaches her "immortal Boy" to "Richly paint the vernal year" (ll. 91, 90). Greece's willing souls are replaced by the English audience able to respond with joy, horror, and perhaps most important, the feelings of the heart. Shakespeare can "ope the sacred source of sympathetic Tears" (l. 94). This renaissance golden age—one that is as much the fruit of liberty as of nature—is no less brilliant when the product of the sublime and poetically supernatural, for Milton, we soon hear, was "Nor second" (l. 95) in his Christian, elevated epic. In fact, Gray adds in a probable contrast of English practice with Greek theory, "He pass'd the flaming bounds of Place and Time" (l. 98) even though he suffered "endless night" (l. 102) as a result of his exalted vision. Dryden, who comes thereafter in this English progress, is "less presumptuous" than Milton but nonetheless roams "o'er the fields of Glory" in his couplet form (ll. 103–104). Gray again turns to Dryden at the beginning of his final paragraph, when he alludes to Dryden's ode and its "Thoughts, that breathe, and words, that burn," and laments—"But ah! 'tis heard no more" (ll. 110–111).

Gray has given us an English epitome of Helicon's "thousand rills," as he cites his own nation's dramatic, epic, and odic forms, and then stops to ask the English lyre divine, "what daring Spirit / Wakes thee now?" (ll. 112–113). That spirit is of course Thomas Gray's as the poem and Gray's own note to "heard no more" make clear. "We have had in our language," he says, "no other odes of the sublime kind, than that of Dryden on St. Cecilia's day: for Cowley (who had his merit) yet wanted judgment, style, and harmony, for such a task. That of Pope is not worthy of so great a man" (p. 207). Here is a genre in which the modern poet can excel, a form little tried and less succeeded in by his forbears and contemporaries. Gray is humble but not humbled, and cautious but not anxious as he adapts his own genius to what he has and has not inherited—not "the pride, nor ample pinion / That the Theban Eagle bear" (ll.

114–115); not the Pindaric ode celebrating victories in athletic war games, but his own ode written by a poet helped by
the Muse even as he was an infant. Such an ode will allow
him to

> . . . mount, and keep his distant way
> Beyond the limits of a vulgar fate,
> Beneath the Good how far—but far above the Great.
> (ll. 121–123)

That is, as "The Progress of Poesy" ends, his sublime ode
will keep him beneath the morally good man in reputation
and value, but above the politically great man, perhaps the
sort celebrated in the classical, or classically inspired, soaring
ode.

Gray has surveyed the movement of poetry and some of
its kinds from free Greece to free England and proclaimed
himself the "daring Spirit" aware of a vacuum in the
nation's literary genres. He aims to fill that gap and does so,
I suggest, in his own sublime ode that follows. "The Bard,"
indeed, begins with its speaker quite literally "far above the
Great" on a crag on Mt. Snowdon, looking down at Edward
I's army twisting its hostile way toward him in order to kill
him and the vestiges of liberty. Here is Gray's Advertisement to his poem: "The following Ode is founded on a
Tradition current in Wales, that EDWARD THE FIRST,
when he compleated the conquest of that country, ordered
all the Bards, that fell into his hands, to be put to death" (p.
18). Gray thus announces that this poem is to deal with an
audience not of "willing" but of unwilling souls in a pre-
Shakespearean era when Albion did not have liberty to help
nurture the Muse. Consequently, we see the death of the
Bards and of poetry, but also, especially in the prophetic
parts of the poem, the considerable discomfort of the tyrant
and enemy to art. He induces tears of pain, where Shakespeare, in "The Progress," induces tears through sympathy.
Gray repeats the same rhyme words to help us see the parallel in his sister poems. In "The Progress" we hear that
Shakespeare can unlock the gates "Of Horrour . . . and

thrilling Fears, / Or ope the sacred source of sympathetic Tears" (ll. 93–94). In "The Bard" not even Edward's virtues can "save thy secret soul from nightly fears, / From Cambria's curse, from Cambria's tears!" (ll. 7–8). Similarly, in line 19 of "The Progress" the Lord of War has "drop'd his thirsty lance at [poetry's] command"; in line 14 of "The Bard" the tyrant untutored by poetry shouts, "To arms! . . . and couch'd his quiv'ring lance."

Gray not only has changed his warlike auditor to someone with an unwilling rather than willing soul; he also has changed his conception of the poet of odes. "The Progress" begins with the poet as external, passive voice, asking, "Awake, Æolian lyre, awake, / And give to rapture all thy trembling strings" (ll. 1–2); near the end of the poem, the poet is more active, but still tentative, as he asks about his own role in the tradition of the ode, and wonders who "Wakes thee now?" (l. 113). In "The Bard," however, the Welsh poet himself is the confident, active, performer who "with a Master's hand, and Prophet's fire, / Struck the deep sorrows of his lyre" (ll. 21–22).

That lyre no longer is Aeolian but Welsh, and the mountain home of the poet no longer is Helicon but Snowdon, for Gray is investigating both his own and his country's place in traditions and individual talents. Hence the southern European myths and names—Helicon, Ceres, Thracia, Cytheria, Venus, Hyperion, Delphi, Maeander, and Latium—surrender to the equally mythic and harmonius Hoel, Llwellyn, Cadwallo, Urien, Modred, Plinlimmon, and Arvon, not to mention the more mundane Edward, Mortimer, Gloucester, and Conway. Gray also investigates the consequences for the poet and poetry of some of these changes—here, the poet's new role as prophet and avenger rather than sovereign calmer and soother. The lone bard views the shades of his murdered colleagues and says:

'I see them sit, they linger yet,
'Avengers of their native land:
'With me in dreadful harmony they join,

'And weave with bloody hands, the tissue of thy line.'
(ll. 45–48)

The poem becomes a prophecy of the decline of Edward and
his Plantagenet dynasty, as Gray's British sublime ode
confidently turns from Pindar's apparent celebration of an
athlete's achievement, to the Bard's celebration of the
decline of tyranny, the restoration of liberty, and the function of poetry in the state. Celebration of the mortal body
yields to celebration of the immortal spirit.

The implications of this prophecy again lead us toward
Gray's uses of literary transmission, for the sublime commonly evoked the epic and Milton. Specifically, the chorus
of ghosts weaves a vocal tapestry that predicts and portrays
the several disasters that Edward's line and the nation are to
suffer because of his aberrations. Edward III, for example,
will be neither pitied nor mourned in death (l. 65) and Britain herself will be subject to "the din of battle bray" and
"Long Years of havock" (ll. 83, 85). Once the ghosts have
led the Bard to this sight of vengeance, they disappear; in
their stead, Mt. Snowdon reveals the equally prophetic
"Visions of glory" (l. 107) that show the restoration of
order, the true king's posterity, and liberty and poetry: "No
more our long-lost Arthur we bewail. / All-hail, ye genuine
Kings, Britannia's Issue, hail!" (ll. 109–110). Gray's note
to the last words again makes his intention clear: "Both
Merlin and Taliessin had prophesied, that the Welch should
regain their sovereignty over this island; which seemed to be
accomplished in the House of Tudor" (p. 211)—and the
noblest of Tudors was Elizabeth, who combined manly
power and virginal grace for the protection of the nation,
freedom, and the arts. Moreover, Gray again offers a parallel to his earlier "Progress," where Queen Venus of classical
myth held her amorous court and induced sexuality and, by
implication, birth; shortly thereafter, the woman becomes
Mother Nature who guides Shakespeare. In "The Bard" the
propagating female force stems from the British poetic arts

and artists around chaste Elizabeth, so that the dead themselves, and with them the mythic past and brilliant future,
are brought to life.

'What strings symphonious tremble in the air,
'What strains of vocal transport round her play!
'Hear from the grave, great Taliessin, hear;
'They breathe a soul to animate thy clay.
'Bright Rapture calls, and soaring, as she sings,
'Waves in the eye of Heav'n her many colour'd wings.'
(ll. 119–124)

At the beginning of "The Progress" Gray asked the Aeolian
lyre "to give to rapture all thy trembling strings" (l. 2); now
Gray images Rapture as actually singing and calling as the
British race is restored and fulfilled through Elizabeth.

He also calls in at least two epic parallels that could not
have been far from his mind or that of his reader—namely,
the prophesies in Book VI of the *Aeneid*, and Books XI and
XII of *Paradise Lost*. Aeneas, protected by the Cumaean
Sibyl, visits the Elysian fields in the underworld and speaks
with the shade of his father Anchises; that benevolent voice
tells him of Rome's checkered future until its greatest
achievements under Augustus, restorer of a golden age to
the republic and peace with law to a recalcitrant world. Over
1600 years later, the Archangel Michael guides Milton's
Adam up "a Hill / Of Paradise the highest" (XI, 377–378),
evokes the many failures and murders within the human
race, and shows it, finally, restored to grace through Christ's
sacrifice. In each case a troubled, diminished world is
fulfilled in the vision of the future, and in each case that
fulfillment is made possible by the presence of a version of
the king of kings, whether Roman, Christian, or British.

Gray of course knew both of these poems, and he probably knew some or all of the more modern epics which used
a similar convention, one especially attractive for Sir Richard
Blackmore. It appears in Book V of his *Prince Arthur* (1695),
Book IX of *King Arthur* (1697), Book VIII of *Eliza* (1705),
and Book VIII of *Alfred* (1723). For Blackmore, Britain's

best aspirations are fulfilled in Elizabeth, William of Orange, or other congenial monarchs. For Voltaire, Louis XIV serves that role, as in Canto VII of the *Henriade* (1728; 1732 in English, pp. 150–159), and for Pope it was George II, the destructive, parodic, completion of Dulness's best hopes in the third book of the *Dunciad* of 1728 and 1729, and the third and fourth books of the final *Dunciad* in 1744.[27] A version of the golden age reappears in each work, and in Gray's "Bard" reappears as a golden age of letters. The destructive wars of Edward are sublimated in the poetic wars of Spenser. The malign Plantagenet tyrant is replaced by the benevolent tyrant poetry, again controlling us for our own pleasure and instruction. Hence Milton's new Eden exemplifies the new world possible with the restoration of Arthur's Welsh dynasty and liberty.

> 'The verse adorn again
> 'Fierce War, and faithful Love,
> 'And Truth severe, by fairy Fiction drest.
> 'In buskin'd measures move
> 'Pale Grief, and pleasing Pain,
> 'With Horrour, Tyrant of the throbbing breast.
> 'A Voice, as of the Cherub-Choir,
> 'Gales from blooming Eden bear;
> 'And distant warblings lessen on my ear,
> 'That lost in long futurity expire.'   (ll. 125–134)

The allusions to Spenser and Milton again urge the epic context of Gray's sublime ode, the genre he has chosen as his own contribution to British letters, which now goes beyond

---

27. Arthur Johnston observes that Gray "certainly knew the prophecies in the Old Testament, in books 6 and 8 of the *Aeneid*, books 11 and 12 of *Paradise Lost*, and book 5 of Sir Richard Blackmore's *Prince Arthur*. Gray's prophecy follows the pattern of that in *Paradise Lost*—a series of disasters followed by a vision of a new age." *Selected Poems of Thomas Gray*, p. 76. Johnston's "Poetry and Criticism After 1740" also remains one of the best introductions to the mid and later eighteenth century. See History of Literature in the English Language, vol. 4, *Dryden to Johnson*, ed. Roger Lonsdale (London: Sphere Books, 1971), pp. 357–395.

him to a "long futurity." But Gray is not content even with
what he thought obvious, and so adds an epic tag—"He
spoke"—and repeats the words "endless night" which he
used in "The Progress of Poesy" for Milton (l. 102). The
conclusion of "The Bard" demonstrates the Welsh Bard's
triumph over Edward and British Gray's triumph over a
Greek literary form, which he has mastered and turned into
a vehicle suitable for his nations's needs and his own. The
Bard cries out to Edward upon completion of the prophetic
vision:

> 'Enough for me: With joy I see
> 'The different doom our Fates assign.
> 'Be thine Despair, and scept'red Care,
> 'To triumph, and to die, are mine.'
> He spoke, and headlong from the mountain's height
> Deep in the roaring tide he plung'd to endless night.
> (ll. 139–144)

Gray's and the Bard's sublime ode end with a reminder of
their Miltonic and British roots, as Snowdon and Conway,
not the Helicon and her springs in "The Progress" supply
the backdrop of mountain and water.

In these quasi-Pindaric sister odes, then, Gray has discussed the origins of poetry and its several species in an
innocent, politically free world of willing souls. Shortly
thereafter, Freedom and the Muses migrate to Britain, where
native genres begin, and Gray determines that his role is to
offer a specifically national ode, as exemplified in his own
"Bard" and its investigation of the relationship between poetry and liberty. Gray thus places us in Wales, where liberty
and poetry temporarily are destroyed in the Bard, but revived
after the collapse of the Plantagenets and the triumph of
Elizabeth Tudor, descendant of Welsh Arthur. Gray thus
changes the ode from Greek praise of an athlete, to British
praise of literature and monarchs. He also associates his ode
with the epic's prophecies of restoration in the *Aeneid* and,
especially, in *Paradise Lost*, so that his poem is part of
"Britannia's Issue." By so writing, Gray embodies the

midcentury reexamination of the past that allowed him to profit from his modernity while changing the tradition he received. In 1751 Samuel Johnson argues that he who "wishes to be counted among the benefactors of posterity, must add by his own toil to the acquisitions of his ancestors, and secure his memory from neglect by some valuable improvement."[28] "Some valuable improvement" added "to the acquisitions of his ancestors"—such terms suggest one fitting description of Gray's attitude toward his own achievement and his varied literary inheritance.

28. *The Rambler*, 154, September 7, 1751, in *Samuel Johnson. The Rambler*, ed. W. J. Bate and Albrecht B. Strauss, vol. 5 of *The Yale Edition of the Works of Samuel Johnson* (New Haven and London: Yale University Press, 1969), p. 58.

ROBERT HALSBAND

Hogarth's Graphic Friendships:
Illustrating Books By Friends

As a painter and draftsman-engraver William Hogarth ranks
high in eighteenth-century British art. As a book illustrator,
although here he expresses a lesser aspect of his genius, he
is worthy of attention as well.[1] When he illustrated works by
comtemporary writers whom he knew personally, we can
examine the illustrations in a biographical context to supplement other relevant contexts. His friendships with writers
cover a wide range, from close intimacy (as with William
Huggins) at one extreme, to that of mere acquaintanceship
at the other. The types of literature he illustrated are likewise varied: a collection of essays; four stage works—an oratorio libretto, a ballad opera, a comic interlude, a burlesque
tragedy; and, most successfully, one of the famous novels of
the century.

The earliest example of Hogarth's work as a literary illustrator for someone he knew is his frontispiece in 1726 for
Nicholas Amhurst's collection of periodical essays *Terrae-*

---

1. I am greatly indebted to two important books by Ronald Paulson:
Hogarth's Graphic Works, rev. ed. (New Haven and London: Yale University Press, 1970) and *Hogarth: His Life, Art, and Times* (New Haven and
London: Yale University Press, 1971), hereafter cited as *HLAT*. My essay
can be regarded as a series of footnotes to Paulson in the sense that it
amplifies minor topics of his large-scale works.

Filius: Or, The Secret History of the University of Oxford.
Amhurst's connection with the university had been stormy:
in 1719, at the age of twenty-two he was expelled—for liber-
tinism and misconduct, according to the authorities; for
Whig principles and opposition to the university's Toryism
and high church sentiments, according to his own self-
defense. He then settled in London as a journalist and in
1721 began a campaign of revenge by issuing *Terrae-Filius*,
pubished twice a week for about six months. In 1726 he collected and republished the essays in two volumes.

Amhurst's earliest connection with Hogarth had occurred
in 1724, when, in his periodical *Pasquin*, he praised
Hogarth's satiric print *Masquerades and Operas*, "representing the bad Taste of the Town," as Hogarth himself
described it, since masquerades, opera, and pantomime had
driven English plays from the theaters.[2] Admiring Hogarth's
work, Amhurst—rather than his printer Richard Francklin,
who was politically oriented—probably engaged him to design
and engrave the frontispiece for *Terrae-Filius*. (Figure 1)

What does the print show? The first number of the
periodical explains that at the Encaenia, Oxford's annual
commemoration of founders and benefactors, an undergraduate in the role of university buffoon—called *terrae-filius*
(or son of the soil)—delivered a mock, satirical oration made
up of university gossip to divert the crowd of spectators, his
"merry oration" being "interspers'd with secret history, rail-
lery, and sarcasm, as the occasions of the times supply'd him
with matter." The setting is the Sheldonian Theatre,
designed by Christopher Wren and opened in 1669, and
today still used for the annual Encaenia (although an oration
by a *terrae-filius* has long since been dispensed with).

In the gallery sit the undergraduates, one of whom is
climbing over the balustrade; they frequently interrupted and
heckled the speaker. Below them sit the masters and doc-
tors. In the center the vice chancellor presides, with a proctor on his right. In the lower right corner stands the other

2. Paulson, *HLAT*, I, 103, 121.

1. Frontispiece to *Terrae-Filius: Or, The Secret History of the University of Oxford* (1726) by Nicholas Amhurst. The Henry E. Huntington Library, San Marino, California.

W.ᵗ Hogarth Inv.   G. V.ᵈ Gucht Sc.

Per Vulnera Servor
Morte tuâ Vivens.   *Virg. Æneid:*

2. Frontispiece to *Judith: an Oratorio; or Sacred Drama* (1733) by William
Huggins. The Henry E. Huntington Library, San Marino, California.

proctor with a copy of *Terrae-Filius* that he has indignantly torn in half—probably because he believes himself slandered in it. But the focus of attention is the *terrae-filius* orator himself, the center figure in the cluster of people. His wig and gown have been torn off by an outraged woman. Others mentioned in his oration surround him menacingly; he is even being attacked by a dog. The print thus reflects the irreverent essays that it introduces.

Hogarth, of course, never studied at Oxford. Unless he attended an Encaenia for the purpose of designing the frontispiece, he could have based his design on a print of the Sheldonian and a description of the *terrae-filius* oration. As to his acquaintance with Amhurst, in 1729 the *Craftsman*, a political paper edited by Amhurst, printed a notice of Hogarth's secret marriage to the daughter of Sir James Thornhill, the painter.[3] The information probably came to Amhurst through his friendship with Hogarth.

In contrast to Amhurst, who could not have known Hogarth intimately, William Huggins was a friend of long standing, and of such closeness that Hogarth addressed him in one letter as "My Dear best Friend."[4] To document their friendship we have engravings, letters, and a vivid little portrait in oils.

Huggins, born in 1696 and almost exactly Hogarth's age, was far from being a hack writer. An Oxford graduate, he was for brief periods a fellow of Magdalen and a functionary at Hampton Court. He also trained for the law, and assisted Hogarth in his campaign (in the 1730s) to persuade Parliament to draft legislation for the copyright of prints. But Huggins' main passion was Italian poetry. He was a pioneer enthusiast in the Romantic appreciation of Italian literature.[5]

His earliest known connection with Hogarth was as the painter's patron. About 1732 he bought from him two important paintings—a version of *The Beggar's Opera* and a

3. Ibid., I, 204.
4. Ibid., I, 263.
5. Roderick Marshall, *Italy in English Literature 1755–1815* (New York: Columbia University Press, 1934), p. 33.

picture of the Bambridge committee of the House of Commons during its investigation of the horrifying conditions in the Fleet prison. (Its warden, Thomas Bambridge, had bought the appointment from Huggins' father, who himself had been notorious for his profitable cruelty.) These two paintings had been intended for a collector, who when he became bankrupt fled England; Huggins generously bought them himself.[6]

About the same time on his own behalf he commissioned Hogarth to design a frontispiece for a literary work he had written. Its title, as published in 1733, was *Judith: An Oratorio; or Sacred Drama*, with music by Willem De Fesch, a Dutch composer recently emigrated to London. On the title page of the pamphlet Huggins modestly listed the author as W— — H— —. Through choruses, recitatives, and airs, Huggins dramatized the central episode of a story taken from the Old Testament Apocrypha. It tells how the beautiful and virtuous Judith, a Hebrew widow, determines to rescue her people from the besieging army of Assyrians. Accompanied by her maid, she goes to the camp of Holofernes, general of the Assyrian army. He is so struck by her beauty, which he hopes to enjoy that night, that he drinks himself into a stupor and falls asleep. Judith then seizes his sword and cuts off his head, which she carries back to the Hebrews. Their army then attacks, displaying the head on a spear, and the Assyrians, demoralized by the loss of their commander, are defeated and flee.

The story had frequently been used by Renaissance and baroque painters, most of whom depict Judith displaying the severed head. But Hogarth chose the less shocking but more suspenseful moment when Judith prepares to carry out her bold and bloody deed. (Figure 2) Pointing to the victim with one hand, she holds his sword in the other. (His helmet and shield, no longer protecting him, lie nearby, symbolizing his helplessness.) Judith's grandly rhetorical gesture seems borrowed from history painting, as though Hogarth has

6. Paulson, *HLAT*, I, 230.

miniaturized the biblical legend.[7] The precise libretto passage
that he illustrated in the frontispiece is Judith's air:

> O God, a manly Strength impart
> To my Hand as to my Heart,
> For thy chosen People's Sake.
> Rush forth thou massy glitt'ring Sword,
> That on thy detested Lord
> My just Vengeance I may take.

The quotation from Virgil printed at the bottom of the plate
constitutes an ironic counterpoint to the picture. Translated
it reads: "saved by these wounds of thine, and living by thy
death." In the *Aeneid* the lines are mournfully uttered by
the Etruscan king when he sees the corpse of his son who
was killed in the battle that has enabled him to survive.

As a specimen of Hogarth's draftsmanship, the design
seems inferior. The heroine's arms are clumsily drawn, for
example. But the weakness may also be blamed on the
engraver, Gerard Vandergucht, who frequently engraved
Hogarth's drawings. What can be said in favor of the composition is that it does reflect the pious fervor of Judith's
heroism.

The oratorio was scheduled to be performed in the theater
in Lincoln's Inn Fields on February 8, 1733, aided by new
painted scenery and magnificent decoration.[8] Cecilia Young,
who was to sing the main part, was one of the best singers of
her time, with a high and unusually flexible soprano. But
the announced opening performance of *Judith* did not take
place, for Miss Young withdrew because of illness, or so she
claimed. Huggins angrily disclaimed responsibility for the
cancellation, blaming it on "the Misconduct and pretended

---

7. Hogarth's design has striking similarities to a print of Judith by Bernard Picart, engraved by Pigne, probably dating from 1710 (Kitto extra-
illustrated Bible, Huntington Library, San Marino, California, vol. 30, f.
5720). Paulson mentions Picart's influence on an earlier work by Hogarth
(*Hogarth's Graphic Works*, I, 31).

8. John Ireland, *Hogarth Illustrated* (London, 1791–1798), II, 526.

Sickness" of Miss Young.[9] (Her frequent illness, Grove's *New Dictionary of Music* states, was attributed by some to intemperance.) A week later the performance took place, with an inferior singer in the leading part. The libretto, whose printing had evidently been arranged by Huggins, was sold only at the playhouse and could not have had a large sale. The performance, conducted by De Fesch, did not catch the town's fancy, and *Judith* was performed only once again, seven years later at a benefit for him.

Yet apart from the frontispiece, Hogarth made use of the oratorio in a curious way. Two months before its first performance, he issued subscription tickets for his own forthcoming large single engraving entitled *A Midnight Modern Conversation.* Most of the small subscription form is filled with a design usually referred to as "A Chorus of Singers." (Figure 3) The conductor, at the top of the heap of people, conducts from a score on which is printed "Judith: an Oratorio; or Sacred Drama by"; in the chorus, consisting of fourteen men and boys, five display their scores on which can be read "the world shall Bow to the Assyrian Throne"—the text of a choral number in Act I, Scene 1, of the oratorio. From the conductor at the top, evidently a caricature of the composer De Fesch, to the choirboys at the foot, the entire engraving has a crude, gutsy vigor about it, especially since all the individuals are characterized with sharp particularity.[10] Hogarth's use of this oratorio chorus as the ornamental design on his subscription ticket can only be interpreted as an advertisement for his good friend's work, then in rehearsal. The oratorio's sacred theme served also as a moral contrast to the vice and debauchery that make up the subject of the engraving.

9. Unless otherwise noted, all references to stage performances are drawn from *The London Stage 1660–1800* (Carbondale: Southern Illinois University Press, 1960–1968), Part 3: 1729–1747, ed. Arthur H. Scouten; Part 4: 1747–1776, ed. G. W. Stone, Jr.

10. For a detailed analysis of the plate, see Frederick Antal, *Hogarth and His Place in European Art* (London: Routledge & Kegan Paul, 1962), p. 62.

3. "A Chorus of Singers" (1732). The Henry E. Huntington Library, San Marino, California.

4. William Huggins (1758). The Hyde Collection, Somerville, New Jersey.

The warm friendship of Hogarth and Huggins continued to flourish. In January 1735 both men were among the group that founded the Sublime Society of Beefsteaks, a social club devoted to convivial pranks. During the next two decades Huggins passed most of his time at his country house busy with literary pursuits. In 1757 he published his anonymous translation of *Orlando Furioso* in two volumes. Soon after that he asked Hogarth to paint his portrait as a companion piece to one of his late father, done by Hogarth in the early 1740s.[11] Hogarth graciously agreed. (Figure 4) The result is an oval portrait showing Huggins, informally dressed in a morning cap looking to the side with an amiable expression as though pleased by what the artist has put in the background. The bust on the left is inscribed on its plinth "Il Divino Ariosto," and on the right a wall plaque lists the three books of *The Divine Comedy*, a translation of which Huggins was working on. Foreseeing its publication, Huggins asked Hogarth to consider illustrating Dante's masterpiece. "What you propose," Hogarth replied, "would be a Noble undertaking which I believe ten or a dozen years agoe I should have Embraced with joy, and would have pleased the Public, if I could have done the Author any degree of Justice, but consider now my dear Friend Sixty is too late in the day to begin so arduous a Task a work that could not be compleated in less than four or five years." In his indolence, he continued, he could only be content with trifles.[12]

Almost two years later in 1760, when Huggins prepared to publish his translation, he asked Hogarth to make an engraving of his portrait to serve as frontispiece. Again Hogarth begged to be excused. He knew from experience, he explained, that he had the devil of a time copying his own work, and he was sure the poorest engraver could perform the task better than he. But, in fact, Huggins employed for the task Thomas Major, who would later be the first engraver

11. Paulson, *HLAT*, II, 263.
12. Ibid., II, 264–265.

elected to the newly established Royal Academy. As for Huggins' translation, except for a very brief excerpt published in a magazine,[13] his ambitious work remained in manuscript (and is now lost), and his engraved portrait intended as a frontispiece was merely struck off in a few copies.[14]

Hogarth's frontispiece to *Judith* was not only a tribute to friendship but also a sign of his interest in the stage. He wished to compose his pictures, he once remarked, as though they were representations on the stage.[15] Of the book illustrations he designed for friends, three others (besides *Judith*), were frontispieces for stage works.

Joseph Mitchell, a Grub Street poet and a member of the Scotch contingent in London, sought the patronage of the Prime Minister so strenuously that he was sometimes called Sir Robert Walpole's poet, although he failed to win Walpole's favor. He courted less exalted patrons as well. In February 1731 he published *Three Poetical Epistles. To Mr. Hogarth, Mr. Dandridge, and Mr. Lambert, Masters of the Art of Painting.* The first epistle, addressed to Hogarth as an "Eminent History and Conversation Painter," praises him extravagantly: "Shakespeare in Painting, still improve / And more the World's Attention move."

Perhaps in gratitude to Mitchell for his flattering notice,[16] Hogarth designed the frontispiece for a ballad opera that Mitchell had recently completed. Entitled *The Highland Fair: or, Union of the Clans*, it was staged at the Theatre Royal in Drury Lane on March 20, 1731. In its brief prologue the supercilious Critick laughs at the notion of a Scotch opera, to which the poet replies: "Why not, Sir, as well as an *English*, *French*, or *Italian* one?" (*The Beggar's Opera* by John Gay, a spectacular success, had started the vogue in 1728.) Mitchell's subtitle—the "Union of the Clans"—sums up the

---

13. *British Magazine*, April 1760, p. 266.
14. One copy is in the Huntington Library.
15. Hogarth, *The Analysis of Beauty*, ed. Joseph Burke (Oxford: Clarendon Press, 1955), p. 209.
16. Paulson, *HLAT*, I, 235–237, 531.

theme of its Romeo and Juliet plot. Three performances the first week and a fourth the next month make up its entire stage history. It was published during the first week, having already been advertised in *The London Evening Post*: "With a curious Frontispiece, design'd by Mr. Hogarth."

What Hogarth depicted in the frontispiece (Figure 5) is the concluding scene of the opera. One clan chief, Colin (on the left) is accompanied by his piper, behind whom can be seen his vassals and servants. Confronting him stands Euen, chief of the enemy clan. Their exact actions are given in the stage directions: "The Chiefs bow thrice as they meet, Colin making the first Steps and Reverences, according to the Ceremonial agreed upon." Both chiefs are armed with nondescript swords and shields, but with Scotch bonnets on their heads and a set of bagpipes to supply local color. The engraver of Hogarth's design was again Gerard Vandergucht, this time less graceless than in the *Judith* frontispiece. The caption under the print, far from reflecting its Scottish setting and story, comes from the *Aeneid*: "Perchance even this [distress] will some day be a joy to recall." In the Roman epic this is how Aeneas consoles his men after they have been storm-tossed onto the shore of Carthage. Similarly, the Scottish clan chiefs, living in peace, will some day recall their former distressful strife. Presumably the Latin tag, like the one printed under the frontispiece to *Judith*, was provided by Hogarth. Yet neither literary work bears any relation to Roman epic or legend. Perhaps Hogarth was recalling his boyhood training, when his father was a schoolmaster and Latin scholar.

Such an ardent theater-goer as Hogarth inevitably encountered David Garrick, the greatest actor and after 1747 the most successful theatre manager of the time. In 1741 at the very beginning of his London career the young actor achieved instant fame as Shakespeare's Richard III. Hogarth must have met him soon afterwards. Unlike previous actors, who postured the role in the traditional declamatory style, Garrick transformed himself into the crafty, mercurial monarch, playing him with naturalistic expression and intensity. The high point of his performance was the tent scene

in the final act, when Richard awakens from his guilty dream
to be confronted by the ghosts of his victims. When
Hogarth painted his portrait of Garrick in 1745 he chose this
dramatic scene. (Figure 6) Huge, life-size dimensions
endow the picture with the sweep and grandeur of history
painting. As Ronald Paulson writes, it is a remarkable fusion
of history painting and intimate portraiture.[17] Evidently not
commissioned by Garrick, it was sold to a private collector,
after being engraved as a print.

Not only actor and manager, Garrick was also playwright
and poet, and he involved Hogarth in both these activities
near the end of Hogarth's life. In March 1762 Garrick wrote
a brief comic interlude in verse for the theatre in Drury
Lane, calling it *The Farmer's Return from London*. In the
preface he modestly claims that he wrote it only as a benefit
for Mrs. Pritchard, one of his favorite leading ladies, and
would not have printed it "had not his Friend, Mr. *Hogarth*,
flattered him most agreeably, by thinking [it] not unworthy
of a Sketch of his Pencil." He was therefore dedicating
"this Trifle" to Hogarth, he writes, to honor him "both as a
Man and an *Artist*."

In his frontispiece (Figure 7) Hogarth has delineated the
homely kitchen-living room in which the farmer—played by
Garrick—tells his family about his visit to London, where he
has seen the coronation (of George the Third and his bride),
attended the theater, and visited Cock Lane, scene of a
recent ghost-hoax. Although Garrick provided the farmer
and his wife with three children, Hogarth put only two into
his design. The cracked wall and coarse furnishings reflect
the rugged simplicity of the farmer, whose Falstaffian figure
and rough costume are in tune with his rustic dialect and
crude sense of humor. The scene glows with earthy realism
of Dutch and Flemish genre paintings.[18] When his children
are out of the room the farmer assures his wife that he has
not succumbed to any prostitutes in London: "I know, as

17. *HLAT*, II, 29.
18. For a detailed analysis of the plate, see Antal, *Hogarth*, p. 71.

5. Frontispiece to *The Highland Fair; or, Union of the Clans. An Opera* (1731) by Joseph Mitchell. The New York Public Library.

6. David Garrick as Richard the Third (1745). The Walker Art Gallery, Liverpool.

Wm Hogarth.delin.   James Basire.Sculp.

The Farmer's Return.

7. Frontispiece to *The Farmer's Return from London. An Interlude* (1762) by David Garrick. The Henry E. Huntington Library, San Marino, California.

W. Hogarth inv^t.   Ger VanderGucht sculp.

8. Frontispiece to *The Tragedy of Tragedies; or, The Life and Death of Tom Thumb the Great* (1731) by Henry Fielding. The Henry E. Huntington Library, San Marino, California.

we sow we must reeap, / And a cunning old ram will avoid rotten sheep." The part of his wife was played not by Mrs. Pritchard, as intended, but by Mary Bradshaw, who won the greatest success of her career in that part.

On the stage the interlude was popular, no doubt for its topicality and robust humor. It played for twelve nights the first season, and three the following. In print, as a thin pamphlet, it went into a second edition the same year. Perhaps Hogarth's frontispiece helped sell it, particularly since the engraver had done the design justice. He was James Basire, who had recently been appointed engraver to the Society of Antiquaries, and who is best known today as William Blake's teacher and master.

The friendship between Garrick and Hogarth was acknowledged after Hogarth's death, when Mrs. Hogarth asked the actor to write an epitaph for her late husband's tombstone. It begins: "Farewell! great painter of Mankind! / Who reach'd the noblest point of Art . . ."[19]

Hogarth's friendship with Garrick runs a curiously parallel course to his relationship with Henry Fielding. Warmly admired by Fielding, Hogarth designed the frontispiece for one of his friend's minor plays and after Fielding's death honored him with the portrait that introduces his collected works.

In his brief career as playwright, from 1728 until the Licensing Act of 1737, Fielding wrote a variety of comedies, farces, and burlesques. When his burlesque *Tom Thumb, A Tragedy* (in two acts) was staged and published in March 1730 he was at least acquainted with Hogarth. A year later, after he had revised and enlarged the play as *The Tragedy of Tragedies; or the Life and Death of Tom Thumb the Great* (in three acts), it bore the frontispiece designed by Hogarth. (Figure 8) Here the artist could display his brilliance as

---

19. George Winchester Stone, Jr. and George M. Kahrl, *David Garrick: A Critical Biography* (Carbondale: Southern Illinois University Press, 1979), p. 105.

caricaturist; and in this plate his customary engraver did justice to his design.

Tom Thumb, the hero, is hardly visible as he struts (in the lower left), dressed in armor with an over-sized plume decorating his helmet. This "little Hero, Giant-killing Boy," as he is called in the play (p. 7) is further described: "Tho' small his Body be, so very small, / A Chairman's Leg is more than twice as large" (1731, p. 4). In the particular scene illustrated in the frontispiece two ladies in rivalry for Tom Thumb's love face each other. The taller one is Glumdalca, the captive Queen of the Giants, who is beloved by King Arthur, and she has just boasted of her amorous conquests to her rival, Princess Huncamunca, the king's daughter. The princess says, as she approaches the rival queen: "Let me see nearer what this Beauty is, / That captivates the Heart of Men by Scores." And as she holds a candle up to the Queen's face she exclaims: "Oh! Heaven, thou art as ugly as the Devil (1731, p. 31). (These lines parody the passage in Dryden's *All for Love*, where Octavia scrutinizes Cleopatra to discover the charms that have bewitched Mark Antony.[20])

In designing the frontispiece Hogarth was apparently guided by the stage representations at the Little Theatre in the Haymarket, where he could have seen the play in rehearsal. (The text, with frontispiece, was published just before the first performance and during the play's run was sold at the theatre.) The background has the look of a stage set: an interior in the Palladian style. Tom Thumb's size in the frontispiece is necessarily subhuman—or, seen in a different perspective, he is human while the two women are superhuman giantesses. In the earlier version of the play Tom Thumb had been played by a girl (Miss Jones). In *The Tragedy of Tragedies* the part was played by a boy, "Young [John] Verhuyck," whose only other recorded stage appearance, two years earlier, had been in *The Beggar's Opera*

---

20. John Dryden, *Four Tragedies*, ed. L. A. Beaurline and F. Bowers (Chicago: University of Chicago Press, 1967), p. 246.

"perform'd by Lilliputians." The high-pitched voice of this diminutive youth would have added a measure of humor to the swashbuckling boasts of Tom Thumb the Great.

That Hogarth was commissioned to supply this amusing frontispiece to the dramatic burlesque implies that Fielding held the artist in high regard; and he was not reluctant to express his admiration explicitly in print. In his periodical *The Champion* he called Hogarth "one of the most useful Satyrists any Age hath produced" (June 10, 1740). In the preface to *Joseph Andrews* (1742) and in the text of *Tom Jones* (1749) as well, he pointedly paid tribute to Hogarth's genius.[21] He continued the compliments by referring readers to Hogarth's prints for characters and scenes in his novels;[22] he modestly assumed that he could only approximate with words what Hogarth so eloquently expressed with brush, pencil, and burin.

An opportunity for Hogarth to exhibit his friendship for Fielding came in 1762, some eight years after Fielding's premature death, when Fielding's publisher issued the first collected edition of his works and needed a frontispiece for the first volume. Fielding had apparently never sat for his portrait. Hogarth designed a suitable sketch, and this was engraved by Isaac Taylor, one of the better engravers of the time. (Figure 9) Whether Hogarth drew the portrait from memory or used a silhouette profile given to him—the facts are disputed—the framed bust is certainly his own creation. Himself nearing the end of his life, he was able to infuse the slight outline with a striking intensity of expression. The prominent nose and chin, the brilliant deep-set eyes, and the receding upper lip, indicating the loss of his teeth (which

21. *Joseph Andrews*, ed. M. C. Battestin (Middletown: Wesleyan University Press, 1967), p. 6, n. 1.

22. Robert E. Moore, *Hogarth's Literary Relationships* (Minneapolis: University of Minnesota Press, 1948), pp. 127–132.

Fielding joked about)[23] —all contribute to the human likeness.

Set in its ornamental frame—designed probably by the engraver—the portrait hangs above various objects and emblems relating to Fielding as writer and lawyer. For the man himself, the sword symbolizes his aristocratic family background; he was a collateral descendant of the Earls of Desmond and Denbigh. The pen and inkwell stand for his literary profession, and as evidence the book titles can be read: *Joseph Andrews, Tom Jones,* and his last novel *Amelia,* opened to its concluding pages. Of the two masks decorated with laurel leaves, only the mask of comedy is placed upright, while the mask of tragedy—a genre Fielding never practised—lies supine and unused. The scales of justice refer to his appointment as justice of the peace; and the *Statutes at Large Vol XIII* is the annual volume of Sessions Acts for 1740 (the thirteenth year of George II's reign), when Fielding was called to the bar and began his legal career. Against the tome leans a bundle of legal briefs, and under it lies a legal document, perhaps a cognizance, unfolded toward the viewer to display a version of Fielding's own signature. His career as lawyer and judge bridged his activities as playwright and novelist: all these phases, placed under his portrait, have the effect of an epitaph. Thus Hogarth memorialized his friend.

Publishers at that time rarely added illustrative plates to contemporary novels, a new genre regarded as relatively ephemeral. Hogarth had once begun to illustrate the classic *Don Quixote,* a model of sorts for *Joseph Andrews,* in which Fielding invoked "the inimitable Pencil of my Friend Hogarth" (1742).[24] But when Fielding's publisher decided to illustrate the third edition with a dozen engraved plates the following year, he did not turn to Hogarth, who would

23. Wilbur L. Cross, *The History of Henry Fielding* (New Haven: Yale University Press, 1918), III, 71–73. For a thorough analysis of Fielding portraiture, see Martin C. Battestin, "Pictures in Fielding," *Eighteenth-Century Studies,* 17 (1983), 1–13.

24. Ed. Battestin (1967), p. 41.

9. Frontispiece to *The Works of Henry Fielding* (1783), vol. I. The Henry
E. Huntington Library, San Marino, California.

10. Frontispiece to *The Life and Opinions of Tristram Shandy, Gentleman* by Laurence Sterne, 2nd ed. (1760), vol. I. The Henry E. Huntington Library, San Marino, California.

presumably have found the task congenial. Instead James Hulett designed and engraved the plates, and they seem feeble compared to Fielding's lusty text. His later novels *Tom Jones* and *Amelia* were not illustrated in any contemporary edition.

Two other novelists, however, both friends of Hogarth, commissioned him to illustrate their work. When *Pamela, or Virtue Rewarded* became a sensational success on its publication in November 1740, Samuel Richardson, its anonymous author and one of its three publishers, determined to have the second edition embellished with a frontispiece for each of the two volumes. He was not unfamiliar with illustrated books, the previous year having himself edited a collection of Aesop's fables that contained many illustrative plates. His purpose in adding plates to *Pamela* was probably to encourage the sale of a new edition, though in this instance it is difficult to understand why any encouragement was needed. Instead of hiring one of the hacks employed in the printing trade, he turned to Hogarth.

By the end of December (1740) Richardson's friend Aaron Hill, playwright and journalist, had heard that he proposed to use illustrations in the new edition. "The designs you have taken for frontispieces," Hill wrote to him, "seem to have been very judiciously chosen; upon presupposition that Mr. Hogarth is able (and if any-body is, it is he), to teach pictures to speak and to think."[25] But when the second edition of the novel was published in February 1741 it contained no plates. In his lengthy introduction to the first volume Richardson explained that "it was intended to prefix two neat Frontispieces"; and that although one was actually finished, there was no time to execute the other because of the pressing demand for the new edition. Besides, he added, the engraving of the finished design, "having fallen very short of the Spirit of the Passages they were intended to represent, the Proprietors were advised to lay them aside." No engraving or even sketch of either frontispiece survives

25. Richardson, *Correspondence*, ed. A. L. Barbauld (London, 1804), I, 56.

as evidence of Hogarth's design and Richardson's disappointment. The publisher did not necessarily disapprove of Hogarth's design, since it was the engraving that he found wanting; and the two men remained friends. But Richardson persisted in his desire to illustrate the novel; and in the following year the sixth edition of *Pamela Part I* was embellished not with two but with fourteen plates by the leading book illustrator of the decade, Hubert Gravelot, and the up-and-coming Francis Hayman. These illustrations need not be discussed here since they do not concern Hogarth, but they demonstrate Richardson's serious intention to have his novel illustrated.

The other novelist with whose work Hogarth was connected, more fruitfully this time, was Laurence Sterne. Of all Hogarth's literary friends and (in a sense) patrons, Sterne stands out as the only one who both studied and practised painting.[26] In *The Life and Opinions of Tristram Shandy, Gentleman* he discussed its craft as well as its aesthetics. When he alluded to Hogarth in the novel he could not have been certain that Hogarth would in fact be its illustrator.

Since Dodsley, the London publisher, had declined to publish *Tristram Shandy* on his terms (in 1760) Sterne arranged for the two volumes to be printed in York, and he shipped some copies to Dodsley to sell in London. The book's instant and striking popularity quickly persuaded Dodsley to publish a second edition.

He signed a contract with Sterne (on March 8, 1760) setting the terms for reprinting the first two volumes and for issuing (at the same time) the third and fourth. The contract was witnessed by Sterne's friend Richard Berenger, a bon vivant and man-about-town. To Dr. Johnson he seemed "the standard of true elegance," and to Hannah More, "everybody's favourite."

---

26. Sterne scholarship has not overlooked this rich topic; see especially William V. Holtz, *Image and Immortality A Study of "Tristram Shandy"* (Providence: Brown University Press, 1970).

He could easily have been a favorite of Sterne's, for before the two parted that day he told Sterne that he would gladly be of service to him. "You bid me tell You all my Wants," Sterne wrote to him later in the day; and then he specified: "no more than ten Strokes of *Howgarth's* witty Chissel, to clap at the Front of my next Edition of *Shandy.*" He then described the scene he wished illustrated: "The loosest Sketch in Nature, of Trim's reading the Sermon to my Father &c; w[oul]d do the Business—& it w[oul]d mutually illustrate his System & mine." Since such a sketch by Hogarth was "not to be bought with money," he tells Berenger, he would ask it as a favor from the artist he so much admired.[27] Berenger's request on Sterne's behalf was successful. On March 25 a newspaper advertisement promised that the new edition of *Tristram Shandy* would appear the following week "with a Frontispiece by Mr. HOGARTH," and on April 3—exactly four weeks after Sterne's request—the illustrated edition was on sale.[28]

Why had Sterne asked for this particular episode to be the subject of the frontispiece? First let us see what he had written about painting and painters (including Hogarth) in these first two volumes—which, one may assume, Hogarth had already read before being solicited through Berenger to provide a frontispiece. In the first volume Sterne had inserted, in chapter 8, a mock-dedicatory letter, which he then defends (in the next chapter) as being a good one, by analogy with the attributes of painting: design, coloring, drawing, and so on. He more pointedly alludes to painting in the second volume (chapter 6), where he draws an analogy between rhetoric, art, and music: "Just heaven! how does the *Poco piu* and the *Poco meno* of the *Italian* artists; —the insensible MORE OR LESS, determine the precise line of beauty in the sentence, as well as in the statue! How do the slight touches of the chisel, the pencil, the pen, the fiddle-

27. Sterne, *Letters*, ed. Lewis P. Curtis (Oxford: Clarendon Press, 1935), pp. 99–100.

28. Kenneth Monkman, "The Bibliography of the Early Editions of *Tristram Shandy*," *The Library*, 5 ser., vol. 25 (1970), p. 22.

stick, *et caetera*,—give the true swell, which give the true
pleasure!'' When Sterne wishes to portray Dr. Slop, the
man-midwife who so clumsily brings Tristram into the world,
he invokes Hogarth by name. "Imagine to yourself," he
writes, "a little, squat, uncourtly figure of a Doctor *Slop*, of
about four feet and a half perpendicular height, with a
breadth of back, and a sesquipedality of belly, which might
have done honour to a serjeant in the horseguards" (vol. 2,
ch. 9). "Such were the outlines of Dr. *Slop*'s figure," he
continues, "which,—if you have read *Hogarth*'s analysis of
beauty, and if you have not, I wish you would;—you must
know, may as certainly be caracatur'd, and convey'd to the
mind by three strokes as three hundred."

How appropriate, then, that the scene Sterne asked
Hogarth to illustrate should include Dr. Slop! (Figure 10)
The entire scene—of Corporal Trim reading the sermon to
Mr. Shandy, Uncle Toby, and Dr. Slop—is sketched verbally
by Sterne as though he were giving directions to the illustrator. As Trim prepares to read, Sterne interrupts: "But
before the Corporal begins, I must first give you a description of his attitude." Not that of a soldier standing in his
platoon ready for action, but as unlike that as could be. "He
stood before them with his body swayed, and bent forwards
just so far, as to make an angle of 85 degrees and a half
upon the plain of the horizon . . . He stood . . . his right-leg
firm under him, sustaining seven-eighths of his whole
weight,—the foot of his left-leg . . . advanced a little,—not
laterally, nor forwards, but in a line betwixt them;—his knee
bent, but that not violently,—but so as to fall within the limits of the line of beauty;—and I add, of the line of science
too"; after which Sterne explains why a scientific as well as
an aesthetic reason authenticates Trim's posture.

Hogarth has stated in the preface to his treatise *The
Analysis of Beauty* (1753) that the serpentine is the "line of
beauty." And to be sure, Trim's figure seen from behind (as
here) is serpentine, in contrast to the gross, swollen caricature of Dr. Slop seen in profile. He has not yet finished out-
lining Trim's posture and proportions: "He held the sermon
loosely,—not carelessly, in his left-hand, raised something

11. Drawing for frontispiece to *Tristram Shandy,* 4th ed. (1760), vol. I. The Berg Collection of the New York Public Library.

12. Drawing for frontispiece to *Tristram Shandy* (1761), vol. III. The Berg Collection of the New York Public Library.

above his stomach, and detach'd a little from his breast"
(vol. 2, chs. 15–17). What Hogarth had to do, then, was to
carry out the directions set down by Sterne; and is it not
plausible that Sterne specified this very scene to be illustrated because he himself had conceived it in graphic (as well
as rhetorical) terms?

This frontispiece to the second edition of the novel was
repeated in the third, but in the fourth edition—published
later in the same year—Hogarth altered it. (Figure 11) Using
his original drawing, he made two conspicuous additions
which were duly copied by the engraver. Centered in the
foregroud a tricorn hat lies on the floor. The justification for
this is clear in Sterne's text: as Corporal Trim prepares to
read the sermon he "laid his hand upon his heart, and made
an humble bow to his master;—then laying down his hat
upon the floor, and taking up the sermon in his left-hand
. . ." and so on. In his former version Hogarth had overlooked the hat; he now gives it a place in the design. But
why the grandfather clock in the corner of the room? It is
unmentioned in this scene. Since the passage of time is so
essential an element of the story, intricately woven into its
texture, a clock serves as its visible presence.[29] In the other
plate—the frontispiece to volume 3—as we shall see, a clock
again stands in the corner of a different room. Neither of
these clocks, we should note, is the one that Tristram's
father had forgotten to wind in the memorable first scene of
the novel; that one stood at the head of the backstairs (ch.
4).

At the end of January 1761 Dodsley issued the third and
fourth volumes of *Tristram Shandy*. In these Sterne again discussed painting and the sister-art of literature. In one passage where he wishes to describe the posture of Tristram's
father, he writes: "his whole attitude had been easy—
natural—unforced: *Reynolds* himself, as great and gracefully
as he paints, might have painted him as he sat" (ch. 2). In

29. Cf. Samuel L. Macey, *Clocks and the Cosmos* (Hamden, Conn.: Archon
Books, 1980), p. 59.

contrast to this sober comparison, Sterne could also be ironic about the art criticism lavished by connoisseurs on grand pictures: "not one principle of the *pyramid* in any one group" (referring to the Italian treatise on painting by Lomazzo, mentioned by Hogarth in *The Analysis of Beauty*).[30] And he then rattles off the flattering clichés applied to such masters as Titian (coloring), Rubens (expression), Raphael (grace); concluding with: "Of all the cants which are canted in this canting world . . . the cant of criticism is the most tormenting!" (ch. 12).

As a frontispiece in the third volume, Dodsley inserted the illustration of a scene from, oddly enough, the fourth volume; and again it was Hogarth who designed it. (Figure 12) Unlike the illustration for the first volume, commissioned (so to speak) by Sterne, this one has no supporting documentation to explain its genesis. By then, since Sterne and Hogarth were on friendly terms, their agreement could have been personal and verbal. The scene chosen is the crucial one of Tristram's baptism. Susannah has been charged by Mr. Shandy to tell the curate to christen the boy Trismegistus, but she garbles the message, and the curate—whose own name is Tristram—bestows it on the infant. Then Sterne continues: "My father followed *Susannah* with his night-gown across his arm, with nothing more than his breeches on, fastened through haste with but a single button, and that button through haste thrust only half into the button-hole.—She has not forgot the name, cried my father, half opening the door—No, no, said the curate, with a tone of intelligence . . . Pish! said my father, the button of his breeches slipping out of the button-hole" (ch. 14). In this drawing the figure of Mr. Shandy—"almost incredibly clumsy for Hogarth," writes the editor of his drawings[31] —stands with clenched fist, as though aflame with anger that his son has been misnamed. The baptismal basin, placed on

30. P. 91.
31. A. P. Oppe, *The Drawings of William Hogarth* (London: Phaidon Press, 1948), p. 55.

13. Frontispiece to *Tristram Shandy* (1761), vol. III. The Henry E. Huntington Library, San Marino, California.

a chair, has been overturned, thus adding an element of disorder and confusion to the scene.

Transferred to the copper plate by the engraver, the design was clearly altered, presumably by Hogarth's direction. (Figure 13) Mr. Shandy holds out his hand as though uttering the pish directed at either Susannah or the buttonhole. This time the baptismal basin rests on a table, unspilled, next to a prayer-book; and instead a pillow, on which the infant had been laid, has fallen to the floor. Both frontispieces in *Tristram Shandy* were engraved by Simon François Ravenet, a French craftsman resident in London. Since he had been employed by Hogarth to engrave two of the plates in *Marriage a la Mode* (1745) he was presumably employed by Dodsley at Hogarth's suggestion.

If Sterne planned that Hogarth should design any additional frontispieces, he could easily have been discouraged by this crude one. In any case, no illustration accompanied any of the succeeding five volumes. Hogarth's involvement in political controversy with Churchill and Wilkes, as well as his poor health, would have discouraged him from any further work for Sterne, and his death in 1764 put an end to his career.

What have we seen in this rapid survey of Hogarth's book illustrations for his friends over a span of thirty-six years? Clearly he was stimulated by the most worthy works: Fielding's burlesque tragedy, Garrick's comic interlude, and Sterne's eccentric novel. His friendship with all these writers added, no doubt, some interest, even enthusiasm, to these illustrations. They are tributes to friendship as well as graphic embellishments. They also demonstrate Hogarth's versatility as an illustrator, a versatility matched in his paintings and various original series of engravings.[32]

32. I am very grateful to the following for permission to reproduce the plates: Mary Hyde (Figure 4), the Berg Collection of the New York Public Library (Figures 11 and 12), the New York Public Library (Figure 5), the Walker Art Gallery, Liverpool (Figure 6), and the Huntington Library (Figures 1, 2, 3, 7, 8, 9, 10, 13).

W. B. CARNOCHAN

Gibbon's Silences

In the summer of 1760, young Edward Gibbon, then in his early twenties, wrote a letter to his father explaining why he thought he was unsuited for the parliamentary career expected of him. When he wrote, he and his father were living in the same place, the family manor house of Buriton. He wrote because he could not bring himself to say directly what he wanted to say: "An address in writing, from a person who has the pleasure of being with you every day may appear singular. However I have preferred this method, as upon paper I can speak without a blush and be heard without interruption."[1] Gibbon's timidity has an appealing honesty to it. Most of us, when we turn to the written word in ticklish private circumstances, claim we only want to be clear. Gibbon is more forthright. He writes to avoid embarrassment and inarticulateness.

By writing rather than telling his father that he is unfit for parliamentary life, he goes far to prove his own point. For what he fears most in Parliament is having to speak in public: "I never possessed that gift of speech, the first requisite

1. *The Letters of Edward Gibbon*, ed. J. E. Norton (London: Casell, 1956), I, 123. Subsequent quotations from this edition are identified in the text.

of an Orator, which use and labour may improve, but which
nature can alone bestow." With a sense of premonitory terror he imagines what the experience would be like: "An
unexpected objection would disconcert me, and as I am incapable of explaining to others what I do not thoroughly
understand myself, I should be meditating, while I ought to
be answering." Moreover, Gibbon finds himself too dispassionate an observer: "never Orator inspired well a passion,
which he did not feel himself" (I, 124–125). Horace has
said the same thing in *Ars Poetica*.[2] On Gibbon's diagnosis,
his case is one of too much anxiety, too little passion.

In fact he was an accurate judge of his own temper and, as
it turned out, too good a prophet. In his late thirties he did
enter Parliament and for a time entertained the hope of
being, at least in a modest way, an orator. Writing his friend
John Holroyd on Christmas Eve 1774, he reported that he
was boning up on American affairs with the pamphleteer
Israel Mauduit and that sooner or later "I mean to think
perhaps to speak for myself" (II, 51). At the end of January
he wrote Holroyd again, announcing that he had become a
zealous yet so far silent friend of the government and then,
suddenly, fancying himself as speaking out in an unaccustomed voice:

if my confidence was equal to my eloquence and my eloquence to
my knowledge, perhaps I might make no very intolerable Speaker.
At all events I fancy I shall try to expose myself.

Semper ego auditor tantum, numquamne reponam?
(II, 57–58)

It is a great leap, self-conscious and partly self-deprecating,
from the anxiety of "I fancy I shall try to expose myself" to
the Juvenalian question: "Must I always be a listener and
never reply?" Inside Gibbon the judicious historian, the
supremely cool ironist, and the timid little fat man, a lean
orator would like to have gotten out. He wished he had had

2. Ll. 102–103: "si vis me flere, dolendum est / primum ipsi tibi."

the talents of Juvenal or of Julian, in some ways the tragic hero of the *Decline and Fall*, whose rhetorical skill he recounts with barely concealed yearning: "The assemblies of the senate . . . were considered by Julian as the place where he could exhibit, with the most propriety, the maxims of a republican and the talents of a rhetorician. He alternately practised, as in a school of declamation, the several modes of praise, of censure, of exhortation; and his friend Libanius has remarked that the study of Homer taught him to imitate the simple, concise style of Menelaus, the copiousness of Nestor, whose words descended like the flakes of a winter's snow, or the pathetic and forcible eloquence of Ulysses."[3] But for Gibbon, reality and fantasy were worlds apart. Never managing to overcome his fears, he never made his maiden speech.

This failure troubled him more than anything else in his life. Despite his adolescent flight into the embrace of the Roman Catholic church and despite some ordinary youthful indiscretions, he had always been and always prided himself on being the dutiful son of his capricious and irresponsible father. Sitting mute in Parliament, Gibbon cannot have escaped the sense that in one last, crucial respect he was failing to live up to Edward Gibbon, Sr.'s, expectations. His failure produces puzzlement, shame, self-reproach. At first he tries to pretend that only the right occasion is lacking. Early in February 1775 he reports to Holroyd "such an inundation of speakers" on two recent occasions that "neither Lord George Germaine nor myself could find room for a single word" (II, 59). Pairing himself with Lord George Germain, twenty years his senior and one of the best speakers in the House, indicates the rhetorical company Gibbon would like to keep, even though he speaks (surely) with tongue at least halfway in cheek. Being silent along with Lord George Germain is no humiliation, especially not if the principals in

3. *The History of the Decline and Fall of the Roman Empire*, ed. J. B. Bury (London: Methuen, 1909–1914; reprinted, New York: AMS Press, 1974), II, 453–454.

the debate are Charles James Fox and Alexander Wedder-
burn, as Gibbon also takes care to report. But he could not
deceive himself long, and these dreams of power and presence fade before the reality of his crippling anxiety.

Two weeks later, again to Holroyd, he confesses, "I am
still a Mute, it is more tremendous than I imagined; the
great speakers fill me with despair, the bad ones with terror." At the same time his defensive instincts have surfaced, and he lodges this confession in an aside, an island of
fear in a quiet sea: "On Wednesday we had the Middlesex
Election, I was a Patriot, sat by the Lord Mayor who spoke
well, and with temper but before the end of the debate, fell
fast asleep.—I am still a Mute, it is more tremendous than I
imagined; the great speakers fill me with despair, the bad
ones with terror.—When do you move? . . . How do you like
your footman?" (II, 61). Is it Gibbon or Wilkes, the Lord
Mayor, who falls asleep? It might be either. In either case,
the effect is similar if not identical. Sharp and sudden
contrasts—Gibbon or perhaps Wilkes himself falling asleep
as the House debates the resolution that had expelled Wilkes
six years earlier; Gibbon in despair and terror; Gibbon
inquiring after his friend's ordinary domestic affairs—mark
his habits of self-protection. He fences off anxiety, assigning
it only an incidental place in the structure of his life. And
he domesticates it by hyperbolizing it. Surely despair and
terror are not exactly despair and terror, being so easily contained? By at once exaggerating the temperature of his emotional life and writing off his true feelings as incidents to the
ordinary, he shields himself from their harsher effects.

Three days later, in a note to Holroyd, Gibbon reports:
"Still dumb." Then he doses his pain with more draughts of
the quotidian: "but see hear, laugh sometimes, am oftener
serious but upon the whole very well amused. Adieu" (II,
62).

A month later he tells his stepmother of his silence, this
time working up his nerve with talk of parliamentary business and of the "agreable" new shape his life has taken, and
only then announcing that "As yet I have been mute. In the
course of our American affairs, I have sometimes had a wish

to speak, but though I felt tolerably prepared as to the matter, I dreaded exposing myself in the manner and remained in my seat safe but inglorious. Upon the whole (though I still believe I shall try) I doubt whether Nature, not that in some instances I am ungrateful, has given me the talents of an Orator, and I feel that I have come into Parliament much too late to exert them" (II, 63). The truth is coming home. Though he manages still to believe he will "try," Gibbon is on the way to resignation and silence. Once again he glimpses a source of the fears that bind him—"I dreaded exposing myself"—and he catches, fleetingly, a sense of the absolute silence of death: he is one with the mute inglorious Milton in Gray's churchyard.

Early in April 1775 he tells Holroyd in a climax of frustration: "I have remained silent and notwithstanding all my efforts chained down to my place by some invisible unknown invisible power" (II, 64). This attribution of his failure to a doubly invisible (the unconscious repetition is striking) unknown power seems mostly to have cured Gibbon of self-recrimination—though he could not altogether let the subject go. In 1779 he tells his friend Georges Deyverdun: "Dans le Senat Je suis toujours demeuré tel que vous m'avez laissé, mutus pecus" (II, 218). And in 1780 he apologizes to Dorothea Gibbon for not having lived up to her hopes: "I can only condole with you that a person, in whose fate and reputation you are perhaps more deeply interested, should still continue a dumb Dog" (II, 241). Gibbon's relationship with his stepmother was more than cordial, but the good will he attributes to her in this case all too closely resembles the peremptory good will of his father. Ten years after his father's death, Gibbon cannot wholly shake his sense of an obligation unfulfilled.

In fact, his reticence and anxiety were a deeply-lodged, immutable aspect of his character from start to finish. Writing Dorothea from Lausanne in late spring 1784, he begins by apologizing for his poor habits as a correspondent, an opening that appears in his letters with remorseless frequency. This time it leads him to wonder why we "are not fonder of letter-writing." After all, letter-writing has the advantage over conversation when it comes to speaking of oneself—and here what seems a recollection of the disclaimer to his father, in that painful letter of 1760, returns unbidden to his mind: "we all delight to talk of ourselves and it is only in letters, in writing to a friend that we can enjoy that conversation not only without reproach or interruption, but with the highest propriety and mutual satisfaction" (II, 409–410; 410). Now in his forties, Gibbon worries as he had almost twenty-five years before about conversational embarrassment. Perhaps he worries even more, now, about being interrupted; having learned to compose in his mind the massive paragraphs of the *Decline and Fall*, he was increasingly accustomed to thinking in large units of discourse. Only the casual circumstances of his life in Lausanne, provincial and undemanding, made it possible for him to live with inhibitions that time had done little to diminish.

In 1739 when Philip Stanhope was seven years old, his father, Lord Chesterfield, wrote him a letter about "the art of speaking well":

LET us return to Oratory, or the art of speaking well; which should never be entirely out of your thoughts, since it is so useful in every part of life, and so absolutely necessary in most. A man can make no figure without it, in Parliament, in the Church, or in the Law; and even in common conversation, a man that has acquired an easy and habitual eloquence, who speaks properly and accurately, will have a great advantage over those who speak incorrectly and inelegantly.[4]

That young Stanhope would utterly fail to become a distinguished orator, inhibited like Gibbon by shyness, seems the appropriate and perhaps predictable result of such strenuous pedagogy. But the art of speaking well was not only a matter of self-interest; it was an insistent social obligation.

---

4. November 1, 1739. *Letters Written by the Late Honourable Philip Dormer Stanhope, Earl of Chesterfield, to his Son* (London: J. Dodsley, 1774), p. 96.

To the socially obligatory character of being able to speak well, the generation after Chesterfield's, especially in the person of Thomas Sheridan, added a grander conception of oratory that helped kindle the rhetorical fires of late eighteenth-century England. In 1756, when Gibbon was nineteen, Sheridan published *British Education* (dedicated to Chesterfield), his extravagant, controversial, and highly successful volume that claimed for oratory the powers of a moral and cultural panacea. What was needed to reform British education, in Sheridan's view, was to recapture the oratorical power of the ancients and ground it on the religious underpinnings of the British state. Carry out such a program and the millennium waits: "would not London be the grand emporium of arts, as she already is of commerce? Would not persons flock hither from all parts of the world to see and admire these works? Does not her situation, and the ease with which her shores are accessible to people from all corners of the earth, give England a natural right in this respect over all other countries in the world?"[5] Sheridan's panacea turns out, like others of its kind, to resemble Johnson's last refuge of the scoundrel. But the fervid patriotism of Sheridan's vision helped to set the stage for the oratorical triumphs of Fox, Burke, and the rest. In such a setting, where oratorical skills became charged with associations of moral value, it was a singularly bad time to be fated, like Gibbon, to be mute.

It was also a bad time to be inept at "manly" conversation, as the pages of Boswell's *Life* make abundantly and sometimes painfully clear. Johnson's and Boswell's reiterated insistence on conversational power as the touchstone of intellectual excellence might surprise any twentieth-century reader who paused over it. Nourished on discriminations between facility and depth, we suppose that deep thinking needs to be mined from below ground. We incline to side with the (perhaps legendary) professor in the

---

5. *British Education; or the Source of the Disorders of Great Britain* (Dublin: George Faulkner, 1756), p. 356.

Harvard Law School who refused to debate a colleague because, he said, he thought only half as fast as that colleague—though twice as well. Johnson was of a different mind. Of a distinguished jurist he said, "I never heard any thing from him in company that was at all striking; and depend upon it, Sir, it is when you come close to a man in conversation, that you discover what his real abilities are."[6] There runs through the *Life* an intellectual, even a moral, grading of persons on the basis of their conversational powers. At the head of the class are Johnson, Burke, and Garrick ("the first man in the world for sprightly conversation" [*Life*, I, 398]). The dunces are Goldsmith and Gibbon: Goldsmith because he was forever anxious to "shine" and too often made a fool of himself; Gibbon because he was shy and because, as if to prove the truth of Sheridan's claims that verbal powers were inseparable from moral character, he was an "infidel."

In fact Gibbon emerges as the principal victim of moral disapproval in the *Life*. Other unbelievers—Rousseau, Voltaire, Hume—were less easy to condescend to: they had to be cudgelled into submission, even in absentia. Gibbon was an easier mark. It was in his temper to submit, and he was nearby. He is Boswell's whipping boy. On one occasion, Boswell tells how Johnson becomes preoccupied with the natural lore of bears, carrying on what amounts to a monologue while others go about their conversational business. Then: "Silence having ensued, he proceeded: 'We are told, that the black bear is innocent; but I should not like to trust myself with him.' Mr. Gibbon muttered, in a low tone of voice, 'I should not like to trust myself with *you*.' This piece

6. *Boswell's Life of Johnson*, ed. George Birkbeck Hill, revised and enlarged by L. F. Powell (Oxford: Clarendon Press, 1934), IV, 179. Subsequent quotations from the *Life* are identified in the text. On the relationship between Johnson's conversation and the habits of traditional rhetoric, see Brigitte H. Carnochan, "The Colors of the Imagination in Swift, Pope, and Johnson" (Ph.D. diss., University of California, Berkeley, 1983), pp. 203–252. On Gibbon and the Johnsonians, see D. M. Low, "Edward Gibbon and the Johnsonian Circle," *New Rambler* (June 1960), pp. 2–14.

of sarcastick pleasantry was a prudent resolution, if applied to a competition of abilities" (*Life*, II, 348). Another time Johnson is scoring some rhetorical points against historians and the writing of history. Boswell reports Gibbon's silence: "Mr. Gibbon, who must at that time have been employed upon his history, of which he published the first volume in the following year, was present; but did not step forth in defence of the species of writing. He probably did not like to *trust* himself with *JOHNSON*!" (*Life*, II, 366). Still another time Boswell records a dialogue between "several eminent men." Among them is Gibbon, who plays only a small part in the exchange, once or twice responsive to others but never opening up new ground. Boswell identifies him by the letter "I," for "Infidel" (*Life*, III, 230ff).

The assumptions that underlie the age's valorizing of speech show up clearly in the *Life*. In the excursions of the spoken word, Johnson, Boswell, and Thomas Sheridan, too, propose an answer to the cultural question that had dominated their century: in what forms of human action could heroism best be preserved? The psychology of conversation in the *Life* is a psychology of spontaneous combat. Gibbon, unwilling to "step forth" in defense of history-writing, is a cowardly knight unwilling to pick up a challenge and enter the lists against a dangerous antagonist.

Like other substitute forms of heroism such as cricket or baseball, verbal aggression has the advantage of seldom killing an opponent. Yet the metaphors of combat describing conversational engagements in the *Life* yield a sense of almost tangible physical violence:

Dr. Adams told us, that in some of the Colleges at Oxford, the fellows had excluded the students from social intercourse with them in the common room. *JOHNSON.* "They are in the right, Sir, for there can be no real conversation, no fair exertion of mind amongst them, if the young men are by." (*Life*, II, 443)

But on the present occasion he had very little opportunity of hearing them [a group of "Scotch literati"] talk, for, with an excess of prudence, they hardly opened their lips, and that only to say something which they were certain would not expose them to the sword of Goliath. (*Life*, II, 63)

Exulting in his intellectual strength and dexterity, he could, when he pleased, be the greatest sophist that ever contended in the lists of declamation; and, from a spirit of contradiction, and a delight in shewing his powers, he would often maintain the wrong side with equal warmth and ingenuity. (*Life*, IV, 429)

And, of course:

Mr. Burke having been mentioned, he said, "That fellow calls forth all my powers. Were I to see Burke now, it would kill me." (*Life*, II, 450)

Boswell has probably conflated separate sayings of Johnson's, as Hill's note points out: "That fellow calls forth all my powers"; and, when Johnson was ill, "Were I to see Burke now, 'twould kill me." The conflation is apt. Boswell picks up the metaphor of conversational struggle and makes it literal. In this hypothetical engagement between Burke and Johnson, the stakes would actually be life and death.

The cult of conversational heroism means, by convention, a cult of "manliness." It is half amusing, half touching to discover Gibbon striking the properly aggressive posture in a letter to Garrick from Paris in August 1777: "Assure Sir Joshua in particular that I have not lost my relish for *manly* conversation and the society of the brown table" (II, 160). The underscoring of *manly* sets Gibbon at a distance from the very assurance he asks Garrick to give Sir Joshua: self-consciousness colors, as though with a blush, his participation in the manly society of the knights of the brown table.

Manliness meant a showing forth of the self. In the *Life* conversation entails display, and Boswell as the recorder of conversation gazes on naked combat or, in our modern approximation of the ancient spectator's role, acts the reporter in the locker room (where the game is nakedly replayed). Let us look back: "They are in the right, Sir, for there can be no real conversation, no fair exertion of mind

amongst them." Or: "something which they were certain
would not expose them to the sword of Goliath." Or:
"from a spirit of contradiction, and a delight in shewing his
powers." Or: "That fellow calls forth all my powers." Or,
from Gibbon: "I fancy I shall try to expose myself." Or:
"I dreaded exposing myself."

At the same time, and in keeping with the latent sexuality
of conversational struggles, Johnson claims that speaking and
thereby showing forth the self signifies a therapeutic overcoming of inhibitions. The only problem is that the claim, in
the form Johnson makes it, turns out to be suspect. *Rambler*
159 (September 24, 1751), Johnson's reflection on the para-
lytic bashfulness of some would-be public speakers, reads
like a prediction of what Gibbon, still a schoolboy in 1751,
would grow up to endure:

> The imbecillity with which Verecundulus complains that the pres-
> ence of a numerous assembly freezes his faculties, is particularly
> incident to the studious part of mankind, whose education neces-
> sarily secludes them in their earlier years from mingled converse,
> till at their dismission from schools and academies they plunge at
> once into the tumult of the world, and coming forth from the
> gloom of solitude are overpowered by the blaze of public life.[7]

What remedy? Admitting that the disease is not easy to
cure, Johnson proposes that "no cause more frequently produces bashfulness than too high an opinion of our own
importance." Because we imagine our listeners "panting
with expectation" and "hushed with attention," the mind is
soon "overwhelmed" by its struggles and "quickly sinks into
languishment and despondency." The cure, then, is to realize that "no man is much regarded by the rest of the world."
The bashful speaker who "considers how little he dwells
upon the condition of others, will learn how little the attention of others is attracted by himself." That will cure us of

---

7. *The Rambler*, ed. W. J. Bate and Albrecht B. Strauss, vol. 5 of *The Yale
Edition of the Works of Samuel Johnson* (New Haven: Yale University Press,
1969), p. 81.

the vain belief that what we "say or do will never be forgotten."[8] But this is the rational, stoic therapist speaking, and the general accuracy of the proposition clashes with some sharp particularities of human experience. It clashes also with some Freudian home truths. It is not just false vanity to suppose that what we say or do will never be forgotten, if we mean never in the lifetime of our hearers or the spectators of our acts. It is not just false vanity to suppose our sexual exposures will never be forgotten if we mean (for example) by the child who watches. And it would not have been false vanity in Johnson to suppose that his words and actions would never be forgotten as long as there were readers of his *Life*. This is one case where the moralist in Johnson runs afoul of actual experience. Perhaps, then, the only remedy for bashfulness is not to try to conquer it but to make the best of it, to compensate for it, or to deny the cultural demands that bring on its humiliations in the first place. Those were Gibbon's remedies, in any event.

Gibbon always made the best of things. By wrapping anxiety in the protective coverings of everyday, by biting his tongue when faced with the aggravations of his father's irresponsibility, by growing the large covering of flesh that hid not only his sexuality from himself but, with it, the watery swelling in his groin that he lived with for some thirty years—by defensive strategies like these he contrived to live the placid life of an observer who put the decline and fall of Rome, as well as his own infirmities, into their proper places.

At the same time, like other shy or inarticulate writers, Gibbon made up in his writing for what he could not manage to say. When Rousseau at the start of the *Confessions* imagines himself being judged on the last day, he comes carrying his story in his hands. It is a summary emblem of the inarticulate writer—Rousseau fills the pages of the *Confessions* with evidence of his verbal shyness and *gaucherie*—who writes down what has to be told because, like Gibbon writing

8. Ibid., V, 84.

his father about his fear of public life, he would be too ill at
ease to speak it out: "Que la trompette du jugement dernier
sonne quand elle voudra, je viendrai, ce livre à la main, me
présenter devant le souverain juge. Je dirai hautement:
'Voilà ce que j'ai fait, ce que j'ai pensé, ce que je fus. J'ai
dit le bien et le mal avec la même franchise.' "[9] Writing contains and protects speech: Rousseau has told the good and
the bad alike. And, in writing rather than speaking of the
self, he fancies he can achieve the goal of total self-
revelation that he holds up so often in the *Confessions*: "Je
veux montrer à mes semblables un homme dans toute la
vérité de la nature."[10] He aims to tell all. Discourse is
discontinuous, fragmentary, approximate: only in writing
may the illusion of completeness be gained.

Indeed, the goal of completeness or, less radically, fullness seems naturally to accompany or to follow from the limitation of verbal reticence. At least that is an inference from
the cases of Rousseau, of Gibbon (whose massive history
aims as much as the *Confessions* to leave nothing out of
account), and of Samuel Richardson, yet another inarticulate
writer of the age, who wrote about his affliction: "When I
was young, I was very sheepish; (so I am indeed now I am
old: I have not had Confidence enough to try to overcome a
Defect so natural to me, tho' I have been a great Loser by
it)."[11] Rousseau's *Confessions*, Richardson's *Clarissa*,
Gibbon's *Decline and Fall*: all three texts aim to tell the
whole story. All three, in different ways, anticipate and
disarm interruption. All three come from writers not adept
at speaking their mind.

---

9. *Les Confessions; Les Rêveries du promeneur solitaire*, ed. Pierre Gros-
claude (Paris: Editions Magnard, [1954]), p. 33.

10. Ibid.

11. To Samuel Lobb, January 31, 1754. Quoted in T. C. Duncan Eaves
and Ben D. Kimpel, *Samuel Richardson: A Biography* (Oxford: Clarendon
Press, 1971), p. 16. On Richardson's "sheepishness," see Steven Young,
"Vanity and Virtue in Richardson's *Clarissa*" (Ph.D. diss., Stanford University, 1982), pp. 1–10.

Gibbon often makes explicit the antithetical relationship between speech and writing. He pleads his case to his father in 1760: "my genius, (if you will allow me any,) is better qualified for the deliberate compositions of the Closet, than for the extemporary discourses of the Parliament" (I, 124). No sooner does he exorcise, by naming, the "invisible unknown invisible power" that has kept him chained in his place than he announces his return to writing with a triumphant emphasis: "I have *resumed my History with vigour*" (II, 64). (It is the annual triumph of the scholar released from the anxieties of wintry exposure into a summer freer from exigencies of speech.) In 1783, his career in Parliament nearing an end, he tells his stepmother, as if to reassure himself: "Your vain hope (a kind and friendly vanity) of my making a distinguished figure in that assembly has long since been extinct, and you are now convinced by repeated experience that my reputation must be derived solely from my pen" (II, 345). And on the earlier occasion when he lost his seat from Liskeard in 1780, having offended his cousin Eliot who held the seat in his disposition, he writes his patron and appeals instinctively to the opposition between speech and writing: "You will not expect that I should justify the grounds of every silent vote which I have given or that I should write a political pamphlet on the eventful history of the last six years" (II, 252). To justify every silent vote would be impossible, for it would be to speak deliberatively of past occasions. To write a political history of the last six years, though perfectly within Gibbon's power, would not answer immediate needs. Speech and writing occupy different temporal realms.

Knowing that he was a writer, not a speaker, finally enabled Gibbon to lay aside with some assurance the values of "manly" conversation.[12] To the Johnsonian ideal of

---

12. At the same time he endowed his writing with a compensatory sexuality, not only describing "the place and moment of conception" of the *Decline and Fall* but ultimately celebrating his "deliverance" (*Memoirs of My Life*, ed. Georges A. Bonnard [New York: Funk and Wagnalls, 1966], pp. 136, 180.) On the *topos* of giving poetic birth, see Terry J. Castle,

sexually athletic exercise and show he proposes an alternative of conversation as an "unbending": "By many, conversation is esteemed as a theatre or a school: but after the morning has been occupied by the labours of the library, I wish to unbend rather than to exercise my mind."[13] This is a ghostly echo thrown off by the debate Gibbon might have had with Johnson about conversation, had he ever mustered the wit or the nerve to do so. Gibbon's ideal shares first in the Horatian tradition of interchange among those removed from worldly care. In this sense he looks back to his Augustan predecessors, Swift and Pope: their conversation, too, was less exercise than unbending. At the same time, the Horatian ideal, which assumes both the intellectual power and intellectual equality of the participants, comes into uneasy contact here with the newer values of self-enclosed domesticity and its implicit intellectual hierarchy. Gibbon goes on: "I wish to unbend rather than to exercise my mind; and in the interval between tea and supper I am far from disdaining the innocent amusement of a game at cards." If the habit of conversational unbending suits the Sabine farm, the game of cards suits the eighteenth-century drawing room. Gibbon may have aimed to be one of Horace's descendants, but in fact he preferred not to share the limelight in provincial Lausanne:

I shall add as a misfortune rather than a merit that the situation and beauty of the Pays de Vaud, the long habits of the English, the medical reputation of Dr Tissot, and the fashion of viewing the mountains and *glaciers* have opened us on all sides to the incursions of foreigners. The visits of Mr and Madame Necker, of Prince Henry of Prussia, and of Mr Fox may form some pleasing

---

"Lab'ring Bards: Birth *Topoi* in English Poetics 1660–1820," *Journal of English and Germanic Philology*, 78 (1979), 193–208. Castle argues that acceptance of the convention wanes in the early eighteenth century; it comes subtly alive in Gibbon.

13. *Memoirs*, p. 178.

exceptions: but in general Lausanne has appeared most agreable in my eyes when we have been abandoned to our own society.[14]

In the linkage of pseudo-Horatian ease with drawing-room domesticity lies the danger of what might be called political deception. Like Richardson, who gathered around him a circle of compliant women to be his listeners, or like Rousseau, whose liaison with Thérèse Levasseur was a singular intellectual mismatch, Gibbon preferred to dazzle others with his fame and his casual chat. His attitude in conversation, as he described it in the first letter (dated 1764) that survives of his long correspondence with Holroyd, was statuesque, almost a self-parody: "my body bent forwards, and my fore-finger stretched out" (I, 174–175). It was an attitude designed to fix attention on himself, and he seems never to have given it up. Tales survive of Gibbon's conversational primping and preening during his last years in Lausanne. Conversation was an art that he never managed wholly to master.

But he did in his way master silence. Behind the thousands of words of the *Decline and Fall* lies the reflective silence of consciousness. That is what endows Gibbon's account of the history's origin with its special power. What persists in his several accounts of the moment of conception are the date, the time of day—it could only have been evening, and the conflict represented in the interpenetrations of silence and sound. The final version is: "It was at Rome on the fifteenth of October 1764, as I sat musing amidst the ruins of the Capitol while the barefooted fryars were singing Vespers in the temple of Jupiter, that the idea of writing the decline and fall of the City first started to my mind."[15] The Franciscans interrupt Gibbon's meditation with their vespers, intruding on the silence of the past as Christianity had intruded on the authority of empire. But the irony is double. Because it is evening, the service enforces a sense of

14. Ibid.
15. Ibid., p. 136 n. For Gibbon's successive versions of the story, see pp. 304–305.

mutability: evensong lingers over the bittersweetness of the temporal. At evening, official religion holds up to uncertainty its own convictions. In the medium of his own musings, Gibbon's Franciscans assert the passing of empire. Mutability solicits silence, and those who grew preoccupied with the wreck of the past accorded silence new power. Henry Fuseli's "Artist Moved by the Grandeur of Ancient Ruins"—the compelling frontispiece of W. Jackson Bate's *The Burden of the Past and the English Poet*—portrays the artist poised between melancholy and reverence.[16] The drawing provides no evidence beyond its title that its central figure is an artist; this is the artist silent in contemplation. Rousseau, who in the *Confessions* had imagined himself appearing before his judge with the written word securely in hand, moves on to the *Rêveries du promeneur solitaire*, in which the written word celebrates meditation and silence. And even Gibbon, far more sociable than Rousseau, came to sense the possibilities while in Lausanne of a private aesthetic of silence. Having lost his seat on the Board of Trade, given up his seat in Parliament, and taken a step in moving to Lausanne that his friends had tried to dissuade him from, Gibbon begins (not unlike Rousseau) to mythologize his story: Lausanne is a quiet Eden, London a tumult, and Parliament a "Pandaemonium," full of noise and deviltry.[17] Some of what the Ile de Saint-Pierre meant to Rousseau, Lausanne meant to Gibbon.

But he came closest to achieving an aesthetic of silence in the public utterance of his history. At its most powerful, the *Decline and Fall*, like other literature of meditation, aims at

16. (Cambridge: Harvard University Press, 1970).

17. For example, to Lady Sheffield, October 22, 1784, about Lausanne: "this delicious paradise" (III, 10); to Dorothea Gibbon, December 27, 1783: "M. Deyverdun's house is spacious and convenient, and his garden . . . unites every beauty and advantage both of town and country. But into this paradise we are not yet introduced." (II, 387); to Lord Sheffield, March 2, 1784: "some great and memorable debate in the Pandaemonium" (II, 400); to Lord Sheffield, May 11, 1784: "I much fear your discontent and regret at being excluded from that Pandaemonium." (II, 405); "the tumult of London" (*Memoirs*, p. 183).

verbal transparency through which appears a visionary world. The form of meditation favored by Gibbon's age was the prospect, and his history is both prospect and narrative.[18] It is as if its author were double: the historian who tells the story and the artist who watches from a high vantage the visual panorama of history unfolding through the "silent lapse of time."[19] The countless prospects of the *Decline and Fall* all lead up to one final outlook on the ruins of Rome in chapter 71, as the story comes to an end. The ending, to any reader familiar with Gibbon's autobiography and his account of the conception of the *Decline and Fall*, recalls how the enterprise began. Now Gibbon remembers the Renaissance humanist Poggio Bracciolini, who ascended the Capitoline in the fifteenth century to meditate, like Gibbon, on "the wide and various prospect of desolation": "This spectacle of the world, how it is fallen! how changed! how defaced!"[20] Poggio had written, "O quantum . . . haec capitolia ab illis distant, quae noster Maro cecinit,

Aurea nunc, olim silvestribus horrida dumis,"

alluding to *Aeneid*, I, 348.[21] Gibbon recalls as well *Paradise Lost*, I, 84–85 ("But O how fall'n! how chang'd / From him, who in the happy Realms of Light . . ."), in which Milton recalls *Aeneid*, II, 274–275 ("Quantum mutatus ab illo / Hectore . . .") and Isaiah 14:12 ("How art thou fallen from Heaven, O Lucifer, son of the morning!"). A simple Virgilian allusion in Poggio ripples outward to embrace ancient and modern, others and ourselves. We watch Virgil, Poggio, Milton, and Gibbon all watching the spectacle of the world: "The art of man is able to construct monuments far more permanent than the narrow span of his own existence; yet these monuments, like himself, are perishable and frail; and, in the boundless annals of time, his life and his labours must

18. In a book about Gibbon, in progress, I consider his use of prospects in the *Decline and Fall*.

19. *History of the Decline and Fall*, VII, 318.

20. Ibid., VII, 313; 314.

21. *Historia de Varietate Fortunae* (Paris, 1723; reprinted, Bologna: Forni Editore, 1969), pp. 5–6.

equally be measured as a fleeting moment."[22] The *Decline and Fall* is always dissolving its own art in silence.

"There is a relationship between silence and faith."
Max Picard, *The World of Silence*[23]

The skeptical Gibbon, "infidel" that he was, intuited sources of a faith that Johnson, despite or because of his fiercest efforts, could not reach. What is silence? Bernard Dauenhauer lists four attributes: "(1) silence is an active human performance which always appears in connection with an utterance, (2) silence is never an act of unmitigated autonomy. Rather, (3) silence involves a yielding following upon an awareness of finitude and awe. The yielding involved in silence is peculiar inasmuch as (4) it is a yielding which binds and joins."[24] Dauenhauer goes on, in a phenomenology of silence, to elaborate the nuances of this list. His subtleties are beyond the reach of this essay. Yet the *Decline and Fall* seems to dramatize such attributes: not only in its interplay of speech and the representations of silence, nor only in its evocation of finitude and awe, but especially in the way it binds together spectators to the passages of time. Does it strain credulity to think of Gibbon, small and fat and awkward, as a forerunner of Keats's Cortez, silent upon a peak in Darien? To this reader of the *Decline and Fall* the odd resemblance marks the way in which silence is a yielding that binds and joins.

22. *History of the Decline and Fall*, VII, 317.
23. Trans. by Stanley Goodman (Chicago: Henry Regnery, 1964), p. 228.
24. Bernard P. Dauenhauer, *Silence: The Phenomenon and Its Ontological Significance* (Bloomington: Indiana University Press, 1980), p. 24.

Statue of Edmund Burke, Bristol, England.

GERALD CHAPMAN

Burke's American Tragedy

In the American capital today Burke is the only eighteenth-
century British statesman with a monument and park all his
own, in fact the only British statesman so honored before
Winston Churchill in the 1960s. The monument (in a grassy
triangle at Massachusetts Avenue and 11th Street NW) is a
standing portrait, bronze, appropriately eight feet high, hand
uplifted, its marble base engraved with a solemn lapidary
sentence, "Magnanimity in politics is not seldom the truest
wisdom"—many readers will know the rest, from the *Speech
on Conciliation with the American Colonies*, March 1775—"and
a great empire and little minds go ill together." The original
of this American replica stands in a parkway at Bristol,[1]

1. Executed by the English sculptor J. H. Thomas at Capri, Italy, in 1864.
Except as indicated, page numbers of *The Works of the Right Honourable
Edmund Burke* refer to the widely available editions published by Little,
Brown & Co., 12 vols. (Boston, 1865–1867) and Bohn's British Classics, 8
vols. (London, 1854–1889)—cited hereafter as Little, Brown and Bohn.
Accidentals, however, are printed from the last edition incorporating
Burke's corrections (London, 1803). The lapidary sentence is in *Works*
(Little, Brown), II, 181; (Bohn), I, 509. The sentence engraved at Bristol
is, "I wish to be a member of Parliament to have my share of doing good
and resisting evil," from "Speech Previous to the Election at Bristol,
1780," *Works* (Little, Brown), II, 421; (Bohn), II, 167.
    A shorter version of this essay was presented to the Late Eighteenth

Britain's second largest city when Burke represented it in the House of Commons (1774–1780). He had won his reputation in Commons, starting with his maiden speech in 1766, as a critic of British errors in the Stamp Act crisis, and so entered into American legend as a sympathizer and charismatic spokesman for liberty. More exactly, he envisioned a free Atlantic civilization developing through its first stages under British dominion but in familial reciprocity: "we might have kept them very easily," he still believed in 1779, but once "the natural Bonds of dominion" were broken, the imperative next best was "a friendship that will hold."[2] An opportunity for a benign world-historical order and greatness, one form it could have taken, was failed for its time by small-mindedness. A later, kinder, and bleaker judgment acknowledged, however, that "Times, *accidents*, the Characters of men, do much, but *accident*, (or an unseen providence for unknown Ends,) does most of all."[3]

From 1771 until the outbreak of war he served as "agent" for the General Assembly of New York, that is, a salaried overseas representative in technical matters, mostly of trade—a little more than friend but less than lobbyist. Even as the Second Continental Congress moved toward war in May 1775, Ben Franklin, another "agent," drafted a resolution of public thanks to Burke, for "generous Endeavours," but kept it back among his papers.[4] They corresponded secretly during the war, and at least once Burke considered a

---

Century Section of the Modern Language Association, New York City, 1976, at the kind invitation of Professor Lawrence Lipking.

2. To Dr. John Erskine, June 12, 1779, in *The Correspondence of Edmund Burke*, ed. Thomas W. Copeland, et al., 10 vols. (Chicago and Cambridge: The University of Chicago Press, 1958–1978), IV, 87—cited hereafter as *Corr.*

3. To Sir Gilbert Elliot, September 3, 1788, *Corr.*, V, 415.

4. Along with the Earl of Chatham (the elder Pitt), David Hartley, and the Bishop of St. Asaph (Jonathan Shipley): see *Letters of Members of the Continental Congress*, ed. Edmund C. Burnett (Washington, D. C.: The Carnegie Institution of Washington, 1921), I, 105.

visit to Franklin in Paris.[5] Like many other Whigs, he came to admire George Washington, whose "character would be transmitted to the latest ages, among the first of heroes and patriots";[6] on occasion he wore the blue frock coat and buff waistcoat (colors of Washingtonian undress) adopted by Foxite Whigs as political uniform and public flout.[7] Endeavoring generously again, after several years' work he freed the captured President of Congress, Henry Laurens, from the Tower, with his own bill for prisoners' exchange. In 1783, with the arrival of peace, Burke met and admired John Adams, and, while the latter resided in London as ambassador, read his *Defense* of the American constitution (3 vols., 1787).[8] He had nothing against a republic, the form of government best now for American needs,[9] although he worried lest "the democratic party threatened to overpower the interests of the Federalists, to whom he gave full credit for wisdom and patriotism."[10] Perhaps he read *The Federalist* when it appeared in 1788. As late as August of that year, a good ten months before the French Revolution, he entertained Tom Paine in his home for a week and escorted him to the country estates of Whig grandees, calling his guest, with whatever reserve of irony, "the great American

---

5. In January 1777: see *Corr.*, III, 310. The surviving exchange of letters dates from late 1781 and early 1782. On Franklin, cf. "An Appeal from the New to the Old Whigs," *Works* (Little, Brown), IV, 100; (Bohn), II, 30.

6. Thomas Somerville, *My Own Life and Times, 1711–1814* (Edinburgh, 1861), pp. 222–223.

7. For example see To Dr. French Laurence, August 18, 1788, *Corr.*, V, 412.

8. Joseph Charles, *The Origins of the American Party System* (New York: Harper Torchbook Edition, 1961), pp. 68–69.

9. *The Parliamentary History of England from the earliest period to the year 1803*, ed. W. Cobbett, 36 vols. (London, 1806–1820), XXVII (December 22, 1788), 821—cited hereafter as *PH*. Cf. *PH*, XXIX (May 6, 1791), 365–366.

10. Somerville, *My Own Life and Times*, p. 223.

Paine."[11] No wonder then if circumstantial evidence convicted him in many minds as factious, even disloyal—one of the "vile agents" in Johnson's (reported) parody of the *Speech on Conciliation*.[12]

Yet surely "the pursuit of happiness," that touchstone, would have aligned Edmund Burke with *Rasselas* or *The Vanity of Human Wishes*, not with Jefferson and "the projectors of independence," as he dubbed them.[13] And though he lived beyond Johnson into a frantic decade when the old Copernican term *revolution* took on everywhere its strange new meaning (and implied Creation myth), "to make a new world, throw out the past and start the world over,"[14] the reality of such a wish he always regarded, as Johnson must have, as a delusion, another ambush of the heart when it was not a fraud, and either way an invitation to the abyss. For all his exasperation (fully returned) with the older man's politics—especially with *Taxation no Tyranny* (1775), in which the "formidable champion . . . summoned all his vigor and eloquence in vindication of a civil war"—even so, the friendship of Johnson, Burke told Commons, was "the greatest consolation and happiness of his life."[15]

Despite the complex originality of Burke's intelligence, in his métier another "great experiencing nature"[16] like Johnson himself, the system of moral ideas he carried into social

11. To Dr. French Laurence, August 18, 1788, *Corr.*, V, 412.

12. The parody is reported in Mrs. Piozzi's *Anecdotes* in *Johnsonian Miscellanies*, ed. George Birkbeck Hill (Oxford, 1897), I, 173–175, parodying *Works* (Little, Brown), II, 114–115; (Bohn), I, 460.

13. *PH*, XVIII (November 16, 1775), 977.

14. Since Copernicus' *De revolutionibus orbium caelestium* the term, astronomical even in Chaucer, had meant an eternal (natural) order of cyclic return in the motions of heavenly bodies. On its changing meaning, see Burke's expression in *PH*, XXVIII (February 5, 1790), 361: "this strange thing, called a revolution in France," whereas "our revolution (as it is called)" in 1688 had been "in truth and substance, and in a constitutional light, a revolution, not made, but prevented."

15. *PH*, XXX (December 15, 1792), 109–110.

16. W. Jackson Bate, *Samuel Johnson* (New York: Harcourt Brace Jovanovich, 1977), p. xix.

analysis owed much to the all-freshening psychiatry of *The Rambler*. The two differed most, perhaps, in their ways of encountering history. For Burke, "America was a new case . . . a nation *sui generis*";[17] he recognized that, for the first time in civilized memory, a new people had invented a government and put it successfully into practice. His thinking can be sampled in process in manuscript notes dating probably from 1782, the year of Lord Shelburne's preliminary articles of peace:

This peace being the *Basis* of a settlement in a *new Order* of things, at the great Crisis of a general Change, is like to be

<   > in the Forests Delphinum Sylvis appingit. Shelburne like the great painters.

decisive on the permanent condition of that Country & the *rank* it is to hold through all succeding generations.

[not a Revolution by his varying the positions of the old Stock.

A *great revolution* has happend, a revolution not made by the shiftings & varied positions of the *old* stock of power portioned in different degrees among the formerly existing States, but by the appearance of a new State, of a new *Species*, in a *new* part of the Earth wch has made as complete a change in the Ballances & gravitations of the other Powers as the coming of a new Planet rushing into the System of the Solar World.

The Birth of this mighty Babe shook every thing—aspice convexo nutantem pondere mundum. Terras tractusq caelumque profundum.

[New Center of Relations

The effect was instantly to produce a *new center of relations* of all countries to that, & of

17. *PH*, XXIII (March 7, 1783), 613.

This Toryism run mad.	all other Countries to one another.

Whether we can inquire into a
Treaty of peace without shaking its
validity. The question is whether
the constitution of this Country
be a good one or not.
this perhaps may be one of the
Articles of the constitutional
reform.[18]

A dislike for Shelburne and the treaty's terms prompts a
mock from Horace, *Delphinium Sylvis appingit* (*Ars poetica*, 30
and its context): like a mad or bad poet hopeful of grandeur
from mere variation, Shelburne "paints a Dolphin in the
Forests." But sarcasm gives way to a Virgilian tragic or post-
tragic consciousness at once religious and practical, a
statesman's consciousness how new scenes for action, new
eras in the destiny of the world, and new duties arise irreversibly from the mystery of events in time, after strange beginnings and inexplicable wastes of suffering.   Then, just as
quickly, Burke queries himself about an article in next year's
Reform Bill.   Sarcasm or wit transcended by visionary or
tragic energy that arches from past to future, then the har-
nessing of both for practical steps in a brand-new here and
now—the combination is characteristic of Burke.   The Virgil
is *Eclogue* IV (the "Messianic" eclogue, in its rhyming
verses 50–51) announcing a golden age by the birth of a
child who shall rid the earth of guilt and dread: "Behold the
world, the expanse of sea and lands, and deep heaven, uncertain [wavering] in its vaulted balance [of power]." Burke's

18. Sheffield City Libraries, Wentworth Woodhouse Muniments, BK
6/164—hereafter cited as Sheffield. My warm thanks to the Director of
Libraries, Mrs. Pat Coleman, and to Trustees of the Fitzwilliam (Wentworth) Estate for their permission to quote. The variant at BK 6/45
specifies "a Planet like Saturn," as if Burke toyed with a pun on *redeunt
Saturnia regna* (Virgil, *Eclogues*, IV.6).   Illegible matter is put in angle
brackets.

quotations many times imply an unstated memory or the original, and Virgil's next verse is "Behold how all things rejoice in the age that is coming." The abyss of history had opened, and after tragic convulsions, gave birth to a new state *in* an new state *of* time. Nothing could be more awesome to Burke than that, or call for more toughly pragmatic acceptance. "A sacred veil [is] to be drawn," he remarked in 1788, "over the beginnings of all governments . . . Time . . . has thrown this mysterious veil over [most of them]; prudence and discretion make it necessary to throw something of the same drapery over more recent foundations."[19]

Despite his Augustan decorum and derisions, Burke had in his temper more than a little of the prophetic visionary, as many in his day recognized, no doubt Johnson among them, but knew no better than Burke himself what to do about such an embarrassment. Sometimes he joked about it—what was wrong with foresight? Friends shrugged it off as wild-Irishism (prevaricating naturally) complicated by Whiggery and/or Christian piety (perhaps too strait in virtue). Enemies adjudged him mad off and on, or, in Blake's cold eyes, not mad enough. And all may have been right. Burke was halfway to Blake in turning an intense spiritual eye on events and in catching the "spirits" of people and situations. "How closely that fellow reasons in metaphor!" goes the well-known remark of one of his audience.[20] Yet, unlike Blake, he subdued his visions to practical prose; and instead of creating his own myths by which to read the times, he appropriated myths in educated public sanction—or, as he might have put it, he "applied his reading," especially of literary classics, to life. My effort here is to glimpse his practical mythology in his writings on the seven-year British struggle and defeat in America, and so pull nearer the light one source of the richness in Burke's style regarded also as a state of mind. My argument is that, dispersed through

19. "Speech in Opening the Impeachment of Warren Hastings: Second Day, 16 Feb. 1788," *Works* (Little, Brown), IX, 401; (Bohn), VII, 159.
20. *Johnsonian Miscellanies*, I, 171 n.

hundreds of pages over many years (but centering here, for illustration, in and around 1775, within speeches, pamphlets, private correspondence, and masses of manuscripts) there is a paradigm or structure of tragedy, especially blood tragedy somewhere between Aeschylus and *Macbeth*, which is not merely ornament or allusion but an authentic way of seeing and feeling what happened: a paradigm, furthermore, that can "apply" again, that has a way of waking up in other times and societies, including our own.

Some such "tragic" side of Burke fed his early nineteenth-century kudos as the Shakespeare of politics— idolizing which, however Anglo-eccentric it may seem now and begrudged by many, had its point. An intuition that "Shakespeare himself has come again"[21] responded to his intelligence and his gift of self-knowledge at a time of cataclysm for Europe before (and after) the Napoleonic wars. George Canning considered Burke's death in 1797 "an event for the world," for the age itself would be distinguished "for all time" as the one in which Burke lived; and, as is well known, many in the Romantic generation—Coleridge, Wordsworth, even Hazlitt—came to see Burke's importance as transcendent. "No one, I suppose, will set Johnson before Burke," Coleridge huffed.[22] But also—Hazlitt is especially sensitive on this score—such an intuition recognized in Burke something inherently dramatic, not formal but performative. Most major Augustans, from perhaps Butler, Swift, and Pope to Johnson and Gibbon, had doubted that any great form of tragedy could mature within contemporary theatre; yet they achieved within the mixed forms of satire,

21. See *Corr.*, VI, 216 n., quoting the wife of the British Minister at Turin, in 1791, but by midcentury the comparison was frequent.
22. *The Table Talk and Omniana of Samuel Taylor Coleridge*, ed. T. Ashe (London, 1896). Canning is quoted in Sir Philip Magnus, *Edmund Burke: A Life* (London: John Murray, 1939), p. 297. For more on Coleridge and Wordsworth, see Alfred Cobban, *Edmund Burke and the Revolt Against the Eighteenth Century*, 2nd ed. (New York: Barnes & Noble, 1961); for Hazlitt, see *The Eloquence of the British Senate* (London, 1808) and passim in his essays.

pensée, and history a quality of vision that is hard to call anything less than "tragic," despite their achieving at other times (and perhaps at their most authentic) a post-tragic humanism for which, to borrow a famous phrase from Jasper, "tragedy is not enough." Burke belongs, at times, in such company, though more engagedly a public man than autonomous writer. As with them, his deepest themes include how to advance or preserve "civil society" (civilization) as such. Yet his being a public man at such a turning point in modern history positioned him as a writer to some advantage: tragedy as first invented had its roots in historic compassion and anxiety for the *polis*, in planned regressions of imagination into large-scale suffering and experience of the worst archaic cruelty or barbarity, curse, mistake, dilemma. Perhaps the tragic is always a possible rediscovery in "political" events, especially great wars when history enters a dead-end wilderness, but also anywhere power goes blind and ordinary human beings are angry. What is even easier to overlook, however, because so simple, is that the eighteenth-century Parliament, especially the House of Commons, was a unique, ephemeral mode of theatre, both as performing art and as playhouse and audience.

St. Stephen's,[23] which burned in 1834, was a fourteenth-century chapel, built by the Edwards to outshine Sainte Chapelle in Paris, in key features the prototype in England of Gothic perpendicular, slightly taller than Sainte Chapelle and in its day as famous for beauty. After the Reformation it was refurbished as a meeting place for Commons—"framed and made like unto a theatre" (a 1571 description)—the "Papist" statues, paintings, and tapestries removed, the stained glass and multifoil tracery replaced with plaster, oak wainscot, and a ceiling, and everything further cut down and remodeled to a neat plain style by Sir Christopher Wren about 1707. But its ecclesiastical foundation was a renewable

---

23. The following paragraph draws freely from Maurice Hastings, *Parliament House* (London: Architectural Press, 1950); and P. D. G. Thomas, *The House of Commons in the Eighteenth Century* (Oxford: Oxford University Press, Clarendon Press, 1971).

memory—one should remember as much when reading the
Speech on Conciliation, with its subtly placed religious
imagery; indeed, the tips of five chapel-arches were visible
on each side in the rarely visited attic. A German Lutheran
pastor visiting Commons in 1782, after the traumas of the
American war, Gordon Riots, and much else had desacral-
ized the House even more, described it as "rather a mean-
looking building," in which some members would arrive
rudely in boots, husk nuts, or sprawl out for a nap, and yet
somewhat like a chapel, the Speaker's Chair towering like a
pulpit, the Great Table and its reposing Mace like an altar,
the surrounding benches "covered with green cloth . . . like
our choirs in churches." Burke's piety when active was Providential, literally so, and he could hardly have not regarded
the House, the place of his (Aenean) duty on earth, as more
than a government building, as indeed a place of sacerdotal
responsibility, a temple—except on all the other occasions
when manifestly it was no such blessed thing. Yet many
likenesses, as they seem now, to either church or theater
were conspicuous: the mysticism of the Mace borne always
shoulder-high by a dazzling Sergeant-at-Arms, other rituals
or pageants (searching the cellars, Black Rod, the oath,
"genuflection" of sorts to the Speaker), the wig and black
silk gown of the Speaker and his robed Clerks-at-the-Table,
rules and taboos, the brilliant Court dress and swords worn
by the Ministry, conflicts, crises, intrigues, and applauses,
awareness of the storied past of famous men and precedents,
the excitement of gathering auditors, even a star system
among speakers, orange girls in the Lobby, and spectators or
petitioners whispering or thronging the Strangers' Gallery
(except when closed, as generally it was in 1771–1777). To
rise to speak upon the floor, for a man unsure of his part,
was to become very alone in a crowd of faces expectant,
bored, or disapproving—several hundred restive people
closeted within a room 57'6" by 32'10" and only a 30' ceiling.
In his maiden appearance Addison was so dizzied by stage
fright and *Hear! Hear!*'s that he could only repeat, "Mr.
Speaker, I conceive . . . I conceive . . . Mr. Speaker . . . Sir, I
conceive . . ." before sitting down—having conceived three

times and brought forth nothing, a voice remarked, followed by crushing laughter.[24] Throughout his eight sessions (1774–1782) coinciding with the American war, Gibbon never dared rise, "notwithstanding all my efforts," he groaned in April, 1775, "chained down to my place by some invisible unknown invisible power"—for years "a Mute," "a dumb Dog."[25]

Yet this was the physical center or showplace of Burke's imaginative life, where together with a repertory of other actors and extras he wrangled, harangued, or just listened, day in day out for almost thirty years. Even between sessions, mulling what to say or do in the House shaped much of his being. The final drama of Burke, to be sure, was his search by language for the truth to be given; but his laboratory where truth could be tested and new evidence gathered was the raw political scene to which celebrity in Commons kept him responsible. As his manuscripts show, he composed much at home for the House and its refractory audience, thinking things out, turning phrases, getting facts, anticipating counter-strategies and sifting options, as a playwright sifts a plot, or as a priest contemporizes his sermon, or as an actor tries on roles or prepares himself for a specific part in a given playhouse—yet in this case, in these open-ended plays (or "happenings"), knowing little of the other actors' lines or whether there would be a plot. Beautifully literate as the few speeches that Burke published are, most if not all of his thousand addresses had to be impromptu or acted out as if impromptu, from memory, whether for ten minutes or three hours. As verbatim fact, much if not most is lost in devouring time, and we find ourselves poring over the mazy manuscripts—or through newspaper accounts, chance notes, diaries, even gossip—to restore some part of what is lost. But the surviving riches establish Burke's medium as not oration or even "literature" in some faddish

24. Norman Wilding and Philip Laundy, *An Encyclopaedia of Parliament* (New York: Praeger, 1968), p. 449.

25. *Letters of Edward Gibbon*, ed. J. E. Norton (London: Macmillan, 1956), II, 61, 64, 241.

sense, but the Commons stage, including its day-by-day pressures and vunerabilities of ego, its roles that become reality, its demands for specific language, together with a busy offstage of back rooms, clubs, and competitive celebrity, long hours of reading and self-rehearsal, stultifying anxiety, and weariness. Yet it was exigency in Commons, and preparations to meet it day after day, that matured Burke's style (while prescribing its limits), gave him authority of "voice" and greatness of subject, including, when needed, a sublime transparency fit for every audience. Without a stage to write for he would have been, if not lost, very different; yet his greatest triumphs would come in his moments of breaking loose from it, gearing his House voice for a stage more permanent.

In Burke, as in ourselves, there can be only limited certainty when allusions and quotes-from-memory, say from Simonides, Ovid, Aquinas, *Hamlet*, or *Hudibras*, imply recollection of the whole of the literary structure to which they belong, or of associated structures in mind but not quoted— as, indeed, what interpretations of those structures, and what coalescence of interpretations, all passing vaguely as an "educated taste." What exactly was in Gibbon's mind when he praised in Burke's speeches a "profuse and philosophic fancy" that "possessed the *sense* and *spirit* of the Classics"?[26] In part, of course, he meant Burke's original-language literacy as such, say in Greek. Though not so fluent as Gibbon, even before his M.A. Burke had taken honors courses in Greek at Trinity College, Dublin, which required of every student a minimum of four years' reading from Homer through Demosthenes and Longinus, including Sophocles' *Oedipus Tyrannus*, *Electra*, and the *Trachiniae*.[27]

---

26. *Edward Gibbon: Memoirs of My Life*, ed. Georges A. Bonnard (London: Funk & Wagnalls, 1966), pp. 212, 248; italics mine.

27. The four-year curriculum is printed in John William Stubbs, *The History of the University of Dublin* (Dublin and London, 1889), pp. 199–200. In 1794 Burke described his Greek as too "worn out" to rival that of his son Richard, who (as Burke saw to it) was "perfectly accurate in that Language. Starting in 1775, Richard studied Aeschylus, Sophocles, Euripides, and Pin-

But "the sense and spirit of the Classics" would also imply an attitude toward reading and the uses of literacy common since Augustan satirists: a turning away from hermeneutics, considered as sufficient already for the purposes of public life, to be left to editors and specialists, toward a praxis of applicability of works in learning's commonwealth. "Reading, and much reading is good," Burke wrote to his son in 1773; "but the power of diversifying the matter infinitely in your own Mind, and of applying it to every occasion that arises is far better. So dont suppress the vivida vis."[28] Implied is an attitude that values subjective energy and considers a reading, say of *Oedipus Tyrannus* or *Macbeth*, as still unfinished—and hence the "meaning" of a phrase, verse, passage, scene, or entire structure as incomplete—until the reader uses it to new purposes of his own. A reader's use for it is part of its meaning, to a practical infinity of uses so long as *Macbeth* or *Oedipus Tyrannus* is meaningful. The reader owes the work a life of its own by remaining open to it, but also he has a life of his own with the work, which assists to insight. In such a praxis, to distinguish mere learning afloat from earned personal vision, or Longinian transumption, can be doubly hard. Which is it, shall one say, in the agonized desire of Sir William Jones, in 1780, "if God preserve his life, to write the history of the American war in the manner of Thucydides, *i.e.*, from his own personal knowledge of many actors in it on both sides, and of the events"?[29]

---

dar in a postgraduate tutorial with a native Greek in London, Mr. Nicolaides, whom Burke befriended and even helped to a pension in 1782—that is, during the years of the American war. It would have been unlike Burke not to peek in, if only to learn something for himself. See Appendix I in *Corr.*, VII, 580–585.

28. To Richard Burke, Jr. and Thomas King (February 4, 1773), *Corr.*, II, 420. For *vivida vis [animi]* see Lucretius I.72.

29. To Lord Althorp, June 16, 1780, Spencer MSS, *Second Report of the Royal Commission on Historical Manuscripts* (London, 1874), p. 13.

The prologue to this tale of the house of Albion opens with an entanglement of family prides by force and counter-force, and with perception of a vital curse which only greatness could remove. Whatever romance young Burke brought with him from Ireland about English vigor and greatness of statesmanship must have suffered early, and one wonders what rescue fantasies he carried into Commons. For years he considered emigrating to America.[30] Deadness of feeling and smallness of mind, failures of imaginative vigor and magnanimity, are his steady complaint, including (in manuscripts dating from the 1760s) "almost all kinds of poetry . . . cultivated with little success" and "particularly in what regards the Theatre."[31] In his first published words at age nineteen, he had aligned himself, a bit unevenly, with Pope's campaign against "the Empire of *Dulness*,"[32] and a *Dunciad*-reading of modern England, as later of modern France, recurred in Burke's imaginative life, though never simple-mindedly so. Estimates of national apathy, overrefinement, and decline were, to be sure, a midcentury commonplace; indeed, most European diplomats from about 1763 to 1780 regarded England, despite its military power, as a self-crippled giant unable to act.[33] Burke could mock the attitude even as he puzzled over the need for it: for example, "Mr Grenville begins to slacken in his attendance [in Commons]; His Language is, I am told, that of despair of the Commonwealth, Prophecies, Omens, ruin, &c. &c. . . .

30. See *Corr.*, I (March 11, 1755), 119; (August 10, 1757), 123; (July 10, 1761), 141.

31. "Hints for an Essay on Drama," *Works* (Little, Brown), VII, 147–148; (Bohn), VI, 177.

32. *The Reformer*, 1 (Thursday, January 28, 1748), [1], young Burke's periodical founded to reform Dublin taste and morals especially by reforming the theater.

33. Michael Roberts, *Splendid Isolation, 1763–1780*, The Stenton Lecture for 1969, University of Reading (1970); cf. W. E. H. Lecky, *A History of England in the Eighteenth Century* (New York, 1878), I, 505 and passim.

Yet all is in an odd way . . . so odd a situation of things."
"We live in a strange time."[34]

In his language and visionary breath, however, as also in
his will to be up and doing, Burke more often sounds like an
early Matthew Arnold, or perhaps Wordsworth in some
moods. From his first Parliament in 1766 he puzzled over
the "Stupor" or "Torpor" which had fallen upon political
England as he saw and felt it, a calamitous slowing down or
halt of vital energies that threatened to change the national
character as he had believed it to be—a "Strange insensibil-
ity," "a sort of troubled sleep" of self-alienation, a "sliding
away from the genuine Spirit of the Country."[35] The majestic *Thoughts on the Cause of the Present Discontents* (1770)
was not only a manifesto for the Rockingham Whigs and a
statement of permanent worth about parties as such but also
a probing of organic custom for the "strange distemper"
which without any "great external calamity . . . pestilence or
famine" "strikes a palsy into every nerve of our free constitution . . . in the same degree benumbs and stupifies the
whole executive power; rendering Government in all its
grand operations languid, uncertain, ineffective."[36] A Providential vitalism runs through all of Burke's thought,
expressed often in thematic images of paralysis or disease,
languor, stagnation, as at other times of shadows, specters,
ghosts, or phantoms. A sacredness attaches to all vital
powers, however wrong-headed their use, and a mystery to

34. To Charles O'Hara, April 8 [1766] and [April 21, 1766], *Corr.*, I,
248–250.
35. For examples, see *Corr.*, I (*post* November 11, 1766), 278; II
(December 31, 1770), 177; II (*post* July 14, 1771), 222; II (June 1, 1772),
305; II (October 27, 1772), 352; II (*post* November 15, 1772); and so on,
for many years.
36. "Thoughts on the Cause of the Present Discontents," in *The Writings
and Speeches of Edmund Burke*, ed. Paul Langford and William B. Todd et al.
(Oxford: Clarendon Press, 1981–), vol. 2, *Party, Parliament, and the American Crisis, 1766–1774*, ed. Paul Langford, pp. 253–254, 283—hereafter cited
as *Writings and Speeches*. In this magnificent edition in process, there has
also appeared vol. 5, *India: Madras and Bengal, 1774–1785*, ed. P. J.
Marshall.

their welling-up or their waning in all things human in individuals, families, traditions, or nations. (Which belief, one
may add, is a sine qua non of tragedy: not a cause but a
necessary condition. Tragedy without vitalism is impossible.
Toward the beginning of Greek tragedy was the Greek smile
and the heartening dance—the fragile, earned, irreducible
yes—and the end of tragic form is to circle back to it by laws
of suffering.) Burke is the political congener of mid-century
British criticism in literature and the arts in his refusals to
countenance formalism, in the sense of forcing prefabricated
forms upon governments, churches, or any vital organization
or institution in history.

At the level of public events, where curses become history, the "first fatal opening," in Burke's phrase, was the
Stamp Act crisis of 1765 "arising from claims, which pride
would permit neither party to abandon."[37] What the British,
dully, considered a benign tutelage was to the Americans as
violence against life and sacred honor. By 1770 "it became a
trial who should yield first," a family stalemate of suspicion
and hardening will.[38] "Our severity has increased their ill
behaviour. We know not how to advance; they know not
how to retreat."[39] Somehow "the unwieldy haughtiness of a
great ruling nation, habituated to command, pampered by
enormous wealth, and confident from a long course of prosperity and victory" had to be reconciled "to the high spirit
of free dependencies, animated with the first glow and
activity of juvenile heat, and assuming to themselves as their
birthright, some part of that very pride which oppresses
them."[40] In short, an adolescent hero soon to be famous for
transcendental gifts and imperial dreams was in angry

37. "Letter to the Sheriffs of Bristol," *Works* (Little, Brown), II, 234;
(Bohn), II, 34.
38. *Sir Henry Cavendish's Debates of the House of Commons during the Thirteenth Parliament of Great Britain Commonly Called the Unreported Parliament*,
ed. J. Wright, 2 vols. (London, 1841–42), II (May 9, 1770), 18.
39. Ibid., I (April 19, 1769), 398.
40. "Letter to the Sheriffs of Bristol," *Works* (Little, Brown), II, 231;
(Bohn), II, 31–32.

rebellion against a regal mother, not finished with building her own empire, indeed just reaching for it with high risk — and yet a civil and progressive imperatrix, this English Clytemnestra, famous for liberties, and jealous of her dignity. Some of the psychohistory of these years, in the language of both sides, is so trans-parent (alas) as to be almost funny, except when a cause to shudder. Page after page of the *Parliamentary History* premises the analogy of mother country and rebellious child, or wicked king/father or stepmother and loyal child, and then spins arguments in happy oblivion of facts.[41] Burke himself explores the analogy, "reasons in metaphor" with it for whatever the jot of truth to be gained—for as he said many times, in national as in family quarrels, the principles can be the same; but he is just as likely to mock the analogy as cant. To what extent such familial projections, and their reversible field of Oedipal energies, may have decided public or even government opinion and action would be fascinating to learn.

The plot thickened with "Intolerable Acts" of 1774, against which, on April 19, Burke made his *Speech on American Taxation*, the first speech he would trouble to publish (nine months later but virtually as spoken) after more than two hundred appearances on the floor. He stopped his ears against the whine of abstract Rights from both sides — meaning by "abstraction" a mere word or sound that nevertheless has the power to arouse passions and whose deeply subjective, often contradictory or unexamined meanings are out of touch with practical life and its tightly coiled possibilities for good or evil—possibilities that are knowable only in the concrete by intelligent watchfulness of step after step.[42]

41. For miscellaneous examples, see *PH*, XVI (January 14, 1766), 90 n.; XVII (March 14, 1774), 1176–1178; XVII (March 28, 1774), 1185–1186, and the American petition on 1191–1192; XVII (April 15, 1774), 1198–1199; XVII (April 19, 1774), 1271.

42. See Burke's discussion of "compound abstract words" in Part V of *A Philosophical Enquiry into the Origin of Our Ideas of the Sublime and Beautiful*, ed. J. T. Boulton (New York: Columbia University Press, 1958), pp.

In the clamor over Rights—Rights of the king or imperial Parliament versus those of colonial assemblies, the prescriptive Rights of history and the British constitution versus the natural Rights of mankind, or of the New World—profound human dilemmas were shrinking into slogans and so were at odds, Burke realized, with the mystery of need in men and nations to take their lives their own way. "It was our metaphysical quarrel about mere words," he would remark five years later, "that had caused the American war . . . We had commenced that war, not to recover a substance, but to possess, what if obtained, would have proved no more than a shadow."[43] Indeed, "the End for wch the War [was] made [was] not *by war* to be accomplished."[44] But words were only the foreground; in the approaching "Theatre of a Civil war,"[45] as he styled it, behind the words and yet released by them was a delusive entanglement of vital energies escalating (into the Aeschylean)—real-life events taking shape awesomely, week by week, month by month, as, literally, a classic. Where others heard juridical arguments on the floor of Commons, or indulged epic futures in the green fields of America, Burke heard with a shudder the stir of Erinyes, dark whines from the bestial floor: "As army clashes with army, so shall what-is-Right with what-is-Right."[46] Passions of righteousness were winging into life from the abyss itself, passions so terrible in permanent nature as to dwarf any possible differences of civilized preference among sane men. As usual, in the name of Right, all distinctions of specific innocence or guilt were no longer remembered or even wanted,

---

163–177—hereafter cited as *Philosophical Enquiry.*

43. *PH*, XX (December 6, 1779), 1211.

44. Sheffield, BK. 6/111.

45. Northamptonshire Record Office, Fitzwilliam MSS, A.xxvii.52—hereafter cited as Northampton. My warm thanks to Mr. P. I. King at Delapre Abbey and to the Trustees of the Fitzwilliam Estate for their permission to quote.

46. Aeschylus, *Choephoroi*, 461 (free translation mine).

"all kinds of people, all sexes, all ages, [confounded] in one common ruin."[47]

Burke had brought to contemporary politics, and into the other great theater of England, an ancient way of seeing, some may suspect a primitive Irish one, reinforced by his study of Greek—a respect for dark, somehow animal powers at the base of history, ferocious if provoked, or else, more hopefully, a just Providence, for as tragic writers from Aeschylus to Shakespeare have shown, the two are not mutually exclusive in tragic feeling. Even the dapper scientism of his *Philosophical Enquiry Into the Origin of Our Ideas of the Sublime and Beautiful* (1757, but almost certainly begun ten years before) trembles at times not only with explicit Christian humility but with apprehensions that if laid open might have been chided, even by Johnson, as "superstitious." Not just the vogue for Longinus, but personality and experience set Burke upon investigating "terror" as "the common stock of every thing sublime" along with other passions (for example, sex) which, however mysterious or grand in their transformations, "merely arise from the mechanical structure of our bodies, or from the natural frame and constitution of our minds," and therefore are primordial, as "they were in the beginning of the world."[48] A glance down his deceptively rational chapter heads (in Part II) can show that he is no more scientific than he is awed by the experience of something immemorial, very likely as old as the race of man or as deep as birth, a coming awake to wildness and danger, as it were to the Mt. Kithairon in things—to Terror, Obscurity, Power, Privation ("Vacuity, Darkness, Solitude, and Silence"), Vastness, Infinity, Magnitude, Difficulty, Magnificence, Light ("light which by its very excess is converted into a species of darkness"), and, then, with a startling shift further outward, Sound and Loudness ("vast cataracts, raging storms, thunder"), Suddenness, Intermitting, The cries of Animals, Bitters and Stenches,

47. *PH*, XVIII (March 6, 1775), 390; cf. XVII (March 25, 1774), 1183.
48. *Philosophical Enquiry*, pp. 45, 50.

Feeling, Pain. One is ready for a flutter of pterodactyls, if
not the cry of Poor Tom, or a Sophoclean or Aeschylean
ode:

> Numberless, the earth breeds
> dangers, and the sober thought of fear.
> The bending sea's arms swarm . . .
> Things fly, and things walk the earth.
> Remember too
> the storm and wrath of the whirlwind.[49]

No wonder if Hardy's reading of the *Enquiry* found its way
into the darknesses of Egdon Heath and elsewhere in *The
Return of the Native.*[50] And no wonder if, ridiculing an old
treason bill revived aganst the American colonists in 1770 as
"this little foundling, this OEdipus, this riddle," Burke
meant by that a combination "of ancient ferociousness with
modern effeminacy."[51] Along the way young Burke had seen
or come to imagine, almost certainly in Ireland, congenital
terrors just under the surface of the present, bearers of
violence and pain, which lowly human beings can only
acknowledge and try not to provoke.

In Part I of the *Enquiry* young Burke, reductively mimetic,
had refused any superiority to tragic fiction over tragic reality: "catastrophe touches us in history as much as the
destruction of Troy in fable." Indeed, "we shall be much
mistaken if we attribute any considerable part of our satisfaction in tragedy to a consideration that tragedy is a deceit, and
its representations no realities. The nearer it approaches the
reality, and the further it removes us from all idea of fiction,
the more perfect is its power. But be its power of what kind
it will, it never approaches to what it represents." The principles of the tragic really exist in nature, or rather within us

---

49. Aeschylus, *Choephoroi*, 585–593.   Reprinted from "The Libation
Bearers," in *Aeschylus I: Oresteia*, trans. Richmond Lattimore, p. 114, in
The Complete Greek Tragedies, ed. David Grene and Richmond Lattimore
(1953), by permission of the University of Chicago Press.

50. See *Philosophical Enquiry*, pp. cxviii-cxx.

51. *Cavendish Debates*, II (May 9, 1770), 19.

and our inborn "sympathy," operating "antecedent to any reasoning, by an instinct that works us to its own purposes, without our concurrence." As the classic habitat for sublime experience, tragedy is a recurring concern in Part I; yet he cites no examples from it, English, Greek, or French. "Art can never give the rules that make an art," he believes, except in ever-weakening copies; the orignal of tragedy, "the origin of our ideas," is to be sought in experience of human nature and historic reality, where Aeschylus or Shakespeare found it, and where a modern tragedian must look.[52] If such an argument is inadvertent witness to the failure of mid-century tragic theater to be as interesting as life, it is nevertheless richly inquisitive in that borderland, unlikely ever to be settled, where reality and art intersect and in-form one another. In *The Reformer* nine years before, Burke had dismissed virtually all tragedy in English except "the divine *Shakespear*," citing heroic plays, Otway's "small spark," Dryden, followed by "the fustian Tragedies of *Lee* and *Young*" and "the *minores Poetae,* such as *Row, Addison,* and those who have wrote Tragedies since then." It follows that if the contemporary stage is defective, and if in addition *Macbeth* is played with "the heavy Jest of the Brooms, the smutty Entendre of the *red hair'd Wench*" and other "choice Buffooneries," then one must seek elsewhere for tragic experience which the human mind requires.[53]

Later, for mature political Burke, the full human struggle to be rational, revering law, and yet have authentic identity and vitality occurs every day—not just in tragic fable—over depths of time in which are stored radical contradictions of justice and life itself. It is madness to stir them by choice, and there are plentiful, everyday ways to stir them blindly. Of "all the contradictions of our most mysterious nature," Burke observed, among the most mystifying is that we retaliate against what we hate by imitating it, even at the cost of

52. *Philosophical Enquiry*, pp. 45–47, 54.
53. *The Reformer*, 2 (Thursday, February 4, 1748), 2–4; 3 (Thursday, February 11, 1748), [1].

self-destruction. A fury, once stirred, multiplies its horrible kind if left to itself. Negotiation, somehow, of a living justice (whether by charity or compromise or tolerance, avoiding the "miserable *petitio principii*" of "You are wrong; I am right; you must come over to me, or you must suffer") is, in the end, the only alternative to somebody's destruction that provokes to other destructions.[54] Hence in part Burke's love for Parliament as an institution (not unlike that of Aeschylus, at least in the play, for the Areopagus Council): for its surrogate wars render unnecessary the real wars that, given human nature, must otherwise occur, and in any country can always return:

> This House is the theatre and stage, on which all the several factions [in English history] have fought their battles: in this House they have exercised their detestable vengeance upon each other: victory, triumphs, defeats, and factions have alternately prevailed: this place has been strewed with bones: here they have dug up the shields, the casques, the helmets, that shew it has been the field of blood.[55]

For such reasons, Burkian practicality often means what one has to do in a given situation to keep the Erinyes silent—no small task when so much of the human capacity for loving finds itself bound to a perhaps equal ferocity and capacity for anger or hate, against oneself or all others. Burkian realism means acting within a given situation so cooperatively as not to release its tragic potential. For, once released, as he believed that it had been in 1774–1775, a mechanism of retributive cause and effect takes over—national character is sapped, leaders see evil delusively as good, innocents suffer, earth is laid waste—as event necessitates event in darker and darker vengeances whose end is unfathomable. People are swept up by events which nevertheless they make, in some huge, blind collaboration, becoming part of that "automaton

---

54. "Tract on the Popery Laws," *Works* (Little, Brown), VII, 331–333; (Bohn), VI, 27–29.
55. *Cavendish Debates*, I (May 8, 1769), 425.

supported and moved without any foreign [that is, outside] help," which Burke once defined as the perfection, the final essence, of drama.[56]

We can follow through his letters and manuscripts a kind of fever chart of mounting recognition, anxiety, and helplessness as the tragedy of Britain in America took on, in his unbelieving eyes, the automatism of form without reason. What is evident now must have been evident to everybody who met him, for even crude reports in the *Parliamentary History*, if extracted and aligned, supply a matching pattern of behavior—plus, indeed, salutary reminders of what is too easily forgotten, his indefeasible comic courage. The notice of May 5, 1774, is common throughout his career: "Mr. *Edmund Burke* [made] a masterly speech of upwards of an hour (at the first part of which the House was in a continual laugh)."

Three days earlier, the Intolerable Acts had called to his mind *The Dunciad*: "light after light goes out & all is Night."[57] Commons had "given punishment & *Govt* in one—Govt given in *Anger*"—yet it felt "no sort of terrour at the awfulness of the situation" in which it had been "placed by providence." He felt himself "shrunk to nothing. Next to that tremendous day, in which it is revealed, that the saints of God shall judge the World," he knew nothing more terrible.[58] Yet as late as September, with Parliament dissolved and new elections underway, including his own try for Bristol, a major constituency which could amplify his voice, he still hoped for no immediate crisis.[59] The first Continental Congress met in Philadelphia; but in his first speech to the new Fourteenth Parliament, December 5, Burke urged new

56. "Hints for an Essay on Drama," *Works* (Little, Brown), VII, 150; (Bohn), VI, 179: drama as invented, of course, by the Greeks, for "there are still parts of the world in which it is not, and probably never may be, formed."

57. Sheffield, BK 27/235.

58. Sheffield, BK 27/229.

59. To the Marquess of Rockingham, September 18, 25, 1774, *Corr.*, III, 30.

members to a remarkable vision of change, of the power of
parliamentary society to transcend the dead past without sev-
ering itself from all that was best. At the same time he
noticed, "a spirit of blindness & delusion prevails[;] we are
preparing to mangle our own flesh."[60] A week later he was
"extremely severes . . . compared the House of Commons to
a dead senseless mass, which had neither sense, soul, or
activity."[61] By mid-January, when he published his earlier
Speech on Taxation, he was lamenting "the present Crisis,"
and though on January 23 "the House was kept in a continual roar of laughter" at first, his speech soon became
"very severe." Even through the blur of a reporter's haste,
jotting on a knee such bits and summary as he could, the pattern in Burke's suffering is visible:

January 26, 1775: "Mr. Burke proceeded to lament the national
calamities about to befal this devoted [that is, cursed] kingdom.
Besides the horrors of a civil war, besides the slaughtered innocents who are to be victimated to the counsels of a ministry precipitate to dye the rivers of America with the blood of her inhabitants;
besides these disasters . . . other shocks . . . were all depicted in the
strongest colours by Mr. Burke . . . . he vowed by all that was dear
to him here and hereafter, he would pursue [the ministry] to condign punishment" *February 2, 1775:* "Mr. *Burke,* who was this
day much indisposed . . . called the present moment the true crisis
of Britain's fate, painted the dreadful abyss into which the nation
was going to be plunged." *February 6, 1775:* "He exerted himself
to deprecate the shameless tyranny we exercised. He abhorred political as much as he did religious persecution. His heart seemed
engaged."[62]

In a weary but powerful speech on March 6, he predicted the
punitive Act for Restraining the Trade of New England
Colonies would soon recall Macbeth's horror: "I am in
blood / Stept in so far, that, should I wade no more /

60. Sheffield, BK 27/231–232.
61. *PH,* XVIII (December 13, 1774), 57.
62. *PH,* XVIII, 189–190, 233, 263.

Returning were as tedious as go o'er." As murder led to
murder in the play:

> he did not doubt but that [this Act] would be productive of the
> very same consequences.
> That this was, in effect, the Boston Port Bill, but upon infinitely
> a larger scale. That evil principles are prolific; this Boston Port Bill
> begot this New England Bill; this New England Bill will beget a Vir-
> ginia Bill; again a Carolina Bill, and that will beget a Pennsylvania
> Bill: till one by one parliament will ruin all its colonies, and root
> up all its commerce; until the statute book becomes nothing but a
> black and bloody roll of proscriptions, a frightful code of rigour and
> tyranny, a monstrous digest of Acts . . .
> But the point on which he rested most was . . . the unheard-of
> power given to governors, of starving so many hundreds of
> thousands at their mere pleasures, of which, he said, no history of
> real, and even no fabulous invention of fictitious tyranny [that is, a
> tragedy like *Macbeth*] had ever furnished an example, he dwelt a
> long time, and placed it in an infinite variety of lights; and kindled
> into such warmth, that he was at length called to order. But he
> continued to repeat the strong terms . . . he hoped they would have
> the benefit of the prayer made for those who alone had done an act
> worse than this, "Forgive them, they know not what they do."[63]

Two days later—the day on which Johnson's *Taxation no
Tyranny* appeared—he was again "warm against the Bill,"
"fine and pathetic" on the subject of famine; a week later
"severe" again, against Lord North's "ruinous and mad
career of violence."[64] Then on March 22 came the great
Speech on Conciliation, whose resolutions for peace were
negatived on the spot. Burke had expected no success from
it; despite its choral hope and common sense, and its luminous rhetoric of prophecy and church ritual (doubly effective
in St. Stephen's), he had written it only to discharge "his
Conscience as a being accountable for his Actions and his

conduct" to Providence.[65] His health had declined severely from the stress since January; he took American affairs "so to heart, that he [was] much fallen away and . . . not at all well," a friend reported;[66] he remained frail into summer. The fact was, he had written another friend some two weeks earlier, March 9: "I confess I grow less Zealous [for the superiority of this Country] when I see the use which is made of it . . . We talk of starving hundreds of thousands of people with far greater ease and mirth than the regulations of a Turnpike . . . My Soul revolts at it. No cruelty, no Tyranny ever heard of in History or invented in Fable has at all equalled it."[67]

The news of Concord and Lexington struck with symbolic finality. "Blood has been shed. The sluice is opend—Where, when, or how it will be stopped God only knows."[68] Now it began: "British blood spill'd by British hands—a fatal aera!"[69] —or error.

By early summer Burke had "sunk into a kind of calm and tranquil despair, that had a sort of appearance of contentment,"[70] but the events of 1775, like madness settled in the bones of both sides, filled him with "anxious horrour & perturbation that does not suffer me to keep quiet night or day[,] a poignant anguish that thrills through my heart on the Crisis that approaches."[71] News of Bunker Hill duly arrived on August 12, and the raw American army had already undertaken its ill-fated and somehow weird invasion of Canada. One of its brilliant young generals, Richard Montgomery, was an ex-British officer and acquaintance, an Irishman who had emigrated only three years before; by

65. To James De Lancey, March 14, 1775, *Corr.*, III, 137; and Richard Burke, Sr., to Richard Champion, March 22 [1775], III, 140.
66. To James De Lancey, *Corr.*, III, 137 n.
67. To Richard Champion, March 9, 1775, *Corr.*, III, 131–132.
68. To Charles O'Hara, [*circa* May 28, 1775], *Corr.*, III, 160.
69. Sheffield, R101–5–3 (another draft exists at R155/9): variant versions of "Address to the King," printed posthumously, *Works* (Little, Brown), VI, 169; (Bohn), V, 467.
70. To the Marquess of Rockingham, August 4, 1775, *Corr.*, III, 183.
71. Sheffield, BK 27/228.

December his body would lie in bloody snow outside Quebec.[72] Why was that? Affairs in America took "entire possession" of his mind, Burke told Lord Rockingham: he could write on nothing else.[73] Situations calling for humility and alertness, compromise, humor, had blundered onto some loftier, ghastly stage of criminal violence and paradox, irreversibly. "We make our war . . . on the *Vital principle* of our own national Strength & on the scource of the publick health and Vigour."[74] "Our Victories can only complete our Ruin." "Our madness passes all conception. Theirs too in some particulars is extraordinary."[75]

With the sort of empathy or double consciousness that came to him in a crisis, he staged the larger madness in himself, testing it from within, rummaging his whole experience in his eagerness and anxiety to understand.

The despair that has seized upon some, and the Listlessness that has fallen upon all, is surprising, and resembles more the Effect of some supernatural Cause, stupyfying and disabling the powers of a people destined to destruction, than anything I could have imagined.[76]

Whom the gods would destroy, they first make mad[77] —or charm by witches, or confront with ghosts. Such a vatic intuition of paralysis, ignorance, and unreality had struck his thoughts in previous April when he warned Commons:

---

72. Burke reports the news of Montgomery's death in a tactful letter to a mutual friend, Richard Champion, [February 22, 1776], *Corr.*, III, 150. Cf. Fox's testimony in *PH*, XXIX (May 6, 1791), 379–380: "During the American war they had together rejoiced at the successes of a Washington, and sympathized almost in tears for the fall of a Montgomery."

73. To the Marquess of Rockingham, August [22,] 23, 1775, *Corr.*, III, 189.

74. Sheffield, BK 27/227: the draft belongs to the speech of March 6, 1775 (*PH*, XVIII, 389ff.).

75. To Charles O'Hara, August [17,] 1775, *Corr.*, III, 185, 187.

76. To Charles O'Hara, p. 186.

77. See to the Marquess of Rockingham, November 11, 1773, *Corr.*, II, 484, where Burke quotes the Greek maxim in Latin from Barnes's edition of Euripides (1694).

"You are therefore at this moment in the aukward situation of fighting for a phantom; a quiddity; a thing that wants, not only a substance but even a name."[78] Within a short time had arrived what he long had feared, "a great Change in the National Character," which now as if stunned was "marching with hasty strides to its utter ruin" without seeing what must come:

The people look back without pleasure or indignation, and forward without hope of fear. No man commends the measures which have been pursued, or expects any good from those which are in preparation; But it is a cold Languid opinion; like what men discover in affairs that do not concern them. It excites to no passion; It prompts to no Action.

Peripety and recognition may not coincide to forms that history makes, but the automaton, once set going, grinds on in silence: "Every event so prepares the Subsequent, that when it arrives, it produces no surprise, nor any extraordinary alarm." Though "impious War" was just beginning, he could extrapolate its end:

If things are left to themselves, It is my clear opinion, that a nation may slide down fair and softly from the highest point of Grandeur and prosperity to the lowest state of imbecillity and meanness, without any ones marking a particular period in this declension; without asking a question about it; or in the least speculating on any of the innumerable acts which have stolen this silent and insensible revolution.[79]

As one might expect of Burke, intuitions of disaster gave way to surges of will to rescue, or at least to justify his conscience in the station given. "We are calld to rouse ourselves," he wrote grimly to Lord Rockingham, "each in his post, by a sound of a Trumpet almost as loud as that which

78. "Speech on American Taxation," *Writings and Speeches*, II, 418.
79. To the Marquess of Rockingham, August [22,] 23, 1775, *Corr.*, III, 190–193; cf. To Richard Champion, December 1, 1777, ibid., p. 405.

must awaken the Dead."[80] But ironies thickened. When the Olive Branch Petition, as it would be known, arrived from Philadelphia two weeks later, Burke was asked, as the great spokesman against tyranny, to join in its presentation to Lord Dartmouth—that is, he was asked to serve as official representative of the Continental Congress, in appealing to George III against the acts of Parliament! Although torn by a perverse wish to do just that, he declined political suicide, not—he assured the American representatives—from any "Craven Scruple or thinking too precisely on the Event": he was no Prince Hamlet.[81] Indeed, within two days of receiving the petition the king declared the colonies in rebellion. To the Duke of Richmond, Burke, momently defeated, urged steps "towards preventing the ruin of your Country; which if I am not quite Visionary, is approaching with greatest rapidity," for, he continued, "a Speculative despair is unpardonable where it is our duty to Act" (here he is recalling Latin *speculatorius*, "just looking on, watching as from a tower").[82] Yet, as he also knew, "In War, *Events* do every thing. Ones *principles* ought not to be led by them; but I fear ones *conduct* must, more or less."[83]

America in 1775 figured in his imagination as "the most beautiful object that ever appeared upon this Globe."[84] "The spirit of America is incredible," he wrote to an Irish friend in August. "Such a Spirit as now animates them, may do strange things."[85] Great men, perhaps greater, were on the American side. "Few things more extraordinary have happend in the history of mankind," he noted in October, thinking of Franklin. "These rebels of ours are a singular

80. To the Marquess of Rockingham, August 4, 1775, *Corr.*, III, 183.
81. To William Baker, [August 23, 1775], *Corr.*, III, 196; cf. To Arthur Lee, August 22, 1775, p. 188.
82. To the Duke of Richmond, [September 26, 1775], ibid., p. 217.
83. To William Baker, [October 12, 1777], ibid., p. 389.
84. To the Duke of Richmond, [September 26, 1775], *Corr.*, III, 219.
85. To Charles O'Hara, August 17, 1775, ibid., p. 187.

sort of people"[86] —a people of Heroes . . . Europe sits as at a Theatre to see this scene of the New world."[87] After an American defeat, probably Howe's victory at Long Island in August 1776, Burke wrote in his private papers:

The Americans, as I have, & do repute them the first of men, to whom I owe eternal thanks for making me think better of my Nature [so I] shall in every circumstance of Fortune be their friend—& though they have been obliged to fall down at the present before the professional Armies of Germany, yet they have afforded a *dawning* hope by the stand they have made that in some Corner of the Globe, at some time or in some Circumstance or other, the *Citizen* may not be the *Slave* of the soldiers.[88]

In short, the Americans had become more nearly the "eager, inquisitive, jealous, fiery people" which he believed the English had been "a very short time ago";[89] in their "free energy of mind," he told Commons, "he feared the Americans were now what we were then [in the seventeenth century]; and were struggling that an insufferable tyranny should not be established over them."[90] If the Americans lost, he brooded, England would risk settling deeper into a military despotism; foundations had been laid for a standing army.[91] Looking back darkly from his last years, he is reported as having wondered if America perhaps had been meant as the "asylum [of European freedom] when it is hunted down in every other part. Happy it is that the worst of times may

86. To Count Patrick Darcy, October 5, 1775, ibid., p. 228.
87. Sheffield, BK 6/113; and cf. "Address to the British Colonists in North America," printed posthumously, *Works* (Little, Brown), VI, 190; (Bohn), V, 480: "Europe . . . as a spectator, beholds this tragick scene."
88. Sheffield, BK 6/47.
89. To the Marquess of Rockingham, August [22,] 23, 1775, *Corr.*, III, 190.
90. *PH*, XVIII (February 6, 1775), 263.
91. Among many examples, see Sheffield, BK 27/235, a draft belonging to the speech of May 2, 1774: "Therefore you must govern with an Army or not at all. Here is laid the foundation of Military government[,] purely and simply a Military Government."

have one refuge still left for humanity."[92] Yet if the Americans won, the cost of victory, without British equipoise and the riches of the British constitution, might be, in time and tragically, a terrible civil war. "He said [in 1785, though he had feared as much in 1777!] that he would not be surprised at the defection of some of the colonies from the Union—I believe he mentioned the southern states."[93] The Erinyes live everywhere, even in the future.

By coincidence a letter survives from July 4, 1776. Having passed a bad night, Burke tried all morning to sleep, his imagination gored by "the hurry and Bustle of the March of the first division and second division of Pennsylvania Troops, of the fortification of Boston, and all the Din of War," including horrible doubts of "what will become of this People" and "to what Providence has destined them and us."[94] The Declaration of Independence was published in London newspapers on August 17; no letter of Burke's survives from that date, but his feelings are known: "On the day that he first heard of the American states having claimed independency, it made him sick at heart; it struck him to the soul, because he saw it was a claim essentially injurious to this country, and a claim which Great Britain could never get rid of: never! never! never!"[95] Lear had lost again his stubborn Cordelia. By some dark irony one of the thirteen gunboats commissioned (in September 1775) for the Pennsylvania Navy had been christened *Burke* in his honor.

---

92. Quoted by Lord Acton in *Essays in the Liberal Interpretation of History: Selected Papers*, ed. William H. McNeill (Chicago: The University of Chicago Press, 1967), p. 386.

93. Somerville, *My Own Life and Times*, p. 222; cf. "Address to the British Colonists in North America," printed posthumously, *Works* (Little, Brown), VI, 191–192; (Bohn), V, 482: "That very Liberty, which you so justly prize above all things, originated here . . . your present union . . . cannot always subsist without . . . this great and long respected Body, to equipoise, and to preserve you amongst yourselves in a just and fair equality . . . a course of war with the Administration of this Country may be but a prelude to a series of wars and contentions among yourselves."

94. To the Marquess of Rockingham, [July 4, 1776], *Corr.*, III, 278.

95. *PH*, XX (December 14, 1778), 82.

The following February it was on station in the snowy Delaware River, some miles below where Washington crossed. When Howe beseiged Philadelphia in the major campaign of 1777, *Burke* went into action, was heavily damaged, and soon had to be junked.[96]

Perhaps the greatest horror of the war, to Burke, was the turning inside out of English public character under the stress of self-violating ironies. And his commonest figure for it was Macbeth—not the slaughtering regicide, the psychopath, who together with Milton's devils would stalk through his imagination of revolutionary Paris in the 1790s, but the refined and natively good man depraved, stumbling from brutality to brutality, morally bewitched, unable to stop until brought to despair and damnation—in general, Macbeth interpreted (with Johnson's textual help) by Burke's friend Garrick.[97] Even nearer Burke's view was that of William Richardson, who in *A Philosophic Analysis and Illustration of Some of Shakespeare's Remarkable Characters* (1774) revealed "how a beneficent mind may become inhuman: and how those who are naturally of an amiable temper, if they suffer themselves to be corrupted, will become more ferocious and more unhappy, than men of a constitution originally hard and unfeeling."[98] In thanks for a presentation copy, Burke expressed particular agreement with Richardson on the

96. See *Naval Documents of the American Revolution* (Washington, D. C., 1966), II, 240–241, 272, 428, 581; III, 202, 1034, 1366, et seq. Apparently *Burke* was sold in December, 1778: John W. Jackson, *The Pennsylvania Navy, 1775–1781* (New Brunswick, N.J.: Rutgers University Press, 1974), p. 336.

97. For Garrick's interpretation, see the full chapter in Kalman A. Burnim, *David Garrick: Director*, 1961 (repr. Carbondale, Ill.: Southern Illinois University Press, 1973).

98. Quoted from the "New Edition" of 1780, or see Brian Vickers, *Shakespeare: The Critical Heritage*, vol. 6: 1774–1801 (London: Routledge and Kegan Paul, 1981), p. 121.

"quite new" approach to "that progress of corruption" in Macbeth "by which the virtues of the mind are made to contribute to the completion of its depravity."[99]

"We are deeply in blood," Burke wrote to a Quaker friend. "We have forgot or thrown away all our antient principles. This view sometimes sinks my Spirits."[100] The very names of affection and kindred, which once were the bond of charity, had become incentives for an "insane joy" of vengeance.[101] People thought him disloyal and dishonest, he knew, because so earnest and so passionate for peace.[102] "Depend upon it," he wrote in November, 1777, "the people of England are not what they were . . . as far as I can see, nothing but the despair of being able perfectly to destroy the people of that [the American] Continent, can effectually root out of the minds of *this* people the desire of doing it. It grows more and more vehement every day."[103] Even hope, the only "principle of activity" for human good, had become "the grand betrayer . . . our sole friend—the great sweetener & great deluder of Life."[104] Among the excuses for savagery was a soon-to-be-modern doctrine of "the rights of War"— meaning anything goes, no limits, no scruples, so long as a declared enemy is hurt—especially mischevious because, as Burke knew: "The State of War [is] a State of Necessity & all its Laws therefore [are] Laws of Necessities—in practical war not easy to judge of the Bounds of Necessity."[105] He tried to keep in public view the true "rights of war recognized by civilised states, and practised in enlightened Europe" as established by the era's "law of nations": a system of limits and rules, often successful, whose purpose had

---

99. To William Richardson, June 18, 1777, *Corr.*, III, 354. Burke used very nearly the same phrasing in notes for an American speech two or three years before; see Sheffield, BK 27/226.
100. To Richard Shackleton, August 11, 1776, *Corr.*, III, 286–287.
101. "Letter to the Sheriffs of Bristol," *Works* (Little, Brown), II, 203; (Bohn), II, 11.
102. To Charles James Fox, October 8, 1777, *Corr.*, III, 384.
103. To William Baker, November 9, 1777, ibid., p. 401.
104. Sheffield, BK 6/110; and cf. 27/243.
105. Ibid., BK 6/84.

been "instead of pushing war to its extremes, to endeavour, by every means in our power, to moderate its horrors."[106] But war, he argued, was no longer waged to

<win over> America; that is given up as desperate but its nature & conduct is to be alterd to make it conform to this New object wch is the *Desolation of the Country*, that one of the fairest parts of the Globe may remain for ever useless to itself, to France, & to the whole race of mankind.

[The] declaration then of English Policy is, that what you cannot govern or conquer is to be destroyd lest somebody else should profit of it.[107]

As the years of war passed, Burke fought in himself a dejection "not to be described," losing slowly to talk of old age, the failure of his life, and retirement, "so compleatly sick I am of this game of politicks"[108] —a dejection that persisted until after the negotiations of 1782 and the exhilaration of new tasks, namely his Reform Bill and the sudden urgency in his imagination of India's people and their suffering.

A public habituation to violence and terror, and, what is so often the opposite to humanity in classical tragedy, a living at random as the animals must, are among his darkest themes in the terrible trough of 1778–1781 when British fortunes were bleak indeed, entangled in a "mad and impolitic war" that nobody could end—this stagnated Pool"[109] —when "it was, and had been for seven years, nothing but American war, American war, American war; and it would be American war to the end of the chapter."[110] No matter what the motives originally—"what nobody is to be praised

106. *PH*, XXII (May 14, 1781), 218, 228–232.
107. Northampton, A. xxvii.12, apparently part of the speech in *PH*, XIX (December 4, 1778), 1399–1400.
108. See To Richard Champion, August [22,] 1779, *Corr.*, IV, 125; To the Chairman of the Buckinghamshire Meeting, April 12, 1780, p. 227; To the Duke of Portland, October 16, 1779, p. 153; and To the Duke of Portland, September 3, 1780, p. 273.
109. To Richard Champion, October 9, 1778, ibid., p. 25.
110. *PH*, XXII (November 27, 1781), 721.

or blamed for"—the war was continued "not from *reason*
but from *habit*—We consider it as a thing *belonging* to us . . .
a thing to exercise our . . . exultation and depression as we
hear what we call good or bad News—but not at all as a
matter of Counsel & deliberation." Even worse, Burke continued, "Whenever we state the desperate condition of our
affairs in America the answer is—very bad indeed—but how
will you get out of it? & this is spoke with a sort of Tone of
Triumph. The Noble Lord exalts his Voice with double
force, expands his chest, throws about his Arms, crows &
chuckles & flutters as if he had laid his adversaries dead at
his feet."[111] Very large appropriations were funded, to
Burke's horror, to arm Indians with "hatchets, tomahawks,
scalping-knives, razors, spurs, &c." which would be used
against noncombatants, and also to stir slaves to
insurrection.[112] It was a policy, in short, of killing "man,
woman, and child, burning their houses, and ravaging their
lands, annihilating humanity from the face of the earth, or
rendering it so wretched that death would be preferable . . .
against those who, conscious of rectitude, had acted to the
best of their ability in a good cause, and stood up to fight for
freedom and their country."[113] His long opposing speech
(February 1778), considered by many among his most
powerful, exists now only in reports and manuscript
fragments;[114] but the quality of his vision of what had happened and must continue after the war's end as a legacy of
habituation—a kind of *Macbeth* in perpetuity, or Erinyes
scattering and spreading—is explicit many times: for example, in the following manuscript, whose actual subject is what
America would have been like in defeat but whose tragic
mirror tilts back an English image no less dark:

111. Sheffield, BK 27/242.
112. *PH*, XIX (March 2, 1778), 971–972.
113. Ibid., (December 4, 1778), p. 1400.
114. Ibid., (February 6, 1778), pp. 694–649. Horace Walpole was much
impressed: see To William Mason, February 12, 1778, *Horace Walpole's
Correspondance with William Mason*, ed. Grover Cronin, Jr., and Charles H.
Barnett (New Haven: Yale University Press, 1955), I, 354–356.

you have left ten trained to arms for one you found so in the
beginning of this contest; ten for one habituated to a military life &
unsettled habits . . . Besides the breaking up of all the conceald
fountains & great Depths of government, the entire subversion for
so long a time of all regal Authority, the Random Speculations of
every individual, the Taste of Wild Liberty to all, & of new
independent power to some . . . will make the return even to the
old order impracticable . . . I know that many among us as well as
elswhere indulge an Idea . . . that the slaughters they shall make by
foreign mercenaries, by savage 'irruption' & revolting servitude,
the pillage & waste of the Country, the confisactions of property, &
the Legal Shambles wch they shall open at the close of the War will
give the people a distaste to any future insurrection. They think so
because they love a government of terror . . . [Yet] it is known as
much as any thing can be known, that the miseries of War do not
indispose men to that state; & that War is much more likely to follow war in any Country than originally to break out in one that is
long composed. The first Breach is terrible to the quiet. Nothing
is dreadful to a man which is habitual to him . . . The manners of
men grow ferocious & their minds desperate . . . Men reconcile
themselves to any thing. They become habituated to a Life of toil
& contention. The ferocity of stubborn spirits is not allayed by
force & Violence—but by care & security.[115]

The sort of behavioral machinery in both good and evil
which renders one the deed's creature is axiomatic in
Burke's moral vision, as in Shakespeare's.

Burke had heard the Erinyes before as a youngster in Ireland, where in the north they still snort and whine. He
would hear their dark groans again, even more terribly after
1789, not just in France and the world, but in himself and
his losses, most terribly in the early death of his son. The
grandeur of his last achievement is in direct proportion to
neurotic terror, hatred, despair, and self-righteousness, overcome, and transformed into numinous wisdom—when it is
transformed. His American tragedy—"the most chargeable,
the most disgraceful & the most calamitous wars, that this

115. Northampton, A.xxvii.87.

nation ever was engaged in,"[116] he summarized in 1782—prepared him well, one may think, for the different and deeper tragedy of Europe (and India) in the years that followed. Indeed, it could be argued that the abysses that opened in Burke's old age have never closed but spread beyond Europe to the edge of history itself. They are today's news. Yet, to end as we began, we have now the Burke monument—meaning, of course, his writings and speeches and the example of his life, even its failures; for there is no political horror that his complex nobility of mind and heart cannot help one to see and endure, and sometimes to change. Not altogether playfully we might remember his statue in Bristol and Washington: striding slightly forward, hand uplifted in what is perhaps cheerful hail of a free posterity he never saw but taught to know itself better—or, as it may be just as firmly, in a sober gesture of warning and stepping back, as from some abyss of blood whose very face paralyses and blinds. Either attitude would express the man.

116. Sheffield, BK 6/157.

JEAN H. HAGSTRUM

"What Seems to Be: Is":
Blake's Idea of God

Blake is unconventionally and excitingly religious. Neither orthodox formulation nor liberal-progressive theology comes close to being adequate to his idea of God. His God is not a wholly other, who directs men by laws or motivates them by externally bestowed grace. Nor is he immanent in nature, traditionally the second book of God, whose glory the heavens declare and whose handiwork the firmament shows forth. Nor is he disclosed in the many inherited religious and philosophical paradoxes or antitheses that juxtapose the one and the many, the moved and the unmoved, the general and the specific, essence and accident. None of the foregoing is sufficiently vivid, poetic, intimate, or pluralistic to meet Blake's spiritual needs. What then can God be said to be? Above all else an intellectual achievement, a product of mental fight, of a suffering psyche. He emerges, not in argument or logic but in existential struggle, as a person, sometimes in historical record, more often in vision. No reader should expect to finish this piece with a clear or precise definition; some sense of what it meant for Blake to believe in God is all that can be asked for.

"Great Eternity": Blake's Heaven

From about 1794, the year in which he may have engraved *The Book of Urizen*, Blake tended to refer to his special version of heaven as Eternity, Great Eternity, or Eden.[1] He continued in letter, lyric, and prophecy to use the traditional term "heaven" in a good sense (a place of beings who surround, support, and inspire his spirit), which we must sharply distinguish from the home of "Angels & weak men," the conventional heaven of *The Marriage of Heaven and Hell*, where hell is the source of a redemptively purging energy.[2] But in this commentary I lay aside that famous and dazzling inversion, which is also present in the Lambeth prophecies and *The Songs of Experience*, and concentrate on Great Eternity, which is a good, though not a conventionally good, place, the environment of Blake's divine being. *Eternity* and *eternal* are noble biblical words, but they are also noble secular words, used by unbelieving or purely humanistic writers to refer to the transcendent both in this life and sometimes even in the next. Thus Shelley refers to Adonais as a star who "beacons from the abode where the Eternal are." Blake's eternity is both secular and spiritual, artistic and religious; and if the two can in any way be separated, it must be said strongly—and, it would seem, in opposition to much contemporary criticism—that the religious is fundamental.

Recognizing that purely moral judgments (as contrasted with religious), along with temporal and spatial conceptions, must be reduced to a minimum, we must nevertheless try to isolate the kind of goodness inherent in this spiritual locality. It is populated by "myriads," who are described as all "the wisdom and joy of Life." It cannot be separated from

1. William Blake, *The Four Zoas* (hereafter abbreviated *FZ.*), 5:29, in *The Complete Poetry and Prose of William Blake* (abbreviated E), ed. David V. Erdman (Garden City, N. Y.: Anchor Press/Doubleday, 1982), p. 303; ibid., 99:1 (E.371).

2. The phrase comes from *America*, 16:14 (E.57) but is fully applicable to the *Marriage*.

Eden, where the unity of all the faculties is perfect and brotherhood is universal. It is a place of sweetness and happiness, the "land of life," a place of "warmth" and "perfect harmony." Above all, it is the place of the "Divine Presence," for it is presided over by Christ, who cannot always or fully be distinguished from "the Eternal Father." Paradoxically, it is at the same time a place of limitation: not of evil, to be sure—for so blatant a contradiction could not be tolerated—but of qualities that suggest the purely human, sometimes the human even in its fallen condition. The Eternals can shudder as Los often does, or petrify like Urizen, both of whom are called Eternals. They and their confreres are often afraid of becoming what they behold, and collectively they can groan in deep trouble, like the whole creation in the Bible as it awaits its deliverance. Eternals lament, weep, rage, separate themselves from their environment, or flee into the deep. They are scarcely a body of palm-bearing, harp-playing resurrected saints or angels adoring eternal majesty in order serviceable.[3]

Can these paradoxes and contradictions (if so indeed they are) be resolved? Not surely by conceiving of Blake's Eternity as an enclosed garden with a sky-god viewing it from above and enforcing immutable laws, nor by considering it as in any way static, formal, abstract, geometrical. But if we try to think of it as Blake did and so experience its force, the co-presence of these kinds of goodness (mostly joy) and of limitation (mostly purely human) becomes at least understandable. For Eternity is infinite and flexible, a place of movement and energy—a place, in fact, of raging, consuming, warring energies. Its people are "drunk with the Spirit, burning round the Couch of death," a condition of intensity doubtless in part caused by their being in the presence of a threat. But no matter what they do or where they are, the Eternals live in "wild flames," which, however (if I may

---

3. For the quotations from and references to Blake in this paragraph, see *The Book of Urizen* (abbreviated *Ur.*), plates 15, 18 (E.78); *FZ.*, 21:1–6 (E.310–311); 12:4 (E.306); 39:10 (E.327); 71a:5 (E.348); 133:26 (E.402); *Milton*, 14:33, 35 (E.108); *Jer.*, 34:8, 21 (E.179–180).

change or mix metaphors lamentably), move like biblical wheels within wheels—not, as in the world of Locke and Newton, like "wheel without wheel, with cogs tyrannic." Like living forms responding to heat and cold—even like sexual organs in amorous activity—beings in Great Eternity contract and expand. Such visionary motion stands in contrast to the perceptions of a corrupt human society, which are "frozen to unexpansive . . . terrors."[4]

So much for what we may call the "climate" of Eternity, its "intellectual pleasures & energies." What about its people and government? It is clearly not a monarchy or an episcopacy; it is without conventional ruler divine or ecclesiastic; God as person or form appears when perceptions contract or expand. If anything, it is a council, Congregational in government, which in its collectivity is called the Divine Imagination—a committee of burning presences who are free to come and go, to divide in opinion from one another, to take separate actions. For example, some choose to "disregard all Mortal Things"; others choose to descend, view mortality more closely, and participate, at the edge of life, in its redemption. Its presences are, in part, Blake's friends and his great predecessors, including Milton, who has lived there about a hundred years and is now driven by his fellow eternals into Blake's earth-hell (Ulro). Another historical person, who has entered Eternity frequently in vision, believes he will also enter it at death, when he goes into "his Own Eternal House . . . into the Mind in which every one is King & Priest." Eternity is a state of mental energy and creation, of heightened self-consciousness, available now to anyone willing to become a prophet; but it is also a *post-mortem* life that continues the strenuous joys that have led to spiritual greatness in time. To and from Eternity not only real people like Milton and Blake come and go, but also reified faculties and cultural forces like the Four Zoas, along

---

4. *FZ.*, 20:12–13 (E.313); 105:16–17 (E.378); *Milton*, 20:44 (E.114); 35:1 (E.135); *Jer.*, 15:18–20 (E.159); 55:3 (E.204).

with other products of imaginative seeing that have taken on the status of real entities.[5]

The Eternals are capable of actions, of which two are particularly notable, even though somewhat grotesque or awkward in their presentation. One is the erection of a tent or tabernacle with pillars and a curtain to separate and enclose unknown space, an unpleasant but necessary action to prevent the ultimate disaster of formlessness, which to Blake is always "Deep, horrible without End." The other action is the dispatching into history of the guardians of man's form, who, considered in a chronological line, constitute epochs of human religious history. It may seem uncouth to commission *eyes* or to embody them in institutions; but the image came to Blake from his source, where the "eyes of the Lord . . . run to and fro through the whole earth" (Zechariah 4:10). In any case, Blake pours out his most intense dramatic and imagistic energies upon the action of the Eternals in sending forth these "seven Spirits . . . into all the earth" (Revelation 5:6), an action that recalls not only the Bible but the commissioning of Christ by God in *Paradise Lost*, Book 3, and perhaps also the debate among the Four Daughters of God over which divine quality will prevail in dealing with man. Blake's Council of Eternals divides in debate, as the minions of Satan do in Milton's hell. Some, the more adventurous, wish to descend and see for themselves the changes in Albion, both the man and the place. Others opt for inaction; these are more cautious, more exclusive, fearful of birth and death and perhaps also of sexuality, and partial to the equality of Eden to which they are now accustomed. But the bold ones prevail, crying out, "Bring forth all your fires! / So saying, an eternal deed was done: in fiery flames."[6]

---

5. *Jer.*, 55:1 (E.204); 68:65 (E.222); Blake's letter to George Cumberland, April 12, 1827 (E.784). The unfortunate absence or subordination of women in Great Eternity cannot be discussed here but will be the subject of discussion in my forthcoming book on the body in Romantic literature.

6. *Jer.*, 55:16-17 (E.204). See also *Ur.*, 19:2-9 (E.78); *FZ.*, 22:39 (E.312); 115:42-50 (E.381); *Jer.*, 55:1-35 (E.204-205).

Such, then, is Blake's heaven, which is less dramatic than
Milton's hell but considerably more interesting than his
heaven, with its fixed hierarchies, or Dante's *Paradiso*, with
its highly formalized fire and light. The very humanity of
Blake's divine place has left its edges loose and its definition
contradictory; its very flexibility makes it conceptually
elusive. And yet these very qualities guarantee not only its
appeal but, for Blake, its redemptive effectuality. His is a
very special and virtually unique communion of saints, of
the noble living and the noble dead in a state of expanded
awareness that thrives upon dynamic change and the interaction of living contraries.

God in History: Urizen the Tyrannical Father

The entrance of the Seven Eyes of God into history was a
mixed blessing at best if we except Christ, the seventh and
last Eye, and S. Foster Damon has summarized their various
failures. The first five need not detain us, since they are
remote from Blake and us; they remain unexplored in the
prophecies. But the sixth Eye, Jehovah of Israel, the
Lawgiver of Sinai, the creator of the patriarchy, impinged on
Blake every day of his life; and grave moral and psychological suffering must reside in the fact that Blake had to call
him "leprous" and even regard the psychocultural condition
over which he presided as "the ancient Leprosy." This
Lawgiver-Father is united in Blake's myth with Urizen, the
Zoa from whom he is not clearly separated until important
revisionary developments in *Jerusalem* and later works
remove the leprosy and the tyranny.[7]

7. S. Foster Damon, *A Blake Dictionary* (Providence, R. I.: Brown
University Press, 1965), *s.v.* "Eyes of God"; *FZ.*, 115:49 (E.381); 108:14
(E.383). For a discussion of Urizen, see John Sutherland, "Blake and
Urizen," in Blake's *Visionary Forms Dramatic,* ed. David V. Erdman and
John E. Grant (Princeton: Princeton University Press, 1970), pp. 244–262.
This paper is intended to resist Sutherland's belief that "Blake was never in
any danger of being dominated by Urizen" (p. 259).

Urizen is surely one of the most impressive symbols created in English Romantic poetry—complexly and broadly conceived but always as palpable and solid as he is suggestively multivalent. He is figured forth as an irresistible natural force like winter (snow, cold, hail, darkness, ice, freezing storms are his natural milieu) or as impenetrable matter like rock, brass, and, especially, iron. He is the original solipsist, a tough and unyielding selfhood, whose master trait is a tyrannous will. His tyranny expresses itself in two related but separable clusters of activity. (1) A personification of the faculty of reason, this Zoa manifests himself in culture as Cartesian or Newtonian, as the *esprit de système*, as the geometer God, as a logocentric maker of legalistic books and tablets, as an abstract logician, analyst, and generalizer, and as an architect who creates impressive but essentially inhuman shapes of metal and stone. (2) He is also the original superego—a *paterfamilias*, king, pope, bishop, priest—the transmitter of religious, social, and national codes. What gives him his essential unity through all these diverse psychological, cultural, and historical manifestations is that he embodies quintessential tyranny, indeed the very tendency itself toward selfish domination; he is maddened by an obsessive desire to be God and proclaim himself as such. Again and again he utters variants of the cry, "Now I am God from Eternity to Eternity," a cry he repeats even when he stands in the midst of his ruined world. That cry is echoed by Los, Tharmas, Vala, Albion, the Spectre of Urthona, and Satan, Urizen's successor in Blake's myth. It cannot be stressed too often that his master trait, the ruling passion that organizes his *Gestalt*, is the will to power—a quality that gives a coherent body, as it were, to this "Schoolmaster of souls," this "great opposer of change," this "dread form of Certainty." And Blake made this quality basic and causal as well as organizing: "A Tyrant is the Worst disease & the Cause of all others."[8]

---

8. *FZ.*, 12:8 (E.307); 79:23–24 (E.355); 119:21, 23 (E.389); Annotations to Bacon for p. 67 (E.625). Compare the phrase that Blake applies to Urizen, "Schoolmaster of souls," with Galatians 3:24, "Wherefore the law

It has long been believed, but not often enough said in our day of understandable timorousness in judging religions, that Urizen is not a parody but a direct representation of what Blake saw as the God of Judaism and Christianity in their codified forms in their Mosaic and Pauline inscriptions. The Jesus of ecclesiastical tradition says, "And I say also unto thee, That thou art Peter, and *on this rock* I will build my church" (Matthew 16:18, emphasis added). Urizen says, "Lo! I unfold my darkness: and *on / This rock* place with a strong hand this book / Of eternal brass, written in my solitude" (*Ur.*, 4:31–32 [E.72], emphasis added). He is called "the Mighty Father" (*FZ.*, 15:12 [E.309]), he creates iron laws that no one can keep even "one moment," and he curses his children for not keeping them. These allusions to the scriptural God are by no means fortuitous: Blake is taking on the patriarchy at its source. But he also attacks the God of his predecessor Milton, who had called nature the creation of "the Great Work-Maister" God (*Paradise Lost*, 3:696). Blake calls Urizen "the great Workmaster" (*FZ.*, 24:5 [E.314]). Urizen, winning a victory over Los, collects himself in "awful pride," attacks the spirit of Jesus as visionary and soft, and proclaims himself "God the terrible destroyer":

> Ten thousand thousand were his hosts of spirits on the wind:
> Ten thousand thousand glittering Chariots shining in the sky:
> They pour upon the golden shore beside the silent ocean.
> Rejoicing in the Victory; & the heavens were filld with blood.
> (*FZ.*, 12:24, 26, 32–35 [E.307])

In *Paradise Lost*, Jesus, riding "the Chariot of Paternal Deitie," attacks his enemies:

> Attended with ten thousand thousand Saints,
> He onward came, farr off his coming shon,

---

was our schoolmaster."

And twentie thousand (I thir number heard)
Chariots of God, half on each hand were seen.
(Paradise Lost 6:750, 767–770)

Unmistakably, Blake views Milton's patriarchal and militaristic Christ as Urizenic, and his own Urizen as an embodiment of supreme paternal power. Blake once said to Crabb Robinson that he did not believe in God's omnipotence,[9] and he declared in annotating John Caspar Lavater, "No Omnipotence can act against order," and in annotating Swedenborg, "There can be no Good-Will. Will is always Evil" (E.593, 602). Blake rarely regarded the will of God as good. What did he do, then, with these traditional qualities of the Godhead, omnipotence and will? He bestowed them on his Urizen in an imaginative act that proclaimed that just as that unforgettable old man is a creature of the poet's mind, so the patriarchal God is a creation of man's collective mind. For all their strutting pomposities or thundering damnations, both alike are creaturely. The perception of that equation is of ultimate importance to Blake and his critic—in healing his own mind and in giving us a clue to the power of his art.

That power appears very strongly in the visual Urizen. The sharply etched but heavy presence of that anti-man (here we refer of course only to his fallen condition) may be said to give him precisely what he sought, a "solid without fluctuation" (*Ur.*, 4:11 [E.71]). From our point of view, we have a haunted and haunting image whose condensation of artistic means and whose realized powers of formal articulation create for it inescapable psychological and aesthetic space. This imaginative body is a *coincidentia oppositorum* in the fullest Romantic sense, combining authority with sentimental pity, strength with weakness, fallen majesty with hints of future redemption. Rising as a counter-revolutionary figure over the Atlantic; sitting in his vegetable

9. G. E. Bentley, Jr., *Blake Records* (Oxford: Clarendon Press, 1969), p. 316.

or rocky cave, weeping (see Figure 1); making mystical signs on his metal books; poising himself on rocks with a dark void below; applying his compasses to the creation of the world; touching the first man with clay (see Figure 2); hovering over Job as a nightmare (see Figure 3)—these direct and indirect portrayals of the tyrant oppress the spirit as they make Blake's point about a tyrant-deity. Such artistic power in the visual medium must surely owe much to the art of the age as well as to Blake's remote ancestor, Michelangelo: to formidable contemporary images of Saturn, Jupiter, Oedipus, Lear, Laocoon, Ugolino, and Nebuchadnezzar, many of whom Blake himself portrayed as Urizenic. To this powerful antigeriatric current in an age of revolution Blake submitted himself early, and he unflaggingly transmitted its energies until his very last days.[10]

The verbal Urizen is at least as impressive, and he is most fully developed as a mythic actor in the book that bears his name and in *The Four Zoas*. It has sometimes been said that Blake in his late great prophecies tired of his anti-man and replaced his evil tyranny with Satan and his redeemable portion with Los.[11] Blake did, to be sure, make some adaptations appropriate to his new attack on Deism and to the direct entrance into his myth of Milton. But if anything is clear it is that Urizen, though not so frequently named or so directly portrayed as before, has not died but lives on as a deeply rooted tendency to tyranny that continues to plague

10. Urizen is anticipated frequently in Blake's first work, *Poetical Sketches*, published in 1783 (in "Winter," in the several warlike tyrants, human and divine, of the dramas); in *Tiriel*, a searing portrait of a political and domestic tyrant; in *The French Revolution*, with its visions of aged terror, full of imagery intimately associated with Urizen. Urizen is of course a presence in both the words and designs of *The Songs of Experience* and the Lambeth prophecies. It should be noted that he appears as a tyrant before he appears as Reason, and there is little doubt that his tyranny is a more basic and important quality than his rationality. In other words, he fits the patriarchy, religious and political, more closely than he fits the Enlightenment and Deism.

11. See Leopold Damrosch, *Symbol and Truth in Blake's Myth* (Princeton: Princeton University Press, 1980), pp. 153–155.

1. *The Book of Urizen,* plate 11. Copy G. Lessing J. Rosenwald Collection, Library of Congress, Washington, D.C.

2. *Elohim Creating Adam.* Tate Gallery, London.

human nature even in post- or anti-religious cultures. Thus Satan speaks like Urizen ("I am God the judge of all") and, as Los and his consort Enitharmon come to know, actually "*is* Urizen."[12] Thus the spectre of Urthona (an imaginative man's negative double), who is defined as the "Reasoning Power / An Abstract objecting power that Negatives every thing" (*Jer.*, 10:13 – 14 [E.153]), says in quintessentially Urizenic fashion, "I am God O Sons of Men!" (*Jer.*, 54:16 [E.203]). And thus even Vala, Blake's Venus, cries out, "I alone am Beauty," "I am Love" (*Jer.*, 29:48, 52 [E.176]). Vala is here following her acknowledged and unacknowledged master Urizen in the most mischievous of his psychic annexations—the strategy of appropriating individuality and erecting logically analyzed and dialectically separated qualities into tyrannous hypostatizations that eat up the winged joys of life and the minute particulars of art.

Blake's Anxiety

Anything as compelling as a drive toward Urizenic tyranny will inevitably cause anxiety in one who recognizes its presence and realizes its evil potential. And in creating Urizen, Blake writes not as an unconscious transmitter of intuitive insights but as a full-bodied Romantic in the noon blaze of an aroused self-consciousness. Blake attributes anxiety even to the Eternals; it is acutely present in Los, when he is working outside eternity in time, to retain vision in periods of great tribulation. Two passages involving Los define two kinds of psychic anxiety. (1) A fearful Los cries out in *Jerusalem*:

> Yet alas I shall forget Eternity!
> Against the Patriarchal pomp and cruelty, labouring incessant
> I shall become an Infant horror. (83:3 – 5 [E.241])

(2) Much earlier, in *The Book of Urizen*,

---

12. *Milton*, 10:1 (E.104, emphasis added); 38:51, 56 (E.139 – 140).

> Los wept howling around the dark Demon [Urizen]: . . .
> Groaning! gnashing! groaning!   (6:1, 7:2 [E.73 – 74])

Why such anguish? Because imagination feels the pains of separation from reason. More remotely and profoundly, because Urizen now is "Unorganized" (6:8), with only a "fathomless void" (6:5) beneath him; and Los realizes that he, like the fellow immortal whose form he must rescue through creation, can also fall into unbeing. The first passage grows out of a profound fear of becoming what one beholds—that is, of becoming a newly reborn Urizenic man with a tyrannous spirit. The second grows out of an even greater fear of the void. This greater fear is harrowingly illustrated in Los's fall, which takes place when he becomes wrathful after his wrenching separation from Urizen and after he has been assigned the task of watching over his fallen companion. His very fury, now objectless, has eaten up all the solidity that once supported him, leaving only a horrid vacuum beneath and around him.

> Falling, falling! Los fell & fell
> Sunk precipitant heavy down down
> Times on times, night on night, day on day
> Truth has bounds. Error none: falling, falling:
> Years on years, and ages on ages
> Still he fell thro' the void, still a void
> Found for falling day & night without end.
> (*Book of Los*, 4:27 – 33 [E.92])

Harold Bloom has said that a poetic text is "a psychic battlefield upon which authentic forces struggle for the only victory worth winning, the divinating triumph over oblivion."[13] The sentence is fully applicable to Blake if we alter the word "oblivion" to "nonentity." But what is nonentity? It must surely be a form of madness whose exact nature cannot at present be recovered. Quite literally—and

13. Harold Bloom, *Poetry and Repression: Revisionism from Blake to Stevens* (New Haven: Yale University Press, 1976), p. 2.

Blake was a great literalist of the imagination—Los has lost his reason in the separation from Urizen that tortures him, and now a profound void gapes before him. Was this the "Nervous Fear" Blake confessed to feeling as the "dark horrors" of the American and French revolutions "passed before [his] face"? Are the groanings of Los those "Perils & Darkness" Blake says he himself "traveld thro" and from which he came out victorious?[14] Doubtless in part, at least. But our aim here is to recover Blake's idea of God, not to psychoanalyze him; and to the fear of the void we shall return in the next section when we try to see how the anxiety of emptiness is cured.

The other fear, expressed in the first passage quoted above, that Los will forget Eternity in his antipatriarchal struggle, is very closely related to our subject—the fear that in creating Urizen he will become his own creature's creature. This fear must have been very real, since Blake regarded the tendency to tyranny as a kind of original sin, present in all of us and perhaps peculiarly clamorous in himself. Generating the debilitating anger we saw in *The Book of Urizen* and *The Book of Los*, and in *The Four Zoas* generating an even more debilitating "furious pride," the struggle against "Patriarchal pomp and cruelty" (*Jer.*, 83:4 [E.241]) leads Los into a vile capitulation to his enemy: "Our God is Urizen the King, King of the Heavenly hosts," he says. "We have no other God but he" (*FZ.*, 48:11, 15–16 [E.332]). This abjectness, this declaration of perverted faith, leads the imaginative artist, who must surely know better and must therefore be full of anxious fear about his degradation, to proclaim his godhood "over all" and even to reduce his own eternal imaginative form of Urthona

14. Letter to John Flaxman, Sept. 12, 1800 (E.708); letter to Thomas Butts, Nov. 22, 1802 (E.720). Blake's own fear of emptiness must have been lifelong. In an amazing letter written to John Linnell in the year of his death, he confesses to a "terrible fear" at the thought of moving, an "Intellectual Peculiarity," as he called it, that left him only these alternatives, to be "shut up in Myself" or to be "Reduced to Nothing" (Feb., 1827; E.782).

to a mere "shadow." How close all this was to Blake's own
spirit can only be surmised, but surely the expulsion from
the psyche of the codified God of Abraham, Isaac, and Jacob
and of the institutional Father of our Lord Jesus Christ cannot have been accomplished without an expense of spirit and
a waste of shame. Los speaks of "Inspiration deny'd;
Genius forbidden by laws of punishment" (*Jer.*, 9:16
[E.152]), showing that patriarchy can enter the very soul of
an artist to frustrate his vocation. But the Established God
in the soul is a pancultural condition, more broadly conceived than loss of artistic faith; the nadir is recorded by
Blake:

> To Sin & to hide the Sin in sweet deceit, is lovely!!
> To Sin in the open face of day is cruel & pitiless. But
> To record the Sin for a reproach: to let the Sun go down
> In a remembrance of the Sin: is a Woe & a Horror!
> A brooder of an Evil Day, & a Sun rising in blood.
>   (*Jer.*, 50:25 – 29 [E.200])

Here is the heart of Blake's patriarchal anxiety; here Blake
weighs fully his own burden of the past.

These then are the two great anxieties of Blake—a fear of
the void and a fear of what God the Father Almighty, Maker
of Heaven and Earth and Creator of the Western Patriarchy,
can do within the soul of man. Is there a connection
between the two? There must surely be. Alberto Moravia
has one of his characters in *1934* say that an "ambiguous
and dissociated condition . . . is characteristic of every
society based on fear" and that "in a regime of terror it's
impossible not only to distinguish truth from falsehood, but
also to distinguish the truth of falsehood."[15] In other words,
where a tyrannous will prevails in all its whimsicality and
unreason, man loses form, distinction, and value. Tyranny
creates the void. It is a pity that Blake himself did not

15. Quoted in a review by Stephen Spender in *New York Review of Books*,
June 30, 1983, p. 26.

explore more fully the relationship between the two great fears of his Los.

Before leaving the fear of an unforgiving, tormenting God, the creator of a fiery hell and of the laws of punishment, it must be emphasized that it is not the power of a really existent, vengeful tyrant in the skies whose judgments Blake fears. He was a man disposed to faith, but he was not superstitious, and he would never have allowed himself to be guided by craven fear. To such a real tyrant he would have cried out with the fiery Orc of his radical political period: "No more I follow, no more obedience pay" (*America*, 11:15 [E.55]). It is rather the devastation wrought by the *idea* of a tyrannical God-Dictator that Blake fears—the damage to the individual and corporate psyche. He also dreads what the very possession of such an idea over so many centuries implies about our nature and about the real danger of a recurring appetite for tyranny. It is not only Christ who is resurrected in Blake; Urizen arises again and again even after, as we have seen, he has lost his name.

Harold Bloom, the most original and brilliant student in our time of poetic sublimity and its relations to anxiety, regularly aestheticizes the fears of poets like Blake. It is not an antecedent God but an antecedent poet who engenders anxiety, particularly if influence has been strong and inescapable. For Bloom the location of the anxiety must largely be a speculative and indirect extrapolation from poetic texts, because he believes that in reality poets "tell continuous lies about their relations to their precursors" and, like all analysts of the mind from Freud on, he regards his poet-patient's resistance to such a theory as evidence for its validity. But do Milton's successors ever betray, directly or indirectly (for all traumatic unworthiness reveals itself somehow), a "sense of trespass" in the presence of their poetic father?[16] (Perhaps William Collins did indeed feel

16. Harold Bloom, *A Map of Misreading* (New York: Oxford University Press, 1975), pp. 10, 78–80. See also *Figures of a Capable Imagination* (New York: Seabury Press, 1976), p. xii.

tremblingly unworthy in his relations to Milton.) There is
no trace of *agon* in Wordsworth, even though the later poet
does call his predecessor's soul "awful." He corrects the
language of *Paradise Lost*, sometimes challenging an idea
here and there with all the relaxation of a Samuel Johnson,
but he usually confirms Hazlitt's judgment that "Milton is
his great idol, and he sometimes dares to compare himself
with him." Nor is there any evidence, overt or covert, of
personal tension or of a large revisionary enterprise at work
in Coleridge's relations to the great poet. Quite the contrary!
Coleridge says, "It is very common—very natural—for men
to *like* and even admire an exhibition of power very different
in kind from any thing of their own. No jealousy arises."
And Coleridge is at his ease when he sets about finding in
the great-souled Milton illustrations of his own theories of
poetry and the imagination.[17] Blake betrays many signs of
sharing the hero-worship of the Romantics for the great of
the past, who were, in his view, the embodiments of the true
God—the only truly available revelation outside the mind of
the seer himself.

But of course Blake's attitude toward Milton is vastly
deeper-going and more strenuously spirit-consuming than
that of his fellow Romantics. Because Milton, like Dante, is
in part a victim of the God-idea of the patriarchate, he
evokes in the bold and ever-challenging Blake a complex and
majestic task of revision that stretches the younger poet's
spirit to the breaking point. The soul of Milton must be
purged—as Blake's own soul must be continually purged—of
the murderous notion of a cruel divinity and also of that
tyrannous tendency in human nature, the selfhood. But
there is no evident jealousy of Milton's power of authority as
a poet, no desire to murder the aesthetic father or to become
his father's father, no desire to displace his predecessor;
there is, rather, an ambition to purge his master's spirit, to

---

17. Joseph A. Wittreich, Jr., *The Romantics on Milton: Formal Essays and
Critical Asides* (Cleveland and London: The Press of Case Western Reserve
University, 1970), pp. 113, 119, 276.

soften his acerbity, to unite him with his emanation and so feminize his psyche, and to enlist his mature and unspoiled genius against the common enemy, Urizen. All of which in fact Blake succeeds in doing! He does not misread Milton — he reads him all too accurately; instead, he revises him — rebuilds him, as Milton himself reconstructs Urizen, removing the clayey dross of the patriarchy and remodeling him in the life-giving red clay (Adam) of the true God.

Can we describe Blake's emotion toward Milton more accurately? It was not Oedipal love-hate but rather profound admiration combined with lamenting tears over a partial betrayal of otherwise shared religious ideals. "Who would not weep if Atticus were he?" Blake must have felt in the presence of patriarchal elements in Milton's thought precisely what he felt whenever and wherever he beheld the tracks of the Urizenic (Satanic) "Wheel of Religion":

> I wept & said. Is this the law of Jesus
> This terrible devouring sword turning every way?
> (*Jer.*, 77:13, 14–15 [E.232])

Thus Bloom, one of the most stimulating of modern critics, seems to have mislocated Blake's *agon*, which arose in a conflict with the God of the patriarchy. But that same critic has perceived, with uncanny insight though without elaboration, that the chariot of fire that Blake himself mounts to wield his bow of burning gold and shoot his arrows of desire, is none other than one of the Old Testament tropes for God, the chariot of Ezekiel, the Merkabah, the very vehicle in which Milton places his Christ.[18] The boldness of Blake's transumption is almost beyond belief, indicating that the cure of his anxiety was as deep-going as his suffering had been intense.

---

18. For Bloom's brilliant survey of the Merkabah image, see *Poetry and Repression*, pp. 83–95.

God the Divine Hand and Jehovah the Good Father

Wordsworth wrote,

> . . . my voice proclaims
> How exquisitely the individual Mind . . .
>   to the external World
> Is fitted:—and how exquisitely, too— . . .
> The external World is fitted to the Mind.[19]

Blake's high argument is of course different, since the polarities are not the same; but the "fit" is equally exquisite. For God removes effectually and precisely both of the fears described in the preceding section: God the Divine Hand removes the anxiety of emptiness, and Jehovah the Good Father removes the anxiety of primal and ever-recurring tyranny, replacing Urizen and annihilating Satan. Blake's God is created within a structure of desire as a projection of our perceptions and as a fulfillment of our needs. He is not a being wholly other, wholly causal, wholly antecedent. He is, in fact, not ontological at all—at least the argument whether he exists does not interest Blake. God belongs magnificently to the environment of integrating energy which is Blake's Great Eternity. We should note in passing that Blake has radically revised yet another great Western doctrine about God, the doctrine of the fitness of ends and means, of divine purpose and natural powers.

The horror of "indefinite space," which, we remember, tortured the Eternals, Urizen, Los, and Blake himself, is erased by the Divine Hand, of God conceived of as limit, as a formal restraint upon both contraction (which would otherwise drive into the concentrated hardness of a cosmic black hole) and opacity (which would otherwise smoke away into airy nothingness). This idea becomes illuminating, though complex, when Los working at his creating forge feels the finger of the Hand Divine over his furnaces, putting a limit

---

19. "Preface to *The Excursion*," ll. 62–68, *Poetical Works of William Wordsworth* (Oxford: Clarendon Press, 1949–1972), V, 5.

to destruction as he uses his divinely given powers which are "fitted [observe again this important theological and Wordsworthian word] to circumscribe this dark Satanic death." Why should Los, just at the moment that he senses that he is being led by brotherhood and mercy, feel terror at this task? Because he senses that in the act of giving form he crucifies Christ afresh, an action that causes him to undergo in his own spirit the bodily passion of his Lord. For by creating bodies of any kind, Blake-Los is reenacting an incarnation, which inevitably leads to a crucifixion and only then to a resurrection. This chain of salvation, requiring that bodies be put on before they are put off, is one of the very few laws of Blake's cosmos. But certainty of Christlike death, particularly since it can be a redemptive death, does not alone explain the fear; the creator is also "terrifd at the shapes / Enslaved humanity put on."[20]

What Blake calls "organization"[21] (one of his truly great words and one exactly expressing the healing of a mind that fears the void) is a divine accomplishment which creates a body for Urizen—a process Blake repeated obsessively—and which transforms that body into energetic creativity. The salvation of the wintry old God-man is told fully in *The Four Zoas* and need not be recounted here—his multiple resurrections from his slimy bed into a restored force in the psyche. But its climax does deserve attention. Los had already

---

20. *Milton*, 13:20–21 (E.107); 23:51 (E.119); *FZ.*, 9:17 (E.305); 56:19–27 and 55b:21–22 (E.338). The cosmic law is what Blake calls "the Universal Dictate"; it is, as articulated by Blake's Milton, to "despise death, not to fear it, and to annihilate the self in mutual love," *Milton*, 21:53 (E.116); 38:34–41 (E.139). From such Christlike incarnation, resurrection results. Blake is never more Christian than in his expression of this universal law of sacrificial, incarnational love.

21. Blake preferred this word to "order," which was closely associated with the dark and sickly dens and towers of the Establishment, although he could use this term in a favorable sense. It was a great evil in Blake's thought to be "disorganized," but to be "organized" was a comparably greater good. To be organized meant to be possessed of minutely articulated parts and to be endowed with living organs. The great organizer is Christ and, after him, the artist.

created Urizen's human, fallen form, which we know so well
(see Figure 1). Now realizing that he must "modulate" his
Orcan fury into which the very idea of Urizen seemed
designed to precipitate him, he embraced his own "raging
flames" and

> . . . drew them forth out of the depths planting his right foot firm
> Upon the Iron crag of Urizen thence springing up aloft
> Into the heavens of Enitharmon in a mighty circle
> And first he drew a line upon the walls of shining heaven
> And Enitharmon tinctured it with beams of blushing love.
>   (*FZ.*, 90:26, 32–36 [E.370])

Mr. and Mrs. Blake are once more in Great Eternity,
together producing illuminations, having sprung up into this
realm in a leap firmly supported by Urizenic iron. Los then
separates Urizen's true image ("shadow," denoting art)
from his warlike patriarchal spectre:

> Startled was Los he found his Enemy Urizen now
> In his hands he wonderd that he felt love & not hate
> His whole soul loved him he beheld him an infant
> Lovely breathed from Enitharmon he trembled within himself.
>   (*FZ.*, 90:64–67 [E.371])

We can now see that the healing of the mind by the
Divine Hand was a complex double process. It began by giving Urizen the body of that familar white-bearded old man,
to resist the suctions of the void. It ended by releasing the
primal energy of this old man into a resurrected form—that
"radiant youth" we see in "naked majesty":

> So Urizen spoke he shook his snows from off his Shoulders & arose
> As on a Pyramid of mist his white robes scattering
> The fleecy white renewd he shook his aged mantles off
> Into the fires Then glorious bright Exulting in his joy
> He sounding rose into the heavens in naked majesty
> in radiant Youth.
>   (*FZ.*, 121:27–32 [E.391])

The paradox of the conquest of fear through form is a deep one, but it is rooted in reality. It is as though one might say: I now realize that what has tortured me for years—and tortured whole cultures for centuries—is a creation of my own mind and of millions like me. I have created the image of that fear as honestly as I can, at whatever cost. I see that it does correspond to what I have feared, and I am free of its terrors, which are now "cathected" to my representation. I am therefore no longer haunted by its freely floating, uncontrolled, demonic energy, and I am now enabled to imagine even the humanly attractive and dynamic form that lay behind what caused my fears and may indeed have given them such potency. For it is apparent that so vigorous and persistent a power as tyranny must have derived from some kind of primal energy. Such is Blake's idea of catharsis, the work of God the Divine Hand.[22]

The other aspect of divine salvation, the salvation from the fear of tyranny in oneself and in society, is the function of the Good Father. It is unnecessary to specify Blake's early, middle, and late alternatives to the bad patriarchy of Jehovah-Urizen, alternatives revealed in his many honorific uses, all through his career, of the word "father" in a good sense and his many portrayals at all periods of benign old men. At no time was Blake without the idea of a good

---

22. In connection with this belief in form, it is interesting to note that Blake felt the need to redefine the term "infinity" in his late works. The word could be a virtual synonym for God. But in *Jerusalem* it is said, "The Infinite alone resides in Definite & Determinate Identity" (55:64 [E.205]), and in *Milton* the sons of Los create forms "with bounds to the Infinite putting off the Indefinite" (28:4 [E.125]). David E. James sees Blake's *Laocoon* (a representation of "Jah & his two Sons Satan & Adam") as portraying a reversal of the fall, beginning the process of regeneration through the assumption of spatial and temporal form. If so, *Laocoon* can be regarded as a manifestation of the Divine Hand at work. See *PMLA*, 98 (March 1983), 226–236. The idea that ultimate reality embraces the principle of limit and form may distress those who dwell too much on Blakean exuberance and who confine measure and boundary to Urizen alone. But neither he nor God can be understood without the idea of the Divine Hand, nor indeed can the idea of contraries, which include both Reason and Energy.

father, even though the concept may have gone partially underground in his revolutionary period. We can therefore absolve Blake of the "psychopathy" that Freud and Alan Harrington have found endemic in modern society, the absence of a superego.[23] Nevertheless, much of Blake's vision is dominated by the cruel father who tortures the mind not least by being an answering image to the inner tendency of human nature to tyrannize. This image must be cast out, and anyone wishing to follow the progress of this purgation should study closely the career in Blake of Jehovah, first the leprous sixth eye of God but finally the Lord Jehovah who creates "merciful Order" (*Jer.*, 49:55 [E.199]) and as Elohim Jehovah proclaims the "Covenant of the Forgiveness of Sins" (*The Ghost of Abel*, 2:24 [E.272]). Once Blake is certain of mercy, he is willing to restore might, omnipotence, law, and will to the divine principle, a fascinating development that must be discussed elsewhere.

One might pause to ask why Blake felt such an urgent need to create in his latest prophetic work a virtually separate ideal of Jehovah and his covenant of mercy. Why would not Christ do, the ever-merciful Lamb of God, the image of the Father and of humanity itself? It may be that Christ had been too intimately associated with Los, with the human imagination, with Blake himself, with youthful energetic humanity. Now that Urizen, the primal old man of history, has himself become a naked youth, a bright preacher of the Everlasting Gospel of life, there is a potential danger of another void. Venerability is lacking. But that quality is restored to human life in Jehovah, the Ancient of Days, healed of his leprosy and now the universal patriarch of a Covenant of Mercy. Jesus can, to be sure, be called "Father & Saviour," but Western man is not fully at ease without Jehovah, the archetypal father.[24]

23. See Thomas McFarland, *Romanticism and the Forms of Ruin* (Princeton: Princeton University Press, 1981), p. 201.

24. *Jer.*, 25:9 (E.170). Leslie Tannenbaum in *Biblical Tradition in Blake's Early Prophecies* (Princeton, New Jersey: Princeton University Press, 1982), pp. 202–208, believes Blake derives a sharp separation between Jehovah

My bones are pierced in me in the night season & my sinews take no rest

My skin is black upon me & my bones are burned with heat

11

The triumphing of the wicked is short, the joy of the hypocrite is but for a moment
Satan himself is transformed into an Angel of Light & his Ministers into Ministers of Righteousness

With Dreams upon my bed thou scarest me & affrightest me with Visions

Why do you persecute me as God & are not satisfied with my flesh. Oh that my words were printed in a Book that they were graven with an iron pen & lead in the rock for ever For I know that my Redeemer liveth & that he shall stand in the latter days upon the Earth & after my skin destroy thou This body yet in my flesh shall I see God whom I shall see for Myself and mine eyes shall behold & not Another tho consumed be my wrought Image Who opposeth & exalteth himself above all that is called God or is Worshipped

WBlake invent & sculp

London. Published as the Act directs March 8. 1825 by Will Blake N 3 Fountain Court Strand   Proof

3. *Job,* plate 11. Department of Prints and Drawings, British Museum, London.

4. *Jerusalem,* plate 99. Copy F, acc. #953. The Pierpont Morgan Library, New York.

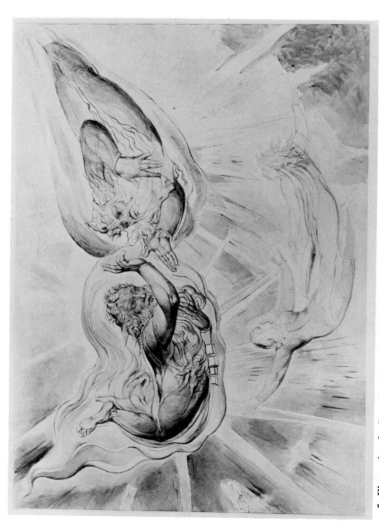

5. Illustration for Dante's *Divine Comedy*, illustration 95 ("St. Peter, Beatrice, Dante with St. James Also"). National Gallery of Victoria, Melbourne. Felton Bequest, 1920.

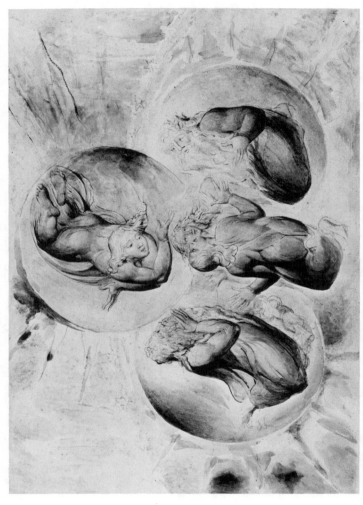

6. Illustration for Dante's *Divine Comedy*, illustration 96 ("St. Peter, St. James, Dante, Beatrice with St. John the Evangelist Also"). Department of Prints and Drawings, British Museum, London.

Three notable visual designs represent the union of mankind with redeemed and restored venerability. On Plate 99 of *Jerusalem* (see Figure 4), God the Father embraces a youthful being (male or female, male-female?) in flames of desire and intellectual energy that recall the flame-plants of the *Songs of Innocence*. The other two appear as illustrations to Dante's *Paradiso*. Both show Saints Peter and James, each bearded but in heart-warming good health and benevolence. In the first (Figure 5), James, a good, sound, decent old man extends a fraternal hand to a truly merciful Peter, whose eyes stream mercy and whose obvious marks of suffering qualify him to give a blessing. In the second (Figure 6), circling energies of love unite, in overlapping roundels, Dante and Beatrice and a youthful Saint John with the older veterans Peter and James. This is an embrace of Great Eternity where there is no longer patriarchal tyranny nor any generation gap whatever. But the patriarchal beards remain to remind us of what has been, what might have been, and what again might be.

Blake lived through a revolutionary period in which, as Edmund Burke said, "sons . . . called for the execution of their parents" and "wretches calling themselves father . . . demand the murder of their sons." Images of castration, mutilation, and cannibalism abundantly mark the relations of fathers and sons. Blake, as we have seen, expressed revolutionary anti-paternalism, but he seldom stooped to such violence. He never descended to the brutality of a Goya, to take but one example, whose Saturn has bitten off the head of a mature being, an adolescent, perhaps even a man.[25]

---

and Elohim from the two distinct narrative accounts in Genesis, Elohim being evil and associated with Urizen, Jehovah being good and associated with Los. The argument is not compelling even for the earlier prophecies; for Blake as a whole it tends to ignore or deemphasize the powerful association Blake establishes between Urizen and Jehovah in their fallen state: both are leprous and Sinaitic; both are thunder-gods and associated with stars; both are patriarchal and accept worship from their suffering victims.

25. See Ronald Paulson, *Representations of Revolution (1789–1820)* (New Haven: Yale University Press, 1983), pp. 31, 363.

Is Blake illuminated by two great father-creations of our own century? He is surely as realistic as Freud in perceiving the mischief that a tyrannical father can do in the psyche of man, but he is not imprisoned in the Freudian realism that sees identification with the father as usually ambiguous, the boy's imaginative sympathy for the father arising only because he wishes to replace him, to attain ascendancy over him, and then to enjoy "a true object-cathexis toward his mother."[26] Jung believed the figure of the "Wise Old Man" to be archetypal, one of the "organizing dominants" of four-fold consciousness; and the Jungian "anima always stands in the relationship of a daughter to the wise old man." But this figure is only a "fragment of the objective psyche," though an "autonomous entity," who appears in all cultures as someone possessing authority, whether as magician, doctor, priest, teacher, professor, grandfather, or even hobgoblin.[27] Jung's archetypal structure, working itself out from the psyche into culture and deriving historically from a primeval teacher of alchemical secrets, is essentially bland compared to Blake's. It lacks the terror Blake finds in omnipotent Urizenic authority and also lacks the intense love the poet bestows upon the Jehovah of the Covenant, the Jesus of mercy, or the redeemed Heavenly Father. Nor is there in Jung the fierce antitheses of cruel patriarch and embracing father, nor the everlasting tensions of warring contrarieties engaged in the mental battle that Blake called the "War & Hunting" of Great Eternity (*Milton*, 34:50; 35:2 [E.134, 135]). Blake believed that redemptive force fully existed only in a divine being who is "The God *of Fire* and Lord *of Love*" (*Jerusalem*, Plate 3, "To the Public" [E.145]).

---

26. Sigmund Freud, *Standard Edition of the Complete Psychological Works* (London: The Hogarth Press, 1955–), XVIII, 105. See also XI, 172–173; XVII, 27–28; XXI, 183.

27. C. G. Jung, *Collected Works*, ed. Sir Herbert Read *et al.* (New York: Pantheon Books, 1955–), V, 333, 391; VII, 109–110; IXi, 215–216; XII, 123.

Conclusion: Regression and Subjectivity?

The most serious charge that can be made against the thought of Blake as it has been presented in this commentary is that it was regressive and entirely subjective. Blake writes after an intense vision,

> I remaind as a Child
> All I ever had known
> Before me bright Shone.[28]

And "return" is everywhere a compulsive imperative; both the lyric and prophetic muses direct this command to the fallen earth, to Jerusalem, and to England itself. But to what are we asked to return? Sometimes to Beulah, that place of pastoral rest between earth and Eden, which Blake mercifully opens to weary earth-travelers and to his knights of mental fight. But most often it is to Eternity that Blake summons us, and can anyone possibly call it a place of narcissistic arrest or infantine peace? Existing in Blake's Eden is rather like what one imagines a great conductor to experience when he is translating *The Rites of Spring* into a performance, churning up a raging energy on which form is being impressed.

Blake's way of destroying error (stop beholding it, and it will burn up) has of course seemed notoriously subjective and easy to some. Subjective it certainly is. But easy? A mind habituated by centuries of powerfully sanctioned beholding is not changed by fiat, and what is to be burned up in a Last Judgment growing out of prophetic vision is a stubborn reality of our culture, however subjectively produced. Centuries of false seeing have been reified into institutions and cultural forms; the idea of God has produced a terribly real and inescapable presence in actual life, as palpable as a mountain, as irresistible as a hurricane.

28. Poem in letter to Thomas Butts, October 2, 1800, ll. 72–74 (E. 713).

> . . . What seems to Be: Is: To those to whom
> It seems to Be, & is productive of the most dreadful
> Consequences to those to whom it seems to Be: . . .
> (*Jer.*, 32:51–53 [E.179])

Blake has expressed the weight of this burden marvelously in the drawing already mentioned (see Figure 3), where a heavy, torturing, self-reflective Urizen-Satan haunts Job on his bed.

It is rather easier to believe that a false vision can create a bad culture than that a good vision can create a good culture. But there is no reason why the mind which produces Los and Christ may not be as consequentially powerful as the mind which produces Urizen-Satan. And one must surely allow some kind of existence to the Divine Hand, which through fashioning bodies heals Blake's mind, and to the good Father, who creates a covenant of mercy and forgiveness of sin and so allays Blake's anxieties. It takes at least two to enter into a covenant. The prophet, Blake's Strong Man, not only rages with inspiration; he "marches on in fearless dependance on the divine decrees," and a decree implies somebody at the other end.[29]

And yet this most antinomian of Christians does not permit us to base his belief upon natural, logical, institutional assumptions, or to derive from his fierce dedication an unmistakable sense of ontological being. He rests his case against Bishop Watson entirely on inner certainty, and it is difficult to resist the conviction that in the end Blake's God, as so many have in the past believed, is a structure, a product, a sublime projection of the "Imagination which is Spiritual Sensation."[30] It is not quite just to call Blake a man of faith; he is, rather, a man of sight—a seer, in the etymological meaning. And the relationship between what he needs to see for his own mental health and what he in fact ultimately comes to see is so close that it is hard to escape an overwhelming sense of subjectively produced truth. And yet

29. A descriptive Catalogue, Number V (E.545).
30. Letter to Dr. Trusler, August 23, 1799 (E.703).

we must remember that *all* affirmations of faith or of vision raise precisely this problem of external objectivity. Samuel Johnson, who tended to regard God as "the great Lawgiver of the universe," a "Creator," and a "Governour,"[31] may have been projecting his own desire for order and social peace on the entire universe. Freud's brilliant and disturbing analysis of the dynamic relations of belief and desire has enormously extended the bounds of the subjective.

But however rational, empirical, or skeptical an investigator may think he has to be, he can surely never deny the flaming force of Blake's final embrace of the good father, Jehovah, whom he saw as a person. However internal or organic the poet's vision—and it was neither Mosaic nor Pauline but Johannine—it is never abstract, general, or purely mystical, fusing bodiless essences in light and fire. In Blake's vision it is clearly outlined identities that unite, as living lovers with bodies do. Blake saw real people, real forms. And God is one such.

We cannot therefore say that Blake has answered the perhaps unanswerable question of *what* God is. But he tells us *where* God is. He is in the very center of the integrating and integrated psyche; there he lives and moves and has his being. Since we have spent so much time on the idea of a false God, it is not irrelevant to ask in conclusion,

Where is the Covenant of Priam, the Moral Virtues of the Heathen
Where is the Tree of Good & Evil that rooted beneath the cruel heel
Of Albions Spectre the Patriarch Druid! . . .
          (*Jer.*, 98:46–48 [E.258])

In other words, where is Urizen? For Blake-Los, he now lives in the "Outward Spheres of Visionary Space and Time," remanded to only the "shadows of Possibility." He

31. See especially sermons 3, 4, and 16 in *Samuel Johnson: Sermons*, ed. Jean Hagstrum and James Gray in *Yale Edition of the Works of Samuel Johnson*, Vol. XIV (New Haven: Yale University Press, 1978), pp. 29, 39, 176. I do not wish to suggest that the supreme being for Johnson was not also a gracious and benevolent father, but to emphasize the dominant qualities.

belongs to "Visions & . . . Prophecy," where we can "Fore-see & Avoid" him, though escape from him is by no means certain.[32] To create such a place for him almost cost Blake his humanity. But through that effort the most ancient heavens became fresh and strong.

32. *Jer.*, 92:17–19 (E.252).

The Novel

RALPH W. RADER

From Richardson to Austen: "Johnson's Rule" and the Development of the Eighteenth-Century Novel of Moral Action

The neo-Aristotelian approach to the novel from which my own approach in part derives—I refer specifically to the work of R. S. Crane and Sheldon Sacks[1] —has tended to identify the novel with the action structure first described by Aristotle and long employed in the drama before its appearance in *Pamela* and, subsequently, in Richardson's later novels and those of Fielding, Burney, and Austen. Since I shall be referring to the action structure throughout, let me define it here by saying, more simply than would my predecessors, that it is an affective structure designed to induce, develop, and finally cathartically resolve in the reader an active concern for a protagonist which results from the tension between what the reader is led to think will happen to the protagonist (his fate) and what he is led to think ought to

---

1. See Crane's "The Concept of Plot and the Plot of *Tom Jones*," in *Critics and Criticism: Ancient and Modern,* ed. R. S. Crane (Chicago: University of Chicago Press, 1952), pp. 616–647; and Sacks's *Fiction and the Shape of Belief* (Berkeley: University of California Press, 1964), esp. pp. 26–27 and 268–269.

happen to him (his desert). Thus stated, the concept corresponds pretty much to what we might call the novel of plotted suspense, and, intelligently applied to such novels, it can yield consistent insight. But it does not provide any really satisfactory basis for analyzing a number of works unequivocally registered as novels—for instance, in the eighteenth century, *Tristram Shandy* and *Humphry Clinker* — and this points to the more general fact that our possession of the intuitive concept "novel" is stronger than our intuitive notion of the action structure. We are more aware of *Tom Jones, Tristram Shandy*, and *Ulysses* as novels than we are of the fact that the first is a novel of plotted suspense while the other two are not.

The plain implication of such reflections is that the action structure is not the definitive characteristic of the novel. The most fundamental thing that Richardson in *Pamela* borrowed from the drama was, I think, not the action structure but, as Mark Kinkead-Weekes has suggested, the dramatic mode itself.[2] In watching a play we seem to see the actors as characters acting out of their own purposes, while more fundamentally our imaginations register and respond to the fact that their actions are fictive, designed to realize the playwright's artistic purpose in the play. Now it is this same kind of illusion that the novel, using mere words and not actors, contrives with largely covert art to present. We may say for the sake of precision and clarity, using Michael Polanyi's helpful terms, that the novel presents to our imagination a focal illusion of characters acting autonomously as if in the real world, within our subsidiary awareness of an underlying authorial purpose which gives their story, virtually real, implicit significance and affective force.[3] This formulation is meant to locate the basis of the universal impression that the novel is "realistic," that it is "dramatic," that it shows rather than tells, or rather tells by

    2. Mark Kinkead-Weekes, *Samuel Richardson: Dramatic Novelist* (Ithaca, New York: Cornell University Press, 1973), p. 395.
    3. See Michael Polanyi, *Personal Knowledge: Towards a Post-Critical Philosophy* (Chicago: University of Chicago Press, 1974), pp. 55–56.

showing, in contrast with earlier narratives which may be said to tell in order to show.

Crane's and Sacks's formulations do not directly express the realistic mode of the novel as independent of the action structure, in large part I think because of their tendency to think of that structure as an integral and unmalleable formal principle and of the transition from the drama to the novel as a mere change in the manner of representation—in drama, in prose—conceived as a repertory of logical possibilities in principle available to artists at any time. This almost structuralist tendency to think in terms of fixed and timeless forms deflected their attention from the evidence which suggests that the novel needs to be conceived as a unique, historically emergent construction, something entirely new under the literary sun. Nevertheless, I believe that the concept of the action structure is accurately applicable to the novel as historically the most important of the subsidiary organizations used to give the realistic surface of novels their significance and force, and I have already implied my agreement with Crane and Sacks that it characterizes the main line of development in the eighteenth-century novel from Richardson to Austen. But the attempt to explain the structural peculiarities of these novels individually and as a developmental sequence immediately again raises the problem whether the action novel, any more than the novel form as a whole, can be thought of as fixed and timeless rather than as mixed and historically adapted to the purposes and preconceptions of its users, specifically in the present instance to the didactic purposes of the eighteenth-century novelists who employed it. Crane was quite sure that didactic aims had no part in actions, the essence of which for him was just that they *were* mimetic and not didactic, and in his famous essay on *Tom Jones* he made no mention of Fielding's explicitly announced didactic intention, just as in his account of neoclassical criticism he tended to think of critics who spoke of incorporating morals into actions as misunderstanding Aristotle rather than as formulating viable conceptions of mixed forms which fell well within the possibilities of free human creation.

Following Crane and clearly recognizing that Fielding's and other eighteenth-century action novels do in fact incorporate didactic material, Sacks redefined the action so as to make the expression of an author's belief not only permissible but necessary. In doing this I think he blurred the distinction between two different claims: (1) that the aesthetic requirements of the action structure put no pressure on an author to falsify his beliefs in building into his work the moral judgments of characters necessary to develop and resolve the tension of suspense; and (2) that the expression of doctrinal or other didactic material was inherently compatible with the action conceived as a strictly integral form. The first claim I take to be indubitable, but the second dubious. Sacks's own demonstration of the brilliantly inventive ways in which didactic material is built into *Tom Jones* and *Amelia* is more easily interpreted to the opposite conclusion, that such material is *not* inherently compatible with the action structure but requires special accommodation. Sacks did not draw this conclusion because he was committed, as I say, to an almost structuralist view that principles of literary form must be conceived as fixed, unitary, and finite if they are to be capable of explaining the facts of our literary experience, but it seems to me just the facts of our literary experience—that *Amelia*, for instance, seems manifestly weakened by formal contradictions—that suggest the usefulness of thinking of literary works not as embodiments of *a priori* principles of literary form but as constructions in which the author's attempt to realize his aesthetic and allied aims may produce conflicts which leave on the works the marks of their solutions.

My specific thesis in this paper is that we can get maximum insight into what I will call the eighteenth-century novel of moral action if we think of its employment of the action structure, with its inherent need to develop and cathartically resolve concern for a protagonist, as under the constraint of a commitment to moral instruction imposed by the most fundamental critical assumptions of the time, assumptions which the novelists shared and positively accepted as the basis of their work. My aim may be considered an intention to explore, in relation to the novel, the concrete critical implications of Ralph Cohen's much larger argument that "neo-classical forms were mixed and interrelated, dominated by didactic models."[4]

Fielding's example shows that ideas and messages as such can be built into action structures, sometimes, as with *Amelia*, at a heavy formal price. But the didactic pressures of the time exerted an even more fundamental influence on the substance of the action structure itself by restricting the novelist's freedom to develop the character of his protagonist solely on the basis of aesthetic considerations, for cathartic effect alone.

In implicit reproof of current novelistic practice, Dr. Johnson asserted in his famous *Rambler* 4, that "In narratives, where historical veracity has no place, I cannot discover why there should not be exhibited the most perfect idea of virtue; of virtue not angelical, nor above probability, for what we cannot credit we shall never imitate, but the highest and purest that humanity can reach, which, exercised in such trials as the various revolutions of things shall bring upon it, may, by conquering some calamities, and enduring others, teach us what we may hope, and what we can perform."[5] Now we may take this prescription not as laying down a principle (let us call it "Johnson's Rule") which the novelists ignored but one which they consciously accepted and attempted to embody in their works, with results, as I shall attempt to show, that have much to do with the problematic qualities of their individual novels and with the progressively different forms which emerged in this series.

I have elsewhere described the specific action structure of *Pamela* by saying that the concern we are made to feel for her is a serious fear which results from the fact that her

---

4. See Ralph Cohen, "On the Interrelations of Eighteenth-Century Literary Forms," in *New Approaches to Eighteenth-Century Literature* (New York: Columbia University Press, 1974), p. 75.

5. Samuel Johnson, *The Rambler*, ed. W. J. Bate and Albrecht B. Strauss, Vol. 3 of *The Yale Edition of the Works of Samuel Johnson* (New Haven: Yale University Press, 1969), p. 24.

desert and fate develop along a line of branching alternatives where one branch always leads to an ethically unacceptable or materially undesirable safety (respectively either refused by Pamela or closed by circumstance), while the other, ethically impeccable and always chosen by Pamela, leads overtly and immediately to greater danger but covertly and ultimately to the most desirable resolution of her difficulties.[6]

It can be predicted from this model that the impeccable moral choices which lead Pamela immediately to her greatest danger but ultimately to her greatest reward will constitute her a moral paragon but will also involve the danger that she will be viewed as a hypocrite, since the dramatic presentation through her consciousness makes the reader's awareness of the potential positive outcome of her morally defensive action seem, contrary to Richardson's intention, part of her implicit calculation; and, indeed, whatever her motivation, the dynamic equation of virtue and reward which the novel offers the reader is inherently ambiguous and vulgar.

I will not detail here the full structural account of *Pamela* which this model can generate, since I have already done so in another essay (see footnote 6) but will turn at once to *Clarissa*, a novel which has as its structural core the same contest between the sexually libertine male and the female paragon, or perfect "exemplar," as Richardson himself calls Clarissa.[7] We may assume that Richardson, sensitive to criticism of the have-your-cake-and-eat-it-too morality of *Pamela*, decided to alter its desert-fate structure so as to create a novel of contrasting moral stringency and grandeur. We may precisely locate the great moral difference within close structural similarity of *Pamela* and *Clarissa* by saying that Clarissa's fate and merit develop along a line of

6. See the author's "Defoe, Richardson, Joyce and the Concept of Form in the Novel," in *Autobiography, Biography, and the Novel* by Will Matthews and Ralph W. Rader (Los Angeles: William Andrews Clark Memorial Library, 1973), pp. 34–35.

7. Preface to *Clarissa; or, The History of a Young Lady*, Everyman Edition, 1902 (reprint, London: J. M. Dent and Sons, 1967), I, xiv. Subsequent references by page number in text.

alternatives where one branch, always refused by Clarissa or closed by circumstance, is defined as ethically acceptable but not as impeccable, and apparently promises earthly felicity, while the other, always chosen by Clarissa, is defined as ethically impeccable and increasingly excludes the possibility of her earthly felicity.

The model appears cold and taciturn, but if we question it in the right spirit it will grow articulate and tell us that *Clarissa* is the story of a woman who is constrained, or constrains herself, to give up all objects of earthly desire in order to remain virtuous, since the only outcome of the sequence envisaged in the model is the heroine's death. Such a story is inherently painful and is made more so by the basic principle of its structure, which forces us to be aware, as Clarissa makes her impeccably virtuous choices, that to make a self-regarding choice would be very easy, since an alternative temptation is always present and defined as ethically acceptable. Our participation in the book may be described by saying that we fully empathize with Clarissa's plight and in a way (a crucial way) feel its pain more sharply than she does, since we are more attracted than she is to the earthly goods she gives up with such relatively clear-sighted ease; she suffers, but she does not suffer agonies of indecision. On the other hand, we are reassured about her sacrificial choices and do not judge them as capricious or overly nice, since we are made more aware than she can be that if she did make the self-regarding acceptable choices, she would not by such means actually achieve earthly happiness. She is restrained by principle alone from choices that full knowledge would define as imprudent. The emotion that develops and is discharged as we witness this struggle is an admiring and indignant pity quite in contrast with the hopeful fear gradually turning to fearful hope with which we follow the career of Pamela.

The inherent moral grandeur of *Clarissa*, however, is not quite the tragic grandeur envisaged by Aristotle and achieved by the Greek tragedians and, in a somewhat altered form, by Shakespeare. Superficially considered, *Clarissa* is that kind of tragedy proscribed by Aristotle when he asserted that in effective tragedy "a good man must not be seen passing from happiness to misery" because such a spectacle "is not fear-inspiring or piteous but simply odious to us."[8] Aristotle has in mind a situation where a good man is externally deprived of the happiness he desires and deserves and that we desire for him, a situation merely frustrating or shocking. But *Clarissa* is not shocking in an aesthetically unpleasant way, because it does not fulfill Aristotle's implicit conditions. Clarissa is not deprived of but, at the behest of an ethical imperative which forbids self-gratification, voluntarily gives up all objects of earthly desire. But more than that, she gives up desire itself; she wills finally, as her commitment to principle demands, not to will, not to desire anything earthly, even life itself. Rather, she actively desires death as a positive, pleasurable good, and we are made to believe in and at an admiring distance to sympathize with that desire. She is not a good person, then, whose desires are frustrated, but a good person whose desires, in a strange way, are fully realized. Unlike the usual tragic situation, Clarissa's involves her conscious, willed choice, at every step along the way, of her own personal moral good, clearly perceived as it is present in the situation in which she finds herself. She *chooses* her fate as the true tragic protagonist does not, without moral mistake (except in a token sense), and she remains ethically impeccable to the end, blaming herself but free of blame.

Despite Clarissa's positive choice of her fate and lack of blame in it, her story would still be unsatisfactory if the reader did not also take satisfaction in the outcome, and to secure that satisfaction was Richardson's primary problem in constructing the ending. His solution was simple: to make it appear that Clarissa would find her full and proper reward in heaven. But this appearance was difficult to achieve within the limits of a form which could display only the phenomena of this world. One dimension of Richardson's solution was

8. Aristotle, *Poetics*, trans. Ingham Bywater, in *The Basic Works of Aristotle*, ed. Richard McKeon (New York: Random House, 1941), p. 1466.

his successful representation of Clarissa's own serene conviction, expatiated upon and dramatized in her long renunciation of life, that her destiny was indeed her Father's house in heaven. But the most brilliant part of the solution was the development of a possibility latent in Richardson's use of the letter form as a story-telling vehicle. By presenting posthumously Clarissa's long will and a number of her letters to various persons, Richardson achieved the wonderful effect of giving Clarissa's afterlife a seemingly concrete manifestation, whereas if her voice had ceased at her death, the effect would have been far different. In her letters she seems to speak fully, easily, and serenely after her death from the achieved perspective of immortality. At the same time that Richardson gives this affective proof of her afterlife, he concurrently represents other characters in a way that will enhance that sense. Even the best of those who remain after her death have no positive happiness, while those responsible for her death are punished with condign severity; everyone seems to have no thought but of Clarissa and her merits and her life beyond, so that the whole world of the novel seems to give a kind of negative testimony to her transcendent significance and existence.

The climax of this aspect of the book is Lovelace's death scene, which is narrated as follows by the valet De La Tour:

> *Blessed*—said he {Lovelace}, addressing himself no doubt to Heaven; for his dying eyes were lifted up. A strong convulsion prevented him for a few moments saying more, but recovering, he again, with great fervour (lifting up his eyes and his spread hands), pronounced the word *blessed*. Then, in a seeming ejaculation, he spoke inwardly, so as not to be understood: at last, he distinctly pronounced these three words, LET THIS EXPIATE! And then, his head sinking on his pillow, he expired, at about half an hour after ten.[9]

The scene is constructed so as to give the most persuasive testimony possible to Clarissa's presence in heaven. Here

9. Samuel Richardson, *Clarissa*, IV, 530.

the great prevaricator—speaking in pain, at the point of death, and only for himself, since he is indifferent to De La Tour's presence—is seen for once to be absolutely sincere. Through Lovelace's words, much more through his gesture and attitude, which imply his thorough and undoubted conviction of Clarissa's presence in beatitude above, the imagination of the reader is led to experience the fact of Clarissa's immortality, all the more since De La Tour does not understand the implications of the scene, which is left to the reader's own active inference and hence to his implicit belief.

Richardson's maintenance of that impeccability in Clarissa's choices which ultimately justifies her apotheosis presented him with some special problems of which I may briefly notice those surrounding first her elopement and then the rape. In order to free Clarissa of fault in the elopement, Richardson first develops a situation where it appears that Clarissa may not be able to resist the nefarious pressures or even forged processes that may be brought upon her to marry Solmes, and thus he makes acceptable but not impeccable the choice Lovelace offers of rescuing her and depositing her in some safe place. But Clarissa decides to withdraw from this choice (more dangerous than she knows, as *we* know) only to be obliged by Lovelace's contrivance to meet him in the garden to revoke her tentative consent in person. Once there, Lovelace tricks her into his carriage by making it appear that her brother and father are about to burst out upon them, to their great danger at the hands of Lovelace. Thus, at last, Clarissa chooses to run away not for her own salvation but for the sake of the others she is bound to hold dear. But now Richardson has contrived to maintain her impeccability while bringing her by choice into the moral bind he needs to generate her fate. From this point on, her freedom, though actual, is almost an illusion; she cannot thereafter really choose to profit by her choice, marry Lovelace, and live, without appearing retrospectively to have made in leaving a self-interested choice and thus being less than impeccable. When she steps into the carriage her doom is, as the melodramatic phrase goes, sealed.

But even as that doom develops against the apparent but always receding possibility that she and Lovelace can accept each other, we become more and more aware of the absolute opposition between their characters that prevents any actual rapprochement. Their characters are designed so as to be mutually exclusive in their potential choices. She will do nothing which, not dictated by principle, has the least hint of self-gratification about it, while he seeks from her, in gratification of his pride, a fearful, self-regarding acknowledgment of his power. (It is important to note that his desire is not basically sensual, as is consistently suggested by the fact that he remains indifferent to the other women available in Mrs. Sinclair's house.) His primary wish is that she show herself less than an angel, acknowledging her fleshliness toward him. He wants to validate in respect of himself the proposition of Satan in *Job* 2:4, "Skin for skin, yea all that a man hath will he give for his life." But she will give nothing, will not violate principle even for her life, and he will not spare her unless she does. For that matter, we understand clearly that he would not spare her even if she did, because she would then be less than perfect, and he would not want her. He can neither accept her perfection without the ultimate test which makes his possession of it impossible, nor would he have been able to accept her had she proved imperfect in the test.

Admiration and pity for Clarissa thus grow as the action leads inevitably toward the rape. But a difficulty for Richardson emerges with and in the rape. It is necessary that the violation which makes it impossible for Clarissa to live be a rape and that she be unconscious while it is perpetrated, or else she might seem in some sense to have assented, which would mar her perfection, as of course would marriage after the fact, an ethically acceptable temptation which all England seems to urge upon her. But in being raped, she emphatically does not choose and maintain her moral responsibility for her fate, and hence the principle of form of the book seems to fail: internal moral development is replaced by melodrama, with Clarissa a passive victim of external force. Richardson's solution is the famous pen-knife scene, in which, after the pathos of Clarissa's postrape situation has been fully developed, Clarissa splendidly faces Lovelace down, persuading both him and the reader that she will take her life rather than suffer further indignity. With this scene she has taken her fate once more into her own hands and afterwards is spiritually free of Lovelace, so that when she escapes the house a few hours later she is henceforward free of his physical presence and control.

This following out of the constructive logic implicit in the formal principle I have hypothesized locates something of *Clarissa*'s moral magnitude and cathartic power. It can also suggest the limits of its effectiveness as they derive from the same source, the need to sustain unto death Clarissa's program of impeccable obedience to principle by means of which she seeks to contravene her natural desires, selfishness, and pride. Her implicit motto is "I will not do what I will; I will not gratify my selfish pride." But that she will not gratify her pride is, of course, just her pride; in its own self-immolation her ego (or rather the reader's) finds the gratification she has pervasively denied herself; her self-denial is the ground of the reader's moral self-indulgence. Clarissa is cut off from responsibility and causally separated from the devastation wreaked by the rocket blast of her ascent to heaven. She forgives Lovelace and does not desire his punishment; she forgives all her enemies. Yet Lovelace dies miserably and they die, satisfying in the reader the vengeance which he has admired Clarissa for giving up. In this sense, *Clarissa* is affectively similar to *Pamela* in that it requires the reader to tolerate in himself a moral ambiguity from which the heroine is represented as being free. But *Clarissa*, though it falls short of the agapemenous sublimity displayed in a Cordelia, achieves grandeur just because, unlike *Pamela*, it does dramatize the full price for moral pride, renouncing the earthly vanities which in *Pamela* are cherished. In essence it is an enactment of the you'll-be-sorry-when-I'm-dead fantasy, but it is the grandest and most scarifying version of it imaginable in the stringency and relentlessness with which it carries the moral will to the extremity of death. It is an epic of righteousness, or rather self-righteousness, with the virtues and defects proper to such a work; but with its defects it is still a novelistic action of nearly incomparable massiveness and power.

Richardson's last novel, *Sir Charles Grandison*, presents for explanation, within the terms I have used to consider its predecessors, the fact of its great critical popularity in its own and immediately succeeding times as compared with its marked neglect in our own era and in contrast with *Clarissa*. Why the great loss in power from the earlier to the later work? Space permits only a brief and schematic answer. Envious as always of Fielding, Richardson had been particularly scornful of *Tom Jones* and of the low and immoral adventures in which Fielding was willing to display his hero. Yet his own Lovelace, though antagonist and not protagonist, fell as much as Tom Jones under Johnson's condemnation of mixed characters whose sympathetic attractions masked vice and made it seem attractive. Looking back on Lovelace and Mr. B., Richardson felt the point of his friends who urged him to paint a truly good man to put Fielding's flawed hero in his proper light. And so, as is well-known, it became Richardson's specific intention in *Grandison* to present "the Example of a Man acting uniformly well thro' a Variety of trying Scenes."[10]

There was only one difficulty with Richardson's plan. His decision to make a perfect hero meant that he could not develop an effective action. In his previous novels he could generate powerfully dynamic action structures through his impeccable heroines' acts of moral resistance to the threatening advances of the male antagonists, thus creating a mounting sense of moral danger registered against a mounting sympathy. But a hero cannot be put in such a posture of passive resistance leading increasingly to danger without making him seem unheroically weak or ludicrous. And to make a successful action out of his positive choices would require either that he make mistakes inconsistent with his

10. Preface to *The History of Sir Charles Grandison*, ed. Jocelyn Harris, 3 vols. (London: Oxford University Press, 1972), I, 4.

moral perfection or that the grounds of his acts be merely external and the action therefore melodramatic and independent of his internal moral state. An action based on a courtship, as Richardson's was, was even more limited: a morally perfect hero can only be attracted by and rewarded with a morally perfect heroine, but between two such paragons there cannot be any morally significant differences that can serve as the dynamic basis of a truly fateful separation between them. Richardson's solution, such as it was, was to separate his hero Grandison from his heroine Harriet Byron by means of a prior semi-commitment Grandison has unblameably made to a third paragon, Lady Clementina della Poretta. The situation is artificial and not productive of morally dynamic action, but it does permit a semblance of action, while the real emotional effect lies in the episodes, Richardson's "Variety of trying Scenes," as occasions for displaying at large Grandison's moral perfection. Richardson does all that he can to offset the inherent and essential dullness of a story in which the principals can make no real mistake and be in no real distress, by using novelistic means to lend interest to his characters and by using the resources of his genius to reconcile, as Jocelyn Harris says, "an inert mass of instruction with the demands of entertainment."[11]

But no degree of genius could truly vitalize an action stultified by its initial commitment to display its leading characters as moral paragons. And saying no more than this, we can find the solution to the first half of the problem noted above: the eighteenth century loved *Sir Charles Grandison* because, triply observing Johnson's Rule, it was so full of beautiful conduct, an orgy of impeccabilities and delicacies, whereas later audiences are wearied by its lack of organic movement. The choices of the characters create and resolve no tension, and there is no catharsis. In short, we may say that its structure is such that eighteenth-century audiences were edified but that we are not delighted.

11. Jocelyn Harris, Introduction to *Sir Charles Grandison*, p. xxiii.

Richardson's tripartite engagement with Johnson's Rule left a distinct problem for his successors: how to construct an effective action in which both male and female protagonists were moral paragons. The solution was begun by Fanny Burney and completed by Jane Austen, with some help from Fielding. Fielding's own struggle with the demands of moral action and related problems requires the attention of another essay, but for my purposes here I may say briefly that in his most relevant work, *Tom Jones*, he did present a hero who, despite the long history of moral complaints about him, was intended as a moral paragon—a man incapable of acts inconsistent with his perfect natural benevolence. The defects of Tom Jones's virtues are flaws sufficient to generate an exemplary moral action of the comic kind, in which those defects are displayed as the partial cause of an apparently adverse fate before the actually happy fate generated by his virtues themselves finally appears. The hero's internal activity is thus made causally integral with his external career, but Jones's defects were too gross to pass muster by most eighteenth-century and even later standards (as already noticed), and the comic attenuation Fielding employs to reduce our sense of the seriousness both of Jones's lapses and his potential fate prevents us from having anything like the close view of his internal moral life that Richardson offers in his novels. But with the resource of the comic action provided by Fielding, new solutions were possible to the dilemma which had stultified *Grandison*. If in a comic novel the fateful issues were made less materially serious than in *Tom Jones*, and the hero and heroine given correlated imperfections not amounting to moral faults, a relative closeness of psychological transcription would be possible which could maintain moral interest and significance without imperiling the sacrosanct status of the paragons. The closer and more sensitive the transcription, the less materially momentous the separating moral issue would have to be to achieve affective balance, and here we see the basis of two apparently contradictory views of the Jane Austen novel as on the one hand a tempest in a teapot and on the other a wonder of fine psychological and moral analysis.

The halfway house to Austen was, of course, Fanny Burney. We need be concerned here only with her first novel,
Evelina, for only in that novel, written in obscure anonymity,
was she able to be free from the burdens of propriety which
increasingly crushed the life out of her late novels. Borrowing from *Grandison* her paragon hero and heroine, Lord
Orville and Evelina, Burney reduced their dignity and the
high seriousness of their moral concerns in a way appropriate
to the reduced scope of the comic action in which she placed
them. In the early stages of the story she allows Evelina's
choices to create her own fate in somewhat the same manner
as Tom Jones's do. We are in general assured that Evelina,
beautiful and impeccable but provincial and naive, will eventually, though we know not how, be rewarded by marriage to
Orville, but in the meantime we are treated to the spectacle
of Evelina in her naivete committing faux pas which would
seem to doom her romantic hopes but which are nevertheless overcome with perfect aplomb by the endlessly con-
siderate Orville. By reducing the heroine's defect to a
merely social ineptitude, Burney is able to present her as a
moral paragon while still organically creating a suspense in
which we closely participate. But this solution was imperfect.
The defect attributed to Evelina was lacking in moral
significance and, accidental and circumstantial as it was,
could not be used to generate the whole action. If Evelina
had continued the line of inept social choices with which the
action so effectively begins, she would increasingly have
seemed a fool, unworthy of Orville's love and the reader's
sympathy. The result was that Burney was forced to relocate
the sources of the separating embarrassments outside the
heroine in the Branghtons, a band of low bourgeois relatives
to whom Evelina is not affectionally committed but whose
association she cannot for various reasons, including those of
propriety, escape. The result is a wonderfully excruciating
series of embarrassments, but the point of her predicament
is that she is *not* responsible for her relatives' vulgarity and
other shortcomings, though she seems doomed to suffer
from them.

The climax of this development comes when the Branghtons, in Evelina's name, crudely demand the use of Lord Orville's carriage from his servants and, after setting her down, become involved in an accident that damages the carriage. The sequel is narrated to Evelina next morning by an egregiously conceited vulgarian cousin, who tells her of his visit to ask Lord Orville's pardon, gaining entree again by use of Evelina's name. Lord Orville receives the visit with characteristic politeness, whereupon the cousin offers a further encroachment as follows:

". . . so it come into my head, as he was so affable, that I'd ask him for his custom. So I says, says I, my Lord, says I, if your Lordship i'n't engaged particularly, my father is a silversmith, and he'll be very proud to serve you, says I; and Miss Anville, as danced with you, is his cousin, and she's my cousin too, and she'd be very much obliged to you, I'm sure."

"You'll drive me wild," cried I, starting from my seat, "you have done me an irreparable injury;—but I will hear no more!"—and then I ran into my own room.

I was half frantic, I really raved; the good opinion of Lord Orville seemed now irretrievably lost; . . . for the rest of my life, he would regard me as an object of utter contempt.[12]

This is as far as the secondary line of development can be taken, and Burney immediately after develops out of this the first of a number of largely external melodramatic devices to maintain and increase suspense until such time as she can dramatize the closing fullness of mutual understanding which Orville and Evelina achieve as a prelude to their union. Thus Burney was able neither to generate her action from within her characters nor to make morally significant the internal dimension of the action which she did manage to realize. Her location of her heroine's embarrassments outside of her control but impinging on her sense of responsibility—she suffers from them because she *appears*

---

12. *Evelina; or, The History of a Young Lady's Entrance into the World* (New York: Norton, 1965), p. 234.

responsible for them—is the characteristic feature of her work. Considering the matter a little more closely, we can see that the external embarrassments through which Evelina suffers constitute an appeal to that side of our self which locates the source of our social insecurities in persons or situations other than ourself. It is not I but the others, my relatives, who are so vulgar (our weaker self says), and I am not responsible for them. The nightmare of social embarrassment is exquisitely realized in the book, but it *is* nightmare and, despite the degree to which it is brought to objective dramatization, requires a kind of indulgence of the insecure, snobbish part of our nature against the other side of mature responsibility. The psyche is flattered but not forced to self-knowledge and confrontation of the submerged moral issues involved, which is why we find *Evelina* today still amusing where it does not seem stilted, but not deeply moving.

We can begin to understand Jane Austen's contribution to the development I have been tracing by setting against the episode of Evelina's outrageous cousin an episode from *Northanger Abbey* remarkably similar in structure but significantly different in quality. The Thorpes in concert with Catherine's brother have renewed plans to visit Blaize Castle but discover that Catherine has engaged herself (for a second time) to walk with Miss Tilney. Her friends urge her to cancel the engagement for the sake of their collective pleasure: "she *must* and *should* retract, was instantly the eager cry of both the Thorpes; they must go to Clifton tomorrow, they would not go without her, it would be nothing to put off a mere walk for one day longer, and they would not hear of a refusal."[13] But Catherine will not be moved: "do not urge me, Isabella. I am engaged to Miss Tilney. I cannot go." Still her friends press her, making every unfair and selfish appeal, and her brother joins his voice strongly to

---

13. *Northanger Abbey and Persuasion*, Vol. 3 of The Novels of Jane Austen, ed. R. W. Chapman (London: Oxford University Press, 1933), p. 97. Subsequent references by page number in text.

theirs. "I did not think you had been so obstinate, Catherine; . . . you once were the kindest, best-tempered of my sisters" (pp. 99–100). "I hope I am not less so now," she replied, very feelingly; "but indeed I cannot go. If I am wrong, I am doing what I believe is right." But external circumstance in the person of John Thorpe intervenes to shape her fate (as he had on the previous day deflected her from her first date to walk with Miss Tilney). He has left the discussion for a few minutes and rejoins them with a gay look, saying:

"Well, I have settled the matter, and now we may all go tomorrow with a safe conscience. I have been to Miss Tilney and made your excuses."
"You have not!" cried Catherine.
"I have, upon my soul. Left her this moment. Told her you had sent me to say, that having recollected a prior engagement of going to Clifton with us to-morrow, you could not have the pleasure of walking with her till Tuesday. She said very well, Tuesday was just as convenient to her; so there is an end of all our difficulties.—A pretty good thought of mine—hey?" (p. 100)

Isabella and James are pleased but Catherine is not. "This will not do," she says, and sets off, despite efforts to restrain her, to find Miss Tilney. "I will go after them," said Catherine; "wherever they are I will go after them. It does not signify talking. If I could not be persuaded into doing what I thought wrong, I never will be tricked into it" (p. 101). The analogy of the scene with that where young Branghton speaks to Lord Orville about the carriage is close, but how different the effect. Austen has built into her scene of social embarrassment a dimension of moral agency and responsibility that serves to integrate a serious moral intention with her need to develop an organic and affectively potent action, and this serves to raise the pleasure of the scene into a range of moral value that Burney never touches but that is Austen's characteristic register.

Further consideration of the principle of structural difference in similarity of the scenes from *Evelina* and *Northanger Abbey* allows us to describe a striking relation between *Evelina* and the first drafted of Austen's novels, *Pride and Prejudice*. The title of Austen's novel is, of course, taken from Burney's second novel, *Cecilia*, a fact that helps us to direct our attention to the initial change which Austen made in the paired paragons she drew from *Evelina* as Burney had taken them from *Grandison*. Darcy and Elizabeth are given imperfections not amounting to moral faults—pride and prejudice, in short but adequate description—which serve as the beginning but not the full substance of their separation, a substance which can be seen to derive so remarkably, not from *Cecilia* but from *Pride and Prejudice*, that one might almost say that *Pride and Prejudice* is *Evelina* transformed according to the principle already specified for the scene in *Northanger Abbey*, namely, that those characters represented as responsible for the paragon's adverse fate but as having no claim upon her affections and thus her sense of moral responsibility, be represented as having such a claim and requiring such responsibility.

Evelina is committed early to the unwanted chaperonage of Mme. Duval, her grandmother, a volubly vulgar, aggressive, and declassé woman, through circumstances scarcely known to Evelina and, except for the fact of kinship, alien to her in every respect. Thus developed, Mme. Duval is calculated to be a powerful source of social embarrassment and distress to Evelina without posing any real threat to her intrinsic status or any real problem in moral accommodation to either Evelina or Orville. Austen modulates the almost surrealistic stridencies of this figure into Mrs. Bennet, a normally vulgar mother whose propinquity Elizabeth must from the first acknowledge and respect, while within that respect ultimately conceding that her mother's deficiencies offer Darcy reasonable grounds for his misjudged advice to Bingley. In parallel fashion, the tradesmen cousins of *Evelina*, the Branghtons, become Elizabeth's city cousins, the Gardiners, but whereas the Branghtons are occasions of embarrassment whom Evelina can snobbishly scorn and reject, the Gardiners exemplify fully the cultivated values on which the evaluations of the book are based, so that the values are thus emphatically defined as more than class values, as Darcy's easy acceptance of the Gardiners underlines. Austen makes the same point from another direction with Lady Catherine de Bourgh, a second upper-class relative of Mme. Duval, whose boorishness also bears witness against the identification made in *Evelina* (though to some extent dramatically qualified) of manners with class, and so provides a full expression of the barriers of class pride which Darcy in moral autonomy must cross to claim Elizabeth. The results of this system of transpositions is, like that in *Northanger Abbey*, to bring within the range of consciousness and dramatized moral responsibility elements of feeling which are repressed in *Evelina* and thus to strengthen probability and morally enrich the suspense structure of the book.

A further borrowing involves the conversion of Sir Clement Willoughby into Wickham. In *Evelina*, Willoughby is used as a melodramatic threat to the heroine, a covert external expression of internal sexual feeling. Wickham's sexual attractiveness to Elizabeth is directly represented in an early episode where her muted physical infatuation is expressed in an implicit but distinct fashion that permits psychological honesty but preserves her status as a paragon. The full reality of Wickham's sexual threat is deflected to expression in his off-stage elopement with Lydia; thus the sexual dimension of courtship is acknowledged without compromising either the moral purity or realistic integrity of the story. And these characters are then nicely reintegrated into the main action as a final barrier to the marriage of Elizabeth and Darcy. By this means Darcy can be presented with an opportunity to display with gratifying probability and surprise the full resources of his moral character and intelligence, as Elizabeth had earlier done in revising, against the grain and in response to good evidence, her mistaken estimate of *him*.

In short, Austen in *Pride and Prejudice* achieves a solution to the problems presented to the action novelist by the didactic demands reflected in what I have called Johnson's Rule. She does this by creating a morally impeccable, yet entirely natural, hero and heroine who are first separated from each other, not by circumstance but by significant misjudgments not amounting to moral error, defects deriving

from appropriate strengths of their splendid characters—
Darcy's pride in his inherited station, and Elizabeth's prejudice against Darcy which arises from a proper pride in herself. Austen then amplifies and supports this original rift by
means of the protagonists' relationships to characters whose
qualities and actions are themselves morally problematical,
without damaging the essential impeccability of the protagonists. She thus achieves a novelistic action which is fully and
honestly edifying and completely delightful.[14]

Austen's other two early novels, *Sense and Sensibility* and
Northanger Abbey, also repay analysis as structures resulting
from conflicts between the action structure and didactic
intentions less specific than those expressed in the requirements of Johnson's Rule. Austen's creative intention in
Northanger Abbey was not to parody the gothic novel but
rather to incorporate in a comic action a reference to it that
would define a corrigible defect in the heroine's understanding of the world so as to measure the realistic or confronta-
tional fantasy of the Austenian novel against the deceptive
and indulgent fantasy of the gothic mode. Though the incorporation of the alien matter is as complete as the nature of
the constructional situation allows, the final effect is to
render the action a bit top-heavy and lacking in the full substance of the other books.[15] *Sense and Sensibility* is a work
with which few of Austen's readers are fully satisfied, yet
whose precise formal deficiencies are hard to define. Some
see the formal rationale of the work in an intention to contrast the systems of thought and value of the two sisters, as
indicated in the title. But this merely didactic or thematic

14. My view of the structure of *Pride and Prejudice* has been significantly
influenced by that of Sheldon Sacks as briefly sketched in his "Golden Birds
and Dying Generations," *Comparative Literature Studies*, 6 (September
1969), 285–287. See also Walter Anderson's cognate but more extended
analysis in "Plot, Character, Speech, and Place in *Pride and Prejudice*,"
Nineteenth-Century Fiction, 30 (December 1975), 367–382.

15. For a cogent and much fuller account of the interrelation of the action
structure and gothic material in *Northanger Abbey*, see Walter Anderson,
"From Northanger Abbey to Woodston: Catherine's Education in Common Life," forthcoming in *Philological Quarterly*, 63 (Summer 1984).

conception does not do justice to the actual dramatic power of the work, which can be analyzed quite effectively as developed in action terms. The precise formal situation can be expressed if we say that, though the work is entirely developed as an action, the first choice of a structural core for the book, the choice of the contrasting sisters, cannot be explained as being inherently appropriate to an action as are the choices of Pamela and Mr. B., for instance, or Elizabeth and Darcy, but only as appropriate to a didactic intention. We have in *Sense and Sensibility*, then, a different kind of example of the impingement upon the action form of the requirement that novels be morally instructive. The idea that Austen in this instance built an action novel on a didactic base I believe can be used to develop an analysis which will explain quite well its feel to us and its puzzlements.

Austen's later novels—except perhaps *Persuasion*, where, eyes to the sea, her art looks toward fresher formal possibilities—are touched in fairly obvious ways by the pressures of eighteenth-century didacticism. After her the action novel was to undergo new lines of development, but the novel of moral action and its concomitant formal problems came to an end with her, partly because the line had reached its perfection, but more largely because later novelists threw Johnson's Rule and related didactic baggage out the window, as Becky Sharp did his *Dictionary*, en route from the restraints of the academy to new and less trammeled pleasures.

Women and the City

"Sir, when a man is tired of London, he is tired of life; for there is in London all that life can afford."[1] So said Johnson to Boswell when the younger man worried lest London might lose its fascination if he actually lived there. For *a man*, eighteenth-century London provided all that life could offer. For a woman, its provision might prove more problematic.

Nineteen years after Johnson made his pronouncement, twenty-one-year-old Jane Austen wrote her sister Cassandra about her difficulties in planning a short trip to London. She cannot go, she reports, unless a respectable family will take her in, and no obvious possibility presents itself. She must also make arrangements for returning home, but this problem she decides to ignore. "My Father," she writes, "will be so good as to fetch home his prodigal Daughter from Town, I hope, unless he wishes me to walk the Hospitals, Enter at the Temple, or mount Guard at St. James."[2] Her brief fantasy of masculine independence, of pursuing a profession forbidden to women—doctor, lawyer, or soldier—

1. *Boswell's Life of Johnson*, ed. George Birkbeck Hill, rev. L. F. Powell, 6 vols. (Oxford: Clarendon Press, 1934), III, 178.
2. *Jane Austen's Letters to Her Sister Cassandra and Others*, ed. R. W. Chapman, 2nd ed. (London: Oxford University Press, 1952), September 18, 1796, p. 17.

exemplifies an imaginative freedom that substitutes for
opportunity in the external world. Women, Austen believes,
cannot be allowed liberty in London because they might
enact forbidden wishes. The titillation of this thought, and
of the resentment she allows herself to hint, must satisfy
her. The London evoked by the writer's imagination provides opportunities unknown to women in the country—and
equally unknown in the real city. The unreal city offers
fulfillment; it may even create new desires. Jane Austen's
father will of course want to "protect" her from it.

The imaginary city of eighteenth-century novels, like
Austen's fantasy-metropolis, encourages female dreams of
self-determination, particularly in sexual matters. As
officially articulated in tracts, sermons, and educational
manuals, the much-reiterated upper-class ideology of sex in
eighteenth-century England left little room for overt female
agency, or even for female desire. Sequentially the property
of fathers and of husbands, women passed from hand to
hand, ideally without inconvenient personal wishes: not
agents but objects of exchange. The hegemony of fathers
often seemed to exceed that of husbands. In a work entitled
A Father's Legacy to His Daughters, for example, the well-
known moralist John Gregory warned young women against
revealing love for, even interest in, a man. "If you love
him, let me advise you never to discover to him the full
extent of your love, no, not although you marry him."[3] Few
women really love a man anyhow (most only feel gratitude),
and love is dangerous for its possessor. "Miserable will be
your fate, if you allow an attachment to steal on you before
you are sure of a return."[4] Such advice implies an assessment of female desire as weakness (or perhaps as threat).
Utter passivity provided women's most acceptable resource.
If never to *show* love strengthened a woman's position,
never to *feel* it might fortify her yet more. Women, in
Gregory's representative view, could participate in no equal

3. 4th ed. (London: W. Strahan, 1774), pp. 87–88.
4. Ibid., p. 105.

emotional exchange; they must remain recipients. Psychically they must preserve their secure roles as daughters, even if they married. Gregory tells his girls repeatedly that no man but he will ever treat them without dissimulation. The moral is clear: Stick to Daddy, at least emotionally.

Although the passion-free woman hardly provides a promising subject for fiction, many eighteenth-century novels celebrate her (and some damn in lurid terms her imagined lascivious sister). Apparently assuming marriage as the proper goal of female existence, fiction nonetheless often stresses the hazards involved in leaving Father. Disapproval of female desire reveals itself both by omission (passion rarely manifests itself distinctly in heroines) and by deflection. Standard plots about women (seduction and betrayal, or attempted seduction and resistance, with *Clarissa* and *Pamela* as the prototypes) displace desire onto men. A supplementary form of displacement locates sexual danger, as well as sexual opportunity, in the city. Pamela suffers and triumphs in rural seclusion, but more typical fictional maidens find their sexual fates in urban settings: settings which, by the multiple temptations and opportunities they provide, may enable young women disastrously or successfully to escape their fathers.

In the moral geography of fictional eighteenth-century England, London supplies a locus for energy. The center of trade, institutional exchange, it serves also as symbolic center of passion: lust, gluttony, wrath, envy, avarice, and profligacy. Samuel Richardson's *Clarissa* (1747–48) and Fanny Burney's *Evelina* (1778) alike use the situation of a young woman in the city to explore personal systems of sexual economics. Both heroines try, or seem to try, to leave their fathers; for both the drama of filial devotion contesting with desire for personal agency assumes central importance. The imagined metropolis provides an arena for their feelings and fantasies to play themselves out, but only behind intricate disguises. These women discover in and through the city temporary means of assertion, yet their efforts end in self-subordination. Trying to make action the instrument of desire, they learn how severely female desire must limit itself, how difficult it proves for women to participate even metaphorically as agents in London's commerce. For novelists to investigate such issues in fictional terms implies at least their preconscious awareness of the psychological difficulties orthodox moralities create for women. External and internal pressures to remain a child contend, in these fictional women, with need for self-determination. The result, important novelists suggest, can hardly prove happy.

The city as symbolic locus has acquired, by the mid-eighteenth century, a fairly well-defined, if self-contradictory, set of associations. As Max Byrd has demonstrated, the century's mythology of the city reveals much ambivalence about the moral implications of symbolic London, an environment calling "to mind irresistible Hogarthian images of vitality," but also "a squalor, a hopelessness, that we cannot easily imagine today."[5] Novels insist on the city's dangers more than its despair: the press gang that captures Tom Jones, the sexual adventurers who threaten Evelina and her fictional sisters. Yet fiction also conveys London's magnetic attraction, particularly for young men.

And young women? They, too, felt the attraction—and often suffered as a result. Minor eighteenth-century novels provide a revealing context for the two works that principally concern me here. Reiterating a few moralistic points about the city, they establish assumptions on which Richardson and Burney draw, and they suggest the restrictive power of those assumptions. Crude and repetitive in plot, they yet help to expose the ideological substructure of more powerful fiction.

The fictional city provides a synecdoche for the "public" realm. For women, the "public" did not imply a locale for commerce or profession, for political or military action. A woman's business was to marry as well as possible. London did not allow women to sit in Parliament, but it provided abundant opportunities for female self-display: there a

5. *London Transformed: Images of the City in the Eighteenth Century* (New Haven: Yale University Press, 1978), p. 3.

woman could go about her "business" by showing herself at theatre and assembly, making herself an object of sexual commerce. Metaphorically, London's space and what goes on in it oppose the familial and the orderly hierarchies of traditional upper-middle-class existence. In a midcentury epistolary novel, the young woman who has chosen the country writes to her city friend, "You, I know, cannot perceive any charms in such a rude retreat, fit to engage the attention of a fine lady. Here are no powdered beaus, or gilt equipages, none of the splendid allurements with which ladies of your vivacity, are apt to be captivated; but for my part, a natural tincture of gravity may possibly make me more easily support the absence of what your gayer disposition may induce you to consider as the very essence of happiness."[6] Felicia, the writer of this letter, goes on to describe the harmonious family life and rational system of education marking her aunt's household. The lover she finds in the vicinity speaks from the heart. "The modest rusticity of my spark," she writes her friend, "so very different from the confident addresses of the town beaus, must make him seem a very odd sort of creature to you, who are so used to hear yourself praised in lofty strains, that you will perhaps be surprised that there should be any other way of touching the heart."[7]

This passage exemplifies several fictional clichés about the city. Women who yearn for metropolitan life thereby convict themselves of superficiality. They prefer flattery to feeling; they dedicate themselves to pleasure. Cultivating, valuing, and valued for their "vivacity," they thus hint at their own sexuality. Their lives lack the stability and the order of rural existence.

One of the city's sinister aspects is its attributed lack of saving community. Imagined as a chaos of unknown people without ties to one another, it cannot protect the defenseless.

6. Mary Collyer, *Felicia to Charlotte*, 2 vols. in 1 (New York: Garland, 1974), I, 3–4. Reprint of 1744 ed., vol. 1; 1749 ed., vol. 2.

7. Ibid., I, 23.

Its very architecture and geography embody threat: whorehouses and madhouses (*Clarissa*), mazes where one loses one's way and encounters menacing men (*Evelina*), crowded theatres and opera houses. Any building may conceal corruption. When young Henrietta Worthy, heroine of a minor novel, ventures to London, she is almost raped in a house rented by a man for the sole purpose of violating young women. Neighbors have "often heard the Cry of distressed Innocence," but because they do not want to get in trouble, they do not interfere.[8] Women lured into such buildings escape, like Henrietta, only by dint of much screaming, much fainting—and good luck or providential intervention.

Like Mrs. Sinclair's establishment in *Clarissa*, this house where women suffer presents a plausible appearance to the world. London is a city of appearances. Women, to be successful there, must concentrate on attractive physical and social self-preservation, thus risking high costs in alienation. Often unable to distinguish between substance and surface, they make bad choices. One frivolous young woman, in a work called *The Auction*, wants nothing to do with the "plain, honest looking Gentleman" who woos her; scorning him as a "Country Booby," she complains, "why he is just like my Father: I should be ashamed to be seen in Town with him."[9] Her belief in the glamour of the "Town" leads her to think social surface the only index of worth; she cannot understand the moral substance her father represents, and she can pretend to escape her father by rejecting her lover, a fantasy for which the narrative voice condemns her.

But even in highly conventional fiction, matters turn out to be more complicated than this example would suggest. *The Auction* also presents a "good" sister, who marries a man enthusiastically endorsed by her father. Shortly before

8. [Edward Kimber], *Maria: The Genuine Memoirs of a Young Lady of Rank and Fortune*, 2 vols. in 1 (New York: Garland, 1974), I, 110. Reprint of 1770 ed.

9. Mrs. A. Woodfin, *The Auction*, 2 vols. in 1 (New York: Garland, 1975), II, 46. Reprint of 1770 ed.

the wedding, she discovers that her fiancé wishes to display her as a prize to London society. "Mr. *Worthy* too said, that next to calling *Fanny* his own, the greatest Pleasure he had any Idea of, would be to appear with her in public, and enjoy the exulting Pleasure of seeing the Croud of envious Beaux adoring his *Fanny*, while he knew himself to be the sole Possessor of her Heart."[10] The man apparently anticipates sexual possession less eagerly than he fantasizes the competitive satisfaction of seeing others see his Fanny as desirable. Neither the narrator nor any character within the fiction conveys the slightest disapproval. The city's marital commerce allows men to express triumph over a profitable transaction; women, only the objects of such transactions, have no such liberty.

What a woman does matters less than how she is seen. Thus a character in Helen Williams' *Julia* deliberately arrives late at a play: "she chose to excite attention by disturbing the performance, and drawing the looks of the audience from the stage to herself . . . [H]er whole mind was occupied in performing her own part gracefully, while she remained an object of general observation."[11] This woman understands social reality. She who presents herself as an attractive commodity can hope to fare well in London's marriage market.

The novels I have cited generally evoke negative aspects of the metropolis as a female environment. The city's appeal to young women's narcissism, its stress on the superficial, its insistent objectification of women, its population of strangers, its opportunities for concealed corruption all endanger. Pope could gently tease a young woman about her boredom in the country, while tacitly approving her preference for urban excitement; Congreve imagined a Millamant both dazzling and virtuous in the city environment. But by the mid-eighteenth century, London's symbolic opposition to orderly family life caused novelists to use it almost entirely as a locus of instability and of danger.

10. Ibid., II, 165.
11. 2 vols. (New York: Garland, 1974), I, 35.

Richardson and Burney, writing about women in the city, on the whole accept as given the urban characteristics evoked by minor novelists. Yet they also acknowledge other possibilities, including that of a woman's growth through city experience. Investigating the problematics of female passivity, they tacitly note the sexual implications of prohibitions on self-directed action, suggesting ingenious possibilities for female self-assertion within a restrictive social context. Finally, however, they reaffirm the necessary subordination of women to fathers.

Both *Clarissa* and *Evelina* use a young woman's interaction with an unfamiliar urban environment to evoke social and sexual dilemmas and solutions. Clarissa, of course, comes to London under peculiar circumstances. Alternately captive and fugitive, she establishes a relationship to the city bearing little obvious resemblance to that of the numerous fictional heroines who journey to London seeking their fortunes in marriage. Evelina belongs to this latter class, although marriage comprises for her no conscious goal: she thinks she wants a father, not a husband. Both young women, defining themselves in an alien setting, discover in the process the means of agency. Yet Clarissa must die to assert herself, and Evelina must suppress her own capacities: their solutions are at best ambiguous.

To achieve agency even briefly, they must deal with their sexuality—if only by finding out how to deny it. *Evelina* as well as *Clarissa* reveals constant submerged reference to the sexual issues which cannot be fully articulated. The city provides a new locus for examining this pattern of reference. Because it encourages literal buying and selling of objects as well as metaphorical trade in people, because it facilitates both passion and calculation, it invites attention to the intersections of feeling and contrivance in the women characters who enter it, and to the sexual and emotional economics they develop.

Clarissa first rejects, then embraces the idea of London as a personal environment. Like Lovelace, she thinks of the city initially as a place of passion, and she fears that in it she will prove unable to control appearances so as to insure the good opinion of others. Finally, though, the city of trade and of churches provides her with the metaphors of successful sublimation.

In an early exchange between Clarissa and Anna Howe over what course the beleaguered young woman should follow to escape a marriage forced on her by her family, Anna observes, "London, I am told, is the best hiding-place in the world."[12] Clarissa rejects such a refuge. "But supposing I could remain there concealed, to what might not my youth, my sex, and unacquaintedness with the ways of that great, wicked town, expose me!—I should hardly dare to go to church for fear of being discovered . . . Who knows but I might pass for a kept mistress; and that, although nobody came to me, yet, that every time I went out, it might be imagined to be in pursuance of some assignation?" (Letter 82, I, 422). Her fantasy about London focuses unerringly on the sexual—but not, as one might expect, on the danger of rape or seduction. Instead, as fearfully as another woman might conjure up images of violation, Clarissa imagines someone else imagining her as a sexual being. She makes her own sexuality a fiction two removes from actuality. In the fantasized environment of the "great, wicked town," unknown people may fancy such things. Clarissa's own leap of the imagination betrays both her intensifying (though not fully acknowledged) awareness of sexual possibility and her decreasing confidence. At the beginning of her correspondence, she declared, "Upon my word, I am sometimes tempted to think that we make the world allow for and respect us as we please, if we can but be sturdy in our own wills, and set out accordingly" (Letter 5, I, 22). Now she no longer believes she can make the world respect her. Poised on the brink of her disastrous escape from home and family, she begins to fear that security depends on familiarity. And

12. Samuel Richardson, *Clarissa*, 4 vols. (London: J. M. Dent, 1932), Letter 81, I, 416. Subsequent references by page number in text.

she responds, before any actual experience of the city, to London as a place of appearances.

If Clarissa thinks of London as an environment where others may speculate dangerously about her, Lovelace believes it a locale for full expression of his own sexuality, a place of licensed self-indulgence and of relentless temptation. He imagines that urban "diversions," particularly the theater, that center of female self-display, will insensibly weaken the moral resistance of a woman unaccustomed to their lures. Since Clarissa fails to yield to temptation, Lovelace resorts to rape, helped by women who embody for him, for Clarissa, and presumably for the reader, all the city's corruption. Clarissa's subsequent frenzy makes her beg her tormentor to lock her up "in some private mad-house about this town; for such it seems there are, never more to be seen" (Letter 33, III, 213). Still concerned with the impression she makes on others, she rejects this form of narcissism by imagining the utter obscurity she now longs for, conjuring up a city of private madhouses, places full of tortured passion like her own.

From the point of view of Clarissa's family, the city's population of strangers guarantees danger. Mrs. Hodges, a family servant, articulates this view: "Won knoes not what company you may have bin forced to keep, sen you went away, you know, maddam. Exscuse me, maddam; but Lundon is a pestilent place" (Letter 77, III, 334). The fact that no one *knows* the city's inhabitants epitomizes London's "pestilence." Unpredictable, unknown people may not share moral or social assumptions of the rural gentry. They may allow themselves forbidden indulgences, introducing those "forced to keep" company with them to dangerous pleasures.

The family's vague projections of moral corruption further contaminate Clarissa in their minds. Her father curses her, wishing her misfortune in this life and the next; the burden weighs heavily on Clarissa's mind. She has defied patriarchal authority in leaving home, but it continues to dominate her; she feels the rape itself as fulfillment of her father's malediction. Lovelace and Mr. Harlowe thus mingle in her consciousness, but after her violation she begins to free herself from both, although she continues to reiterate her wish that her father should repeal his cruel decree.

As her psychic state changes, her own projections onto the city alter; she ceases to feel alien. Fleeing the emotional chaos of Mrs. Sinclair's establishment, she finds shelter with a man named Smith "—a glove-*maker*, as well as *seller*. His wife is the shopkeeper. A dealer also in stockings, ribbands, snuff, and perfumes. A matron-like woman, plain-hearted, and prudent. The husband an honest, industrious man. And they live in good understanding with each other: a proof with me that their hearts are right" (Letter 92, III, 386). In the Smith family she can remain private; from her refuge there she can escape to church, no longer concerned, she explains, about her appearance, no longer worried about what strangers think of her. Others have become adjuncts to her private drama rather than shapers of it. Although in fact strangers' false speculations, reported to her parents, postpone familial reconciliation, her attention focuses now on other matters. Clarissa continues to explain her downfall as partly occasioned by the fact that she "knew nothing of the town, or its ways" (Letter 121, III, 505). But—"This great town," she writes Anna Howe, "wicked as it is, wants not opportunities of being better; having daily prayers at several churches in it; and I am desirous, as my strength will permit, to embrace those opportunities" (Letter 7, IV, 27). She believes that she can more readily cultivate her piety in London than in her friend's vicinity.

Clarissa's ability to accept so serenely existence in the wicked town declares her sublimation of sexual feeling after Lovelace's violation. Before the rape, her shifting responses to Lovelace's machinations registered his erratic manipulativeness, but also her self-contested passion, revealing itself in glimpses only to be once more repressed. Lovelace encourages Clarissa's intense anxiety; reality justifies it. The city terrifies her. She can depend on no one; unfamiliar physical surroundings correspond to moral and emotional perplexity. Clarissa's uprooting from the familial setting and from the countryside that comfortably contains the gentry

symbolizes her more fundamental uprooting from the non-
sexual role of good girl, grandfather's favorite. Solmes'
repulsiveness, Lovelace's attraction, draw her into acting—
without full involvement of her will—on the basis of her
own sexual response.

Important English novels in the eighteenth century, examples of a genre frequently linked by historians with the growing middle class, virtually ignore the commerce that created
this class, of makers and sellers, one of whom comforts
Clarissa. Defoe almost alone writes of trade and its analo-
gues in crime and colonization. Tom Jones, Tristram
Shandy, Amelia's husband—none works for a living, except
at soldiering. The Smiths are minor figures in the complexities of *Clarissa*.[13] Yet one may wonder why Richardson has
Clarissa seeking asylum with tradespeople rather than, say,
with the conventional impoverished widow who rents rooms
to eke out a scanty inherited income. The Harlowes are
often said to represent bourgeois consciousness; the Smiths,
however, much more directly epitomize the rising bourgeoisie.

In a strange scene late in the novel, Lovelace comes to
seek Clarissa at the Smiths' and finds her absent. He falls
into a kind of manic fit stimulated by the shop and shopkeepers. First, he pretends to be a customer, demanding
washballs, snuff, and gloves. In a typical act of phallic
aggression, he attempts to tear out one servant's teeth to
replace another's, assuring the victim, "I will pay thee a
good price, man: don't struggle thus!" (Letter 55, IV, 130).
He waits on a female customer, telling her that he would

13. Previous commentators have ignored the Smiths. Ian Watt, *The Rise
of the Novel* (Berkeley: University of California Press, 1957), initiated attention to class structure as an issue in *Clarissa*, but he does not concern himself with the Smiths. Even Terry Eagleton's recent *The Rape of Clarissa:
Writing, Sexuality and Class Struggle in Samuel Richardson* (Oxford: Basil
Blackwell, 1982) neglects the role of Clarissa's London experience in her
development. Two important recent studies, Terry Castle *Clarissa's Ciphers*
(Ithaca: Cornell University Press, 1982), and William Beatty Warner, *Reading Clarissa* (New Haven: Yale University Press, 1979), concentrate on
problems of interpretation in reading such a text.

have treated her had she not been so homely. Then a pretty woman attracts his attention. He flirts with her through various purchases, first refuses, then accepts the sixpence she offers him, finally seizes her hand and beseeches "her to walk into the back shop with me" (IV, 132). At last he flings down money and departs, "the people about the door seeming to be in good humour with me; one crying, A pleasant gentleman, I warrant him!" (IV, 133).

Lovelace considers shopkeeping something to be mocked, parodied, overthrown, not merely an object of aristocratic disdain. The scene of small trade arouses all his aggressive instincts. Something more complicated than snobbery has awakened his passion.

At a profound level, the concept of trade might well trouble Lovelace. Something given, something gained, fair exchange; to a man yearning to have his status as "emperor" universally acknowledged, a man even in love far more deeply concerned with power than reciprocity, a man embodying the principle of male domination—selling snuff for sixpence embodies all he detests. When he converts trade itself into aggressive power, assuring a servant of a good price for his teeth, he can enjoy himself; or when he openly sexualizes it, as in his exchange with the two female customers. He desperately declares control, even as he loses Clarissa (away at church when he appears at the Smiths') and loses his ability to make everything happen as he would have it. The world of trade threatens not only his aristocratic but his patriarchal assumptions.

At the center of the novel seethes the struggle between Clarissa's increasing spiritual power and Lovelace's diminishing psychic and physical power. In the background the Harlowe family, dominated by tyrannical father and brother, insist on their false economics, their perverted mode of exchange with Clarissa as chief commodity. Clarissa flees from dehumanizing patriarchal economics to equally dehumanizing patriarchal totalitarianism. After Lovelace "can go no farther" (Letter 29, III, 196), Clarissa finds a more comforting London centered in the tradespeople's dwelling, where man and woman live in marital harmony and share commercial activity. The Smiths' healthy commerce opposes the Harlowes' perverse counterpart; their reliance on exchange contrasts with Lovelace's energy of appropriation. Lovelace's effort to mock, threaten, and disorganize their little economy creates only temporary disorder. The Smiths hardly protest; bystanders smile at the whims of a "gentleman," someone who does not know any better. The order these shopkeepers generate through their modest trade survives Lovelace's depredations, facilitates Clarissa's self-spiritualization, empowers them more securely than Lovelace can ever empower himself, and establishes the tone for Clarissa's final benign vision of London.

In Richardson's mythology of the city, then, the metropolis incorporates contrasting meanings. It represents, and by its manifest danger criticizes, the disorder of uncontrolled individual passion, embodied in the throng of strangers. It menaces women in particular with sexual energies they have learned to deny in themselves; onto its unknown inhabitants, women, like novelists, project inadmissible feelings. But the potential of a city meeting a woman's needs (at least Clarissa's idiosyncratic needs: it provides opportunities to buy a coffin, sell clothes, attend church any day at virtually any hour; and to remain concealed)—this benign potential also exists, emblemized in the uprightness of petty trade. As a place of indulgence, London embodies threat; as a place of business, security. The fair trade of the Smiths, moreover, provides a metaphor for the crucial exchange Clarissa finally initiates: one father for another.

With the Smith family, Clarissa for the first time achieves a measure of control over her own life and escapes male domination: the goal Jane Austen fleetingly imagined in such different terms. She can express her independence, given her tragic circumstances, only by orchestrating her own dying, but she makes of that dying a dramatic triumph, through it substantiating also her psychic dominance over all who know her. In London, where appearance reigns, she has perfected a mode of self-presentation superbly adapted to her purposes; she has discovered her own form of agency, insistently asexual, yet above all a response to her sexual situation and experience and to the system of sex as commerce. As Clarissa develops her means of self-support, she achieves ironic mastery, no longer the victim of other people's manipulations, only of her own. At last she successfully manages to be seen exactly as she chooses.

The Smiths have little apparent effect on Clarissa's operations; they belong to the supporting cast. Their way of life, however, provides a model of balanced exchange. Selling clothes, buying a coffin, making her peace with her family, trading her father for another Father, Clarissa establishes her form of commerce and her quiet triumph. Lovelace's autocracy and her father lose power; the young woman's humility helps her achieve self-sufficiency.

That Clarissa can dramatize herself and control her destiny only by dying suggests the severe limitation of spiritual economics as a resource in a materialist society. To be sure, Lovelace loses more unequivocally than does Clarissa, never truly possessing the woman he wants, no longer able to believe in his own utter supremacy, essentially deserted by his closest male friend, rejected by his family, finally dead and (presumably) damned. Clarissa, on the other hand, dies acclaimed virtually as a saint, arranging the details of her passing for maximum dramatic effect, loved and mourned by all who know her: a Christian triumph. Nonetheless—she dies. She cannot survive her sense of violation, outrage, and spiritual as well as physical damage; she cannot survive her father's curse. Her society provides no appropriate place for a woman so damaged. Alive, she would possess little power, even of choice. Dying, then dead, she exercises enormous force.

Clarissa's death criticizes her society not only as the spiritual criticizes the material but as the oppressed criticizes the oppressor. The Smiths provide a model of cooperative, productive marriage and of fair trade. The city supplies churches, good people, a refuge, and many watchers, for Clarissa's apotheosis as well as for her violation. But, like the country, it offers Clarissa no opportunity for balanced relationship, no fair exchange. Its whorehouses and madhouses after all tell a profound truth: women who

believe they can make the world respect them take large
risks. The world will, however, readily respect them in their
dying. Richardson's novel, daring in its imagining of a
woman determining terms of exchange, draws back from
exploring the full possibilities of such imagining.

The connection of commerce, sex, and female agency
emerges more emphatically in *Evelina*, in which the central
character discovers her powers quite specifically by struggling
to separate herself from the realm of commercial energy.
Pitting the middle and the upper classes against one another,
the city demands of Evelina complicated and perplexing
choices.

Toward the end of the novel, the fool Lovel mocks Captain Mirvan for supposing London "a mere *show*, that may
be seen by being *looked at.*"[14] As usual, this idle fop reveals
more truth than he knows. More stringently than *Clarissa*,
Evelina investigates implications of social class in urban life,
and it concentrates on the woman's experience of urban
problematics.[15] It does not, however, provide images of commerce, nor does it imagine any way for women to escape
fathers.

14. Fanny Burney, *Evelina, or The History of a Young Lady's Entrance into
the World* (New York: Norton, 1965), p. 379.

15. Until very recently, commentary on *Evelina* has followed the lead of
Joyce Hemlow, "Fanny Burney and the Courtesy Books," *PMLA* 65
(1950), 732–761, and *The History of Fanny Burney* (Oxford: Oxford University Press, 1958). Hemlow considers the novel a form of conduct book,
instructing readers in propriety. Michael Adelstein's volume in the Twayne
series, *Fanny Burney* (1968), which calls its subject "Fanny" throughout,
apparently assumes the naiveté of her novelistic characterizations. In
"Ev'ry Woman Is at Heart a Rake,'" *Eighteenth-Century Studies*, 8 (1974),
27–46, I examined Evelina's use of innocence as a form of sexual attraction; in *Imagining a Self* (Cambridge: Harvard University Press, 1976), I
investigated Evelina's passivity in terms different from those of the present
study. Rose Marie Cutting, "Defiant Women: The Growth of Feminism in
Fanny Burney's Novels," *Studies in English Literature*, 17 (1977), 519–530,
argues for the importance of Mrs. Selwyn as the type of the forceful woman
of whom Burney essentially approves.

Before Evelina reaches London, her guardian's epistolary comments recall a familiar mythic view of the city. Mr. Villars evokes a city devoid of physical reality but embodying threat: physical, moral, and psychological. Most of all, he worries about London's possible effects on Evelina's imagination.

> But can your ladyship be serious in proposing to introduce her to the gaieties of a London life? Permit me to ask, for what end, or for what purpose? A youthful mind is seldom totally free from ambition; to curb that, is the first step to contentment, since to diminish expectation is to increase enjoyment. I apprehend nothing more than too much raising her hopes and her views, which the natural vivacity of her disposition would render but too easy to effect. (p. 8)

To diminish expectation is to increase enjoyment. Precisely the contrary is true. In fact Villars wishes to *decrease* Evelina's possibilities of enjoyment. Far from severe as a father-surrogate, he yet insists on remaining in control. Enjoyment implies possible self-indulgence, perhaps an escape from compliance, perhaps boredom with the country. Enjoyment provided by Lord Orville allows Evelina to experience the triumph of imagination over reason. When the girl leaves London for the first time, her guardian writes,

> Your evident concern at leaving London is very natural, and yet it afflicts me. I ever dreaded you being too much pleased with a life of dissipation, which youth and vivacity render but too alluring; and I almost regret the consent for your journey, which I had not the resolution to withhold.
> Alas, my child, the artlessness of your nature, and the simplicity of your education, alike unfit you for the thorny paths of the great and busy world . . . Not only my views, but my hopes for your future life, have ever centered in the country. Shall I own to you, that however I may differ from Captain Mirvan in other respects, yet my opinion of the town, its manners, inhabitants, and diversions, is much upon a level with his own? Indeed it is the general harbour of fraud and of folly, of duplicity and of impertinence; and I wish few things more fervently, than that you may have taken a lasting leave of it. (pp. 104–105)

Mr. Villars then fantasizes about Evelina's safe future as "the ornament of her neighbourhood" and demands her assurance that "this one short fortnight spent in town has not undone the work of seventeen years spent in the country" (p. 105).

This clergyman's description of the city as the harbor of fraud and of folly has a weight quite different from that of the traditional Horatian contrast between corrupt city and virtuous country. The guardian's "work" in the country has made Evelina securely his own; his ardent wish to keep her in rural retirement speaks his concern for preserving an exclusive relationship. More than once he alludes to his fantasy of "closing these joy-streaming eyes in [Evelina's] presence, and breathing my last faint sighs in her loved arms!" (p. 387)—a fantasy that he does not abandon at the prospect of the girl's marriage but that nonetheless retains a distinctly sexual character.

Indeed, although Villars barely alludes to the sexual menace of the city, all his anxieties have sexual bearing. His reiterated concern that Evelina's "vivacity" makes her vulnerable, like his eagerness to confine her "expectation," suggests his desire to prevent her awareness of her own sexuality. The dreaded stimulation of the city involves heightening of sexual consciousness, enlargement of sexual possibility. To keep a young woman in the country keeps her safe from, among other things, excessive self-knowledge.

The city Evelina actually experiences, less completely sexualized than Villars' imagining of it, threatens and instructs her both through the commercial middle class and the upper classes. Evelina's ambiguous social position gives her a foot in both worlds. Her father, an aristocrat, refuses to acknowledge her; she therefore cannot quite claim membership in the upper classes. Moreover, she has a vulgar grandmother, Mme. Duval, a woman of dubious social origins (at the time of her marriage a barmaid) and of reprehensible social behavior. Like other novelistic heroes and heroines, Evelina aspires upward. Her detestation of her shopkeeping relatives and of her aggressive grandmother emphasizes her desire to separate herself utterly from everything they represent.

Evelina's interest in the city focuses entirely on its aristocratic aspects. The assemblies and balls of the upper classes provide for a young woman places of opportunity as well as of danger: opportunity to attract a man into the marriage which will establish her social security. For good or for evil, the city is the place to meet men. If the aristocratic city thus associates itself with sex, however, it also relies heavily on an intricate and, for the outsider, virtually incomprehensible code of manners, a code readily distinguishing those who "belong," a kind of behavior designed partly to conceal the sexual. Never fully articulated, therefore difficult to master, this code is taken as an index of morality as well as of good breeding. The men commenting on Evelina's deviations use emphatic moral language; her self-castigation for errors of decorum sounds even more extravagant. She experiences the social code always as restriction; its chief law is never to act from feeling. All Evelina's mistakes stem from responding to her own immediate emotional needs. Thus she refuses to dance with one man, only to accept another, violating the rules of proper behavior; she flees her vulgar relatives and finds herself dangerously alone in a carriage with Sir Clement; she insults a fop by laughing at him. As she learns better behavior, she learns to spend more time in silence, to cultivate her "innocence," to proclaim to Lord Orville her inability to act and think for herself. When Lord Merton seizes her hand, Evelina responds by declaring her helplessness: "Would to Heaven . . . that I too had a brother!—and then I should not be exposed to such treatment" (p. 296). So she proves her eligibility; Lord Orville repeatedly and positively responds to her expressed desire to be taken care of.

The aristocratic city (which extends metaphorically to Bristol and Bath) educates Evelina in an unWordsworthian wise passiveness. Her relations with men emphasize the need for repression and denial; she must protect herself against verbal and physical assault by showing no vulnerability. Her guardian warns her severely against her open

emotional response to Lord Orville. She learns to present
herself as a frightened child, and she gets her reward.

From the city of the commercial middle class she learns
different lessons—but not the lesson of fair trade. The early
readers of *Evelina* responded with enthusiasm to the terrific
vitality of Mme. Duval, the former barmaid; the Branghtons,
who run a silversmith's shop; Mr. Smith, renter of the room
above the shop; and Captain Mirvan, a seafaring man of vulgar propensities. These people appear to have no code of
manners at all. They act from impulse, expressing immediate feelings with no effort at control. Siblings quarrel in public; Evelina's grandmother articulates violent anger on every
conceivable occasion; people frequently use one another;
Captain Mirvan plays sadistic practical jokes. Evelina feels
only revulsion at such conduct (thus proving, presumably,
her aristocratic nature). The very aspect of London changes
when she has to associate with the vulgar: "Indeed, to me,
London now seems a desert" (p. 157). Most of the serious
trouble she gets into results from her contact with these people. Even Sir Clement's attempted seduction follows
Evelina's effort to escape Mme. Duval and the Branghtons;
the insulting letter allegedly from Lord Orville responds to
her written disclaimer of responsibility for her relatives'
behavior.

Nonetheless, these middle-class vulgarians have an important effect on Evelina: *they make her act.* Although to Lord
Orville she professes helplessness, in response to her unat-
tractive relatives and their associates, she does things, right
or wrong. She rescues Macartney; she refuses Mr. Smith's
invitation (commenting on his surprise at her spirit); she
rejects young Branghton, despite her grandmother's pressure;
and more actively, she uses her letters to Villars to formulate
judgments of these people in vivid terms.

The two social classes composing Evelina's city, then, call
attention to opposed aspects of the heroine's development.
To fit herself for an aristocratic husband, she insists on her
helplessness and passivity and her need for guidance and
help. In contrast, her association with the vulgar demands of
her active judgment and literal action to dramatize her

separation from and opposition to them. She grows up, in effect, by spending time with the middle classes, but she remains childlike, innocent, fearful, and passive in relation to the upper classes.

Evelina reverses the symbolic equations of *Clarissa*. The aspects of London under Lovelace's symbolic aegis include whorehouse, madhouse, and prison: places of passion uncontrolled and punished; the shopkeeping Smiths create an urban order of predictability and restraint. In Burney's novel, on the other hand, shopkeepers indulge in indecorous displays of violent feeling, and aristocrats, dealing with their own kind, follow a demanding and restrictive code. (The aristocratic assaults on Evelina's virtue derive from ignorance of her true birth. While she remains a "nobody," she constitutes fair game.) Locating polarized qualities in opposed social spheres, both novels use London and its class structure as ways of rendering internal division. Impulse toward indulged passion and desire for restraint, these contrasted sides of female nature find correlatives in the fictional city.

But the two works convey different views of the relation between action and passion. Evelina can escape her foster-father's submerged sexuality only by allying herself with a man happy to play a father's role as well as a husband's and by locating her original father and winning his devotion. She must obscure to herself and to others the fact that she actively wishes marriage; she must deny her sexuality in order to find the opportunity to express it. Although she grows up, escapes her guardian's smothering benevolence, and gets the man she wants, she achieves these ends only by pretending to remain a child. Her life in the city indeed enlarges her imagination, as Villars feared it would; her encounters with the vulgar help her discover the capacity to act. But she fears the power that Mrs. Selwyn, the independent woman of good birth and powerful tongue, embodies; she will not, like that aggressive older woman, herself choose to act forcefully in the aristocratic context. The city teaches her incompatible lessons, but neither she nor the writer who created her appears to recognize their incompatibility. Evelina retreats to her aristocratic marriage as though she had never encountered the Branghtons, evidently rejecting all she has learned by means of the urban bourgeoisie as though their violence, anger, and unrestraint belonged only to her unconscious. Like Jane Austen's father, Evelina's father-husband restores her to psychic confinement.

Clarissa's more definitive fate implies more serious social criticism. She, too, feels at the outset subordinated to a father who, unlike Villars, claims utter power over her. When she defies that claim, she brings destruction on herself. Her struggles to repress her sexuality end only in her rape; her subsequent sublimation and self-spiritualization, occurring in the context of her life with tradespeople, cannot solve the problem of her relation with her father. Her flight with Lovelace involved no full commitment of her will; her flight to death, on the other hand, constitutes concerted action. Unlike Evelina, she makes a conscious choice to exchange fathers, but she, too, can only escape one father by finding another: that divine Father to whose house, as she explains to Lovelace, she proposes to go. The extremity of her solution suggests the desperation of the female situation. Clarissa must die to escape paternal possessiveness (possessiveness, in this case, of a financial rather than a sexual object). The city has taught her the impossibility of living: she cannot survive the chaos of Lovelace's London, she cannot achieve the simple clarity of the Smiths'.

Clarissa and *Evelina* alike suggest at least buried realization of the severe psychic confinement to which women are destined and the inability or unwillingness fully to imagine alternative destinies. But their use of the city, and particularly of the commercial middle class, exemplifies different degrees of imaginative freedom or daring. Richardson makes sexuality his explicit subject and then allows a woman character to transcend it. He first celebrates the moral order of fair trade and then conceives a young woman who initiates her own significant and subversive trade: one father for another. Burney, on the other hand, considers social class as more a matter of style than of action. She never imagines her silversmith actually dealing in silver. Commerce has no place in *Evelina*, a novel which avoids economic issues. Evelina has plenty of money for her needs, and she acquires more and more. Her metaphorical economics, too, involves not exchange but accretion. Never defying women's traditional family role, Evelina simply accumulates fathers, literal and metaphoric. Her exploration of agency implies no threatening consequences, no real challenge of the status quo. If, like Clarissa, she temporarily substitutes the city for her father's house, she does so only to return to a father's house. The city implies an alternative to traditional patriarchal arrangements, but Burney finally evades that alternative. And even Richardson, by shifting the level of discourse to the spiritual, does not quite fully confront the implications of the female dilemma he has brilliantly evoked.[16]

16. I am greatly indebted to Margaret Ferguson, Mary Poovey, and Aubrey Williams for reading and commenting on drafts of this essay.

MAX BYRD

Sterne and Swift: Augustan Continuities

It is possible to speak of the advantages of influence as well as the anxiety. In recent theoretical speculations, elaborating what might be called the poetics of neurosis, Harold Bloom has proposed a view of literary history as a series of baroque, subliminal psychic rivalries between modern poets and their predecessors. "Belated" modern poets, he contends, are at once inhibited and inspired by the accomplishments of earlier writers; they fall back from the challenge of an overpowering tradition and can free themselves to write only by taking arms against a sea of fathers. They take arms and by "misreading" end them. To find his own voice, that is, the filial poet must distort or reinterpret the "precursor" who tyrannizes his imagination, much as Blake recasts *Paradise Lost* to make Satan the hero and Milton the poet of the devil's party. What Bloom calls "anxiety" W. Jackson Bate more accurately and dramatically terms "the burden of the past," using as example the specific historical situation of mid- and later eighteenth-century England, when "originality" and "novelty" for the first time become conscious critical ideals and young writers feel an urgent pressure to differ from earlier writers, by sheer force of singularity if nothing else.[1]

Laurence Sterne's extravagant assault upon literary convention has sometimes caused him to be placed among these anxious experimental writers—among pre-Romantics like Ossian, Chatterton, and Blake—but Sterne's originality, for all its subversion of convention, has finally more to do with eccentricity than experiment. He belongs in the main to an earlier generation of writers; his point of view and, so far as we can judge them, his intentions are profoundly conservative, hard to distinguish from those of Johnson, Pope, or Swift. In spite of the celebrated "oddness," Sterne seems less like someone striking out a new path than like someone cartwheeling back and forth across familiar terrain, merely capering to absurd extremes. Indeed, in his self-absorption, in his effort to use the novel to establish or clarify his own identity, Sterne scarcely looks up to see what is being written around him; his letters and books are striking for their lack of reference to contemporary literature, and he seems unaware even of the existence of his immediate predecessors, Fielding and Richardson. His glance instead turns automatically to the past, to the writers of what D. W. Jefferson has called "the tradition of learned wit"; and his use of these writers—his cockeyed imitation of their best voices and gags—conveys nothing at all of anxiety, everything of irreverent glee.[2]

Of all the writers of that tradition, Swift appears to have exerted the most extensive influence upon Sterne. In what follows, however, I attempt not to trace the categories of

---

1. Harold Bloom, *The Anxiety of Influence: A Theory of Poetry* (New York: Oxford University Press, 1973); W. Jackson Bate, *The Burden of the Past and the English Poet* (Cambridge: Harvard University Press, 1970).

This essay is adapted from material in chapters 2 and 3 of my volume *Tristram Shandy*, to appear in the Allen and Unwin Critical Library. It is printed here by kind permission of Allen and Unwin and the general editor of the series, C. J. Rawson.

2. "*Tristram Shandy* and the Tradition of Learned Wit," *Essays in Criticism*, 1 (1951), 225–248.

that influence in detail, only to suggest how thematic continuities tie Sterne, loosely but by a line of wit, to Swift and to certain Augustan preoccupations.

The fundamental difference between Sterne and Swift may be felt in their characteristic images for the brain—that extensive, pleasant ocean in the Sternean scheme which can accommodate a flotilla of thoughts like Dr. Slop's "without sail or ballast . . . millions of which, as your worship knows, are every day swimming quietly in the middle of the thin juice of a man's understanding, without being carried backwards or forwards, till some little gusts of passion or interest drive them to one side."[3] Sterne, indeed, makes a leitmotiv of such images: no writer has ever described the inside of our heads so literally. In *Tristram Shandy* the "spare places of our brains" are capacious beyond all imagination (III, xx). They can contain a city square of nerves, converging on the cerebellum like streets and alleys (II, xix); Toby's head can be like the inside of a Savoyard's box or filled with wet tinder or, more wonderfully still, "like a smoak-jack;—the funnel unswept, and the ideas whirling round and round about in it, all obfuscated and darkened over with fuliginous matter" (III, xix). "Such a head!" Tristram exclaims, identifying the real setting of the novel: "—would to heaven! my enemies only saw the inside of it" (III, xxxviii).[4]

By contrast, Swift does not simply arrive at this inner space in the flicker of a simile. His entry is accomplished by the officious Reason, "with Tools for cutting, and opening, and mangling, and piercing."[5] And when the brain is finally

3. Laurence Sterne, *The Life and Opinions of Tristram Shandy, Gentleman,* ed. James Aiken Work (New York: Odyssey Press, 1940), III, ix. Cited hereafter parenthetically by volume and chapter in the text.

4. David Thomson discusses this image pattern in *Wild Excursions: The Life and Fiction of Laurence Sterne* (London: Weidenfeld and Nicolson, 1972), pp. 12–24.

5. *A Tale of a Tub,* ed. A. C. Guthkelch and D. Nichol Smith, 2nd ed. (Oxford: Clarendon Press, 1958), p. 173. Cited hereafter parenthetically by page number in the text.

laid open and dissected, he draws our attention not to its spaciousness but to its disappointing "Defects . . . in Number and Bulk" (pp. 173-174). Or if we consider ideas to be like the mist that rises from a dunghill, then, contends the narrator of *A Tale of a Tub*, "it will follow, that as the Face of Nature never produces Rain, but when it is overcast and disturbed, so Human Understanding, seated in the Brain, must be troubled and overspread by Vapours, ascending from the lower Faculties, to water the Invention, and render it fruitful" (p. 163). Elsewhere, in the course of explaining the usefulness of quilted caps, he repeats "the Opinion of Choice *Virtuosi*, that the Brain is only a Crowd of little Animals, but with Teeth and Claws extremely sharp, and therefore, cling together in the Contexture we behold, like the Picture of *Hobbes*'s *Leviathan*, or like Bees in perpendicular swarm upon a Tree, or like a Carrion corrupted into Vermin, still preserving the Shape and Figure of the Mother Animal" (p. 277).

Every comparison of Swift and Sterne turns into a contrast like this, in which an initial similarity of purpose collapses, as here Sterne's vividly distinct images, his rapidfire fantasy, shrivel before Swift's relentless development of simile into monstrous analogy. Sterne himself makes comparisons with Swift into contrasts: unlike Swift, he tells one correspondent, he has not yet been persecuted by his enemies into great fame; unlike Swift, he tells another, who has warned him against indecent humor, he will be cautious—"I deny I have gone as farr as Swift—He keeps a due distance from Rabelais—& I keep a due distance from him—Swift has said a hundred things I durst Not Say—Unless I was Dean of St. Patricks."[6] But this is not to say that Swift exerts no influence on him. To the contrary, in a general way Sterne clearly identifies with him, seeing himself as a second Anglo-Irish clergyman frustrated by the politics of the

---

6. *The Letters of Laurence Sterne*, ed. Lewis Perry Curtis (Oxford: Clarendon Press, 1935), pp. 132 and 76. Cited hereafter parenthetically by page numbers in the text.

church, too clever for his own good, writing himself out of favor and into scandal as Swift did in *A Tale of a Tub*. He describes proudly to Eliza how old Lord Bathurst, the former patron of Pope and Swift, came up to him in London and declared, "Despairing ever to find their equals, it is some years since I have closed my accounts, and shut up my books, with thoughts of never opening them again: but you have kindled a desire in me of opening them once more before I die; which I now do; so go home and dine with me" (*Letters*, p. 305). The *Journal to Eliza* itself appears to have been inspired by Swift's *Journal to Stella*, which was published in 1766, the year that Sterne met Eliza.

As a writer, Sterne responded chiefly to *A Tale of a Tub* (*Gulliver's Travels* seems hardly to have interested him), and what he responded to is very clear: of all the major works usually cited as Sterne's sources—*Gargantua and Pantagruel, Don Quixote*, Montaigne's *Essays*—the formal elements of *Tristram Shandy* are most nearly replicated in the *Tale*. No other source so closely resembles it in details of structure and device—the digressions piled precariously upon digressions, the mock-scholastic parodies of literary decorum (Swift's endless Apology, Dedication, Preface, and Introduction), the volleys against critics, the proposals for other books, and the division of emphasis between actual narration and the encroaching personality of the narrator. Even certain recurrent images of the *Tale*—brains, horses, noses—appear again in *Tristram Shandy*. At the most general level these resemblances disappear, of course—Swift is writing a satire and Sterne a novel—but similar forms sometimes have a way of generating similar themes. Sterne's bawdry, his interest in language as a subject of interpretation and corruption, and his view of madness undoubtedly have many sources, including most importantly his own enigmatic and self-afflicting personality; but his predispositions to those themes are surely mobilized by Swift's example, even if from a common starting point they tend to go racing in utterly different directions.

"Walter is wise, he is witty, he is humane," writes John Traugott, "—and he is mad."[7] "Is Uncle Toby mad too?" John Preston asks, comparing him to Swift's demented Jack.[8] All of the inhabitants of Shandy Hall, observes V. S. Pritchett, "live shut up in the madhouse of their own imaginations, oysters itching voluptuously upon the pearl within."[9] "The real point about Walter and Toby," says Michael DePorte, "is not so much that Sterne thinks them mad, or even that most contemporary readers would have thought them mad; the point is rather that given the psychiatric criteria of the day they *are* mad."[10]

This is not true, of course. Swift's Hack narrator in the *Tale* is a genuine madman by eighteenth-century criteria, a self-confessed "student" of Bedlam, a projector whose "imaginations are hard-mouth'd, and exceedingly disposed to run away with his *Reason*, which I have observed from long Experience, to be a very light Rider, and easily shook off" (*Tale*, p. 180). His actual madness reflects a cultural crisis of enormous proportions to Swift's mind, a destructive folly that is willful, poisonous, and sinful, and it will serve as an image of self-deception and blindness throughout Swift's career, from the Calvinist Jack and the raging Peter to the Bedlamite Yahoos of *Gulliver's Travels*. But if "madness" is a term almost unavoidable in a discussion of Swift's work, it occurs to few contemporaries of Sterne, who prefer instead to see his eccentric heroes as Rabelaisian humorists rather than as madmen.[11] It is true that Tristram describes himself as subject to the changes of the moon and finds that he, too,

7. John Traugott, *Tristram Shandy's World: Sterne's Philosophical Rhetoric* (Berkeley and Los Angeles: University of California Press, 1954), p. 59.

8. John Preston, *The Created Self: The Reader's Role in Eighteenth-Century Fiction* (London: Heinemann, 1970), p. 171.

9. V. S. Pritchett, *Books in General* (London: Chatto and Windus, 1953), p. 175.

10. Michael V. DePorte, *Nightmares and Hobbyhorses: Swift, Sterne, and Augustan Ideas of Madness* (San Marino, Calif: The Huntington Library, 1974), p. 116.

11. See the evidence assembled in *Sterne: The Critical Heritage*, ed. Alan B. Howes (London: Routledge and Kegan Paul, 1974).

will be led astray by his "pads" (hobbyhorses): "sometimes, to my shame be it spoken, I take somewhat longer journies than what a wise man would think altogether right" (I, viii). And "Shandy" is Yorkshire dialect for crackbrained, addled. But to be long on the road, to be addled, not to be wise—these confessions hardly bear comparison with the tragic madness of Swift's fools. And in any case, the literal degradation of eighteenth-century insanity—the shocking excremental squalor that so intensifies the figurative energy of Swift's satire—plays no part in Sterne's vision, which domesticates folly to mere eccentricity or humor, the harmless single-mindedness that he and his readers intend when they speak of "Cervantick satyr." By contrast, Swift's madmen are not only degraded, but destructive: drawing upon the ancient tradition of madness as a link to supernatural power, he presents the mad world as dangerous and revolutionary; his madmen in the *Tale* are murderous princes and generals like Henry IV, subversive philosophers like Hobbes, dissenting enthusiasts like the Puritans; and as any English reader with a memory of the Civil Wars would understand, they daily threaten the stability of church and state. Against this vision of public crisis, Sterne can only set the private impotence of Toby and his monomania, a sentimental saint, like Don Quixote insane in just one way and all the more virtuous in every other.

Nonetheless, if the idea of madness in Sterne's works is primarily a critical metaphor imposed from without and not a thematic motif as in Swift, it is imposed so often because it discloses a moral issue central to both writers. The association of ideas that Sterne took from Locke and made into a comic device occurs in a context of irrational behavior that verges, as many readers have felt, on madness: Locke's gallery of victims who are tyrannized by their fixed habits of association—as Tristram tells us his parents are—grows progressively more bizarre, until the principle of association becomes a kind of "unreasonableness" that is, Locke says with unusual anger, perhaps our "greatest" source of "error."[12] Such "unnatural" and habitual associations as we all develop are at the "root" of madness, he declares, adding, "I shall be pardoned for calling it by so harsh a name as madness, when it is considered that opposition to reason deserves that name, and is really madness; and there is scarce a man so free from it, but that if he should always, on all occasions, argue or do as in some cases he constantly does, would not be thought fitter for Bedlam than civil conversation" (*Essay*, II, xxxiii, 4).

In Locke's hands this unreasonableness constitutes a criticism of human nature. In Sterne's hands it constitutes a criticism of reason. Or rather, of the view that makes reason sovereign over human nature. For no principle of logic, no "natural" connection, is strong enough to penetrate Walter's mesh of theory or Toby's bunkers, or to make Tristram follow an orderly pattern of narration; even that notorious eighteenth-century symbol of divine and human reason, the clock, takes its place in a wildly unnatural association of ideas. If we object that Sterne is merely describing obsession or the Renaissance psychology of "humors," his explicit references to Locke's *Essay* still complicate what would otherwise be familiar techniques of comedy, and encourage us to speak seriously, even philosphically, of Shandean eccentricity, as we cannot, for example, of Sir Epicure Mammon's greed or Lord Emsworth's dottiness about pigs. The emphasis Sterne brings to bear on language and interpretation, moreover, connects his work to the Cervantic tradition, in which madness becomes not a matter of reason or unreason but a matter of point of view. (It can be no accident that the Shakespearean play to which *Tristram Shandy* most often alludes is *Hamlet*, where themes of interpretation, illusion, and madness are paramount.) Neither Cervantes or Sterne, of course, goes so far as to say that reason has no part in our makeup; but in the mirror of Toby's monomania,

---

12. John Locke, *An Essay Concerning Human Understanding*, ed. A. C. Fraser (Oxford, 1894; reprint, New York: Dover, 1959), II, xxxiii, 18. Cited hereafter parenthetically by volume, chapter, and section in the text.

in Walter's approximately plausible theories, and the Don's ready explanations of enchantment, they obviously parody its operation and its claims; and at extreme moments their parody raises the possibility that reason bears no necessary relationship to reality at all. "Herein seems to lie the difference between idiots and madmen," Locke says: "that madmen put wrong ideas together, and so make wrong propositions, but argue and reason right from them; but idiots make very few or no propositions, and reason scarce at all" (*Essay*, II, xi, 13). The difference, that is, lies finally between Locke's thoroughly Augustan position that madness is "wrong"—the moral connotations of his language recall Swift, who holds his Bedlamites accountable for choosing to be "well-deceived"—and Sterne's more equivocal suggestion that every consciousness contains a fiction, every subjectivity a truth.

The issue, finally, may be put into the classical terms of the age. The great criticism of Swift, Johnson, and Locke is that although reason enables us to apprehend reality, imagination blinds us to it. "There is no man whose imagination does not sometimes predominate over his reason," Imlac insists in Johnson's moving portrait of a madman's delusion, "who can regulate his attention wholly by his will, and whose ideas will come and go at his command. No man will be found in whose mind airy notions do not sometimes tyrannise, and force him to hope or fear beyond the limits of sober probability."[13] It has been argued that Sterne's view of imagination is sufficently esemplastic to include him in the coming generation of writers, like Blake, Coleridge, and Wordsworth, who would transform the imagination into a creative principle, a moral and aesthetic standard higher than sober reason.[14] But in his sermons, those indispensable

13. *The History of Rasselas, Prince of Abyssinia*, ed. George Birkbeck Hill (Oxford: Clarendon Press, 1887), ch. 44, p. 140. Cited hereafter in the text parenthetically by page number.

14. See especially Robert Alter, "*Tristram Shandy* and the Game of Love," *American Scholar*, 37 (1968), 316–323. The broader topic is the subject of James Engell, *The Creative Imagination: Enlightenment to Romanticism*

commentaries on his fiction, Sterne speaks of imagination in a voice that we can hardly distinguish from Johnson's: "Will the coolest and most circumspect say, when pleasure has taken full possession of his heart, that no thought nor purpose shall arise there, which he would have concealed?—In those loose and unguarded moments the imagination is not always at command—in spite of reason and reflection, it will forceably carry him sometimes whither he would not."[15] ("All power of fancy over reason," Imlac declares, "is a degree of insanity" [*Rasselas*, p. 140]). And in his whole comedy of hobbyhorses, which carry Tristram (like Swift's loose rider) "whither he would not," we are still very far from the prevailing value of sensibility, the belief that irrationality releases some inward power and guides us toward a higher consciousness. In his literal pictures of the brain—as in Swift's—we are even further from something like Wordsworth's vision on Mt. Snowdon of "the perfect image of a mighty mind, / Of one that feeds upon infinity," a mind that resembles the highest possibility of the poet's mind.[16] For Sterne's vision of mind reaches no higher than hobbyhorses or the "several receptacles, cells, cellules, domiciles, dormitories, refectories, and spare places of our brains" (III, xx).

Sterne's presentations of madness lead no one toward an elevated consciousness or a profounder reality. Or to put it more positively, we might say that Sterne, like Johnson, displays the classic Augustan faith that human nature is primarily social, that reality (not hell) is other people. If his idea of community is sentimental and nonhierarchical, in contrast to the usual Augustan view, he nonetheless shares the impulse that makes Imlac advise the mad astronomer to forsake his solitude and to correct his madness by

---

(Cambridge: Harvard University Press, 1981).

15. "The House of Feasting and the House of Mourning Described," in *The Sermons of Mr. Yorick*, in *The Writings of Laurence Sterne* (Oxford: Basil Blackwell, 1927), VI, 19.

16. *The Prelude*, ed. Jonathan Wordsworth et al. (New York: Norton, 1979), 1805 ed., Book XIII, 70–71 (p. 460).

conversation and society. Thus, there is misunderstanding in every social exchange in *Tristram Shandy*, but not alienation. There is subjectivity, but not solitude. A sense of human limitations, given in an elegiac tone and defined by the familiar Augustan terms of time and death, crowds his characters together and renders them foolish and mad only in the ordinary human sense. From another point of view Sterne, like Swift, is simply drawing on a view of madness traditional among preachers: like other Augustans, he is writing a comic version of Ecclesiastes.

On two occasions, however, Sterne does describe actual madness. The account of Maria, the peasant madwoman whom Tristram meets near Moulins, belongs to a subgenre invented and perfected in "the age of sensibility": the portrait of madness designed to elicit neither scorn nor awe, but quivering, tearful pity.[17] This is the same Maria who afterward triggers Yorick's apostrophe to "sensibility" in *A Sentimental Journey* and whose sisters the Man of Feeling visits in dreamlike Bedlam cells: a stock figure of bathos, adumbrated perhaps in Richardson's *Clarissa*, grotesquely distorted in the madwomen of Gothic fiction to come. In Maria the idea of madness as willful, blamable folly has disappeared; the manic energy, at once menacing and obscene, of Swift's madhouses has given way to passivity and melancholy. Unfettered, she roams far from the uproar of both Shandy Hall and Bedlam. Sterne does, however, connect her tenuously to the supernatural by the fact that, although no one has taught her to pipe, she has somehow learned the service to the Virgin Mary. And she combines this hint of literal inspiration with the eroticism that is never far from such feminine vulnerability: "she was beautiful; and if ever I felt the full force of an honest heart-ache, it was the moment I

---

17. I take this phrase from Northrop Frye, "Towards Defining an Age of Sensibility," in *Fables of Identity* (New York: Harcourt, 1963), pp. 130–137. See also Laurence Sterne, *A Sentimental Journey Through France and Italy by Mr. Yorick*, ed. Gardner D. Stout, Jr. (Berkeley and Los Angeles: University of California Press, 1967), pp. 268–279.

saw her" (IX, xxiv). Maria appears to exist primarily, in fact, to provoke the repressed sexuality of her admirers (she is herself frustrated in love). Yorick will collapse in self-ravishment, vibrating to the great "Sensorium" of feeling that her madness has revealed. More typically, Tristram will retreat to a disarming psychological distance, calling his initial heartache by that most Augustan of pejoratives, "my enthusiasm," and breaking her spell with a crude, insensible joke:

> MARIA look'd wistfuly for some time at me, and then at her goat—and then at me—and then at her goat again, and so on, alternately—
> —Well, *Maria*, said I softly—What resemblance do you find?
>
> (III, xxiv)

Madness, in short, turns to bawdry, as does everything else in Sterne's world, releasing suggestion if not meaning. In this regard, Sterne may be said to occupy a position halfway between Rabelais and the Victorians: if the subject of sex is never more than a page away in his work, yet it is never rendered steadily or directly. The element of fantasy present in everyone's sexuality appears to suffuse Sterne's: he imagines strangely bodiless flirtations, concentrated with excruciating sensitivity on extremities, tips of fingers, pulses. In such jokes as Toby's bewilderment over the "right end of a woman," we encounter Sterne's characteristic combination of bravado and impotence (II, vii), in the tremulous indecencies of *Journal to Eliza* and *A Sentimental Journey* a prolonged but superficial hysteria. Swift obviously stands far closer to Rabelais: there is nothing of the nudging elbow in his humor, nothing of Sterne's characteristic wink and snigger. But there is little of Rabelais' gaiety, either. Swift's indecent humor, when it concerns sexuality, strikes most readers as coarse rather than direct, without pleasure. And when it grows scatological, most readers pull back from the grim anger it discharges, an anger that sometimes seems directed at the sheer inescapable fact of the human body's functions. In his account of the Aeolist priests, for example,

Swift's Hack first explains that large funnels stuck up their posteriors bring on the inspiration of strong winds and eloquent eructations. More impressive still, he adds, are the "*Female* Officers, whose Organs were understood to be better disposed for the Admission of those Oracular *Gusts*, as entring and passing up thro' a Receptacle of greater Capacity, and causing also a Pruriency by the Way, such as with due Management, hath been refined from a Carnal, into a Spiritual Extasie" (*Tale*, p. 157). This sardonic refinement ("refined" is surely the most common adjective in the *Tale*) has long been recognized as Swift's version of sublimation, the displacement of psychic effects from an appropriate to a disguised object, although Swift states it in Aristotelian rather than psychological terms: "the Corruption of the Senses is the Generation of the Spirit" (*Tale*, p. 269). Nor does he limit its application to female pruriency. As the Hack narrator of the *Tale* undertakes to survey the uses of madness in a commonwealth, he begins with the case of a "certain Great Prince" (Henry IV of France), who suddenly raises a mighty army and fleet and threatens universal conquest. "It was afterwards discovered, that the Movement of this whole Machine had been directed by an absent *Female*, whose Eyes had raised a Protuberancy, and before Emission, she was removed into an Enemy's Country . . . The very same Principle that influences a *Bully* to break the Windows of a Whore, who has jilted him, naturally stirs up a Great Prince to raise mighty Armies, and dream nothing but Sieges, Battles, and Victories" (*Tale*, pp. 163–165).

Whatever the remoter origins of Uncle Toby—the sentimental memory of Sterne's soldier-father or the eccentric Captain Robert Hinde proposed by some scholars—it is impossible to avoid seeing Swift's version of sublimation at work in him, spurring the hobbyhorse of siegecraft, his "Fancy . . . *astride* on his Reason" as firmly as any Bedlam inmate's (*Tale*, p. 171).[18] ("Most Kinds of Diversion in

18. For Captain Hinde, see C. J. Rawson, "Two Notes on Sterne," *Notes & Queries*, N. S., 4 (1957), 255–256.

Men, Children, and other Animals,'' Swift sardonically
observes, ''are an Imitation of Fighting.'')[19] Sterne makes
the connection between repressed sexuality and warfare
almost as plain, in fact, as Swift does: when Trim utters the
words ''A Rood and a half of ground to do what they would
with,'' Toby blushes immoderately, and a moment later Tristram draws the necessary comparison, adding only a teasing
note on the importance of privacy to miniature warfare:
''Never did lover post down to a belov'd mistress with more
heat and expectation, than my uncle *Toby* did, to enjoy this
self-same thing in private . . . The idea of not being seen,
did not a little contribute to the idea of pleasure pre-
conceived in my uncle *Toby*'s mind'' (II, v).

For Sterne this displacement of erotic energy apparently
represents no more than a joke on human nature, a Shandean variation on a topos that, one way or another, stretches
back to the *Iliad*. For Swift, however, the joke is made
through clenched teeth. Its serious point is that our politics
derive from our illogical psychology, that our collective
corruption has its source in the ease with which our lower
faculties control our higher. More seriously still, such sublimation reveals a moral error: the preference of illusion to
truth; for we know these things about ourselves, or ought to,
and yet choose to remain mired in appetite, willfully blind to
realities. Swift makes the consequences of this self-deceit as
violent and repellent as he can; he pitches it all in the place
of excrement, and with the climactic image of Bedlam hospital and its iron bars he makes clear that when we choose this
way we choose to be enslaved, not to be free. But Sterne
simply turns away from the satiric possibilities implicit in the
preference of illusion over truth. His voice returns no echo
of Swift's fierceness. Toby's mock warfare leaves flies
unharmed and widows unravished. Apart from that rood and
a half of sublimation, in fact, Sterne's bawdry far more than

---

19. Jonathan Swift, ''Thoughts on Various Subjects,'' in *The Prose Works
of Jonathan Swift*, ed. Herbert Davis (Oxford: Basil Blackwell, 1939–1968),
IV, 247.

Swift's depends upon ambiguity and ambivalence, matters for linguistic rather than moral interpretation.

At the practical, larcenous level from which novelists usually regard other fiction, Sterne unquestionably discovered in Swift's allegory of the brothers Martin, Peter, and Jack the problem of interpretation in its most suggestive form.[20] For their father's will had, of course, expressly commanded the three brothers never to alter the appearance of their inherited coats; but motivated by lust—by their desire to court three grand ladies—they concoct a series of sophistic rereadings of the will that begins with shoulder knots and oral tradition, proceeds to gold lace and Aristotle's *de Interpretatione* ("which has the Faculty of teaching its Readers to find out a Meaning in every Thing but it self" [*Tale*, p. 85]), and concludes with satin linings and sheer forgery. And though Swift's satiric target here is primarily the Roman Catholic church, he makes the same general point throughout his career: words have at once a single meaning and endless meanings. Like Locke, he holds to the view that words should mean definite things, precisely and obviously. ("There are some poets, Kipling for example," writes W. H. Auden, "whose relation to language reminds one of a drill sergeant: the words are taught to wash behind their ears, stand properly at attention and execute complicated maneuvers, but at the cost of never being allowed to think for themselves.")[21] But unlike Locke, who finds the problem in the inherent ambiguity of language itself, Swift blames instead its corrupt users—the politicians, priests, and rabble who pervert what can and should be clear. "*I charge and command my said three sons,*" booms the will, "*to wear no sort of* Silver Fringe *upon or about their said Coats* . . . However, after some Pause the Brother so often mentioned for his Erudition, who was well Skill'd in Criticisms, had found

20. Sterne's *A Political Romance* (York, 1759), in its first version called "The History of a Good Warm Watch-Coat," employs a mildly licentious imitation of Swift's inherited coat allegory in the *Tale*.

21. *The Dyer's Hand and Other Essays* (New York: Vintage, 1968), p. 22.

in a certain Author, which he said should be nameless, that
the same Word which in the Will is called *Fringe*, does also
signifie a *Broom-stick*" (*Tale*, p. 88).

Sterne, no one has ever doubted, delights in the ambiguity that so discourages Swift. In Sterne's world, words
never stand still for a single meaning: they dart continually
like seabirds into our subconscious, returning every moment
with fresh and outrageous evidence of our disposition to pervert. And while Swift directs his satire at the brothers' willingness to make words mean whatever they want—in the
service of power, vanity, and illusion as well as lust—Sterne
limits the alternative meanings to a single kind: whatever we
say, we are thinking of sex.

> —Here are two senses, cried *Eugenius*, as we walk'd along,
> pointing with the fore finger of his right hand to the word *Crevice*,
> in the fifty-second page of the second volume of this book of
> books,—here are two senses,—quoth he.—And here are two roads,
> replied I, turning short upon him,—a dirty and a clean one,—which
> shall we take?—The clean,—by all means, replied *Eugenius*.
> *Eugenius*, said I, stepping before him, and laying my hand upon his
> breast,—to define—is to distrust. (III,xxxi)

Crevices, whiskers, noses: fanned by the south winds of the
libido, every word turns gently over to reveal another meaning. So infectious, in fact, is Tristram's habit of sexualizing
his language that after a time no word at all seems innocent.
Scholars read with dictionaries of slang open beside them
("toby" means "penis"), hobbyhorses turn stud, and a sentence justifying digressions can bring explication to a blush-
ing halt: "when a man is telling his story in the strange way
I do mine, he is obliged continually to be going backwards
and forwards to keep all tight together in the reader's fancy"
(VI, xxxiii).[22] Tristram says, quite truthfully, that he
depends "upon the cleanliness of my readers' imaginations"
(III, xxxi).

---

22. See, for example, Frank Brady, "*Tristram Shandy*: Sexuality, Morality, and Sensibility," *Eighteenth-Century Studies*, 4 (1970), 41–56.

Swift indulges in no such trust. If Sterne offers us a choice of meanings, either possible, for his part Swift insists that interpretation aims at nothing less than truth. Peter, having locked away the will and seized power over his brothers, thrusts a piece of bread before them and, in a parody of transubstantiation, calls it mutton. They protest that the mutton strangely resembles a twelve-penny loaf. "*Look ye, Gentlemen*, cries Peter in a Rage, *to convince you, what a couple of blind, positive, ignorant, wilful Puppies you are, I will use but this plain Argument; By G—, it is true, good, natural Mutton as any in* Leaden-Hall Market; *and G— confound you both eternally, if you offer to believe otherwise.* Such a thundring Proof as this, left no farther Room for Objection: The two Unbelievers began to gather and pocket up their Mistake, as hastily as they could" (*Tale*, p. 118). This is Quixotic madness gone sour; fiction turned to lies. Worse still, it is a moral failing for which language is not responsible. Here, of course, Swift assigns responsibility for misrepresenting truth to his characters, the mad Peter and his cowardly brothers, and by extension to the religious factions they represent. But as so often happens in his work, the page never contains his anger. Elsewhere and generally throughout the *Tale*, responsibility for misinterpretation widens to include not only the Hack and his puppets, but also the "Gentle Reader" and flawed human nature, torn perpetually between the state of being a knave or a well-deceived fool. "I am wonderfully well acquainted with the present Relish of Courteous Readers," says the Hack in an ostensible compliment to us; "and have often observed with singular Pleasure, that a *Fly* driven from a *Honey-pot*, will immediately, with very good Appetite alight, and finish his Meal on an Excrement" (*Tale*, p. 207).

Sterne may have taken from Swift the technique of reaching out thus to include the reader in the "conversation" of the book, but he never duplicates the suffocating intimacy Swift so ferociously achieves: his clowning references to "Madam" and "Sir" and "Your Reverences" create only a curiously impersonal familiarity. Nor does he duplicate the technique of irony that places so crushing a burden of interpretation on the reader. For Swift's irony finally extends the question of interpretation beyond the action or the texts within his texts: it challenges the reader directly to understand the writer himself, as a person, as a character, and it works to ensure that he cannot. The relationship between author and reader is the ultimate question of truthful interpretation that Swift raises, and raises only to deny. Beneath Tristram's mad dashes, the chatter and puppyish cajoling, we detect a self in the making, a self engaged, as Sterne declared to David Garrick, in an act of self-portrait, a personality that we (and Sterne) can eventually "read" (*Letters*, p. 87). A far stronger self lies beneath Swift's metamorphoses—a face glimpsed and lost at every moment—but it is the last illusion to think that we can know him.

The issue of truth in interpretation, however, may be seen in another way, through the memorable vividness of a stylistic interest shared by both writers. Readers have long noticed that Swift's brilliant use of metaphor is not without a characteristic tension between literal and figurative meanings. There is, for example, the absurdity of Peter's claim that bread is mutton, which mocks one metaphor with another and plays them both against our literal experience of bread and meat. There is, as well, the absurdity of effect when dunces take a figurative expression and act upon it literally, so that Jack, having described a skin of parchment (the Bible) as "Cloth," wraps it about his head "for a Night-cap when he went to Bed, and for an Umbrello in rainy Weather" (*Tale*, p. 190). Or when the sages of Laputa carry about great packs of implements and things to display in place of speech. Or when the tailors of the *Tale* mistake a metaphor for reality and thus hold "the Universe to be a large *Suit of Cloaths*" (*Tale*, p. 77). Swift's practice, moreover, is to allow his misreaders to carry their literalizations as far as possible, to construct systems from them, and to fashion a metaphorical reality that at best misleads, at worst blasphemes. Hence the Aeolists, taking etymology literally, misunderstand completely the spiritual expression "inspiration" and transform it into the belchings and eructations of

Dissent. Hence too the metaphorical "devouring" of Ireland that so offends the Modest Proposer leads him to advocate a literal cannibalism. In all of these collisions between metaphor and truth, we are encountering Swift's wonderful, surreal inventiveness, but we are also encountering an obvious moral challenge to sift through metaphor to correctness.

Few readers can have gone far in *Tristram Shandy* without recognizing that Sterne writes as one of the incontestable masters of the comic image. I have in mind not only those precise visual images he continually creates ("a number of tall, opake words, one before another, in a right line" [III, xx]), but also the explicit comparisons that pop suddenly around the corner of the most ordinary syntax:

others on the contrary, tuck'd up to their very chins with whips across their mouths, scouring and scampering it away like so many little party-coloured devils astride a mortgage. (I, viii)

Humph!—said my uncle *Toby*;—tho' not accented as a note of acquiescence,—but as an interjection of that particular species of surprize, when a man, in looking into a drawer, finds more of a thing than he expected. (II, xvii)

He pick'd up an opinion, Sir, as a man in a state of nature picks up an apple. (III, xxxiv)

There is a wealth of pleasure in such silliness. We can respond to the cleverness of the allusions to Hobbes' state of nature and to Swift's runaway horse "astride" a mortgage; we like the irrepressible bawdry by which "drawer" metamorphoses into an undergarment; or we take simple pleasure in the childlike literalness with which Sterne revitalizes abstractions like mortgages and opinions. But absent completely is that Swiftian tension between literal (that is, true) and figurative meanings, between moral correctness and self-deception.[23] Absent, too, is Swift's habit of

23. I draw on two excellent discussions: Kathleen Williams, "Restoration Themes in the Major Satires of Swift," *Review of English Studies*, N. S., 16

developing a metaphor into a system. Sterne's images come
in a random, unpredictable fashion and disappear like bubbles. Even where Sterne does exploit the tension between
literal and figurative, it is not for any moral purpose: Toby
misunderstands every possible expression that touches upon
siegecraft—"As *Yorick* pronounced the word *point blank*, my
uncle *Toby* rose up to say something upon projectiles" (IV,
xxvi). He is the true Lockean man, who takes all words in
one sense only, literally or figuratively according to the inap-
propriateness of the context ("You shall lay your finger
upon the place—said my uncle *Toby*.—I will not touch it,
however, quoth Mrs. *Wadman* to herself" [IX, xx]). But he
is also and undeniably the good man, the very opposite of a
dunce or hack, the man of sentiment whose instinctive compassion transcends all verbal language. And though his constant misinterpretations are as complete and systematic as
any in the *Tale*, he follows them virtually alone, with the
single disciple Trim, not as part of a mob (to use the word
Swift so disliked). And in any case, there is always someone
present to correct his misinterpretation and to readjust the
context.

When Tristram develops a metaphor on his own, moreover, his interest in the literal is limited to the creation of
those numerous personifications that are such a feature of
his style; and he proceeds ordinarily not by a rigorous and
obvious logic, but by a skittering process of free association.
Thus he begins a chapter with a reference to Momus'
famous complaint that Hephaestus' model of a man lacks a
window in his breast, where his desires and secrets can be
seen; he goes on to imagine Momus' window installed in real
people, then in the inhabitants of the planet Mercury, who
must be turned entirely to glass by the heat of the sun. But
at the end Tristram himself interposes to correct the metaphor and to insure that we do not take it literally: "But this,
as I said above, is not the case of the inhabitants of this

(1965), 258–271; and Maurice J. Quinlan, "Swift's Use of Literalization as
a Rhetorical Device," *PMLA*, 82 (1967), 516–521.

earth;—our minds shine not through the body, but are wrapt up here in a dark covering of uncrystalized flesh and blood; so that if we would come to the specifick characters of them, we must go some other way to work" (I, xxiii). A faint preacherly tone of voice can be heard here, of course. But in general Sterne's comic images rarely raise questions of interpretation and deception as Swift's do. Rather than moral urgency, they communicate something like that delight in nonsense which is never quite unalloyed in Swift. They communicate a simple, playful joy in the manipulation of unreal words—or in W. K. Wimsatt's phrase, in the cheerful manipulation of a "heightened unreality" characteristic of the Augustan wits. Wimsatt adds, "The peculiar feat of the Augustan poet was the art of teasing unreality with the redeeming force of wit—of casting upon a welter of unreal materials a light of order and a perspective vision."[24] To the extent that this is a moral enterprise—redeeming, ordering—Sterne's kinship may be in some doubt, despite his frequent protests that he had written nothing but moral works. To the extent, however, that Sterne, like Pope in his freest moments, simply cuts loose from literal meaning and delights in that chaotic unreality, the kinship is secure.

> Nonsense precipitate, like running Lead,
> That slip'd thro' Cracks and Zig-zags of the Head.
> (*Dunciad*, I, ll. 123–124)[25]

> As when a dab-chick waddles thro' the copse
> On feet and wings, and flies, and wades, and hops;
> So lab'ring on, with shoulders, hands, and head,
> Wide as a wind-mill all his figures spread.
> (*Dunciad*, II, ll. 63–66)

24. "The Augustan Mode in English Poetry," in *Hateful Contraries: Studies in Literature and Criticism* (Lexington: University of Kentucky Press, 1965), p. 155.

25. Alexander Pope, *The Dunciad, in Four Books*, ed. James Sutherland, Twickenham Edition (London: Methuen, 1963), V, 279. Cited parenthetically by book and line in the text.

—my father could never subscribe to it by any means; the very idea of so noble, so refined, so immaterial, and so exalted a being as the *Anima*, or even the *Animus*, taking up her residence, and sitting dabbling, like a tad-pole, all day long, both summer, and winter, in a puddle. (*Tristram Shandy*, II, xix)

But it is the measure of Swift's seriousness—and sometimes of his grimness—that he so infrequently turns his back on the literal and verisimilar, that reality so implacably encroaches on his fantasies. If he could have known it, Sterne's uncritical pleasure in the irrational would only have seemed to him without moral weight and tension. Or as C. J. Rawson observes in a genuinely Shandean speculation about literary influence, "what the *Tale of the Tub* is really parodying is Sterne, in advance."[26]

26. C. J. Rawson et al., "Sternian Realities," in *The Winged Skull: Papers from the Laurence Sterne Bicentenary Conference at the University of York*, ed. Arthur H. Cash and John M. Stedmond (London: Methuen, 1971), p. 92.

MELINDA ALLIKER RABB

Engendering Accounts in Sterne's
A Sentimental Journey

The balance of sentimental commerce is always against the expatriated adventurer.

I confess I do hate cold conceptions, as I do the puny ideas which engender them.

Sterne, *A Sentimental Journey*

As a traveler, Yorick is "apt to be taken with all kinds of people."[1] People form his real itinerary. Places, in country or town, matter only as backdrops for human encounters. Sterne prefers to focus his narrator's attention on the tip of a lady's thumb, while great cultural monuments pass by without stirring the slightest interest. Such eccentric sightseeing may be understood in part as a contrast to Smollett's empirical thoroughness and to the *Travels'* profusion of "unentertaining detail" (Letter II) among the "observations [he] had occasion to make upon this town and country" (Letter

---

1. All quotations and page-citations from *A Sentimental Journey* refer to Laurence Sterne, *A Sentimental Journey Through France and Italy by Mr. Yorick*, ed. Gardner P. Stout, Jr. (Berkeley and Los Angeles: University of California Press, 1967). Cited hereafter by page number in the text.

IV).[2] Or Sterne may be partly understood in contrast to a "romantic and itinerant character" like Hazlitt, who likes to go a journey alone: "I laugh, I run, I leap, I sing for joy," he says in sublime communion with nature.[3] One of Hazlitt's most revealing remarks about travel as a means of self-fulfillment alludes critically to the voyage motif in Sterne's works: "'Let me have a companion of my way,' says Sterne, 'were it but to remark how the shadows lengthen as the sun goes down.' It is beautifully said; but in my opinion, this continual comparing of notes hurts the sentiment."[4] But it is precisely "this continual comparing" of oneself and others that transforms Yorick's encounters—even the momentary meeting of his finger with a lady's thumb—into a metaphorical and inner journey. His itinerary also consists of the path of his own thoughts and feelings, his desires and fears. The beautiful *Grisset*'s pulse throbs for a few protracted seconds. But it is Yorick's pulse, ever fluctuating with his own sensations, that quickens or slows the narrative. Although Sterne's metaphor of the journey has not excited as much scholarship as other motifs and figures, Morris Golden aptly notes that "it may be even closer to the core of the world he sensed."[5] Most recent critics of Sterne agree that his

2. Tobias Smollett, *Travels Through France and Italy*, ed. Frank Felsenstein (Oxford: Oxford University Press, 1981), pp. 12, 21.

3. William Hazlitt, "On Going a Journey," in *The Complete Works of William Hazlitt*, ed. P. P. Howe (London and Toronto: J. H. Dent and Sons, 1931), VII, 182. Hazlitt, it should be noted, partly retracts his exuberance about solitude in the final paragraphs of the essay, in which he admits that an English-speaking companion might be welcome in a foreign country. However, in his own travels through France, he "did not feel this want or craving [of companionship] very pressing once." He was content to have "breathed the air of general humanity."

4. Ibid., pp. 188–89.

5. "Sterne's Journeys and Sallies," *Studies in Burke and His Time*, 16:47. In a footnote to the introductory essay for his edition of *A Sentimental Journey*, Stout also observes, "In Yorick's travels, Sterne brought to its fullest realizaton the metaphor of life and of writing as a journey which is central to *Tristram Shandy* and to the *Sermons*," (p. 47, n.64).

Studies of *A Sentimental Journey* that focus on other major motifs include John Dilworth, *The Unsentimental Journey of Laurence Sterne* (New York:

experience consists of "the continually interrupted, inadequate moment of words, gesture, and feeling, quite apart from the world of things."[6] Yet the world outside the individual sensibility does, as Yorick attempts to record, matter. Alan Dougald McKillop and many subsequent readers have noted Yorick's double awareness of experience as simultaneously witty and sentimental.[7] Yet another kind of double awareness informs his responses, and this is his consciousness of experience, not simply as sexual, but as distinctly masculine and feminine.

Yorick's response to each person he meets thus varies "according to the mood [he] is in, and the case—and . . . the gender too, of the person" (p. 33). Relationships, and the kind of self-knowledge they provide, depend upon these distinctions; Sterne's puns on "case," "mood," and "gender" suggest a special grammar of thought and feeling with which the narrative is written and by which it may be read.[8] In particular, the inseparability of language and sexuality affects both the literal and metaphorical meanings of the journey as writing, life, and self-awareness. The episodes of *A Sentimental Journey* describe a series of male and female

XXX, 1948); Joseph Chadwick, "Interpretation in Sterne's *A Sentimental Journey*," *Eighteenth-Century Studies*, 12 (1979) 190–205; Martin C. Battestin, "*A Sentimental Journey* and the Syntax of Things," *Augustan Worlds*, ed. J. C. Hilson, M. M. B. Jones, and J. R. Watson (New York: Barnes and Noble, 1978), pp. 223–39; Henri Fluchère, *Laurence Sterne: From Tristram to Yorick*, trans. Barbara Bray (London: Oxford University Press, 1965), esp. pp. 354ff.

6. John Dussinger, *The Discourse of the Mind in Eighteenth-Century Fiction* (The Hague: Mouton, 1974), p. 173.

7. *The Early Masters of English Fiction* (Lawrence: University of Kansas Press, 1956), pp. 215–216.

8. Barbara Johnson observes in *The Critical Difference*: "[I]f literature could truly say what the relations between the sexes are, we would doubtless not need much of it . . . It is not the life of sexuality that literature cannot capture; it is literature that inhabits the very heart of what makes sexuality problematic for us speaking animals. Literature is not only a thwarted investigator but also an incorrigible perpetrator of the problem of sexuality." See *The Critical Difference: Essays in the Contemporary Rhetoric of Reading* (Baltimore: Johns Hopkins University Press, 1980), p. 13.

interactions that test and define Yorick. He cannot simply
laugh, run, leap, and sing for joy. His desires must negotiate
with a world of complicated urges for power and love, money
and sex, domination and dependence. As a "single man,"
he cannot simply say, "*Me voici! mes enfans*—here I am—."
His self-portrayal must be indirect and protracted: "There is
no more perplexing affair in life to me, than to set about telling anyone who I am—for there is scarce any body I cannot
give a better account of than myself" (p. 221). In "The
Passport" he points directly to his name on a page of *Hamlet*, but confusion follows: the Count de B**** completely
misperceives the thin stranger in the black silk breeches. "I
have often wished I could do it in a single word—and have
an end to it," Yorick laments unconvincingly. No single
mood, case, or gender adequately will name his complex self.

Another kind of difference influences the progress of
Yorick's journey. The people he is "taken with" constantly
participate in "sentimental commerce" (p. 78). They sell,
spend, give, or take. In these terms, connections between
language, sexuality, and money develop as the narrative
proceeds. The reader quickly discovers that the "great, great
Sensorium of the world! which vibrates, if a hair of our
heads but falls upon the ground" (p. 278) also is a great
emporium, which registers, as on a Dow Jones of sentiment,
the exchange of even a single *sou*. Aptly, Yorick wears
Eliza's portrait—female and symbolic of emotional power—
around his neck, while he carries the king's portrait—male
and symbolic of economic power—on the coins in his pocket.
In the world's vast marketplace, financial transactions are
both gender-related and language-related. The symbolic
action of *The Temptation. Paris.*" (pp. 235–36), for example,
derives first from writing: Yorick's trembling pen ("the devil
was in me") approaches the *fille de chambre*'s preferred
inkwell ("she offer'd it so sweetly"), and he wishes to
"write it, fair girl! upon thy lips" but "durst not." When
the characters move from the desk to the bed, their terms of
desire shift to commerce: "I'll just shew you, said the fair
fille de chambre, the little purse I have been making to-day to
hold your crown."

Yorick's awareness of difference, as a means of self-awareness, is oriented, obviously, toward a male perspective. Even the narrative's central metaphor of the journey is particularly masculine in the eighteenth century. Yorick has many contemporary fellow-travelers in many genres. Epic and mock-epic heroes, picaros and satiric *naifs*, philosophers and adventurers, pilgrims and historians, pack their valises and set out on the road. The ambulatory male, factual and fictionalized, appears at every turn.[9] *Tristram Shandy* offers two important paradigms. Tristram mounts his hobbyhorse to ride the king's highway. And, Slawkenbergius' Tale, Diego (or rather, Diego's metaphoric nose) mounted on a dark mule and "arrayed . . . in a crimson-satin pair of breeches" moves from town to town. In Yorick's catalogue of travelers, each "class" is masculine. He specifies "delinquents travelling under the direction of governors" and "young gentlemen transported by the cruelty of parents" (p. 79). Whether idle, vain, lying, proud, splenetic, or inquisitive, they are "these men I speak of" and "these gentlemen." To be expatriate is to be male; indeed, the journey of life seems framed by the grand tour at the start of manhood and the journey to a mild climate during the illnesses of old age. Like a descendant of Odysseus or Aeneas, the eighteenth-century traveler tests his identity abroad, while his Dido languishes in a village and his Penelope waits at home. Even more directly like a descendant of Don Quixote, the sentimental traveler discovers and leaves a Dulcinea at every inn. Yet Yorick's testing of himself in a foreign world presses him against the limits of this familiar figurative

9. On the subject of eighteenth-century travel writing see Charles Batten, *Pleasurable Instruction: Form and Convention in Eighteenth-Century Travel Literature* (Berkeley and Los Angeles: University of California Press, 1978). The general importance of the traveler, however, exceeds the scope of a single work. Accounts of journeys by women exist, of course, such as those by Lady Mary Wortley Montagu and Mrs. Piozzi. But such women are not free solitary travelers, nor do they match their male counterparts in number. Indeed, most familiar male writers of the century contribute in some way to "travels": Defoe, Swift, Boswell, Johnson, Gibbon, Smollett, Fielding, and Gray head the list.

shaping of life. The limitation of the journey metaphor is a limitation of gender; Yorick must transform his own metaphor in order to articulate what is feminine in the world and in himself.

Women are much less likely to sally forth alone.[10] They seldom venture independently because their movements are circumscribed by male relationships. Even a feisty and mobile figure like Moll Flanders stays close to home when unattached. Or she furtively wanders the streets, often in disguise. A paradigm of the female traveler would be the Austen heroine who walks from the house to the shrubbery and back, only if the weather is fine. Women who make excursions in *A Sentimental Journey* (with one exception to be discussed later) have male-determined motives for leaving home or are headed back into a male-determined role: they are wives, sisters, widows, and daughters whose presence on the road merely represents a transition back into stasis. Eliza joins her husband.[11] The lady in Calais meets her brother and only then is named as the sister of Monsieur de L***. Maria would go to England "as a daughter." No wonder the French captain does not wait for an answer to his rhetorical question: "*Et madame a son mari?*" (p. 108). And not surprisingly, the female reader disappears from the narrative. Tristram's careful projection of "Madam" and "Sir" as implied readers seems less relevant in the predominantly male context of the journey. Yorick, much more exclusively than Tristram, is a learned wit and thus belongs to the world of classically educated gentlemen from which women largely

10. In his letters, Sterne occasionally mentions women travelers as members of a group or with a chaperon. See, for example, *Letters of Laurence Sterne*, ed. Lewis Perry Curtis (Oxford: Clarendon Press, 1935), No. 221, p. 403. For a general discussion of the relationship of eighteenth-century women to male institutions, see John Richetti, "Women in Eighteenth-Century Literature," *What Manner of Woman: Essays on English and American Life and Literature*, ed. Marlene Springer (New York: New York University Press, 1977), pp. 65–97.

11. Yorick does not confront the fact of Daniel Draper explicitly in *A Sentimental Journey*.

were excluded.[12] Sterne must rework the feminine presence, not so much as implied audience, but as a force to be integrated into the understanding of Yorick as a man and writer.

With this problem of gender difference to solve, Sterne further elaborates the journey metaphor with details that constantly suggest the multiple concerns of language, sexuality, and money. For the attentive reader, words, objects, and actions hold several meanings simultaneously. And the trip—either through France or through Yorick's mental landscape—moves forward with the energy generated by these meanings and the tensions between them. With imagery as erudite as that of Pope's "Cave of Spleen," yet as common as that in eighteenth-century pornography, bits of scenery take on sexual identities and functions.[13] Purses, gloves, pates, doors, and snuffboxes, or swords, coins, pens, goats, and cockpits, set off trains of association. The hired vehicles that carry Yorick through France acquire case, mood, and gender. The *Desobligeant* is single, male, and antisocial until Yorick writes the Preface and thus moves it and himself back into the possibility of relationship. The *bidet* and the *vis-à-vis* have sexual connotations for La Fleur who has trouble straddling the *bidet* and goes "*pour faire le galant vis a vis de sa maitresse.*" The *Remise*, which contains both male and female, receives the fullest treatment of all its possible meanings: a hired coach; the act of putting back (the lady's hand); feelings of forgiveness (the monk); and a financial bargain or discount ("I never finished a twelve-guinea bargain so expeditiously in my life," says Yorick of

12. The exclusion of women from "male" classical education is discussed by Irene Tayler and Gina Luria in *What Manner of Woman*, pp. 98–133. Ian Watt assumes this exclusion, too, in *The Rise of the Novel* (Berkeley and Los Angeles: University of California Press, 1965), p. 151.

13. I assume that Sterne draws on conventions of seventeeth- and eighteenth-century libertine and pornographic literature. A differing view of the significance of Sterne's subtext is A. Franklin Parks, "Yorick's Sympathy for the Little: A Measure of his Sentimentality in *A Sentimental Journey,*" *Literature and Psychology* 28 (1978), 119–124.

its hire). Three important actions—writing, spending, and dying—become double and triple *entendres.* Ordinary actions—trying on gloves, putting away a book, passing someone in a hall, looking at a purse, feeling a pulse—are recounted in language rife with innuendo: "[I]f it is the same blood which comes from the heart, which descends to the extremes (touching her wrist) I am sure you must have one of the best pulses of any woman in the world—Feel it, said she holding out her arm. So . . . I took hold of her fingers in one hand, and applied the two forefingers of my other to the artery" (p. 164). Even philosophical statements transform themselves suggestively: "[T]he greatest they knew of, terminated in a general way, in little more than a convulsion." Frames of reference shift and blend, so that the articulation of their ostensible subject quietly is contradicted, often enriched, by others. As one meaning engenders another, so any object, action, or expression may acquire gender.

One must assume that the world of unstable and multiple meaning in *A Sentimental Journey* approximates the unsteady course of Yorick's self-understanding. If a man's desires and fears are expressed in terms of language, sexuality, and money, where does the journey of life lead? And can the available systems for evaluating life—the biblical wisdom of a sermon, the love of a "pure" woman like Eliza, a good bargain in the marketplace—be reconciled? The starling episode explores these questions. The bird (evoking the Latin pun on the author's name, *sturnus*) is one of several alter-egos for author and protagonist.[14] Locked in its cage, like the traditional symbol of the winged soul within the body, it "can't get out." Its confinement represents Yorick's threatened imprisonment in the Bastille and also his pent-up sexual energy, for he has "sworn to [Eliza] eternal fidelity." Both the bird and its owner are bound by the limitations of language. The single refrain, "I can't get out," is

14. See Stout's account of the starling as an emblem for Sterne and Yorick, *A Sentimental Journey*, pp. 205–206.

no more effective than Yorick's "single word." Finally, both are enclosed in the economic forces of sentimental commerce, which are always against them. Symbolically caught in unrelenting systems of language and money, the starling is alphabetically traded: "Lord A begg'd the bird of me—in a week, Lord A gave him to Lord B—Lord B made a present of him to Lord C—and Lord C's gentleman sold him to Lord D for a shilling—Lord D gave him to Lord E—and so on—" (pp. 204–205). The potential for such commerce to devalue the individual object (ultimately the starling has "little store set by him") relates to Yorick's persistent problem of ascertaining his own identity: "It is impossible but many of my readers must have heard of him; and if any by mere chance have ever seen him—I beg leave to inform them, that the bird was my bird—or some vile copy set up to represent him."

The starling's loss of value and identity has ominous implications for the traveler in the journey of life. Translation through language, exchange through money, and generation through sexuality fill the world of *A Sentimental Journey* with desire and fear of loss or gain. The bird's English words are misunderstood in France; it is given away and sold. It remains alone and so creates no genuine offspring but only "vile" copies. In contrast, Yorick recalls another bird, a libidinous cock-sparrow that has been observed engendering with vast procreative energy in an open window (p. 228). The sparrow has no problem with those animal spirits that "go cluttering [away] like hey-go-mad" on the first page of *Tristram Shandy*. Bevoriskius, who watches the sparrow and who is a learned writer like Yorick, is thus ironically distracted from authoring a "commentary upon the generations from Adam." The starling and the sparrow suggest that Sterne's principle metaphor of life (and writing about life) as a journey rests on an inevitable paradox, the same paradox that underlies *Tristram Shandy*, Book 7: Tristram leaves England to escape death, but with every passing moment approaches it more nearly. The "son of a whore" knocks on his door in France. *A Sentimental Journey*'s figurative elaboration of the paradox allows Sterne to explore the problem with greater concentration and depth. The journey of life, whatever its twists and turns, always leads to the same final destination, in which narrow place all unique personalities, all differences, merge. Yorick's reluctance to approach the end—or any kind of ending—is everywhere apparent, despite his supposed eagerness to reach fuller knowledge of his "heart." Repeatedly, he exclaims, "May I perish, if I do," reminding us that he certainly will perish in any case. His "quiet journey of the heart" may follow "the illusions of an imagination which is eternally misleading [him]" into "dirty thoughts," "melancholy," and eventually to that son of a whore. Dying, in one or the other of its senses, frequently weighs on his mind. His cough may make him "pale and sickly." Or he may think of sexual dying because he is "almost every hour . . . miserably in love with some one." Like the starling, he has little hope for the kind of immortality achieved by the engendering of the cock-sparrow. Human progeny, in direct contrast to the constant living memory of Tristram as a child, are a rare commodity in Yorick's world.

Reluctance to expend his manhood has a counterpart and substitute in Yorick's careful expenditure of capital, another commodity in short supply. Dying and spending, as in the bedroom scene with the *fille de chambre* or the glove-buying scene with the *Grisset*, arouse his conflicting emotions. Critics have found Sterne's epithet for the *Journey* (his "work of Redemption") a puzzling, "curious phrase."[15] Yet the phrase aptly combines spiritual with worldly gain and suggests the narrative parallel between dying and spending. Money is a common detail in travel accounts; many a bill of fare has found its way to publication. But rarely do these details acquire the metaphorical power inherent in Yorick's

15. John Dussinger, *Discourse of the Mind*, p. 175. Dussinger considers the word as a religious, not an economic term: "Redemption implies some former guilt, something concealed that the reader is to discover with Yorick's confession; yet the elusiveness continues in all the most intimate details revealed." My view is that Yorick's pun on redemption consistently reinforces the narrative's use of money to chart the progress of the soul.

distribution of guineas, crowns, and *sous* into purses, hands, pockets, and snuffboxes. Money becomes a measure of human relationship and a kind of life-force.[16]

Yorick begins *A Sentimental Journey* by imagining his own death (in this case, from indigestion) in terms of the *droits d'aubaine.* On the one hand, loss of life concurs with loss of wealth: Eliza will be "torn from [his] neck" and his pockets, emptied. On the other hand, while his living "arteries beat cheerily together," money flows, too. The healthy man may spend freely: "[He] pulls out his purse, and holding it airily and uncompress'd, looks around him, as if he sought for an object to share it with—In doing this, I felt every vessel in my frame dilate—the arteries all beat cheerily together, and every power which sustained life . . ." (p. 68). Stinginess is a "base passion" that makes him feel "very ill": "It must needs be a hostile kind of world, when the buyer . . . cannot go forth with the seller." Denying money to the monk and niggling with Monsieur Dessein put Yorick "into the same frame of mind . . . as if he was going along with him to Hyde-park corner to fight a duel," that is, as if he were facing death. Generosity signifies "power which sustain[s] life," according to a kind of spiritual currency. The "little bargains of honour" and "tribute . . . [he] could not avoid paying to virtue" invigorate him: "I never gave a girl a crown in my life which gave me half the pleasure" (p. 189), he says when he "has bought nothing.—Not one earthly thing" (p. 242). Sterne's "earthly" redemption through "sentimental commerce" also is accomplished by the writing and selling of the book; these boost his income while sales of *Tristram Shandy* lag. More figuratively within the narrative, Yorick's redemption (the "account" he must give to the "great Governor of nature") is negotiated through the

16. A comparable treatment of money as sentimental commerce occurs in the *Letters.* Sterne describes offering Lydia "ten guineas for her private pleasures." Her refusal, he writes, "affected me too much": "No, my dear papa, our expenses of coming from France may have straiten'd you—I would rather put an hundred guineas in your pocket than take ten out of it'—I burst into tears." No. 224, pp. 406–407.

currencies of charity, passion, and words as they are exchanged with men and women.

He overlaps these currencies in many ways, most interestingly through images of *hands*, engaging in all kinds of transactions. Hands that grasp, pay, write, and touch function as synecdoches for the intricacies of sentimental commerce. Typical of the narrative's synecdochic focus is "In the Street. Calais.": "[B]ase, ungentle passion! thy hand is against every man, and every man's hand against thee—heaven forbid! said she, raising her hand up to her forehead . . .—Heaven forbid indeed! said I, offering her my own—she had a black pair of silk gloves open only at the thumb and two forefingers, so accepted it without reserve—and I led her up to the door of the Remise" (p. 90). Most of the important "events" of the journey are enacted by hands: exchanging snuffboxes, trying on gloves, feeling a pulse, holding a sword, wiping away a tear, pulling a cord, pointing to *Hamlet*, distributing *sous*, stretching out from bed, or, of course, holding a pen. Hands connect in relationships expressing shifting modes of power: a hand that gives must be met by one that takes. Most moments of contact define one or more kinds of difference, so that the fleeting pressure of a finger momentarily establishes who commands and who yields. With these versatile synecdoches, the narrative gestures toward self-knowledge by showing (and writing, too, in Yorick's case) the boundary between the individual and the world.

The cultural systems toward which Yorick reaches out with pen, coin, or caress organize and control the distribution of power. If the central metaphor of the journey is masculine, the central concept in Yorick's masculine experience is the *father*. From the father ensue social, political, and economic hierarchies. The related ideas of *pater, patria* (or *ex patria*), and patrimony figure repeatedly in most episodes; they mark a distinct change from the preoccupation with fathers and fathering in *Tristram Shandy*. It is as difficult to imagine Tristram without a childhood, as it is to imagine Yorick with one, for Yorick always seems adult and knowing. He cares not at all about the differences between himself as child and man, but a great deal about the differences among men. He is far from home, but still moves within a social order based on paternal hierarchy and inhabited by citizens who variously possess and lack the father's potency, wealth, and knowledge. The individual's position on the scale of power generates both his self-image and his relationships. Yorick's first words invoke these assumptions by echoing a common sermon theme: "They order these matters better in [Heaven]."[17]

The heavenly Father, also the ultimate Author, engenders divine and human affairs, as he contains and metes out authority. His mundane counterparts, in the narrative, begin with king and descend through the aristocracy to common heads of households. Yorick realizes in the first episode that the king's secular law may deprive him of a legacy and a hypothetical heir. The implicit comparison between the good father in heaven and the bad one in France strongly influences Yorick's personal views. "Now I was a king of France," he imagines at the end of the episode, ". . . what a moment for an orphan to have begg'd his father's portmanteau of me!" The father's potential *largesse*, as the emanation of godly benevolence, casts a long shadow over *A Sentimental Journey*. None of its characters surpasses the parental ineptitude of Walter Shandy, but many test the adequacy of paternal ideals. Yorick's comic and self-conscious responses to the other male characters—and his dubious celebration of his own manhood—chart an uncertain course for the male journey to maturity.

Yorick's treatment of the beggars in Montreuil ("Montriul"), like his treatment of Maria, casts serious doubt on the efficacy of paternalistic behavior. Self-mocking, self-

17. John Stedmond, *The Comic Art of Laurence Sterne: Convention and Innovation in* Tristram Shandy *and* A Sentimental Journey (Toronto: University of Toronto Press, 1967), p. 143. Stedmond calls *A Sentimental Journey* "the critical commentary on the Sermons" and points out that the superiority of divine over human order is a common sermon theme. For further elaboration of the relation between Yorick's narrative and the Sermons, see pp. 132–160.

indulgent, Yorick undercuts his own benevolent role. He surely receives more than his eight-*sous* worth of obsequious flattery from the "sons and daughters of poverty" who lavish "My Lord *Anglois*" on him. And despite his protective sentiments toward Maria, his fancied "daughter" is left behind in the market at Moulines. The power to give and withhold brings Yorick virtuous pleasure in "The Conquest." But power proves an ambiguous force of unequal distribution, despite his wishful assertion, "as if man to man was not equal, throughout the whole surface of the globe." "If" becomes a crucial word, along with other phrases like "wast thou" and "I would." Most of his imagined egalitarianism or generosity is speculative, as in the highly conditional terms of his benevolence toward Maria (p. 273). Authority and dependency determine who he is and how he behaves; sentimental commerce cannot operate without such distinctions. The balance sheet sometimes is clearly in his favor.

Yorick as expatriate also must explore the liabilities of lost power: "I should not like to have my enemy take a view of my mind," he says on his way to the Duc de C*****, "when I am going to ask protection of any man." Subservience makes his thoughts "dirty" and his heart "servile." An even more painful lesson in the interaction of power and dependency follows his misinterpretation of "The Riddle." Yorick wrongly believes that flattery will allow him to control others. But by indiscriminately allying himself to every affluent member of French society, he is enslaved. "For three weeks together, I was of every man's opinion I met," he says, and, by means of sycophancy, "could have eaten and drank and been merry all the days of my life." At first, his submissiveness merely earns him the patronizing epithet "un bon enfant," rightly reminding him that he is *ex patria*. But soon the "bon enfant" has become a prostitute: "[O]ne night, after a most vile prostitution of myself to half a dozen different people," he confesses, "I grew sick—went to bed" (p. 266). In terms of sentimental commerce, in which money is a life-force, "'twas a dishonest reckoning" and a dangerous one, too. Yorick's disillusionment with the power of flattery is deeply felt, for he had exaggerated the solution to the riddle as "a secret at least equal to the philosopher's stone." The flattering beggar, after all, had hoped only for a twelve-*sous* piece. Yorick's extreme servility of imagination in Parisian society makes him feel like a pampered child and like a whore, but not like a man in the image of the Father.

Similar themes are viewed differently in "The Captive." After solving the riddle, Yorick utterly suppresses his own ideas and caters to the fantasies of other people. In contrast, fear of the Bastille makes him "[give] full scope to [his own] imagination." Here he savors a fantasy in which he subjugates another man to his power. As Yorick pulls the strings, so the captive twitches with pain: "I took a single captive, and having first shut him up in his dungeon, I then look'd through the twilight of his grated door to take his picture" (p. 201). Like a cruel father locking up an innocent child, Yorick afflicts the captive with his own worst fears: sickness, solitude, and hopelessness. Fittingly, the captive is a grieving father: "his children—" thinks Yorick as his "heart began to bleed." The captive even becomes a crude kind of writer: "with a rusty nail he was etching another day of misery to add to the heap." But this extreme exercise of authorial power also proves fruitless, and Yorick "could not sustain the picture of confinement which [his] fancy had drawn" (p. 203).

The systems generated from the father—*pater, patria*, and patrimony—and their manifestations in language, sex, and money, provide a coherent standard for most of the male population of *A Sentimental Journey*. Yorick inevitably thinks in these terms. The monk, a poor celibate, irritates him instinctively. Only after he learns the monk's history as soldier and lover, does he become "the good monk" and, finally, "Father Lorenzo." The narrative includes absent fathers (the captive), dead fathers (Maria's), the first father (Bevoriskius' Adam), and unnatural fathers (Yorick says of the mourner near Nampont, "I thought by the accent, it had been an apostrophe to his child; but 'twas to his ass" [p. 138]). The public derides Monsieur l'Abbe: "*Quelle grossierte*," agrees Yorick. Male heads of households include the ineffectual husband of the beautiful *Grisset* and the hen-pecked notary. A *chichesbeo* seems to wait for every matron, and, in the city, Yorick finds "[e]very third man a pigmy": "[W]hat struck me the moment I cast my eyes over the *parterre* . . . was, the unaccountable sport of nature in forming such numbers of dwarfs." He remembers Toby Shandy's opinion that the siring of such diminished examples of manhood is "worse than getting nothing." In Paris the identities of man and child become confused. Yorick helps "a little boy" across a gutter, but "turning up his face to look after him, [he] perceived that he was about forty."

The stories of the Chevalier de St. Louis and the Marquis de E**** receive special attention: they "reflect light upon each other" and upon the cultural systems generated from the idea of the father. Both are good men who fall on hard times. Loss of patrimony drives both into "no resource but commerce." Both are denied fertility: the chevalier has no children; the Marquis' "successful application to business" means "smiting the root forever of the little tree his pride and affection wish'd to see reblossom." Yet patriarchal power saves both. A stronger father, the king, gives the chevalier a new patriarchy in the form of 1500 livres a year. "About nine months later," Yorick specifies, the soldier is reborn into a new life. The Marquis, who bears the sins of his noble ancestors through twenty years of business, also renews his manhood. The ceremony of the unmistakeably phallic patriarchal sword, lost but regained, prompts Yorick's effusive, "O how I envied him his feelings!" Money effectively redeems a man's life in these stories. The balance of sentimental commerce is always against the expatriated adventurer. But for these exceptional characters, real commerce leads to repatriation; they are not spent but saved.

The stories of the Chevalier and the Marquis have happy endings that illustrate the benevolent aspect of the paternal hierarchy. Indeed, the fact that they have endings at all suggests their significance in Yorick's metaphorical journey. Most stories in *A Sentimental Journey*, including the narrator's, flagrantly lack closure. "The Fragment." is an obvious example: both stories, the notary's and the dying gentleman's, break off abruptly. "And where is the rest of it, La Fleur?" asks Yorick. Other fragments of language are scattered along his route: among them, the starling's repetitive chirps, the captive's forlorn scratches, and the German's sighs. Madame L*** "had been prevented from telling [him] her story." Maria's account of "how she had born it, and how she got supported, she could not tell." Yorick himself tries "to return back to the story of the poor German and his ass—. . . and could no more get into it again." He tries to complete two letters but fails: "I begun and begun again . . . throwing the pen down despairingly" (p. 151). "I took up a pen—I laid it down again—" (p. 235). Unfinished stories, like incomplete transactions of money and unconsummated sexual acts, are part of the testing of personal power within the patriarchal hierarchy. The metaphor of the journey of life and of writing makes language a source of power; it, too, flows concurrently within life. Yorick tries to convince himself that the terror of the Bastille "is in the word," that with "pen and ink and paper and patience, albeit a man can't get out, he may do very well within" (p. 196). But often he is forced into "unsaying." Sometimes he searches vainly for "a single word," at others he is frustrated by "saying too much," at still others, by silence ("where is the rest of it?"). Each fragment, retraction, and omission suggests that language (like other systems of power) is for any man a problematic way to achieve self-completion and continuity. Despite Yorick's considerable prowess with words, often flamboyantly displayed, he urges us to notice the times when his page stays blank or blotted. What the heavenly Father says, is so. But for Yorick, "[t]here is no more perplexing affair in life, than . . . telling."

On his masculine journey, then, Yorick meets other men whose finished and unfinished stories shed light on his own. They express both desire and fear about what the hierarchy of the father may mean for the individual, especially when he is cast out from the world of *patria*. The old gentleman in "The Fragment," wants to tell a narrative about who he is, a parallel to Yorick's efforts to give an account of himself. All this testing culminates in Yorick's final encounter with a man and suggests that he has made a certain progress. "The Supper." and "The Grace." bring him to an idealized earthly patriarch: "The family consisted of an old grey-headed man and his wife, with five or six sons and sons-in-law and their several wives, and a joyous genealogy out of 'em" (p. 281). Yorick feels "magick" and "an elevation of spirit," for the old man gives the expatriate a new home: "I sat down at once like a son of the family," says Yorick, as he joins their "feast of love." Earlier, he was falsely "un bon enfant"; now he honestly becomes "like a son."

Symbolic actions reinforce the climactic feeling of union and integration. The group gathers around the table, while Yorick borrows the old man's knife to cut a loaf of bread. A shared flagon of wine consecrates the meal. Earlier meetings with false or inadequate fathers are now transcended by a joyous epiphany. Former "illusions of an imagination which is eternally misleading [him]" now bring him the blessings of paternal grace. As the old man presides over the family's traditional dance, Yorick soars to visionary rapture: "In a word, [he] thought [he] beheld *Religion* mixing in the dance" (p. 284). Although *Tristram Shandy* includes a comparable epiphany of country joy (Book 7, chap. 43, pp. 537–538), Tristram's vision centers on a "Nut Brown Maid."[18] Yorick, on the other hand, responds most fully to the ideal patriarch who reminds him of the Heavenly Father of his *Sermons*: generous, engendering, and above the limitations of language. "[The old man] said, that a chearful and contented mind was the best sort of thanks to heaven that an illiterate peasant could pay—Or a learned prelate either, said [Yorick]" (p. 284).

The encounter brings the traveler a moment of equipoise in which the antithetical forces generated by the patriarchal system seem reconciled. The hands that join in the dance share in rhythm and movement. Differentiating relationships of power and submission, freedom and bonds, seem

18. Even more precisely, Tristram fixes on the slit in the skirt (*Tristram Shandy*, Book 7, chap. 43, pp. 537–538).

harmonized, so that the festive scene might end a comedy. The scene does not, however, conclude *A Sentimental Journey*, nor does the father sufficiently give meaning to the expatriate's experience. His world, literally and metaphorically, is also female. And women inspire his "continuing comparing" according to other kinds of difference. No maternal deity shares the throne with the Heavenly Father. Although Nature is feminine, even "she" must yield to the masculine authority of the "great Governor of Nature." Mothers of any kind rarely cross Yorick's path and never absorb the main focus of his attention. Rather, the other focus of the narrative is on love ("teach us to love one another better than we do") as a special "branch of [sentimental] commerce," with its own specialized currency of money, tears, and words.

The primary metaphor associated with women is the circular "ring of pleasure."[19] Its enclosed shape contrasts directly with the linear configuration of the "male" metaphor of the journey. For Yorick, the ring holds an enigma from which he often feels excluded and which is crucial to his attempts at self-understanding. When he is "left solitary and alone in [his] own chamber," he looks out on Paris as a waking man might look into his own dreams. He sees a fantasy of sexual attraction that intensifies his own feelings of foreignness, of being, for a moment, a self-reflective outsider in a world hypnotically driven by desire: "I walked up gravely to the window in my dusty black coat, and looking through the glass saw all the world in yellow, blue, and green, running at the ring of pleasure . . . all—all tilting at it like fascinated knights in tournaments of yore for fame and love" (pp. 155–156). In the "glittering" male world, not only "the young in armour bright," but even "the old with broken lances" attempt the female ring. The presence of the old, "broken" knights in the game suggests a lifelong urge toward the enigmatic circle, and a lifelong frustration of

---

19. See Stout's explanation and background information on the ring of pleasure in chivalric lore and as a slang term, p. 156, n.14.

lasting union. If the father organizes Yorick's experience of men, the ring of pleasure connects his experience of different women. If he feels the problems of *ex patria*, he also feels the problems of being outside the circle. The fantastic scene below his window, for example, makes him feel "reduced" to a solitary "atom." He knows he must go down and enter the tournament, too.

Yorick tries hard to respond fully to women on his "journey of the heart." He prolongs the descriptions of female encounters with the smallest details of look, gesture, and dialogue, as he tilts metaphorically at the ring of pleasure in the form of letters, purses, inkwells, gloves, and hands. Each episode is a kind of trial, and he often approaches women in his role of the quixotic knight, armed with stereotypes of male desire. Usually, these provide a neat compliment to the paternal ideal: power and submission in terms of money, sex, and language. Wryly and self-consciously, Yorick discovers the inadequacy of his approach.

False pretexts about women disrupt the text that Yorick is trying to write about himself. Every time he assigns a woman to a conventional role, he must adopt a reciprocal role. As one convention begins to contradict another, or is contradicted by experience, the instability and artificiality of the roles becomes apparent. For example, a woman as an "angel of light" or divine "goddess" requires an adoring apostle who dispenses good deeds in her name. Yorick tries to "conceive every fair being as a temple" (p. 219) and to worship at "the pure taper of Eliza." He also relies on the stereotype of a heroine-in-distress who requires a romance hero to protect her. The lady in Calais promises a "melancholy adventure" that suits Yorick in his role of Knight of the Woeful Countenance. Yorick reads some women according to the paradigm of Eve. Maria, who has yielded to temptation yet bears some traces of past innocence, requires an understanding companion in a postlapsarian world of sin and death. Like the illustration to Bevoriskius' commentary—a "queer little plate of Death enclosing Adam and Eve in his net while Eve offers the apple to her spouse"[20]—the daughter of Eve appeals to Yorick in his role as Parson and sermon-writer. Finally, the seductress requires a man who is capable of carnality. While the *Grisset*'s eyes flash "Most willingly, monsieur," or while she lays "her hand on [his] own to detain [him]," Yorick struggles to protect his virtue: "Whatever . . . the trials of my virtue—whatever is my danger— . . . let me feel the movements which rise out of it, and which belong to me as a man" (pp. 237–238).

Each account of a woman also produces an account in the currencies of sentimental commerce: a story, a financial transaction, a physical exchange of touch or tears. In this way, Yorick tries to merge his identity with the women he meets. It is a kind of engendering that works best when he knows as little as possible about his partner, and thus meets little resistance to the imposition of his cultural assumptions. "When your eyes are fixed upon a dead blank—you draw purely from yourselves," he justly observes. Like blank pages to be filled with his own imaginings, women seem interchangeable to the sentimental lover. Yorick has "been in love with one princess or another almost all [his] life." One princess (Eliza) keeps him sexually virtuous, or provides a good excuse. Another princess (the anonymous lady) keeps him from mean actions toward the monk. Eliza is oddly and casually depersonalized into a remote presence, burning like one distant star within a galaxy. Sounding a little like Browning's duke, Yorick describes "[his] last flame happening to be blown out by a whiff of jealousy on the sudden turn of a corner" (p. 146). Typically, it is the "pleasurable ductility" of the lady in Calais that attracts him. Before she has name, history, or even a face ("'twas not material"), Yorick's "drawing was instantly set about" (p. 92).

In fact his comically stubborn determination to avoid the "real" woman in favor of the imaginary "type" puts him through some amusing maneuvers: "I had got ground enough for the situation which pleased me—and had she

20. Ibid., p. 350.

remained close beside my elbow until midnight, I should
have held true to my system, and considered her only under
that general idea" (p. 107). The "general idea" or cultural
cliché of woman and the particular woman repeatedly collide.
Before he sees the lady's face, he fits her out as a goddess.
When she draws aside her veil to reveal a face "not critically
handsome," he switches her to the role of widow in distress.
When he holds her hand, she is transformed into a lover: "I
could have taken her into my arms and cherished her." No
sooner has he "settled the affair in [his] fancy" that she is
bereaved, than her first words jestingly bespeak her sense of
humor, *"C'est bien comique,* 'tis very droll, said the lady
smiling" (p. 110). When he decides that his offer of sharing
the *Remise* would shock her, she lets him know she would
have accepted. He renders her lonely; she meets her
brother. He persists in making her his "poor lady,"
although we find that she is sister to a count. Only when
Yorick gets her safely out of the way, before she has had a
chance to tell her own story, can he fully indulge his version
of the damsel in distress: "with what a moral delight will it
crown my journey," he complacently imagines, "in sharing
the sickening incidents of a tale of misery told to me by such
a sufferer? to see her weep! . . . what an exquisite sensation
is there still left, in wiping them from off the cheeks of the
first and fairest of women, as I'm sitting with my handkerchief in my hand in silence the whole night beside her" (p.
146). By reverting to his original vision of the unseen "goddess," now restored to "the first and fairest of women," he
cancels out the intervening episodes. He remains true to his
"system" and amusingly false to experience.

He perceives Maria through even more pretexts about
female types. First, she is literally lifted out of the pages of
another book, *Tristram Shandy*: "The story [Tristram] had
told of that disorder'd maid affect'd [Yorick] not a little in
the reading" (p. 269). Maria might also be found on the
pages of the book Yorick encounters in Paris, *Les Egarments
de Coeur et de l'Esprit* (p. 188), in which she would be a perfect wandering heroine. Yorick weeps, then, but at Maria's
actual story, for she is conveniently out of her mind and

inarticulate. He responds to other versions of her: Tristram's, her mother's, countless other romance-writers', his own. He is startled by her physical presence: "And is your heart still so warm, Maria?" he asks. The dripping handkerchief, the faithless goat, the virginal white dress, the song played on the pipe, Maria's long hair and silken net, her "scarce earthly" looks—all of these details suggest that Yorick is constructing an elaborate pastiche of literary symbols to cover the improbability of Maria. Her artificial pathos, and the comic extremes to which Yorick must resort to maintain it, are epitomized in the sign "S" (Shandy but also Sterne): "[S]he took the handkerchief out of her pocket to let me see it; . . . on opening it I saw an S mark'd in one of the corners" (p. 272). With this authorial mark, which somehow has wandered from *Tristram Shandy* onto a page of *A Sentimental Journey*, Sterne claims Maria as a transferable convention, as a space on which to write. It is not surprising to learn that eighteenth-century female-readers could laugh at such hyperbolic portrayals of women. Mrs. Thrale describes her daughters' unsophisticated but healthy reaction: "I remember many years ago, when Susan and Sophia came home one Time from Kensington School . . . they used to repeat some Stuff in an odd Tone of Voice, & to laugh obstreperously at their Own Ideas—upon Enquiry we found out that 'twas the pathetic Passages in *Sterne's Maria* that so diverted & tickled their Spleen."[21] Yorick may indulge in another protective fantasy of his power to care for a weak and handsome damsel, but he leaves Maria to find her own way home.

The most comic example of this propensity to substitute pretextual accounts of women for particular women is the letter from Jacques Roque that Yorick uses in place of his own to Madame L***. "*Chaucun a son tour*," he ironically admits, "*Vive l'amour! et vive la bagatelle!*" (p. 153). He

21. *Thraliana; the Diary of Mrs. Hester Lynch Thrale (later Mrs. Piozzi) 1776–1809*, ed. Katherine M. Balderston (Oxford: Clarendon Press, 1942), II, 823–824.

errs when he depends upon pretexts about women and when he loses himself in fantasies of wish-fulfillment. Corrective parallels and echoes within the text of *A Sentimental Journey* redress some of these mistakes and expose inappropriate clichés. Yorick imagines himself sitting devotedly by "the fountain of [Madame L***'s] tears." But he later "serve[s] at [Madame Rambouliet's] fountain," where he is reminded that a "tender flower" also may "[p]luck [a] rose" (p. 183).[22] Similarly, his revery about Maria first generalizes her toward an ideal: "she was feminine—and so much was there about her of all that the heart wishes, or the eye looks for in a woman" (p. 275). These musings conclude with a biblical allusion, that "she should not only eat of my bread and drink of my own cup, but Maria should lay in my bosom, and be unto me as a daughter." But the same biblical passage, here tenderly evoking sentiment for the shorn lamb, has also been applied in Nampont to the dead ass that blocks the road (p. 139). Yorick's fairy tale princesses refuse to stay quietly in towers of literary convention.

Other female stereotypes lead to other kinds of resistance. When Yorick is not dewy-eyed with empathy, he may be riveted by the smallest detail of the female body. The narrative slows almost to a standstill while he concentrates on the throb of an artery, the pressure of a palm, or the warmth of a tear. He is fascinated by the sensations that women arouse in him and the comic/sentimental challenge of controlling them. He sublimates the back-and-forth movement of love-making with Madame L***, the Marquesina di F****, the *Grisset*, the *filles de chambre*, and Maria. These women typically draw him into self-contradiction when he relies on the problematic "general idea" of who they are. They seem to hold out the apple, perhaps in the shape of an inkwell or a purse, and they never say no, only "*tres voluntiers*". Yorick thus thinks of dying, spending, shame, and guilt, and of the link between sexuality and mortality. Genteelly, he arouses

---

22. For the background of these idioms for excretory functions, see Stout, pp. 182–184.

"dirty thoughts"; and while paying a "tribute to virtue," he is symbolically lewd. He claims that he cannot bear the least indecent suggestion, yet he suggests indecencies. Through feelings of consanguinity for the *fille de chambre* and of pity for Maria, he mingles blood and tears instead of bodies. He knows that "some threads of love and desire" cannot be removed from the "whole web" of human interactions, but neither can he follow these threads to their ends. He idealizes communion, but he is governed by difference.

If encounters with women challenge Yorick's disembodied ideal of the "fair spirit," they also end in comic realizations about women as flesh and blood. As a group they are vital, kind, pleasant, and good. He feels tempted by them, yet, like the *Grisset*, they seem "really interested, that [he] should not lose [him]self." He tries to imagine that he could perform some important service for them, but they all manage to get along without him. They never seem as worried about their own virtue or decorum as Yorick seems worried for them. "Such were my temptations" is, ironically, his assessment.

The sensorium of Yorick's world vibrates with every contact with female anatomy (of which *A Sentimental Journey* has numerous examples), and, indeed, physical contact becomes the crucial mechanism by which spiritual progress and self-knowledge occur. Women make Yorick aware of his own body, and moments of physical sensation make him cry, "I am positive I have a soul." The desire to touch is transmuted from temptation to spiritual renewal, according to a doctrine proposed in his *Sermons*: the "strict correspondence which is held between our souls and our bodies."[23] The *Sermons* argue that "this strict correspondence" is essential to "the frame and mechanism of human nature" which has "need of all [the] external helps which nature has made the interpreters of our thoughts." Thus "men cloathed with bodies . . . cannot be touched or sensibly affected, without producing some corresponding emotion in

23. Ibid., pp. 162–163.

[the soul]." By means of this ingenious explanation, sexual arousal becomes a reminder of the spirit; it is a positive good promising redemption. But Yorick's female clichés make this doctrine problematic. Who stirs him—angel or Eve? The desire to touch reminds him of his immortal soul, or rather, of the difference between immortal soul and mortal body. He is in no hurry to unclothe the naked spirit that moves when the *fille de chambre* "pass[es] her hand across [his] neck," nor does immortal longing seem uppermost in his thoughts. Rather, he frequently reminds us that all of a man's little deaths will be followed by a long, and fearfully anticipated, one. And, in keeping with Sterne's metaphors, all a man's expenditures will lead to a final, also feared, redemption.

The inconsistencies among Yorick's ways of understanding women lead to the problem of his difficult confrontation with what is female in himself. He may call his fancy "a deceiving slut" and he may apologize if tears make him "as weak as a woman." Yet when he makes his "eloge" on love as "the passion" solely responsible for "all generosity and goodwill" and (when love wanes) for increases of "Misery" (pp. 128–129),[24] he sounds less like Cervantes' masculine Don Quixote and more like Charlotte Lennox's female Quixote, Lady Arabella: "She was taught to believe, that Love was the ruling Principle of the World; that every other Passion was subordinate to this; and that it caused all the Happiness and Miseries of Life."[25] Further, Yorick seems implicitly to recognize that, in addition to the capacity to be "always in love," what is most valuable in himself is most closely related to the engendering power of women: his creative powers as writer, even as a writer of a male journey. This incipient androgeny—a more satisfactory reconciliation of difference than his uneasy and contradictory responses— underlies his instinctive testing of cultural clichés about what

24. The entire passsge (pp. 128–129) is of interest as a feminizing of the quixotic notion of romance and love.

25. Charlotte Lennox, *The Female Quixote*, ed. Margaret Dalziel (London: Oxford University Press, 1970), p. 7.

is female. As an author, he desires to—and in a sense does—contain both genders within himself. Aptly, Sterne describes the writing and publication of *A Sentimental Journey* by metaphorically transforming himself into a pregnant woman: "I am going to ly in; being at Christmas at my full reckoning . . . [and] shall have the honour of presenting . . . a couple of as clean brats as ever chaste brain conceiv'd."[26] The fascination with the female ring of pleasure is its creative function of renewal and birth; it offers another metaphor of life as the "little span" (p. 114) that might be breached by the author's pen.

In his last episode, following the paternal resolution of "The Grace," Yorick enters a completely female world. La Fleur disappears, and the companions who accompany him are the hostess at the inn and two other women. Thus the episode's gender is female, and its case, he specifies, is delicate ("The Case of Delicacy."). After passing various alter egos and projections of himself along the road, he meets a lady-traveler who, like himself, is unattached and unassigned to any pretext or cultural cliché. She has no male-relationship to define her. The chamber she and Yorick eventually share has, as in the symbolism of a dream, two identical beds ("parallel" and "very close together") separated by a "flimsy transparent curtain" which divides male and female halves. The atmosphere is "full of difficulties every way," all resulting from an acute awareness of the difference between them. Equally they make claims and concessions as they debate the comic "treaty of peace." This makes a verbal prelude to Yorick's "ejaculation" and "asseveration," actions made possible by the inseparability of language and sexuality. Another silent female presence lurks between them, and, when Yorick tries to break the

26. *Letters*, No. 233, p. 405. This passage is quoted by Stout, *A Sentimental Journey*, p. 1. Sterne uses the birth metaphor again in Letter 229, with reference to the publication of *A Sentimental Journey*. Although metaphorical pregnancy is not unique to Sterne among male writers (Sidney's Astrophel, for example), Sterne typically is self-conscious and emphatic in his re-use of any conventional figure of speech.

barrier, this is what he enounters with his famous gesture:
"when I stretch'd out my hand, I caught hold of the *fille de
chambre*'s   ." His outstretched hand, catching hold of
the empty space on the page should remind the reader of the
knights and the empty ring.[27] Yorick fancies himself as a
traveler who has "eyes to see, what time and chance are perpetually holding out to him as he journeyeth on his way."
But his narrative stops at a moment when he cannot see at
all and when "time and chance" have held out something
that he finds literally unaccountable. Thus he remains,
reaching out to what is female, beyond himself, and beyond
the power of language and money. It is Sterne's joke on
himself to have found his "End" in the same anatomical
place where he began. The world is big with jest, and
Sterne, too, would be in that interesting condition.

The metaphor of the journey—of life, of writing, of self-
knowledge—seems to reach an impasse. In his encounters
with women, Yorick does not experience a bright epiphany
like the celebratory scene of patriarchal benevolence and harmony in "The Grace." A more difficult task of integration
remains, and death still draws near. Sterne's solution to
these dilemmas is suggested in the letter he wrote about the
"birth" of his travels. "Being at Christmas at [his] full
reckoning," the delivery of *A Sentimental Journey* will evidence a second miraculous conception, a mysterious joining
of the Father in heaven with the author's pregnant but
"chaste brain." In this ultimate incorporation of sentimental
commerce, male and female successfully combine. By leaving Yorick in the dark bedroom at the inn and obscurely
joining his hand with "the *fille de chambre*'s   ,"
Sterne does engender an unending account that earns him
immortality.

27. For a different and interesting interpretation of the final unfinished
sentence, see Jonathan Lamb, "Language and Hartleian Association in *A
Sentimental Journey*," *Eighteenth-Century Studies*, 13:285–312.

ALEX PAGE

"Straightforward Emotions and Zigzag Embarrassments" in Austen's *Emma*

Why does Emma Woodhouse take up with Harriet Smith so impetuously? Why are there so many parlor games in this novel, so many playwrights at work? Why is there so much playacting? The possible answers seem to me to have a strong bearing on Emma's psychic development. This development does not proceed—whose does?—in a straight line. Its major strand is the "awakening of a normal, intelligent, young woman to the possibilites of physical love," but there are impediments of all sorts, some of which do not show above the surface.[1]

Listing the ostensible reasons for Emma's befriending Harriet so expeditiously may help answer our questions and will certainly rekindle our admiration for the rich web of motives and implications in which Jane Austen envelops her people as they live through a hypercharged year:

Emma is at loose ends, having just "lost" her friend and former governess Miss Taylor to marriage, and therefore is on the lookout for a quasi replacement.—She is convinced that it was she who

---

1. Joseph M. Duffy, Jr., "Emma: The Awakening from Innocence," *English Literary History*, 21 (1954), 40. This seminal essay claims that the conflict in *Emma* is between fancy and nature, with the heroine letting go of the former and embracing the latter, namely, reality.

engineered the marriage and, returning home in a flush of triumph, hatches the plan of doing Mr. Elton, the young vicar of Highbury, a like favor.—She is bored, or she knows that she will be bored after the wedding has faded, with Highbury society; in one of those electric shocks of revelation we are told that she "used to despise the place";[2] Harriet offers a welcome diversion; She means to prove to Knightley that her success in arranging the Weston marriage was no fluke.—It is commensurate with her position of empress of Highbury to "notice" a promising member of the lower orders, to be "useful" to her, and to "raise" her socially a notch or two.—To remind her subjects of her exalted status, Emma engages, as only an absolute monarch may, in what is taboo to others.—Emma basks in the flood of gratitude that flows so richly from Harriet.

These motives rumble and clank in what I called a hypercharged year. For the Weston marriage has released an inordinate amount of sexual energy. Before it, Emma's life, we are given to understand, was an unusually sheltered one— "there is nobody hereabouts to attach her; and she goes so seldom from home," Knightley remarks to Mrs. Weston ambivalently (p. 41). He is jealous, presently Emma will be jealous, and so will Jane Fairfax; there is the Emma-Churchill flirtation, the Elton marriage, a scandalous (imagined) affair, not to mention "Emma's delight in matching wills with Mr. Knightley," according to one commentator who goes on to say: "This sexual energy is channelled into social forms but not contained by them."[3] Surely this burgeoning of sexual energy accounts in large measure for the emotions at play when Emma meets Harriet for the first time: "[Harriet] was a very pretty girl, and her beauty happened to be of a sort which Emma particularly admired. She was short, plump, and fair, with a fine bloom, blue eyes,

2. *The Novels of Jane Austen*, ed. R. W. Chapman, 3rd ed. (Oxford: Oxford University Press, 1933), p. 221. All subsequent quotations are from this edition with page numbers given in the text.

3. Jan S. Fergus, "Sex and Social Life in Jane Austen's Novels," in *Jane . Austen in a Social Context*, ed. David Monaghan (Totowa, N. J.: Barnes & Noble, 1981), p. 83.

light hair, regular features, and a look of great sweetness; and before the end of the evening, Emma was as much pleased with her manners as her person, and quite determined to continue the acquaintance" (p. 23). Harriet's conversation is undistinguished, but she is so "engaging," "grateful," and "artlessly impressed" that "encouragement should be given." And then "those soft blue eyes and all those natural graces should not be wasted on the inferior society of Highbury" (p. 23). Why, Emma has fallen in love at first sight, or at least is suddenly infatuated. Harriet's beauty does it, especially "those soft blue eyes," the seat of libidinal power since time immemorial.

It is worth reminding ourselves that the novel does not begin "Emma Woodhouse, beautiful, clever, and rich," but "*handsome*, clever, and rich." Nobody calls Emma beautiful except Mrs. Weston (p. 39), and she is far more partial to Emma than the narrator. Emma prides herself on "penetration," that is, quickness, depth, and accuracy of understanding, and very early she is led to conclude that Harriet has next to none. Emma is a consummate manager and organizer. A woman of twenty-one, she runs a sizable household with exemplary efficiency and has done so since she was twelve; she can deal effectively with virtually everyone in Highbury. To watch her handle her father is to watch a renowned surgeon do a quadruple bypass. Can one not say there is a slight, yet unmistakable, masculine component in her temperament? On a masculine-feminine scale we should find Harriet way over at the feminine end while Emma would be a bit further toward the masculine pole, further than any other woman in the novel (excluding Mrs. Elton), or for that matter any heroine in any Austen novel.

No sooner has Emma "appropriated" Harriet than she hastens to match her with Mr. Elton. What is the rush? It takes little more than ten pages and two weeks before Emma has made Harriet cast Robert Martin aside and put forward the vicar. If there is any truth to Emma's being in love with Harriet, why would she be so eager to do away with one suitor only to line up another, ignoring for the moment the inferior social status of the first? Would she not want to keep

Harriet to herself?[4] There is some feverish haste in promoting the Elton match, a haste which is not sufficiently accounted for by Emma's customary dispatch in managing things. I suggest that the erotic feelings she has for Harriet are to her a source of confusion, uncertainty, insecurity, and perhaps danger, and the best way she can allay them is by doing the "natural" and socially most near-at-hand thing—find her a respectable husband. But if that is so, why would not Robert Martin do? Here the class distinction is relevant, not as an abstract principle but as a day-to-day practicality: Emma could not be with her beloved if she became Mrs. Martin. (This will cease to be an issue later when she is sure that "their friendship must change into a calmer sort of goodwill" [p. 482].)

But class difference isn't everything. The courtship between Harriet and Martin has ripened to a point at which an offer of marriage has been made—in short, the most interesting part of the courtship (to Emma) is over. Nothing more lies waiting than either marriage or rejection. This is not the case if Mr. Elton is the suitor. There the courtship from inception to fruition lies shining all before her, and the assiduous organizer of it may be in the very midst of its ups and downs, may be the prime observer with a front-row seat. The object of her observation is to see "how it is done," how a courtship progresses and culminates in a union—a most understandable curiosity in a vivacious, nubile, clever, yet wholly inexperienced, young woman. In short, she enjoys through Harriet "an experimental relationship with a man."[5]

Then how does such a clever young woman *not* see that Elton directs his attention to her, using Harriet merely as a bridge? It is a convenient, involuntary blindness on her part in order to remain the uninvolved spectator. However, she is more than that; she is the writer and director of this play.

---

4. She uses these very words (p. 66) when she hoodwinks Knightley into believing she has given up matchmaking.

5. Duffy, "Emma," p. 45.

Emma achieves two goals: her homoerotic feelings are safely channeled into a sanctioned activity—matchmaking— while at the same time she learns the how-to's of courtship. Harriet remains the beloved while serving as a decoy, a stand-in. Emma is passing through an androgynous phase; she is not altogether clear about her sexuality and yet terribly eager to find out all she can. Such a stage is not unusual for female teenagers in a patriarchial society to pass through, and Emma at twenty-one seems to us, in that particular respect, like someone whose adolescence has been delayed. Of that she is aware and thus all the more eager to make up for lost time.

Let us glance briefly at the conversation, as amusing as it is revealing, between Harriet and Emma on the subject of spinsterhood (pp. 84–86). I claim it supports the view presented of Emma's current state. "If I were to marry, I must expect to repent it," she says. Harriet is shocked: "Dear me!—it is so odd to hear a woman talk so!" Emma offers her reasons: there is no one "very superior" around; she has never been in love; she is rich, has status, is cherished by her father, has employment aplenty (drawing, reading, music, carpet-work), and as "objects for the affections" there will be a swarm of nieces and nephews. Does she mean it, or is she whistling in the dark? Her assertions must have sounded far more radical in her day than they do in ours. Harriet can hardly believe her ears; she remains wholly unconvinced, though she is easily talked into everything else. Emma wants to get some kind of a rise out of her. The truth is that by this time Emma is becoming rather exasperated with Harriet's denseness and would not be above teasing her out of it. But as so often happens in Austen, this conversation does heavy double duty: it is necessary for Emma not to commit herself just yet to the *charivari* rituals of courtship. Extolling affluent spinsterhood provides a more or less plausible defense of noninvolvement. I think it confirms her present androgyny, her need to stay outside but close up (in that order) to satisfy her curiosity, to learn, and to be ready when Mr. Right is discovered.

This role of observer, however, goes up in smoke when Elton mortifies Emma by declaring his love. Keeping one's distance, remaining on the outside, maintaining so-called objectivity in a situation of this kind may be a self-delusion, the novel would seem to suggest. What agitates Emma so when "the hair was curled, and the maid sent away, and [she] sat down to think and be miserable" (p. 134) is that the marriage she tried to orchestrate turned into a lopsided triangle with her at the precarious apex. Yet she has learned from the episode not merely that she must go easy in directing other people's lives; she has learned to examine her feelings more carefully. At least the "straightforward emotions left no room for the little zigzags of embarrassment" vis-à-vis Harriet.

The opportunity to apply her new knowledge comes when Frank Churchill courts her and she responds. It is no more than a lukewarm response because he is such a mercurial suitor. The following passage beautifully shows Austen giving her heroine a chance to rethink her attitude to Churchill. "[She] continued to entertain no doubt of her being in love," is how it begins. Then, switching to the first person, she thinks, "I certainly will not persuade myself to feel more than I do," and concludes: "Every consideration of the subject, in short, makes me thankful that my happiness is not more deeply involved. — I shall do very well again after a little while — and then, it will be a good thing over; for they say every body is in love once in their lives, and I shall have been let off easily" (pp. 264–265). She can balance her warm feelings for Churchill and the pleasure she takes in his lively company against his quirky behavior. She senses something superficial in him. Thus she cautions herself to be on guard against leading him on, as she vainly believes she can, because his effect on her has not been very deep. It also shows her making a sour-grapes denial of love not uncharacteristic of a young person's fear of love — fear of inadequacy, fear of what a commitment to love may entail.

Immediately after Emma has clarified her feelings to herself and in essence rejected Churchill, she turns her attention to the problem of Harriet. Churchill's timely rescue of the latter from the importuning gypsies, as well as his cursory reference to her in his letter to Mrs. Weston ("Miss Woodhouse's beautiful little friend" [p. 266]) are enough to conjure up a new candidate for her protegée's hand. To her credit, Emma checks herself immediately: "I know the danger of indulging such speculation" (p. 267). In any case, getting Harriet properly yoked has lost some of its erotic content after the Elton debacle. Emma's interest in her abates gradually because the feelings awakened by her have been redirected to a male. When she tells herself that "it was well to have a comfort in store on Harriet's behalf" (p. 267)—meaning Churchill, to make up for her mistake with Elton—it sounds more as though she were looking after a charity case than a lover. Her teenage androgyny is turning into a clear-eyed sense of herself as a young woman considering (even if, in Churchill's case, rejecting) possible male partners.

There is another chapter in Emma's see-sawing psychic development. Emma has grown up without a role model. Of her mother's "caresses" she has no more than "an indistinct remembrance" (p. 5). Who else is there in all of Highbury? Mrs. Weston would be a natural, but we are told that she early assumed the role of sister and friend owing to the "mildness of her temper" (p. 5). She is about ten years older than Emma, but even so Emma unquestionably dominated her. Emma's sister Isabella? Hardly, for she is so "wrapt up in her family; a devoted wife, a doating mother" and so resembles their father in her hypochondria (p. 92) that she becomes a parody figure difficult to take seriously. Who else is there? No aunts, no grandmother, no valued female family friend, such as Lady Russell in *Persuasion*, are in sight, who might fulfill the office of guiding her over the shoals of adolescence, courtship, wifehood, and motherhood, and help her form her values. She is surrounded by a bevy of well-meaning Goddards and Bateses to whom *she* might

6. In fact, Miss Bates has a mild claim. In the conversation on spinster-

rather be a role model.[6] There is no one.[7] Emma grows up a poor little rich girl; she is entitled but underprivileged. Is it not likely that such a girl will be willful, spoilt, a snob, that she will leap before she thinks, and make glaring faux pas?[8] One should not be overly surprised if one keeps remembering that she grows up virtually an orphan.

There are no proper role models, but there are two women who when the events of the novel take place, approximate that function in a curious way—one setting an example of a positive role, surrounded by many ifs and buts, the other, a spine-chilling warning of what to avoid. The first surely is Jane Fairfax. She is touted as the most accomplished young lady of Highbury; she has no peer in singing, at the pianoforte, or with the needle. The stick-to-itiveness that Emma lacks she has. Well-spoken and beautiful, she is often described as elegant, a term of richer connotations than we allow it today, that is, gracious, and refined, rather than merely well-dressed. What she lacks is a sense of humor, as well as Emma's blooming health. And, certainly,

---

hood discussed above, Emma says Miss Bates is "too silly to suit" her (p. 85) but quickly goes on to admit her implacable good nature, her generosity, and the fact that "nobody is afraid of her"—the last a curious item. All the more surprising then that the only female who does have a modest part as Emma's role model should suffer such a severe rebuff in the Box Hill episode. Then again, is it so surprising? I propose that Emma's outburst rises in part from anger and from disappointment that Miss Bates is not a *more* powerful, *more* generally admirable role model for her, not one whose effectiveness is undercut by her logomania. For a thorough discussion that takes, however, a different tack, see Bernard J. Paris, *Character and Conflict in Jane Austen's Novels: A Psychological Approach* (Detroit: Wayne State University Press, 1978), p. 85.

7. It has long been pointed out that there are no effective, strong mothers in any of the Austen novels. In *Emma* there is not even a questionable one—the hostility against mothers has become absolute.

8. Helen Storm Corsa describes "the freeing of [the] heroine from the frozen state of a kind of infantile and primary narcissism to the emotionally aware and warmly feeling young adult" in "A Fair but Frozen Maid: A Study of Jane Austen's *Emma*," *Literature and Psychology*, 19 (1969), 103. She is particularly enlightening on the psychological tempests at Box Hill, pp. 111–122.

money. Owing to the scenario Frank Churchill has devised for her, she must also do without the chance to be more freely herself.[9] But this we do not know until very far along. Emma is expected to like her and admire her, but she cannot bring herself to do either because Jane keeps her at such a distance. Or can Emma not abide being constantly reminded of how much better she herself ought to be, how much she falls short of her role as an upperclass heiress? Does Jane Fairfax inundate Emma with too many oughts and shoulds? Is she too much like a superego?

At the other end lives the crass Mrs. Elton. Numerous critics have pointed to the resemblances between her and Emma. Both are snobs, both vie for the first place in Highbury, both acquire protegées rather to their own advantage than the latter's; both like to direct, control, and offer snap judgments, and both have a strong materialistic bent. What is kept under wraps, more or less, in Emma is blared forth raucously in Mrs. Elton. Emma is in a red-hot fury after their first meeting. She calls her an "insufferable woman . . . a little upstart, vulgar being" (p. 279). After Emma and her father have discussed her visit, and after he has bewailed the state of marriage once again—and endorsed it unintentionally by asserting that "a bride . . . is always first in company," an endorsement not lost on Emma—"her mind returned to Mrs. Elton's offences, and long, very long, did they occupy her" (p. 280). Significantly, Emma is not able to exercise her wit on Mrs. Elton because she sees or fears to see the egocentric impulses they share. She distances herself from Jane Fairfax though she knows she ought not to; she tries to free herself from the strident vulgarities of Mrs. Elton and finds it difficult. There is a short-circuiting in her relations with both women—Jane as her superego, Mrs.

---

9. "She has not the open temper which a man would wish for in a wife" (p. 288), says Knightley, much to Emma's satisfaction. He is unaware that her standoffishness is not a character flaw but an adjustment to a bad situation.

Elton as her id.[10] I am well aware of using these terms imprecisely, but some such pull in this comic novel gives us the feeling that Emma's agitations in her development are both familiar and serious.

If there are no genuine female role models, then are there possible male ones? Her father, whom one hesitates to group among the males, must be dismissed out of hand. It is interesting to note that his palpable androgynousness reappears in his daughter, albeit in a far more natural form. Mr. Weston is a cheerful, prancing nonentity. Nor does John Knightley count even though he is sharp-eyed and well-intentioned, but he is just not around enough and besides is a little choleric. There is only George Knightley.[11] He very much plays the role of a father or older brother. He watches Emma closely, criticizes her, praises her, and gives her a periodic reckoning of how she is doing. Not flawless, he may nevertheless be the moral norm of the Highbury world, the embodiment of schooled common sense. Emma learns to prize these qualities too but not without a struggle. The struggle matters more than the fact that at the end of the story she is ready to acknowledge his superiority. The struggle sharpens her wits, develops her critical acumen and prevents her—fortunately—from ever turning into another homebody of homebodies, another Isabella. In short, Knightley does act as a role model of sorts, imbuing her, however, with the "harder" virtues of the male rather than the "softer" ones of the female: self-control against showing affection, rationalist versus "imaginist," independence versus dependence.[12] The hard edge to Emma's character,

10. To complete the triad, who could reflect Emma's ego better than mild, tolerant, rational Mrs. Weston?

11. In the encounter between Emma and Mrs. Elton referred to above the latter's worst offense was to speak of him familiarly as Knightley and to intone fruitily, "Knightley is quite the gentleman" (p. 278).

12. Here is a radically different view: "Knightley will keep her wayward impulses under control, but he will not help her to grow . . . To satisfy his own pride, he needs at once to exalt Emma and to keep her inferior to him . . . It is difficult to see Emma, under Knightley's tutelage, outgrowing her dependency" (Paris, *Character and Conflict*, p. 92). As a rejoinder I would

without which she is simply not Emma, is owing, I believe, to the general shortcomings of her role models. That ought to remind us, moreover, what a hard row she has to hoe, privileges of birth notwithstanding. No wonder she zigzags, no wonder she doesn't live up to her own and others' high expectations of her.

Finally, I should like to raise again my original questions that pertain to Emma's wavering development. Why are there so many games in this novel—card games, parlor games, word games, board games, improvised games (as at Box Hill)—more games than in any of Austen's other novels? Why do we have two major episodes, and one imagined one, that bear the characteristics of plays rather than narratives, if plays may be considered as a species of game?[13] I refer to the Harriet-Emma-Elton courtship, to Frank Churchill's concealment of his engagement to Jane, and to the Fairfax-Dixon "affair." The first point to be made is that the profusion of games testifies to the confinement of Highbury society and provides a major source of "home-entertainment." Games dispel boredom, are a pretext for mounting a sociable evening, or, conversely, are what a sociable evening declines to. Does not the ubiquity of games contribute to the impression, so aptly described by Lionel

---

like to quote an interchange between Emma and Knightley on the occasion of the dinner at the Westons. They are concerned about conveying the jittery neurasthenic Mr. Woodhouse home during a half-inch snowfall.

"Your father will not be easy; why do not you go?"

"I am ready, if the others are."

"Shall I ring the bell?"

"Yes, do." (p. 128)

Why does Austen inflict such an atypically drab dialogue, if not to show two people who relate to each other in a mature, straightforward fashion as the occasion requires.

13. I am omitting the purest form of game or play, the dance, which also has an important role in the novel. See Raymond F. Hilliard, "*Emma*: Dancing Without Space to Turn In," in *Probability, Time, and Space in Eighteenth-Century Literature*, ed. Paula Backscheider (New York: AMS Press, 1979). He suggests that the "most conspicuous expression" of vitality in the novel is "playfulness" (p. 277).

Trilling, of Highbury as an idyll? There is not much else our cast can do with their plentiful spare time.

Secondly, games provide acceptable ways of dealing with the sexually-charged atmosphere.[14] They make the needed role-playing possible. There is Harriet's collection of riddles and charades to which Elton makes his labored contribution; there is the anagram game, which Knightley, his suspicions aroused, watches eagle-eyed. He decides that "these letters were but the vehicle for gallantry and trick. It was a child's play, chosen to conceal a deeper game on Frank Churchill's part" (p. 348). It is a shrewd guess, and he is nearly right.

By design, games are win-or-lose propositions, and so is a play if it is seen as a game in which psychological gains or losses occur. The game that Emma plays in setting up Harriet for Elton to pursue has the highest stakes one can find in a comedy, the overcoming of the fear of love and the matching of more or less appropriate partners. There are at least three vividly realized scenes that lend themselves to easy staging: Harriet sitting for her portrait, Emma infiltrating Harriet into the vicarage by a ruse, and Elton vainly declaring his cold love in a cold carriage. Emma's game turns out to have three losers and no winners, though all three will present themselves for a return engagement with new partners. As producer-playwright, Emma is the quickest to turn her loss into a partial victory, for she realizes the cause of the fiasco. The importance of the three well-realized scenes lies in the opportunity they offer for role-playing: for instance, Emma the string-puller and observer, Harriet the passive love object and decoy, and Elton the heavy-footed, hard-breathing suitor. They are given "as if" blank checks as tryouts for different roles, and role-playing is a necessary activity for a young person to engage in before she or he can settle into one that promises the best satisfactions of his or

---

14. The distinction between card games and word games is explored in an illuminating essay by Alistair M. Duckworth, "Spillikins, Paper Ships, Riddles, Conundrums, and Cards: Games in Jane Austen's Life and Fiction," in *Jane Austen: Bicentenary Essays*, ed. John Halperin (Cambridge: Cambridge University Press, 1975).

her needs. Emma has played god in a sort of spoilt-brat syndrome, a role she reluctantly abandons when she thinks through her part in the debacle as she sits before her mirror. However, the sexual excitation that comes with the exercise of power is not likely to leave her.

The imaginary affair Emma makes up out of whole cloth for Jane Fairfax and Mr. Dixon gives us an inkling of what rich sexual fantasies occupy her: clandestine courtship, seduction, adultery, dangerous sexual encounters—she imagines a mighty, perhaps ungovernable, emotion. Emma ascribes Jane's melancholy debility to guilt over the affair, which may be another way of saying that she is both terrified by, and attracted to, sex—not an abnormal combination for a young woman on the threshold of physical love.

The stakes are different, the setting is different, and the very tone is different in the play staged by Frank Churchill in order to keep both his fortune and his fiancée—in that sequence. In Emma's Harriet-Elton play we are in on the secret from the beginning; in the other we must unravel the mystery. In the first Emma uses Harriet by making her into a decoy, while that is exactly what happens to Emma in the second—it is when the shoe is on the other foot that she is all for having everything "decided and open" (p. 460). Churchill's concealment of his engagement to Jane Fairfax puts the latter into a very trying position and no doubt contributes to her air of malaise. He derives sadistic pleasure from her discomfort, just as his pleasure derived from flirting with Emma—his cover—comes from his awareness that he is playing a double game. He walks a thin line, he courts discovery, both associated with being sources of perverse excitation. (It might not be amiss to remind ourselves of the psychological and moral havoc brought about by the theatricals in *Mansfield Park*.) Luckily Emma is never fully drawn in because in her quickness and her ability to think things through she realizes that there is some playacting and much insincerity in his professions. To Knightley, who often expresses Emma's thoughts on the next higher level of abstraction, falls this remark, as suggestive as any in Austen: "The gallant young man [Churchill] ... seemed to love

without feeling" (p. 348). His self-exculpatory letter to Mrs.
Weston (pp. 436–443), but addressed as much to Emma and
the entire Highbury commmunity, sounds better than it is,
as again Knightley takes pains to point out. The pleasure
with which Churchill devised the whole scheme is now
matched by making such a dramatic clean breast of it. He is
the showman still, claiming exorbitant credit for his
newfound penitence and humility. There is a brief scene
near the end wherein the two playwright-directors, Emma
and Churchill, have a last word and beautifully sum up the
roles they have played.

The company gathers at the Westons' house. Emma and
Churchill contrive a private talk while they are watching Jane
who is out of earshot. It would hardly occur to Churchill
that this is another scene in a play to which he adds ominous
overtones. " 'Is not she looking well?' said he, turning his
eyes towards Jane," and a few moments later: "Did you
ever see such a skin?—such smoothness! such delicacy! . . .
dark eye-lashes and hair . . . a most distinguished complexion . . . Just colour enough for beauty." Emma interrupts
but he is in full spate: "Observe the turn of her throat.
Observe her eyes" (pp. 477–79).[15] And more of the same
for the ensuing lines. How utterly consistent and how full of
foreboding. Churchill really has not grown at all; he reveals
again his peeping-Tom inclinations, his preoccupation with
surface and appearance. One fears for Jane; it is in the cards
that he will bluster through life, the eternal adolescent playing hurtful games and leaving his victims with a shrug or a
tear by the roadside. A child of fortune, indeed.

Emma's interruption of Churchill's encomium of Jane
neatly adverts to my present theme. Emma says: "I do
suspect that in the midst of your perplexities at that time,
you had very great amusement in tricking us all.—I am sure
you had.—I am sure it was a consolation to you." He denies

---

15. A fuller discussion of this important scene appears in Irvin Ehrenpreis,
*Acts of Implication: Suggestion and Covert Meaning in the Works of Dryden,
Swift, Pope, and Austen* (Berkeley: University of California Press, 1980), pp.
121–123.

it and assures her he was "the most miserable wretch." She continues:

> "Not quite so miserable as to be insensible to mirth. I am sure it was a source of high entertainment to you, to feel that you were taking us all in.—Perhaps I am the readier to suspect, because, to tell you the truth, I think it might have been some amusement to myself in the same situation. I think there is a little likeness between us."
> He bowed. (p. 478)

But she qualifies the likeness instantly: "If not in our dispositions . . . in our destiny" inasmuch as they will each marry "two characters so much superior to our own" (p. 478). The difference is that Emma has profited by her experience in role-playing while Churchill is destined to reenact his role over and over again. Further, I believe that Emma, as she moves toward marriage, resolves to abandon role-playing altogether as she recalls her own unsuccess and Churchill's perversities. Whether she can pull it off is another matter.

One of the many achievements of this novel is that we grow so familiar with Emma, so partial to her, admitting the while that we will never know her fully—that "There is an anxiety, a curiosity in what one feels for Emma" (p. 40) is as true for Knightley as for the reader—that we cannot help but speculate on her future. Will she wear the pants in the family? Will she be on the lookout for other lives to meddle with? Or will she turn into the submissive, complaisant wife that the last pages point to? I can see her resolve these questions on paper, for with her brightness, her drive, her "predilection for creativity,"[16] with her Johnsonian clarity of mind which enables her to look within and benefit therefrom—plus a little acquired "steadiness"—she has all

---

16. Susan Siefert, *The Dilemma of the Talented Heroine: A Study in Nineteenth-Century Fiction* (Montreal: Eden Press, 1978), p. 130. Ms. Siefert remarks astutely that Emma's "harmless reveries" must be balanced against her "social manipulation" and that she needs to "refine and channel her imagination" (pp. 130–131).

the makings—what more likely!—of an Early Victorian novelist.[17]

17. This thought is not original with me, and I regret that I cannot locate its source. This may be the place to acknowledge that some of the ideas presented here arose in enlightening talks with Katherine Boland, a bright student of more years ago than it seems worth computing.

Contributors

LAWRENCE LIPKING
 Northwestern University

MARTINE WATSON BROWNLEY
 Emory University

JOHN RIELY
 Boston University

W. H. BOND
 Harvard University

GWIN J. KOLB
 University of Chicago

JOHN H. MIDDENDORF
 Columbia University

JAMES G. BASKER
 Harvard University

BERTRAND H. BRONSON
 University of California
 at Berkeley

JOHN D. BOYD, S.J.
 Fordham University

EMERSON R. MARKS
 University of Massachusetts
 at Boston

JAMES ENGELL
 Harvard University

JOHN L. MAHONEY
  Boston College

MARY HYDE
  Four Oaks Farm

HOWARD D. WEINBROT
  University of Wisconsin
  at Madison

ROBERT HALSBAND
  University of Illinois

W. B. CARNOCHAN
  Stanford University

GERALD CHAPMAN
  University of Denver

JEAN H. HAGSTRUM
  Northwestern University

RALPH W. RADER
  University of California
  at Berkeley

PATRICIA MEYER SPACKS
  Yale University

MAX BYRD
  University of California
  at Davis

MELINDA ALLIKER RABB
  Brown University

ALEX PAGE
  University of Massachusetts
  at Amherst